Encyclopedia of Modern China

Encyclopedia of Modern China

VOLUME 4
U–Z, INDEX

David Pong

EDITOR IN CHIEF

CHARLES SCRIBNER'S SONS
A part of Gale, Cengage Learning

GALE
CENGAGE Learning

Detroit • New York • San Francisco • New Haven, Conn • Waterville, Maine • London

GALE
CENGAGE Learning™

Encyclopedia of Modern China

David Pong, Editor in Chief

For product information and technology assistance, contact us at **Gale Customer Support, 1-800-877-4253.**
For permission to use material from this text or product, submit all requests online at **www.cengage.com/permissions.**
Further permissions questions can be emailed to **permissionrequest@cengage.com**

Library of Congress Cataloging-in-Publication Data

Encyclopedia of modern China / David Pong, editor in chief.
p. cm. --
Includes bibliographical references and index.
ISBN 978-0-684-31566-9 (set : alk. paper) -- ISBN 978-0-684-31567-6 (v. 1 : alk. paper) -- ISBN 978-0-684-31568-3 (v. 2 : alk. paper) -- ISBN 978-0-684-31569-0 (v. 3 : alk. paper) -- ISBN 978-0-684-31570-6 (v. 4 : alk. paper) -- ISBN 978-0-684-31571-3 (e-book)
1. China--Civilization--1644-1912--Encyclopedias. 2. China--Civilization--1912-1949--Encyclopedias. 3. China--Civilization--1949---Encyclopedias. I. Pong, David, 1939–.

DS755.E63 2009
951.003--dc22

2009003279

Gale
27500 Drake Rd.
Farmington Hills, MI 48331-3535

ISBN-13: 978-0-684-31566-9 (set)   ISBN-10: 0-684-31566-1 (set)
ISBN-13: 978-0-684-31567-6 (vol. 1)   ISBN-10: 0-684-31567-X (vol. 1)
ISBN-13: 978-0-684-31568-3 (vol. 2)   ISBN-10: 0-684-31568-8 (vol. 2)
ISBN-13: 978-0-684-31569-0 (vol. 3)   ISBN-10: 0-684-31569-6 (vol. 3)
ISBN-13: 978-0-684-31570-6 (vol. 4)   ISBN-10: 0-684-31570-X (vol. 4)

This title is also available as an e-book.
ISBN-13: 978-0-684-31571-3 ISBN-10: 0-684-31571-8
Contact your Gale sales representative for ordering information.

Printed in the United States of America
1 2 3 4 5 6 7 13 12 11 10 09

Editorial Board

Contents

List of Maps

U

UNIT (*DANWEI*)

The term *unit* (*danwei*) commonly refers to the workplace in urban China after 1949. The unit was ubiquitous: Until the mid-1980s, government and party organizations, state-owned enterprises, financial institutions, and educational establishments were all designated as units. With few exceptions, unit employees were entitled to lifetime employment. Typically, a unit provided its employees with housing, education, health care, recreational activities, rationed goods, pensions, and so forth. For many, the distinguishing feature of a unit was a lifetime social-welfare system from cradle to grave, and a network of relationships encompassing work, home, neighborhood, and political membership. Thus, many scholars trace the origins of the unit variously to the Communist free-supply system from the 1930s, the heritage of labor protest, and the evolution of labor-management institutions.

BEFORE 1949: ORIGINS

Still, the unit is best understood as a part of the prevailing administrative system embracing virtually all government, business and financial, as well as educational institutions in urban China after 1949. Such a definition emphasizes that these institutional entities were integral parts of the overall state administrative structure, a character that cannot be explained by any of the above-mentioned traditions or institutions.

The evidence suggests that the origins of the unit in the sense of China's prevailing administrative system can be traced to the Nationalist struggle to rationalize the administrative bureaucracy during the Second Sino-Japanese War (1937–1945), when the Nationalists used the term *unit* to designate political, economic, and administrative organizations. Beginning in the early 1940s, the government and state-owned enterprises routinely used the term *unit* to identify various organizations, as well as subordinate entities, within those organizations. Even the term *work unit* (*gongzuo danwei*), which for decades has been the standard although erroneous translation for the term *danwei*, was carefully defined in 1943 to refer to the head of a department (*ke*) within the administrative unit of a division (*chu*) and the technical personnel of various constituent parts with the rank of a department head. Thereafter the term was used regularly in Dadukou Iron and Steel Works, the largest state-owned enterprise in Nationalist-controlled areas during the war. Shortly after that, the term *work unit* simply referred to the department as an administrative unit. At the same time, the term *management unit* (*guanli danwei*) was used to refer to the larger administrative unit known as division.

Those same units also acquired some of their defining characteristics during the Sino-Japanese War, including unit provision of social services and welfare. Studies have shown, for example, that the war witnessed the formation of self-contained enterprise-run service and welfare communities. Employees lived in factory apartments and dormitories, bought their daily necessities at factory cooperatives, purchased vegetables grown at factory farms, and went to factory clinics and hospitals for medical treatment. Employees' children received their education in factory schools. When employees died, they sometimes were buried in factory cemeteries. To put it differently, the unit designation of political, economic, and administrative organizations and unit provision of social services and welfare predate the Communists' rise to power.

1949 TO 1980: EXPANSION

After 1949, the unit became part of urban China's administrative system, expanded its function as the provider of social services and welfare, and developed new characteristics such as party control, permanent employment, and labor immobility. As a part of the prevailing urban administrative system, a typical unit had administrative departments or divisions that matched their counterparts in pertinent administrative bureaucracies at a higher level. For example, a typical unit had a finance department or division that coordinated with the finance department or division of a municipality and ultimately with the ministry of finance of the central government. An inevitable consequence of the unit's incorporation into the overall administrative structure was the loss of autonomy on the part of unit leaders or managers over issues such as wages and personnel.

In addition, a typical unit offered its employees housing, recreation, and health-care facilities, schooling for their children, ration coupons for food, and pensions and burial funds. The unit also engaged in a variety of political activities under party leadership and supervision, including political campaigns, which were typically carried out unit by unit. In fact, the unit represented an extension of the Communist Party, as the unit had within it either a party committee or commission, depending on the unit's size. Under the party committee or commission were the party secretary's office, the organization department, the propaganda department, and the discipline inspection department. Such an organizational structure was designed to match the organizational structure of the Communist Party at a higher level. Finally, the unit was characterized not only by permanent employment but also labor immobility. Very few employees obtained permission to transfer from one unit to another.

SINCE 1980: MODIFICATION

The reforms initiated by the Communist Party during the early 1980s have brought about significant modification, if not transformation, of the unit system. Within the unit, the labor contract has replaced permanent employment as the basis of employment for a majority of employees. Material incentives have replaced ideological and psychological ones in an effort to promote labor productivity. Many units no longer provide employees comprehensive social services and welfare. The party-state has also relaxed what had been the rigid administrative and political control that various units exercised over their employees. Employees can transfer from one unit to another with relative ease.

Within state-owned enterprises, which had been a core component of the unit system, profit came to be recognized as essential for enterprise survival and growth beginning in the early 1980s. At the same time, the weakening of the welfare feature of the unit went hand-in-hand with the strengthening of managerial control and profit orientation by the latter half of the 1990s. On one hand, the withdrawal of state financial support and the competitive disadvantages of state-owned firms in the marketplace removed the foundation for welfare paternalism. On the other hand, those firms' increasing autonomy within an increasingly market-oriented economy meant that managers not only acquired the power to dismiss workers but also had to devote their energies toward increasing productivity and profit. At the same time, the reforms have permitted the development of privately owned, joint-venture, and collective enterprises, which are not extensions of the government apparatus. Within those new enterprises, entrepreneurs and managers have introduced practices of scientific management designed to enforce labor discipline and maximize profits.

Despite their market orientation and profit motive, some private firms that developed during the 1980s actually reproduced many features of the *unit* system. For instance, a recent study suggests that during the early 1990s, many high-tech firms located in Haidian District in Beijing were a key source of housing, medical care, social security, and other welfare needs of their employees, despite considerable variation between them. In fact, in the large and more profitable firms, the level of provision was often on a par with, and even surpassed, that of state-owned enterprises. A major factor for the reproduction of the features of the *unit* system was the existence of intense competition for skilled labor in high-tech firms, which motivated managers to provide attractive benefits packages to employees. Another factor was the absence or inadequacy of alternative sources of social services and welfare outside the workplace, which necessitated provision by the firm of those services and welfare.

On balance, however, the reforms have not only weakened the traditional unit system, they have had profound implications for the reconfiguration of urban Chinese society. In response to the tremendous social and economic changes, notably the massive unemployment resulting from the reform and privatization of state-owned enterprise units and the influx of millions of migrant workers to the cities, the party-state in the 1990s introduced experiments that led to the creation of new urban "communities" (*shequ*) under government control and supervision and with jurisdiction over clearly demarcated urban space. The responsibility of the community is no longer confined to the provision of social services and welfare; it includes functions ranging from social-service and welfare provision to culture, health, education, morality, policing, and grassroots democracy. Specifically, the community is expected to provide a range of services to the resident population irrespective of occupation. Second, the community is charged with the responsibility for managing aspects of urban health care and sanitation. Third, the community is expected to organize a wide range of educational and cultural programs. Fourth, the community plays an important role in the local coordination of security work. Fifth, the community is required to coordinate and liaise between various organizations.

The fulfillment of those functions rests with full-time salaried officials with the help of community volunteers. Most of those communities feature a community center that was erected close to the center of the territory that it serves. Although the future of those communities is unclear at the dawn of the twentieth-first century, it appears that they may eventually replace the unit as the basic social, political, and administrative organization in urban China.

SEE ALSO *Education: Education since 1949; Education: Kindergarten; Housing; Labor; Life Cycle: Old Age; Medical Care since 1949; Social Welfare; Urban China: Urban Housing; Urban China: Urban Planning since 1978.*

BIBLIOGRAPHY

Bian, Morris L. Building State Structure: Guomindang Institutional Rationalization during the Sino-Japanese War, 1937–1945. *Modern China* 31 (2005): 35–71.

Bian, Morris L. *The Making of the State Enterprise System in Modern China: The Dynamics of Institutional Change.* Cambridge, MA: Harvard University Press, 2005.

Bian, Morris L. How Crisis Shapes Change: New Perspectives on China's Political Economy during the Sino-Japanese War, 1937–1945. *History Compass* 5 (2007): 1091–1110.

Bray, David. *Social Space and Governance in Urban China: The* Danwei *System from Origins to Reform.* Stanford, CA: Stanford University Press, 2005.

Bray, David. Building "Community": New Strategies of Governance in Urban China. *Economy and Society* 35, 4 (2006): 530–549.

Francis, Corinna-Barbara. Reproduction of *Danwei* Institutional Features in the Context of China's Market Economy: The Case of Haidian District's High-Tech Sector. *China Quarterly* 147 (1996): 839–859.

Frazier, Mark W. *The Making of the Chinese Industrial Workplace: State, Revolution, and Labor Management.* New York: Cambridge University Press, 2002.

Lee Ching Kwan. From Organized Dependence to Disorganized Despotism: Changing Labour Regimes in Chinese Factories. *China Quarterly* 157 (1999): 44–71.

Lü Xiaobo and Elizabeth J. Perry, eds. *Danwei: The Changing Chinese Workplace in Historical and Comparative Perspective.* Armonk, NY: Sharpe, 1997.

Morris L. Bian

UNITED FRONT WORK

United-front work (*tongyi zhanxian gongzuo*) consists of "rallying all who can be rallied" to common strategies, to tactical causes, against a common enemy, or for a common goal. Building support for such causes usually involves making political concessions, using strong emotional appeals, and providing material rewards of some sort. The key constraint is the need to maintain party organizational independence. In the case of communist parties, collaboration across class lines was always done with the long-term strategy of using allies today to secure victory in the revolution intended to eliminate the economic and social basis of those same allies. The groups allies formed were also infiltrated or controlled by communists who kept their party affiliations secret while seeking to use their positions to advance the greater revolutionary cause. In most cases communists abandoned such alliance immediately or soon after seizing power.

The Chinese Communist Party (CCP) stands alone among communist parties in its development of united fronts to not only help achieve key political and military victories in the lead up to the final seizure of power by force, but also to assist in the subsequent economic, political, and social transitions to communism. The success of this work is reflected in relatively smooth and very rapid changes that occurred in China between 1949 and 1956. In China's case, this success was also a spur to revitalizing united front work to aid the post-Mao economic reforms and the subsequent social and other changes that ensued.

The United Front Work Department of the CCP remains central to debates and policies ranging from working with the Guomindang (Nationalist Party) and bringing Taiwan under direct Chinese sovereignty, to working with overseas Chinese, liaising with businesses, monitoring and controlling religious believers, handling relations with China's ethnic minorities, and building support for China among non-Chinese foreigners. As part of the CCP, it is also integrated with the government and other parts of society by means of party cells from the Central Committee down to the lowest levels, but the effectiveness of those charged with this work depends much on the attitude of the leaders at each level and place.

BEFORE 1949

The Comintern (Communist International), the organization directing communist revolutionary efforts worldwide, imposed the first United Front (1923–1927), during which the new, tiny, and fragmented CCP was forced into a bloc-within alliance with Sun Yat-sen's then radical and revolutionary anti-imperialist Guomindang. Communists joined the Guomindang to strengthen its revolutionary tendencies and win over Guomindang members to communism. This first period of cooperation between the CCP and Guomindang ended in April 1927, when Chiang Kai-shek (Jiang Jieshi) purged known and suspected Communists within his party and the cities under Nationalist control. Nevertheless, this first alliance helped party membership grow to thousands and enabled Communists to develop personal relations with Guomindang soldiers and officials in organizations such as the Whampoa Military Academy (Huangpu Junxiao) that proved invaluable in later years.

The CCP's subsequent soviet period (1927–1936) was initially marked by "Red Terror," violent class warfare and confiscation of property, policies that alienated potential supporters. Refugees fled to the Guomindang, and the CCP then had to divert soldiers to fill economic and administrative roles. These factors and increasing Guomindang military pressure led to the collapse of the economy of the Chinese Soviet Republic and culminated in the CCP's Long March retreat to Yan'an in October 1934. Contact with many minority groups during the march highlighted the need for good relations with them.

In 1935 the Comintern responded to the rise of fascism by promoting cross-class cooperation to build an antifascist united front. To forestall a Japanese attack on the Soviet Union, Soviet agents also began negotiating with the Guomindang and the CCP for a Communist-Guomindang united front against the Japanese. By the time of the Xi'an Incident in December 1936, when the Manchurian warlords Zhang Xueliang (1901–2001) and Yang Hucheng (1893–1949) kidnapped Chiang rather than launch another attack on surviving communist forces, the basis for the second United Front had been decided.

With the new United Front, the CCP could again operate legally in the cities and seized the opportunity to build a much broader united front, targeting students, teachers, bureaucrats, business owners, and overseas Chinese. This united-front work developed propaganda and activities aimed to, at the very least, neutralize support for the Guomindang by portraying it as undemocratic, corrupt, and unable, even unwilling, to defend China from Japanese aggression. While winning more support for the CCP was one aspect of successful action, simply increasing the numbers of those who withdrew active

support for the Nationalists was perhaps more important in the short term. United-front work also invoked patriotism and personal ties to Guomindang officials and officers to gather intelligence and weaken or prevent actions against the CCP.

Among the major targets of united-front work between 1936 and 1949 were the many small political groups and activists outside of Guomindang and CCP control because these had significant and ready access to the press, government, and key social groups, and hence a disproportionate influence in urban areas. The National Anti-Japanese Salvation Association and the groups that later fused to become the Democratic League of China were perhaps the most important of these. After Japan attacked Pearl Harbor in December 1941, the CCP's united-front work focus rapidly shifted to become increasingly aimed at organizing for an eventual open political and military struggle with the Guomindang.

After Japan's defeat, united-front workers created seven new groups to put more pressure on the Guomindang to delay as much as possible, the Nationalists' inevitable open anti-Communist military action and to prepare for elections to a National Assembly, should these be called. These minor parties and groups were the China Association for Promoting Democracy, the China Democratic National Construction Association, the Chinese Peasants and Workers Democratic Party, the Taiwan Democratic Self-Government League, the China Zhigong (Public Interest) Party, the Jiusan (September 3rd) Society, and the Revolutionary Committee of the Nationalist Party. These groups worked together as part of the CCP's second front in urban areas to undermine Guomindang legitimacy while some also worked to prevent the emergence of any "third force" in Chinese politics that might complicate the communist rise to power. When in 1948 Chiang eventually banned the minor parties and groups and the Democratic League of China, he handed the CCP a major political victory, seemingly proving the Guomindang's dictatorial nature and incompetence and demonstrating the need to choose one armed party or the other.

UNITED FRONT WORK AFTER COMMUNIST VICTORY

After 1949 and as part of Mao's New Democracy, the United Front Work Department redirected its efforts to create a People's Democratic United Front, designed to reassure key social groups and promote rapid economic reconstruction. The wartime Political Consultative Conference, the original united-front government, was replaced by the National People's Congress as the highest official organ of state. The conference itself became the Chinese People's Political Consultative Conference, the highest embodiment of united-front work, under the direct control of the United Front Work Department but without any official power.

After 1949 the minor parties and groups were used to model, encourage, and help the implementation of thought reform so that CCP-approved proletarian thinking would replace bourgeois thinking and Western ideas like liberalism and idealism would be renounced. In 1953 the All-China Federation of Industry and Commerce was established to foster control and transformation of small enterprises and artisans. To aid in this revolution, the CCP launched the Three-Anti's and Five-Anti's Campaigns of 1951–1952 to discredit private business and bourgeois thinking.

The United Front Work Department also developed policies to incorporate China's many ethnic minorities, officially recognizing fifty-five and allowing these representation in the Chinese People's Political Consultative Conference. Religious believers were put under enormous pressure to recant or to join churches under control of the State Religious Affairs Bureau. China's many Christian groups were reorganized into the Three-Self Patriotic Movement of Protestant Churches (the three self's being self-governance, self-support, and self-propagation) and the Chinese Patriotic Catholic Association. The United Front Work Department also appealed to overseas Chinese to return and help build a new China, a call heeded by thousands.

In 1957, under the direction of Li Weihan (1896–1984), the United Front Work Department worked hard to encourage largely cowed united-front allies to criticize the CCP as part of Mao Zedong's Hundred Flowers campaign to rectify party shortcomings. When after much work by the United Front Work Department these allies began criticizing the CCP and then even Mao in ever more strident tones, Mao launched the Anti-Rightist Campaign against them. Almost all united-front allies except those protected by secret party membership were eventually labeled rightists. United-front work fell increasingly into disrepute, and the United Front Work Department and Li Weihan came under intense criticism.

Only after the failure of Mao's Great Leap Forward (1958–1960) was united-front work partially revived, this time to get the minor parties and groups and non-party individuals to assist in economic rebuilding as part of the so-called Second Hundred Flowers campaign (1961–1964). Mao Zedong, however, was now only interested in class struggle, and as his Great Proletarian Cultural Revolution unfolded, united-front work was largely abandoned. The minor parties and groups, other united-front allies, and the United Front Work Department all entered serious decline or were effectively disbanded.

Even before Mao Zedong died in 1976, the United Front Work Department was being revived, but after his death it became an important part of the CCP's efforts to realize the Four Modernizations in agriculture, industry, science and technology, and national defense. The

department developed a new Patriotic United Front campaign to win support for reinvigorating the motherland. By the early 1980s this line was reformulated as Deng Xiaoping's New Era United Front, but patriotism remained the key appeal for stimulating support for party goals.

In 2002 the CCP launched a New Century United Front. This largely internally directed campaign emphasizes using united-front work to integrate China's newly emerging classes of businesspeople and other interest groups into the political system to maximize social harmony and resolve social tensions. Externally, united-front work is directed at bringing about a peaceful world environment conducive to China's economic development.

BIBLIOGRAPHY

Groot, Gerry. *Managing Transitions: The Chinese Communist Party, United Front Work, Corporatism, and Hegemony.* New York: Taylor and Francis, 2004.

Leung, Beatrice. China's Religious Freedom Policy: The Art of Managing Religious Activity. *China Quarterly*, no. 184 (December 2005): 894–913.

Van Slyke, Lyman P. *Enemies and Friends: The United Front in Chinese Communist History.* Stanford, CA: Stanford University Press, 1967.

Gerry Groot

UNITED KINGDOM, RELATIONS WITH

After the founding of the People's Republic of China (PRC) in 1949, Great Britain became one of the first European countries to recognize the new state. Britain did so largely to protect its interests in Hong Kong, which, with the exception of the World War II period (1937–1945), had been an overseas British territory since the nineteenth century.

For most of the first decade of the PRC's existence, the British government followed an official trade embargo against China, instigated largely by the United States, though informal trade links were established by private businesspeople after a delegation led by Lord Boyd Orr (1880–1971) and the Cambridge economist Joan Robinson (1903–1983) visited in 1953. By the end of the 1950s, to all intents and purposes, trade between the two countries was largely tolerated. Rolls-Royce invested in China in the early 1960s, selling spare parts for aircraft, and in the 1970s allowing the Chinese to purchase Spey aircraft engines and to manufacture some components in China. Shell and British American Tobacco also maintained a presence in China. This presence was interrupted from 1966 to 1976, during which period the British legation in Beijing was attacked by Red Guard groups in

A Chinese official awaiting the arrival of Chinese President Hu Jintao, London, England, November 8, 2005. Though the British initially recognized the People's Republic of China quickly after its inception, diplomatic ties became strained during China's Cultural Revolution after Red Guard units threatened the British embassy in Beijing. Since the British handover of Hong Kong in 1997, relations between the two countries have improved, with both sides engaging in robust trade and investment. © **LEON NEAL/REUTERS/CORBIS**

1968, and Britain was lumped with the United States as a major enemy. The attack on the legation left a particularly negative legacy, with representation in Beijing scaled down till the early 1970s. There were also public scuffles at the embassy in London during this period, instigated by overzealous radicals serving there.

The rapprochement with the United States following the visit of President Richard Nixon (1913–1994) in 1972 opened the way for the United Kingdom to upgrade its relationship to ambassadorship level from chargé d'affaires in 1972. Prime Minister Edward Heath (1916–2005) visited China in 1973, beginning a regular series of top-level visits. However, it was not until 1999, when President Jiang Zemin traveled to the United Kingdom, that Britain saw its first visit by a Chinese head of state. Queen Elizabeth visited China in 1986 on the first (and, as of 2008, only) visit by a British head of state to China.

THE ISSUE OF HONG KONG AND ITS RETURN TO CHINA

After the reemergence of Deng Xiaoping in 1978, the key issue in Sino-British relations was the return of Hong Kong. Initial overtures in 1980 and 1981 to suggest an

extension of Britain's ninety-nine-year lease on the territory were dismissed by the Chinese. Prime Minister Margaret Thatcher seriously considered retaining possession of Hong Kong Island in 1984, but realized that its reliance on the mainland for water, food, and energy made this prospect untenable. For the next fifteen years, torturous negotiations took place over what political model Hong Kong might follow after reversion in 1997. The Tiananmen Square massacre in June 1989 only increased concerns in Hong Kong and the United Kingdom that the Chinese government would clamp down in Hong Kong and that the mainland government posed a significant threat to the civil, legal, and press freedoms enjoyed in the territory.

A Basic Law (a de facto constitution) was approved in 1990, guaranteeing Hong Kong "a high degree of autonomy" over domestic issues, while the Beijing government took responsibility for defense and foreign affairs. This arrangement was dubbed by Deng Xiaoping the "one country, two systems" solution. It was agreed that Hong Kong would retain its currency, and that a limited franchise would be established for the legislative council, with a chief executive being appointed, and then elected.

Beginning in 1992, the last British governor of Hong Kong, Chris Patten, made several bold moves to open

6

Hong Kong further to democracy, extending the franchise and holding elections that were immediately dismissed by China after 1997. Critics of Patton's actions pointed out that the British had not made such moves toward democracy in the decades before the imminent handover, and that to do so at this time was irresponsible. However, fears that the reversion of Hong Kong to China on June 30, 1997—in a ceremony attended by the British prime minister Tony Blair and the Chinese president Jiang Zemin—would lead to a crackdown in the newly established Special Administrative Region (SAR) have so far proved unfounded.

Hong Kong suffered badly during the Asian financial crisis in 1997 to 1998, when property prices and stock values plummeted. But Hong Kong has bounced back, and in 2008 stands as one of the most successful and dynamic economies in the region. It is still not a democracy, with universal suffrage not promised until 2017, at the earliest.

RELATIONS SINCE 1997

Since 1997, the United Kingdom's perceived closeness to the United States has been a continuing source of tension with China. This became particularly acute in 2003 and 2004, when the European Union considered lifting the arms embargo placed on China in 1989. Some argued that such an embargo was now largely symbolic and that the sale of military equipment to China was restricted by other legislation. The Chinese government was keen to see the embargo lifted, and the United Kingdom initially supported the move. In the end, the anticipated lifting of the embargo did not occur due to the passage in March 2005 of China's Anti-Secession Law, which claimed the right to the use of force to prevent Taiwanese independence.

Britain and China have also focused on their trade relationship. Britain remains China's largest investor among countries of the European Union, with almost $25 billion invested, most concentrated in coastal areas. The largest British investments are from BP ($5 billion), Shell ($5 billion), and Vodafone ($4.5 billion), with other British investors including Tesco, Rolls-Royce, and the retailer B&Q, which has over seventy outlets in China. Britain's financial-services sector has also been active in China, playing to the strengths of the U.K. economy, with the Royal Bank of Scotland taking a share in a Chinese bank, and the insurer Prudential being granted licenses in China. As of 2007, there were six thousand British-Chinese joint ventures in almost every province and autonomous region. Reversing the trend, in 2007 the China Development Bank took a 3 percent stake in one of Britain's largest banks, Barclays. By 2008 there were more than three hundred Chinese investments in the United Kingdom, and over fifty Chinese companies listed on the London Stock Exchange.

Since China's entry into the World Trade Organization in 2001, most of the bilateral trade issues have been delegated to the European Union, with such issues as market access, the trade deficit, and quality standards addressed there. The United Kingdom has been successful at attracting Chinese students (about 70,000 by 2006) and Chinese tourists (about 125,000 per year). Britain has four diplomatic posts in China—in Beijing, Shanghai, Chongqing, and Guangdong. Increasing numbers of British universities are also offering courses in Mandarin Chinese, expanding an academic field opened up by Cambridge and Oxford in the late nineteenth century. These many ties are strengthened by a significant Chinese diaspora. Approximately 200,000 British citizens of ethnic Chinese descent live in the United Kingdom, many of them originally from Hong Kong or Guangzhou.

SEE ALSO *Hong Kong.*

BIBLIOGRAPHY

Bickers, Robert A., ed. *Ritual and Diplomacy: The Macartney Mission to China, 1792–1794.* London: Wellsweep, 1993.

Brown, Kerry. *The Rise of the Dragon: Inward and Outward Investment in China in the Reform Period, 1978–2007.* Oxford, U.K.: Chandos, 2008.

Cradock, Percy. *Experiences of China.* London: Murray, 1994.

Hoare, J. E. *Embassies of the East: The Story of the British and Their Embassies in China, Japan, and Korea from 1859 to the Present.* London: RoutledgeCurzon, 1999.

Macartney, Lord. *An Embassy to China: Being the Journal Kept by Lord Macartney during His Embassy to the Emperor Ch'ien-lung, 1793–1794,* ed. J. L. Cranmer-Byng. London: Longmans, 1962.

Martin, Michael F. *Hong Kong: Ten Years after the Handover.* Congressional Research Service, Report for Congress, June 29, 2007.

Kerry Brown

UNITED NATIONS DEVELOPMENT PROGRAM (UNDP) HUMAN DEVELOPMENT REPORT ON CHINA, 2005

SEE *Economic Development: UNDP Human Development Report on China, 2005.*

UNITED STATES, RELATIONS WITH

The first visit to China of a U.S. ship, the *Empress of China* in 1784, marked the beginning of Sino-American trade relations. Since then, relations between China and the United States have undergone many changes, in mutual attitude and in levels of involvement, politically and economically. Americans dreamt of opening the "China market" and firmly establishing a presence in Asia. China's response reflected its long struggle to attain national independence and reestablish territorial integrity after decades of national humiliation. When the People's Republic of China (PRC) was founded in 1949, the hopes for a China fully open to economic and political relations with the United States seemed to disappear.

EARLY MUTUAL DISTRUST AND WAR, 1949–1955

Well into 1949, the United States maintained its involvement in the civil war between the Chinese Communist Party (CCP) of Mao Zedong and the government of the Nationalist Party (Guomindang, or GMD) led by Chiang Kai-shek. Ultimately, Chiang's regime was too corrupt and incompetent to maintain power, and in defeat it retreated to the island of Taiwan, thereby continuing the civil war. The United States followed an interim policy of withholding quick recognition of the PRC. This did not last, however, and soon the United States withdrew from China since it did not wish to recognize the new "communist" government. From this point to 1971, the only China that the United States recognized was the Republic of China in exile on Taiwan.

The PRC signed a mutual friendship treaty with the Soviet Union in February 1950, thereby "leaning to one side" in the Cold War struggle between international communism and the "Free World." China's policy on the United States was unclear until June 1950, when North Korea invaded South Korea. This prompted U.S. president Harry S. Truman (1884–1972) to reverse efforts to extricate the United States from China's continuing civil war; instead, he sent the U.S. Seventh Fleet into the Taiwan Strait to prevent a possible PRC attack on Taiwan.

As a result of its military involvement in the Korean War, China was branded an "aggressor nation" by the United Nations (UN). The United States then took a stronger stand against recognition of the PRC, using the UN's rhetoric as a pretext for extending full diplomatic relations and economic and military aid to the Republic of China (ROC), or Taiwan. In February 1955 Congress eventually ratified a mutual defense treaty between the ROC and the United States.

LEARNING TO "RECOGNIZE" CHINA, 1954–1972

The first diplomatic setting in which the United States and the PRC were major participants was the Geneva Conference of 1954. The PRC played an important role in getting Ho Chi Minh's forces to accept partial victory in Vietnam, demonstrating to the world China's potential as an international actor. In 1955 ambassadorial-level talks began between the United States and the PRC in Geneva. These continued for years in Warsaw.

Taiwan was the central obstacle in any improvement of relations. The United States had major military bases there, and was providing economic and military aid. In 1958 the PRC began intermittently shelling the offshore islands of Quemoy (Jinmen) and Matsu (Mazu), heightening the tension every once in a while. This is where things stood until the election of Richard Nixon (1913–1994) to the U.S. presidency in 1968.

President Nixon and his national security adviser, Henry Kissinger (b. 1923), set out to improve relations with the PRC in order to put further pressure on the Soviet Union in the context of the long-running Sino-Soviet split, and, perhaps more important, to seek China's aid in pressuring North Vietnam to negotiate an end to the Vietnam War. In July 1971 Nixon was invited to visit China. In October 1971 the United States no longer opposed PRC entry into the UN; this shift led to the departure of the ROC from the UN. In February 1972 the world watched as Nixon shook hands with Premier Zhou Enlai and Chairman Mao Zedong, turning a new page on U.S.-China relations. The Shanghai Communiqué that came out of their meetings established a U.S. position favoring a "One-China" policy. That would be the cornerstone of improved China-U.S. relations going forward.

THE TWISTED PATH TO NORMALIZATION, 1973–1979

Liaison offices were established in Beijing and Washington. Exchanges between the United States and the PRC increased, but the push for more formal relations lost its momentum. The Nixon administration was hamstrung by the Watergate scandal at home. Then, with the deaths of Premier Zhou Enlai and Chairman Mao in 1976, succession issues in China hampered progress. Trade actually declined from 1974 to 1976. China also was concerned about the Ford administration's moves toward détente with the Soviet Union and how that might affect its own relationship with the United States. And there was lack of clarity over what role the United States would play in Asia after its defeat in Vietnam in 1975.

A new administration under President Jimmy Carter (b. 1924) in 1977 reaffirmed the goal of normalizing relations with the PRC. The United States had to deal with Vice Premier Deng Xiaoping, then the major figure at the center of China's day-to-day affairs though he was not "officially" in charge of PRC affairs. Deng was not chairman of the CCP, nor was he premier of the State Council or president of the PRC. He had a base of support, however, due to his revolutionary history and his having survived the Cultural Revolution and the Gang of Four's attempts to remove him in 1976. In December 1978 Deng put the PRC on the road to major economic reforms, setting the framework for an ambitious policy of opening China to the outside world. The United States welcomed the changes and was ready to fully take part. The U.S.-PRC relationship now had economic as well as political and geostrategic elements, and both sides assumed they would benefit in the long term.

U.S. negotiators found Deng difficult, especially over the issue of Taiwan. After many months of secret negotiations and mutual recognition of the need for a "peaceful reunification" between the PRC and the ROC, the deadlock was broken. On December 15, 1978, President Carter announced the establishment of diplomatic relations between the United States and the PRC as of January 1, 1979. This resulted in an official state visit by Deng Xiaoping to the United States, the first "official" visit, though Deng had spoken before the UN in 1974. Television coverage of Deng wearing a cowboy hat at a Texas rodeo signaled a new day in U.S.-China relations.

RELATIONS IN THE PERIOD OF REFORM, 1979–1989

In the first year of this new relationship, many things happened very quickly. Consular offices were opened in major cities. The U.S. Congress, protesting the new friendship with the PRC, passed the Taiwan Relations Act specifying future U.S. obligations to the island and establishing the American Institute in Taiwan (AIT) to handle future relations and serve as an unofficial "embassy" on Taiwan. A trade pact was signed between the United States and the PRC, and the United States offered $2 billion in Export-Import Bank credits over a five-year period. This first year also saw a series of cultural agreements signed between the two countries.

After the Soviet Union invaded Afghanistan in December 1979, China and the United States agreed to take mutual actions to counter Soviet influence around the world. Some saw this relationship as approaching the status of an alliance. During this period, Congress also approved a U.S.-PRC trade agreement that granted China most-favored-nation (MFN) treatment. China could purchase air-defense radar, helicopters, and transport planes, and U.S. companies were authorized to build electronics and helicopter plants in China. At the same time, however, China vigorously protested the United States' continued sale of defensive military equipment to Taiwan.

The 1980 presidential election brought the Taiwan issue to the fore again. Ronald Reagan (1911–2004) angered the PRC with his campaign promise that he would restore official relations with Taiwan. After his inauguration, and following a wave of protests and denunciations from Beijing, President Reagan backtracked on the issue and announced that he would honor the agreements made at the time of normalization. By August 17, 1982, the PRC and the United States had come up with a new joint communiqué in which the PRC confirmed that "peaceful reunification" with Taiwan was its fundamental policy, and the United States pledged not to increase its arms sales to Taiwan, either in quantity or quality.

In large part, the relationship continued on this way for the next seven years. There were more economic agreements between China and the United States, always with some tension regarding Taiwan and the continued U.S. arms sales there. PRC leaders protested, but there was no serious break in the fundamental relationship. Sometimes human rights issues came up, but mutual economic interests always prevailed. This changed drastically with the events at Tiananmen Square in early 1989.

NEW TENSIONS, 1989–2001

Prior to the Tiananmen Square incident in June 1989, tensions with the United States centered mainly on the Taiwan issue: As long as that was managed, even precariously, relations moved forward. After June 4, 1989, when the Chinese military violently crushed the Tiananmen prodemocracy protests, this could no longer be the case.

President George H. W. Bush (b. 1924), a self-avowed friend of China and former chief of the U.S. Liaison Office under President Ford, had to show solidarity with the prodemocracy movement. All high-level official exchanges with the PRC were cancelled; weapons exports were suspended; trade and investment programs were cancelled; and the U.S. Congress legislated serious sanctions against the PRC. With the new focus on human rights, the United States took the lead in getting Western countries to push for greater political reforms in China.

The United States and China never looked at their relationship in the same way again. China did the United States a favor in 1991 when it did not veto UN Resolution 687 on the use of force to remove Saddam Hussein from Kuwait, and this somewhat softened tensions. But mutual distrust had become the core of the relationship. The U.S. Congress continued to hold up any significant improvement of economic relations between the two countries, and there were annual debates over whether or not to grant most favored nation status to the PRC.

Chinese fighter jet flying near a U.S. spy plane, January 30, 2001. *Diplomatic relations between the United States and the People's Republic of China became tense after the midair collision of an American surveillance plane and a Chinese F-8 fighter jet. While the Chinese pilot perished in the accident, the crew of the U.S. plane landed safely on the island of Hainan and were detained for two weeks before the U.S. government secured their release.* © **REUTERS/CORBIS**

When President Bill Clinton (b. 1946) was elected in 1992, the United States and China seemed ready to resume a more expansive and active relationship, with both sides willing to consider better relations after the disenchantment that set in following Tiananmen in 1989, though the arguments over improved economic relations continued. There was growing pressure from a new "China lobby" led by U.S. business interests fearful they would be left behind by the PRC's massive growth. Annual growth rates in China were in the range of 12 to 13 percent. The argument that "engagement" with China—including better economic relations—would eventually have a beneficial effect on human rights there became the basis for an improved relationship. Eventually, by 2000, China was granted permanent normal trading relations (PNTR) status, which eventually led to its entry into the World Trade Organization (WTO) in 2001.

Taiwan was still an obstacle, however. In 1996, just before the first democratic elections for president of the ROC on Taiwan, the PRC conducted military exercises in the Taiwan Strait. The message was clear: Any election in Taiwan that might result in a proindependence government

would be a threat to China's territorial integrity. President Clinton ordered two carrier groups to the Taiwan Strait. The ROC's president Lee Teng-hui (Li Denghui, b. 1923), who was also chairman of the GMD, made it clear that he was not interested in promoting independence from China. In March 2000 Chen Shui-bian (b. 1950), the leader of the proindependence Democratic Progressive Party (DPP), was elected president of Taiwan. Tensions rose again.

In 1999 and early 2001 two more incidents strained U.S.-PRC relations. During Operation Allied Force in the former Yugoslavia in May 1999, NATO bombs struck the Chinese embassy in Belgrade, killing three Chinese citizens. Huge demonstrations against the United States took place in major cities across China. Eventually, the United States agreed to make financial reparations to the families of those who died and those who were injured. A strong sense of Chinese nationalism was rising.

In April 2001 a U.S. spy plane collided with a PRC jet fighter near the PRC island province of Hainan, resulting in the loss of the Chinese plane and its pilot. The national anger that had erupted during the Belgrade episode again spread across the country. The crew of the U.S. spy plane was held by China for nearly two weeks, inflaming passions in the United States and provoking calls for military action. The notion of a "China threat" began to attain a wider audience.

U.S.-PRC RELATIONS SINCE 9/11

China's international prestige rose when in July 2001 it was announced that Beijing would host the 2008 Olympics. Human rights and the status of Taiwan continued to be points of tension with the United States, but the terrorist attacks of September 11, 2001, pushed these issues aside temporarily. Both countries recognized the need for PRC-U.S. cooperation to counter terrorism. Fears of a "China threat" subsided. However, the U.S. decision to go to war with Iraq in 2003 was not fully supported by China, though it had accepted the U.S. campaign in Afghanistan after 9/11.

North Korea and its nuclear program became a major security issue for the United States, which felt that China was not doing enough to restrain its ally. Ultimately, China showed that it could use its influence in a positive way. Because the North Korean regime needed support from the PRC, given its isolation from much of the rest of the world, Chinese leaders were able to play a significant role in defusing the conflict between the United States and North Korea over nuclear weapons. Of course, China expected the United States to show its thanks with better economic relations and continuing support for the PRC position on the question of Taiwan.

China's military spending has long been a concern for the United States, especially as it relates to the continuing issue of Taiwan's security. The PRC's anti-satellite test in 2007 raised fears of a potential connection with cyberwar tactics in the new era of asymmetrical warfare. Rumblings of the "China threat" resurfaced.

The significant trade imbalance between the United States and the PRC, which has hovered around $200 billion since 2005, added more strain. Compounding this, at the end of 2007 product safety became big news when it was discovered that toys imported to the United States from China were unsafe because they contained lead paint. This opened anew the confluence of issues concerning overall trade imbalance, quality control, trade subsidies, currency valuation, and the fact that China holds a large portion of the U.S. national debt. In late 2008 it was estimated that China held nearly $600 billion in U.S. Treasury bonds.

Human rights came to center stage again with China's harsh repression of protests in Tibet in March 2008 and in connection with the 2008 Olympics. On its traditional pre-Olympics journey around the world, the Olympic torch was met by protests and counter protests. The Western media's criticisms of China's actions in Tibet brought strong denunciations from PRC leaders and from Chinese all over the world. This raised the specter of an increasingly militant Chinese nationalism and greater tension between the PRC and the United States.

Finally, there may have been an unwelcome echo in Taiwan when, after eight years of rule by the Democratic Progressive Party, political power was returned to the GMD under Ma Ying-jeou (Ma Yingjiu, b. 1950) in March 2008. In fact, it was reported that the turnover prompted a great sigh of relief among U.S. policy makers because they believed that the GMD would help ease the tension between Taiwan and China. After all, calm in the Taiwan Strait has been a core concern of U.S.-China policy since its beginning.

SEE ALSO *Foreign Policy Frameworks and Theories: One-China Policy and "One Country, Two Systems"; Snow, Edgar.*

BIBLIOGRAPHY

Cohen, Warren I. *America's Response to China: A History of Sino-American Relations.* 4th ed. New York: Columbia University Press, 2000.

Dumbaugh, Kerry. *China-U.S. Relations: Current Issues and Implications for U.S. Policy.* Washington, DC: Congressional Research Service, 2008.

Greis, Peter Hays. *China's New Nationalism: Pride, Politics, and Diplomacy.* Berkeley: University of California Press, 2004.

Han, Nailong, ed. *Diplomacy of Contemporary China.* Hong Kong: New Horizon Press, 1990.

Macmillan, Margaret. *Nixon and Mao: The Week That Changed the World.* New York: Random House, 2007.

McCormick, Thomas J. *China Market: America's Quest for Informal Empire, 1893–1901.* Chicago: Quadrangle Books, 1967.

National Intelligence Council. *Tracking the Dragon: National Intelligence Estimates on China During the Era of Mao, 1948–1976.* Washington, DC: National Intelligence Council, 2004.

Peck, James. *Washington's China: The National Security World, the Cold War, and the Origins of Globalism.* Amherst: University of Massachusetts Press, 2006.

Joseph T. Miller

URBAN CHINA

This entry contains the following:

OVERVIEW

In the nineteenth and early twentieth centuries, China was an agriculture-based country with small-scale home industries and little industrialization and urbanization. While late-Qing officials boasted of two thousand walled cities and towns, these served as centers of governance and administration, sites of cultural activity, and market centers for rural hinterlands, as well as entrepôts for long-distance interregional trade. Beginning in the mid-nineteenth century, a small number of treaty ports was established, influenced in design and cultural activities by the West. Although a few of these cities were large by world standards, they encompassed only a very small proportion of the total population. The fall of the Qing dynasty, the rise of the Republic, the Japanese invasion, and the civil war marked a long interval of continued low urbanization, as did the triumph of Mao Zedong in 1949. While the 1950s experienced rapid urban population growth as part of the "big-push" investment in heavy industry under the First Five-Year Plan, the following twenty years saw the overall level of urbanization decline, with the famine of the early 1960s and the Cultural Revolution (1966–1969).

Apart from intense industrialization of cities, two key features marked urban China during the Maoist period. First, China developed an extraordinary rural-urban social and economic divide, which persists in some dimensions today. In 1978, at the dawn of reform era, the countryside was almost exclusively agricultural, with little of the rural industry typically found in other countries. State economic and social policies sharply curtailed rural-urban interaction and the traditional role of cities as regional market centers. Population movements were very limited and tightly regulated by the household-registration or *hukou* system. Urban per capita consumption was at least double that of the rural sector.

Second, Chinese cities were structured very differently than cities in much of the rest of the world. Service activities, including retailing, restaurants, and personal and business services, were at a minimum. Cities were dreary production machines, with workers housed near their workplace in tiny state-provided concrete walkup apartments or rundown, crowded traditional courtyards. Urban infrastructure, including road development, parks, and cultural activities, was neglected.

Starting in the late 1980s, Chinese cities transformed rapidly to emerge in function and appearance more like cities in other countries. Urban social life resumed with the rapid growth of retail outlets, cultural activities, restaurants, and personal services. Reforms in planning and land and housing markets had dramatic effects; per person urban consumption of space quadrupled within twenty years. Cities developed highway systems and transit, and population and industry deconcentrated to suburban areas. Housing built in the Maoist period was torn down to be replaced by modern condominiums separate from the workplace. Traditional courtyard neighborhoods were sometimes gentrified, but often they were bulldozed to make way for the modern city. The biggest cities invested heavily in statement architecture and urban design on a world scale.

In the reform era, Chinese cities and towns experienced strong population growth as migration restrictions deriving from the *hukou* system were relaxed in stages, inducing rural-to-urban in-migration. With population and economic growth, Chinese cities increasingly face the social problems of poor environmental quality, congestion, urban slums, and high levels of inequality that plague cities in many developing countries. Despite relaxations, China is still marked by a continued institutional rural-urban divide, with urban versus rural *hukou* status dividing the population socially and economically. This plays out in cities. While, under relaxed migration, one-third of the urban workforce in 2000 had rural *hukou*, these migrants are denied citizenship rights in larger cities. They are forced to live separately from urban residents, increasingly in informal settlements that are essentially urban slums. They have few effective rights for their children to attend state schools and their families to obtain basic social and health benefits. This is a challenge for the future.

SEE ALSO *Treaty Ports.*

BIBLIOGRAPHY

Brandt, Loren, and Thomas Rawski, eds. *China's Great Economic Transformation.* Cambridge, U.K.: Cambridge University Press, 2008.

Chan, Bernard. *New Architecture in China.* New York: Merrell, 2005.

Deng, F. Frederic, and Huang Youqin. Uneven Land Reform and Urban Sprawl in China. *Progress in Planning* 61, 3 (2004): 211–236.

Fujita Masahito, J. Vernon Henderson, Kanemoto Yoshitsugu, and Mori Tomoya. Spatial Distribution of Economic Activities in China and Japan. In *Handbook of Regional and Urban Economics,* Vol. 4: *Cities and Geography,* eds. J. Vernon Henderson and Jacques-François Thisse, 2911–2977. New York: North-Holland, 2004.

Henderson, J. Vernon. *Urban Development: Theory, Fact, and Illusion,* chap. 11. New York: Oxford University Press, 1988.

Kwong, Julia. Educating Migrant Children: Negotiations between the State and Civil Society. *China Quarterly* 180 (2004): 1073–1088.

Logan, John R., ed. *Urban China in Transition.* Malden, MA: Blackwell, 2007.

Lyons, Thomas. P. *Economic Integration and Planning in Maoist China.* New York: Columbia University Press, 1987.

Naughton, Barry J. *The Chinese Economy: Transitions and Growth.* Cambridge, MA: MIT Press, 2007.

Oi, Jean C. Reform and Urban Bias in China. *Journal of Development Studies* 29, 4 (1993): 129–148.

Paine, Suzanne. Spatial Aspects of Chinese Development: Issues, Outcomes, and Policies, 1949–1979. *Journal of Development Studies* 17 (1981): 132–195.

Perkins, Dwight. Completing China's Move to the Market. *Journal of Economic Perspectives* 8, 2 (1994): 23–46.

Ruan Xing and Patrick Bingham-Hall. *New China Architecture.* Singapore: Periplus, 2006.

World Bank, East Asia and Pacific Regional Office. *China: Socialist Economic Development.* Washington, DC: Author, 1982.

J. Vernon Henderson

ORGANIZING PRINCIPLES OF CITIES

The Chinese word for city (*chengshi*) literally means "walled market" or "wall and market." Used in English-language scholarship, the term formerly referred to the walled capitals of administrative divisions (provinces, prefectures, departments, and counties) that pertained under the imperial system of government. Some towns (*zhen*, i.e., noncapitals), located at strategically sensitive spots, also had walls, but are not referred to as *cities* in English-language writings on China because they lacked an allotted place in the field administration. By the end of the twentieth century, the walls of nearly all settlements had disappeared, with one or two exceptions, and administrative structures had changed. In consequence, the term *city* is difficult to apply with consistency over time. According to the 2007 Urban Development Report of China, China in that year had 656 cities (actually municipalities), which accounted for 45 percent of the population. In 1800, by contrast, there were more than 1,300 cities (i.e., walled capitals), although the total urbanization rate did not exceed 5 or 6 percent.

Most nineteenth-century walled cities were physically no more than a few hundred years old, although the sites may have been occupied for many more centuries again. In other words, the walls and probably most of the dwellings within the walls dated from the Ming dynasty (1368–1644) or later. The shape of the walls was square or rectangular in the case of northern cities, tending toward circular or irregular in the south, depending on the lie of the land and whether or not the walls had been added to a preexisting settlement. In cities of regular dimensions (square, rectangular, or circular), it was common to have four main gates, one for each of the cardinal directions, and for opposite gates to be linked by a straight thoroughfare. The favored orientation, both for the city as a whole and for important buildings within it, was south. The underlying principle of urban design was cosmological. The main canonical reference for urban planners in imperial China was a chapter in the *Rites of Zhou* (*Zhou li*), a work to which dynastic founders and their advisers over a period of around two millennia were likely to refer when building or reconstructing a capital city.

The area enclosed by the walls varied according to the position of the city in the administrative hierarchy. A county city was likely to be smaller than a prefectural city, which in turn was usually smaller than a provincial capital. The area within the walls of Beijing was around 25 square miles. The walls of Pingyao County in Shanxi Province, which are still intact, enclose an area of less than 2 square miles. Occasionally, a city low in the hierarchy grew unusually large due to market forces, and a wall was added to protect the populous city suburb, thus effectively extending the intramural area. Walls demarcated the city from the surrounding countryside, and were a visual reminder of the power and authority of the imperial government. In an influential article, Frederick Mote (1922–2005) emphasized the lack of a distinctive urban style to the built environment of Chinese towns, arguing in essence for an urban-rural continuum (Mote 1977). This position has yet to be pointedly rebutted, but is not supported by more recent research (e.g., Gaubatz 1996) and should be cited with caution.

The spatial organization of the city was binuclear. Typically, the busy commercial center of a city was separate from the administrative center. The latter was defined principally by the yamen or official quarters of the magistrate or prefect, together with the temple to the city god, where the magistrate performed rites to ensure the smooth management of administration, and the school-temple, which was a temple to Confucius as the patron of literacy. The commercial quarter included the residences of merchants, as well as their shops, together with temples, guild or native-place halls (*huiguan*), restaurants, and a variety of other commercial institutions. Shops were clustered according to the nature of the trade, a practice arising from tax arrangements. The open shop-fronts typical in southern cities presented passersby with dazzling displays of goods.

REFORMED CITIES OF THE REPUBLICAN ERA

Parks, public gardens, plazas, and other sorts of space where people might assemble freely were largely lacking in cities before the early twentieth century, although some of the

City Wall of Xi'an, Shaanxi province, China, October 3, 2005. *With a rapid expansion of the economy in the late 1900s, many large cities in China struggle to preserve ancient structures amid a need for more housing, factories, and office space.* © **LIU LIQUN/CORBIS**

functions of such spaces were served by marketplaces, tea-houses, temples, and incidentally vacant land. The reformed or "improved" (*gailiang*) city of the early Republic incorporated these features, which were seen as a mark of civilization (*wenming*) and progress (*jinhua*). In Beijing, for example, former imperial gardens and temple grounds were transformed into public parks during the Republican era. Public schools, libraries, and museums were other institutions where people from all quarters of a given town might rub shoulders, even if in most cases, including parks, entry fees were usually charged. In Guangzhou and Shanghai, department stores and cinemas emerged as major examples of private enterprise leading to the same end.

The copybook example of urban modernization is Nantong, a city in eastern Jiangsu, on the north side of the Yangzi River. The hometown of one of China's leading early industrialists, Zhang Jian (1853–1926), Nantong was remolded under his direction into a model of Chinese industrial modernity, complete with factories, modern schools, a public clock tower, a museum, a public library, newspapers, and

film companies. By the 1930s, various combinations of these institutions were to be found in many major centers, attesting to the widespread aspirations of local elites to modernize their hometowns. Most of these modernizers were inspired by the foreign concessions in Shanghai, where high-rise buildings, wide roads, mechanized transport, street lighting, running water, and a sewage system set the benchmark for urban "civilization."

"OLD CITIES OVERHAULED"

In 1949 the newly installed Communist government declared Beijing the capital of the People's Republic of China (PRC) and launched a new set of urban reform measures. Some of these measures, such as slum clearance and new residential housing, duplicated the Nationalists' efforts under new names. The demolition of city walls, again commenced in the Nationalist era, proceeded apace across the country. Soviet advisers presented the new government with urban plans that placed administration at the city center, and replaced old residential areas with integrated industrial work-residential complexes, which became the familiar *danwei* (work units), a hallmark of urban organization in the Mao years. In Beijing, these developments were accompanied by the enlargement of Tiananmen Square, permitting the massive rallies with which the square is now indelibly associated. This impressive center belied the segmented character of the city, which was a product of the *danwei* system. Envisaged as productive centers of industry filled with workers, cities in Mao's New China lost many of the institutions that had once defined them, including sites of leisure such as teahouses, restaurants, cinemas, and luxury retail outlets. Commerce, to the extent that it was countenanced, failed to keep pace with the growth of the urban population.

One of the consequences of urban planning in the twentieth century was the destruction of old towns right across the face of China. Each new regime yielded new urban forms. From a patchwork of walled cities and market towns with their one- and two-storied houses and shops lining narrow laneways, urban China was transformed over the course of a century into so many plantations of five-storied apartment blocks, factories, and state-owned stores. In the PRC, the phrase *jiu cheng gai zao* (old cities overhauled) became, and largely continues to be, the guiding principle of urban development. In Beijing, an alternative vision of urban change was early articulated by Liang Sicheng (1901–1972) and his collaborator Chen Zhanxiang (1916–2001) but failed to win favor. Neglect and poverty rather than planning led to the survival of some old cities or parts thereof. In Shanxi Province, a few walled cities remained intact until the 1980s. Little of this built heritage was to survive the reform era.

SEE ALSO *Gardens and Parks; Special Economic Zones; Treaty Ports.*

BIBLIOGRAPHY

Campanella, Thomas J. *The Concrete Dragon: China's Urban Revolution and What It Means for the World.* New York: Princeton Architectural Press, 2008.

Carroll, Peter J. *Between Heaven and Modernity: Reconstructing Suzhou, 1895–1937.* Stanford, CA: Stanford University Press, 2006.

Dong Yue (Madeleine Yue Dong). *Republican Beijing: The City and Its Histories.* Berkeley: University of California Press, 2003.

Gaubatz, Piper Rae. *Beyond the Great Wall: Urban Form and Transformation on the Chinese Frontiers.* Stanford, CA: Stanford University Press, 1996.

Lipkin, Zwia. *Useless to the State: "Social Problems" and Social Engineering in Nationalist Nanjing, 1927–1937.* Cambridge, MA: Harvard University Asia Center, 2006.

Mote, Frederick. The Transformation of Nanjing, 1350–1400. In *The City in Late Imperial China*, ed. G. W. Skinner, 101–154. Stanford, CA: Stanford University Press, 1977.

Qin Shao. *Culturing Modernity: The Nantong Model, 1890–1930.* Stanford, CA: Stanford University Press, 2004.

Skinner, G. W., ed. *The City in Late Imperial China.* Stanford, CA: Stanford University Press, 1977.

Tsin, Michael. *Nation, Governance, and Modernity in China: Canton, 1900–1927.* Stanford, CA: Stanford University Press, 1999.

Yang Dongping. *Chengshi jifeng: Beijing he Shanghai de wenhua jingshen* [City monsoons: The cultural spirit of Beijing and Shanghai]. Beijing: Xinxing chubanshe, 2005.

Antonia Finnane

CITIES AND URBANIZATION, 1800–1949

Urbanization is the process of spatial differentiation of a population between town and country. It is usually described as an outcome of market forces. This might seem counterintuitive in the case of Qing China, an agrarian empire where the administrative functions of the walled town appear to have had a formative influence on the pattern of urban development. Market forces, however, are central to the influential model of Chinese urbanization developed by the American anthropologist G. William Skinner (1925–2008), as described below.

THE SKINNERIAN MODEL

In a series of studies first published in 1977, supported by ongoing research till the time of his death in 2008, Skinner drew on central-place theory to account for the pattern of Chinese urbanization as revealed in nineteenth-century data. Central-place theory predicts that in a given urban system organized on flat terrain, the logic of communications will yield a hierarchy of urban, service-providing places, spatially organized in a concentric pattern, yielding an even distribution of a few large, many medium, and multiple smaller central places. In the Skinnerian application, physiographic features such as mountains and bodies of water help shape the actual configuration because of the way such features impede or facilitate communications.

The driving force behind urbanization in this agrarian empire (although not the only variable) was the commercialization of agriculture, leading to the proliferation of market towns in response to cash-cropping, cottage industry, and regional specialization. Skinner found that the pattern of urbanization over China as a whole did not suggest an integrated economy. Rather, China (excluding the far West and the Northeast) could be divided into eight regions, which he termed *macroregions*. The most heavily urbanized were those covering southeast China, from the Lower Yangzi Delta, down the coast to the border of Vietnam. Yun-Gui (incorporating much of Yunnan and Guizhou provinces) was the least urbanized.

A street scene from Guangzhou, China, c. 1880. *At the beginning of the nineteenth century, the vast majority of the Chinese population lived in rural settings, primarily engaged in agricultural pursuits. However, as trade with the West increased after the Opium Wars, some Chinese migrated to the newly-prosperous port cities, though large scale urbanization would not occur in China until the late twentieth century.* © MICHAEL MASLAN HISTORIC PHOTOGRAPHS/CORBIS

Around 1843—that is, before the impact of the Opium War (1839–1842) could be manifested—there were around 292 cities of 10,000 or more residents across the eight regions. The largest cities in the empire, with populations of above half a million, were also major centers of government: Beijing, the imperial capital; Guangzhou, the provincial capital of Guangdong and the designated port for foreign trade; Suzhou, the provincial capital of Jiangsu and the major entrepôt in the Lower Yangzi Delta; and Wuhan (incorporating Wuchang, Hancheng, and Hankou) in the middle reaches of the Yangzi. Skinner explained the governmental factor as a case of the bureaucratic apparatus being attuned to the natural economic order, and its operations to some extent as influencing that order.

Whatever the merits of that view, most substantial towns were seats of government. In official records it is often difficult to distinguish these seats of government from the areas under their jurisdiction. The names by which cities were known were county or prefectural names: Unlike a market town, an administrative town did not have a highly specific place name.

THE POLITICAL ECONOMY OF URBANIZATION

In a critique of the Skinnerian model, anthropologist Hill Gates describes urbanization, or the movement of people into cities, as "essential to the operation of China's political economy" (Gates 1996, p. 63). Gates sees a *tributary mode of production* (TMP) in China as coexisting with a *petty capitalist mode of production* (PCMP), the two serving as "China's motor," and the interplay between them as shaping urbanization in China. Where "Skinner sees administration," Gates is inclined to see "tributary political economy," that is, the organized extraction of surplus by the political class from the producers (Gates, p. 69).

Analyzing urbanization in China from this perspective, she notes the low commercial importance of cities (i.e., county capitals) across the North China Plain; the contrasting high level of commercial importance of urban centers in the Lower Yangzi, where there were too many towns for all to be county capitals; and above all "the near-absence of cities on the nineteenth-century northern coast" in consequence of TMP-based interventions in the natural environment (Gates, p. 72). These three features draw attention in different ways to what Gates views as an ongoing "struggle between a hegemonic TMP and a structurally more dynamic PCMP" (Gates, p. 78). In essence, while Skinner downplayed the role of the state in urbanization, Gates keeps it firmly in view.

THE CHANGING FACE OF URBAN CHINA

Regionally, and within China as a whole, the Opium Wars of the nineteenth century and a series of internal rebellions had a pronounced impact on the pattern of urbanization in China. Massive population loss, the destruction of many significant cities, the establishment of the treaty ports, and the growth of foreign trade skewed urban growth toward the expansion of a few large cities on the coast. The most obvious example is Shanghai, a county capital that became a treaty port by virtue of the Treaty of Nanjing (1842), experienced massive population growth during the Taiping Uprising (1851–1864), and in the second half of the nineteenth century supplanted nearby Suzhou as China's leading commercial city. In the south, Guangzhou, another treaty port, lost out to Shanghai when it ceased to be the sole designated port of foreign trade. But Guangzhou enjoyed dynamic relations with the emerging city of Hong Kong, which was established as a British colony 1842, and in the longer term was a major determinant of intensive urbanization on the Guangdong coast.

The growth of treaty-port cities, especially on the coast, was matched by the decline of many inland cities in consequence of changing patterns of trade and modes of transport. Steamer shipping along the coast and the Yangzi diverted trade from lesser inland waterways. The decline of the Grand Canal, China's main north-south waterway, led to the decline also of a number of significant towns along its route, especially in northern Jiangsu and Shandong. Rural migrants bypassed once-prosperous towns—Jining, Yangzhou—for Shanghai. Treaty-port status alone, however, did not determine a city's fortunes. Ningbo, one of Qing China's great centers of commercial activity, was adversely affected by the rise of Shanghai. Ningbonese merchants shifted their capital, and often their families as well, to the new center of action, joining their Cantonese counterparts to become Shanghai's new elite.

Skinner calculated that circa 1893 there were over forty thousand "central places" in China, of which nearly two-thirds were standard market towns with hinterlands of between fifteen and thirty villages. The overall urbanization rate in his estimate was around 6 percent. In the first half of the twentieth century, the urbanization rate may not have changed greatly. Although there is some evidence of overall economic improvement up to the time of World War II (1937–1945), especially during the Nanjing decade (1927–1937), political instability meant that population movements between town and country were unsteady and unpredictable. In the 1930s, the agricultural economist John Lossing Buck (1890–1975) gave an urbanization rate of 21 percent for China as a whole, but this untenably high figure resulted from the weighting of his sample toward highly urbanized counties. While some individual cities grew enormously, so did the rural population.

TOWN AND COUNTRY IN THE REPUBLICAN ERA

During the Republican era, the relationship between town and country changed in a number of respects. First, the technological gap between urban and rural areas changed, particularly on the coast, as industrialization brought major changes to daily life, including in sources of energy, communications, and working environments. Sanitation facilities, utilities, running water, macadamized roads, and mechanized transport transformed city life. Factories attracted labor from the countryside. Work opportunities for women, especially in spinning mills, lowered the gender ratio in urban environments, where the number of men had once been overwhelmingly superior.

Second, the range and scale of urban services grew. Education is an obvious example. The small private schools and academies that served the old education system, designed to prepare candidates for the civil service examination, gave way to an extensive, mixed education system providing for students of both sexes from primary school to university. Boys who were once taught by tutors at home were sent in growing numbers to boarding schools and colleges in capital cities, and their sisters were soon following suit.

Third, a cultural gap opened up between town and country. Biographical materials suggest that modern education contributed to an urban-rural gulf that graduates found difficult to bridge. In particular, quarrels over arranged marriages and the many documented cases of young men abandoning their village wives in favor of companionate alliances with educated girls show new value systems being produced by life in China's modern cities.

Local government is another area of obvious change in urban-rural relations. Under the old regime, the jurisdictions of town-based officials of the field administration (*difang guanyuan*) invariably extended beyond the urban area to the limits of the country, department, or prefecture of which the city was capital. Prefectural seats, moreover, were sometimes divided into two counties, with administration of the urban area devolving to two different county magistrates, not necessarily in communication with each other. This was even more common among provincial capitals. Under the Qing, Suzhou had three county magistrates, while Beijing was "simultaneously under the jurisdiction of the Capital City, Daxing and Wanping Counties, and Shuntian Prefecture" (Dong 2003, p. 46).

In the Republican era, a new perception of the city as a social and economic unit resulted in experiments with municipal government, moving Chinese administrative practices into closer accordance with international trends. Particularly worth noting is the historically unprecedented recognition of an urban area as a discrete administrative unit, separate from the surrounding countryside. This commenced with Guangzhou in the 1920s, initially in connection with plans for self-government. Although self-government was not realized, a sequence of administrative adjustments under the Nationalists left the designation *Guangzhoushi* (Guangzhou city) intact. Among these adjustments was the creation of a category of special cities (*tebieshi*), anticipating the system of independent municipalities (Beijingshi, Shanghaishi, Tianjinshi, Chongqingshi) in the People's Republic of China.

Changes in local government in the Republican era also signified ambivalence as to the proper place of cities in relationship both to the center and to the countryside. The Anti-Japanese War (1937–1945) and succeeding civil war prevented these relationships from being clarified and stabilized under the Nationalists. The Nationalist government may even have curtailed urban growth through taxation measures unfavorable to the growth of manufacturing and trade. Yet given the combination of internal conflict, Japanese aggression, and the Great Depression, growth of appreciable dimensions in this period was anyway unlikely. During the Anti-Japanese War, the most obvious changes in the urban sector nationally involved Kunming and Chongqing, inland cities that experienced a population explosion as a consequence of the wartime relocation of government and educational institutions. After the war, this population movement was reversed, but there was virtually no time for the major urban centers to stabilize before the country was plunged into civil war that would result in an entirely new set of negotiations between town and country.

SEE ALSO *Gardens and Parks; Housing: Housing, 1800–1949; Special Economic Zones; Treaty Ports.*

BIBLIOGRAPHY

Dong, Madeleine Yue. *Republican Beijing: The City and Its Histories.* Berkeley: University of California Press, 2003.

Esherick, Joseph, ed. *Remaking the Chinese City: Modernity and National Identity, 1900–1950.* Honolulu: University of Hawai'i Press, 2002.

Fitzgerald, John. The Province in History. In *Rethinking China's Provinces,* ed. John Fitzgerald, 11–40. London: Routledge, 2002.

Gates, Hill. *China's Motor: A Thousand Years of Petty Capitalism.* Ithaca, NY: Cornell University Press, 1996.

Skinner, G. William, ed. *The City in Late Imperial China.* Stanford, CA: Stanford University Press, 1977.

Antonia Finnane

URBANIZATION SINCE 1949

After the establishment of the People's Republic of China in 1949, the government embarked on a program of collectivization and nationalization of businesses, land, and housing. Under the influence of Soviet advisers, the government in the 1950s also embarked on a program of extensive investment in heavy industries in key cities. Up until the mid-1970s, China continued with episodes of big-push investments in heavy industry in key locations, which strongly influenced the nature of cities in the Maoist period.

The big push of the 1950s was accompanied by a mass movement of people to cities, the urban population growing at a rate of about 8 percent a year in the first ten years. After the failures of the Great Leap Forward and the resulting famine, migration policy changed and a sharp urban-rural divide emerged in various dimensions. From 1960 to 1978, the level of urbanization declined. The establishment of the household-registration, or *hukou*, system in 1958 to regulate migration created a sharp divide of the population and their birthrights along urban and rural lines. The huge rural sector, containing over 80 percent of the population organized in communes, became almost strictly agricultural, with little of the rural industry and services found in other countries. Cities were divorced economically and socially from their hinterlands. Urban residents in 1978 enjoyed over twice the per capita consumption of rural residents, and China's degree of personal-income inequality was at least as great as India's.

Cities in the Maoist period were manufacturing centers organized into units (*danwei*), such as state-owned industrial enterprises. Initial investment favored coastal cities and cities in the resource-rich northwest, with "third front" cities in Sichuan, far from the coast and the Soviet Union. Besides jobs, work units provided housing and basic services for their workers. Economic planning emphasized production at the expense of consumption, with the result that cities had few restaurants, no markets, no shopping centers, few cars, poor urban transport facilities and infrastructure, and no suburbs.

Workers lived either in crowded traditional courtyard housing or in new concrete walk-up apartment buildings, usually next to or forming part of the workplace. Living space was minimal, a little over 3 square meters per person in major cities by 1978. While urban design emphasized a cellular approach organized around work units, with fairly flat density gradients and little commuting, there was some semblance of neighborhoods in cities, with party elites, professionals, managerial personnel, and workers tending to live in different sectors of the city. People's standards of living did vary modestly within cities, but differences were largely invisible, hidden behind compound walls.

Cultural development and urban aesthetics were neglected. The state rejected both the culture of the past (the Four Olds) and western influences ("spiritual pollution"). Cultural activities shrank to praise of the state, elevation of Mao, and indoctrination. Residential neighborhoods were tightly regulated, organized into residential committees, which were the eyes of the party. Residential committees worked with city authorities in regulating crime, birth control, migration, and dissent. Architecture emphasized Soviet-style functionality and large, dreary public venues. Isolated from much of the world, mainland China had no cities serving as windows to the world, places of international cross-fertilization in ideas and culture.

Despite the heavy hand of the national government, economic planning was carried out at the provincial and prefectural levels. There was little interprovincial or even intercity trade. Larger cities, encouraged to be self-sufficient, tended to produce an entire range of economic products. This configuration—weakness of the center and operational strength in the cities—was a continuation of the past and persists today.

CITIES IN THE REFORM PERIOD

Reforms starting in 1978 and continuing through today have radically changed the nature and role of cities. Early reforms were carried out in the rural sector, including development of a vibrant industrial sector consisting of town and village enterprises. From the 1990s, however, cities became the engines of growth. National policy emphasized investment and a shift in fiscal resources toward cities, as well as development of foreign direct investment and special economic zones in cities, all at the expense of the rural sector. Urban production shifted more to consumer-oriented products, markets were reestablished, and shopping centers and a vibrant restaurant sector were developed. After the mid-1990s, reforms emphasized growth of the business and financial-service sectors.

On a national scale, certain features mark China's overall urbanization of the last twenty years. The household-registration system continues to maintain the sharp urban-rural divide. There were 300 million workers in agriculture in 1978, with perhaps 200 million of these 300 million being "surplus workers." Those absolute numbers remain the same today, although there has been substantial growth of the urban population, at a rate of about 4 percent a year. The divide in urban versus rural consumption has only increased, and the rural sector faces declining relative quality of education and other services. Urbanization policy set in place in 1982 intended rural-urban migration to be local, with short-distance moves. Up until the late 1990s, urbanization was accomplished in large part by transforming former rural townships into cities, in-place urbanization, as opposed to urbanization through longer-distance migration to cities. Research suggests that this diffuse urbanization has resulted in many economically undersized cities with insufficient economies of scale. Research also suggests that China remains under-urbanized vis-à-vis its continued surplus agricultural labor force. Yet as the household-registration system has weakened in the last ten years, youth in agriculture have increasingly migrated to the largest cities as soon as they finish high school. In 2000, one-third of urban workers had a rural household registration.

Another feature of national urban policy is that cities operate in a strict administrative hierarchy, with cities at the top of the hierarchy enjoying greater fiscal and investment advantages. There are municipalities, regional-level cities, county-level cities, and township-level cities. This administrative hierarchy also translates into a hierarchy of size and per capita wealth and income. Within the hierarchy, rural-urban migration is much freer at the bottom than at the top. In part, migration restrictions at the top restrain these favored cities from becoming overpopulated megacities.

Reforms within cities have changed urban life. Work units no longer dominate the scene as providers of work and housing. Land and housing markets developed after the late 1980s transformed housing from welfare to a commodity. Almost the entire formal urban-housing market has been transformed into a private "ownership" market (seventy-year leaseholds that can readily be sold). Per capita living space in the cities has more than quadrupled since 1978. With this rapid development, the role of residential committees as the eyes of the state has diminished. Planning and massive investment in urban transport infrastructure and public utilities have hollowed out the crowded city centers. The locations of workplaces and residences have been divorced, and both industry and residences have undergone massive suburbanization. In many cities, much of the housing built during the Maoist period is gone. Pre-Liberation housing in older, traditional neighborhoods has gentrified in some cases or continued to house lower-income urban residents. But in many cases such neighborhoods have been bulldozed to make way for modern buildings. The struggle between preserving and reconstructing old-heritage neighborhoods and tearing down the old to make way for the new plays out with different outcomes in different cities. Underlying that struggle is a process of defining Chinese culture in the modern age and China's image in the world.

A great and visible Chinese accomplishment since the 1990s is China's urban construction: massive building of roadways, transit lines, bridges, apartment, and office buildings. Most visible in the biggest cities are innovative architectural and technology pieces, usually designed by Western architects yet unique nonetheless. Just as the reconstruction of Manhattan in the 1950s was based in part on demonstrating the triumph of America to the world in the Cold War era, the reconstruction of, say, Beijing and Shanghai symbolizes China's entry onto the world stage. The physical transformations are astonishing, making Chinese cities unrecognizable in comparison to the 1990s. With rejection of the Maoist period and ambivalence toward encouraging traditional culture, with political suppression of dissent, control of religion, and censorship and tight regulation of the Internet, commercial cultural development has focused on buildings and venues, rather than on people—artists, writers, performers, and musicians freely expressing themselves.

Similarly, while key Chinese cities struggle to become global cities, lack of reform along certain dimensions limits the possibilities. Global cities are financial, business-service, and headquarter centers. Development of these sectors in urban China is hindered by slow development of the rule of law and slow reforms in the financial sector. Global enterprises must struggle to engage in the social and economic networking system (*guanxi*) and to cultivate party and political contacts to resolve contract disputes.

Policy makers in Chinese cities also struggle under limitations. Mayors are evaluated on their ability as economic managers, not as service providers. In addition, environmental regulation is still in its infancy in China; data suggests that 16 of the 20 most polluted major cities in the world are in China. Another major issue is the presence in the largest cities of a huge disenfranchised underclass, rural migrants. In the largest cities, migrants live in dorms or increasingly in informal-housing districts, in enclaves typically on the city outskirts but also dotting the more central parts of some cities. Many such enclaves are essentially slums, with poor water and sewerage, whose governance is not well integrated into the city. Migrant children in cities are largely denied access to state schools. Semi-legal underground schools are set up by migrants, but often face regular closings by city governments. Migrants have little access to social services, health insurance, or job-training programs. Faced with the potential time bomb of a huge disenfranchised population in large cities, the government must deal with a well-articulated dilemma. Large cities are favored fiscally and in capital markets and more generally in job creation, and these advantages attract migrants. Yet opening the doors to migrants and integrating them into urban society would only encourage more migrants and the development of huge megacities.

BIBLIOGRAPHY

Au, Chun-Chung, and J. Vernon Henderson. How Migration Restrictions Limit Agglomeration and Productivity in China. *Journal of Development Economics* 80, 2 (2006): 350–388.

Brandt, Loren, and Thomas Rawski, eds. *China's Great Economic Transformation*. Cambridge, U.K.: Cambridge University Press, 2008. See especially the papers by Chan, Henderson, and Tsui and by Cai, Park, and Zhou.

Chan, Kam Wing. *Cities with Invisible Walls: Reinterpreting Urbanization in Post-1949 China*. Oxford: Oxford University Press, 1994.

Ding, Chengri, and Yan Song. *The Evolution of Land and Housing Markets in the People's Republic of China*. Cambridge, MA: Lincoln Institute of Land Policy, 2005.

Fujita, Masahisa, Tomoya Mori, J. Vernon Henderson, and Yoshitsugu Kanemoto. Spatial Distribution of Economic Activities in China and Japan. In *Handbook of Regional and Urban Economics*, vol. 4: *Cities and Geography*, ed. J. Vernon Henderson and Jacques-François Thisse. Amsterdam: North-Holland, 2004.

Henderson, J. Vernon. *Urban Development: Theory, Fact, and Illusion*. New York: Oxford University Press, 1988. Chapter 11.

Iredale, Robyn, Naran Bilik, and Fei Guo. *China's Minorities on the Move: Selected Case Studies*. Armonk, NY: M. E. Sharpe, 2003.

Kwong, Julia. Educating Migrant Children: Negotiations between the State and Civil Society. *China Quarterly*, no. 180 (2004): 1073–1088.

Logan, John R. ed. *Urban China in Transition*. Oxford: Blackwell Publishers, 2007.

Naughton, Barry J. *The Chinese Economy: Transitions and Growth*. Cambridge, MA: MIT Press, 2007.

Oi, Jean C. Reform and Urban Bias in China *Journal of Development Studies* 29 (1993): 129–148.

Perkins, Dwight. Completing China's Move to the Market. *Journal of Economic Perspectives* 8 (1994): 23–46.

Ruan, Xing. *New China Architecture*. Singapore: Periplus, 2006.

Watts, Jonathan. Satellite Data Reveal Beijing as Air Pollution Capital of the World. *Guardian*, October 31, 2005. http://www.guardian.co.uk/news/

World Bank. *China: Socialist Economic Development*. 3 vols. World Bank report no. 3391. Washington, DC: World Bank, 1983.

Wu, Weiping. Cultural Strategies in Shanghai. *Progress in Planning* 61 (2004): 159–180.

Zhang, Li. *Strangers in the City: Reconfigurations of Space, Power, and Social Networks within China's Floating Population*. Stanford, CA: Stanford University Press, 2001.

J. Vernon Henderson

URBAN PLANNING
SINCE 1978

Under the centrally planned economy of China's pre-1978 period, urban planning was perceived as a tool to realize the socialist ideology of planned development and to translate the goal of economic planning into urban space. This approach was abandoned after economic reforms were launched in 1978. The reemergence of property rights from housing and land reforms in the late 1980s led to a further burst of vested interests in the development of urban space. Such projects required urban planning to ensure that development was suitable to a market economy (Yeh and Wu 1996, 1999).

The adoption of growth-oriented development and decentralization, along with the injection of foreign capital, means that urban planners have to accommodate a development environment characterized by fewer restrictions on the land-use demands of commercial and industrial projects. The shock waves generated throughout these processes and the subsequent restructuring of interests, along with demands for land and urban space, undermined the confidence of planners (Wu, Xu Jiang, and Yeh 2007). China's urban planners were not ready for these shocks during the early reform period, and signaled an urgent need to improve the legal foundation of the country's urban-planning system. This led to the passage of the City Planning Act in 1989 by the National People's Congress.

The 1989 act stipulated the comprehensive function of urban planning and delegated a wide range of powers to municipalities, from plan making to development control. In contrast to past practices, after 1989 prior permission was required for all development projects. Before granting permission, city planning departments require "one report and two permits": that is, a site-selection recommendation report, a land-use planning permit, and a building-construction permit. City planning departments also make discretionary judgments on development proposals on the basis of considerations formulated in development plans and other requirements of government (Xu Jiang 2001).

There are two major types of development plans, namely, a *master* plan and *detailed* plans. The master plan is statutory in nature. Along with defining the broad land-use zones, the master plan spells out a wide range of urban-development strategies and land-use policies regarding such factors as transportation and open space. Land-use policies are set out in detailed plans that define the boundaries of each construction project within the designated plot. The detailed plans also address indexes such as floor-area ratio, building density and height, general layout, and utility engineering, as well as the three-dimensional site design. However, detailed plans are not statutory in nature, and development control is difficult, if not impossible (Xu Jiang and Ng 1998; Xu Jiang 2001). Planning regulations are often subverted by local officials, flawed enforcement, and interference from higher levels of administration. As land leasing becomes an essential source of government income, planners are pressured to apply less regulation in land development so as to encourage economic growth and urban expansion.

Since the late 1990s, the hunger for capital has intensified intercity competition and encouraged place-based entrepreneurial efforts by local governments (Xu Jiang and Yeh 2003, 2005). In such circumstances, planning has become more than merely refusing or constraining externalities. Urban planning has increasingly served to promote a locale and enhance its competitiveness. In many cities, development plans focus on face-lifting projects—such as airports, deep-water ports, underground rails, and convention and exhibition centers—as a means of addressing economic and social problems, and projecting new and dynamic city images in the era of globalization. Hundreds of cities in China, large and small, are competing to complete major projects that are branded by the world's top architects and planners. In addition, much city-led comprehensive residential development has evolved into full-fledged campaigns to transform the urban structure through various economic and technological development zones, industrial parks, and other special zones. In this way, cities appear more "modern," with Manhattan-like skylines that look down on multilane highways leading to growing new urban areas.

The outcome is twofold. On the one hand, the promotion of a locale presents an opportunity for Chinese cities to stimulate business and lure investment. On the other hand, building an entrepreneurial city brings to the fore the question of the validity of the local government's planning approach to city building. Such an approach not only diverts public-sector resources away from basic services that the city's disadvantaged groups depend on; it also creates urban spaces that cease to be socially meaningful and functional. As a result, the distinctive qualities of Chinese cities have gradually disappeared. The understanding of cities as a collection of cultural and physical layers is missing in the urban planning of today's China (Soule 2005).

These questions are further exacerbated by rapid urbanization. China's urban population is expected to reach 1.0 to 1.1 billion by 2050. Urbanization at such a scale and speed has overwhelmed the efforts of Chinese governments at various levels to manage urban areas. The flood of rural-to-urban migration has worsened the infrastructure burden of cities, and led to tremendous growth of urban areas where millions of migrant workers lack adequate access to basic services. There is also a pressing need to address the problems of widespread misuse of land, urban sprawl, traffic congestion, and poor sanitation and living environments in all Chinese cities, especially those that are threatened by rapid and uncontrolled growth, inadequate and poorly maintained infrastructure, industrialization, and increasing vehicle ownership. Some experts believe that these problems can be partially addressed by improving the country's urban-planning system.

On October 28, 2007, the National People's Congress promulgated the Urban and Rural Planning Act, which came into force on January 1, 2008. The act stresses the "rural" element to ensure a better spatial coordination of urban and rural land uses and to avoid massive agricultural land loss and unauthorized land development in cities, towns, and villages. The act also curbs the discretion of local governments and key officials in the decision-making process, while encouraging public participation. It is expected that the act will help to create a qualitative and sustainable transformation of both urban and rural landscapes.

BIBLIOGRAPHY

Soule, Jeffrey L. Beijing's Urban Form Should Reflect Its History. *China Daily*, July 30, 2005. http://www2.chinadaily.com.cn/english/doc/2005-07/30/content_464723.htm

Zhonghua renmin gonghe guo chengxiang guihua fa [Urban and Rural Planning Act of the People's Republic of China]. *Jiangsu chengshi guihua* [Jiangsu urban planning] 1 (2008): 4–9.

Wu, Fulong, Xu Jiang, and Anthony G. O. Yeh. *Urban Development in Post-reform China: State, Market, Space*. New York: Routledge, 2007.

Xu Jiang. The Role of Land Use Planning in the Land Development Process in China: The Case of Guangzhou. *Third World Planning Review* 23, 3 (2001): 229–248.

Xu Jiang and Mee Kam Ng. Socialist Urban Planning in Transition: The Case of Guangzhou, China. *Third World Planning Review* 20, 1 (1998): 35–51.

Xu Jiang and Anthony G. O. Yeh. Guangzhou: City Profile. *Cities* 20, 5 (2003): 361–374.

Xu Jiang and Anthony G. O. Yeh. 2005. City Repositioning and Competitiveness Building in Regional Development: New Development Strategies of Guangzhou, China. *International Journal of Urban and Regional Research* 29, 2 (2005): 283–308.

Yeh, Anthony G. O., and Fulong Wu. The New Land Development Process and Urban Development in Chinese Cities. *International Journal of Urban and Regional Research* 20, 2 (1996): 330–353.

Yeh, Anthony G. O., and Fulong Wu. The Transformation of Urban Planning System in Midst of Economic Reform in PRC. *Progress in Planning* 51 (1999): 167–252.

Anthony G. O. Yeh
Xu Jiang

URBAN HOUSING

It is perhaps not entirely accurate to characterize the Chinese housing system under the planned economy as based on public housing, because a large proportion of what is known as "public housing" was built and owned by state work units (*danwei*). This approach to housing provision maintained a relatively high level of social mixing, because households with different socioeconomic status usually lived within the same compound or residential area. The involvement of *danwei* in housing development and allocation also meant that housing inequalities unfolded along dimensions different from those of a market economy. Institutional factors such as the *hukou* (household registration) system and such attributes of the workplace as rank and size matter in the allocation of housing (Logan et al. 1999).

In the 1980s, various experiments were carried out to raise rents and promote the sale of public housing. But they remained experiments. The major change in housing policy was to expand investment sources by including workplace and personal contributions so as to solve the housing-shortage problem. Before 1998, housing reform proceeded cautiously and in an ad hoc manner, leading to continuing and increasing involvement of workplaces in housing production and allocation (Wu 1996). In fact, most housing stock in China was built after reform.

The Asian financial crisis of 1997 created a challenge for the Chinese government in its effort to maintain economic growth. The government had to rely on domestic demand. A "radical" approach to housing was adopted, according to which in-kind allocation of public housing based on the state work-unit system was abolished, with the hope of developing a market-based housing system to boost domestic demand.

Since then, housing development has been used as an instrument to promote economic growth and absorb surplus capital. Through commodification of housing provision and the privatization of public housing, China became a nation of homeowners. According to the State Statistics Bureau, homeownership in cities and towns reached 87 percent in 2007. In addition, luxury apartments and villas are being built in the style of secure gated communities, leading to increasing residential segregation.

Although it is difficult to give an accurate figure, house prices in major cities by 2008 had more than doubled since 2000, and housing affordability became a topic of everyday conversation. Unlike the original design of housing reform in 1998, public rental housing is residualized, dwindling into a residual sector. Despite efforts to develop "social rental housing" (*lian zhu fang*), the sector is underdeveloped. Rapid growth in commodity housing is attributed to increasing personal wealth, higher expectations for housing quality, the view that housing

GATED COMMUNITIES

There is no equivalent Chinese term for what are known in English as "gated communities." The closest may be *fengbishi xiaoqu*, meaning "enclosed communities" or "communities of enclosure," a term that refers more to the enclosed style of property management. In fact, many residential areas in China are gated. Gating is not limited to luxury residences, and gates appear in various neighborhoods ranging from low to high quality.

Under the socialist work-unit (*danwei*) system, living quarters were often developed by the workplace, and gated residences became common. But in these gated communities, there is a relatively high level of social mixing, because people of different social strata, but from the same workplace, live within the same compound. Because of the integration of living and work space, the gated living quarters under the *danwei* system enhanced collective control. This system became the microscopic foundation of political control, which does not necessarily resort to modern coercive measures.

Gated commodity housing estates are more pure living spaces. These residences are more socially homogenous because of the price hurdle. But compared with their North American counterparts, most Chinese gated communities for the middle-range housing market are heterogeneous. For China's up-market villa-style gated communities, mostly in the suburbs, the allure is not the gated form per se but rather the anonymity and luxury such communities provide.

Despite talk of community building, the sense of place-bound community is waning in these gated communities. The aim to "build communities" in a conventional mold poses an ever greater challenge to the authorities. However, because residents of gated communities are homeowners, there is also an increasing awareness of property-based interests. Although *danwei* compounds and commodity housing estates share the gated form, there is a substantial difference in terms of alienation. Gating reinforces trends toward sharper social stratification.

Fulong Wu

Because housing is linked with financial risk and affordability, the issue of housing has become politicized in China. The central government has promulgated a series of policies to curb the inflation of house prices, but by 2007 there had been no obvious sign of cooling, because the development of land and housing is driven by various interests, including that of local governments serving as de facto landlords.

In addition to the urban poor, a challenge for the government is housing provision for rural migrants. So far, their housing needs have mostly been filled by "informal" private rentals, especially in the "urban villages" or "villages in the city" (*cheng zhong cun*), because migrants are not entitled to public housing.

BIBLIOGRAPHY

Logan, John R., Bian Yanjie, and Bian Fuqing. Housing Inequality in Urban China in the 1990s. *International Journal of Urban and Regional Research* 23, 1 (1999): 7–25.

Wu, Fulong. Changes in the Structure of Public Housing Provision in Urban China. *Urban Studies* 33, 9 (1996): 1601–1627.

Wu, Fulong, Xu Jiang, and Anthony Gar-On Yeh. *Urban Development in Post-Reform China: State, Market, and Space.* London: Routledge, 2007.

Fulong Wu

DEVELOPMENT ZONES

There are a variety of development zones in contemporary urban China, including special economic zones (*jingji tequ*), economic-technology development zones (*jingji jishu kaifaqu*), high-tech development zones (*gaoxin jishu kaifaqu*), border economic-cooperation zones (*bianjing jingji hezuoqu*), and reform experiment zones (*gaige shiyanqu*). All development zones are independent from local administrative management and enjoy tax and financial benefits. At the beginning of the reform era, the central government established the development zones to attract foreign investments and to guarantee that the country's vested interests would not be damaged by the experimental nature of the reforms.

The development of various zones in the 1980s and 1990s contributed greatly to China's accelerating urbanization process and successfully established venues for the country's economic development. However, due to the massive scale of development over a short period of time and the multiple conflicts created among various administrations, the central government limited the number of zones in order to eliminate the "fever" created by such an urban-development strategy.

can be a form of saving and investment, and an inflow of overseas "hot money" into China with the expectation of the revaluation of the renminbi.

DEVELOPMENT-ZONE FEVER

During the 1980s, after its success in establishing four special economic zones, the state opened fourteen coastal cities and established thirty national economic-technology development zones, fifty-two national high-tech development zones, thirteen free-trade zones (*baoshuiqu*), thirteen border economic-cooperation zones, and eleven national holiday resorts (*guojia lüyou dujiaqu*). By the end of 1993, there were 119 national-level development zones with a total geographic area of 1,149.5 square kilometers. At the local level, 8,700 development zones were established by governments at all levels.

The effort toward establishing an effective method of developing the domestic economy led to numerous problems. An oversupply of cleared land and an overconversion of farmland, for example, led to wasted national resources. According to statistics published by the Land Management Bureau, the total combined area of development zones established by local governments reached 15,000 square kilometers in 1993, exceeding China's total city area. This frantic overdevelopment produced a real-estate bubble between 1992 and 1994 and led to one-third of nonperforming loans in the banking industry.

REASONS FOR THE DEVELOPMENT-ZONE FEVER

The development-zone "fever" arose for several reasons. First, all development zones enjoyed tax benefits since the 1980s. The tax rate for general enterprises was 33 percent in urban China; in national high-tech zones and national special economic zones, however, it was 15 percent. In coastal economic zones and coastal special economic zones, the tax rate was 24 percent. For foreign businesses, the enterprise value-added tax had a 75-percent refund rate, compared to only 25 percent in normal urban areas. All development zones also benefited from a high retention rate for annual income. With such attractive financial benefits, all local governments became interested in establishing development zones to increase annual income. Meanwhile, development zones also provided numerous employment opportunities for local populations.

Second, in most developed countries, urban construction and maintenance expenses are covered by real-estate taxes, urban land-use taxes, land value-added taxes, and other taxes. In the United States, for example, state and federal real-estate tax income is relatively high. In China, the rate is much lower. In 2001 China's real-estate tax income at the local and national level was only 8.79 percent and 4.18 percent, respectively. As a result, total tax income could not cover urban construction and maintenance expenses.

Third, to recoup the costs of urban construction, maintenance, and further investment, local governments had to rely on fees collected from land-use rights transactions. According to the Treasury Department, 60 percent of a land-use transaction fee was retained at the local level, while 40 percent belonged to the state. Of the 40 percent collected by the state, 87.5 percent was later refunded to the locality, which meant that a total of 95 percent of the land-use transaction fee belonged to the local government, and the state only collected 5 percent. With such attractive financial benefits, transferring land-use rights immediately became a favored source of "second income" in well-developed local areas.

Fourth, in established urban areas, local governments engaged in urban renewal had to cover the costs of demolition, relocation, and debris removal. Rural land could be converted more efficiently and at less expense. This might be another reason local governments rushed to establish development zones on the urban fringe.

Fifth, the opening of development zones had the advantage of extending the administrative reach of local governments, sharply increasing the number of institutions and jobs within a given region. In many areas, there were more administrative officials working in development zones than in conventional urban centers. The state also gave enhanced administrative authority to government officials in development zones so that they could manage daily work more effectively, especially through greater powers to negotiate with foreign investors and regional administrators. For example, the special economic zones, such as Shenzhen, were granted deputy-provincial administrative rank, signifying that the senior official ranked second only to the provincial governor. This ranking increased administrative costs, which were in part offset by the fact that most civil servants hired in the development zones were young, and the financial burden of retirement pensions and medical insurance was correspondingly light. At the same time, to fill the few high-paying leadership positions, the newly developed zones could select and hire distinguished civil servants with track records of innovation to build a new management culture.

The high rank of development zones signified greater legislative and administrative rights than pertain in normal subprovincial administrative units. Zone administrators could simplify administrative processes, reduce administrative costs, increase efficiencies, and exercise greater legal power. This approach allowed for the retention of most economic benefits within the locality itself, guaranteed the negotiation leverage of the local government, and added more power for the regional officials in general. Local administrators benefited most: There were more official positions for cadres and more opportunities for promotion; cadres enjoyed special compensation and higher income; and finally, because most zones were located outside of the cities, cadres could receive an additional allocated apartment. Many regional administrators took advantage of this system to avoid supervision from their superiors. They could assign their direct subordinates to establish development zones that enjoyed higher administrative rank and independent rights so that their own immediate supervisors could not interrupt economic management.

Finally, according to the law, the subprovincial administrative system had the authority to rearrange local administrative regions and administrative organizations. Such adjustments needed to be legally ratified only at the provincial level and above. In other words, legal officials had no right to regulate or inspect the management of development zones. The Hainan Special Economic Zone is an exception, because the zone is coterminous with the province, and any administrative adjustments have to comply with the requirement of legal ratification. Below the provincial level, local cadres faced no such restraints.

TWO EXAMPLES OF DEVELOPMENT ZONES

China-Singapore Suzhou Industrial Park (Zhongguo-Xinjiapo Suzhou Gongye Yuan) was established in 1994. It was built on the joint efforts of the two governments to develop an "internationally competitive high-tech industrial park and a modern, gardenlike township." The park focuses on developing three major industries: semiconductors, optical electronics, and electrical mechanics. It is invested with great authority and a high degree of independence. Suzhou Industrial Park can approve all foreign-invested projects, as long as they are in line with national policy. It has an independent customs regime, a bonded logistics center, its own export-processing zones, and its own security system, as well as the power to approve official overseas trip applications. Goods entering the logistics park from within China are treated as exports and are entitled to a tax rebate.

As a new model for economic and technological cooperation, the China-Singapore Suzhou Industrial Park allowed Chinese partners to learn management skills from their Singaporean counterparts, while both countries benefited from foreign direct investment (FDI). During the first few years, the success of "little Singapore" was impressive and encouraging. With an average annual growth rate of 20 percent for both fixed committed investments and a number of companies choosing to locate in the park, the park's efficiency, professional management, lack of corruption, and superior infrastructure were praised on all sides. However, because of the Asian financial crisis, local competition, and the flexibility of FDI, in June 1999 the government of Singapore announced its disengagement from Suzhou Industrial Park. One of the main lessons that developers and investors learned from the experience was never to underestimate the capability and power of provincial and city-level administration in running development projects. Developed in collaboration with the central government in Beijing, the Suzhou Industrial Park received the strongest political support from the state. In the end, however, daily management rested with the local government and FDI investors.

The largest free-trade zone in the North and Northwest is Tianjin Port Free-trade Zone (Tianjin Gang Baoshuiqu), which includes Tianjin Airport Industrial Park and Tianjin Airport International Logistics Zone. The zone prioritizes the development of high-tech manufacturing and international logistics industries. The administrative committee for the zone is in charge of enterprise registration, land planning, and construction. The Airport International Logistics Zone focuses on shortening the processing time in the largest airfreight base in northern and northwestern China. By developing the logistics industry, which involves the integration of information, transportation, inventory, warehousing, material-handling, and packaging, Tianjin successfully transformed itself from a heavy industrial center to a strategic business hub in northern China, with international connections to Korea, Japan, Hong Kong, and more distant regions.

SEE ALSO *Companies: Joint Ventures; Economic Development; Foreign Investment since 1949; Socialist Market Economy; Special Economic Zones.*

BIBLIOGRAPHY
Hong Kai, Jiang Hua, Li Enyuan, and Shi Weidong. Zhongguo "Jingji Kaifaqu Re" de Zhidu Fenxi [The systematic analysis of China's "development zone fever"]. *Mei Zhong Jingji Pinglun* [USA-China business review] 4, 3 (2004):13–17.
Pereira, Alexius. The Suzhou Industrial Park Experiment: The Case of China-Singapore Governmental Collaboration. *Journal of Contemporary China* 13, 38 (2004): 173–193.
Yang, Daniel You-Ren. Dilemmas of Local Governance under the Development Zone Fever in China: A Case Study of the Suzhou Region. *Urban Studies* 45, 5–6 (2008): 1037–1054.
Zweig, David. *Internationalizing China: Domestic Interests and Global Linkage.* Ithaca, NY: Cornell University Press, 2002.

Wang Danning

REAL ESTATE MANAGEMENT

The development of China's urban real estate market started as the state's effort to deal with the urban housing shortage. In 1982 state policies required local governments, state-owned enterprises, and individuals to contribute to housing investment. As part of the decentralization process, work units were allowed to retain profits to invest in housing development, and subsequently to distribute subsidized housing to their employees (Wu 2002, p. 156). The Land Administration Law of 1988 was issued to facilitate rural-urban land conversions that gradually commercialized the land-use right and its transaction. This land reform created a "dual land market"—the central government made land available through administrative allocation or by leasing land through paid transactions. Lease terms are typically forty years for commercial use, fifty years for industrial use, and seventy years for residential use. The Ministry of Land Resources, which has included the Land Management Bureau since 1998, is responsible for pricing land, approving rural-to-urban conversion plans, and allocating land to work units.

Since 1998, land-use rights can be obtained through negotiation, competitive bidding, and auction with the appropriate city government. Urban industries and other state agencies whose land was administratively allocated without charge but occupied good locations can now benefit greatly by leasing their land to the highest bidders for other uses. The profits derived from leasing land-use rights can be extremely high, because the difference between the market value and the value set by negotiations can be substantial (Ma 2003, pp. 242–243).

A significant black market has emerged as work units transfer rights to developers for secretly negotiated fees. In the absence of a straightforward land-taxation system, municipal governments also rely heavily on one-time revenues from leasing land-development rights, or they make land available to developers in exchange for in-kind contributions of road construction, public amenities, and other infrastructure. The combination of the dual land market and public revenues from one-time payments, often in-kind, has produced inefficiencies, opportunities for corruption, and challenges for long-range planning.

By 1997, the Chinese economy had transformed from a shortage to an over-accumulation regime. Faced with a lack of effective demand, profits and capacity utilization began to fall. The Asian financial crisis in 1997 further exacerbated the problem, as the strong currency compared with other Asian currencies began to hurt the export sector. As a result, real estate development has been chosen as a new growth pole. It was hoped that housing consumption would stimulate domestic demand, thus supporting the economic growth target. In 1998 the central bank supported an increase in housing credit and encouraged commercial banks to release mortgages to households. Under the new mortgage scheme, about 100 billion yuan was ready for the borrowers (Wu 2002, p. 161).

However, both inner-city redevelopment and the development of the urban fringe are extremely controversial because they benefit local government agencies and developers at the expense of residents and villagers who are dislocated. Dislocation removes people from their livelihoods and basic services. It also involves disputes over appropriate levels of compensation (Abramson 2006, p. 204). In inner-city redevelopment, increasing amounts of space are dedicated to the exclusive use of transportation; poorer residents are resettled farther from the city center; and older, demographically and socially diverse, or poorer neighborhoods are replaced with more exclusive, uniform, and expensive neighborhoods or commercial projects. The new public spaces are inhospitable to pedestrians, and off limits to street vendors and those who provide inexpensive services to residents. Market-driven growth has dominated the real estate management, and the lack of community-based, nonprofit, and resident-friendly social networks has become a serious issue in the new neighborhoods.

BIBLIOGRAPHY

Abramson, Daniel Benjamin. Urban Planning in China Continuity and Change. *Journal of the American Planning Association* 72, 2 (2006): 197–215.

Ma, Laurence J. C. Economic Reforms, Urban Spatial Restructuring, and Planning in China. *Progress in Planning* 61 (2004): 237–260.

Wu, Fulong. Real Estate Development and the Transformation of Urban Space in China's Transitional Economy, with Special Reference to Shanghai. *The New Chinese City: Globalization and Market Reform.* Ed. John R. Logan, pp 153–166. Oxford: Blackwell, 2002.

Wang Danning

SMALL-TOWN CHINA

In the Chinese context, a small town means more an urban place than a rural settlement. Therefore the status of "town" is designated by the Ministry of Civil Affairs (MCA). According to MCA, in 2005 there were 19,522 designated towns. The criterion of designated towns is the location of county government, or a settlement with a population under 20,000 but having more than 2,000 nonagricultural population, or a settlement with above 20,000 population and more than 10 percent of nonagricultural population. Although before the mid-1990s China had an "urban policy" to strictly constrain the growth of super large cities, reasonably develop medium-sized cities, and actively promote the growth of small cities, the policy has never been effectively implemented. This is because regulating city size cannot be readily achieved at the aggregate level. There is no mechanism to allocate resources and projects into small cities.

However, in the 1980s and early 1990s, small towns in the coastal region experienced rapid growth, especially in terms of the numbers of towns. Their growth was driven by the release of surplus laborers in agriculture and the boom of township and village enterprises (TVEs), a process known as "urbanization from below" (Ma and Fan 1994).

In the 1980s, Fei Xiaotong (1910–2005), the renowned Chinese sociologist, foresaw the shift of agricultural to non-agricultural population in densely populated rural areas and emphasized the need to build more small towns. He argued that the small town is a big question and proposed a model for peasants to leave the agriculture sector without leaving the rural areas. Hence, more small towns would need to be built to accommodate China's increasing nonagricultural population.

The original purpose of developing small towns was to absorb surplus rural population and thus intercept their flow into super large cities. However, in reality, the small towns did not achieve such a goal. Migrants continue to flow into big cities, where there are more job opportunities. Since 1990, the dominance of large cities has become increasingly apparent (Lin 2002).

However, along with the deepening of market reform, some small towns began to gain a new role in market distribution, and have become specialized in particular markets. For example, Yiwu in Zhejiang Province is a major market town for small consumer products.

Overseas investment also stimulates the growth of small towns, especially those in the Pearl River Delta, into industrial towns. Investment in labor-intensive manufacturing products is located in small towns in the city of Dongguan, for example. This pattern of scattered growth resembles the so-called *desakota* model of Southeast Asia, originally proposed by Terry McGee (McGee and Robinson 1995).

Since 2005, a major driving force for small-town development has been the construction of "new countryside," which aims to extend urban infrastructure into rural areas. There are also attempts to consolidate scattered villages into designated towns.

Within metropolitan areas, the growth of small towns originates from their role in industrial development under the planned economy. Small towns were built by state investment as industrial areas. But these industrial "satellite towns" failed to attract population because of the lack of infrastructure and services. Since the implementation of land and housing reform, the growth of small towns has increasingly been driven by urban sprawl, population decentralization, and industrial relocation (Wu 1998). Some real-estate projects take the form of *dapan* (mega-estates). These mega-estates are huge residential districts built by developers, usually in modern styles. They are in fact new towns but privately built. Many are in South China, for example, Panyu in the Pearl River Delta. They are so large that they are virtually small towns. *Dapan*

developers also provide a wide range of services, including schools and shopping centers.

In addition, the development of small towns in the megacity regions represents an effort to develop a polycentric urban structure. According to its new master plan, Beijing aims to develop eleven new towns, including the three towns of Yizhuang, Shunyi, and Tongzhou. In Shanghai, the so-called one city and nine towns plan aims to give each newly built town a distinct European style. For example, Anting will be designed as a German town because it is a location of automobile production supported by German investment.

BIBLIOGRAPHY

Fei Xiaotong. *Notes on Small Towns*. Beijing: Xinhua Press, 1985.

Lin, George C. S. The Growth and Structural Change of Chinese Cities: A Contextual and Geographic Analysis. *Cities* 19, 5 (2002): 299–316.

Ma, Laurence J. C., and Fan Ming. Urbanisation from Below: The Growth of Towns in Jiangsu, China. *Urban Studies* 31, 10 (1994): 1625–1645.

McGee, Terry G., and Ira M. Robinson, eds. *The Mega-Urban Regions of Southeast Asia*. Vancouver: University of British Columbia Press, 1995.

Wu, Fulong. The New Structure of Building Provision and the Transformation of the Urban Landscape in Metropolitan Guangzhou, PRC. *Urban Studies* 35, 2 (1998): 259–283.

Fulong Wu

URBAN EMPLOYMENT TO 1949

At the beginning of the nineteenth century Qing China was a predominantly rural economy. China's urban residents amounted to a mere 6 percent of China's total population, no more than twenty-five million. Thus, the urban workforce comprised fewer than ten million people at any given time before 1912.

Even on the southeast coast, where commercial growth was the strongest, the old domestic pattern of the internal division of labor between farming by male members and textile production (mainly cotton) by female members remained unchanged. As a result, much of China's handicraft was retained in the rural sector. This sector was tiny: During the 1930s China's traditional handicraft workers amounted to just twelve million, not counting rural housewives.

China's urban handicrafts were mainly silk weaving and the production of metal and porcelain. Information on the scale and scope of these industries has remained patchy. Regarding silk weaving, in the early 1850s, before the Taipings' killing and looting, Nanjing was estimated to have had 170,000 silk weavers with 50,000 silk looms to produce two million bolts of silk cloth a year. Suzhou's silk production was believed to have been on a similar scale, so China's urban silk weavers were at least 340,000. Visual records suggest that they were mainly male. China's metal and porcelain industries were much smaller and found mainly in the Pearl River Delta. The annual metal and porcelain trade values were 6 million *liang* and 5 million *liang*, respectively. Given that 30 to 40 *liang* of silver a year was what the elite Manchu soldiers were paid, the number of metal workers is likely to have been 200,000 and the porcelain workers, 167,000. Statistics on other urban productions such as tailoring, furniture making, and construction are unknown.

Before 1912 the largest single urban employer was the Eight Banner Corps and the Green Standing Army, whose soldiers were customarily stationed in urban centers. Their total number varied from time to time around the one million mark. These soldiers, especially the Manchu, stayed in the army for life. With their families, their population was likely to have been five million. Additionally, there were fewer than 30,000 civilian officials and military officers on the Qing payroll.

To support the urban population of twenty-five million, the service sector employed people ranging from hairdressers to rubbish collectors. The most important group had to be urban commercial dealers of various kinds. To take pawnshops as an example, in the 1810s, China had more than 23,100 of them, hiring perhaps 100,000 people. In 1900 Shanxi native banks had 650 branches empire-wide, which were likely to have hired no more than 100,000 people. The number of Qing salt merchants was much smaller: The Qing government registered only 425 with licenses for the whole empire (as in the 1790s). Qing export merchants under government license were fewer still: no more than 100. Then, there were long-distance traders who were mobile between rural and urban sectors. During the Qing, there were ten major merchant groups, stemming from Huizhou, Shanxi, Shaanxi, Shandong, Ningbo, Guangdong, Fujian, Longyou, Dongting, and Jiangyou. Evidence suggests that each group often had fewer than 100 members. So, at most, they may have had a total membership of 10,000. In major cities there were also sectoral associations for the market agents of the same business. In the early twentieth century the largest sectoral associations had 3,000 members, the smaller ones only a few dozen. Overall, the number of urban and semiurban merchants probably remained under one million.

However, there was a new breed of merchant, the compradors, as a result of the Nanking Treaty of 1842. Unlike the traditional *cohong* merchants, the compradors did not need government approval. The formation of the group was dictated entirely by the market itself. Also, compradors were the most enthusiastic learners of doing business in the Western capitalist way. By 1900 China had over 10,000 compradors with an aggregate wealth of 500 million *liang* of silver.

China's modern industry began earlier than Japan's if one counts the Qing Self-strengthening movement that began in 1861, when China's first modern factory, the Anqing Arsenal, was built to produce modern firearms. By the end of the movement during the 1890s China had a total industrial urban workforce of just over 90,000 that was evenly divided between Qing state-run enterprises, Chinese private enterprises, and foreign enterprises. Their share in China's urban workforce of ten million was a negligible 0.1 percent. By 1913, however, China's modern industrial workforce may have reached 900,000, although the figure includes those in the mining industries located outside urban areas. In the 1920s, within the manufacturing sector, China's traditional handicrafts still claimed over 80 percent of the sectoral GDP, leaving only 20 percent of the GDP to the modern factories.

The real growth occurred in the Nanjing decade (1927–1937), when China's modern workforce increased to three million. The main growth sectors were in modern transport, especially railways, and light industry, especially cotton textiles. Geographically, new workers were concentrated in a handful of coastal cities, of which Shanghai was the largest. Even so, in 1930 Shanghai had no more than 750,000 factory workers in a city of three million people. In the deep South where Guangzhou and Hong Kong were situated, modern transport had a very strong showing. In addition, in Japanese-controlled Manchuria, some growth occurred in railway construction, mining, and iron and steel production. There, the modern workforce was a few hundred thousand.

By this time, the majority of workers were rural migrants. A great proportion of these migrants were illiterate women and children. As a result, China's urban population increased to forty-one million (in 1936) and China's urbanization rate increased to 8.6 percent (in 1938), which was marginally higher than in 1911; the structure was anything but modern.

Even so, much of the modern industry in China was destroyed by the eight-year invasion and conquest by Japan and the following four-year-long Communist-Republican civil war. In Manchuria much of the modern industrial equipment was taken by the Soviet Union as war reparations for its victory over Japan. In 1949 China's economy was distinctively rural or pre-industrial.

BIBLIOGRAPHY

Cao Shuji. *Zhongguo Yimin Shi* [A history of migration in China]. Fuzhou, China: Fujian People's Press, 1997.

Hao, Yen-P'ing. *The Commercial Revolution in Nineteenth-century China* Berkeley: University of California Press, 1986.

Pong, David. Government Enterprise and Industrial Relations in Late Qing China. *Australian Journal of Politics and History* 47, 1 (March 2001): 4–23.

Sun Yutang. *Zhongguo Jindai Gongyeshi Ziliao* [Materials on modern industries in China]. Beijing: Science Press, 1957.

Wu Chengming. *Zhongguode Xiandaihua: Shichang Yu Shehui* [China's modernization: market and society] Beijing: Sanlian Books, 2001.

Xu Dixin and Wu Chengming, eds. *Zhongguo Ziben Zhuyi Fazhanshi* [A history of capitalist development in China]. Beijing: People's Press, 1985.

Xu Tailai. *Yangwu Yundong Xinlu* [Re-examination of the westernization movement]. Changsha, China: Hunan People's Press, 1986.

Xu Xinwu, ed. *Jindai Jiangnan Sizhi Gongye Shi* [A history of silk-weaving industry in early modern Yangzi delta]. Shanghai: Shanghai People's Press, 1991).

Yan Zhongping. *Zhongguo Jindai Jingjishi Tongji Ziliao Xuanji* [Selected statistical materials of economic history of early modern China]. Beijing: Science Press, 1955.

Kent G. Deng

URBAN EMPLOYMENT AND UNEMPLOYMENT SINCE 1949

During the first eight years after the 1949 founding of the People's Republic of China, the government carried out a socialist transformation of production ownership and set up a number of basic industries. This process led to urban growth, which came to a halt with the launch of the Great Leap Forward in 1958. From that time through the decade of the Cultural Revolution (1966–1976), the political environment became unstable, with a serious impact on urban development and employment. During the Cultural Revolution, thousands of young people were sent to the countryside to receive reeducation from the peasant class, causing a tide of "reverse urbanization." Table 1 shows the low level of the tertiary-employment structure during this period.

Nevertheless, Chinese cities made progress during this period, a trend marked by two features: (1) large and medium-size cities developed considerably, with small cities and towns appearing to decline; and (2) a great number of new cities were built in the middle and western parts of China, balancing the traditional spatial pattern of urban development (Zhu Zhenguo and Yao Shimou 2000).

In 1978 the Third Plenary Session of the Eleventh Central Committee of the Communist Party adopted a policy of economic reform. By this time, Deng Xiaoping's agricultural reforms of the late 1970s and early 1980s were succeeding. Thus, urbanization accelerated, and the

Structure changes of employment in China (1952–1978)

Year	Primary industry	Secondary industry	Tertiary industry
1952	83.5	7.4	9.1
1957	81.2	8.9	9.9
1962	82.0	7.8	10.1
1965	81.5	8.3	10.2
1970	80.7	10.1	9.2
1975	77.1	13.3	9.6
1978	70.5	17.4	12.1

SOURCE: *China Statistical Yearbook*, 1994; Lu Huapu. Review of the Urban Growth over the Past Twenty Years and Prospects for the Next 2 or 3 Decades. Qinghua University, 2002. From: http://www.ville-en-mouvement.com/articles/lu_huapu03.pdf.

Table 1

Development of Chinese cities (1952–1978)

City scale	1952	1957	1965	1978
Super city (population over 1,000,000)	9	10	13	18
Big city (between 500,000–1,000,000)	10	18	18	27
Medium-size city (between 200,000–500,000)	23	36	43	60
Small city (below 200,000)	115	114	97	92
Organizational town	5400[1]	3621[2]	About 3000	About 2600

Notes: 1. 1954 data; 2. 1956 data

SOURCE: Lu Huapu. Review of the Urban Growth over the Past Twenty Years and Prospects for the Next 2 or 3 Decades. Qinghua University, 2002. From: http://www.ville-en-mouvement.com/articles/lu_huapu03.pdf.

Table 2

tide of rural-to-urban migration swelled, due also to an improved food supply in the cities.

Urban migrants (known as the "floating population") emerged as a new status group with the opening of markets. In 2000 the size of the floating population reached seventy-nine million. The 2000 census defines the floating population as individuals who have resided at their place of destination for at least six months without local household-registration status. China's coastal regions, such as the province of Guangdong, have witnessed the largest increase in the size of their floating population. According to Liang Zai and Ma Zhongdong (2004), the floating population in Guangdong nearly tripled between the 1990 and the 2000 censuses. It is generally believed that the income level of these migrants exceeded their former incomes at their place of origin.

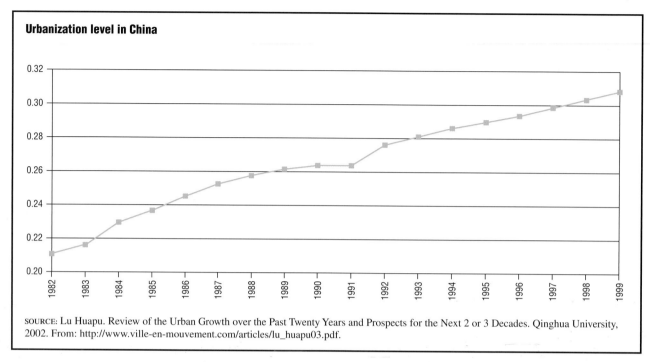

Urbanization level in China

SOURCE: Lu Huapu. Review of the Urban Growth over the Past Twenty Years and Prospects for the Next 2 or 3 Decades. Qinghua University, 2002. From: http://www.ville-en-mouvement.com/articles/lu_huapu03.pdf.

Figure 1

The floating population was a heterogeneous group, including both migrants whose residence was more stable and those who were transient on a longer-term basis, such as vagrants and *mangliu* ("blind drifters" who roam from place to place to seek their fortunes) (Wong 1994). In the 1980s, the authorities took control of this kind of internal migration using various new residence regulations. In particular, the State Council Notification on the Question of Peasants Entering Towns and Settling (1984) gave farmers the opportunity to obtain nonagricultural registration in market towns, albeit with restrictions. This policy change signaled the government's growing pragmatism in handling internal migration. By this time, internal migration had become a fact of life (Solinger 1999). Further, the government had to permit more mobility because surplus agricultural workers continued to appear under the agriculture-responsibility system. Introduced in the late 1970s, the household-responsibility system quickly proved successful, because it increased efficiency and promoted incentives on the part of farmers while at the same time reducing the need for labor.

Continuous migration of rural workers who, under the strict residence-registration system, had no authorization to live in cities, resulted in migrants having to eke out a living under abject conditions. Importantly, their social insurance needs have not been adequately met, and they are not given the full benefits of citizenship. Their well-being has become a major source of concern for local governments and policy analysts (Liang Zai and Ma Zhongdong 2004). Episodes of contentious collective action involving laid-off workers have erupted throughout China in recent years. Chinese migrants are often viewed by urban dwellers as "foreign."

URBAN GROWTH SINCE THE LATE 1980s

Urbanization has risen steadily since the late 1980s as a result of the mainland's political and economic development. There are several characteristics to this process: (1) a greater number of large cities; (2) rising urbanization levels—China's level of urbanization reached 30 percent or more in the late 1990s, higher than the average level for low-income countries (see Figure 1); (3) rising levels of tertiary-industry employment—from 1990 to 2003, the proportion of those employed in tertiary industry rose steadily from 18.5 percent to 29.3 percent, with the number of employees reaching 218.09 million; correspondingly, the proportion of those employed in primary industry dropped from 60.1 percent to 49.1 percent (see Figure 2).

URBAN EMPLOYMENT

At the end of 2006, China's total population reached 1.31 billion. The number of employed individuals totaled 764 million, of which 283.1 million were urban and 480.9 million were rural. The urban registered unemployed population in 2007 was 8.47 million, with an official

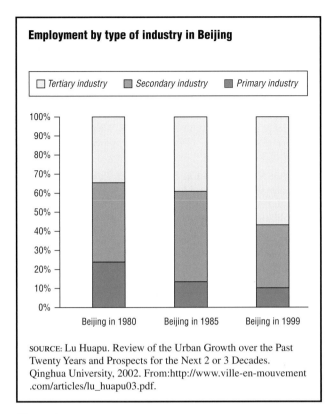

Employment by type of industry in Beijing

□ Tertiary industry   ▨ Secondary industry   ▨ Primary industry

SOURCE: Lu Huapu. Review of the Urban Growth over the Past Twenty Years and Prospects for the Next 2 or 3 Decades. Qinghua University, 2002. From:http://www.ville-en-mouvement.com/articles/lu_huapu03.pdf.

Figure 2

urban unemployment rate of 4.1 percent (*China Statistical Yearbook* 2007). The term *urban registered unemployment* refers to those who: (1) possess nonagricultural residence cards; (2) are at least sixteen years of age but not old enough to retire; (3) are able to work but are not actually doing so; and (4) want to work and have registered at the local labor exchanges.

According to the *China Labour Statistical Yearbook* (2005), at the end of 2004 China's total population of formal employees was about 111 million. The term *formal employees* refers to those who work in (and receive income from) units with state ownership, urban collective ownership, joint ownership, shareholding-stock ownership, or limited-liability corporate ownership, as well as units funded by foreigners and investors from Hong Kong, Macau, and Taiwan, or other ownership and their affiliated units. More than 30 million worked in manufacturing, which accounted for 27.5 percent, the highest subset, of the working population. The average annual salary in 2004 was 14,251 renminbi, earned by those working in manufacturing, while other industries ranged from 7,494 renminbi per annum (farming) to 33,449 renminbi per annum (information technology, computers, and software). Given such diversity, employees in high technology, a tertiary industry, can easily find salaries four or five times the pay of those performing physical labor. The disparity between "brain workers" and manual workers is real.

Urban formal employees worked 42.4 hours per week on average in 2004, a statistic that varied when broken down by industry. Wholesale and retail working hours were the longest, reaching 50.1 hours per week. By contrast, working hours for those employed in education, public management, and social organizations were the shortest, with 41.1 hours per week on average. Those doing physical labor usually exceeded the average number of hours per week.

By and large, urban employees are protected by social insurance (pension insurance, unemployment insurance, employment-injury insurance, and maternity insurance). According to the Ministry of Labor and Social Security, some 0.2 billion employees received pension insurance in 2006, but the other four types of insurance covered fewer employees in urban areas. Among them, employment-injury insurance was the least prevalent.

THE UNEMPLOYMENT SITUATION IN CITIES AND TOWNS

During the second half of the 1990s, the official (registered) unemployment rate ranged from 2.9 to 3.1 percent before rising in 2001 and 2002 to 4.0 percent. Official statistics count as unemployed only those individuals who register for unemployment benefits with local governments, a total not based on representative sample surveys. Thus, the official figures are questionable because they overlook millions of workers who were laid off with no expectation of reemployment or who lost jobs but did not register with local governments (Giles et al. 2005). While scholars have advanced other estimates based on various sources, including survey data, these should be taken with some caution because sample sizes are usually not large.

One thing is certain: Urban unemployment has been increasing since economic restructuring began in 1978. This is reflected even in official explanations. According to the *China Labour Statistical Yearbook* (2004), the reasons for unemployment in urban areas are many, including inability to find a job after graduation, bankrupt enterprises, lay-offs, reassignment, and expiration of contracts and land requisitions, to name just a few. Lay-offs are the main factor causing unemployment, with 36.0 percent of the unemployed having lost jobs. State-owned enterprises have been laying off (*xiagang*) a large number of redundant workers to increase efficiency (Deng Guangliang and Ngan 2008). In the forty-five to fifty-nine age group, over 60 percent of unemployed had been laid off. However, in the sixteen to nineteen age group, 87.7 percent of unemployed had been unable to find a job after graduation. The thirty to thirty-nine age group constituted 31.9 percent of the entire urban unemployment population.

The *China Labour Statistical Yearbook* (2004) reports that among the unemployed, 49.3 percent had a middle-school education and 34.8 percent had finished high school. Among those unemployed due to lay-offs, 49.3 percent had only completed middle school, with another 37.8 percent having completed high school. There is little gender difference when it comes to unemployment and educational background. But for the thirty to thirty-nine age group, unemployed females (36.7%) outnumbered males (27%), perhaps because women in this age group are often required to assume the responsibility of caring for the family and are less sought after by employers. Manufacturing workers (35.6%) topped the unemployed population, while workers from international organizations accounted for only 0.1 percent.

In response to urban unemployment, China has developed a variety of plans to help displaced workers find employment or reemployment. In addition, new forms of employment, such as part-time and temporary jobs, have cropped up, as have jobs in foreign-invested firms.

DEVELOPMENTS SINCE WTO ACCESSION

China's accession to the World Trade Organization (WTO) in 2001 has repercussions not only for its foreign trade and investment regime but also for its employment environment. WTO membership exposes China's economic development and employment scenario to external influences. In the early 2000s, the government was optimistic that WTO accession would result in the long term in increased employment opportunities, which would arise from China's integration with the world economy. Although the government predicted that short-term unemployment would rise due to industrial restructuring, early findings show differential impacts. The obvious change after accession was an increase in employment in the apparel and textile sectors. However, trade reforms caused a decrease in employment in some agricultural and manufacturing sectors.

SEE ALSO *Labor: Unemployment; Standard of Living; Women, Employment of.*

BIBLIOGRAPHY

Chang Sendou. Modernization and China's Urban Development. *Annals of the Association of American Geographers* 71, 2 (1981): 202–219.

Chen Qingxiu. Estimation on the Employment Trends of China. *Scientific Decision Making* 10 (2003): 33–37.

Deng Guang Liang (Tang Kwong-leung) and Raymond Man-hung Ngan. China: Social Security in the Context of Rapid Economic Growth. In *Social Security, the Economy, and Development*, eds. James Midgley and Deng Guangliang, 137–159. New York: Palgrave Macmillan, 2008.

Giles, John, Albert Park, and Zhang Juwei. What Is China's True Unemployment Rate? *China Economic Review* 16, 2 (2005): 149–170.

Gose, Ajit K. *Employment in China: Recent Trends and Future Challenges.* International Labour Office: Economic and Labour Market Analysis Department. 2005. http://www.ilo.org/public/english/employment/strat/download/esp2005-14.pdf

Koop, Marissa. Urbanisation and Urban Development in China. 2001. http://www.accci.com.au/koop.htm

Liang Zai and Ma Zhongdong. China's Floating Population: New Evidence from the 2000 Census. *Population and Development Review* 30, 3 (2004): 467–488.

Liao Danqing and Guo Huiling. Urbanization Is an Effective Way to Improve the Situation in China. *Chinese Rural Economy* 3 (2004).

Liu Weide. A Study on the Question between Population Urbanization and Employment of City and Rural in China. *Economic Geography* 21, 3 (2001).

Lu Huapu. *Review of the Urban Growth over the Past Twenty Years and Prospects for the Next 2 or 3 Decades.* 2002. http://www.ville-en-mouvement.com/articles/lu_huapu03.pdf

National Bureau of Statistics of China. *China Statistical Yearbook.* Beijing: China Statistics Press, various years.

National Bureau of Statistics of China. *China Labour Statistical Yearbook.* Beijing: China Statistics Press, various years. http://www.molss.gov.cn/images/2006-11/16/271103161537 62520791.pdf

Office of the State Council of the PRC. *China's Employment Situation and Policies.* White paper. 2004. http://www.china.org.cn/e-white/20040426/index.htm

Solinger, Dorothy J. China's Floating Population: Implications for State and Society. In *The Paradox of China's Post-Mao Reforms*, eds. Roderick MacFarquhar and Merle Goldman, 220–240. Cambridge, MA: Harvard University Press, 1999.

Wong, Linda. China's Urban Migrants: The Public Policy Challenge. *Pacific Affairs* 67 (1994): 335–355.

Zhu Zhenguo and Yao Shimou. New Patterns of Urban Development in China. *Chinese Geographical Science* 10 (2000): 20–29.

Tang Kwong-leung (Deng Guang Liang)

V

VIETNAM, RELATIONS WITH

After the victory in 1949 of the Chinese Communist Party (CCP) in the Chinese civil war, China began providing the Vietminh, a Vietnamese nationalist group, with invaluable support in the anticolonial war against the French. China's support contributed to the Vietminh victory in that conflict in 1954. Thereafter, relations between China and Vietnam were officially close until the end of the Vietnam War in 1975.

RELATIONS BETWEEN 1954 AND 1975

After Vietnam regained full independence from France in 1954, relations between China and the Democratic Republic of Vietnam (DRV) were close. China provided the DRV with extensive economic and military assistance and sent thousands of advisers to help the Vietnamese in the agriculture, industrial, and defense fields. China also provided Vietnam with considerable assistance during the Vietnam War. However, irritants developed relating to different perceptions of the Soviet Union and divergent views on relations and negotiations with the United States. After the Paris Agreement in 1973, Vietnam claimed that China had advised it to diminish the level of the fighting in the South for a few years. China rejected this claim.

CHINA-VIETNAM RELATIONS FROM 1975 TO 1991

Following the end of the Vietnam War in late April 1975, relations between China and Vietnam went through dramatic changes from seemingly good and normal relations in 1975 to open war in early 1979. Relations deteriorated over a number of issues. First, there were continuing differences concerning the Soviet Union and China's uneasiness about Vietnam's relations with that country. Vietnam's relations with the Soviet Union grew stronger during this period, particularly in 1978, as relations with China deteriorated.

Second, there were conflicting interests in Cambodia. China's gradually increasing support for Cambodia and its shift to open support from early 1978 in the deepening conflict between Vietnam and Cambodia was of major concern to Vietnam. The Vietnamese military intervention in Cambodia in late December 1978 caused further tension after a Cambodian government with close relations with China was overthrown.

A third issue was the situation of the ethnic Chinese living in Vietnam and the way in which the Chinese minority was treated. China complained about what it perceived to be discriminatory treatment of Chinese in Vietnam. A mass migration of ethnic Chinese from Vietnam in the spring of 1978 officially led to the public deterioration of bilateral relations between the two countries.

A fourth issue related to territorial disputes along the land border, in the Gulf of Tonkin, and in the South China Sea. The clashes that occurred along the border were an indication of divergences with regard to other issues and of the overall deterioration of relations, rather than an important disputed issue in itself. The maritime disputes became increasingly publicized in 1979 when the conflict was already evident. The overall deterioration of

Chinese militia forces pledging support for the Vietnamese, Beijing, July 30, 1966. *After first supporting the Vietminh to overthrow the French in 1954, China maintained close relations with their neighbor to the south until the end of Vietnam's war with the United States. By 1979, the first of a series of continuing border conflicts between China and Vietnam erupted, resulting in an uneasy coexistence at the beginning of the twenty-first century.* © BETTMANN/CORBIS

relations led to a militarized conflict that escalated into China's attack on Vietnam in February and March 1979.

The 1980s were characterized by continued tension along the land border and also by a naval clash in the South China Sea in March 1988. Thereafter, tension receded. The normalization process began with low-level contacts in the mid-1980s and expanded to high-level meetings from early 1989. The increased diplomatic interaction paved the way for a high-level summit in November 1991, during which bilateral relations were fully normalized.

CHINA-VIETNAM RELATIONS SINCE FULL NORMALIZATION IN LATE 1991

During the 1990s the relationship between China and Vietnam was characterized by two contradictory trends: one positive, with expanding contacts and cooperation in many fields, and the other negative, with continued differences relating primarily to territorial disputes. The positive trend was prevalent throughout the decade, but was at times slowed by the fluctuating levels of tension relating to the border disputes, in particular those in the South China Sea area. In the early 2000s, collaboration expanded while tension relating to territorial issues receded.

Expanding political, cultural, economic, and military contacts between the two countries illustrate the positive trend in improving and expanding bilateral relations, and there is a strong political willingness to strengthen and deepen the overall relationship. A number of bilateral agreements have been signed. The expansion of economic relations is evident from the growth in bilateral trade—up to 1 billion U.S. dollars in 1996, 2 billion in 2000, and 10.4 billion in 2006, with a considerable imbalance in China's favor. China is also providing loans and assistance to upgrade Chinese-built factories in northern Vietnam.

Relations and collaboration at both government and provincial levels have also been considerably expanded, thus facilitating trade relations and border management, as well as people-to-people interaction as reflected in the growth of tourism, in particular from China to northern Vietnam. In the political field, the relationship between the two ruling parties—that is, the CCP and the Communist Party of Vietnam—has deepened through a steady stream of exchange visits at various levels within the two parties. The combined relations at government and party levels contribute to generating extensive collaboration between the two countries. Contacts between the two countries' armed forces have also expanded through regular visits and through joint initiatives to improve security both along the land border and in the Gulf of Tonkin.

Tension in bilateral relations has primarily been caused by differences relating to territorial disputes and to a lesser degree by problems relating to cross-border smuggling. After late 1991, particularly between May and November 1992, sharp differences relating to all the territorial disputes—overlapping claims to the Paracel and Spratly archipelagos, to water and continental shelf areas in the South China Sea and in the Gulf of Tonkin, and to areas along the land border—were prevalent. Differences relating to oil exploration in the South China Sea arose in 1994, 1996, and 1997. In 1998 there was no extended period of tension relating to the border disputes.

In 1999 the focus was on reaching a settlement in the land-border dispute, and this effort resulted in the signing of a Land Border Treaty on December 30, 1999. In 2000 negotiators focused on settling the Gulf of Tonkin disputes, resulting in the signing of the Agreement on the Demarcation of Waters, Exclusive Economic Zones, and Continental Shelves in the Gulf of Tonkin on December 25. Following negotiations on a supplementary agreement on fisheries completed in 2004, the ratification of the 2000 agreement on maritime delimitation in the Gulf of Tonkin was completed.

Since 1999 tension has generally been avoided, but official protests have been issued in response to a limited number of actions carried out in or in relation to the South China Sea. Thus, the land-border and Gulf of Tonkin disputes have been resolved, while the disputes in the South China Sea remained unresolved. But the level of tension has been considerably reduced.

Relations during the second half of the twentieth century were characterized by periods of close collaboration and a period of deep conflict. Near the end of the first decade of the twenty-first century, cooperation prevailed, following the improvement of relations during the 1990s and expansion of relations in the early 2000s. In the future, the relationship between China and Vietnam will be determined by how successfully the two sides handle disputes. Deepening bilateral cooperation in different fields and expanding economic interaction contribute to building a more stable bilateral relationship, and progress in managing territorial disputes has contributed to the prospect of long-term stability in the relationship between China and Vietnam.

SEE ALSO *ASEAN, Relations with; Geographical Regions, Natural and Human; Russia, Relations with; South China Sea; Southeast Asian States, Relations with; United States, Relations with.*

BIBLIOGRAPHY

Amer, Ramses. Sino-Vietnamese Normalization in the Light of the Crisis of the Late 1970s. *Pacific Affairs* 67, 3 (1994): 357–383.

Amer, Ramses. Sino-Vietnamese Relations: Past, Present, and Future. In *Vietnamese Foreign Policy in Transition*, ed. Carl A. Thayer and Ramses Amer, 68–130. Singapore: Institute for Southeast Asian Studies; New York: St. Martin's Press, 1999.

Amer, Ramses. *The Sino-Vietnamese Approach to Managing Boundary Disputes.* Durham, NC: International Boundaries Research Unit, University of Durham, 2002.

Amer, Ramses. Assessing Sino-Vietnamese Relations through the Management of Contentious Issues. *Contemporary Southeast Asia* 26, 2 (2004): 320–345.

Gilks, Anne. *The Breakdown of the Sino-Vietnamese Alliance, 1970–1979.* Berkeley: Institute of East Asian Studies, University of California, 1992.

Hervouet, Gérard, ed. *Le dialogue Chine-Viêt-Nam dans un contexte de sécurité multilatérale en Asie Orientale* [The China-Vietnam dialogue within the context of multilateral security in East Asia]. Quebec: Institut québéquois des hautes études internationales, Université Laval, 1997.

Ross, Robert S. *The Indochina Tangle: China's Vietnam Policy, 1975–1979.* New York: Columbia University Press, 1988.

Womack, Brantly. *China and Vietnam: The Politics of Asymmetry.* Cambridge, U.K.: Cambridge University Press, 2006.

Woodside, Alexander. Nationalism and Poverty in the Breakdown of Sino-Vietnamese Relations. *Pacific Affairs* 52, 3 (1979): 381–409.

Ramses Amer

VILLAGES SINCE 1800

Chinese dynasties changed hands frequently for more than two thousand years, but some basic features of village life remained unchanged. One such feature is that many rural residents were *zi geng nong*, self-reliant family-unit farmers, tilling either their own land or rented land. Most farmers paid high rent to a landlord, and a farming family's livelihood usually had to be supplemented by handicrafts, such as the raising of silkworms or the production of textiles, agricultural tools, or furniture, organized within the family or the village. Handicraft products were made for family use, as well as for selling at the market. Several villages would usually serve one market or market town, which in turn served as an urban-rural interaction point and offered related commercial functions.

Traditional Chinese urban life and commerce were very much dependent on and closely related to the village economy: When the rural economy was better, commercial activities flourished and urban life was more prosperous. This was particularly the case in the Yangzi River and Pearl River Delta areas. However, there were rural areas where villages had no access to town centers. This was true especially of walled villages in remote mountainous areas of Yunnan and Guizhou and in some areas in the northwest. In such places as Gao village in Jiangxi Province near the fertile Poyang Lake, there was no market town for hundreds of kilometers and very little commercial activity, so handicraft products were mostly made for family consumption.

ECONOMIC SCARCITY AND SELF-SUFFICIENCY

Historically, the level of prosperity in Chinese villages has been related to the land-population ratio. The glaring lack of land resources for China's huge population is a factor that differentiates Chinese rural society sharply from its counterparts in many other parts of the world. According to one estimate, per capita arable land in 1990 in China was 0.08 hectares, compared to 0.11 for Japan (the next lowest), 0.12 for the United Kingdom, and 0.20 for India. By 2030, when China's population is expected to be 1.6 billion, there will still be 800 million Chinese living in villages, even if the urbanization rate reaches 50 percent. The very fact of this shortage of land under such tremendous population pressure has determined that rural life in China transpires under the strain of an economy of scarcity in which rural existence, past and present, is not a lifestyle that one may choose, but a means of survival.

Typically, Chinese villagers lived at a subsistence level during times of high population pressure or during natural disasters such as large-scale droughts or floods, but village life could be comfortable and even prosperous at other times. Several golden periods of rural prosperity followed large-scale wars that dramatically reduced the size of the population.

In many parts of the rural heartland, particularly in such provinces as Anhui, Henan, Jiangxi, Hunan, and Sichuan, self-sufficiency—that is, relative independence of commercial exchange—was a feature of life up to the late 1960s and early 1970s. Before the reform-era phenomenon of rural-to-urban migration involving hundreds of millions of people, the majority of villagers in China's rural heartland produced most of their own tools, clothing, sugar, wine, soy sauce, furniture, and daily necessities such as shoes, fans, hats, and raincoats.

HEALTH CARE AND EDUCATION

Dramatic changes in village education and health care took place in the Mao era. State-run primary schools were unknown in China before the twentieth century. Children were taught by private teachers in their own or a nearby village. Girls would not attend school at all, nor would the majority of children from poor families. Occasionally, a village clan might support a poor boy's education, but most people in nineteenth-century China were illiterate. Education reform was underway even before the Republic was established in 1911, but a massive campaign to promote literacy among the poor did not start until the People's Republic of China (PRC) was established in 1949. The period of most rapid expansion of rural education was also the most radical period of the Mao era, from the late 1960s to the early 1970s. Though education in rural China still lags behind urban China, where the literacy rate is nearly 100 percent, China's rural literacy rates are among the best of any in developing countries.

Rural life expectancy was also low before the establishment of the PRC: In 1949 rural life expectancy was around thirty-nine years. This is hardly a surprising statistic given the eight-year Anti-Japanese War, the three-year civil war between Nationalist and Communist troops, and the lack of access to most medical technology in rural China. Peace, medical technology, and sheer political will by the PRC raised village life expectancy to around sixty by the late 1970s. One example of effective and affordable medical care for the rural poor was the barefoot doctor system developed during the decade of the Cultural Revolution. This system was dismantled in the 1980s, leading to a sharp deterioration in the provision of health care in the villages.

CLAN CULTURE AND VILLAGE CONFLICT

Many Chinese villages are clan or lineage communities, with all residents belonging to a single clan and all bearing the same surname. Consequently, much of the cultural and religious life in a village focuses on clan activities, and has always done so. Likewise, internal village politics usually involve different branches of the clan, while cross-village conflicts usually involve clan disputes.

One development has led to a weakening of the lineage tradition in the minds of Chinese villagers. Many young Chinese who migrate to work in urban areas far from their hometowns have come to consider lineage and clan ideas backward and outdated. A substantial number of migrant workers meet and marry villagers from other provinces, a trend that further dilutes the concept of a clan village.

RELIGION AND CUSTOMS

The lineage helps shape village religious and ritual life through the fostering of ancestor worship. Another major religious force in much of rural China is Buddhism. Sometimes villagers do not differentiate ancestor worship from Buddhism. They might attribute historical figures with godlike status, call them *pusa* (buddha), and pray and make offerings to them. The cult that developed around Guan Yu (d. 219 CE) is an example of this process.

Woman carrying children in Guizhou province, China, 1988. *Although the majority of China's population lives in rural areas, large scale migration to urban areas at the turn of the twenty-first century continues to transform village life. As many migrants tend to be young people looking for employment and educational opportunities, many villages throughout the countryside have suffered from the loss of this productive generation.* © **KAZUYOSHI NOMACHI/CORBIS**

Even during the most radical period of the Mao era, when such practices and beliefs were considered "feudalistic" and "backward," villagers covertly continued these traditions. Since the post-Mao reforms, this mixing of elements of different beliefs for spiritual sustenance or—more often—for commercial gain has been revived and strengthened. In many parts of China, rural residents have turned Mao into a religious figure.

Other traditions persist as well. Chinese New Year, officially renamed Spring Festival by the Communist government, remains the most important and festive occasion in village life. Although Chinese rural residents have created a rich material culture, the villagers have always lived very frugally and often at subsistence level. For this reason they work hard and save all year, but they spend whatever is saved on clothing, food, and consumables such as fireworks during the Spring Festival. In addition, during the festival period, people travel hundreds and thousands of miles and go through hardship and difficulties to be with their families. The Chinese New Year of the Rat in February 2008 was one of the coldest on record, with widespread snow even in the south. Despite power lines collapsing and trains coming to a halt, the Chinese transport system eventually managed to move a staggering 200 million people to their family homes for the New Year.

THE GENDER ISSUE

As in all premodern societies, there was serious gender discrimination in traditional Chinese society, with women suffering sexual exploitation and humiliation. In rural China, discrimination was more marked in affluent families, due primarily to two factors. First, men in affluent families might desire several concubines, as well as a wife. In these families, the life of a concubine could be miserable. Secondly, because women from poor families were involved in economic activities, they often enjoyed greater influence in the family than their more affluent peers.

In the early twentieth century, a national movement for women's liberation reached rural China, but without penetrating deeply. Women's liberation took root in rural China with the Communist revolution in 1949. Gender equality was promoted on a large scale, and practical measures were taken to encourage the education of women and their participation in political and production activities. It was this goal that partly inspired the formation of commune canteens during the Great Leap Forward years in the late 1950s, so that women were not bound to the kitchen. Though the experiment was soon abandoned as the Great Leap Forward disaster unfolded, much of the philosophy of gender equality was retained in Communist ideology. Further campaigns to realize gender equality were undertaken during the decade of the Cultural Revolution from 1966 to 1976.

As the commune system was refined and enhanced after the Great Leap Forward, rural women's participation in production activities (outside of the family) increased to the extent that they worked in the field as much as men, except when they had to care for children. In general, women were paid less in the commune system, mainly because they usually did less physically demanding work. Women were responsible for most of the housework, including cooking, cleaning, and child care. Men did more farmwork in the collective and on their private plots than women did, but because of their participation in production, women did grow more assertive and had a greater say in family matters.

Many of the gains in women's liberation were eroded by the post-Mao reform policies. The one-child per family policy, in particular, gave rise to discriminatory attitudes toward female babies, with a family more likely to abort an unborn girl or to give a female child away for adoption. New patterns of crime included the sale of women in rural areas and the employment of rural women as prostitutes in urban centers, practices that were previously unknown in the PRC. Education offers another example. In the new era of opportunity, many families would allow a girl to become a migrant worker so that her brother could receive an education from the money she sent back home.

FURTHER REGIONAL DIFFERENCES

The difference between village life and city life constitutes one of the starkest contrasts in contemporary China, one that is partly reflected in urban-rural differences in gender discrimination. Within rural China, however, a number of other variables affect the differences in the quality and pattern of life. Among these is the regional differentiation between north and south. The north is characterized by a great expanse of level dry land that is good for crops such as wheat. In the south, the land is full of hills, mountains, rivers, and lakes. Most of the rice crop is produced in the south.

These kinds of differences have important implications for rural life and village organization. Villages in southern China are more clan conscious than are northern villages, perhaps due to a greater need than northern villages to protect limited resources. There is very little intravillage mobility in southern China, whereas it is not uncommon to find recent migrants settling down in a northern village. As a result, religious activities in southern villages tend to be more closely related to clan relations. Another consequence of the geographical difference is that the mechanization of farming on the plains of northern China progressed more quickly, even during the Mao era. Finally, as southerners will readily claim, the natural fertility of the south has allowed a much greater diversity of diet, both in ingredients and in the style of cooking.

SEE ALSO *Education: Education in Rural Areas; Land Tenure since 1800; Peasantry, 1800–1900; Poverty; Taxation and Fiscal Policies, 1800–1912.*

BIBLIOGRAPHY

Crook, Isabel, and David Crook. *The First Years of Yangyi Commune.* New York: Humanities Press, 1966.

Elvin, Mark. *The Pattern of the Chinese Past.* Stanford, CA: Stanford University Press, 1973.

Endicott, Stephen. *Red Earth: Revolution in a Sichuan Village.* London: Tauris, 1988.

Gao, Mobo. *Gao Village: A Portrait of Rural Life in Modern China*. London: Hurst; Honolulu: University of Hawai'i Press; Hong Kong: Hong Kong University Press, 1999.

Hinton, William. *Fanshen: A Documentary of Revolution in a Chinese Village*. New York: Monthly Review Press, 1966.

Hinton, William. *Shenfan: The Continuing Revolution in a Chinese Village*. New York: Random House, 1983.

Huang Zongzhi (Philip C. C. Huang). *The Peasant Economy and Social Change in North China*. Stanford, CA: Stanford University Press, 1985.

Huang Zongzhi (Philip C. C. Huang). *The Peasant Family and Rural Development in the Yangzi Delta, 1350–1988*. Stanford, CA: Stanford University Press, 1990.

Parish, William, and Martin King Whyte. *Village and Family in Contemporary China*. Chicago: University of Chicago Press, 1978.

Potter, Sulamith Heins, and Jack M. Potter. *China's Peasants: The Anthropology of a Revolution*. Cambridge, U.K.: Cambridge University Press, 1990.

Unger, Jonathan. *The Transformation of Rural China*. Armonk, NY: Sharpe, 2002.

Zhu Ling. *Rural Reform and Peasant Income in China: The Impact of China's Post-Mao Rural Reforms in Selected Areas*. London: Macmillan, 1991.

Mobo Gao

VOCATIONAL EDUCATION

Originating from apprenticeship in the Middle Ages, vocational education first emerged in the European industrialized countries in the late seventeenth century, parallel with universal education. The history of modern vocational education in China can be traced back to the late Qing dynasty (1840–1912), when the Chinese imperial government was looking for strategies for survival and self-strengthening against the Western powers, but it was not until the early twentieth century that the modern vocational educational system began to emerge.

BEFORE 1949

The first few modern educational institutes were set up in the late nineteenth century, and most of them were actually vocational schools. For example, the Peking Foreign Language School (Jingshi Tongwen Guan) and the Shanghai Foreign Language School (Shanghai Guangfanyan Guan) were established in 1862 and 1863, respectively, for training diplomats and translators. Also, various arsenal schools such as Fuzhou Naval School (Fuzhou Chuanzheng Xuetang) in 1866 were set up for training skilled workers in a modern manufacturing environment. In China's first legislation for a modern school system in 1902 to 1904, vocational schools were established as a key independent subsystem, from elementary apprentice schools to vocational colleges. In the legislations of 1912 to 1913 and 1922, vocational education was further developed, first opening its doors to women around 1910, and being linked with regular and teacher education from the early 1920s.

In this period, vocational education was seen as a practical yet important component in China's national school system. For example, in the guidelines of educational aims officially set by the Chinese central government from the early twentieth century up to 1949, vocational education was always positioned as a top priority in terms of national initiatives, new establishments, and reform efforts. At the same time, pioneer practitioners actively promoted vocational education by opening experimental vocational schools, establishing professional associations, and publishing influential articles. As one of the founders of China's modern vocational education, Huang Yanpei (1878–1965) in 1916 created the first academic society for research on vocational education, the Subsociety on Vocational Education under the Jiangsu Education Society. One year later he cofounded the National Association of Vocational Education of China (NAVEC) in Shanghai. With these efforts of both individuals and government, by 1949 there were 561 specialized secondary schools, with a total enrollment of 77,095 students (Li 1994, pp. 544–545).

BETWEEN 1949 AND 1978

The vocational education system that developed after the founding of the People's Republic of China (PRC) in 1949 followed the Soviet model closely. With the enactment of the *Guidelines on Reorganizing and Developing Secondary Technical Education* in March 1952, the secondary vocational education system was set up based on the adjustment and restructuring of the old system before 1949. In the 1950s and 1960s there were two main types of vocational education in China: secondary specialized schools that offered four-year programs, and technical middle schools that focused on three-year programs. The secondary specialized schools aimed at training technicians, whereas the technical middle schools trained skilled workers for state-owned factories or industrial enterprises.

Unlike regular schools, which were under educational authorities at national, provincial, or local level, vocational schools were administered by the respective authorities at different levels but were all were overseen by the Ministry of Higher Education. The exception was normal schools, which were set up for training elementary schoolteachers and were under the leadership of local educational authorities and overseen by the Ministry of Education.

In the late 1950s the vocational education system was fully coordinated with the economic development plans through four major types of secondary schools: agricultural schools, industrial schools, normal schools, and part-time vocational high schools. All the graduates from vocational schools were assigned jobs in state- or collective-owned factories or industrial enterprises, or in public schools. By 1965 there were 871 secondary specialized schools with 392,443 students, 400 technical middle schools with 183,419 students, 61,626 vocational middle schools with 4,433,400 students, and 394 normal schools with 155,004 students (Li 1994, pp. 544–552).

Further development of China's vocational education system was seriously hampered by the ten tumultuous years of the Cultural Revolution, starting in 1966. The situation remained chaotic until 1978, when Deng Xiaoping returned to power.

AFTER 1978

After China opened its door to the outside world in 1978, its vocational education system revived step by step along with the gradual restoration of the national educational system, and various reforms were launched to transform the vocational education system. These included transforming some general secondary schools into vocational schools, establishing an educational network for vocational education and training, increasing annual budgets for vocational schools, and other changes designed to increase enrollment and support. Meanwhile, curricula and teaching in vocational schools were tailored to meet the demands of the radical changes in China's economic structure and rapid innovation of technologies. More importantly, serious attention was directed to the quality and efficiency of vocational schools. The size of the vocational education system was also greatly expanded. In 1980, there were 3,314 vocational middle schools, enrolling 454,000 students. Among them, there were 2,924 agricultural schools that were restored or newly opened, with 320,000 students accounting for 70 percent of the total enrollment of vocational middle schools (Li 1994, p. 358).

On May 9, 1983, the *Opinion on the Structural Reform of Urban Secondary Education and the Development of Vocational Education* was signed jointly by four ministries. This policy laid out new tasks, goals, and strategies for the development of the vocational education system in the 1980s. Additionally, the *Decision on Education System Reform* was promulgated in 1985. This document clearly stated that vocational education was one of the key fields of educational reform. It called for the secondary education structure to be adjusted and the vocational education system to be ambitiously expanded. Meanwhile, training millions of skilled and knowledgeable workers for industry, agriculture, and commerce was set as the primary goal of the vocational education system. Up to 1985, 1.16 million students were enrolled in 8,070 vocational secon-

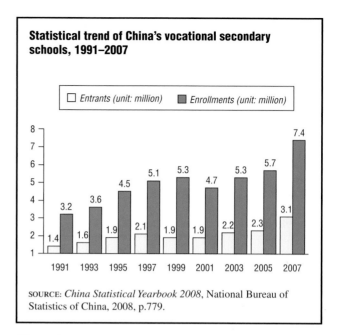

Statistical trend of China's vocational secondary schools, 1991–2007

SOURCE: *China Statistical Yearbook 2008*, National Bureau of Statistics of China, 2008, p.779.

Figure 1

dary schools (National Bureau of Statistics of China 2008, pp. 777–778). By 1988, the percentage of students registered in vocational middle schools jumped from 7.6 percent in 1978 to 44.8 percent of the total enrollment of secondary schools (Li 1994, p. 355). In other words, the structure and system of secondary schools took a significant shift within the ten years.

On May 15, 1996, the Law of Vocational Education, the first law focusing on vocational education in China after 1949, was formally promulgated and implemented. This law was a milestone for the new round of vocational education reform in China, serving as a legal basis for redefining the role, school structure, managerial system, and financial resources for vocational education. Since its implementation, the social status of vocational education has been raised to meet the needs of the socialist market economy and China's radical social change. From the early 1980s to the late 1990s, the secondary vocational school system continued its rapid growth. At the turn of the new century its growth slowed briefly, but by the mid-2000s vocational secondary schools were reenergized and again developed dynamically, as shown in Figure 1.

Meanwhile, China's higher vocational education system has made significant progress in expansion. New student admissions in vocational colleges increased by 3.7 times, from 430,000 in 1998 to two million in 2003, accounting for 52.3 percent of the total recruitment of college students in same year (Wang 2005, p. 6). Among these vocational colleges, private vocational colleges have

Statistics of China's vocational education system, 2007

	Junior secondary	Senior secondary	Colleges	Total
Number of schools	275	5,916	1,015	7,206
Enrollment	152,955	7,252,485	N/A	N/A
Number of teachers	8,699	308,660	307,443	624,802

SOURCE: *China Statistical Yearbook 2008*, National Bureau of Statistics of China, 2008, pp. 775–776.

Table 1

played a more and more important role in the expansion since the late 1990s, as most private higher educational institutions have focused on vocational programs. According to the Ministry of Education's *Annual Statistical Communiqué 2003–2007*, nonpublic higher educational institutions increased from 173 in 2003 to 297, plus 318 second-tier colleges, in 2007. The booming expansion has made it possible to have at least one vocational college in each metropolitan area. Meanwhile, the vocational education system was also diversified in terms of various majors and training programs provided.

The Chinese government at both the central and local levels has played a critical role in the development of the vocational education system since 1978. Early in 1980 the State Council passed the *Report on Secondary Education Structure Reform*, which provided practical strategies for secondary education reform. In 1991 the State Council publicized the *Decision on Energetically Developing Vocational and Technical Education*. In 1993 the *Outline on Reform and Development of Education* was promulgated by the Communist Party of China Central Committee and the State Council, providing a better environment for vocational education development. The *Outline* urged that vocational education schools at all levels must actively meet the needs of local development and the socialist market economy. In 1994 the National Working Conference on Education supported the expansion of experimental vocational education schools based the German Dual System, expecting to promote the quality of the workforce and prioritize the development of vocational education.

Since 2001, China's vocational education system has seen an unprecedented period of development. The State Council in July 2002 hosted the Working Conference of National Vocational education in Beijing. One month later, the *Decision on Vigorously Advancing Vocational Education Reform and Development* was officially promulgated by the State Council. The new policy urged that local governments must allocate an increasing rate of their

yearly budget for vocational education schools or institutions, and that the proportion for vocational education budget must be no less than 15 percent of educational expenditure in urban areas and no less than 20 percent in the areas where nine-year compulsory education has been universalized. In 2004 the Joint Seven Departments of the State Council held the new Working Conference of National Vocational Education in Nanjing, and later publicized the *Opinions on Further Strengthening Vocational Education*. All these policies in recent years have shown that China's government has made firm and persistent efforts for the reform and development of vocational education. These policy actions have shown that the Chinese government once again made vocational education development a national policy priority, and it expects that the enrollment in senior vocational education systems by 2010 will reach eight million, which will be equal to that in regular senior high schools.

The Chinese government has tried hard since the 1980s to rebuild a nationwide vocational education system suitable for the socialist market economy with Chinese characteristics. Many policy actions have been taken to transform the old Soviet model of vocational education, and the outcomes are encouraging. The obstacles and dilemmas in vocational education reform and development, however, remain perplexing. For example, the recent development of secondary vocational education schools is slowing down, compared with that of higher vocational education colleges; the vocational education structure is imbalanced in terms of school types and levels; the vocational education administrative system does not meet the demand of the market; the teacher workforce is not appropriate in terms of quantity or competent in terms of quality; applicants for admission to vocational education schools have much lower academic achievement than those to regular schools. One more major obstacle is that the annual state budget for vocational education expenditure is not sufficient, and as a result, the campus facilities for vocational education schools are unsatisfactory. In addition, great contrasts persist nationwide among different parts of the vocational education system (key schools and disadvantaged schools), different geographical areas (the west and the east), and regions of differing economic resources (the urban and the rural). These obstacles and problems pose serious challenges to Chinese policy makers.

The development of China's vocational education shows how a centralized administration employs multiple policy actions to build up a nationwide vocational education system. The advantages of such a model include the ability to upgrade an old system by collective policy players and behaviors, compulsory participation and involvement, and the optimizing of various resources. But the disadvantages are also obvious: a rigid and hierarchical educational structure, very limited flexibility, little school autonomy, asymmetrical communication between policy makers and school implementers, and so on. In addition, it is definitely difficult for the Chinese government to find a place where the relationship between central control and decentralization is appropriately balanced. This problem challenges Chinese policy makers and practitioners of vocational education as they develop new policy actions in the future.

SEE ALSO *Education.*

BIBLIOGRAPHY
Editorial Board of *Educational Almanac. Dierci zhongguo jiaoyu nianjian* [The second almanac of China's education]. Shanghai: Commercial Press, 1948.

Fallon, Peter R., and Gordon Hunting. China. In *Vocational Education and Training Reform: Matching Skills to Markets and Budgets*, ed. Indermit Singh Gill, Fred Fluitman, and Amit Dar, 161–181. Oxford, U.K.: Oxford University Press, 2000.

National Bureau of Statistics of China. *China Statistical Yearbook 2008*. Beijing: China Statistics Press, 2008.

Li, Lantian. *Zhongguo zhiye jishu jiaoyu shi* [A history of China's vocational and technical education]. Beijing: Higher Education Press, 1994.

Shi, Weiping. *Bijiao zhiye jishu jiaoyu* [Comparative study on vocational and technical education]. Shanghai: East China Normal University Press, 2001.

Sun, Deyu, Lu, Jingwen, and Li, Jun. New Policy Actions and Government Roles: China's Reconstruction of TVET Systems since the 1980s. In *International Handbook of Education for the Changing World of Work*, vol. 3, ed. Rupert Maclean and David Wilson. Dordrecht, Netherlands: Springer Publishers, 2009.

Sun, Peiqing. *Zhongguo jiaoyu shi* [A history of China's education]. Rev. ed. Shanghai: East China Normal University Press, 2000.

Wang, Haobo. Qianxi woguo zhongdeng zhiye jiaoyu zhi fazhan [On the development of China's secondary vocational education]. *China Science and Technology Information* 12 (2005): 225–226.

Wang, Jiping. Wguo zhiye jiaoyu de xingshi he fazhan silu [The situation and development plan of Chinese vocational education]. *Journal of Henan Vocation-Technical Teachers College* (Vocational Education Ed.). 1 (2005): 5–9.

Jun Li

W

WADE, THOMAS
1818–1895

Thomas Francis Wade was a London-born diplomat and linguist whose career began when he became one of the first British consuls to be appointed after the opening of treaty ports following the first Opium War (1839–1842). When Wade arrived in China in 1841 with the British expeditionary force, he began to study Chinese and eventually left the army to take up a position as interpreter to the supreme court of Hong Kong. Later, he became Chinese secretary to the superintendent of trade, John F. Davis (1795–1890). By 1852 Wade was in Shanghai serving as vice consul. There he assisted Rutherford Alcock (1809–1897) in the negotiations that led to the creation of the Imperial Maritime Customs, and he served as the first inspector in 1854, a role later taken over by Robert Hart (1835–1911). The following year, Wade returned to the position of Chinese secretary in Hong Kong, where he began to develop a Chinese-language training program.

INTERPRETER AND DIPLOMATIC ADVISOR

During the Second Opium War (1856–1860), Wade served, along with Horatio Nelson Lay (1832–1898) and Harry Parkes (1828–1885), as an interpreter for Lord Elgin (James Bruce, 1811–1863), the British high commissioner to China. Wade was involved in the negotiations for the Tianjin Treaty (1858) and was instrumental in making the English-language text of the treaty the official version. He and other interpreters also developed the diplomatic aspects of what would come to be called "gunboat diplomacy." They advised Elgin that it was important to maintain a

firm stand against Qing negotiators and be prepared to back it with force. Anything else, they argued, would be seen as a sign of weakness by the Chinese.

Wade was also instrumental in developing a stern line against Chinese "obfuscation" and delays in the negotiating process. He and the other linguists scrutinized captured Qing official correspondence for material to be used against court agents, either to humiliate them or to catch them out in "falsehoods." The object was to convince Qing officials that they could no more avoid British penetration of their official correspondence system than they could avoid British arms. This confrontational approach remained a mainstay of British diplomacy in China for the next two decades.

CHINESE-LANGUAGE PROGRAM

At the newly established British legation in Beijing (1861), Wade, now the Chinese Secretary, formalized the Chinese-language program. He hired native speakers to tutor student-interpreters in conversational Chinese. To supplement these drills, he organized a textbook in Chinese grammar and usage, *Yu-Yen tzu-ehr Chi: A Progressive Course of Colloquial Chinese* (1867), as well as a textbook of documentary Chinese, *Wen-chien tzu-ehr Chi: A Series of Papers Selected as Specimens of Documentary Chinese* (1867). In the documents course, student-interpreters learned the finer points of the Qing bureaucracy and its communication system and were introduced to key documents in Anglo-Chinese relations. Upon completion of the two-year program, student-interpreters were either given a position in Beijing or assigned as consuls to one of the treaty ports. Wade's accomplishments as a linguist also included the creation of an orthographic system for rendering Chinese ideograms into the Roman alphabet.

WADE'S APPROACH TO DIPLOMACY: THE IMPERIAL-AUDIENCE QUESTION AND MARGARY AFFAIR

As Chinese secretary, Wade was at the hub of the interactions between the Zongli Yamen, the Qing foreign office created after the Second Opium War, and the British government throughout the 1860s. He was, in a sense, the indispensable man, not only because of his language skills, but because of his tireless commitment to forcing the Qing to accept the imperatives of the dominant though still-evolving Western international order that was transforming power politics in East Asia. Once he became minister plenipotentiary at Beijing, Wade was involved in a number of critical engagements with the court. In these encounters, Wade sought not only to further British interests in China, but to teach the court how to behave in the contemporary world of competing nation-states. This pedagogical approach to diplomacy was probably best exemplified in Wade's handling of the imperial-audience question and the Margary affair.

Regarding the audience question, Wade was convinced that until European diplomats were received in a formal audience by the emperor, the state of "perfect equality" stipulated by the Tianjin Treaty would not be fully realized. Once Wade became minister, he pressed this point, but Qing officials put him off on the grounds that the emperor would not come of age until 1873. Rallying other European diplomats around the issue, he kept pressure on the Qing to schedule a date for an audience. When officials came up with other reasons for delay, Wade cited precedents from his formidable library of Chinese-language historical materials and Qing records to counter their arguments. Eventually, an audience occurred on July 29, 1873. European ministers bowed at the waist before the emperor and presented their credentials. But because the audience was not in one of the main halls in the Forbidden City, Wade considered the objectives of the treaty only partly achieved.

Two years later, Wade exploited the Margary affair as an opportunity to settle Anglo-Chinese diplomatic issues and teach more lessons. Augustus Margary (1846–1875), one of the graduates of Wade's language program, was sent up the Yangzi to meet an expedition that had mapped the territory between northeast Burma (Myanmar) and Yunnan. While passing through Yunnan, the expedition was attacked by local people and Margary was killed. Wade not only demanded an official investigation and indemnity for the Margary family, but opened questions about travel, trade, taxes on foreign imports, and diplomatic protocol in Beijing. When the Qing government did not immediately respond to his satisfaction, Wade took a belligerent stance, threatened force, and withdrew the British legation to Shanghai. Robert Hart was asked by the court to intervene, and he was able to persuade Wade to open negotiations with Li Hongzhang, the Chinese plenipotentiary, at Chefoo (Zhifu, now Yantai). The result of these meetings was the Chefoo Convention of 1876, which settled the Margary affair and many associated issues.

RETIREMENT AND LEGACY

Wade's approach to diplomacy in China, his aggressive combining of coercion and pedagogy, seems to have taken a toll by the middle of the 1870s, and he began showing signs of mental fatigue. Much of this was brought on by the massive amount of correspondence to the Foreign Office, a large part of it self-imposed, that Wade generated as Chinese secretary and minister and by the frequent turnover of competent linguists in the diplomatic and consular service. The strain led to some kind of breakdown. Wade stopped answering correspondence to London and the treaty ports and frequently claimed to have lost documents that were later discovered in his office by subordinates. Efforts to induce him to catch up on correspondence were only partly successful. His recall to London in 1882 probably had as much to do with his inability to continue to perform his duties as it did with policy disagreements. After his retirement from the diplomatic corps, Wade was appointed the first professor of the Chinese language at Cambridge University in 1888, a position he held until his death in 1895.

Wade's legacy is mixed. His approach to diplomacy with the Qing court reflected the general tenor of British action toward all regimes that appeared benighted. In China, he became a symbol of Western imperialism and China's century of humiliation. Yet, his methods, however objectionable by today's standards, have also been seen as a necessary stimulus for China's "entry into the family of nations." Perhaps his most significant legacy lay in his linguistic efforts. The Chinese-language training program he began continued to operate, with some updating, in the Beijing legation to the eve of World War II (1937–1945), and his Qing documents course may be seen as a precursor to postwar British and American training programs for historians of modern Chinese foreign relations. Lastly, Wade's orthographic system, later modified by Herbert Giles (1845–1935), became a standard for transliterating Chinese. For over a century, the Wade-Giles system served as the primarily means for organizing and cataloging information about China in the English-speaking world.

SEE ALSO *Chinese Maritime Customs Service; Hart, Robert; Margary Affair, 1875–1876; Opium Wars; Sinology.*

BIBLIOGRAPHY

Coates, P. D. *The China Consuls: British Consular Officers, 1843–1943.* Hong Kong and New York: Oxford University Press, 1988.

Cooley, James C. *T. F. Wade in China: Pioneer in Global Diplomacy, 1842–1882*. Leiden, Netherlands: Brill, 1981.

Fairbank, John King, Katherine F. Brunner, and Elizabeth M. Matheson, eds. *The I.G. in Peking: Letters of Robert Hart, Chinese Maritime Customs, 1868–1907*. Cambridge, MA: Belknap Press, 1975.

Hevia, James L. *English Lessons: The Pedagogy of Imperialism in Nineteenth-Century China*. Durham, NC: Duke University Press, 2003.

James Hevia

WALEY, ARTHUR
1889–1966

Arthur Waley ranks as the best-known and most important translator of traditional Chinese literature into the English language, from World War I (1914–1918) until the early 1960s. Altogether, he wrote forty books, translating texts of a staggering variety, ranging from ancient and medieval poetry and works from the philosophical canon to vernacular fiction from the Tang (618–907) and Ming dynasties (1368–1644). In addition, he published studies of ancient Chinese philosophy, biographies of literary figures from the Tang and Qing (1644–1912) dynasties, and historical accounts of the Chinese side of the Opium War (1839–1842). Japanese literature also drew his attention, and his celebrated translations of Noh plays and the eleventh-century *Tale of Genji* played critical roles in making these texts part of the global canon. He also composed more than 130 articles, dealing with East Asian art, literature, drama, and religion. Waley wrote for the general reader, and some of his works were translated into Dutch, German, Italian, Polish, Spanish, and Swedish, as well as Japanese.

Waley was born Arthur David Schloss (Waley was his mother's maiden surname, which he adopted in 1914) into a well-to-do Jewish family, known for its commitment to education and progressive causes. He studied at King's College at Cambridge University, reading in classical and modern languages and graduating in 1910. Evidence suggests that translations of Chinese poetry encountered at Cambridge or shortly after sparked his interest in Chinese literature, and he began teaching himself, with remarkable results, classical Chinese upon receiving a position in 1913 at the British Museum cataloguing East Asian artifacts. He worked at this post until 1929 and became one of the writers and thinkers collectively known as the "Bloomsbury circle." During World War II (1939–1945), he worked in the Ministry of Information as a censor in the Japan section. After 1945, he taught intermittently at the School of Oriental and African Studies at the University of London. Despite his lifelong immersion in East Asian literature, Waley famously never traveled to China or Japan.

Waley's career as a scholar and translator of Chinese might be divided into three phases. The first (1916–1919) featured his renditions of ancient and medieval Chinese poetry, which won wide acclaim, drew praise from Ezra Pound and T. S. Eliot, and appeared later in numerous reprinted editions. In the second phase (1934–1941), Waley turned from Japanese literature to the Chinese canon, translating the *Daodejing* (1934), the *Book of Songs* (1937), and the *Analects* (1938), as well as publishing a study of pre-Qin philosophy, *Three Ways of Thought in Ancient China* (1939). In his last twenty-five years, he took up, most notably, vernacular literature, with abridged translations of *Journey to the West* (published in 1942 as *Monkey*) and Tang narratives (published in 1960 as *Ballads and Stories from Tunhuang: An Anthology*), along with biographies of Bai Juyi (1949), Li Bai (1951), and Yuan Mei (1956).

In his lifetime, Waley's works won a devoted audience. His limpid, graceful prose, uncanny attention to the particular, and sensitivity for his subject transformed the distant world of dynastic China into a place that readers might understand and even savor. Chinese literati often appeared as refined gentlemen, suspicious of the martial and fanatic, and mindful of the passage of time and its inevitable sorrows. As Chinese studies underwent professionalization after World War II, Waley's reputation slipped somewhat. Although many continue to regard highly his *Analects* translation and Bai Juyi and Yuan Mei biographies, some critics faulted him for avoiding philological problems and glossing over cultural differences. That being said, in the twentieth century, no one did more to make traditional China accessible to the West than Arthur Waley.

SEE ALSO *Interpreters of Things Chinese to the West.*

BIBLIOGRAPHY

Johns, Francis A. *A Bibliography of Arthur Waley*. New Brunswick, NJ: Rutgers University Press, 1968.

Johns, Francis A. Manifestations of Arthur Waley: Some Bibliographical and Other Notes. *British Library Journal* 9, 2 (1983): 171–184.

Morris, Ivan, ed. *Madly Singing in the Mountains: An Appreciation and Anthology of Arthur Waley*. New York: Walker, 1970.

Spence, Jonathan. The Explorer Who Never Left Home: Arthur Waley. *Renditions* 5 (1975): 32–37. Reprinted in Jonathan Spence, *Chinese Roundabout: Essays in History and Culture*, 329–336. New York: Norton, 1992.

Mark Halperin

WANG ANYI
1954–

Wang Anyi, one of the most important contemporary Chinese writers, was born in Nanjing on March 6, 1954, and raised in Shanghai. Her mother, Ru Zhijuan (1925–1998), was also a famous writer, and her father was a playwright who was labeled as a rightist in the late 1950s. After Wang graduated from junior high school in 1969, during the Cultural Revolution (1966–1969), she was sent with other educated urban young people to the countryside in Anhui Province to receive "re-education" from the peasants. Wang managed to leave the commune by joining a local performing arts troupe as a cellist in 1972. She began publishing stories in the mid-1970s. After the Cultural Revolution she returned to Shanghai in 1978 to work as an editor for the magazine *Ertong shidai* (Childhood Times). In 1980 she became a member of the Chinese National Writers' Association, in 2001 she was elected chairperson of the Shanghai Writers' Association, and in 2006 she was elected vice president of the Chinese National Writers' Association. The winner of many national literary prizes for fiction, Wang is a versatile and prolific writer, and her work is at the literary forefront.

Her stories from the 1970s and early 1980s are explorations of subjective perspectives, as in the collection *Yu, shashasha* (Gentle Rain, 1981), which focuses on young women's sense and sensibility in facing the social changes and transition from a planned economy to a market economy. Wang's early writing was fresh and sentimental, as was typical of the youth writing of the day—"educated youth literature."

In 1983 Wang Anyi and her mother spent five months at the University of Iowa international writing workshop, exchanging ideas with other writers from around the world. This experience encouraged Wang to take a broader view of the world and to reflect more deeply upon her cultural roots. She soon shifted her literary concerns toward broad social issues, as in the novella *Baotown* (1984). In a nonsentimental way, Wang portrays human aspirations, social destitution, starvation, and vagrancy, and traditional mores in a small village during the whole period of Mao Zedong's rule and the first years after his death. Wang tackles the social and cultural issues in the village, as well as the individual lives there, in a clear matter-of-fact style that combines realism with light allegory. *Baotown* is regarded as a representative work in the "searching for roots" literary movement of the 1980s, and it established Wang's leading role among her contemporary writers.

Wang subsequently expanded her exploration to the largely taboo area of sexuality by publishing three novellas on the theme of love—*Jinxiugu zhi lian* (Brocade Valley, 1986), *Xiaocheng zhi lian* (Love in a Small Town, 1986), and *Huangshan zhi lian* (Love on a Barren Mountain, 1986). Naming the main protagonists in her three novellas simply "he" and "she," Wang Anyi provides long introspective monologues alongside descriptions of the physical attractions of her characters. Her story "Dixiongmen" ("Brothers," 1989) examines female same-sex associations and the hostile social environment that stifles such possibility. Wang

Anyi was the first woman writer to write at any length about sex and other private bodily functions. She paved the way for the intimate and sexual narrative strategy adopted by many young women writers in the mid-1990s, and "body politics" in Chinese literature more broadly.

In the 1990s Wang's narrative styles and perspectives took a new direction in her construction of grand epics combining surrealism and myth with extended family history, as in the novels *Shangxin Taipingyang* (Grieving Over the Pacific Ocean, 1992) and *Jishi he xugou* (Reality and Fiction, 1993). Other important works in the 1990s include *Shushu de gushi* (A Story of an Uncle, 1990), a satirical account of a revolutionary hero seen through the eyes of a young generation, and *Changhen ge* (1995; *The Song of Everlasting Sorrow: A Novel of Shanghai*, 2008), a saga of a former Shanghai beauty queen whose life mirrors many changing phases in modern China.

In the twenty-first century Wang Anyi continues to be productive, usually at the pace of one to three novels a year. She published a series of novels focusing on the inner feelings and strong will of female characters living at the bottom of society in Shanghai, and while critics were categorizing Wang as a specialist in female characters, she published a novel on the underground masculine culture in Shanghai, *Biandi xiaoxiong* (Rebels Everywhere, 2005), depicting urban crime, violence, and brotherhood in Shanghai.

Wang Anyi is a Shanghai writer *par excellence* and often is compared with another female writer from Shanghai, Zhang Ailing (Eileen Chang, 1920–1995), whose writing was popular in Shanghai during the Japanese occupation in the 1940s. The stories of both writers often are set in Shanghai, and contain vivid and informative descriptions of the city itself. Like Zhang Ailing, Wang pays meticulous attention to the details of everyday Shanghai life: clothes, fashion, food, *longtang* alleys, markets, means of transportation, and local customs of interaction. And both writers excel at deep psychological portrayals of their female characters. But unlike Zhang Ailing and many others who have written on Shanghai with an eye to its past, Wang Anyi focuses on contemporary Shanghai. The bulk of her work might be described as a social history of contemporary Shanghai presented through the psychology of its inhabitants.

Wang Anyi constantly challenges her own writing, pushing the limits and broadening her themes and styles. She is never content with what she has previously achieved. It is foreseeable that she will leave a large legacy in the history of Chinese literature.

SEE ALSO *Root-Searching Literature.*

BIBLIOGRAPHY

Wang Anyi. *Love in a Small Town.* Trans. Eva Hung. Hong Kong: Renditions Paperbacks, 1988.

Wang Anyi. *Baotown*. Trans. Martha Avery. Harmondsworth, U.K.: Viking, 1989.

Wang Anyi. *The Flow*. London: Facsimile Publications, 1989.

Wang Anyi. *Love on a Barren Mountain*. Trans. Eva Hung. Hong Kong: Renditions Paperbacks, 1991.

Wang Anyi. *Brocade Valley*. New York: New Directions, 1992.

Wang Anyi. *Selected Stories by Anyi Wang*. Beijing: Foreign Languages Teaching and Research Press, 1999.

Wang Anyi. Brothers. Trans. Jingyuan Zhang. In *Red Is Not the Only Color: Contemporary Chinese Fiction on Love and Sex Between Women, Collected Stories*, ed. Patricia Sieber, 93–141. Boulder, CO: Rowman Littlefield, 2001.

Wang Anyi. *Lapse of Time*. Trans. Dai Naidie. Beijing: Foreign Languages Press, 2005.

Wang Anyi. *The Song of Everlasting Sorrow: A Novel of Shanghai*. Trans. Michael Berry and Susan Chan Egan. New York: Columbia University Press, 2008.

Jingyuan Zhang

WANG GUOWEI

1877–1927

Wang Guowei (courtesy name Jing'an; assumed name Guantang) was a poet, literary critic, epigrapher, and historian. Born into a merchant family in Haining, Zhejiang Province, near Hangzhou, the provincial capital, Wang received a solid early education and showed an aptitude for study when young. His interest was encouraged by his father who, though a merchant, hoped his son would succeed in the civil-service examinations and reclaim the literati status for the family, which had produced several well-respected scholar-officials in previous centuries.

STRADDLING THE OLD AND NEW IN EDUCATION

In 1892, having passed the county-level examination at age fifteen, it seemed that Wang might indeed be able to fulfill his father's wishes. However, Wang's subsequent attempts to pass the provincial examination met with repeated failure. Frustrated and disheartened by China's shattering defeat by Japan in the Sino-Japanese War (1894–1895), he decided to give up studying for the examinations. He traveled instead to Shanghai, a port city that had been opened since the 1840s to foreign influence, where he began pursuing New Learning (*xinxue*), which emphasized the academic subjects taught in Western schools (mathematics, science, foreign languages, and philosophy).

Working as a petty clerk and proofreader for *Current Affairs* (*Shiwubao*), a popular periodical launched and edited by reform-minded scholar-officials, Wang enrolled in the Eastern Language Institute (Dongwen Xueshe) founded by Luo Zhenyu (1866–1940), where he studied both Japanese

and English, as well as a cluster of other subjects (e.g., chemistry, physics, mathematics, and geography) taught by Japanese teachers. But Wang's passion remained the humanities, thanks to which he made a strong impression on Luo, eventually becoming his protégé. With Luo's help, Wang was able to complete and excel in his study. He also befriended several Japanese scholars, who inspired him to engage in a serious study of German philosophy and aesthetics. In 1901 Wang was given a chance to study in Japan, though his time in Japan was cut short when he developed beriberi, a disease he struggled with later in his life.

PHILOSOPHY, AESTHETICS, AND LITERARY THEORY

Wang Guowei was arguably the most important scholar of his generation. He introduced modern scholarship—ranging from philosophy, aesthetics, and literary theory to archaeology and history—to China. Most of his peers were at a loss after the Qing court terminated the civil-service examination in 1905, a move that deprived them of a motive for study. Wang Guowei, by contrast, appeared quite at ease in pursuing new knowledge from abroad. Indeed, he was one of the first Chinese scholars to develop an earnest interest in and a sound understanding of such modern German philosophers as Arthur Schopenhauer (1788–1860), Immanuel Kant (1724–1804), and Friedrich Nietzsche (1844–1900). Drawing on their philosophical ideas, Wang mounted a sharp criticism of the ongoing educational reform unleashed by the Qing court, which he condemned for its myopic design and narrow focus. He also developed his own aesthetic theory and applied it to studying Chinese lyrics, novels, and drama. Wang's research on the drama of the Song and Yuan periods paralleled similar studies by Japanese scholars Kano Naoki (1868–1947) and Aoki Masaru (1887–1964), whom he met during his second sojourn in Japan (1911–1916).

Inspired by Schopenhauer's metaphysical pessimism, Wang Guowei set out to analyze the *Dream of the Red Chamber* (*Hongloumeng*) by Cao Xueqin (c. 1715–1763), a great novel about the rise and fall of a distinguished mandarin family in the Qing period. In contrast to the established approach, which focused on uncovering the novel's intended political message and its resemblance to the author's own life and family, Wang chose to assess the novel's aesthetic value. He considered the work a great tragedy, a masterpiece that attested to "tragic beauty" (*beiju mei*). To him, the novel was marked by a relentless, if unsuccessful, search for the meaning of existence on the part of the author and the characters he created.

Wang's development of aesthetic theory was best shown in his examination of the tradition of poetic and lyric compositions, which resulted in his *Remarks on the Lyrics of the Human World* (*Renjian cihua*; 1910), a seminal work in modern Chinese literary criticism. Wang argued that the beauty of a poem or a literary work lies in whether or not it creates or envisions a "realm" (*jingjie*) that can resonate with the reader's emotion and experience. And the poet can take two different approaches to effecting this realm: one is to create the realm with self-involvement, or to "have a self" (*youwo*) in the realm; the other is to create it without self-involvement, or "without a self" (*wuwo*). From another perspective, Wang stated that the realms can be created either "transparently" (*buge*) or "opaquely" (*ge*). All these concepts, which Wang distilled by making syncretic use of modern Western theories and Chinese literary traditions, have had a lasting influence in shaping the development of literary criticism in modern China.

HISTORY AND ARCHAEOLOGY

Despite his modern scholarly approach, Wang became increasingly conservative in his political views. Throughout his life, he remained loyal to the Qing dynasty, even after its demise in 1912. He also became increasingly uneasy about the cultural iconoclasm that characterized the New Culture movement in the May Fourth era (1915–1925). As scholars of the younger generation continued to dispute the validity of the Chinese historical tradition, Wang strove to validate it by comparing existing written records with newly discovered material evidence. One source of such evidence was the oracle bones from the Shang period (c. 1600–1046 BCE) that had surfaced in his time and been collected and cataloged by Luo Zhenyu and others. Armed with his rich knowledge of ancient texts, Wang was able to decipher oracle-bone inscriptions and piece together enough information to corroborate the historical record concerning the line of succession of the Shang throne. His success impressed many, for at the time the reliability of the historical records was being seriously challenged, and the historicity of China's high antiquity, of which the Shang was an essential period, was also being questioned. But Wang proved that it was premature to refute the legitimacy of the corpus of historical literature formed in the imperial period.

His ability to combine both written and material evidence in historical research, praised as a "method of coalescing dual evidence" (*erchong zhengjufa*), inspired students of history during his time and after. Despite his political conservatism, Wang was admired as a "pioneer of new/modern historiography" (*xinshixue de kaishan*), commanding respect among historians of different political persuasions and cultural positions.

Wang's research on ancient Chinese history was conducted after he had forsaken his studies of philosophy, aesthetics, and literary criticism and assumed a prestigious position teaching history at the newly founded research institute at Qinghua (Tsing-hua) University in Beijing.

His colleagues were well-respected scholars and many of his students later became eminent scholars in modern China. Though Wang had become a towering figure in China's burgeoning academic world, he remained unhappy and, at times, intimidated by the cascade of revolutionary ideas sweeping over the country in the wake of the Qing's fall. His unfaltering loyalty to the fallen regime was shown in his eagerness to offer service to the dethroned Qing emperor, Puyi (1906–1967). The same loyalty also eventually led to his untimely death. In 1927, fearful of the ongoing political upheavals in China, he committed suicide by throwing himself into Kunming Lake near the Summer Place (*Yihe yuan*), a former Qing imperial garden.

SEE ALSO *Classical Scholarship and Intellectual Debates: Debates, 1900–1949.*

BIBLIOGRAPHY

PRIMARY SOURCES

Wang Guowei. *Wang Guowei xiansheng quanji* [Complete works of Mr. Wang Guowei]. Taibei: Datong Shuju, 1976.

Wang Guowei. *Wang Guowei quanji: Shuxin* [Complete works of Wang Guowei: Correspondences]. Ed. Wu Ze. Beijing: Zhonghua Shuju, 1984–.

SECONDARY SOURCES

Bonner, Joey. *Wang Kuo-wei: An Intellectual Biography.* Cambridge, MA: Harvard University Press, 1986.

Rickett, Adele Austin. *Wang Kuo-wei's Jen-Chien Tz'u-Hua: A Study in Chinese Literary Criticism.* Hong Kong: Hong Kong University Press, 1977.

Satō Taketoshi. *Ō Kokui no shōgai to gakumon* [Wang Guowei's life and scholarship]. Tokyo: Kazama Shobō, 2003.

Ye Jiaying and Yeh Chia-ying. *Wang Guowei jiqi wenxue piping* [Wang Guowei and his literary criticism]. Taibei: Guiguan, 1992.

Yuan Yingguang. *Xinshixue de kaishan: Wang Guowei pingzhuan* [The pioneer of new historiography: An intellectual biography of Wang Guowei]. Shanghai: Shanghai Renmin Chubanshe, 1999.

Zhou Yiping and Shen Chaying. *Zhongxi wenhua jiaohui yu Wang Guowei xueshu chengjiu* [Wang Guowei's scholarly accomplishment in light of cultural exchanges between China and the West]. Shanghai: Xuelin Chubanshe, 1999.

Q. Edward Wang

WANG JINGWEI
1883–1944

Wang Jingwei was a top Guomindang (Nationalist Party) leader and the leading collaborator with Japan during the Anti-Japanese War (1937–1945). He was born in Sanshui, Guangdong Province, to an educated family of Zhejiang origin. In 1903 he went to study in Japan on a government scholarship, and two years later he joined the Revolutionary Alliance (Tongmenghui), led by Sun Yat-sen

Wang Jingwei (left) with two Japanese officers, Shanghai, China, November 11, 1939. *Wang Jingwei earned the contempt of many Chinese for his collaboration with Japan during World War II. Looking to balance Chiang Kai-shek's control of the Guomindang, Wang led a puppet-state in areas of China occupied by Japan, eventually becoming regarded as a traitor at war's end.* © BETTMANN/CORBIS

(Sun Zhongshan). His political life thus commenced in Japan, in the cause of the anti-Manchu revolution. Although later acclaimed as a national hero for his failed attempt to assassinate the Manchu prince regent Zai Feng on the eve of the 1911 Revolution, Wang retreated from politics after the revolution and went to Europe with his wife, Chen Bijun.

CONFLICT WITH CHIANG KAI-SHEK

Returning to China in 1917, Wang became a trusted follower of Sun's when in 1923 the Guomindang was reorganized and an alliance was made between the Guomindang and the Chinese Communist Party, known as the first United Front. A contender for the Guomindang leadership after Sun's death in March 1925, Wang took office as chairman of the Nationalist Government (*Guomin zhengfu*), established in Guangzhou in July 1925. His chairmanship was short-lived, however, because of the March 30, 1926, military coup by Chiang Kai-shek, Wang's lifelong contender for the leadership. Wang resigned from his post and left for Europe.

In the course of the Northern Expedition to unify the country, a conflict developed in December 1926 between Chiang and the Guomindang left over the location of the government's new capital and its policy toward the United Front. Chiang had wanted to establish the new capital at

Nanchang (later Nanjing) and suppress the Communists, whereas the Guomindang left preferred Wuhan as the capital and supported the United Front. It was at this juncture, on April 1, 1927, that Wang returned to China and subsequently supported the Guomindang left. The bloody anti-Communist coup of April 12 was Chiang's reaction. Meanwhile, the Communist-led peasant movements in the Wuhan-controlled area left Guomindang control. This concerned Wang, who preferred keeping them under control. Wang finally ended the alliance with the Communists in July 1927. However, he was defamed by a political attack claiming that he had supported the Communists, especially after the Canton Commune of December 1927. Wang again retreated to Europe and held grudges against the Communists and Chiang.

Between 1928 and 1931 Wang led the "opposition to Chiang" (*fan Jiang*) movement, which culminated in the establishment of a separatist government in Guangzhou (Canton) with warlords. Wang was also the de facto leader of the reorganization clique (*gaizu pai*), the former Guomindang leftists who opposed Chiang's dictatorship. However, Japan's invasion of Manchuria in 1931 and its subsequent establishment of the puppet state of Manchukuo there melted down the party's internal divisions, and as a result Wang formed a coalition with Chiang. As head of the Executive Yuan and the minister of foreign affairs,

Wang handled internal and external affairs, most important among them, the Japanese invasion. Unpopular, however, was his appeasement policy toward Japan, which eventually impaired Wang's position as a national leader and almost cost him his life in an attempted assassination in November 1935. His collaboration with Chiang since 1932 abruptly ended, and he headed to Europe for medical treatment.

COLLABORATION WITH THE JAPANESE

The December 1936 Xi'an Incident, in which Chiang was held hostage by his pro-resistance generals reversed the appeasement policy and led to the Guomindang's second alliance with the Communist Party for a united resistance against Japan, the second United Front. Yet Wang, returning from Europe, still favored the same policy of appeasement and was not convinced of Chiang's support for an all-out war with Japan and the alliance. When Nanjing fell into Japan's hands and Changsha was scorched to the earth, Wang, uncertain of the nation's fate, defected with a group of peace advocates (*heping pai*) to Hanoi to propose a peaceful resolution to the military conflict with Japan. His proposal was unheeded by Chiang, and an attempt to assassinate him decisively drove Wang toward the "peace movement," which resulted in establishing a nationalist government in Nanjing under Japan's sponsorship, of which he became chairman. To the resisters, he was a traitor (*hanjian*), but he and his associates never thought so.

Established with the slogan of "national reconstruction with peace and anticommunism," Wang's collaborationist government controlled the lower Yangzi area from March 1940 to August 1945. His collaboration went athwart his purpose to stop the war and set up a reorganized, autonomous nationalist government under a new internal and external order. This is palpable evidence that Wang's government was a puppet (*wei zhengquan*) of Japan. Nevertheless, his emphases on the state's wartime role as protector of the people and on the intimate Sino-Japanese relationship suggest a rethinking of his version (not to be taken at face value) of nationalism, pan-Asianism, and the Three Principles of the People, which was elevated to the status of the Wang Jingwei doctrine (*Wang Jingwei zhuyi*) by his followers. For example, Wang believed the state under Chiang had been unable or unwilling to protect the people during the war, which was a point of departure he used to argue against the charge of treason and for the usefulness of collaboration with Japan, "a natural friend," on behalf of an ineffective, passive state.

Wang's failed collaboration with Japan was a product of the complex wartime situations of the 1930s and 1940s and the Guomindang's political culture, which presumably made him believe that "he is playing the accepted game of Chinese politics" (Linebarger 1941, p.208). Throughout its existence, his government constantly faced difficulties and limits, mainly because it was a Japan-sponsored government but also because it suffered, like its counterpart in Chongqing, from factionalism, corruption, and a lack of qualified personnel and efficient administration. Judging Wang's political life and activities, both as a leader of the Guomindang left and as the leading collaborator with Japan, may require a further examination of the complexities and political culture of the Guomindang. Wang died in December 1944 in Nagoya, Japan. His wife, sentenced after the war to life imprisonment, died in jail in Shanghai in 1959.

SEE ALSO *Anti-Japanese War, 1937–1945; Nationalist Party.*

BIBLIOGRAPHY

Boorman, Howard L. Wang Ching-wei: China's Romantic Radical. *Political Science Quarterly* 79, 4 (1964): 504–525.

Boyle, John H. *China and Japan at War: Politics of Collaboration.* Stanford, CA: Stanford University Press, 1972.

Bunker, Gerald E. *Peace Conspiracy: Wang Ching-Wei and the China War, 1937–1941.* Cambridge, MA: Harvard University Press, 1972.

Cai Dejin. *Wang Jingwei pingzhuan* [An evaluative biography of Wang Jingwei]. Chengdu: Sichuan Renmin Chubanshe, 1988.

Hwang, Dongyoun. Wartime Collaboration in Question: An Examination of the Postwar Trials of the Chinese Collaborators. *Inter-Asia Cultural Studies* 6, 1 (2005): 75–97.

Linebarger, Paul M. A. *The China of Chiang K'ai-shek: A Political Study.* Boston: World Peace Foundation, 1941.

Dongyoun Hwang

WANG MENG
1934–

Wang Meng is a prominent Chinese fiction writer and cultural figure, who served for a brief time from 1986 as minister of culture. Although he is from a family registered in Nanpi County, Hebei Province, Wang Meng was in fact born in Beijing in 1934. When he attended middle school he took part in underground Communist Party work, but did not formally join the Communist Party until 1948. After 1949 he worked with the Communist Youth League. He published his first fictional work, the short story "Qingchun wansui" (Long live youth), in 1953, and later developed it into a full-length novel published in 1956. In 1955 his short story "Xiao Dou'er" (Sprout) was published in the journal *Renmin wenxue* (People's literature); it is sometimes described as his first "representative work." In 1956, during the Hundred Flowers campaign, he published a novel, *Zuzhibu laile ge nianqingren* (The young newcomer in the organization department), which tells the story of a young Youth League member who is thwarted in his new job by the "bureaucratism" of the work unit's leadership. The theme was topical—it conformed to Mao Zedong's denunciation of habits of "bureaucratism" within the Communist

Party, yet the work provoked political controversy. In January 1957 the Chinese Writers Association convened a meeting at which the short story was condemned. The controversy continued until March; the story was banned eventually, as was Wang Meng's earlier work, "Qingchun wansui." Wang Meng was labeled a "rightist," expelled from the party, and sent to a labor camp outside Beijing. In 1962 he was released from detention and taught for a year at Beijing Normal College (Beijing Shifan Xueyuan), but in 1963 he was exiled to Xinjiang, where he remained until 1978. In 1963 he published *Chun man Tulufan* (Springtime in Turfan), his last work to be published until 1978. In Xinjiang he was exiled to the Bayandai Commune in Yining County, outside Yining City in the far west of Xinjiang. He studied the Uygur language and worked as a translator after 1973.

After the fall of the Gang of Four in 1976, Wang Meng was transferred in 1978 to work at the Beijing Writers' Association, and in 1979 he was politically rehabilitated. He published several short stories in 1978, including "Duizhang shuji yemao he banjiekuai de gushi" (The story of the brigade chief's secretary, the feral cat, and half a chopstick) and "Zui baogui de" (The most precious thing), which later was awarded a prize as the most outstanding short story of 1978. Later in 1978 he became chief editor of *Renmin wenxue*. He won a number of national literary awards over the next decade, and also rose quickly up the cultural political ladder, becoming deputy-chairman of the Chinese Writers' Association, a member of the Central Committee, a member of the Chinese People's Political Consultative Conference (CPPCC), and head of the CPPCC's Literature History and Study Committee (Quanguo Zhengxie Wenshi he Xuexi Weiyuanhui).

In the decade before he relinquished the post of minister of culture in 1989, Wang wrote prolifically, producing short stories, novellas, reportage, poetry, essays, literary theory and critique, and studies of the Chinese classic *Honglou meng* (*Dream of the Red Chamber*). Although he continued to comment on political abuses, Wang's writing focused more on social and cultural satire. In much of his work of this period, Wang experimented with narrative techniques and attempted to develop a "stream of consciousness" style. Examples of this style are "Ye de yan" (Eyes of the night), "Hudie" (Butterfly), "Chun zhi sheng" (Voices of spring), "Fengzheng piaodai" (Kite streamers), and "Hai de meng" (Dreams of the sea). These five short stories, as well as "Bu Li" (Bolshevik's salute), were anthologized in *Wang Meng xiaoshuo baogao wenxue xuan* (Selected novellas, stories, and reportage of Wang Meng), published in Beijing in 1981. "Ye de yan," published in the October 21, 1979, issue of the newspaper *Guangming Daily*, broke with the realist style that typified much of the literature published in the post-1976 period, including scar literature. The plot focuses on the encounters of a single night in the life of the protagonist, a writer who returns to the city where he once lived to attend a creative writing workshop after twenty years of banishment to the countryside. Through an indirect inner monologue, the author comments on the changes in post-Mao society. "Chun zhi sheng" (1980) also focused on the mental activities and consciousness of the protagonist, and "Hai de meng" (1980) foregrounds the mental anguish of a rehabilitated specialist in Western literature who is on vacation by the sea. Many critics disliked the stream of consciousness style that Wang was pioneering in Chinese, charging that his stories were excessively modernist and lacking in narrative sequence and plot. According to the scholar William Tay, Wang Meng was not the first to attempt the stream of consciousness style in Chinese; a number of Taiwanese writers had made use of the technique, as had Wang Zengqi in 1945, and of course the device was known to Chinese readers from translations. However, when Wang's stories were translated into English, as most were, his use of the device seems contrived. Many other innovations he pioneered were taken up and subsequently mastered by young writers of the Chinese avant-garde in the 1980s and 1990s.

Wang Meng is celebrated for the witty observations on Chinese society and cultural habits that typify the best of his fiction. In addition to *Long Live Youth* (1979), he has published several other full-length novels: *Huodong bian renxing* (*Activities Deform*, 1986), *Lian'ai de jijie* (*Season of Love*, 1992); *Shitai de jijie* (*Season of Loss*, 1994); *Ansha—3322* (*Assassination—3322*, 1994); *Chouchu de jijie* (*Season of Vacillation*, 1995); and *Kuanghuan de jijie* (*Season of Ecstasy*, 1999). He is, however, better known for his short stories and novellas.

In the two decades since 1989, he has remained a prolific writer, venturing into studies of the Tang dynasty poet Li Shangyin and travel writing, and translating the writings of others. He has been active as a university lecturer, teaching at many prominent Chinese universities and appearing as a guest lecturer on foreign campuses. He has traveled extensively and is often called upon to comment on the state of contemporary Chinese literature at international conferences and cultural events. Two multivolume anthologies of his writings have been published, and in 2006 to 2007 he published two volumes of autobiography, *Bansheng Duoshi* (An eventful half-life) and *Dakuai Wenzhang* (A large slab of essays), which have been best-sellers. His works have been translated into English, Russian, Japanese, German, Korean, Uygur, and other languages.

SEE ALSO *Avant-garde Fiction; Scar (Wound) Literature.*

BIBLIOGRAPHY

PRIMARY WORKS

Wang Meng. *Snowball.* Vol. 2 of *Selected Works of Wang Meng.* Trans. Cathy Silber and Deirdre Huang. Beijing: Foreign Languages Press, 1989.

Wang Meng. *The Strain of Meeting.* Vol. 1 of *Selected Works of Wang Meng.* Trans. Denis Mair. Beijing: Foreign Languages Press, 1989.

Wang Meng. *Wang Meng wenji* [Collected works of Wang Meng]. 10 vols. Beijing: Huayi Publishing House, 1993.

Wang Meng. *Wang Meng wencun* [The writings of Wang Meng]. 23 vols. Beijing: People's Publishing House, 2003.

SECONDARY WORK

Tay, William. Wang Meng, Stream-of-Consciousness, and the Controversy over Modernism. *Modern Chinese Literature* 1, 1 (1984): 7–21.

Bruce Doar

WANG SHIWEI
1906–1947

Wang Shiwei (originally Wang Sidao, courtesy name Shu Han), a radical Chinese writer who was arrested and later executed for his critical essays about Communist rule in Yan'an, was born in Huangchuan, Henan Province. His father's income as a humble schoolteacher was insufficient to support a family of eight children, often requiring Wang to drop out of school for lack of funds. He was active in the 1919 student movement and in 1925 entered Beijing University, but he left after a year. In 1926 he joined the Communist Party. He suffered from unrequited love of a fellow student, Li Fen, who was executed as a Communist in 1928. Two years later Wang married her close friend Liu Ying, with whom he had two children.

From 1927 Wang made a meager living by teaching and writing. His translations included works by Karl Marx, Friedrich Engels, and Leon Trotsky and plays by Eugene O'Neill and John Galsworthy. Like many other idealistic young intellectuals, in 1937 Wang went to Yan'an, at that time the Communist headquarters, but was disappointed to find hierarchy and privilege entrenched there. In a critical essay, "Yebaihehua" (Wild lilies), which he said was inspired by the memory of the martyred Li Fen, he denounced the revolutionary capital's inequalities and bureaucracy. He implied that the essay, like the wild lily itself, with its beautiful flower and slightly bitter-tasting but medicinal bulb, might offer a cure for Yan'an's ills. Soon after the publication of the essay in 1942 he was arrested. At his trial, held during the Yan'an rectification campaign (1942–1944), he was accused of Trotskyism and attacked for his criticisms of Stalin's excesses. He was summarily executed in 1947 during the civil war.

In 1962 Mao noted that Wang Shiwei had been wrongly accused. This admission, not made public until 1986, provided a basis for Wang's formal rehabilitation in 1991. His widow, who had long campaigned for this, was offered "consolation money." She first refused to accept it but later gave it to a fund for young writers.

Western scholars have seen Wang Shiwei as the Chinese Communist Party's first real dissident. In China the radical investigative journalist Dai Qing looked into his case even before Wang's rehabilitation and wrote a book presenting him as a courageous intellectual who had argued for greater democracy. Much of Wang Shiwei's work was reprinted in China in the 1990s.

SEE ALSO *Classical Scholarship and Intellectual Debates: Debates, 1900–1949; Mao Zedong; Trotskyism; Yan'an Forum.*

BIBLIOGRAPHY

Benton, Gregor, and Alan Hunter, eds. *Wild Lily, Prairie Fire: China's Road to Democracy, Yan'an to Tian'anmen, 1942–1989.* Princeton, NJ: Princeton University Press, 1995.

Cheek, Timothy. The Fading of Wild Lilies: Wang Shiwei and Mao Zedong's Yan'an Talks in the First CPC Rectification Movement. *Australian Journal of Chinese Affairs* 11 (January 1984): 25–58.

Dai Qing. *Wang Shiwei and "Wild Lilies": Rectification and Purges in the Chinese Communist Party, 1942–1944.* Ed. David E. Apter and Timothy Cheek. Trans. Nancy Liu and Lawrence R. Sullivan. Armonk, NY: M. E. Sharpe, 1994.

Wang Shiwei. Yebaihehua [Wild lilies]. *Jiefang Ribao* [Liberation daily], Yan'an, March 13 and 23, 1942.

Delia Davin

WANG SHUO
1958–

Wang Shuo, one of the most popular and controversial writers in contemporary China, is extraordinarily prolific, turning out volumes of fiction, film, television scripts, and cultural commentary. His works are striking for their astute observations of a rapidly changing society and iconoclastic "players of the world" sporting an irreverent attitude toward established norms and values. His chief contribution to contemporary literature lies in his unique language, an incongruous and hilarious blend of Beijing dialect, current street slang, and Communist Party sloganeering.

LIFE AND WORKS

The son of a high-ranking military commander growing up in a walled compound in the capital, Wang Shuo belongs to the second generation of the Communist elite. He spent his childhood and teenage years, which coincided with the decade of the Cultural Revolution (1966–1976), playing hooky from school, reading contraband literature, and loitering in the streets of Beijing. After graduating from high school, he entered the navy, a coveted profession open only to the sons and daughters of the military elite. After four years of service, he was discharged and worked briefly at a pharmaceutical job. Beginning in 1983, he became a professional writer.

Wang Shuo published his first short story in 1978 while serving in the navy but really made his name in 1984 with his popular novella *Kongzhong xiaojie* (Air stewardess). Although framed as a romantic tragedy between a former navy soldier and an air stewardess, to most readers of that time, it was a mystery and romance. Yet in the male protagonist there is already a hint of a disillusioned drifter, a figure that would become far more developed in his 1986 novellas *Yi ban shi huoyan, yi ban shi haishui* (Half flame, half seawater) and *Xiangpi ren* (Rubber man).

From 1986 to 1994 Wang Shuo's popularity was at its peak. In 1988 alone he published three short stories, two novellas, and a collection of fiction, in addition to having four of his fictional works turned into films. In 1989 he came out with two novels: *Wanr de jiu shi xin tiao* (*Playing for Thrills*) and *Qianwan bie ba wo dang ren* (*Please Don't Call Me Human*). The year 1991 saw the publication of another novel, *Wo shi ni baba* (I'm your father). In 1992 four volumes of his collected works were published, an honor usually reserved for literary masters. In 1994 the film *Yangguang canlan de rizi* (*In the Heat of the Sun*), based on his novel *Dongwu xiongmeng* (Wild beasts), was released. In 1998 he published *Kanshangqu hen mei* (It looks beautiful), a novel from the perspective of a preschool young rebel. After a hiatus, in 2007 he came out with *Wo de qiansui han* (My millennium), a work that subverts the conventional definition of fiction and self-consciously experiments with the Chinese language. A significant departure from his earlier fiction, this pastiche in six parts consists of, among other things, historical fiction about an imperial empress, a rewrite of Buddhist hagiography, and personal notes on Stephen Hawking's *A Brief History of Time*.

ANTIHEROES

Wang Shuo created an entire gallery of antiheroes in his fiction. These characters, often from an elite Communist background, are urban drifters. Usually young and restless, they oppose tradition, especially the tradition that they themselves are a privileged part of. While they may spout profanity at every opportunity, there is a glimpse of deeply disillusioned idealism. They jeer at cultural pretension and moral values, tear down social norms and ideals, and are often self-destructive. Figures of authority—fathers, teachers, party leaders—furnish targets for attack; innocents, typically virgin ingenues, not unlike the air stewardess in his early novella, are targets to seduce.

His protagonists perpetually speak in a mocking tone, in one breath blending hyperbolic Communist propaganda speak with scatological jokes. This deflating parody turns what was previously sacrosanct, such as quotations from Chairman Mao or even broad humanistic values, into hysterical comedy. Unlike many writers, who seek to restore truth to language, Wang Shuo's antihero, in the face of language thoroughly polluted by totalitarianism, espouses a complete distrust of language. Thus in *Playing for Thrills*, the male protagonist Fang Yan instructs his girlfriend, "Remember: whatever [they] say, just listen and say yes. When it's

over, it's over. Never take it seriously. Otherwise you'll always be dissed. . . . And myself, seventy or eighty per cent of what I say can't be taken seriously" (Wang Shuo 1998).

THE WANG SHUO PHENOMENON

What makes Wang Shuo a phenomenon, in addition to his popularity, is the intense intellectual debates his works generated in the 1990s. While some critics described him as representative of decadent "hooligan literature" or a complete sell-out to the commercial market, others praised his works as the vanguard of postmodernism: a carnivalesque deconstruction of all established political authorities and aesthetic conventions. To these critical debates, Wang Shuo sometimes lent his own voice, making astute and provocative comments on a range of cultural phenomena such as himself, the pop-cultural icon Jin Yong, and the modern writer turned ideological icon Lu Xun. Wang Shuo was thus a point of convergence for many important cultural debates of the late twentieth century, whether they be on the value of urban pop culture or the state of the spirit of humanism.

SEE ALSO *Literature since 1800; Root-Searching Literature; Scar (Wound) Literature.*

BIBLIOGRAPHY

WORKS BY WANG SHUO

Playing for Thrills: A Mystery. Trans. Howard Goldblatt. New York: Penguin, 1998. A translation of *Wanr de jiushi xin tiao*.
Please Don't Call Me Human. Trans. Howard Goldblatt. New York: Hyperion East, 2000. A translation of *Qianwan bie ba wo dang ren*.
Jiang Wen, director. *Yangguang canlan de rizi* [*In the Heat of the Sun*]. Hong Kong: Xincheng Yinxiang Gongsi, 2000.

SECONDARY WORKS

Barmé, Geremie. *In the Red: On Contemporary Chinese Culture.* New York: Columbia University Press, 1999.
Ge Hongbing, and Zhu Lidong, eds. *Wang Shuo yanjiu ziliao* [Research material on Wang Shuo]. Tianjin: Tianjin Renmin Chubanshe, 2005.

Hu Ying

WANG ZHEN (WANG YITING)
1867–1938

Wang Zhen (Wang Yiting, Bailong shanren, Jueqi, Meihuaguan zhu, Haiyunlou zhu) was a leader in Chinese business, politics, Buddhism, and philanthropy, as well as a leading artist of the Shanghai school, an influential patron of the arts, and a substantial contributor to Sino-Japanese cultural exchange.

Buddhist Sage *by Wang Zhen, 1928.* THE METROPOLITAN MUSEUM OF ART, GIFT OF ROBERT HATFIELD ELLSWORTH, IN MEMORY OF LA FERNE HATFIELD ELLSWORTH, 1986. (1986.267.156) IMAGE © THE METROPOLITAN MUSEUM OF ART

Born in Shanghai, Wang pursued a lengthy career in business. From 1902 to 1931 he worked as a comprador for Japanese firms in the city. He also founded Chinese banks and companies and directed many businesses and chambers of commerce, becoming one of Shanghai's most influential capitalists. He served on the Chinese city of Shanghai's City Council, supported Sun Yat-sen (Sun Yixian or Sun Zhongshan) and the Republican revolution, and in 1912 became the director of the Shanghai branch of the Nationalist Party (Guomindang). When Yuan Shikai sought to crush Sun and his supporters in 1913, Wang withdrew from open involvement in politics. He continued to support the Nationalist cause, however, bankrolling the Nanjing government of Chiang Kai-shek (Jiang Jieshi).

Wang Zhen was a committed philanthropist and supporter of Buddhism. He organized the sale of his and other artists' work for charity, and he directed numerous philanthropic societies. After 1913 Wang became a devout Buddhist and helped lead a national revival of the religion. One of the most important lay supporters of the influential monastic reformer Taixu (1890–1947), Wang headed local and national Buddhist associations, raised money for the construction of temples, organized Buddhist presses and publication projects, and supported Buddhist charitable activities.

Wang is now best known as a leading painter and calligrapher of the later Shanghai school who synthesized the popular subject matter and compositions of Ren Bonian (1840–1895) with the calligraphic brushwork of his teacher and close friend Wu Changshi (1844–1927). Particularly adept at rendering birds, flowers, and human figures, Wang was a prolific painter of auspicious subjects, figures from popular religion, and Buddhist themes. He also painted portraits of friends and associates. Although he executed some works for sale, donating his proceeds to charity, Wang produced much of his oeuvre on social occasions and for the purpose of cultivating personal relationships. Wang was also a patron of the arts. He was instrumental in orchestrating the economic success of Wu Changshi, and he supported other Chinese artists by leading traditionalist art societies and serving on the board of the Shanghai Art Academy (Shanghai Meizhuan).

Although he was committed to China's political and cultural integrity, Wang Zhen energetically advocated friendship with Japan. Through such endeavors as the China Industrial Development Company, which he helped found in 1913, he established connections with many Japanese business and political leaders. He also engaged Japan through charity and Buddhism, organizing prayer vigils and shipments of relief supplies for victims of the 1923 Tokyo earthquake and helping lead the Chinese delegation at the 1925 East Asian Buddhist Conference in Tokyo. From the late 1910s through the first half of the 1930s, Wang met with numerous Japanese artists, scholars, politicians, dignitaries, and Buddhists. He mounted solo art exhibitions at the Takashimaya Kimono Shop, cofounded such artistic groups as the Sino-Japanese Art Society (Chinese: Zhong-ri Meishu Xiehui; Japanese: Chūnichi Bijutsu Kyōkai), and helped organize Chinese and Japanese joint art exhibitions in the 1920s and early 1930s.

Wang Zhen's engagement with Japan, along with his capitalist and Nationalist activities, caused him posthumously to run afoul of ideological orthodoxy in the People's Republic of China, where he disappeared from public awareness until the 1980s. With the reestablishment of the art market in China, renewed ties between China and Japan, and renewed interest in art of the Republican period, Wang has reemerged as an important modern artist and subject of historical study.

SEE ALSO *Chinese Painting (guohua); Huang Binhong; Wu Changshi (Wu Junqing).*

BIBLIOGRAPHY

Andrews, Julia F., and Shen Kuiyi (Kuiyi Shen). *A Century in Crisis: Modernity and Tradition in the Art of Twentieth-Century China.* New York: Guggenheim Museum, 1998.

Cao Xingyuan (Hsing-Yuan Tsao). A Forgotten Celebrity: Wang Zhen (1867–1938), Businessman, Philanthropist, and Artist. In *Art at the Close of China's Empire,* Phoebus VIII, ed. Chou Ju-hsi, 94–109. Tempe: Arizona State University Board of Regents, 1998.

Davis, Walter B. Wang Yiting and the Art of Sino-Japanese Exchange. Ph.D. diss., Ohio State University, 2008.

Ruan Yuan (Aida Yuen Wong). *Parting the Mists: Discovering Japan and the Rise of National-Style Painting in Modern China.* Honolulu: Association for Asian Studies and University of Hawai'i Press, 2006.

Shen Kuiyi (Kuiyi Shen). Wang Yiting in the Social Network of 1910s–1930s Shanghai. In *At the Crossroads of Empires: Middlemen, Social Networks, and State-Building in Republican Shanghai,* eds. Nara Dillon and Jean C. Oi, 45–64. Stanford, CA: Stanford University Press, 2008.

Walter B. Davis

WAR CRIMES

International laws regulating the conduct of war, known collectively as the Geneva Conventions, were developed through meetings (conventions) beginning in 1863, starting with the founding of the International Committee of the Red Cross in Geneva, Switzerland. These agreements uphold the principle of *jus in bello*: that even in war, there are laws protecting combatants, prisoners of war, and civilians. Soldiers may not be killed or injured except in battle, nor may they be harmed when surrendering. Prisoners of war may not be killed, tortured, inhumanely treated, or arbitrarily punished, nor may they be forced to serve or work for a hostile power. Civilians may not be attacked, confined, deported, taken as hostages, or used as shields. Though *jus in bello* derives from European traditions, the protections these rules afford are, at least formally, universally recognized.

The international military tribunals convened in Nuremberg and Tokyo in 1946 enlarged the scope of war criminality by creating two additional categories of war crimes. Crimes against peace are wars waged to infringe national territory, impair state sovereignty, or violate a peace treaty. Crimes against humanity consist of the state-sponsored persecution or genocide of a group of people, enshrined in 1948 as the Convention on the Prevention and Punishment of the Crime of Genocide. The Statute of Rome was negotiated in 1998 to create an International Criminal Court (ICC) in order that war crimes and crimes against humanity may be prosecuted in cases where national courts are unable or unwilling to do so. Crimes against peace are beyond the remit of the court, which lacks the authority to determine whether a war has been justly initiated (known as *jus ad bellum*). All other war crimes it can try.

China participated in the negotiations leading to these conventions, and has acceded to most, including the Convention on Genocide. The exception is the Statute of Rome. China is not the only world power that refuses to accept the ICC. Like Israel, India, and the United States, China fears that the court's choice of cases to prosecute will be subject to political influence. More fundamentally, China regards the court's mandate as an infringement on the principle of national sovereignty, and uses international diplomacy to thwart the judicial investigation of crimes against humanity. When the United Nations Security Council referred the situation in Sudan to the prosecutor of the ICC in March 2005, for instance, China quietly resisted the initiative and chose to abstain from the vote that authorized the court to investigate crimes against humanity that the Sudanese government was alleged to have committed in Darfur.

CHINA'S EXPERIENCE OF WAR CRIMES

The Chinese tradition of warfare understood that war should be guided solely by the imperative to prevail; thus it had no explicit counterpart to *jus in bello*. Soldiers could

Japanese general Akira Muto during his war crimes trial, Tokyo, Japan, December 2, 1947.
At the end of World War II, China played a role in the International Military Tribunal for the Far East, sending Mei Ru'ao to represent the nation as a judge. One of twenty-five on trial, Japanese general Akira Muto received a death sentence for his participation in crimes against the civilian population in China and the Philippines. © BETTMANN/CORBIS

be punished, but for breaches of discipline and not for the mistreatment of combatants, civilians, or prisoners, who were regularly executed. If strategists urged that civilians be protected, it was from the concern that civilian suffering might compromise the success of a campaign. When the Red Army famously issued its "Three Rules of Discipline and Eight Points for Attention" in 1928 banning the expropriation of property and the abuse of civilians, it did so to court popular support, not to uphold the rights of civilians vis-à-vis soldiers.

Between the end of the Qing in 1912 and Japan's defeat in 1945, China had almost no experience in prosecuting war crimes. This was not because soldiers in China did not act criminally. They assuredly did, but did so in the context of civil war, which lay beyond the jurisdiction of international law. The Red Cross was intermittently involved in providing relief from war suffering during these years; its efforts even inspired Chinese Buddhists to organize an indigenous alternative, the Red Swastika Society, to deal with war casualties. But no efforts were made to bring those who committed atrocities before tribunals.

At the conclusion of Japan's eight-year military occupation of China (1937–1945), China became actively involved in the international prosecution of war crimes through its participation in the International Military Tribunal for the Far East (1946–1948) in Tokyo. The tribunal was convened to try selected Japanese political and military leaders for waging war illegally (*jus ad bellum*), for failing to observe international norms of war conduct (*jus in bello*), and for committing crimes against humanity. China's interests at the trial focused on demonstrating the illegality of the invasion and on punishing those it regarded as responsible for the atrocities Japanese soldiers committed in China, especially at Nanjing. Like the ten other nations that participated in the Tokyo trial, China appointed a judge to the bench. Mei Ru'ao (1904–1973) agreed with all but the Indian judge that individuals could not evade responsibility for war crimes by hiding behind the states they served. He also argued that Japanese emperor Hirohito (1901–1989) should have been put on trial, an indictment that American geostrategic interests blocked. Of the twenty-five leaders judged, three of those sentenced to death were found guilty in part on the strength of the massive evidence the prosecution compiled of their complicity in war crimes in China.

The Tokyo trial addressed Japan's use of enforced military prostitution without, however, distinguishing it as a war crime. To seek judicial redress for the "comfort women" who were forced into sexual slavery, a Women's International War Crimes Tribunal was convened in Tokyo in December 2000 and in The Hague in December 2001.

It found that Japan's system of military prostitution constituted a crime against humanity.

WAR CRIMES TRIALS IN CHINA

In the postwar trials it conducted inside China, the government was concerned to demonstrate justice and not revenge. Adapting an adage from the *Daodejing*, Chiang Kai-shek (Jiang Jieshi) declared that China would "respond to indignation with virtue" in its treatment of Japanese war criminals. China was as good as Chiang's word. Of the 517 Japanese soldiers tried in military tribunals between 1946 and 1949, fifty-nine were acquitted for lack of evidence, and only 148 were executed. In addition, an undetermined number of Japanese were tried for crimes of a nonmilitary nature in district courts. Nonetheless, by 1949, over a thousand Japanese soldiers remained in custody without trial. The backlog was cleared in 1956, when forty-seven of their number were quickly tried and found guilty of war crimes and then repatriated along with the rest to Japan.

Accusations of war criminality were made against all parties in the Korean War (1950–1953), but no tribunals were convened. Since the 1980s, some Chinese have turned their attention back to Japanese war crimes, arguing that the postwar tribunals failed to address such crimes as biological warfare, military prostitution, and forced labor. Despite lawsuits, conferences, and protests, neither the Japanese nor the Chinese government has wanted to face the diplomatic costs of reopening the issue.

SEE ALSO *Anti-Japanese War, 1937–1945; Wars and the Military, 1800–1912; Wars since 1800.*

BIBLIOGRAPHY
Brook, Timothy. The Tokyo Judgment and the Rape of Nanking. *Journal of Asian Studies* 60, 3 (2001): 673–700.
Lary, Diana, and Stephen MacKinnon, eds. *Scars of War: The Impact of Warfare on Modern China.* Vancouver: University of British Columbia Press, 2001.
Matsui Yayori. Women's International War Crimes Tribunal on Japan's Military Sexual Slavery: Memory, Identity, and Society. *East Asia: An International Quarterly* 19, 4 (2001): 119–142.
Pritchard, R. John, and Sonia Zaide, eds. *The Tokyo War Crimes Trial: The Complete Transcripts of the Proceedings of the International Military Tribunal for the Far East.* New York: Garland, 1981.

Timothy Brook

WARLORD ERA (1916–1928)

The worst fear of central governments of China has always been chaos (*luan*), by which is meant any situation ranging from the devolution of central control over the regions of the vast nation, to complete breakdown of the state into its regions. This process was seen from the center as chaos, completely undesirable anarchy. Such breakdowns have occurred many times in Chinese history, usually at the end of dynasties and continuing in the interregnum before another dynasty emerged. Chaos re-emerged in 1916.

PERIODIZATION

The massive breakdown started five years after the Xinhai revolution. The failure of Yuan Shikai's imperial ambitions, and his subsequent death, removed China's last strongman and led to the devolution of power to the provinces and to levels below the province. The period saw the emergence of large numbers of regional rulers, almost all of them military men. These men called themselves military governors (*dujun*), but were called warlords (*junfa*) by those who bemoaned the loss of central power and the chaotic conditions that the warlords fostered. This convention has stuck; all men who controlled a region below the level of the state are referred to as warlords.

The period of warlord dominance is usually measured from 1916 to 1928, when a new national government was established by the Guomindang in Nanjing. For some parts of China, however, regional rule ended later; residual warlordism lasted until the Japanese invasion in 1937. The exact number of warlords can only be estimated. The number of senior figures was in the hundreds, but this number includes men whose star shone very briefly. Since the warlords engaged in frequent hostilities, and even more frequent betrayals, the duration of an individual warlord's rule might be brief. Very few warlords enjoyed a continuous period of rule; most were thrown out at least once during their careers.

WARLORDISM AND INSECURITY

Warlordism brought a state of chronic insecurity to China's society and economy. Civilians were never secure. Fighting might break out at any moment, endangering lives and property. Cities and lines of communication were particularly vulnerable to military activity. The warlords created few jobs, except in their armies; the number of soldiers burgeoned during this time, climbing into the millions. The economy was fragmented, and little new investment was possible.

Warlordism undermined all the central institutions of China, with the exception of the Post Office. There was no longer a single unified currency; numerous local and even foreign currencies were in circulation within China. There were no functioning national-level legal institutions, no effective central bank. The collection of customs revenues remained under foreign control. Above all there was no central government that could claim legitimate control over China, and therefore no government that could negotiate

effectively with foreign governments. The warlord era laid China open to foreign predation, especially from Japan. It also enhanced the status of foreign enclaves such as Shanghai, Hong Kong, and Tianjin. Many Chinese despaired of the insecurity of China and moved parts of their property and their business operations into the relative safety of foreign-controlled areas.

THE CHARACTER OF WARLORDS

The warlords are sometimes portrayed as vivid, colorful characters, swashbuckling men who lived hard and dramatically. The truth was more mundane and much sadder. The warlords ranged from educated men who had passed at least one stage of the traditional examination system (Wu Peifu), to commanders in the Qing or Republican armies or modern military school graduates (Feng Yuxiang, Yan Xishan), to former bandits (Zhang Zuolin). Some warlords ruled over vast regions, for long periods. Zhang Zuolin, for example, was the ruler of Manchuria, a vast, cold region, for twelve years until his assassination in 1928. Yan Xishan ruled the single province of Shanxi for even longer, from 1912 to 1949. Some warlords were cultivated, some brutish. Some were untouched by modern ideas, others were strongly influenced by the West; Feng Yuxiang, for example, was known as the "Christian general," because he had his troops baptized by a foreign missionary. Most warlords were strongly committed to the region they ruled, especially if it was their home region. The nation of China came a distant second.

MILITARISM

The overwhelming impact of warlordism was the dominance of the military. The warlord era put an end to the concept of civilian rule in China. The military was supreme, and there were only military solutions to problems of control and governance. There were no other mechanisms in play for the change of power, or for the introduction of new systems of government. Military men became the dominant figures in politics and government. The Guomindang, which brought many warlords into its revolutionary movement, came to power as a result of a military campaign, the Northern Expedition (1926–1928). It continued the practice of military dominance right through the resistance war and (on Taiwan) into the 1980s. The Communists came to power largely as a result of their battlefield success in the civil war (1946–1949), though they soon reestablished civil authority over the military.

THE DEVOLUTION OF POWER

Ironically, the loss of central authority had positive effects on China's cultural and intellectual worlds. In the absence of central control, the control of thought and intellectual and artistic production also disappeared. The 1920s and early 1930s were a period of enormous energy and creativity

58

in the intellectual and academic worlds, the movement fueled often by a nationalist passion to see China recover its national pride, and to see an end to the divisiveness of warlordism.

The warlords were not without their own claims to legitimacy. They tapped into a countercurrent to national pride: regional pride. The warlords promoted local and regional interests, hired their own fellow locals (*tongxiang*), retained tax income that should have gone to the central government, and in the process often became local heroes. These men are remembered now in their home regions not as venal characters, but as local celebrities; their homes have been turned into museums, and their descendents honored. In Shenyang, for example, the mansions of Zhang Zuolin have been lavishly restored by the city government, while Yan Xishan is almost the patron saint of Shanxi.

The fatal flaw of warlordism was the effect it had of weakening China. Few of the warlords were actually, as Communist historians have claimed, "running dogs" (*zougou*) of imperialism, but all were complicit in weakening China to the point that Japan was encouraged in its ambitions for expansion in China. These ambitions increased through the 1930s as Japan extended its hold over North China. Although Chiang Kai-shek (Jiang Jieshi) brought the last of the regional holdouts on board in early 1937, after the formation of the United Front between the Guomindang, the Communists, and the residual warlords, it was too late to stave off the full-scale Japanese invasion that came in July.

SEE ALSO *Federalism.*

BIBLIOGRAPHY

Ch'en, Jerome. *The Military-Gentry Coalition: China under the Warlords.* Toronto, ON: Joint Centre on Modern East Asia, 1979.

Gillin, Donald G. *Warlord: Yen Hsi-shan in Shansi Province, 1911–1949.* Princeton, NJ: Princeton University Press, 1967.

Lary, Diana. *Region and Nation: The Kwangsi Clique in Chinese Politics, 1925–1937.* Cambridge, U.K.: Cambridge University Press, 1975.

Sheridan, James. *Chinese Warlord: The Career of Feng Yü-hsiang.* Stanford, CA: Stanford University Press, 1966.

Waldron, Arthur. *From War to Nationalism: China's Turning Point, 1924–1925.* Cambridge, U.K.: Cambridge University Press, 1995.

Wou, Odoric Y. K. *Militarism in Modern China: The Career of Wu P'ei-fu, 1916–39.* Folkestone, U.K.: Dawson, 1978.

Diana Lary

WARS AND THE MILITARY, 1800–1912

During the nineteenth century, the late Qing dynasty (1644–1912) came under the twin pressures of foreign invasion and domestic rebellion. The foreign wars beginning with the Opium War (1839–1842) against Britain and followed by the Arrow War of 1856–1860, the Sino-French War (1884–1885), and the Sino-Japanese War (1894–1895) exposed China's weakness in defending itself. Internally, the Qing state was convulsed by a series of rebellions: the Taiping Uprising (1851–1864) in the south; the Nian Uprising (1851–1868) in the border regions of southwest Shandong, northwest Jiangsu, east-central Henan, and northern Anhui, and the Muslim revolts (1855–1873) in Yunnan on the Burma (Myanmar) border and in Xinjiang. The Taiping Uprising alone, led by the pseudo-Christian Hong Xiuquan (1813–1864), who established the Heavenly Kingdom of Great Peace with its capital in the walled city of Nanjing, ravaged much of China and left twenty to thirty million people dead or injured before it was put down by local militia units (*tuanlian*), particularly the Xiang Army (*Xiangjun*) raised by Zeng Guofan (1811–1872) and the Anhui Army (*Huaijun*) formed by Li Hongzhang (1823–1901). The role of the militia units reflected the startling ineptitude and debilitation of the traditional regular Qing forces.

MILITARIZATION OF CHINESE SOCIETY

Rebellions and their enemies led to the increasing militarization of Chinese society. Contributing to this phenomenon were increasing population pressure upon the land, growing economic competition in rural society, a bankrupt peasantry in certain areas, communal feuding, and a general breakdown of law and order. Local communities took steps to protect themselves by raising militia. As local militarization strengthened local and regional power, it posed some acute problems for the Qing court, but there was no disintegration of the imperial state, because militarization tended to crystallize along axes of existing political and social organizations that remained loyal to the throne during the remainder of the nineteenth century.

THE SELF-STRENGTHENING MOVEMENT

The Western intrusion, combined with domestic rebellion, created an unprecedented situation, forcing Qing rulers to launch the Self-strengthening movement (1861–1894), which put great emphasis on arsenals, shipbuilding, and the acquisition of Western military technology. The Jiangnan Arsenal was established in Shanghai in 1865, followed by the Navy Yard at Mawei (near Fuzhou) in 1866, and by the Nanjing Arsenal in 1867. In 1880 the viceroy of Zhili, Li Hongzhang, established the Tianjin Naval Academy. A great deal of attention was given to naval development until China's ignominious defeat at the hands of the Japanese in 1894 to 1895.

Fallen soldiers at the North Dagu Fort near Tianjin, China, during the Second Opium War, c. 1860. *Conditions imposed on the Qing government after the Second Opium War further angered many Chinese who felt humiliated by the dominance of Western powers. In response, China developed the Self-strengthening movement, a nationalistic plan to overhaul the country's antiquated military system.* © **HULTON-DEUTSCH COLLECTION/CORBIS**

THE NEW ARMY

The preoccupation with naval development rendered army reforms during the Self-strengthening period haphazard and piecemeal. In the north, Li Hongzhang and others developed the Beiyang armies, with their officers' training schools, staff colleges, foreign instructors, and modern armaments. Most notable among these schools was the Beiyang Military Academy, which would produce the Beiyang clique of officers that dominated Chinese politics after 1911. During the Sino-Japanese War, the first modern-drilled Pacification Army (*Dingwujun*) was raised by an official named Hu Yüfen (d. 1906) at Xiaozhan, about 35 kilometers southwest of Tianjin. In 1895 the command and training of this army were taken over by the then- governor of Shandong, Yuan Shikai (1859–1916), who renamed it

the Newly Created Army (*Xinjian lujun*). The next year, Zhang Zhidong (1837–1909), then acting viceroy of Liangjiang, created the Self-strengthening Army (*Ziqiangjun*) in Nanjing, based on the German model. Before the century was over, the Military Defense Army (*Wuweijun*) was formed in Zhili, with Ronglu (1836–1903), a grand secretary and superintendent of the Northern Ports, as commander in chief.

During the early 1900s, in the aftermath of the eight-power invasion of Beijing, a concerted effort was made to establish the New Army with leadership from the Qing court. An edict of August 29, 1901, abolished the traditional military exam to clear the way for modern military education. Another decree (September 1) recognized the value of trained officers by directing all provinces to establish military schools as soon as possible. A third decree issued the next day ordered the division of army units into standing armies, first-class reserves, and gendarmeries. Military reform began in earnest under Yuan Shikai, the viceroy of Zhili. His Newly Created Army was transformed and expanded into the Right Division of the Military Defense Army (*Wuwei youjun*), which, 7,850 strong by 1902, was the most outstanding of all the modern-drilled troops in the country. About 5,500 of the men were quartered in Beijing and the Summer Place, while a large proportion of the Left Division of the Military Defense Army (*Wuwei zuojun*) and the Valiant Army (*Weiyijun*) were within 50 kilometers of the capital.

In Hubei, meanwhile, there were about 9,500 modern-drilled troops; the bulk of them furnished the nucleus of the Wuchang bodyguard, consisting of two infantry regiments and one battalion each of cavalry, artillery, and engineers. The progress made in Zhili and Hubei prompted the Qing court in 1902 to direct the other provinces to reorganize the troops under their control. The next year, a beginning was made in the formation of standing armies in the provinces. To standardize training and to achieve efficiency, the Commission for Army Reorganization, with Prince Qing (1836–1918) and Yuan Shikai at its head, was established in Beijing in December 1903. By 1905 six northern divisions had been formed. Thereafter, the standing armies in the provinces were transformed into new divisions or brigades, a development that led the Qing court to order in April 1906 the creation within ten years of thirty-six divisions to be distributed among the provinces. Meanwhile, the Board of War was reorganized into the Ministry of War, into which the Commission for Army Reorganization was merged. A Manchu officer, Tieliang (1863–1938), was appointed president of the ministry, served by two deputies, the Manchu General Yinchang (1859–1934) and the Mongol bannerman Shouxun.

The date of the completion of the thirty-six divisions was later advanced to 1912, but this proved to be impracticable due to financial constraints. On the eve of the 1911 revolution, only fourteen divisions, excluding the Imperial Guard Corps (composed of former bannermen), of more or less full strength had been completed, to which were added eighteen mixed brigades and two brigades of varying strength. The actual total fighting strength was about 190,000.

The six Beiyang divisions, including the First Manchu Division, were the best trained and equipped. Still, their armaments were of a mixed kind. The 1888-model Mauser rifle manufactured at the Hanyang Arsenal was widely used. The cavalry was armed with the same model carbine. The infantry also used the 6-millimeter Japanese rifle and had Japanese accoutrements, while the cavalry and the artillery had 6-millimeter Japanese carbines and 75-millimeter Japanese Arisaka field guns, respectively. German arms were used too, such as the 75-millimeter Krupp mountain gun, the Vicker-Maxim, and the Schneider-Canet (Creusot) of the same caliber.

MODERN MILITARY EDUCATION

An important aspect of the army reform was the introduction of modern military education aimed at training a competent officer corps. Initially, a number of preparatory schools and schools for commissioned officers were established on a provincial basis. Later, in 1904, the Commission for Army Reorganization recommended the establishment over a period of seven to ten years of a hierarchy of military schools and staff colleges modeled on the Japanese system. There were to be primary schools in all the provinces and Manchu garrisons, four provincial secondary schools, one officers' school, and one staff college (both in Beijing). The recruits were to come principally from the provincial senior (civil) primary schools and partly from the existing military schools founded before 1905. Admission was all by exam. By 1907 military primary schools had been established in all the provinces except Xinjiang, Heilongjiang, and some Manchu garrisons. Two years later, four military secondary schools came into being in Beijing, Wuchang, Nanjing, and Xi'an. Before the opening of the Staff College, planned for 1916, temporary staff-training colleges were opened in Tianjin, Mukden, Wuchang, and Nanjing. In addition to these, there was a preparatory staff college at Baoding, which offered two separate courses, one for officers commanding battalions or squadrons, and the other for company officers. The former course was of one-and-a-half-years duration and the latter three years. All the officers were from the Beiyang and the Eighth and Ninth Divisions.

On the eve of the 1911 revolution, there were twenty-seven primary schools and four secondary schools, as well as Baoding's Preparatory Staff College and the Nobles' College located in Beijing. This last college was intended for members of the imperial clan and the sons or other relations of the highest officials. Over the years, the quality of the officer corps was improved, if still not up to Western standards. By 1911 a new officer corps had emerged, made up of at least three cliques of officers. Graduates of the Seijo Army School (Rikugun Seijo Gakkō) in Tokyo formed the so-called Shikan clique, as distinct from the Beiyang clique. A third broad category of officers who had graduated from schools in Central and South China had to compete with both of the two other cliques. Rivalries and mutual jealousies among them were rife.

CHANGE OF SOCIAL ATTITUDE

Traditionally, the Chinese soldier, illiterate and coming from a very poor background, was held in disdain in a society that extolled civil virtues. There was no military profession in a

Western sense, only a low-paid job to eke out a living for the sluggard and the vagabond. New Army reformers sought to change that by recruiting men who were educated or at least literate to a certain extent, especially into the secondary schools and officers' schools, and by improving conditions—better pay, better food and clothing, smart uniforms, and prospects for promotion. Promising students were sent to Japan, where they attended Tokyo's Seijo Army School and Officers' School (Shinbu Gakkō). Consequently, an increasing number of young men were attracted to the New Army, especially after the abolition in 1905 of the civil-service exam, which had for centuries been the only route to officialdom and the only means of personal advancement for the men of ability. The military profession offered a new career path and a new channel of upward social mobility, while rising nationalism gave it new purpose.

Of course, not every new soldier was educated and not many rose to officer rank. But a good many literate young men did respond favorably to the calling. Members of the new officer corps were in the main from good family backgrounds, many combining a junior traditional degree with a modern military education. A product of the reform era, their rise reflected the changing attitude toward soldiering by the ruling elite and society. Military virtues were now considered as important as civil virtues. The military profession was more respected and gaining popularity. Great progress had been made in instilling a military spirit in the Chinese mind, and the power accruing to a nation proficient in military knowledge and skills was fully appreciated. In 1909 the Qing court recognized the standing of the military profession by introducing a table of precedence for civil and military officials whereby the latter were accorded surprisingly high comparative rank.

THE 1911 REVOLUTION AND AFTER

The New Army played a decisive role in the 1911 revolution. The Wuchang Uprising on October 10 was the work of middle-ranking officers in the local garrison, which had been infiltrated by revolutionary elements. The immediate success of the uprising prompted the New Army divisions elsewhere to respond, leading to the replacement of local authorities by a military-gentry coalition in most provinces. But the Beiyang divisions, commanded by Yuan Shikai, who had been recalled from "retirement" to defend the dynasty, remained loyal to the Qing court until negotiations eventually led to the abdication of the emperor and to the installation of Yuan as the president of the new Republic.

For the most part, the New Army was disorganized by the revolution, with the troops becoming a source of trouble. The country teemed with soldiers, estimated at between 50,000 and 1 million men, many of them new recruits and unruly elements who had been refused enlistment a year or two before. The New Army deteriorated rapidly after 1911 to the point that regional militarists took practically anybody they could get into what soon became their personal armies. The public image of the new soldier that the late Qing had arduously created was greatly tarnished. Now the troops posed acute problems for law and order. Throughout 1912 and for the better part of 1913, there were numerous cases of army mutiny, disturbances, and unrest, not helped by the conflict between the north and south. The inability or unwillingness of the authorities to disband surplus troops was indicative of the ascendancy of the military, which challenged the centuries-old principle of civil supremacy. Over the next few decades, as Mao Zedong put it, political power grew out of the barrel of a gun.

SEE ALSO *Army and Politics; Military Culture and Tradition; War Crimes; Wars since 1800.*

BIBLIOGRAPHY

Chu, Samuel C., and Liu Guangjing (Liu Kwang-ching), eds. *Li Hung-chang and China's Early Modernization.* Armonk, NY: Sharpe, 1994.

Feng Zhaoji (Fung, Edmund S. K). *The Military Dimension of the Chinese Revolution: The New Army and Its Role in the Revolution of 1911.* Vancouver: University of British Columbia Press, 1980.

Graff, David, and Robin Higham, eds. *A Military History of China.* Boulder, CO: Westview, 2002.

Hatano Yoshihiro. The New Armies. In *China in Revolution: The First Phase, 1900–1913,* ed. Mary C. Wright, 365–382. New Haven, CT: Yale University Press, 1968.

Kuhn, Philip A. *Rebellion and Its Enemies in Late Imperial China: Militarization and Social Structure, 1796–1864.* Cambridge, MA: Harvard University Press, 1970.

MacKinnon, Stephen R. *Power and Politics in Late Imperial China: Yuan Shi-kai in Beijing and Tianjin, 1901–1908.* Berkeley: University of California Press, 1980.

McCord, Edward A. *The Power of the Gun: The Emergence of Modern Chinese Warlordism.* Berkeley: University of California Press, 1993.

Powell, Ralph L. *The Rise of Chinese Military Power, 1895–1912.* Princeton, NJ: Princeton University Press, 1955.

Spector, Stanley. *Li Hung-chang and the Huai Army: A Study in Nineteenth-Century Chinese Regionalism.* Seattle: University of Washington Press, 1964.

Edmund S. K. Fung (Feng Zhaoji)

WARS SINCE 1800

The wars of nineteenth- and twentieth-century China are best divided analytically into *civil* wars as opposed to *defensive* wars provoked by a foreign invader. The "foreign" wars were fought in defense of sovereignty, meaning at first the sovereignty of the Qing (1644–1912) empire and then increasingly that of the Chinese nation-state in a modern sense. The domestic wars were peasant uprisings against the Qing or, later, Communist-led uprisings against the Nationalist government of Chiang Kai-shek (Jiang Jieshi). Until the devastating mid-twentieth-century War of Resistance (1937–1945) and the civil war (1946–1949) that followed, the earlier wars—domestic and foreign—were limited geographically in scope of fighting and in their impact on the population and economy.

FOREIGN AND DOMESTIC WARS OF THE LATE QING PERIOD

Often these wars, domestic and foreign, occurred as simultaneous threats to the Chinese state. The first such wars occurred in the middle of the nineteenth century. The most devastating in terms of immediate impact was an internal "civil war" called the Taiping peasant rebellion (1851–1864). It is thought to have cost the lives of twenty-five million people and destroyed much of the economy of Central China. The final siege and massacre at the Taiping capital of Nanjing ended a decade of attacks and counterattacks that swept up and down the Yangzi Valley, bringing a level of violence and suffering to the people that was unprecedented in Chinese history. This occurred in part because of the growing use by both sides of Western weaponry. Smaller-scale peasant rebellions bedeviled China through the 1860s and 1870s in other regions, particularly in Anhui and Henan provinces (Nian rebels). There were also large-scale Muslim-led uprisings in the far northwest provinces.

The Qing dynasty survived these internal threats by reorganizing itself militarily. Slowly, the emperor and his advisers, after devastating losses in the 1850s, recognized the inadequacy of the traditional Manchu-led "banner" units. By default, new regional armies were raised locally to fight the rebels. These were led by Confucian scholar-generals like Zeng Guofan, Li Hongzhang, and Zuo Zongtang. These armies finally suppressed the peasant uprisings and ensured the dynasty's survival into the twentieth century.

Less traumatic at the time, but more disastrous in the long run, was the series of foreign wars that the dynasty had to fight along the China coast. In the West, these wars— usually referred to as the Opium Wars—are better known than the peasant rebellions because they involved Western powers knocking on China's door in the most unpleasant of manners. The casus belli was the insistence by Western (and later Japanese) imperialist powers on exercising increasing control over Chinese coastal trade. Initially, the issue was the right to trade opium openly on the Chinese market.

These were limited wars, beginning with losses in the Opium War (1839–1842), which started in the Guangzhou Delta area of South China, and ending with the sacking of Beijing and its Summer Palace in 1860 by the French and British. But the consequences of these wars were serious because of the direct challenge to Chinese

sovereignty that the loss of sovereign rights represented. By the 1860s, the Chinese state in the form of the Qing dynasty was forced to accept and abide by the infamous unequal treaty system. By 1900 this system undermined sovereignty throughout China by privileging foreign commercial, missionary, and military interests beyond the one hundred coastal and inland "treaty port" cities.

The most shocking loss in the series of foreign wars that punctuated the last half of the nineteenth century came in 1894 and 1895, when China was defeated on land and sea in a war with Japan—a war that began with a conflict over control of Korea. In a humiliating peace treaty signed in Shimonoseki, the Qing court was forced to cede suzerainty over the province of Taiwan, grant special rights to the Japanese in Manchuria, and relinquish all influence over Korea. The Chinese high minister in charge at the time, Li Hongzhang, once a hero for successfully suppressing peasant rebels, was forced to resign in disgrace.

Immediately thereafter, in 1899, another domestic uprising broke out in Shandong and Zhili provinces in North China. Cleverly, or so it seemed at first, the ill-fated Boxer peasant rebels were redirected by a xenophobic Qing court into attacking the foreign community throughout these two provinces, especially missionaries. By early 1900 Boxers were terrorizing the diplomatic community in Beijing. The result proved even more disastrous than the loss to Japan had been. For almost two years, from 1900 to 1902, Beijing and Tianjin were sacked and then occupied by an Allied expedition force of eight powers—forcing the empress dowager Cixi and the Guangxu emperor (1871–1908) into exile, until Cixi signed a humiliating peace treaty and protocol. The latter mortgaged away the budgets of Chinese governments for decades to come.

The first decade of the twentieth century unfolded inauspiciously with more foreign humiliations. Japan and Russia went to war in 1904 to 1905 over control of Manchuria in China's Northeast—leaving the court in Beijing watching helplessly from the sidelines. In terms of the use of firepower, weaponry like the machine gun, and deployment of land and naval forces, this war anticipated World War I in Europe. It also weakened the czar, setting off a series of events that many argue led to the Russian Revolution in 1917. And in terms of Chinese history, the Russo-Japanese War pushed the Qing state to adopt drastic reform measures, which ultimately upended the dynasty. These included the creation of a modern military force (known as the Beiyang Army), advanced officer-training programs, and munitions factories. Politically, the state moved toward a constitutional monarchy, sent students abroad in significant numbers, and initiated state-financed industrial and infrastructural projects, such as railroad construction.

THE REPUBLICAN AND
WARLORD PERIODS

But the losses of sovereignty to foreign powers had already greatly weakened the dynasty and undermined its legitimacy, spawning the antidynastic reform and revolutionary movements of Sun Yat-sen, Liang Qichao, and others that ultimately forced the collapse of the Qing dynasty after the death of the empress dowager in 1908.

Unfortunately, the establishment of the Republic of China in 1912 led to more disunity and more wars—domestic and foreign. The 1911–1912 revolution that overthrew the dynasty was relatively bloodless (in part out of fear of foreign intervention), but the aftermath led to a disintegration of the state into an ever-growing number of regional satrapies controlled by militarists (later more pejoratively called *warlords*). The number of men under arms quadrupled in less than a decade. The availability of more-destructive weapons led to sudden, arbitrary devastation for local populations caught in the crossfire of wars between militarists. Eventually, by the late 1920s, a popular reaction developed in the form of the organization of competing "revolutionary" armies—Nationalist- and Communist-led—who aimed at crushing the warlords (and each other). This meant that throughout the 1920s and 1930s armies swept back and forth across China in a complicated civil-war pattern, pitting warlord against warlord (especially in North China) and Communist against Nationalist forces in southern provinces like Jiangxi. The exception was a brief period when the Nationalists and Communists united in the Northern Expedition of 1925 to 1927 against regional militarists in control of central and northern China.

Between the Russo-Japanese War and the Japanese occupation of Manchuria and attack on Shanghai in 1931 and 1932, there were no further foreign-initiated conflicts on Chinese soil. But the pressure continued from imperialist powers under the treaty-port system, especially from an increasingly demanding Japanese empire. Regional militarists were dependent on arms and funds from a variety of competing foreign interests. Moreover, the state of constant civil war in the hinterland thrust the treaty-port city of Shanghai forward. During this period, Shanghai reached the height of its influence as a center of intrigue, commerce, and modernism in a cultural sense. In contrast, throughout the first half of the twentieth century, the former capital, Beijing, declined in importance politically, and struggled to survive under the thumb of various competing warlords or militarists.

THE WAR OF RESISTANCE
AGAINST JAPAN

The rampant warlordism of the 1910s, 1920s, and early 1930s drove Chinese rural elites to take refuge and reinvent themselves economically and politically in major cities like Shanghai, Wuhan, and Chengdu. But the *longue durée* of the War of Resistance against Japan and the brutal civil war that followed transformed China—socially, politically, and culturally—for better or worse.

In 1931 the Japanese army seized Manchuria, soon declaring the region to be the independent state of Manchukuo (Manzhouguo), with the last Qing emperor, Puyi (1906–1967), as its puppet ruler. In the spring of 1932, the Japanese navy bombed and assaulted Chinese-controlled portions of Shanghai. The Chinese organized a spirited defense and the Japanese withdrew, but not before sending the Nationalist government in Nanjing a strong message that Central China was vulnerable. What followed was an uneasy truce and a series of "incidents" in North China, which the Japanese used to nibble away at Chinese sovereignty. By 1937 the Japanese had moved troops south to the outskirts of Beijing. On July 7, 1937, the final "incident" occurred, when Chinese and Japanese troops clashed at Marco Polo Bridge in the suburbs of Beijing. From this point on to 1945, it was total war—declared by the Chinese side, though labeled an "incident" by the Japanese.

The turning point in the War of Resistance, or the Second Sino-Japanese War, was the fighting that occurred between 1937 and 1939. During the fall of 1937, the highly mechanized Japanese Imperial Army, supported by heavy bombing raids, quickly swallowed North China and moved south, laying siege to Shanghai by the end of August. The battle for Shanghai was fierce, with the Japanese prevailing by November and soon thereafter closing in on the Chinese Nationalist capital at Nanjing. Chiang Kai-shek had committed his crack units to the defense of Shanghai, where he lost half of his well-trained officer corps. In December, in rapid succession, Jinan in Shandong and then Nanjing fell. Using massive firepower and terror tactics, most famously on the population of Nanjing, the Japanese expected to chase what remained of Chiang's disorganized fleeing armies into the central Yangzi Valley and deliver the knockout blow that would force Chiang's surrender, end the war, and leave most of China under Japanese occupation by March 1938.

Instead, the unexpected happened. A variety of regional armies under the command of various militarists came to the rescue of the Chinese nation. Around Wuhan, these regional forces assembled and regrouped with Chiang Kai-shek's central army units fleeing from Shanghai. Under the reorganization, Chiang Kai-shek and former militarist rivals like Bai Chongxi (1893–1966), Li Zongren (1890–1969), and Feng Yuxiang (1882–1948) formed a new combined leadership. As a result, a surprisingly effective last stand was made around Xuzhou and then at Wuhan in Central China. There, during the spring and early summer of 1938, the revitalized Chinese armies blunted the firepower and mobility of the Japanese Imperial Army using human-wave tactics and night attacks and flooding Japanese mechanized units by blowing up the dikes of the Yellow (Huang) River at Huayuankou (near Kaifeng). By the end of October 1938, the Chinese had lost

Chinese soldier captured by a Vietnamese troop, Cao Bang, Vietnam, February 28, 1979.
Responding to Vietnamese aggression against Cambodia's Khmer Rouge regime, China launched an invasion into northern Vietnam in 1979. The hostilities ended quickly, however, as the more experienced Vietnamese troops pushed back the Chinese, ending the conflict in one month's time.
© BETTMANN/CORBIS

both Xuzhou and Wuhan. But in the battle for the central Yangzi Valley, both sides exhausted themselves. And most important, the Chinese side, despite having won few battles, had succeeded in turning the war into a protracted affair that would last until 1945.

The next stage of the war was much slower in pace. The Nationalists moved their capital to Chongqing in mountainous Sichuan in 1939, and with the Communists under Mao Zedong they began to organize guerilla-warfare campaigns from their cave headquarters in the Northwest (Yan'an). There was still fighting, but not on the same scale. For instance, Changsha, the capital of Hunan Province, was captured and reoccupied by both sides three times between 1939 and 1941. And of course at the end of 1941, the Sino-Japanese War became part of a much larger world war with the attack on Pearl Harbor and the American entry into the Pacific and European wars. Chiang Kai-shek (and the Communists) now had a new partner, the United States, permitting both to wait out the war. With the exception of the Japanese Ichi-Go offensive of 1944 (when the Japanese pushed into Jiangxi and Guangxi provinces), the field positions of the opposing armies in China remained roughly stationary for the rest of the war.

But the military facts only tell part of the story. The importance to modern Chinese history of the eight years of total war from 1937 to 1945 is difficult to overestimate, be it in social, cultural, economic, or political terms. The cost in lives lost and property destroyed made this war even more devastating than the war in Europe, a fact not widely acknowledged in the West. Throughout the coastal provinces, from north to south, the atrocities committed by Japanese troops were monstrous. In due course, more than one hundred million homeless refugees (almost a quarter of the population) fled to the interior. Over twenty million civilians lost their lives. Families were torn asunder. Countless women were left to fend for themselves, some alone and others destitute with children, after their husbands and brothers were forcibly pressed into service. Many men died on the battlefield, others succumbed to wounds left untreated, and yet others to starvation and disease.

THE CIVIL WAR AND SUBSEQUENT BORDER DISPUTES

The civil war that followed from 1946 to 1949 between the Communists and Nationalists was fought from Manchuria to Guangzhou. The Communists scored a surprisingly quick victory, but not without further devastation of the countryside in the process. Thus, by the middle of the twentieth century, at least half of the Chinese population had been through a refugee experience. The agonies and uncertainties of being a refugee or living in occupied China led to the long-term traumatization of a generation. There was no question by 1949 that two decades of nearly total war had altered the cultural and political landscape. China would never be the same. These wars (both civil and anti-Japanese) generated a series of mass movements or mobilization efforts. These would become inescapable after "liberation" in 1949, shaking Chinese society to its roots with wave after wave of campaigns that lasted through the 1950s, 1960s, and 1970s.

With the triumph of the Communists in 1949, the closest China came to another civil war was during the height of the Cultural Revolution from 1966 to 1969. But mobilization for war continued, and the new government of the People's Republic of China fought a series of border wars. The first came immediately and was relatively successful, with Chinese troops intervening in the Korean War in late 1950 and fighting the technically superior U.S. troops to a standstill by 1953. The second military intervention, China's brief border war with India in 1962, was also successful. An inconclusive third border war broke out with the Soviet Union in 1969, producing no concrete results for either side. One effect of these border wars was to further isolate the People's Republic internationally.

Another military adventure on Beijing's part was the failed invasion of Vietnam in 1979. The Chinese units that crossed the border into North Vietnam were soon outmaneuvered by the North Vietnamese Army and forced to retreat. In the future, if there is to be a new border war launched from Beijing, it will probably involve an air and sea operation launched against Taiwan.

SEE ALSO *War Crimes; Wars and the Military, 1800–1912.*

BIBLIOGRAPHY

Dreyer, Edward. *China at War, 1901–49.* London: Longmans, 1995.

Fay, Peter. *Opium War, 1840–42.* Chapel Hill: University of North Carolina Press, 1998.

Graff, David and Robin Higham. *Military History of China.* Boulder, CO: Westview, 2002.

MacKinnon, Stephen. *Wuhan, 1938: War, Refugees, and Making of Modern China.* Berkeley: University of California Press, 2008.

Schobell, Andrew. *China's Use of Military Force.* Cambridge, U.K.: Cambridge University Press, 2003.

Spence, Jonathan. *God's Chinese Son: The Taiping Heavenly Kingdom of Hong Xiuquan.* Boston: Norton, 1996.

Stephen R. MacKinnon

WEI YUAN
1794–1857

Wei Yuan was a scholar-official activist who played a prominent role in the critical review of Qing governing institutions and scholarship in the first half of the nineteenth century. He was associated with a prestigious circle of scholar-advisers and prominent officials serving in Liangjiang province who sought to adjust Qing governing institutions to cope with daunting challenges that resulted from long-term social, economic, and demographic change and from the political crisis generated by the fall of Heshen in 1799.

Wei was born to a modest gentry family in Jintan village, Shaoyang County, in south-central Hunan. He ranked first in the 1810 prefectural exam, achieved the *bagongsheng* degree in 1813 that enabled him to study in Beijing, and passed the provincial exam in 1822. He was hired that year by He Changling (1785–1848) to compile and edit the important *Essays on Qing Imperial Statecraft* (*Huangchao jingshi wenbian*, 1826) that defined the critical governing issues of the day, and he continued to serve as an adviser-publicist for leading provincial officials in Liangjiang province until 1844, except for a brief period from 1829 to 1831 when he held a purchased secretarial position in the Grand Secretariat. Wei began his official career in 1844 after passing the metropolitan exam, holding three positions in Jiangsu Province: acting magistrate of Dongting County (1845), magistrate of Xinghua County (1849), and magistrate in Gaoyou Department (1851–1853), where he helped to organize local defenses against the Taiping rebels. Retiring in 1854, he spent his last years at a Pure Land Buddhist monastery in Hangzhou.

SCHOLARSHIP

Wei Yuan shared the Qing literati's view that classical Confucian scholarship provided the moral foundations for personal development and public service, and his scholarly interests were wide ranging and eclectic, including the study of Confucianism, as well as Daoism and Buddhism. His Confucian studies began with youthful forays into Ming Neo-Confucianism, followed by explorations of the Song "learning" approach to the Confucian moral-political mission. He acquired the research techniques of the Han school of textual research from Hu Chenggong (1776–1832), who introduced him to the controversy over the Old and New Text versions of the Confucian classics and commentaries of the early Han period (206 BCE–23 CE) that were just beginning to arouse scholarly interest. Wei also investigated the esoteric, or hidden, readings of the New Texts with Liu Fenglu (1776–1829), producing important works on the *Book of History* and the *Book of Poetry*. These studies provided the moral-political foundations of his view of the Qing moral mission and informed his practical activism as he and his circle of scholar-officials searched for new ways to address the problems that faced the Qing dynasty in the early nineteenth century.

CAREER AS POLITICAL ANALYST

Wei Yuan began a remarkable career from 1822 to 1844 as a political analyst and publicist who addressed governing problems, primarily in Liangjiang, that centered on the destruction of the Grand Canal, the consequent breakdown of canal transport of capital grain supplies, and dysfunction in the Lianghuai salt monopoly. He worked with a circle of like-minded literati activists, such as Bao Shichen (1775–1855), who assisted prominent Liangjiang officials, including Qishan (d. 1854), Tao Zhu (1779–1839), and He Changling, in the solution of these problems. Their efforts led to the successful reconfiguration of hydraulic facilities on the south side of the Grand Canal–Yellow River junction near Huai'an (1825–1827); the experimental use of sea transport to ship tax-grain from Shanghai to Tianjin in 1826; and the creation of the salt-ticket system in the Lianghuai salt fields (1832–1850). Wei Yuan wrote individual essays on these issues, and he helped compile *The Complete Records on Jiangsu Sea Transport* (*Jiangsu haiyun quan'an*) in 1826, which contained key edicts and memorials tracing the steps in the planning and implementation of sea transport from early 1825 to 1826. This work also provided the blueprint for the sea-transport regulations that were included in the 1845 revision of the Board of Revenue's administrative code governing grain transport (*Qinding Hubu caoyun quanshu*).

Wei Yuan and his circle also undertook a broad review of Qing administration under the Six Boards that is contained in *Essays on Qing Imperial Statecraft*, noted above. This work contains a unique expression of the practical, down-to-earth approach to administrative problem-solving and innovation that defines early nineteenth-century "statecraft" (*jingshi*). The first fourteen chapters consider the essentials of moral learning (*xueshu*) and administrative fundamentals (*zhiti*) that the compilers believed were the foundations of effective governance. This is followed by a discussion of the mission of each of the Six Boards, the particular challenges they faced in the early nineteenth century, and institutional adjustments to overcome these challenges (chaps. 15–120). Each chapter contains a collage of excerpts from the writings of scholars and officials from the late Ming to the 1820s that are arranged to highlight the concerns and institutional innovations advocated by the compilers. It is, in sum, a work of advocacy that expresses the moral-social worldview and the practical idealism of statecraft scholars and officials who sought to adjust, fine-tune, and thus strengthen the basic operations of Qing government. Wei Yuan's seventeen contributions to the work included essays on Confucian learning, rites, and military questions ranging from a discussion of the military thinker Sunzi, to city garrisons, the northwest frontier, and the pacification of the Miao in Hunan.

THE MARITIME CRISIS

Wei Yuan's involvement in the critical review of Qing governing institutions prepared him for his analysis of China's maritime crisis during the Opium War (1839–1842). His work on sea transport, in particular, had alerted him to the geography, sailing conditions, and maritime defenses on the northeast coast, as well as the collaborative role of private merchant organizations in the Qing administration of trade, port management, and maritime customs in the four southeastern coastal provinces. Entreated by the disgraced Lin Zexu (1785–1850) to analyze and publicize the new maritime threat, Wei compiled *The Illustrated Treatise on the Sea Kingdoms* (*Haiguo tuzhi*, 1844, 1847, 1852), the first influential Chinese work to warn of the growth of Western commercial and naval power in maritime Asia (Nanyang) and to argue for the reassertion of Chinese overlordship in this region to counter its disruptive effects. The work contains new information drawn from translations of Western works about world geography and the global dimensions of Western power, but most important is its geopolitical analysis of China's historic ties with the Nanyang and its call to reorient the Qing strategic vision to take account of global maritime communications and Western power.

During the maritime crisis, Wei turned his attention to Qing military history, border defenses, and a reconsideration of the history of the Yuan dynasty—issues that he had begun to investigate earlier in his career. He completed *The Military History of the Qing Dynasty* (*Shengwuji*) in 1842, which celebrates the past military achievements of the Qing, but also advocates reforms in military training and local and coastal defenses. Shortly before his death, he began rewriting the history of the Yuan dynasty, examining its achievements and reflecting on the reasons for its decline, as if to discover parallels with the Qing experience.

LEGACY

Wei Yuan was an extremely important transitional figure whose career as a political analyst, pragmatic problem solver, and publicist expressed the practical idealism of statecraft scholar-official activists who lived and worked during the transitional period between the High Qing and the desperate times of the late nineteenth century and who believed that timely, innovative adjustments to administrative practice would solve the problems of Qing governance.

SEE ALSO *Gong Zizhen; Lin Zexu.*

BIBLIOGRAPHY

Hummel, Arthur W., ed. *Eminent Chinese of the Ch'ing Period, 1644–1912.* Washington, DC: U.S. Government Printing Office, 1943–1944.

Leonard, Jane Kate. *Wei Yuan and China's Rediscovery of the Maritime World.* Cambridge, MA: Council on East Asian Studies, Harvard University, 1984.

Leonard, Jane Kate. Timeliness and Innovation: The 1845 Revision of *The Complete Book on Grain Transport* (*Caoyun quanshu*). In *Chinese Handicraft Regulations of the Qing Dynasty: Theory and Application,* eds. Hans Ulrich Vogel, Christine Moll-Murata, and Song Jianze, 449–464. Munich: Iudicum, 2005.

Leonard, Jane Kate. The Qing Strategic Highway on the Northeast Coast. In *The Perception of Maritime Space in Traditional Chinese Sources,* eds. Angela Schottenhammer and Roderich Ptak, 27–39. Wiesbaden, Germany: Harrassowitz Verlga, 2006.

Metzger, Thomas A. *The Internal Organization of the Ch'ing Bureaucracy: Legal, Normative, and Communications Aspects.* Cambridge, MA: Harvard University Press, 1973.

Qi Sihe (Ch'i Ssu-ho). Wei Yuan yü wan-Qing hsueh-feng [Wei Yuan and late Qing scholarship]. *Yen-ching hsueh-pao* [Yenching journal] 39 (1950):177–226.

Wang Jiajian (Wang Chia-chien). *Wei Yuan nien-p'u* [Wei Yuan: A chronological biography]. Taibei: Academia Sinica, 1967.

Wei Yuan. *Wei Yuan ji* [Collected works of Wei Yuan]. 2 vols. Beijing: Zhonghua, 1983.

Jane Kate Leonard

WEIGHTS AND MEASURES

The systems of weight and measurement in use in China during the Qing dynasty (1644–1912) included *yingzao* (length), *caohu* (capacity), and *kuping* (weight). Generally, the units were based on the decimal system, with some exceptions (see Table 1). To standardize the vessel for tax (mainly in the form of grain) collection, the Kangxi emperor (r. 1661–1722) set the vertical length of a grain of millet as the basis for forming one standard length (*yingzao chi* or *bu chi*), which equaled the sum of the horizontal length of 100 medium-sized millet grains (approximately 1 foot or ⅓ meter, see Table 1). One standard unit of capacity (*caohu sheng*) was 3.16 cubic *chi.* One standard unit of weight (*kuping jin*) was the weight of 1 cubic *cun* (1 *cun* equaled 0.1 *chi*) of pure gold. The early Qing emperors (Shunzhi, Kangxi, and Qianlong) took the units seriously and issued decrees of standardization. They also issued standard iron measuring instruments to provincial governments, which reproduced them for taxation and metrological policing.

In practice, this system was difficult to maintain. First, it was difficult to accurately replicate standard measuring instruments in sufficient numbers for distribution all over China. Even when officially approved instruments were available, they were subject over time to wear and tear and thermal expansion and contraction. Second, metrolog-

ical policing was lax, not least because government officials were themselves not serious in keeping to standard. Local officials might even alter the size of measuring instruments for the sake of collecting more taxes, despite strict penal codes against such behavior. Third, local variations were common. For example, *caiyi chi, luban chi,* and *liangdi chi* were length units used in the trades of tailor, carpenter, and builder, respectively. The *caiyi chi* was longer than the *luban chi* and the *liangdi chi.* There were also different systems in different localities, such as the *jing chi, guang chi, guan chi,* which were used in Beijing, in Guangdong, and in areas where maritime customs were followed. Some systems were not necessary decimal. For example, in the carpenter's trade, 9 *cun* amounted to 1 *luban chi.*

By the nineteenth century, some uniformity was imposed by the treaties that the Qing government signed with Western powers. Some treaties stipulated standard conversion for Chinese units. The Imperial Maritime Customs Service, whose duty it was to regulate foreign trade, produced the Haiguan (Maritime Customs) system (*guanping*), which was the basis on which import and export duties were revised. Nevertheless, the Haiguan system did not have an impact on the standardization of measurement in other areas.

In 1905, among other reforms, the Qing court issued an edict of standardization, which introduced Western scientific principles to the traditional *yingzao-kuping* system. The government ordered from France a set of iridium measuring instruments denoted in *yingzao-kuping* units. However, the 1911 revolution ended that effort. The Republican government made another standardization attempt by promulgating a metrological law in 1915. It introduced the commonly used *shiyong* system, which largely followed the old *yingzao-kuping* system. Yet, because of a lack of qualified policing institutions and personnel, standardization proved difficult to achieve. In 1929 the Nationalist government in Nanjing

---

Qing Chinese units of weight and measurement

Length:
5 *chi* = 1 *bu*
360 *bu* = 1 *li*
10,000 *li* = 1,000 *fen* = 100 *cun* = 10 *chi* = 1 *zhang*

Area:
10,000 *li* = 1,000 *fen* = 100 *mu* = 1 *qing*
1 *fen* = 24 *bu*

Capacity:
100 *sheng* = 10 *dou* = 1 *shi*
5 *dou* = 1 *hu*

Weight:
1,000 *li* = 100 *fen* = 10 *qian* = 1 *liang*
16 *liang* (tael) = 1 *jin* (catty)
100 *jin* = 1 *dan* (picul)

Table 1

Conversion table

	Shiyong	Metric	*Yingzao-kuping*	Imperial
Length	1 *shi chi*	0.3333 meters	1.0417 *chi*	1.0936 feet
	1 *shi li*	0.5 kilometers	0.8681 *li*	0.3107 miles
Area	1 square *shi chi*	0.1111 square meters	1.0851 square *chi*	1.1960 square feet
	1 square *shi li*	0.25 square kilometers	0.7535 square *li*	0.965 square miles
	1 *shi mu*	6.667 acres	1.0851 *mu*	0.1644 acres
Capacity	1 cubic *shi chi*	0.0370 cubic meters	1.1303 cubic *chi*	1.8078 cubic feet
	1 *shi sheng*	1 liter	0.9657 *sheng*	0.22 gallons
Weight	1 *shi liang*	31.25 grams	0.8378 *liang*	1.023 ounces
	1 *shi jin*	0.5 kilograms	0.8378 *jin*	2.2046 pounds
	1 *shi dan*	50 kilograms	83.7779 *jin*	0.9842 hundredweight

SOURCE: *Zhongwai do liang heng bizhi biao* (Conversion tables of Chinese and foreign systems of units and weights, measurement, and currency), pp. 3–5, appendix section of *Cihai* (Dictionary of words), Shanghai: Zhonghua, 1948.

Table 2

promulgated a new metrological law that adopted the metric system but recognized the *shiyong* system. The government also established a National Institute of Metrology to be in charge of producing metrological instruments, training personnel, and policing. The Second Sino-Japanese War (1937–1945) impeded these efforts to achieve standardization.

The end of the civil war in 1949 and the establishment of a strong central government made the standardization work easier. The Communist government adopted the metric system and abandoned the *shiyong* system. In 1955 it established a new National Institute of Metrology to oversee standardization work. The institute set up branches in the provinces and trained personnel in metrological research. The disruptions of the Cultural Revolution and its aftermath (1966–1976) slowed progress. Work resumed after 1977, and the government began issuing a series of regulations regarding metrological standardization. In 1985 a metrological law was promulgated. With more effective policing, executed by metrological institutions and better scientific education, China's units of weight and measurement are on the track of standardization.

BIBLIOGRAPHY

Currency and Measures in China. *Journal of the China Branch of the Royal Asiatic Society*, n.s. 24 (1889–1890): 48–135.

Qiu Guangming. *Zhongguo wulixue shi daxi: Jiliang shi* [A great series of the history of physics in China: Metrology]. Changsha, PRC: Hunan Jiaoyu Chubanshe, 2002.

Wu Chengluo. *Zhongguo duliangheng shi* [A history of metrology in China]. 1st ed., 1937. Taibei: Shangwu, 1970.

Zhongwai do liang heng bizhi biao [Conversion tables of Chinese and foreign systems of units of weights, measurement, and currency], 3–5. *Cihai* [Dictionary of words]. Shanghai: Zhonghua, 1948.

Wang Hsien-Chun

WEN JIABAO
1942–

Wen Jiabao, a member of the ruling Politburo Standing Committee (PBSC) of the Chinese Communist Party (CCP) since 2002 and head of the State Council since 2003, may leave his mark in history as a "people's premier" much along the same lines as his hero, Zhou Enlai. Wen was born in September 1942 in the old treaty port of Tianjin, the son of schoolteachers. He attended the renowned Nankai Middle School, the same institution that Zhou attended in the 1910s. Wen's most traumatic experience as a child was shuddering in the arms of his mother when Tianjin was invaded by the Japanese Imperial Army. It is typical of the premier's pragmatism, however, that such bitter memories did not stop him from playing a sizable role in improving ties with Japan, notably during his high-profile visit to Tokyo in 2007.

EDUCATION AND EARLY CAREER

After high school, Wen studied geology at Beijing Geological University from 1960 to 1968. Unaffected by the Cultural Revolution, he was sent as a geological technician and structural engineer by the Ministry of Geology and Natural Resources (MGNS) to hardscrabble Gansu Province in the northwest. The idealistic young man stayed there until 1982, rising to the number-two position in the Gansu Province Geological Bureau. While in Gansu, Wen never met Hu Jintao, who became president in 2003 and had worked in the field of hydraulic engineering and economic planning from 1968 to 1982. But both Wen and Hu benefited from the patronage of party elder Song Ping, who was party secretary of the province from 1977 to 1981. It was at Song's recommendation that Wen was able in 1982 to return to

Chinese Premier Wen Jiabao addressing stranded passengers at a train station in Changsha, Hunan province, January 29, 2008. *As premier of China, Wen Jiabao has earned a populist reputation among many Chinese, partially reinforced by his advocacy of greater government support of the rural poor. Some critics, however, suggest that some of Wen's policies have allowed corrupt politicians and business owners to control much of the nation's wealth, leaving workers vulnerable to future exploitation.* © YAO DAWE/XINHUA PRESS/CORBIS

Beijing and work as a senior cadre in the MGNS's Department of Research and Law. Wen became vice minister a year later, when he was barely forty-one.

Wen's big break came in 1985, when he was selected as one of only several cadres in their forties to be groomed for possible leadership positions in the party and state. (Other officials similarly picked for fast-track career paths included Hu Jintao, Wu Bangguo, and Wang Zhaoguo.) Wen became a vice director of the General Office of the CCP Central Committee, the nerve center of the party. As General Office director from 1986 to 1993, Wen was a close aide to three general secretaries, Hu Yaobang, Zhao Ziyang, and Jiang Zemin. During this tumultuous period, the troubleshooter and drafter of documents was best remembered as the mournful-looking cadre who accompanied Zhao to Tiananmen Square in May 1989 to apologize to the students who were on hunger strike.

There has been no official explanation as to how Wen managed to survive the purge of Zhao's close associates after the June Fourth massacre. Yet it did not come as a surprise to those who knew him well: almost from the day he started

work within the Zhongnanhai party headquarters in Beijing, Wen distinguished himself as a consummate *mishu* (secretary) and administrator who was ready to serve his bosses—of whatever faction and ideological stripe—and to advance the interests of the party above all else. He made himself indispensable to Jiang soon after the former Shanghai party secretary's arrival in Beijing. Jiang—and Deng Xiaoping behind him—promoted Wen to the Politburo in 1992. From 1993 to 2002, he was secretary of the CCP Secretariat, which was in charge of policymaking as well as the dissemination of major documents throughout the party. In this capacity, he became an able assistant of executive vice premier and PBSC member in charge of the economy, Zhu Rongji, as well as of Jiang's successor, Hu Jintao.

ASCENT TO PREMIERSHIP

Wen began his apprenticeship in the art of running China's complex economy when he served as vice premier under "Boss Zhu" from 1998 to 2003. Although he was outranked by Executive Vice Premier Li Lanqing and Vice Premier Wu Bangguo, Wen was Zhu's de facto right-hand man—and he was given the crucial portfolios of agriculture and finance. The soft-spoken, scholarly-looking Wen won nationwide acclaim as the commander in chief of flood control during the disastrous "once-in-half-a-century" deluges that hit the mighty Yangzi and its tributaries in the summer of 1998. He also laid the groundwork for the resuscitation of China's big four commercial banks, which were piling up nonperforming loans that were the equivalent of up to 50 percent of the gross domestic product (GDP). At Zhu's insistence, Wen became prime minister in 2003.

The Sixteenth Congress of November 2002 marked the beginning of the collaboration of Hu and Wen, perhaps the most like-minded and compatible team of party chief and premier in CCP history. As the PBSC member in charge of economic and social issues, Wen was responsible for a series of policies that constitute what is often known as the Hu-Wen *xinzheng* (Hu-Wen New Deal). These have included the "scientific outlook of development" and the campaign to "construct a harmonious society." Efforts were made to ensure that "disadvantaged sectors," including workers and peasants, would benefit more from the fruits of economic progress. The agriculture tax was abolished in 2006. The social-security net—including *dibao*, or a "subsistence-level payout" for the chronically unemployed—was being extended from the cities to the countryside. Overall, more attention was being paid to the "software" aspects of reform, including boosting education and public health, as well as taking care of the environment.

ASSESSMENT

Certainly Wen, who is expected to serve as head of the State Council until March 2013, deserves credit for ensuring a high GDP growth rate of 10 percent or more since the late 1990s. At the same time, he and his cabinet members have been faulted for failing to exert adequate control over irrational exuberance in such sectors as the stock and real-estate markets. Inflation became so serious in early 2008 that Beijing had to resort to price controls over commodities ranging from meat to cooking oil. This reimposition of old-style fiats, coupled with the State Council's procrastination over financial reforms such as making the yuan fully convertible, has raised doubts about the premier's commitment to market principles. Moreover, Wen has failed to adequately tackle the so-called "marriage of [political] power and business," which has resulted in vast areas of the economy being controlled by conglomerates run by relatives or cronies of senior officials.

While throughout his career, Wen's portfolios have always been economic in nature, the prime minister may have to share part of the blame for the stagnation of political reform during the 1990s and early 2000s. One of the manifestations of the moratorium on liberalization is the monopolization of the nation's wealth by the new class of cadre-businessmen. And this is perhaps the key reason why the broad masses of farmers and workers—who are supposed to be the main beneficiaries of the "put the people first" credo of the Hu-Wen team—may continue to be exploited by what critics have called the "red aristocracy."

BIBLIOGRAPHY

Downie, Leonard, Jr., et al. Interview with Wen Jiabao. *Washington Post*, November 21, 2003. http://chinese-school. netfirms.com/wen-jiabao-interview.html.

Lam, Willy Wo-Lap. Wen Jiabao: A Reformer at Heart? *China Brief* (Jamestown Foundation) 2, 7 (March 28, 2002). http:// www.jamestown.org/china_brief/article.php?articleid= 2373040.

McCartney, Jane. You Can't Rush Democracy, Says Chinese PM. *Times* London, September 5, 2006. http://www.timesonline. co.uk/tol/news/world/asia/article628722.ece

Wen Jiabao. Our Historical Tasks at the Primary Stage of Socialism and Several Issues Concerning China's Foreign Policy. *People's Daily*, February 27, 2007. http://www. chinaelections.net/newsinfo.asp?newsid=1221.

Wen Jiabao. Report on the Work of the Government. Delivered at the Fifth Session of the Tenth National People's Congress on March 5, 2007. http://news.xinhuanet.com/english/2007-03/16/content_5857166.htm.

Wong, John, and Lai Hongyi, eds. *China into the Hu-Wen Era: Policy Initiatives and Challenges.* Hackensack, NJ: World Scientific, 2006.

Willy Wo-Lap Lam

WENZHOU

Located on China's coast in the southeastern corner of Zhejiang Province facing the East China Sea on the south bank of the Ou River, Wenzhou is one of eleven provincial subregions or prefectural-level cities (*diji shi*) in Zhejiang. Designated a prefecture in the early Tang dynasty (618–907) and renamed for its mild (*wen*) winters, *Wenzhou* currently encompasses both the urban core (*shiqu*) and the larger administrative region, typically referred to as a prefecture or municipality (*shi*). Wenzhou Municipality has jurisdiction over three districts (Lucheng, Longwan, and Ouhai) making up the urban core, two county-level cities (Ruian and Yueqing), and six counties (Yongjia, Pingyang, Cangnan, Dongtou, Wencheng, and Taishun).

Always one of the country's most densely populated regions, Wenzhou Municipality had a population of 7.7 million in 2007, with 642 people per square kilometer (Wenzhou Tongjiju 2007). Because mountains comprise over 70 percent of the territory, limiting arable land, Wenzhou was always less conducive to rice cultivation than the northern plains of Zhejiang. The population thus turned to the production of tea, fruit, marine products, and handicrafts. Migration was another economic strategy, and many Wenzhounese became itinerate traders, plying local products. International migration was limited until after the mid-nineteenth century by an official ban on foreign ships and trade in the region.

LOCAL IDENTITY AND ROOTS OF ECONOMIC DEVELOPMENT

Wenzhou's contemporary economic success is often seen as emerging from impoverishment, which gave rise to a strong entrepreneurial drive, but historically Wenzhou has been characterized as much by prosperity as by poverty. In the Song dynasty (960–1279), Wenzhou was a flourishing commercial hub with a thriving shipbuilding industry, an international port, and a cultural center. Not a peripheral area in any ordinary sense, the rugged mountains created gaps between the coastal trading centers and the hinterlands, eventually setting the prefecture apart from the rest of the province. The combination of easy access to the sea, difficult terrain, and dense population fostered a distinctive development pattern, a strong sense of local identity, and a reputation for independence.

Wenzhou's local identity is marked by the Wenzhou language (*Wenzhou hua*). A subdialect of the Wu language that is inflected with the *Min* dialect, *Wenzhou hua* is incomprehensible outside the prefecture. The region's distinctiveness can also be seen in the local intellectual traditions, particularly the Yongjia Utilitarian School (Yongjia Shigong Pai) as represented by scholar Ye Shi (1150–1223), who became Wenzhou's godfather of entrepreneurship. Ye offered a counterhegemonic interpretation of Confucianism, praising wealthy merchants as responsible members of society and calling for an end to burdensome government intervention (Lo 1974).

The nineteenth century brought economic stagnation, civil strife, war, and decline to the region. Although Wenzhou escaped the devastation of the Taiping Uprising (1851–1864), natural disasters, hunger, and high rents gave rise to local unrest, including the Gold Coin Uprising (*Jinqianhui qiyi*) in 1858, which mobilized a peasant army of 10,000 before being put down by the Qing forces (*Wenzhou cidian bianweihui*, 1995, p. 454). Instability and hardship further spurred migration as a household survival strategy. International migration became more common after the Opium Wars brought foreign ships to port. In the 1860s, impoverished farmers from Pingyang were recruited as "coolies" to work in Cuba, South Africa, and Europe. In 1876 the Chefoo Convention (*yantai tiaoyue*) made Wenzhou a treaty-port city, leading to increased opportunities for migration. It was not until after World War I (1914–1918), however, that significant numbers of migrants left in search of work and business opportunities overseas, making Wenzhou one of China's officially recognized *qiaoxiang* or "homeland of overseas Chinese" (*Wenzhou shizhi* 1998, pp. 404–406; Hu Fangsong et al. 2005, pp. 114–116).

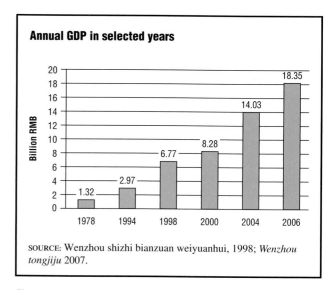

Figure 1

AFTER 1949

With the founding of the People's Republic of China (PRC) in 1949, ideological and policy changes further isolated the region and undermined the viability of Wenzhou's local economy. With little central investment, Wenzhounese were forced to rely on local initiative, including petty commodity production and trade, as well as private finance from such sources as money houses (*qiangzhuang*). Though subdued by harsh campaigns against "tails of capitalism" and "speculation and profiteering" Wenzhou's private economy reemerged and after 1978 grew in scale without official sanction.

In 1985 Shanghai's influential *Liberation Daily* featured a story touting the successful development of wealth-generating household industries in the area and dubbed it the "Wenzhou model." With the term "model" (*moshi*), the newspaper inevitably drew comparison with the Sunan model, which was characterized by collectively owned rural industries. Wenzhou thus became a key symbol in a national debate about the nature of socialism and the limits of reform. The debate was summarized by the pointed question, "Is it socialist or capitalist?" (*xing she, xing zi?*). After 1992, Wenzhou was deemed ideologically acceptable because it advanced productive forces. In the twenty years between 1978 and 1998, Wenzhou's average annual gross domestic product increased at a rate of 15 percent (*Wenzhou shizhi bianzuanhui,* 1998, p. 1032), and the debate about the suitability of Wenzhou's pattern of development had subsided by 2001, when private business owners were welcomed into the Chinese Communist Party and China entered the World Trade Organization.

Migration played an important role in the local economy throughout the reform era. In 1978 half of the people in Pingyang County were migrants (*Wenzhou shizhi bianzuan hui* 1998, pp. 1031–1032). By the end of 2006 there were over 1.7 million Wenzhounese migrants doing business all over China (Wenzhou Tongjiju 2007), often congregating in self-sufficient "Zhejiang villages," but also setting up larger-scale industrial and commercial enterprises (Zhang Li, 2001). Wenzhou has also become integral to Chinese globalization. While still low in comparison with larger port cities, utilized FDI (foreign direct investment) increased 29.6 percent to $463 million in 2006, and exports increased 25.9 percent, with 57 percent of total exports coming directly from private companies (Wenzhou Tongjiju 2007). With more than 425,000 Wenzhounese living abroad in over eighty countries and a growing number of overseas Wenzhou chambers of commerce around the country and the world, the diaspora represents a growing a source of FDI into Wenzhou and creates international bases for the marketing of Wenzhou specialties, such as lighters, shoes, and glasses in the European Union, India, and Africa, as well as the far reaches of the PRC.

With its early revival household business, rapid growth and now more than 240,000 small-scale, individually owned businesses and 130 private enterprises, as well as the creation of active chambers of commerce and local-place organizations both in and outside of Wenzhou, the "Wenzhou Model" is often understood as rooted in a unique local tradition of entrepreneurialism and a natural proclivity for doing business and working hard, (Jin Hui and Li Yang 2002; Hu Fangsong et al. 2005). Yet, Wenzhou's development has been shaped by a complex set of tensions: Though an international port, Wenzhou has also been insular and remote; it is part of the Confucian mainstream but iconoclastic; it is at the forefront of modernizing reform, yet rooted in traditional practices; it is both core and periphery. Thus, it may be best, as Zhang Li argues, to avoid an essentialist interpretation of the local culture, and instead understand this development as a set of practices that were created and recreated by successive generations in response to their historical conditions (Zhang Li 2001, p. 50).

SEE ALSO *Chinese Overseas: Diaspora and Homeland; Chinese Overseas: Emigration and Globalization; Urban China: Cities and Urbanization, 1800–1949; Urban China: Organizing Principles of Cities; Urban China: Urban Planning since 1978; Zhejiang.*

BIBLIOGRAPHY

Hu Fangsong, Yin Fang, and Xu Liu. *Wenzhou pingpan* [Wenzhou evaluation]. Shanghai: Wenhui Chubanshe, 2005.

Jiefan ribao [Liberation daily]. Wenzhou sanshiwan ren congshi jiating gongzuo [In Wenzhou 300,000 people undertake household industry]. May 12, 1985.

Jin Hui and Li Yang. *Kepa di Wenzhou Ren* [Frightening Wenzhounese]. Beijing: Zuojia Chubanshe, 2002.

Lo, Winston Wan. *The Life and Thought of Yeh Shih*. Hong Kong: Chinese University of Hong Kong, 1974.

Wenzhou cidian bian weihui, ed. *Wenzhou cidian* [Wenzhou dictionary]. Shanghai: Fudan Daxue Chubanshe, 1995.

Wenzhou People's Government. Di er jie shijie wenzhouren dahui chuding 10 yue zhaokai [The second world congress of Wenzhounese is preliminarily set to open in October]. *Jinri wenzhou* [Wenzhou today]. April 30, 2008. http://www.wenzhou.gov.cn/col/col3/index.html

Wenzhou shizhi bianzuanhui, ed. *Wenzhou shizhi* [Wenzhou gazetteer]. Beijing: Zhonghua Shuju, 1998.

Wenzhou Tongjiju. 2006 nian Wenzhou shi, guomin jingji he shehui fazhan tongji gong bao [Wenzhou economic and social development statistical report for 2006]. *Wenzhou Tongjiju* [Wenzhou statistical bureau], March 23, 2007. http://www.wzstats.gov.cn/infoshow.asp?id=6062.

Zhang Li. *Strangers in the City: Reconfigurations of Space, Power, and Social Networks within China's Floating Population*. Stanford, CA: Stanford University Press, 2001.

Kristen Parris

WESTERNIZATION

Generally, Westernization involves direct copying of European or American ideas, customs, technology, or fashions. But the term is not used consistently: it can be used in positive or negative ways, with "the West" signifying different concepts. Moreover, the meaning of the term changes over time when the alternatives to Westernization change. On the assumption that modernity was created in the West, some thinkers equate Westernization with modernization. However, an argument heard more often is that each culture develops its own form of modernity based on its own traditions and circumstances, and that therefore Westernization is merely imitation of superficial characteristics.

Japan and India entered the debate over Westernization versus modernization earlier than China. Beginning during the Meiji restoration (1868–1912), the Japanese copied Western institutions and ways ranging from constitutions and newspapers to ballroom dancing and silk hats. The young Mohandas Gandhi, the leader of the Indian independence movement, studied law, wore a suit and bowler hat, and at one point forced himself to eat beef on the grounds that the manly, carnivorous eating habits of the British helped them conquer India. Both countries then reacted against Westernization and drew distinctions between cultural fashions and basic change.

Following the Opium Wars (1839–1942), Qing dynasty (1644–1912) officials tried a succession of strategies, each of which implied a different attitude to Westernization. The Self-strengthening movement (*ziqiang*; 1861–1894)

assumed that "the way of Confucius is the way of mankind" and that importing Western cannons, telegraphs, and warships would be enough to save China. The abstract formula *Zhongxue wei ti, Xixue wei yong* ("Chinese learning for values, Western for use") was useful in separating values from technology, but it was no longer persuasive after defeat in the Sino-Japanese War in 1895. The radical reformer Kang Youwei (1858–1927) avoided the problem entirely with his eccentric claim that modern values had always been inherent in the Confucian classics; Westernization was beside the point. Students and reformers looked to Japan for models (they did not, however, call their program "Easternization"). In the last years of the Qing, the government adopted Western institutions, especially legal codes and court systems; yet "Westernization" was not their objective but rather "reform" in the sense of putting new wine into old bottles.

INTENSIFIED DEBATE

The call for "new bottles" came after the quick frustration of the Republic of 1912—an institution imported from the West. Intellectuals of the New Culture era (1915–1925) debated fiercely how to save the country. To many patriots, Westernization, now explicitly called by that name, seemed desirable or at least inevitable. The debate was dominated by "returned students," mainly those who had studied in the West. The German-trained Chen Duxiu (1879–1942) called for Chinese to kick out "Mr. Confucius" and usher in "Mr. Science" and "Mr. Democracy," two European gentlemen. Hu Shi (1891–1962), who had earned his doctorate in the United States, at one point had no compunction in calling for *quanpan Xihua*, "total Westernization," to cure China of traditional ills. Of course, when examined more closely, his call was less sweeping than it appeared. Hu, like many of this generation, assumed that "Western" values, such as

Former U.S. President Bill Clinton's image on a pamphlet advertising a beauty mask, Beijing, February 6, 2004. This pictured advertisement featuring the image of a former U.S. president provides an example of an early twenty-first century marketing technique that uses a famous Western figure to promote a Chinese product, often without the subject's consent. **AP IMAGES**

science and democracy, were actually universal and that the key was to use Western methods to change China.

Those who opposed Westernization were diverse and too often lumped together under the label "conservative" or even "reactionary." Not all opponents rejected ideas simply because they were Western. Some, like Liang Shuming, for instance, rejected Westernization but not modern values in themselves; he wanted them to grow from Chinese experience and take Chinese forms. Others argued that the barbarism of World War I ended Europe's claim to rationality. Chinese conservatives and, paradoxically, Western critics charged that the returned students had become deracinated: they ate with knives and forks, not chopsticks, and wore Western suits and ties. Returned students, or so the joke went, thought that even the moon was brighter in the West. In the 1920s a reaction set in. One returned student "woke up" to the fact that he had become "Shanghai-fied"—"rushed, vulgar, and commercial"—and put away his Western suits and ties in favor of Chinese-style gowns. Few returned students would refer to themselves as "Westernized" without irony, for they came to believe that to be such was to be out of touch with China and to betray their mother culture.

Both Westernizers and their many opponents accepted the New Culture assumption that there was a zero-sum opposition between modernity and tradition, Western and Chinese, so that to become more modern was to become less Chinese. But the next generation went on to use Western models for inspiration rather than as blueprints, freely mixing old and new, East and West.

By the 1930s the city of Shanghai tested the distinction between modernization, tradition, and Westernization. The "Paris of the East" was fashionable, rich, and cosmopolitan, and although critics called it Westernized, it saw itself instead as modern. The *cheongsam*, a woman's dress that was neither entirely traditional Chinese nor Western, was a symbol of Shanghai modernity, along with Shanghai art deco architecture and films. These forms were considered Shanghai modern. Shanghai Chinese looked down on their country cousins as well as on other cities. Critics in turn saw Shanghai as Westernized in the bad sense—parasitic, debauched, and colonialist.

PRIDE AND IDENTITY

War with Japan in the 1930s transformed the argument and revealed the paradox that national humiliation created cultural pride. Both Nationalists and Communists mixed traditional cultural forms with Western technology to mobilize patriotism, though China's authentic tradition was assumed to be in the countryside. Mao Zedong's 1940 speech "On New Democracy" called "wholesale Westernization" mistaken but called for using Marxist principles to select from both foreign and feudal culture.

After 1949 European and American influences were rejected as imperialistic, while Soviet models were defined as socialist, not Western, but after the break with the Soviet Union in the late 1950s, Mao insisted that China produce its own socialist culture. The New Model Operas of the Cultural Revolution, for instance, used stories of peasant revolution, but the orchestra combined Chinese and Western instruments played in Western scales. For better or worse, this new opera was found neither in Europe nor in pre-1949 China and represented neither pure tradition nor Westernization.

Westernized imports revived quickly following Mao's death. Writers and artists worked in a global, not merely Western, framework. But in popular culture Western fashion and ideals of feminine beauty were popular, with some Chinese women, like their sisters in Japan, using plastic surgery to achieve Western-looking eyes and noses. Pop culture from Taiwan, Japan, and Korea attracted the hearts of the young and the spleen of conservatives. But again, these were global rather than specifically Western styles.

The philosophical debate over Westernization revived New Culture themes. The 1988 television documentary *Heshang* (River elegy) once again treated China and the West as opposites, and in the 1990s the philosopher Li Zehou (b. 1930) called for Westernization of the economy to create a base for eventual democracy. New Left thinkers such as Wang Hui (b. 1959), however, denied that the West had a monopoly on modernity and advocated a socialist alternative to both Maoist revolution and Western neoliberal capitalism. Others argued that Singapore, Korea, and Taiwan had been effective in modernizing based on authoritarian "Asian values"—that is, non-Western values. But even advocates for a revived Confucianism cast Confucius as a nationalist hero rather than a symbol of a history cleansed of Western influence.

BIBLIOGRAPHY
Bonnett, Alastair. *The Idea of the West: Culture, Politics, and History.* Houndmills, Basingstoke, Hampshire, U.K., and New York: Palgrave Macmillan, 2004.

Ch'en, Jerome. *China and the West: Society and Culture, 1815–1937.* Bloomington: Indiana University Press, 1979.

Wang, Jing. *High Culture Fever: Politics, Aesthetics, and Ideology in Deng's China.* Berkeley: University of California Press, 1996.

Wang, Y. C. *Chinese Intellectuals and the West, 1872–1949.* Chapel Hill: University of North Carolina Press, 1966.

Zhang, Xudong. *Chinese Modernism in the Era of Reforms: Cultural Fever, Avant-Garde Fiction, and the New Chinese Cinema.* Durham, NC: Duke University Press, 1997.

Charles W. Hayford

WHITE LOTUS

China's White Lotus tradition originated in the lay Buddhist sects that began emerging outside the monastic mainstream during the Southern Song period (1127–1279). These autonomous groups pursued spiritual salvation in hopes of entering the future Pure Land of Western Paradise. With its rich mix of doctrinal, ritual, and congregational elements drawn from popular Buddhism, Daoism, shamanism, and folk religions, syncretistic White Lotus faith usually coexisted quietly with the established order and its commitment to Confucian ethics, support of family, and loyalty to the throne.

During times of economic distress, social upheaval, and misgovernment, however, these groups often turned to physical salvation, transferring their loyalty to heaven-sent messiahs who promised to destroy the prevailing order in an apocalyptic battle between good and evil. The messiahs would then install a this-worldly Pure Land of justice, peace, and prosperity under benevolent rulers. By late imperial times, this eschatological vision inspired, organized, and sustained a quickening series of rebellions.

DEVELOPMENT

The Mongol rulers of the Yuan dynasty (1279–1368) banned White Lotus sects as "heterodox" for claiming that Mongol oppression disclosed "cosmic decay" at the end of the second of three historical epochs, or *kalpa*s. They insisted that the imminent destruction of the second epoch, now deemed evil, would yield the emergence of the Maitreya Buddha of the Future who would deliver his true believers into the final *kalpa*. This new dispensation was to be presided over by the Persian-inspired Manichaean King of Light, who would restore virtuous Han Chinese rule under the symbol of a white lotus. In the name of these two saviors, Han Shantong (d. 1351), leader of one White Lotus sect, precipitated the abortive Red Turban Uprising (1351), which sought to supplant the Mongol monarchs with Chinese emperors. The first such emperor was to be the messianic Lesser King of Light (who was, in fact, Han Shantong's own son). After Han's death, his disciple, Zhu Yuanzhang (1328–1398), a former Buddhist novice, succeeded in overthrowing the Mongols. But instead of installing a Pure Land utopia after ascending the throne, Zhu proscribed White Lotus faith, reasserted the state's traditional prerogative to control religion, and restored Confucian orthodoxy as the basis of his Ming dynasty (1368–1644).

As it was driven farther underground, White Lotus religion was energized by devotion to a new kind of savior: the Eternal Mother, universal creator and paramount bodhisattva (Buddhist deity). Tearfully seeking her earthly children's spiritual and physical salvation, this compassionate matriarch promised to dispatch the Maitreya Buddha to redeem the suffering faithful and preside over a millennium of "equality and comfort" in the final *kalpa*. In 1774 Wang Lun (d. 1774), a White Lotus teacher of meditation, fasting, and martial arts, proclaimed himself the reincarnated Maitreya Buddha and raised the banner of revolt against the Manchu emperors of the Qing dynasty (1644–1912). Believing they were invulnerable to imperial weapons and occasionally led by Wang's concubine, these rebel warriors were fierce fighters.

WHITE LOTUS REBELLION
(1796–1804)

During the corruption-plagued twilight years of the Qianlong emperor (r. 1736–1796), the White Lotus reached its most combustible stage. The government had only recently opened the hardscrabble borderlands of Hubei, Shaanxi, and Sichuan provinces to land-hungry settlers in the effort to feed China's burgeoning population (which had more than doubled since the Qing's founding) by opening new land to cultivation. Economic hardship and grievances over excessive taxation and other official abuses sharpened the migrants' longings for an earthly Pure Land as traveling preachers disclosed revelations, contained in "precious scrolls," of the Eternal Mother's sympathy for her children's plight. Congregations formed around mystical initiation, group confession, penitential rites, chanting of sutras (Buddhist precepts), faith healing, spirit possession, divination, vegetarianism, and martial arts. They also practiced self-sufficiency through property sharing, promoted women to leadership roles, and proclaimed loyalty to past Ming emperors.

Local officials began persecuting White Lotus adherents, condemning their filial devotion to the Eternal Mother, formation of new communities not on the basis of kin, and gender equality for undermining Chinese tradition. The faithful, in turn, saw government repression as a portent that the third *kalpa* was at hand and concluded that salvation depended on urgent cooperation among the congregations—facilitated through teacher-disciple ties—for armed insurrection. Certain that only the sectarian "elect" who believed in the Eternal Mother would survive the forthcoming "cosmic typhoon," the congregations prepared for combat by stockpiling supplies and forming militias, sometimes in cooperation with outlaw gangs. As they got ready to kill the "unbelievers" who opposed them, the rebels were told not to fear the death that would unite them with their Eternal Mother in her "original home" of "true happiness" in Western Paradise.

At the outbreak of hostilities in 1796, effective guerrilla tactics in the rugged frontier terrain enabled the rebels to overwhelm Qing forces. Only after the Jiaqing emperor (r. 1796–1820) turned back official corruption were imperial troops able to receive needed supplies and reinforcements from southwest China and Manchuria. They also began pacifying the population and starving the rebellion of food and new recruits by erecting walled sanctuaries around loyalist villages and granting amnesty to White Lotus defectors. By the time the rebellion was suppressed in 1804, at a cost of 200 million ounces of silver (the equivalent of five years' state income), the throne was nearly bankrupt and its military severely compromised.

In subsequent decades White Lotus groups continued to rise up. In August 1813 the White Lotus–related Eight Trigrams rebelled when Lin Qing (1770–1813), an apothecary and day laborer, proclaimed himself the Maitreya Buddha and rose up against the Manchus. Before they were annihilated later that year, Lin's rebels had invaded Beijing's Forbidden City, where they intended to assassinate the emperor. More modest White Lotus risings ensued during the 1820s and 1830s. The Nian Uprising (1851–1868), which swept across the North China plain, had White Lotus roots and called for distributive justice and egalitarianism. And the Boxer Uprising of 1900, sparked by anti-Western and anti-Manchu resentments, echoed White Lotus mystical notions in its belief that Boxer insurgents were invulnerable to the foreign expeditionary forces' bullets. By the time the Republic of China was founded in 1912, the Way of Former Heaven sects had spread throughout China and Southeast Asia. Driven underground after Mao's ascendancy in 1949, they thrive in Taiwan in the twenty-first century.

WHITE LOTUS LEGACY

The enduring White Lotus experience in China demonstrates the power of religion to reinforce imperial Confucianism while also offering an alternative reality and a counter-community that challenged established assumptions of family and state, incited mass insurrections, and enacted such radical innovations as elevating women's status. In twenty-first-century China, millennial visions continue to elicit government opposition. Two examples are Falun Gong, with its massive popular following and organizational potential, and the numerous countryside eruptions led by charismatic figures who hark back to millennial ideals of distributive justice and virtuous government.

SEE ALSO *Religious Organizations; Religious Policy; Secret Societies.*

BIBLIOGRAPHY

Liu, Kwang-Ching. Religion and Politics in the White Lotus Rebellion of 1796 in Hubei. In *Heterodoxy in Late Imperial China*, ed. Kwang-Ching Liu and Richard Shek, 281–320. Honolulu: University of Hawai'i Press, 2004.

Naquin, Susan. *Millenarian Rebellion in China: The Eight Trigrams Rising of 1813.* New Haven, CT, and London: Yale University Press, 1976.

Overmyer, Daniel L. *Folk Buddhist Religion: Dissenting Sects in Late Imperial China.* Cambridge, MA: Harvard University Press, 1976.

Ter Haar, B. J. *The White Lotus Teachings in Chinese Religious History.* Leiden, Netherlands, and New York: E. J. Brill, 1992.

P. Richard Bohr

WING ON DEPARTMENT STORES

The Wing On Department Store opened its doors with a dozen or so employees in August 1907 as a modest one-store front in Hong Kong. Its initial capital, at HK $160,000 (Hong Kong dollars), was many times larger than the usual retail business would need. Two brothers, Guo Luo (Guo Le, 1874–1956) and Guo Chuan (Guo Quan, 1879–1966), raised the funds with the help of eleven business associates. They had high ambitions for this enterprise. Their innovative vision was to organize a "universal provider" bringing a full range of high-end goods from all over the world for urban families who desired a modern style of living. This included a grand display of the goods in elegant well-lit halls, to be sold at fixed prices by knowledgeable and unfailingly courteous staff.

EARLY YEARS AND DYNAMIC GROWTH IN HONG KONG

The Guo brothers had considerable business acumen and social connections, which they had gained while working at—and later owning—fruit retail outlets and plantations in Australia and Fuji. From their ancestral home in the Pearl River Delta's Zhongshan County, they had gone to Australia to join relatives and find work. They were impressed by the rags to riches story of the Australian entrepreneur, Anthony Hordern (1819–1876), who rose from street peddler to owner of Sydney's largest department store, employing thousands of workers. They wanted to emulate Hordern, but they also realized that his marketing practices stood in stark contrast to those used in China. For example, reputable Chinese piece-goods stores would keep their fine fabrics upstairs, in rooms to which only their well-connected rich clients would be invited, while low-end items were displayed downstairs where customers could haggle over prices with the store's junior clerks. In the end, it was Guo Luo who, being more visionary and more inclined to risk-taking than his younger brother, took the lead in convincing his partners that Western-style business practices could be successfully adapted to the Chinese setting. They were also heartened by the success of a similar department store, the Sincere Company, which, having opened a few years earlier in Hong Kong, was beginning to do well after experiencing some difficulties.

Within a few short years, Guo Luo was proven right. The Wing On store grew rapidly. It outgrew its original space in two years and moved to new quarters. In 1910 its capital was increased to HK $600,000 as fellow Zhongshanese and kinsmen in Hong Kong, Zhongshan, and Australia bought up new shares. The store then registered with the Hong Kong government, first as a private, then as a public, limited liability company. Yet, by controlling the board and by spreading the stock ownership widely, the Guo brothers and their family, who at no time owned more than 8 or 10 percent of the company stock, retained absolute control of the company. Rapid expansions through reinvestment of earnings continued, so that by 1916 its capital rose to HK $2,000,000. In 1930 each share was split into two. In 1942 Wing On's capital doubled again to HK $8,000,000. Meanwhile, the expansion and improvements of display floors continued as the company gradually and purposefully bought up all the contiguous lots on two street fronts, until the company owned thirty lots measuring almost an acre.

EXPANSION BEYOND HONG KONG

From its early years, as the Hong Kong store became profitable, the Guo brothers made plans to open a new affiliate store with a separate and even larger capital in Shanghai, a city that already had a large Chinese clientele with both sufficient wealth and exposure to Western ways of living. At the same time, the Guo brothers opened branch stores in Guangzhou, Macau, Fuzhou, Hankou, and Wuzhou, and started related lines of businesses such as banking, subsidiary production facilities, hotels, and warehousing, as well as unrelated lines, such as real estate, insurance, wool knitting, and cotton-textile mills in Hong Kong and Shanghai.

The most successful of these ventures turned out to be Shanghai's department store. When the capital goal of HK $2,000,000 was oversubscribed by HK $500,000, the two brothers erected a new European-style edifice on Shanghai's most fashionable shopping street; its grand opening in September 1918 set the standard of opulence and up-to-date fashion for all of urban China. Nine years later, its reserves from retained profits exceeded its original capital, allowing its board of directors to double its authorized capital by splitting each share into two. This was repeated five years later. Thus, by 1932, the Shanghai company's paid-up capital had increased fourfold and reached HK $10,000,000.

These successes came despite several incidences of strong labor unrest, boycotts against foreign imports, and violent anti-Western demonstrations during the 1920s. Even greater crises arose in the 1930s, as the Nationalist government squeezed the company for contributions in the midst of a depressed economy, while Japanese aerial bombardments razed several of its properties. Around 1933 its textile operation in Shanghai almost went under from deflated cotton prices and dumping practices by larger Japanese-owned competitors. It was saved only by Wing On's abundant liquidity and the Guo brothers' strategic decision to divert almost HK $10,000,000 of company funds to its aid. It worked, and the Wing On mills prospered until they became, for a time during the late 1940s, the largest Chinese-owned textile producer in China.

For the pre–World War II period, the early 1930s marked the high point of the Wing On department stores. The combined capital of the Wing On corporate group reached several tens of millions of Hong Kong dollars, and it became one of China's largest businesses. It also established a reputation for promoting a modern professional spirit among its employees and for adopting modern management techniques.

DISTINCTIVE COMPANY CULTURE

Wing On was among the first Chinese businesses to provide organized activities for its employees outside their work hours. It began with the owners—who had become Christians while in Australia—requiring their employees to attend church services on Sunday mornings. The company also organized social clubs, sport teams, music bands, and theatrical troupes, as well as English classes and a reading room in the dorms. Many junior staff lived in company dormitories because the Guo brothers preferred to hire fellow Zhongshanese. These paternalistic practices were, however, adapted to modern goals as the brothers reorganized the traditional partnership into a multitiered corporate structure that included a board of directors and several administrative divisions that were subdivided into supervisory clusters of departments, and then further divided into individual departments. They were also adaptive to cultural embeddedness. Thus, while the staff, from managers to sales clerks, was mostly Zhongshanese, the company would hire those who could pass several tests and show proof of having attained appropriate levels of formal education. Wing On also retained consultants to look into the company accounting system, and until several of the owners' sons and nephews returned from Britain and America with textile and other professional degrees in the 1930s, they kept a British-trained engineer as manager of their textile plants.

Their sustained success owed much to the complementary characters of the two brothers: Guo Luo had the intuitive ability to seize on big ideas and to lay out new strategies in broad strokes. However, his brashness and impatience made him less suited to manage the day-to-day operations. Those tasks fell to Guo Chuan, whose attention to detail, sharp analytical mind, and willingness to improvise kept the company running smoothly.

Guo Chuan worked equally hard at putting the corporate group's finances on a sound, modern footing. Even though the new Shanghai department store raised its own capital, the two stores remained affiliated because they owned each other's stocks and had several overlapping board members. This pattern was followed as new companies in other lines of business were established, such as Wing On Life Insurance in 1925 and the Wing On Bank in 1931. Later, as the need arose to fight off market difficulties and financial crises affecting the various affiliates, the brothers would move various reserves around so the companies could help each other. During such crises, even when senior members of the Guo family had disputes over policy, once a decision was made, everyone would fall into line. In contrast, Wing On's main competitor, the equally modern Sincere Department Stores, did not do well. Although its principal owner, Ma Yingbiao (1864–1944), was as bold and visionary as Guo Luo, he and his partners lost control of the company to the Hong Kong and Shanghai Bank by the mid-1930s.

THE POST-1949 PERIOD

Hard times continued during the 1940s as Wing On survived China's occupation by Japan, civil war, and hyperinflation until 1949, when a new socialist government took over the Chinese mainland and nationalized all businesses. Since the majority of Wing On's business was on the mainland, its loss was not just in financial and human resources, but also in its social networks and cultural bearings. Back in Hong Kong, the company soldiered on: The post-1950 period marked a new era as the reins of authority passed to Guo Chuan's sons and grandsons. As Hong Kong grew into a major financial and manufacturing metropolis during the 1970s, the company prospered and branched out into real estate. However, poor market timing and family discord took a toll on the property investments. By the mid-1980s, the company lost control of Wing On Bank when a new management team from a different branch of Guo Chuan's family took over. Wing On tried to reclaim or at least revitalize its Shanghai store as the Chinese economy reemerged strongly in the 1990s, but to little avail.

More recently, the company was enthusiastically welcomed at the Guo family's ancestral home in Zhongshan County, and has set up offices and retail outlets there. While the Hong Kong headquarters still considers the Wing On Department Store to be its core business, it has grown again to become a transnational corporation, with many divisions, including one selling auto parts in southern California. In 2007 the company organized several public events to celebrate its centenary. Given China's turbulent modern his-

tory, it is rare for any Chinese family-owned company to last this long, especially one of Wing On's size and stature.

SEE ALSO *Chinese Overseas: Returned Overseas Chinese; Shops; Sincere Department Stores.*

BIBLIOGRAPHY

Chan, Wellington K. K. The Origins and Early Years of the Wing On Company Group in Australia, Fiji, Hong Kong, and Shanghai: Organization and Strategy of a New Enterprise. In *Chinese Business Enterprise in Asia*, ed. Rajeswary Ampalavanar Brown, 80–95. London: Routledge, 1995.

Chan, Wellington K. K. Personal Styles, Cultural Values, and Management: The Sincere and Wing On Companies in Shanghai and Hong Kong, 1900–1941. *Business History Review* 70, 2 (1996): 141–166.

Guo Chuan (Philip Gockchin). *Yong'an jingshen zhi qi faren qi changcheng shilue* [A brief history of the origin and development of the spirit of Wing On]. Preface. 1960.

Guo Luo (James Gock Lock). *Hui'yi lu* [Memoirs]. Dedication. 1946.

Institute of Economics, Shanghai Academy of Social Sciences, comp. *Shanghai Yong'an gongsi di chansheng fachan wo gaizao* [The birth, development, and reconstruction of the Shanghai Wing On Company]. Shanghai: Renmin Chubenshi, 1981.

Lian Lingling (Lien Ling-ling). Qiye wenhua di xingcheng yu juanxing: yi minguo shiqi di Shanghai Yong'an gonsi weili [The shaping and transformation of business culture: The Wing On Company in Shanghai in the Republican period]. *Jiandai shi yanjiu suo jikan* [Journal of the Institute of Modern History, Academia Sinica] 49 (2005): 127–173.

Xianggang Yong'an youxian gongsi ershiwu zhounian jinianshi [The Wing On Company Limited of Hong Kong: In commemoration of the twenty-fifth anniversary, 1907–1932]. Preface. Hong Kong, 1932.

Wellington K. K. Chan (Chen Jinjiang)

WOMEN, EMPLOYMENT OF

In late imperial China women were rarely employed outside their family homes. In the home, besides being responsible for housework and child care they might work on the family land or in household textile production, garment making or embroidery, or family businesses. The limited sources of employment for women outside the home included domestic service, prostitution, and the entertainment industry. Rather than being autonomous waged workers, women in these occupations were often bonded to an employer who assumed quasi-parental rights over them, for example in arranging their marriages.

Beginning in the late nineteenth century, feminists and reformers demanded employment for women and education to prepare them for independent careers. Waged and salaried employment for women began to develop in the early twentieth century in the urban areas as a result of these demands as well as the changes brought about by urbanization and industrialization and political and social revolution. During the Republican period (1928–1949), educated women established themselves in most of the professions in the great cities while large numbers of young rural women were drawn to the cities for unskilled factory work. At this point contestation gradually shifted from whether women should be employed to whether they should be employed in the same fields, and on the same terms, as were men. From 1949 the People's Republic promoted paid employment for women as a means to bring about gender equity. Increasing numbers of women found employment, but women's jobs tended to require less skill and were less well-paid than men's. After the economic reforms of the 1980s, the gendered division of labor became more pronounced: women were disproportionately affected by layoffs and faced other problems of discrimination.

LATE QING AND REPUBLICAN PERIODS

Elite women rarely worked outside the home prior to the twentieth century. Only men undertook formal education, the preparation for employment in the civil service. Late-nineteenth-century reformers began to argue that women's education was a prerequisite to making them better mothers and thus to strengthening the nation. Many girls' schools, whether government- or missionary-run, stressed conservative values and saw their task as training competent household managers rather than career women. Yet women educators and women students quickly developed their own women's rights agenda, arguing that women must be more than wives and mothers and must achieve independence. Increasingly independence meant acquiring education so as to be able to take up a profession and earn one's own living.

The number of women affected by these changes was at first very small. In 1909 less than 0.1 percent of female children in China attended school. At the time of the 1911 revolution, tens of thousands of elite Chinese men had studied in Japan, compared with perhaps 200 women. Yet this small number of women whose education gave them entry to the public realm had a disproportionate influence. In their writings and in the newspapers they published, they argued that women could become effective only through education and financial independence. Their ideas were taken up in the early Republic and developed into the radical ideas of gender equality and citizenship for women that became broadly accepted among young intellectuals in the May Fourth movement. In 1920 women began to be admitted to higher education, and more women began to train for careers.

The earliest training for women doctors was provided by mission schools and foreign education. One of the first Chinese women doctors of Western medicine was Jin Yunmei (Yamei Kin, 1864–1934), who qualified in 1885 when medical education for women in the United States and Great Britain was still controversial. She trained at the Women's Medical College in New York (founded by Elizabeth Blackwell, the first American woman doctor) and later practiced in Tianjin, where she became vice president of the city's Red Cross in 1911. In the next generation, China's best-known gynecologist, Lin Qiaozhi (1901–1983), trained at Beijing's Union Medical College, another mission establishment. The mission colleges that offered medical training for women in China from the last years of the Qing dynasty were joined by government establishments under the Republic. By the 1930s, 26 of the 28 medical schools in China admitted women, 16.9 percent of their graduates were women, and there were approximately 550 qualified women physicians. Many of the medical schools also ran training courses for nurses and midwives.

Women also worked in the civil service, law, publishing, journalism, and business. One woman even founded a bank for women in Shanghai, a successful business that functioned from 1924 to 1953. Above all women became teachers, working in girls' schools and colleges to train the next generation of professional women. Many pioneers had to struggle for the education that they believed would afford them a career in place of an early arranged marriage. Zheng Yuxiu, also known as Madame Wei Tao-ming (1891–1959), a lawyer who took a doctorate from the Sorbonne and was responsible for the comparatively favorable treatment of women in the family law of the Chinese republic, had to fight to be allowed to attend school. Xie Bingying (1906–2000), who joined the Nationalist army in the 1920s, refused to eat when her mother withdrew her from school. Gradually, however, after women in professional employment became a small but established social category, elite families, at least in the cities, assumed that they should allow their daughters an education, and many modern young women worked for a living. The employment of married women remained more controversial, especially during Chiang Kai-shek's New Life movement of 1934, which promoted women's domestic roles with the slogan "good wives and virtuous mothers."

The numbers of urban laboring women also increased in the first half of the twentieth century but for different reasons. As industry developed, young rural women, most of them poorly paid contract workers frequently under the control of gang masters, were attracted to the cities to work in factories; their cash wages were enough to support themselves and often also to help their families. The largest concentration of women workers was in the Shanghai textile mills, but women also worked in sweatshops, the retail trade, and offices. Most young workers retained strong

Female enrollment in education, 1952–2002						
	Primary school		Secondary school		Tertiary education	
	Female enrollments	% of total enrollments	Female enrollments	% of total enrollments	Female enrollments	% of total enrollments
1952	12,061,000	28.0	585,800	23.5	4500	23.4
1976	68,233,000	45.5	23,571,000	40.4	186,000	33.0
1987	58,218,000	45.6	20,186,000	40.8	647,000	33.0
2002	57,381,000	47.2	38,702,000	46.7	3,970,000	44.0

SOURCE: *China Statistical Yearbook*, 2003; *Statistical Materials on Chinese Women*, compiled by the Research Institute of the All-China Women's Federation. Beijing: China Statistical Publishing House, 1991.

Table 1

loyalties to their home villages and often returned for visits or to marry and settle down.

As the cities grew, so did the demand for women's labor. The growing middle class employed more maids and nannies. Many of the men in cities were young and single or had left their wives in their hometowns, creating a high demand for prostitutes. Considerable numbers of women worked at all levels of this trade: courtesans in luxurious houses that catered to wealthy merchants and officials, the poorest women in accommodations little better than the shacks of the migrant workers who were their clients.

MAOIST PERIOD

Beginning in 1949 the government of the People's Republic of China promoted the employment of women as a path to liberation. Workplace child care made it easier for mothers to take jobs. Women who grew up in Maoist China were educated for the workforce and assumed that as adults they would be employed outside the home. Table 1 shows both that education was greatly expanded for the total population and that female enrollment grew as a proportion of the total.

In principle, urban women enjoyed the same employment opportunities and social security and health benefits as did men. In practice, they were disadvantaged both by their inferior educational levels and by assumptions about the work that was suitable for women. There was considerable gendered division of labor, with women being assigned to lower positions and less skilled work. Thus in textile mills, for example, almost all the shop floor workers would be female whereas the technicians and managers would usually be male. Driving was seen as a man's job, whereas kindergartens and nurseries were staffed exclusively by women. Men had a better chance of employment in state industry, leaving women disproportionately employed in collective industry, where pay and welfare benefits were inferior. Gendered expectations were challenged during the years of the Cultural Revolution (1966–

1976), when, with the slogan "women hold up half the sky," young women demanded entry to high-profile male preserves such as train driving, erecting high-voltage electricity wires, and mining. But for most of the Maoist period, job assignments were influenced by assumptions about gender.

THE REFORM PERIOD

The economic reforms after the death of Mao in 1976 transformed the urban labor market in China. Although urban workers were still better off than rural residents, their jobs became less secure, and workers were no longer able to rely on the state to supply employment. In the decades that followed, the opinion was often voiced that women are less able or productive than men and too easily distracted by their domestic responsibilities, thus perpetuating discrimination against women in hiring and firing. Good posts were often advertised as open only to men, and women were commonly channeled into junior office posts, the service sector, or professions regarded as suitable for either sex, such as teaching and medicine. State industry and state employment contracted severely, leading to many layoffs. Over 60 percent of layoffs were of women, usually those in their thirties and forties who found it hard to obtain new employment outside the informal sector, which offered greatly reduced wages and benefits. The number of female urban employees dropped from 58.89 million in 1995 to 37.8 million in 2002, representing a fall in women's share of urban employment from 38.6 percent to 37.8 percent.

The millions of new jobs in poorly paid, repetitive assembly-line work created by the prodigious growth of export industries since the economic reforms have tended to attract young female migrants from the countryside rather than urban women. The newly privatizing economy has also provided opportunities to entrepreneurs. Many women have started their own businesses or joined with their husbands in family businesses. Office work accounts for much of the employment created by the new economy for urban women. Those with language skills have been able to find well-paid, white-collar jobs with private or foreign-funded companies (the stereotype that women are better than men at languages working to women's advantage). In office work as in the rapidly expanding employment areas associated with leisure or sexual services, youth and attractiveness play a significant role in hiring. Like escorts, hostesses, or call girls, "white collar beauties," as such office workers are dubbed, are paid in accordance with their looks and can lose their jobs when no longer considered young and pretty enough.

Despite gains in the general acceptance of the employment of women, discrimination has continued in the labor market. Women are often still relegated to jobs that offer lower pay and less prestige than those for men.

SEE ALSO *Education: Women's Education; Prostitution, History of; Women, Status of.*

BIBLIOGRAPHY

China Statistical Yearbook 2003 [Zhongguo tongjinianjian]. Compiled by the National Bureau of Statistics. Beijing: China Statistical Publishing House, 2003.

Edwards, Louise. *Gender, Politics, and Democracy: Women's Suffrage in China.* Stanford, CA: Stanford University Press, 2008.

Gilmartin, Christina. *Engendering the Chinese Revolution: Radical Women, Communist Politics, and Mass Movements in the 1920s.* Berkeley: University of California Press. 1995.

Hershatter, Gail. *Women in China's Long Twentieth Century.* Berkeley: University of California Press, 2007.

Hsieh Ping-ying (Xie Bingying). *Autobiography of a Chinese Girl: A Genuine Autobiography.* Trans. Tsui Chi. London: G. Allen and Unwin, 1943.

Statistical Materials on Chinese Women [Zhongguo funu tongji ziliao]. Compiled by the Research Institute of the All-China Women's Federation. Beijing: China Statistical Publishing House, 1991.

Wang, Zheng. *Women in the Chinese Enlightenment: Oral and Textual Histories.* Berkeley: University of California Press, 1999.

Wang, Zheng. Gender, Employment and Women's Resistance. In *Chinese Society: Change, Conflict and Resistance,* ed. Elizabeth J. Perry and Mark Selden. 2nd ed. London: RoutledgeCurzon, 2003.

Wei Tao-ming, Madame (Zheng Yuxiu). *My Revolutionary Years: The Autobiography of Madame Wei Tao-Ming* New York: Scribner's Sons, 1943.

Delia Davin

WOMEN, STATUS OF

In the nineteenth century, the vast majority of Chinese women received no schooling and were economically dependent on men. Their lives were circumscribed by patriarchal Confucian ideology, according to which the ideal woman was confined within the private sphere, where she served, and was subservient to, first her father and then her husband and his family. In the late nineteenth and twentieth centuries, however, Confucian values and institutions eroded, radical new discourses on women emerged, and major improvements in women's status were achieved.

EARLY FEMINISM, 1890–1920

In the last two decades of the Qing dynasty (1644–1912), elite nationalist reformers called for improvements in women's status, especially for an end to foot binding and for women to be educated. In comparison with the modern Western nations, they reasoned, China was weak and lacked respect on the international stage, in large measure because men were both physically and intellectually crippled by having been brought up by women who were themselves hobbled by lack of education, as well as foot binding. As a result of their efforts, the practice of foot binding was banned by the Qing court in 1902. Earlier, in the nineteenth century, girls' schools were opened, first by Western missionaries and private Chinese groups and later by the government. In the early years of the twentieth century, these schools published the first women's magazines and were the centers of feminist and anti-Qing activities (Croll 1978, pp. 45–79).

During the May Fourth period (1915–1925), feminist concerns took center stage in elite nationalist discourse and debate about how to modernize and strengthen China in the face of invasion and humiliation from foreigners. Heavily influenced by Western liberalism, feminists, both women and men, saw existing norms on womanhood as a central part of an oppressive Confucian family system that prevented the freedom of the individual and the progress of the nation. Calls for freedom in love, sex, and marriage and for the achievement of "independent personhood" (*duli ren'ge*) among women, as well as men, became the hallmarks of feminism in this period (Wang Zheng 1999; Barlow 2004, pp. 64–189).

This period also saw profound changes in elite urban women's lives and consciousness. A new category of "career women" emerged, coeducation was established in secondary schools, and numerous young women went overseas to study and joined political associations of various persuasions (Wang Zheng 1999, p. 115). These changes were, however, almost entirely limited to a tiny urban, educated elite—they did not reach the vast majority of the population in the countryside. Neither was there significant interaction between feminists and female industrial workers in this period, despite the growing economic and political significance of the latter group and the obvious social problems they faced. Over the late nineteenth and early twentieth centuries, thousands of young rural women were

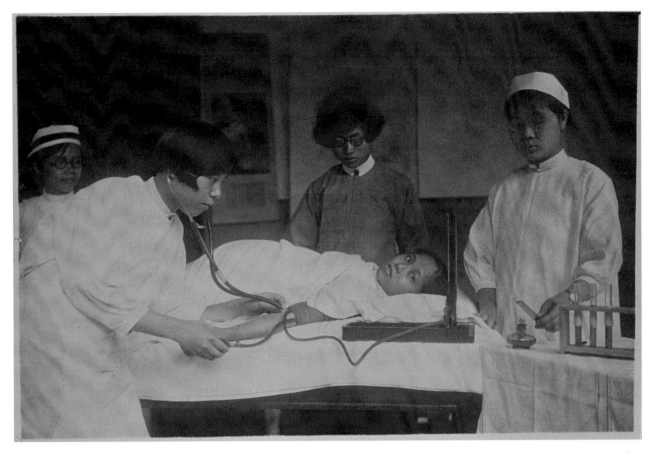

Female Chinese doctors. *Prior to the late 1800s, few women received a formal education in China, as they were expected instead to stay at home and care for family members. By the turn of the twentieth century, however, an increasing number of women began attending school, with a select few earning degrees by studying at universities abroad.* **THE SCHLESINGER LIBRARY, RADCLIFFE INSTITUTE, HARVARD UNIVERSITY**

drawn into work in the silk, cotton, and other factories being established in small but rapidly increasing numbers in Shanghai and other coastal cities. These women organized and were involved in strike actions, but they did so as workers, demanding improved wages and working conditions, not in order to gain rights as women (Croll 1978, pp. 73–74, 102–116). Only in the 1920s did intellectual activists, influenced by Marxism, begin to make connections with women workers and, later, peasants.

THE NATIONALIST PARTY, THE COMMUNIST PARTY, AND WOMEN'S ACTIVISM, 1921–1948

Under the 1924–1927 alliance between the Chinese Communist Party (CCP), which had been founded in 1921, and the Nationalist Party, the women's movement flourished. In Guangdong and in the areas traversed during the Northern Expedition, activists established women's unions in villages and towns, to which large numbers of women from all walks of life were recruited, by means

of cultural performances and other propaganda activities, to fight both for the Nationalist cause and for women's emancipation. However, in the wake of the split between the Nationalist Party and the CCP, and as part of the Nationalist military offensive against the CCP after 1927, the women's unions were disbanded and thousands of women activists were brutally tortured, raped, and shot (Croll 1978, pp. 117–152; Gilmartin 1995).

Subsequently, as part of the New Life movement launched in 1934, the Nationalist government urged and trained women to become "useful citizens" by improving their housekeeping skills and by devoting themselves to the traditional ideal of being good wives and mothers. In many respects, this was a low point for women's emancipation. However, feminists also won important, albeit mostly symbolic, victories. The new Civil Code of 1930 granted women freedom of marriage and divorce and equal rights with men in property ownership and inheritance. However, little effort was put into implementing the code. In 1931 China's suffragists, who had been campaigning for the vote since the first years of the Republic, finally succeeded, with equal political rights for women and men written into the constitution. This was a small victory, for electoral structures had yet to be put in place (Edwards 2008, pp. 176–181). Nevertheless, this constitution, as well as the Civil Code, represented and contributed to a broader historical shift in gender discourses and expectations.

Through the 1930s and 1940s, the CCP continued efforts to mobilize, organize, and emancipate worker and peasant women. During this period, the party accorded women equal rights to vote and hold office, and introduced a Land Law and a Marriage Law. Under the former law, which codified land-reform practices through which land was taken from landlords and distributed among peasants, peasant women and men were to have equal rights to land allotments. The 1931 Marriage Law was similar to the Nationalist Marriage Law. Unfortunately, senior officials gave little priority to these laws, and sometimes discouraged their implementation, citing war needs and resentment from the male peasantry as justification (Johnson 1983, pp. 37–89).

WOMEN UNDER MAOISM, 1949–1978

Since its inception, two themes had characterized CCP policy on women. The first was that women's emancipation could not be achieved without the emancipation of the worker and poor peasant classes from class oppression, and all efforts toward the first goal were to be subsumed under the second. The second theme was that, as Friedrich Engels (1820–1895) had argued, women's emancipation was to be achieved with women's large-scale involvement in public production. In practice after 1949, the first theme meant a repeated marginalization of efforts directed at improving the status of women and a lack of authority for the body responsible for "woman-work," the All-China Women's Federation (ACWF) and its members. Ultimately, during the Cultural Revolution, the ACWF was criticized as "revisionist" and as undermining the class struggle, and was disbanded.

The second theme lent justification to the marginalization of efforts to improve women's status, which did not relate directly to increasing their involvement in public production and political support of the CCP. This meant, for example, that serious efforts to implement the new Marriage Law of 1950 in the countryside were short-lived. In the face of peasant resistance, rural marriage reform was put in the "too-hard basket," and even today, arranged or semiarranged marriages remain the norm in rural areas, divorce is difficult and rare, and women have far from equal rights to land and other property.

Even the goal of increasing women's involvement in the public sphere was not always emphasized by the CCP. Rather, women were treated as a "reserve army" of labor, the importance of whose involvement in the public sphere was emphasized or downplayed according to perceived needs and pressures in the economy, and the degree to which class struggle and political mobilization was prioritized. Thus, in the years 1953 to 1957, 1961 to 1965, and the period following reforms in 1978, the CCP and the ACWF downplayed the importance of women's participation in nondomestic production. In contrast, the Great Leap Forward and the Cultural Revolution were periods when women were mobilized into public production and political activity on a large scale.

Women's entry into employment and their contribution to the family income was important in helping to improve their bargaining power in the family. Yet even with a policy of equal pay for equal work, women earned considerably less than men, largely because they worked at different tasks and in different occupations and rarely gained leadership positions. In the Great Leap Forward and to an even greater extent in the Cultural Revolution, there were efforts to break down the gender division of labor in employment with the argument that "what men can do, women can do too," the promotion of female labor models and "Iron Girl teams," and media portrayals of women in previously masculine jobs, such as tractor driving and machine operation. In practice, gender divisions in the workforce were altered less than the propaganda might suggest. At the same time, though, the claim that "what men can do, women can do too" put women under enormous pressure, and was sometimes exploited by factory managers and agricultural team leaders, who pushed women beyond their physical endurance.

The other problem with the Engelsian emphasis on the mobilization of women into public production was the neglect and trivialization of women's contribution to the "private" sphere of housework and the care of children and other family members. This reached a peak during the Cultural Revolution, when women were still expected to undertake domestic work and childcare, but there was no recognition of the "double burden" that this placed them under or of the value of such work. This was combined with a desexualization of women's image through the virtual prohibition of all such "bourgeois" trappings as lipstick and permed hair, and the imposition of the drab, loose, male "Mao suit" on the whole population. In short, the implication of the famous slogans of the Cultural Revolution era—"what men can do, women can do too" and "women hold up half the sky"—was that women should become like men, only work twice as hard (for further discussion of women under Maoism, see Davin 1976).

WOMEN IN THE POST-MAO PERIOD, 1979–

After Mao's death, and with the instatement of a new CCP regime under the leadership of Deng Xiaoping, ideals of

84

A prostitute talking on the phone between customers, Beijing, July 23, 2003. As large areas of the Chinese countryside remain impoverished, thousands of rural women migrate to urban areas in search of work. However, limited opportunities for legal employment force some women into the sex trade, often to earn money for struggling family members back home. © GILLES SABRIE/CORBIS

gender and womanhood shifted once more, with a widespread rejection of the Iron Girl image and a renewed emphasis on sexual difference. This was engineered, in part, by the new party leaders, who sought to bolster their power in the late 1970s by repudiating both the previous regime's efforts at political mobilization and its attempts to disrupt the "natural" gender order. In addition, with the rise of a commodity economy and consumerism, the image of woman as sex object has been manipulated by the advertising industry in much the same way as it has been in the West. But the shifts in gender discourse have also had popular support, including from many women who felt the removal of Cultural Revolution ideology on gender was far more liberating than the ideology itself had been (Jacka 1997, pp. 40–42; see also the writings of the famous post-Mao feminist, Li Xiaojiang, discussed in Barlow 2004, pp. 253–301).

The ACWF was rehabilitated in 1978, but in other respects, women's political status and the number of women appointed or elected to positions of formal political power declined dramatically in the post-Mao period. With regard to women's economic and social status, the most obvious effect of post-Mao reforms has been an increase in differences and inequalities in status *between women*. The starkest inequalities, apparent across all spheres of life, are between rural and urban women. The much lower status and severe problems faced by rural women can only partially be explained by the CCP's claim that such problems are due to "feudal remnants" and the "backward" attitudes of peasants. The blame must also be laid with the CCP, which, in its all-out pursuit of market-oriented economic growth, has not only failed to challenge entrenched gender values and institutions, but has also not responded adequately to problems for rural women newly arising as a result of commercialization and of state policies, for example, on family planning.

Perhaps the most egregious example is the rise of trafficking in women and children. Rooted, as it is, in long-standing patriarchal values, this practice has been exacerbated by the reemergence of the custom of paying bride-prices and the CCP's failure to combat steep increases in the amount of money that rural men and their families are forced to pay for a wife. It has been further exacerbated by the CCP's one-child policy, which has resulted in imbalances in the sex ratio and a high demand for marriageable women. The promulgation of new legislation, including the Law on the Protection of Women and Children (1992) has done little to combat this.

In addition to large and growing inequalities between rural and urban women, the post-Mao period has seen increases in the inequalities between women within rural areas and within urban areas, and between women and men within both rural and urban areas. In rural areas, market-oriented economic growth and industrialization

Computer information technology festival, Haidian Park, Beijing, September 12, 2005. *At the end of the twentieth century, many Chinese women took advantage of new opportunities after attending college to join the professional work force. However, many women frequently earn lower wages and experience greater levels of unemployment than their male counterparts.* © **GIDEON MENDEL/ CORBIS**

have been accompanied by huge movements of people out of agriculture into local industry and businesses, and, since the late 1980s, to jobs in urban centers and the export-oriented industries of the special economic zones. The first to shift out of agriculture have been men, and to a lesser extent young, unmarried women. Consequently, there has been a "feminization" of agriculture, such that today, agricultural labor, which is low in status and poorly remunerated compared with most other paid work, is dominated by middle-aged and older, married women (Jacka 1997, pp. 120–142).

Nationally, 70 percent of rural-to-urban migrants are men, but in the special economic zones, the workforce is heavily dominated by young, single migrant women. Migrants work in appalling conditions and earn wages considerably lower than those of urban workers. In addition, migrant women generally earn less than migrant men (Jacka 2006).

With regard to urban residents, 60 percent of the unemployed are women. Among those in employment, women are concentrated in relatively low status and poorly paid industries and occupations. Furthermore, both occupational segregation and the wage gap between women and men have been increasing (Jiang 2004).

In the 1980s, the ACWF was criticized for its inability to respond to the problems facing women. Since that time, however, members of the ACWF have shown a high degree of willingness to take on new ideas, to support the newly established field of women's studies, and to work with other feminists, both overseas and in a host of new Chinese civil-society groups. Post-Mao market-oriented reforms and globalization have presented numerous challenges for women, but they have also opened new opportunities to organize and act for improvement in women's status (see Xiong Pingchun, Jaschok, and Milwertz 2001).

SEE ALSO *Education: 1800–1949; Education: Women's Education; Family: Infanticide; Family: One-Child Policy; Gender Relations; Law on the Protection of Women and Children; Life Cycle: Marriage; Rape; Sex Ratio; Sexuality; Women in Politics; Women in the Arts; Women, Employment of.*

BIBLIOGRAPHY

Barlow, Tani E. *The Question of Women in Chinese Feminism.* Durham, NC: Duke University Press, 2004.

Croll, Elisabeth. *Feminism and Socialism in China.* London and Boston: Routledge & Kegan Paul, 1978.

Davin, Delia. *Woman-Work: Women and the Party in Revolutionary China.* Oxford: Clarendon Press, 1976.

Edwards, Louise. *Gender, Politics, and Democracy: Women's Suffrage in China.* Stanford, CA: Stanford University Press, 2008.

Gilmartin, Christina K. *Engendering the Chinese Revolution: Radical Women, Communist Politics, and Mass Movements in the 1920s.* Berkeley: University of California Press, 1995.

Jacka, Tamara. *Women's Work in Rural China: Change and Continuity in an Era of Reform.* Cambridge, U.K.: Cambridge University Press, 1997.

Jacka, Tamara. *Rural Women in Urban China: Gender, Migration, and Social Change.* Armonk, NY: Sharpe, 2006.

Jiang Yongping. "Employment and Chinese Urban Women under Two Systems." In *Holding up Half the Sky: Chinese Women Past, Present, and Future,* ed. Tao Jie, Zheng Bijun, and Shirley L. Mow, 207–220. New York: Feminist Press, 2004.

Johnson, Kay Ann. *Women, the Family, and Peasant Revolution in China.* Chicago: University of Chicago Press, 1983.

Wang Zheng. *Women in the Chinese Enlightenment: Oral and Textual Histories.* Berkeley: University of California Press, 1999.

Xiong Pingchun (Ping-Chun Hsiung), Maria Jaschok, and Cecilia Milwertz, eds. *Chinese Women Organizing: Cadres, Feminists, Muslims, Queers.* Oxford and New York: Berg, 2001.

Tamara Jacka

WOMEN IN POLITICS

In accordance with Confucian gender ideology, in imperial China, women were not allowed to sit the official examination and therefore held no positions in Chinese government. There were a few elite exceptions, such as the Empress Dowager Ci Xi (1835–1908), the de facto ruler of China from 1861 to her death in 1908, but even she spoke to her officials from behind a screen. Other than the few exceptions, women played political and military roles only in heterodox revolutionary movements such as the Taiping and the Boxer uprisings.

WOMEN IN REFORM AND REVOLUTION

From the final years of the nineteenth century, reformers argued that China's backwardness was related to the backwardness of Chinese women; national strengthening required the education of women and their participation in public affairs. Before and after the 1911 Revolution women activists campaigned for equal political rights and specifically for the vote. Women were active participants in political lectures before 1911, and women's associations were founded in many cities. In 1912 suffragists stormed the new parliament in Nanjing, and in 1921 they forced their way into the provincial assembly in Guangzhou. In the following years several provincial assemblies gave women the right to vote. Suffragist leaders such as Tang Qunying (1871–1937) also emphasized educational and work opportunities for women to prepare them for political authority. Suffragists encountered fierce opposition from social conservatives. Even Sun Yat-sen asked them to wait because he thought that the women's rights movement threatened the stability of the Republican movement. Ultimately, however, the idea that women's rights were essential to modernizing and strengthening China made the cause widely acceptable.

The Guomindang (GMD) Constitution of 1928 gave equal political rights to women, but because it envisaged a period of "tutelage" before elections could be held, women's suffrage remained an aspiration. The 1936 constitution also recognized women's rights, but elections were again delayed. Women did participate in the People's Political Council, a nonelected advisory body set up by the Guomindang in 1938. This provided a political forum in which they developed political skills. They also campaigned for a minimum quota of women in any future parliament, a concession written into the constitution of 1946 that was subsequently implemented in Taiwan.

The elite women in the early movement for women's rights were professionals such as lawyers, doctors, school principals, and teachers. They were well educated and often single or widowed, making them free of family restraints. They devoted themselves to the nationalist and feminist causes, which they saw as closely linked. Qiu Jin (1875–1907), the revolutionary leader who was executed for her part in a rising against the Manchu dynasty, was followed by many other women who took up arms and fought both in the 1911 Revolution and in the Nationalist revolution of 1925 to 1928.

From the 1920s women were voting and being elected to office in local and regional assemblies. Women's movement leaders of the 1920s began to think of Chinese women of all classes as their constituency, and to focus on how improve the status of all women. Both the Guomindang and the Communist Party expected and encouraged women to be active in party politics, and both had women's sections. In the Republican period women also were active at the grassroots level in major social, political, and nationalist movements such as the May Fourth movement, the labor movement, the Northern Expedition, and the National Salvation Association (Jiuguohui).

EMINENT INDIVIDUALS

The two most prominent female political figures in Republican China both achieved fame through marriage. Song Qingling (1893–1981), the widow of Sun Yat-sen, and her sister, Song Meiling (1897–2003), the wife of Chiang Kai-shek, both U.S.-educated, pioneered public roles as politicians' wives. In the 1930s Song Qingling,

Chinese Vice Premier Wu Yi (center), at the opening ceremony of a Strategic Economic Dialogue with the United States, Xinghe, Hebei province, December 11, 2007. Despite averaging around twenty percent of the seats in the National People's Congress in the final decades of the twentieth century, few women in the People's Republic of China have risen to the top levels of leadership. However, these few high-ranking women, such as Wu Yi, have earned international respect for their political accomplishments. **GUANG NIU/GETTY IMAGES**

unassailable as Sun's widow, led opposition to Chiang Kai-shek's appeasement of Japan. Song Meiling was a member of the Legislative Yuan 1930 to 1932, and from 1934 headed the conservative New Life movement concerned with raising public morals, imposing modest dress, and upholding women's family roles. From 1937 the sisters worked together mobilizing women for the war effort. With her excellent English, Song Meiling was invaluable to Chiang in his relations with the United States, and in 1943 she became the second woman and the first Chinese national ever to address the U.S. Congress.

Many other women became well known on the national political scene in the Republican period. He Xiangning (1879–1972), the widow of the assassinated GMD leader Liao Zhongkai (1877–1925), was a member of the GMD Central Committee and headed its Women's Department. In the 1930s she joined the National Salvation Association in urging resistance to the Japanese, and in 1948 she was a

founding member of the Revolutionary Committee of the GMD, which was formed to oppose civil war with the Communists. Also prominent in the National Salvation Association was the lawyer Shi Liang (1900–1985), one of the "seven honorable gentlemen" (*qi junzi*) arrested by Chiang Kai-shek for their campaign against appeasement; she later served as the first minister of justice in the People's Republic of China (PRC). Wu Yifan (1893–1985), China's first female university principal and chair of the National Christian Council, and Liu Wang Liming (1897–1970), a veteran suffragist and national president of the Women's Christian Temperance Union, also were active in the National Salvation movement.

WOMEN IN THE COMMUNIST MOVEMENT

Many prominent Communist women leaders such as Xiang Jingyu (1895–1928), Cai Chang (1900–1990) and Deng

Yingchao (1904–1992) first became politically active in the May Fourth movement. Until the Communist movement retreated to the countryside in 1928, they were involved in educating and mobilizing urban working women for political action; later, they were again deployed to mobilize rural women. They campaigned to implement land and marriage reform in the interests of women, to promote women's education, and to organize women to take part in production. However, women activists in the Communist areas who seemed to prioritize women's rights over other political goals, or who criticized the Communist Party in relation to women, were sometimes accused of bourgeois feminism, as the writer Ding Ling (1904–1986) was.

WOMEN AND POLITICS IN THE PRC

Women's liberation (*funü jiefang*) was said to be a priority goal for "New China." The All-China Women's Federation (Quanguo funü lianhehui) was entrusted with mobilizing women to take public roles in politics, urban and village government, production, education, and campaigns for marriage and family reform. Women were most active in local politics, especially on the neighborhood committees that provided a level of informal community government in the cities. Most prominent women leaders, whether Communists such as Deng Yingchao and Cai Chang who had spent years in the Communist rural bases or nonparty radicals such as Song Qingling and Liu Wang Liming who had stayed in the cities controlled by the Guomindang, were encouraged to put their energies into family reform, women's issues, and welfare work, largely through the Women's Federation. Even Kang Keqing (1911–1992), the famous soldier wife of General Zhu De (1886–1976), was assigned to children's welfare. The Women's Federation was able to ensure that gender equality remained on the policy agenda, but despite its efforts, women remained underrepresented in government, especially at the higher levels.

The Women's Federation was closed down during the Cultural Revolution (1966–1969). Under the slogan "women hold up half the sky," women's representation in bodies such as the National People's Congress increased temporarily. At the instigation of Mao Zedong's wife, Jiang Qing (1914–1991), essays about famous Chinese women rulers and about women's capacity to rule were published. For a while, Jiang herself was the most powerful woman in China. Unfortunately, support for women's political activism was discredited by its association with the ideological extremism of the Cultural Revolution. There was less rhetoric about women's liberation in the Reform period, and little improvement in women's political representation in party and state organs.

Twelve percent of the delegates to the First National People's Congress (NPC) in 1954 were women. This rose to 17.8 percent at the Third NPC in 1964 and, affected by the Cultural Revolution, to 22.6 percent at the Fourth NPC in 1975, its highest level (at the Eleventh NPC in 2008 it was 21.33). Women's membership in the NPC's Standing Committee was 4 percent in 1954 and 27.1 percent in 1975; in the 2000s it has ranged between 9 and 13 percent. No woman has ever chaired the Standing Committee. Female membership in the Communist Party rose from 14.2 percent in 1989 to 17 percent in 1999 and 31 percent in 2007. But in 2007 only 13 of the 204 members of the Central Committee were women, and only one of the Politburo's 25 members; all nine of its Standing Committee members were male. In 2008 the state president, the premier, and all four vice premiers were men, as were four of the five state councilors.

Women's political representation in China has not significantly improved since the beginning of the Reform period in 1978—decades that saw considerable change elsewhere in the world. China's NPC ranked twelfth in the Inter-Parliamentary Union in 1994 for representation of women, twentieth in 1999, and fifty-second in 2005.

Unlike the generation of revolutionary activists, prominent women politicians in the Reform period typically were trained in the sciences and began their careers as technocrats. Outstanding women include:

- Chen Muhua (b. 1921), who graduated from Jiaotong University in building construction; served as vice premier (1978–1982) and alternate or full member of the Central Committee (1973–1993); and held numerous government posts in foreign trade, banking, and birth planning;

- Wu Yi (b. 1938), who graduated from Beijing Petroleum College; and served as minister for foreign affairs (1982–1988), foreign trade minister (1993–1998), alternate or full member of the Central Committee (1997–2007), and vice premier (2003–2008), before retiring in 2008;

- Chen Zhili (b. 1942), who graduated in physics from Fudan University; and served as a member of the Central Committee (1997–), minister of education (1998–2003), state councilor (2003–2008), and vice chair of the Eleventh Standing Committee of the NPC (2008) and

- Liu Yandong (b. 1945), who graduated from Jilin University in political science and Tsinghua University in engineering chemistry; and served as deputy head (1991–2002) and head (2002–2007) of the United Front Committee under the Central Committee and alternate or full member of the Central Committee (1997–), member of the Politburo (2007–), and state councilor (2008).

Despite the considerable achievements of these exceptional women, women are still poorly represented in government. Women officials are often relegated to areas perceived as women's concerns, such as education, health, and welfare.

SEE ALSO *Cixi, Empress Dowager; Ding Ling; Song Qingling; Women, Status of.*

BIBLIOGRAPHY

Davin, Delia. *WomanWork: Women and the Party in Revolutionary China*. Oxford, U.K.: Clarendon Press, 1976.

Edwards, Louise. Constraining Women's Political Work with "Women's Work": The Chinese Communist Party and Women's Participation in Politics. In *Chinese Women—Living and Working*, ed. Anne E. McLaren, 105–124. London: RoutledgeCurzon, 2004.

Edwards, Louise. *Gender Politics and Democracy: Women's Suffrage in China*. Stanford, CA: Stanford University Press, 2008.

Gilmartin, Christina. *Engendering the Chinese Revolution: Radical Women, Communist Politics, and Mass Movements in the 1920s*. Berkeley: University of California Press, 1995.

Hershatter, Gail. *Women in China's Long Twentieth Century*. Berkeley: University of California Press, 2007.

Wang Zheng, *Women in the Chinese Enlightenment: Oral and Textual Histories*. Berkeley: University of California Press, 1999.

Delia Davin

WOMEN IN THE VISUAL ARTS

Throughout Chinese art history there have been talented women painters, a few accorded considerable recognition, most relegated to peripheral roles by critics and historians in favor of the male masters whose talents have been more widely acclaimed. The important contributions of women as painters, teachers, collectors, and connoisseurs in traditional China have been the subject of considerable scholarship since the 1990s. In the modern period, the number of women working as artists has increased, as have their roles in expanding ideas of what constitutes Chinese art. Still less numerous than the legions of male cohorts, women artists have increased their visibility and viability to become a presence on the world stage.

In pre-twentieth-century China, women painters came from a variety of social classes. Women who were exposed to education either through family disposition or for professional enrichment were the most likely to learn painting and calligraphy. Gentry women and courtesans, for example, are represented in the history of Chinese painting. The career of Guan Daosheng (1262–1319), wife of the artist Zhao Mengfu (1254–1322), is one example of the extraordinary achievements of a painter of the gentry class, and

the extant works of the Ming dynasty courtesan Xue Wu (c. 1573–1620) attest to her skills in painting and calligraphy. Daughters from painter families also were known to have carried on the artistic traditions of their fathers, occasionally earning reputations of their own. At the pinnacle of society were female members of the imperial household, many of whom were trained in the arts of the brush.

In the modern period, the contributions of women artists continued on a much larger stage. No longer confined to China, female artists found wide-ranging audiences who supported their efforts. In the Qing dynasty, Zhang Lunying (1798–c. 1868) earned an international reputation, but her fame outside of China reached only as far as Korea and Japan. A century later, the reputations of Chinese women artists are truly global.

THE MODERN PERIOD: AFTER 1911

Late Qing and early Republican China saw extraordinary changes in its educational system. Reforms in education during the early twentieth century targeted not just men. Women, who traditionally had been denied access to regular tuition, became the beneficiaries of evolving attitudes toward women and their roles in the changing socioeconomic scene. Schools for women opened and opportunities abounded. Women artists were among the leaders in this charge: The artist Huang Shizheng, wife of the educator Cai Yuanpei (1868–1940), taught painting and calligraphy at a school Cai founded in 1903, and the revolutionary Zhang Mojun (1884–1965) founded a girls' school in Shanghai whose curriculum included both Chinese and Western-style art, including drawing and oil painting. Throughout the second decade of the twentieth century, reforms that affected women's education continued, legitimizing educational opportunities for women, and leading to coeducation after 1919. Prospects for women who wished to pursue art education expanded during this period. The Shanghai Art Academy accepted its first female applicants in 1919.

Study overseas was another avenue newly opened to women interested in developing their artistic talents. Japan was an attractive early destination, offering the adventurous student a relatively nearby opportunity to study Western art, albeit Western art filtered through Japanese teachers. He Xiangning (1878–1972), Guan Zilan (1902–1986), and Qiu Ti (1906–1958) all studied painting in Japan. Slightly later, opportunities opened up for women to study in Europe: Fang Junbi (1898–1986) and Pan Yuliang (1902–1977) went to Paris, Cai Weilian (1904–1940) to Belgium and France. Modernists were not the only ones to study overseas. He Xiangning (1878–1972), who was renowned for her *guohua*-style flower painting, studied in Japan.

During dynastic times, women trained in brush and ink were generally expected to paint subjects considered appropriate for women. Flowers, birds, and female figures were especially popular subjects for women's brushes. Rarely did women painters depict the subjects more properly associated with male literati painters, such as landscape and bamboo. During the late Qing and early Republican periods, this convention continued among women artists. Wu Shujuan (1853–1930) and Ren Xia (1876–1920) were both from artistic families and both continued and expanded the tradition of painting the subjects associated with women. Wu was a *guohua* painter who first specialized in flowers, especially in the style of the Qing dynasty master Yun Shouping (1633–1690). However, she also became skilled at painting large landscapes, which led to her fame as one of the two Wus of Shanghai, paired with the male painter Wu Changshi. Ren Xia, daughter of Ren Yi (Ren Bonian, 1840–1895), continued the traditions of the Four Rens whose works dominated Shanghai school painting of the nineteenth century. Her works closely followed the styles and subjects of her famous father.

Women artists participated in great numbers in the first National Art Exhibition of 1929, and subsequently played an important role in the revival of traditional Chinese painting that took place in the 1930s. Members of the Beijing-based Lake Society were prominent exhibitors in 1929. In 1934 a group of successful women artists in Shanghai led by Li Qiujun (1899–1973), a student of Wu Shujuan, Gu Qingyao (1901–1978), granddaughter of a prominent Suzhou literati painter, and Yang Xueyao, principal of the East City Girls' School, established the Women's Calligraphy and Painting Society, which promoted the practice and exhibition of these traditional arts and the professional careers of their female practitioners. Many of its members, such as Lu Xiaoman (1894–1965), Zhou Lianxia (1908–2000), and Chen Xiaocui (1907–1968), were also famous in their day as writers.

Western-style art education spread in China in the early twentieth century, and with it the ideas, theories, and techniques of Western art. The training of most women painters began with traditional Chinese brush and ink painting, but a number of women were drawn to more modern expressions, which meant learning drawing, still-life, watercolor, and sketching outdoors. Some were able to extend their studies by traveling to Japan or Europe, others were dependent upon the stimulating artistic atmosphere of home and like-minded colleagues to advance their interests.

Pan Yuliang (1895–1977) took full advantage of the evolving educational opportunities open to her. She was in the first group of women accepted to study at the newly coeducational Shanghai Art Academy in 1919, and is the best known among the group of pioneering modernist women artists. The biographical details of her life are well recorded. She studied in France in the 1920s,

and although she returned to China for several years, she felt marginalized for her commitment to modernism. She returned to Paris to make her reputation as a painter and sculptor. Her painted works combine Chinese techniques and media with Western subject matter—female nudes painted with brush and ink, for example—but her oil paintings and sculptures are decidedly Western in conception and execution.

As a teenager, Fang Junbi (1898–1986) moved to France, where she continued her education. Much of her life was spent between China and France. In 1920, Fang became the first Chinese woman admitted to the École nationale supérieure des beaux arts; a few years later she studied under Nabis painter Pierre Bonnard (1867–1947). Although her reputation rested on her Western-style works, she was also comfortable working with Chinese media, in which she incorporated Western elements such as perspective.

Guan Zilan (1903–1986) studied Western art in both Shanghai and Japan. In Tokyo, she associated with leading figures in the introduction of Western art to Japan and had a very successful exhibition career. Her works show decided influence from the Fauves, whose styles were popular among Japanese modernists.

The modernist credentials of Cai Weilian (1904–1940) emanated from both her parents, but certainly were developed in her education abroad. Her father Cai Yuanpei was minister of education and chancellor at Beijing University, and her mother Huang Shizheng a painter and teacher. Cai Weilian's training included study in Brussels and France, and she was best known for historical paintings and portraits. Upon her return to China, she taught Western painting at the Hangzhou Academy of Art, where her students included Zhao Wuji (b. 1921), Zhu Dequn (b. 1920), and Wu Guanzhong (b. 1919).

POST-1949

The generation after Pan Yuliang nurtured a group of talented, successful painters whose careers took them to the top of their profession. Although the post-1949 socialist realist art establishment was male-dominated, a small number of female oil painters, some of whom worked in collaboration with their painter-husbands, were recognized in the People's Republic of China (PRC) and became professors at institutions such as the Central Academy of Fine Arts. Among them are Deng Shu (b. 1929) and Pang Tao (b. 1934), daughter of the modernists Pang Xunqin (1906–1985) and Qiu Ti (1906–1958). Women excelled in every area of art in this period, though they were still far fewer than men.

Many of this generation, particularly those who left China proper, are noteworthy for their commitment to the ideals of traditional Chinese painting. Most were born in China at a time of momentous change and share experiences of war and revolution, as well as adult careers in the diaspora. For those who emigrated around 1949, working overseas offered creative stimulus and increased chances for recognition through exhibitions, publications, and the interest of Western collectors and scholars.

The painting and calligraphy of Fang Zhaoling (1914–2006) evokes a traditional feel, in spite of her cosmopolitan life. Experiences living and traveling in China, the United States, and Europe informed her artistic development, as did her commitment to higher education. Postgraduate study in the 1950s at the University of Hong Kong and Oxford University enabled her intellectual and artistic interests to develop in tandem. With the exception of a short diversion into oils and abstraction in the 1960s while living in London, Fang was primarily a painter of landscape and genre scenes that were deeply rooted in the *guohua* traditions of the past but modern in outlook.

Zhang Shangpu (Constance Chang, b. 1928) was a student at the Zhejiang Academy of Fine Arts, but achieved fame in China as an actress. It was not until after 1948, when she settled in Hong Kong, that she turned seriously to painting. For many years she studied with Lingnan school master Zhao Shao'ang (1905–1998), and then with Huang Banruo (Wong Po-yeh, 1901–1968) and Lü Shoukun (1919–1975). Painting in traditional media and styles, her works evolved from close copies of the old masters to more simplified, abstract evocations of landscape. She moved to San Francisco in 1974.

Zhou Lüyun (b. 1924), a Shanghai native and graduate of St. John's University, settled in Hong Kong after 1949. There she studied with Zhao Shao'ang, under whose tutelage she displayed her accomplishment with the naturalistic manner and skillful technical style of the Lingnan school. In 1968 Zhou joined the New Ink Painting movement spearheaded by Lü Shoukun. Under Lü's guidance, Zhou revolutionized her approach to painting. Her works became more personal and experimental. Her most innovative works are complex, metaphysical compositions that draw on traditional painting principles, and their patterns convey the pulsing energy of the universe. Since 1991 she has made her home in Australia.

Zeng Youhe's (Tseng Yuho's) artistic reputation was established early in China. She was in the first class of women admitted to study art at Furen University, where her teachers were painters steeped in the most conservative styles of Chinese painting, including Pu Jin (1893–1966), Pu Quan (1913–1991), and Qi Gong (1912–2005). In 1949 she settled in Honolulu. Through the early 1950s her works were deeply informed by the influence of her teachers in China. In Hawaii, however, Tseng's creativity soared, and the painting–mixed media technique she developed—*dsui hua*, literally "assembled painting"—resulted in a style

that blended traditional and modern, Chinese and Western. She returned to China in 2006.

Innovation and modern expressions are not the only interests among this talented group of expatriate Chinese artists. Zhang Chonghe (b. 1914) continues the tradition of literati pursuits in a context remote from her native Anhui. Painter, calligrapher, collector, and seal-carver, Zhang's daily practice of calligraphy and study of past masters mark her as a modern-day literata. For many years she taught calligraphy at Yale University, and nurtured a number of private students in calligraphy and seal-carving. In collaboration with her husband, the Chinese literature scholar Hans Frankel (1917–2003), Zhang's academic interests in calligraphy are preserved in annotated translations of Sun Guoting's and Jiang Kui's treatises on calligraphy.

At the end of the Cultural Revolution, some women artists emerged in the forefront of new, post-socialist styles of art. Zhou Sicong (1939–1996), a successful socialist realist figure painter in Beijing, cast this manner aside and experimented in various modes of ink painting. Some of her most lyrical works are her late paintings of lotuses in puddled, highly abstract ink and pale color. The Sichuanese printmaker A Ge (b. 1948), after studying abroad in Europe, broke with conventions of socialist realist woodblock prints and pioneered new styles in the black and white format.

POST-MAO, POST-DENG

The period of rapid social and cultural change in the post-Mao and post-Deng years in China was dominated by the generations of artists who were born after the founding of the PRC in 1949, and especially by the generations who came to maturity during the period of the Cultural Revolution or in the decades since. There are a number of ink artists whose generational cohort lies between the Fang Zhaoling–Zeng Youhe generation, including Dong Yangzi and Yang Yanping, who have many similarities in terms of art and biography. Dong Yangzi (Grace Tong, b. 1942) was born in Shanghai and has lived most of her life in Taiwan, where she launched her reputation as a calligrapher. Yang Yanping (b. 1934) followed a different path. Born in Nanjing, she received her college education in Beijing, where she was associated with the prestigious Central Academy of Fine Arts. In 1986 she moved to the United States. Yang's works are lush, richly colored and textured evocations of lotus and landscape, drawing on her traditional training and understanding of Chinese art history, but also modern and accomplished in Western techniques.

Women have been involved in radical art movements in the modern period since Qiu Ti joined the avant-garde Storm Society in 1932. A half-century later, women artists continued to have a role in moments of dramatic change in the art world, although until recently they still have been far outnumbered by their male colleagues. In the post-Mao period Li Shuang (b. 1957) and Shao Fei (b. 1954) were among the artists who participated in the oppositional Stars movement of 1979 to 1980. Ceramicist, papermaker, and installation artist Hou Wenyi (b. 1958) was a prominent figure in the '85 New Wave movement. Even more notorious was Xiao Lu (b. 1962), who fired a gun into her installation at the 1989 China Avant-Garde exhibition, shocking the art establishment in China and leading authorities to temporarily close the exhibition.

Women painters in the modern period have pursued artistic expressions ranging from traditional-style painting to new forms and media. The decorative traditions of *gongbi* painting and *guohua* have continued to provide inspiration, as has the emergence of new forms of creative expression. Lin Tianmiao (b. 1962) and Yin Xiuzhen (b. 1963) favor installation works using various media (clothing, thread, photography) to explore issues of cultural and gender identity. Oil painting, photography, video, and sculpture have expanded the forms of artistic expression for women artists, who are no longer confined to a narrow range of subjects or expected to conform to a strict cultural ideal.

SEE ALSO *Pan Yuliang; Ren Yi (Ren Bonian); Wu Changshi (Wu Junqing); Wu Shujuan (Wu Xingfen).*

BIBLIOGRAPHY

Andrews, Julia F., and Kuiyi Shen. Traditionalism as a Modern Stance: The Chinese Women's Calligraphy and Painting Society. *Modern Chinese Literature and Culture* 11, 1 (spring 1999): 1–29.

Chang, Chung-ho, and Mimi Gardner Gates. *Fragrance of the Past: Chinese Calligraphy and Painting by Ch'ung-Ho Chang Frankel and Friends.* Seattle, WA: Seattle Art Museum, 2006.

Lim, Lucy. *Six Contemporary Chinese Women Artists.* San Francisco: Chinese Culture Foundation of San Francisco, 1991.

Sullivan, Michael. *Art and Artists of Twentieth-Century China.* Berkeley: University of California Press, 1996.

Weidner, Marsha Smith. *Views from Jade Terrace: Chinese Women Artists, 1300–1912.* Indianapolis, IN: Indianapolis Museum of Art, 1988.

Quatre artistes chinoises contemporaines: Pan Yu-Lin, Lam Oi, Ou Seu-tan, Shing Wai. Paris: Musée Cernuschi, 26 mars-30 avril 1977.

Thompson, Melissa. Gathering Jade and Assembling Splendor: The Life and Art of Tseng Yuho. PhD diss., University of Washington, 2001.

Walt, Melissa J., Michael Knight, and Kazuhiro Tsuruta. *Fang Zhaoling: A Life in Painting.* San Francisco: Asian Art Museum— Chong-Moon Lee Center for Asian Art and Culture, 2005.

Werner, Chris, and Ping Qiu. *Die Hälfte des Himmels: chinesische Künstlerinnen der Gegenwart* [Half of the sky: contemporary Chinese women artists]. *10 Juni–4 Oktober 1998, Frauenmuseum Bonn; April 1999, Künstlerkreis Offenburg.* Bonn: Frauen Museum, 1998.

Melissa J. Walt

WOODBLOCK PRINTING (XYLOGRAPHY)

The eighteenth century was remarkable in China for the scope and scale of its woodblock printing and book production. In addition to the expansion of private and commercial publishing, voluminous works were published in large numbers by the court, especially under the Qianlong emperor (r. 1736–1796), and many were reprinted in the provinces. The Qianlong emperor was renowned for the *Siku quanshu* (Complete library of the four treasuries) project, which resulted in the production of seven manuscript libraries, each comprising about 3,500 individual titles in nearly 36,000 physical volumes. The sources for the manuscript copies included thousands of rare printed books submitted by enthusiastic collectors. These activities further stimulated publishing throughout the country, and by 1800 there were few places in China that had not engaged in woodblock printing. During the Jiaqing (1796–1820) and Daoguang (1821–1850) periods, scholars and book collectors, inspired by the likes of Huang Pilie (1763–1825) and Gu Guangqi (1766–1835), produced numerous bibliographical works. It also was popular to publish xylographic facsimile reprints of Song (960–1279) and Yuan (1279–1368) editions. For example, the Yangzhou scholar Ruan Yuan (1764–1849) published dozens of works in his lifetime, including critical notes to the *Shisan jing zhushu* (Thirteen classics with commentary) in 1808; a facsimile edition of *Gu Lienüzhuan* (Biographies of exemplary women of the past) based on a Song edition he possessed; and the *Huang Qing jingjie* (Imperial Qing annotations on the classics) in 1829, a set of nearly 360 volumes of commentaries on the classics. By the end of the 1830s this exuberant wave of xylographic publishing began to decline, probably owing to economic downturns and the chaos of the Opium Wars and the midcentury Taiping Uprising.

The Taiping armies that swept across a wide swath of central and southern China in the 1850s destroyed countless book collections and disrupted book production for more than a decade. This brought about an extensive need for compensatory publishing that could only be met by xylographic printing. Indeed, voluminous reprint collections (*congshu*) were a prominent feature of publishing in the second half of the nineteenth century. Official printing offices (*shuju*), established in many provincial cities (e.g., Jinling Shuju, later Jiangnan Shuju, set up in Nanjing in 1864 by Zeng Guofan, 1811–1872), fostered large-scale printing projects. Overlapping with native publishing was a new demand for printed matter made by Protestant missionaries, and although they promoted letterpress printing, xylography proved to be a practical and economic means of producing some of their texts. It

A wood block carver at work, Shanghai, China. *Printing books through the use of carved wood blocks, or xylography, remains a respected traditional art in Chinese culture. Enthusiasts continue to create reprints of historical texts using antique wood blocks, while other artists carve new blocks for contemporary works.* © **DEAN CONGER/CORBIS**

was not until the end of the nineteenth century that alternative technologies, such as lithography and Western-style movable-type printing, began to compete successfully with xylography and finally came to dominate after the Republican Revolution of 1911.

Publishing at the end of the Qing period (1644–1912) resembled the final decades of the Ming (1368–1644) in some ways. For example, there was a resurgence of fiction and picture-book publishing. Many of these popular categories began to be printed by the new method of lithography, but initially these publications were associated with port cities such as Shanghai and thought of as foreign. In the rest of the country, xylography remained the norm for printing pictures and text, even for songbooks (*changben*) and ephemeral publications. After the advent of photolithography in China from around 1880, many lithographic editions were based on woodblock editions. Yet the best picture books of the period, such as *Honglou meng tuyong* (Portraits of characters from *Dream of the Red Chamber*) of 1879, depended on traditional technology and the xylographic aesthetic.

LETTER PAPER

Another late-nineteenth-century interest was decorated letter paper (*xinjian*), the development of which is also associated with the Ming period. Woodblock printed stationery can be divided into monochromatic and polychromatic styles, and the best was based on the designs of well-known artists, and printed and sold by famous stationers. As in the late Ming, it was popular to publish bound volumes of beautifully printed specimens, such as the *Wenmeizhai baihua shijianpu* (Hundred flowers poetry-writing paper from Wenmei Studio), published in two volumes in 1911 by the Tianjin stationer Wenmei Studio. Poetry stationery (*shijian*) is another name for letter paper, which continues to be printed by woodblock in China and is especially prized by traditional calligraphers. The most prominent shops are Rongbaozhai in Beijing and Duoyunxuan in Shanghai. In 1934 Rongbaozhai began a meticulous facsimile edition of the famous late-Ming letter-paper publication *Shizhuzhai jianpu* (Decorated letter paper from the Ten Bamboo Studio), completed in four volumes in 1944. New woodblocks were engraved in 1952, and this

NIANHUA (NEW YEAR PICTURES)

Chinese *nianhua* (new year pictures) is a genre of woodblock printing (xylography) that belongs to the category of *minjian banhua* (popular woodcuts). Woodblocks were used as early as the Eastern Han (25–220 CE) to print decorations on textiles. Popularization of papermaking around the same time provided a convenient surface for the transfer of pictures and designs of impressed ink and pigments. Pictorial woodcuts developed together with textual woodblock printing from the Tang dynasty (618–907) onward. By the Song period (960–1279) economic prosperity and artistic development made the printing of woodcuts depicting popular deities for religious and secular festivals rather commonplace. Xylographic color printing techniques and regional decorative styles evolved from Ming (1368–1644) to Qing (1644–1912).

Although generally eschewed by the scholar class, new year pictures were an important part of Chinese traditional culture, especially in the nineteenth and twentieth centuries. Popular religion and domestic culture merged and came to coexist in the form of the stove god (*zaoshen*) and the god of wealth (*caishen*), among others. The new year season is a time of renewal, and household rituals included the changing of pictures, such as of the stove god, usually displayed in proximity to the kitchen hearth. Because China was an agricultural society, these pictures often incorporated calendars. Other auspicious pictures, such as of the god of wealth, were used as door gods (*menshen*), to be pasted directly on main entry doors. In imitation of spring festival couplets (*chunlian*), pairs of matching new year pictures, in a vertical format, were pasted on both sides of a main entry gate, on both panels of a double door, or on a wall on either side of an iconographic or narrative *nianhua*. Iconographic new year pictures show a pantheon of popular deities, and narrative ones depict didactic and symbolic images, such as scenes of domestic harmony and abundant offspring, of boys as scholars (*zhuangyuan*) and girls as beauties (*meiren*). Opera and theatrical scenes as *nianhua* reflect the fact that new year performances are typical of holiday entertainments. In the twentieth century, especially after 1949, new year pictures also have been used to reflect and promote economic, social, and political movements.

The polychromatic woodcut (*taoyin banhua*) is the main medium for new year pictures. In its most primitive form, a single woodblock is used, and different colors are applied separately and printed successively. Most commonly, however, the outline of a single composition is printed in black from a key block, and colors are added by one or a combination of the following techniques: printing from small woodblocks, one or more for each color (*douban*); applying by stencil over small areas of the print (*moban*); or painting on the surface by brush (*shouhui*). Yangliuqing in Hebei, Weifang in Shandong, Suzhou in Jiangsu, and Mianzhu in Sichuan are among the many important production centers in China. The nature of xylography permits the storage of woodblocks that can be used many times before they wear out, and some blocks from the Qing dynasty are still in use today. Lithography and offset printing have been used for new year pictures in recent decades, but they never have been as well received as traditional xylographic prints.

BIBLIOGRAPHY

Laing, Ellen. *Art and Aesthetics in Chinese Popular Prints*. Ann Arbor: University of Michigan, Center for Chinese Studies, 2002.

Wang, Shucun. *Zhongguo nianhua shi* [History of Chinese new year pictures]. Beijing: Beijing Gongyi Meishu Chubanshe, 2002.

J. S. Edgren

beautiful polychromatic woodblock edition has been kept in print since then. Polychromatic woodblock printing also thrived as a source for *nianhua* (New Year's pictures).

ANTIQUARIAN PUBLISHING

In the first half of the twentieth century, woodblock printing persisted in conservative segments of society. Individual scholars such as Chen Yuan (1880–1971) published essays and monographs by woodblock. Xylographic rare-book catalogs such as *Shuangjianlou shanben shumu* (Shuangjianlou, i.e., Fu Zengxiang, rare-book catalog) and *Guoli Beiping Tushuguan shanben shumu* (National Library of China rare-book catalog) were published in 1929 and 1933 respectively. After the Japanese invasion of China several major university faculties removed to the southwest of China. On occasion, xylography was used in the absence of modern printing facilities. For example, in 1939 Nanjing

University published *Changsha guwu wenjianji* (Changsha antiquities news) by woodblock in Sichuan as part of a series previously published by letterpress.

COLLECTIONS OF WOODBLOCKS

After 1949 woodblock printing was upheld as an important Chinese invention and a national cultural asset by the new government. Several organizations in China have large collections of woodblocks and have continuously used them to reprint xylographic editions. This has made it necessary to support artisans trained in skills such as calligraphic transcription, block cutting, hand printing, and traditional binding. It has also maintained a demand for various grades of handmade paper. Collections of woodblocks are found at the Gugong Bowuyuan (Palace Museum) and Zhongguo Shudian (Cathay Bookshop), both in Beijing. The Jinling Kejing Chu (Jinling Woodblock Sutra Institute) in Nanjing has Buddhist woodblocks. The Zhejiang Library in Hangzhou has a collection of woodblocks from the former Zhejiang Printing Office (Zhejiang Shuju), which it combines with the large collection of woodblocks donated by Liu Chenggan (1882–1963), and keeps at the Liu Chenggan Library, Jiayetang, in Huzhou.

The collection of woodblocks in Yangzhou belongs to the Guangling Shushe (Guangling Publishing Company), which has deposited a large part of them at the newly established Zhongguo Diaoban Yinshua Bowuguan (China Block Printing Museum) in Yangzhou. After 1949, blocks were acquired from local booksellers, especially Chen Henghe Shulin (Chen Henghe Bookshop). Guangling Shushe has mostly reprinted older works from original woodblocks with the addition of replacement blocks if necessary. In 1981 they embarked on a project that took twenty years to complete. Two scribes and more than ten block cutters collaborated to produce woodblocks for *Litang daoting lu* (Litang's scholarly notes), based on Jiao Xun's (1763–1820) original manuscript held by the National Library of China in Beijing. When the forty-volume work was finally published in 2001, it was hailed as a unique achievement in textual xylographic printing.

SEE ALSO *Folk Art; New Print Movement.*

BIBLIOGRAPHY

Brokaw, Cynthia. *Commerce in Culture.* Cambridge, MA: Harvard University Asia Center, 2007.

Edgren, Sören. Chinese Rare Books and Color Printing. *East Asian Library Journal* 10, 1 (2001): 24–52.

McDermott, Joseph. *A Social History of the Chinese Book.* Hong Kong: Hong Kong University Press, 2006.

Reed, Christopher. *Gutenberg in Shanghai.* Honolulu: University of Hawai'i Press, 2004.

J. S. Edgren

WORKERS, INDUSTRIAL, 1860–1949

Industrial workers emerged as a social group in China in the last decades of the nineteenth century, first in the foreign-owned shipyards and then in the official and foreign industrial enterprises that were set up in the 1860s and 1870s. Most industrial enterprises were in the treaty ports, where from 1895 foreigners were permitted to engage in manufacturing. In the 1920s nearly half of all China's industrial workers were employed in foreign-owned enterprises. Although the numbers of industrial workers remained small compared to the total population, their concentration in Shanghai and a few other large cities made their role disproportionately significant when the labor movement was at its height in the 1920s. From the 1920s to the 1940s, the Chinese Communist Party, the Guomindang, and Shanghai's notorious gangs vied for influence in workers' organizations.

DEMOGRAPHICS OF THE INDUSTRIAL WORKING CLASS

Estimates of the numbers of industrial workers in China during this period can be only approximate. Most recorded figures are for particular industries or regions, and the definitions used vary. A best guess has the industrial workforce increasing rapidly from about 100,000 in 1894 to 661,000 in 1912 (Bastid-Bruguière 1980, p. 572). Jean Chesneaux produced what he called a very rough estimate for the early 1920s of more than 1.5 million workers—less than 0.5 percent of the Chinese population at the time. This figure included 300,000 workers in the cotton and silk industries, 60,000 in food processing, 50,000 in tobacco, and 50,000 in metallurgy. It also included unmechanized industrial labor and workers involved in transport rather than manufacturing, including 200,000 dock workers, 115,000 ocean transport workers, and 150,000 rickshaw pullers (Chesneaux 1968). A 1933 census of industrial workers in Chinese-owned enterprises counted 435,257 workers. Because this figure covered mechanized enterprises employing thirty or more workers and excluded both foreign-owned enterprises and industry in Japanese-occupied northeast China, it is probably compatible with Chesneaux's estimate, allowing for some growth in the intervening years. All estimates confirm that industrial workers were a tiny proportion of the Chinese population in this period.

The vast majority of industrial workers were concentrated in six widely separated centers:

1. the Shanghai area and its Jiangnan hinterland (where about half of China's industry was located in the early 1930s), a center for trade, textiles, and light industries including food processing, tobacco, matches, and leather;

2. Guangzhou, Hong Kong, and the Pearl River Delta, where industrial employment was concentrated in the silk industry, trade and transport enterprises, cement works, tobacco and match factories, and printing works;

3. the industrial area of Hubei and Hunan provinces, famous for the Hanyeping Company, an industrial combine whose interests included iron and coal mines and a steelworks, and for the cotton, oil, and flour mills and tobacco factories in Wuhan and Changsha;

4. Shandong, which had cotton, flour, brick, cement, and match and tobacco factories, many of which were Japanese controlled, as well as railway workshops and a state arsenal;

5. the Beijing–Tianjin region, where Chinese, British, and Japanese-owned enterprises included cotton mills, food processing, carpet and tobacco factories, and shipyards, as well as a major coal mine at Tangshan; and

6. northeast China, a heavy industrial region dominated by Russian capital in the north and Japanese in the south, where enterprises included blast furnaces at Anshan and oil mills, brickworks, and match factories, most of which were sited close to the two principal rail routes.

Even within each region, China's industrial workers were divided by loyalties of native place, secret society affiliation, and clientelism, as well as by trade, gender, and skill levels.

Before industrialization, the laboring poor in Chinese cities had included artisans, transport workers, petty traders, construction workers, entertainers, and servants. Other marginalized urban groups were beggars and local toughs. The poorest and most marginalized groups were recent arrivals from the countryside, especially refugees from wars, rebellions, natural disasters, and famine. The established urban population tended to work in secure artisanal occupations, whereas newcomers found openings wherever they could, usually with the help of people from the same native place. Skilled industrial workers from the cities tended to have more education, confidence, and job security, and they were fully involved in urban culture. Unskilled workers recruited from the countryside regarded their sojourn in the cities as temporary and retained much of their rural culture. They visited their home villages regularly and traveled home for the harvest. Men sought wives in their home communities. After a few years in the mills, women often returned to the villages to marry and bring up children. Such returnees were succeeded by younger cohorts.

Many of the highly skilled early industrial workers were recruited from among Cantonese shipyard and handicraft artisans. In 1872, when Zuo Zongtang set up an arsenal in Lanzhou in northwest China, he recruited workers in Guangzhou, over 1,000 miles away. Population figures show that in 1885 Cantonese made up 20 percent of Shanghai's Chinese population, but only 4 percent by 1935. In the early twentieth century, textile and food processing enterprises began to dominate the industrial scene. The low-skilled workers these industries needed in great numbers could be drawn from the rural hinterland of the industrial cities.

RECRUITMENT AND CONDITIONS

Unskilled workers were recruited in their villages by labor contractors who painted a rosy picture of their future lives. The contractors guided them to the city and found them jobs and accommodation, services for which the workers paid dearly. Contractors recruited in regions where they had ties, and brought their clients to gang masters or factory overseers with whom they also had native place connections. Entry to the factories was controlled by gang masters and factory overseers. The result of this pattern of recruitment was that particular workshops and occupations came to be dominated by people from the same native places. In Shanghai, the hardest and lowest skilled work was done by workers from Subei (an area north of the Yangzi often afflicted by famine). The higher skilled workers came from Jiangnan or from south China. Occupational distinctions were reinforced by cultural differences of dialect, eating habits, and clothing.

Wages were low and working hours long. Highly mechanized factories usually worked two shifts of 12 hours each. Less capital-intensive ones worked a single shift that could be 16 or even 18 hours. There was one rest day per fortnight. Work discipline was severe, and workers could be fired for illness or pregnancy. The numerous child workers enjoyed no legal protections. Housing was overcrowded, with whole families occupying one or two rooms. Many lived in shantytown huts without water or sanitation facilities. Others slept in primitive dormitories in the factory compound; this provision, widely favored in East Asian industrialization, gave management 24-hour control over its labor force. Young single rural migrants accepted dormitories because no other accommodation was available to them.

ORGANIZED LABOR

From the time of the 1911 Revolution, labor unions began to appear alongside older organizations such as guilds, secret societies, and gangs. In the 1920s, at the height of the labor movement, the Guomindang and the Chinese Communist Party cooperated and competed to organize the workers. Despite profound divisions in the working class, the labor movement demonstrated surprising strength. Skilled workers had the greatest capacity for organization and sustained activity, but there was mass participation by unskilled workers in anti-imperialist actions such as the great stoppage directed against the British in Hong Kong and Guangzhou in 1922, and the general strike that followed the shooting of demonstrators by British-officered police in Shanghai in May 1925. These events marked the peak of the labor movement's prominence in national politics. After the 1927 break between the Guomindang and the Chinese Communist Party, many labor leaders and activists were killed and the trade unions were severely weakened. In Shanghai, Chiang Kai-shek's Guomindang allied with wealthy industrialists made use of the mafia-like Qing Bang (Green Gang) to repress the unions. Subsequently, the Green Gang extended its control over many aspects of Shanghai life, including industrial worksites and unions.

Industry showed modest growth in the 1930s, as did the numbers of industrial workers. The Green Gang effectively controlled the Shanghai unions on behalf of the Nationalist government. Labor protests continued, and strikes for better conditions sometimes succeeded, but the labor movement had become much less important on the national scene.

During the war with Japan (1937–1945) China's industrial base shrank. Much industry was transferred to southwest China and came under state control. In some of these state factories the wartime Guomindang government developed a system of enterprise-administered labor management and welfare that resembled the post-1949 *danwei* system. In Japanese-occupied China, especially in Shanghai, organized labor again became politicized. The Communist Party rebuilt its underground organization in industrial Shanghai and successfully won over some gang members. Worker unrest was partly a manifestation of nationalist anti-Japanese sentiments, and partly a protest against inflation. By 1942 the workers' cost of living in Shanghai had risen to ten times what it had been in 1937.

Unionization developed rapidly after the war. Membership in official unions in Shanghai grew from 228,000 in 1945 to 527,500 in early 1947 (Perry 1993, p. 121). Guomindang attempts to suppress Communist influence in the labor movement were largely unsuccessful. Like most of the urban population, industrial workers suffered terrible privations and insecurity during the hyperinflation of the late 1940s and their increasing disaffection with the Guomindang government eased the Communist takeover of the cities from 1948 to 1949.

SEE ALSO *Labor; Migrant Workers; Urban China: Cities and Urbanization, 1800–1949.*

BIBLIOGRAPHY

Bastid-Bruguière, Marianne. "Currents of Social Change," in John K. Fairbank and Kwang-Ching Liu, eds., *The Cambridge History of China*, vol. 11, *Late Ch'ing, 1800-1911, part 2.* Cambridge, U.K.: Cambridge University Press, 1980.

Chesneaux, Jean. *The Chinese Labor Movement, 1919–1927.* Stanford, CA: Stanford University Press, 1968.

Frazier, Mark W. *The Making of the Chinese Industrial Workplace: State, Revolution, and Labor Management.* Cambridge, U.K.: Cambridge University Press, 2002.

Hershatter, Gail. *The Workers of Tianjin, 1900–1949.* Stanford, CA: Stanford University Press, 1986.

Honig, Emily. *Sisters and Strangers: Women in the Shanghai Cotton Mills, 1919–1949.* Stanford, CA: Stanford University Press, 1986.

Perry, Elizabeth. *Shanghai on Strike: The Politics of Chinese Labor.* Stanford, CA: Stanford University Press, 1993.

Pong, David. Government Enterprises and Industrial Relations in Late Qing China. *Australian Journal of Politics and History* 47, no. 1 (March 2001): 4–23.

Rowe, William T. *Hankow: Conflict and Community in a Chinese City, 1796–1865.* Stanford, CA: Stanford University Press, 1989.

Delia Davin

WU CHANGSHI (WU JUNQING)
1844–1927

Wu Changshi (often pronounced Wu Changshuo), whose career best represents the evolution of artistic patterns from late imperial China to the modern era, was the most innovative painter and calligrapher in China during the early twentieth century. Born into a declining scholarly family in Anji, Zhejiang Province, Wu experienced almost all the major chaotic events of the last phase of the Qing dynasty (1644–1912). In his early years he sought an official career, as did most Confucian scholars. But societal circumstances and his personal temperament forced him to give up this career trajectory, and he turned instead to art.

Wu was best known for his calligraphy in the seal (*zhuan*) and stone-drum (*shigu*) scripts. His lifelong practice of stone-drum script and seal carving enabled him more naturally and spontaneously to produce epigraphic effects in his painting. He learned painting in his middle thirties, but like many Chinese painters of earlier times, his work did not mature until old age. Wu studied briefly in middle age, during the 1880s, under Ren Yi (1840–1895), but was mostly self-taught as a painter. The subject matter of his paintings is relatively narrow, usually flowers and rocks, but he realized the ultimate ideal of literati painting: combining poetry, calligraphy, and painting. His greatest contribution to the development of Chinese art lies in his full integration of the aesthetics of poetry, calligraphy, and seal carving into a form of painting that was recognizably modern. Bronze and stone epigraphic styles (*jinshiqi*) greatly enriched his painting and calligraphy, which, based on premodern principles of calligraphic design, and combined with an almost romantic affection for the lyrical qualities of erosion, patina, and the effects of time, produced qualities of authenticity and abstraction in his brushwork that were in tune with modern aesthetic tastes of the twentieth century. Although he was not the first to introduce epigraphic tastes to painting, a tendency equally strong in the works of Jin Nong (1684–1764) and Zhao Zhiqian (1829–1884), his contribution was unique. He realized the ultimate ideal of literati painting: combining poetry, calligraphy, and painting. His style features powerful brushwork, with evident vigor, spontaneity, and a feeling of simple, awkward, primitive innocence (*zhuo*). Wu's paintings are to be viewed not as images from nature but as arrangements of plants and rocks in an abstract space.

During the second half of his career, Wu lived in Shanghai, selling paintings to make a living. His patrons were either wealthy, educated people, including former Confucian officials, or merchants and middle-class urban residents. In his painting, although he tried to maintain and reinvigorate traditional literati tastes, he also incorporated some elements of popular urban tastes, including bright color and overtly auspicious subject matter. Because his intention was to revive the best of China's ancient culture, such novelty was not his goal, and he would have preferred to be called a revivalist rather than an innovator. He thus rejected the delicacy long associated with court painting and sought to convey power in the individualistic cultural vocabulary of the scholar.

Later observers refer to a "Shanghai school" of painting, supported by the nouveau-riche merchants of the treaty port, and which was characterized more by themes taken from popular culture and vivid appealing color than by any uniformity in style. Although a frequent visitor to the city in earlier years, Wu settled permanently in Shanghai in 1912. He had a remarkable knack for satisfying a range of different kinds of patrons with art that basically adhered to elite standards. His innovations inspired many emulators during the last fifteen years of his life, and in some sense, his work marked a turning point in the Shanghai school. The style of bird-and-flower painting practiced by his many followers is sometimes referred to as the "late Shanghai school," but actually influenced artists all over China, the most famous of whom was Qi Baishi in Beijing.

Wu's painting, with its literati themes, epigraphic essence, and unrestrained boldness, may be seen as intuitively expressing the psychological aspirations of his generation of Confucian scholars—men who continued to believe that China's traditional culture was powerful enough to overcome any obstacle, but that the corruption and chaos of the contemporary period had left it pathetically weak. This was a time when refined beauty had little meaning. The forcefulness of Wu's brushwork, then, may be viewed as the challenge of an individual to the societal conditions that had conspired to destroy his hopes. It

would not be overinterpreting to see in his straightforward vigor and strength the protest of a Confucian scholar who had seen his ideals destroyed by the forces of history but would never quietly surrender.

SEE ALSO *Calligraphy; Chinese Painting (guohua); Epigraphic School of Art; Shanghai School of Painting.*

BIBLIOGRAPHY

Andrews, Julia F., and Kuiyi Shen. *A Century in Crisis: Modernity and Tradition in the Art of Twentieth Century China.* New York: Guggenheim Museum and Abrams, 1998.

Brown, Claudia, and Ju-hsi Chou. *Transcending Turmoil: Painting at the Close of China's Empire, 1796–1911.* Phoenix, AZ: Phoenix Art Museum, 1992.

Cahill, James. The Shanghai School in Later Chinese Painting. In *Twentieth-Century Chinese Painting*, ed. Mayching Kao, 54–77. New York: Oxford University Press, 1988.

Go Shōseki, Sei Hakuseki [Wu Changshi, Qi Baishi]. Vol. 10 of *Bunjinga suihen* [The essential masters of literati painting]. Tokyo: Chūō Kōron Sha, 1986.

Kuiyi Shen

WU HUFAN
1894–1968

One of the most influential connoisseurs and outstanding collectors of Chinese calligraphy and painting in the Republican period, Wu Hufan (style names: Yujun, Dongzhuang; sobriquets: Chou Yi, Qian'an; studio names: Meijing Shuwu, Si Outang) was also an important painter of Chinese painting (*guohua*), as well as a calligrapher and lyricist. A native from Suzhou and the scion of an old scholar-class family with a rich art heritage, he was adopted by his prominent grand-uncle Wu Dacheng (1835–1902). After his marriage with Pan Jingshu (1892–1939), a niece of the collector Pan Zuyin, Wu Hufan moved to Shanghai in 1924. Partly on account of his mentor Ye Gongchuo, Wu participated in the organization of such important exhibitions in the Republican era as the First National Exhibition of Art in Shanghai (1929), Chinesische Malerei der Gegenwart (contemporary Chinese painting) in Berlin (1934), and the International Exhibition of Chinese Art in London (1935/36). Among Wu Hufan's students, the collector Wang Jiqian (C. C. Wang) and the painting expert Xu Bangda were the most prominent. After the Communist takeover, Wu Hufan had to reduce his activity as a connoisseur-collector. He lived on the income from his paintings and supported his family by selling items from his art collection. In 1956 he was designated as the first director of the Shanghai Painting Institute (Shanghai Zhongguo Huayuan). The suggestion was dropped, however, as a result of criticism that his elitist family background made him not suitable for the position. In the anti-rightist campaign of 1957, Wu Hufan was branded an "enemy of the people." His fragile state of health and his maltreatment by the authorities during the Cultural Revolution eventually led to his tragic suicide on August 11, 1968. Wu Hufan was officially rehabilitated in 1978.

As an artist, Wu Hufan became best known for his misty blue-green landscapes and his monochrome paintings of bamboo. His elegant painting style was based on his study of the brushwork of Yuan dynasty literati paintings, filtered through the aesthetic notions of subsequent Suzhou artists. The sometimes bright color scheme and refined brush manner of his works is influenced by later artists active in Suzhou, including Lu Hui (1851–1920). A major thematic shift can be seen in his paintings after he became a teacher at the Shanghai Painting Institute in the early 1960s. Remarkable are his *Red Flag on the Mount Everest* (1960), *Celebration of the Atomic Bomb Explosion* (1965), and *Red Bricks* (*Hong Zhuan*). In the latter, Wu Hufan made use of a pun to satirize the constant Communist demand that painters be "both red and professional" (*you hong you zhuan*). Wu Hufan's calligraphy of the 1920s is written in a graceful and elegant regular-script style (*kaishu*). It evolves into a more vigorous running-script style (*xingshu*) in the mid-1930s. Wu occasionally also practiced the archaic seal script (*zhuanshu*). A major shift in his calligraphy occurred during the Mao era, when he emulated the cursive-script style (*caoshu*) of the monk Huaisu (737–799) of the Tang dynasty, a script style advocated by Mao Zedong.

Wu Hufan inherited parts of his art collection from Wu Dacheng, his maternal grandfather Shen Shuyong (1832–1873), and Pan Zuyin. Among the most precious items were a Song dynasty rubbing album from the Huadu Temple Reliquary Engraving (*Huadusi taming*) by the Tang court calligrapher Ouyang Xun (557–641) and the *Meihua xishenpu* (Manual of plum-blossom likenesses) by Song Boren, printed in 1261. In addition, Wu acquired the hanging scroll *Furong yuanyang tu* (Hibiscus and mandarin ducks) by Zhang Zhong (fl. fourteenth century), from the former imperial collection, and the hitherto lost opening section *Shengshan tu* (literally "surviving mountain") of the *Fuchunshan ju tu* (Dwelling in the Fuchun Mountains) handscroll by Huang Gongwang, dated 1350.

Wu Hufan left numerous inscriptions on Chinese paintings and calligraphy that he identified, authenticated, or judged. Some of them reveal his accurate and systematic research. Before the scholarly article became ubiquitous, Wu Hufan published some of his inscriptions in journals. To make his point he even mounted photographic reproductions and printed texts directly on the works of art, or asked a foreign scholar to contribute to the research with a comment to be written on the work proper. Wu Hufan's

authoritative statements have gained him recognition in the international community of art scholars, curators, and the art market. He thus contributed to transforming art history from traditional connoisseurship to a modern discipline. Equally important, the quality of his painting and scholarship contributed to the survival of traditional Chinese painting amid China's modernization.

SEE ALSO *Chinese Painting* (guohua); *Collections and Collecting; Connoisseurship.*

BIBLIOGRAPHY

Andrews, Julia F. *Painters and Politics in the People's Republic of China, 1949–1979.* Berkeley: University of California Press, 1994.

Dai Xiaojing. Yanyun gongyang, taoxie jiangshan: Wu Hufan zhuanlüe [Nurtured by clouds, painting fine streams and mountains: A short biography of Wu Hufan]. *Duoyun*, no. 10 (May 1986): 138–160.

Spee, Clarissa von. *Wu Hufan: A Twentieth Century Chinese Art Connoisseur in Shanghai.* Berlin: Reimer, 2008.

Clarissa von Spee

WU SHUJUAN (WU XINGFEN)
1853–1930

Wu Shujuan (Wu Xingfen, Xingfen Nüshi, Xingfen Laoren) was a traditionalist artist who was highly esteemed in Shanghai in the early twentieth century. Wu Shujuan was a native of She County, Anhui Province. She first learned to paint under her father, Wu Hongxun (Wu Zijia), who was an adviser to Zeng Guofan (1811–1872) and a painter of orchids, bamboo, and landscapes. She also studied the family art collection of her husband, Tang Kunhua (Tang Guangzhao), an official who spent his retirement enjoying poetry, calligraphy, and painting with Wu Shujuan. Early in her career, Wu mastered bird-and-flower painting in the manner of Yun Shouping (1633–1690). She was a confident painter of landscapes, which she rendered in a number of styles that were popular in Shanghai, and contemporary writers, impressed by the vigor with which she traveled to famous places, took particular note of her topographical works. Wu also painted human figures in styles similar to those of Qian Huian (1833–1911) and Ren Bonian (1840–1895), and she was well known for her connoisseurship.

Wu Shujuan was active in the modern Shanghai art world. She was a member of the Tingyun Shuhuashe (Unmoving Clouds Calligraphy and Painting Society), and with Wu Changshi (1844–1927) and Wang Yiting (1867–1938) she headed the national essence (*guocui*) section of the

Tianmahui (Heavenly Horse Society). Wu Shujuan painted for such modern ends as charity, exhibiting works in Europe in 1918 to raise funds for victims of the war. She also sought to bridge the Chinese and Japanese art worlds, supporting the Sino-Japanese Art Society (Zhong-Ri Meishu Xiehui) by offering readers of its *Sino-Japanese Art Monthly* (*Zhong-Ri meishu yuebao*) the opportunity to purchase her paintings at half their market price. In addition, she exhibited paintings in Tokyo at the 1922 Sino-Japanese Art Exhibition and the 1929 Modern Sino-Japanese Painting Exhibition. Wu Shujuan presented her work to a domestic audience as well, exhibiting at China's First National Exhibition of 1929, and she promoted traditional Chinese painting by teaching younger students, both male and female. These included Tang Xiong (1892–1935), her son, and Li Qiujun (1899–1973), one of Shanghai's best-known, younger female painters.

Wu Shujuan was a highly successful artist. One of her works, which was selected to represent China at an international exhibition in Rome in 1910, captured the imagination of the queen of Italy and was purchased for the royal collection. When Tang Xiong published some of Wu's better paintings in 1915, many Asian and Western art lovers purchased the catalog. By the 1920s, Wu's contemporaries were likening her to Chen Shu (1660–1736), a famed female artist of the Qing dynasty (1644–1912). However, Wu Shujuan was not viewed merely as a woman who could paint. Along with Wu Changshi she was known as one of the "two Wus" of Shanghai, and her accomplishments were such that many Chinese and Japanese artists and dignitaries came to her home to celebrate her seventieth birthday, with a number of Shanghai's best artists producing collaborative works in her honor.

SEE ALSO *Art Exhibitions Abroad; Art, National Essence Movement in; Chinese Painting (guohua); Women in the Visual Arts; Wu Changshi (Wu Junqing).*

BIBLIOGRAPHY

Weidner, Marsha, ed. *Views from Jade Terrace: Chinese Women Artists, 1300–1912.* Indianapolis, IN: Indianapolis Museum of Art; New York: Rizzoli, 1988.

Zhong-Ri meishu yuebao [Sino-Japanese art monthly] 1, no. 1 (March 1922): 5–8.

Walter B. Davis

WUHAN

Wuhan, the capital of Hubei Province, is one of the largest cities in China. The Wuhan metropolitan area is composed of three towns: Wuchang, Hankou, and Hanyang. The name *Wuhan* is formed from combining the initial character *wu* from the first of these place names with the character *han* from the other two.

Wuhan is located at the intersection of the Han River with the middle reaches of the Yangzi, and the area has long been known as the "thoroughfare of nine provinces." It represents a center of communication for almost three-quarters of China's territory. Wuhan is a major transportation hub with dozens of railways, roads, expressways, and waterways connecting the east with the west, channeling the north to the south, and linking Central China with the seas. Wuhan is well connected with the major cities of different regions of China, including the national capital, Beijing, Shanghai in eastern China, Guangzhou in southern China, Chengdu in western China, and Xi'an in northwestern China. All these cities lie within a 1,000-kilometer radius of Wuhan.

INDUSTRIAL AND ECONOMIC DEVELOPMENT

Occupying a site first settled more than three thousand years ago, Wuhan has long been a busy port. In 1861, after China's defeat in the Second Opium War (1856–1860), Hankou was opened as a treaty port and became the site of British, French, German, Russian, and Japanese concessions and consulates. By the early 1920s, Hankou was second only to Shanghai in importance as a financial center in China, boasting branches of more than seventy banks, including eighteen foreign banks. The number of permanent residents in the tri-city complex had by that time reached over one million, including three thousand foreign residents (Rowe 1984).

Wuhan was also one of the birthplaces of China's modern industry, earning it the nickname the "Chicago of China" (Weyl 1918). The Hanyang Steel & Iron Company, established in 1891, was one of the first modern manufacturing operations in China and the largest of its kind in Asia at that time. Its manufacturing productive capacity ranked second in China after Shanghai, accounting for 14 percent of the national total.

Politically, Wuhan was one of the most sensitive areas in twentieth-century China. It was the Wuchang Uprising in 1911 that precipitated a nationwide revolution, leading to the downfall of the Qing dynasty (1644–1912) and the establishment of the Republic of China. In the early stages of the Nationalist revolution in 1926, the Guomindang government relocated its capital from Guangzhou to Wuhan, which briefly provided a leftist alternative to the right-wing regime established by Chiang Kai-shek (Jiang Jieshi) in Nanjing the following year. Four decades later, in July 1967, Wuhan was the site of one of the most violent and destabilizing incidents of the Cultural Revolution, when around one million people became caught up in a factional struggle that approached the dimensions of a civil war.

Modern municipal government in Wuhan was created during the city's tenure as the Nationalist capital, when the three towns were combined and administered by a unified government. After the pre-1930 golden age of economic development, the three towns split apart due to war and frequent flooding. During the invasion of the Japanese after the fall of Shanghai and Nanjing in 1937, Wuhan was used by China as the "centerpiece of an emerging strategy" of defense against the Japanese (Mackinnon 2008, p. 17). The city fell and was in ruins by the end of 1938, resulting in the exodus of more than a million people. The population fell from about two million before the war to 0.31 million in 1940. Demographic and economic recovery did not become evident until the late 1950s.

The flat terrain and difficult hydraulic environment have historically rendered Wuhan highly vulnerable to flooding. Devastating floods in 1931 almost entirely destroyed the tricity complex, leaving some 36,000 people dead and around half a million homeless (Song Ruhai 1931). However, Wuhan has also taken advantage of the natural water resources of the Yangzi River, which is the third-largest river of the world, as well as the Han River, its largest tributary, and the 189 lakes in the basin. The average water resource per person in Wuhan far exceeds that available to most of the world's larger cities.

CIRCUMSTANCES AFTER 1949

Wuhan's three towns have functioned as a powerful combination under a single administrative municipal government since the formation of the People's Republic of China in 1949. Their integration was reinforced by infrastructural development, including construction of two bridges across the Han River and the "First Bridge" across the Yangzi, which was built in the 1950s. On account of its strong economic potential and regional advantage, Wuhan was selected as one of the "key cities" for socialist development in the First Five-Year Plan (1953–1957), a designation that involved hosting China's major manufacturing projects (in particular, those sponsored by the Soviet Union). These included the Wuhan Steel Corporation, Wuhan Dockyard, the Heavy Machine

A flooded park in Wuhan, Hubei province, August 2, 2007. *Situated at the convergence of the Yangzi and the Han rivers, the city of Wuhan serves as a major transportation hub in China. Despite a well-established industrial infrastructure, however, Wuhan has lagged behind coastal Chinese cities enjoying increased economic activity after market-based reforms instituted in the 1980s.* © ZHOU CHAO/EPA/CORBIS

Factory, and the Thermoelectric House. The revived economic importance of the city was manifest in the growth of employment in the state sector from 124,000 personnel in 1950 to 844,000 in 1960. In 1981 Wuhan ranked as the fourth-largest industrial center in China, next to Shanghai, Beijing, and Tianjin (Liu Shengjia 2000).

Since the economic reforms launched in 1978, Wuhan has experienced rapid economic growth and urban transformation. Its metropolitan area covers 8,494 square kilometers. Its population increased from 5.5 million in 1978 to 9.1 million in 2006, with around 6,100,000 residents in the city's built-up urban area. Three development/industrial urban districts have been established: Wuhan Economic and Technology Development District, Donghu New Technology District, and Wujiashan Taiwan Investment District. These districts have attracted more than one-third of total French investment in China, making Wuhan China's most significant beneficiary of French business interests (*People's Daily* 2005).

Host to thirty universities and more than seven hundred scientific research institutes, Wuhan ranks third after Beijing and Shanghai in scientific and educational capacity. In 2006 its gross domestic product (GDP) reached about 260 billion renminbi and approximately 30,200 renminbi (about $4,000) per capita (Wuhan Bureau of Statistics 2007). Wuhan's major sectors include a modern manufacturing industry with optic-electronic information, automobile and steel manufacturing, pharmaceutics, biological engineering, and new materials industries, including Wuhan Iron & Steel Company and Dongfeng-Citroën Automobile Company. The city's commercial activities are also thriving. Wuhan's Hanzhen Jie has emerged as one of the largest and most dynamic commercial districts in Central China.

However, compared with other cities in China, Wuhan's economic-growth pace has been relatively slow since the adoption of the open-door policy. To some degree, Wuhan and its associated region—Central China—have become forgotten corners. The coastal cities were the first to benefit from special policies and privileges encouraging development, while the more recent "go west" policy and the program of "revitalization of the Northeast" bypassed Wuhan and Central China. Although still the largest transportation hub and distribution center in Central China, Wuhan has declined in the urban hierarchy in terms of economic importance. Its ranking dropped from fourth in the early 1980s to sixteenth in 2006 in terms of GDP. It is outranked by such open coastal cities as Guangzhou and Shenzhen (in Guangdong), large cities such as Chengdu (in Sichuan) and Chongqing in the west, and even by small and medium-sized cities such as Dongguan (in Guangdong), Suzhou (in Jiangsu), and Ningbo (in Zhejiang). "When will it be Wuhan's turn?" is not just an economic question, but also a political issue for the central government to answer.

SEE ALSO *Hunan and Hubei; Revolution of 1911; Treaty Ports; Urban China: Cities and Urbanization, 1800–1949; Urban China: Organizing Principles of Cities; Urban China: Urban Planning since 1978.*

BIBLIOGRAPHY

Liu Shengjia. Wuhan chengshi fazhan zhanlue dingwei tiaojian yanjiu [A study on Wuhan's urban development strategy]. *Changjiang Luntan* [Yangtze tribune] 1 (2000): 26–29.

Mackinnon, Stephen R. *Wuhan, 1938: War, Refugees, and the Making of Modern China.* Berkeley: University of California Press, 2008.

People's Daily. Wuhan Absorbs Most French Investment in China. October 25, 2005.

Pi Mingxiu and Yong Wu. *Hankou wubai nian* [500 years of Hankou]. Wuhan, PRC: Hubei Education Publishing, 1999.

Rowe, William T. *Hankow: Commerce and Society in a Chinese City, 1796–1889.* Stanford, CA: Stanford University Press, 1984.

Song Ruhai. *Hankou luchenji* [Record of Hankou's submerge]. Hankou, PRC: Hankou Ziyou Xibao, 1931.

Weyl, Walter. The Chicago of China. *Harper's Magazine* (October 1918): 716–724.

Wuhan Bureau of Statistics. *Wuhan Statistical Yearbook.* Wuhan, PRC: Wuhan Publishing, 2007.

Mark Y. L. Wang

XI'AN

Xi'an is the capital of Shaanxi Province in central China. *Xi'an* literally means "western peace," although the city has had different names during its long history, and before the Ming dynasty (1368–1644) was called Chang'an. The earliest evidence of human activity in the area dates back half a million years. The Banpo site, a short distance from modern Xi'an, is a Neolithic settlement dating back 5,000 years. Xi'an served as the capital of at least thirteen dynasties, and in the Tang (618–907) ranked as the world's greatest city, with, according to visitors, a population of over a million people. Located on the Silk route, the main trading route between Europe and East Asia, Xi'an enjoyed a highly international population, with Japanese, Buddhists from Inner Asia, and merchants from India, Persia, and the Middle East. This diversity created an extraordinarily vibrant, open culture that had a major impact on the centuries that followed.

GEOGRAPHY AND CLIMATE

Geographically, Xi'an is located an average of approximately 400 meters above sea level on the Guanzhong Plain. The city is served by eight rivers, the most significant of which is the Wei River. Xi'an enjoys hot summers (with a high of 88 degrees Fahrenheit, 30.6 degrees centigrade in July) and cold, dry winters (with a low of 25 degrees Fahrenheit, minus 3.9 degrees centigrade), with most rain falling between August and October. Its 2008 population stood at 7.4 million, with the city divided into a number of subdistricts. Over 99 percent of Xi'an's population are Han, with a small population of Hui Muslims, many of them living around the ancient mosque in the city center.

HISTORY

The greatest material remnant of Xi'an's significance in the history of ancient China and the construction of the modern Chinese nation was not discovered till 1974, toward the end of the decade of the Cultural Revolution, when farmers digging for wells uncovered the remains of the vast burial memorial to the first emperor, Qin Shi Huangdi (259–210 BCE). Hundreds of individually crafted terra-cotta warriors standing guard over the entrance to the emperor's tomb were painstakingly excavated over the following years. This find transformed Xi'an into a major international tourist destination, with heads of state, presidents, and more than 800,000 tourists visiting the city each year.

Xi'an's other major tourist sites include the tomb of the empress Wu Zetian (625–705), the only woman ever to have ruled China as empress; the Big Wild Goose Pagoda; the remains of the Ming dynasty city walls; and the Huaqing hot springs, where the young general Zhang Xueliang (1901–2001) was to kidnap Chiang Kai-shek (Jiang Jieshi), head of the Nationalist Army, in 1936, demanding that he create a Second United Front with Mao Zedong's Communists to fight against the Japanese. Zhang succeeded in the task, though he was to spend the next five decades under house arrest as a punishment from Chiang.

Xi'an remained relatively unscathed during World War II (1937–1945), with only sporadic air attacks from the Japanese army. But during this period, the city took in a large number of migrants, expanding its population. With the founding of the People's Republic of China in 1949, there was a brief period during which Xi'an was considered as the capital of the new country, though in the end Beijing's superior strategic position (near the massive port of Tianjin and the Russian and Mongolian borders) won out.

In the 1950s and 1960s, Xi'an figured in China's strategic defense plan when major aviation, aero-engine, and national-defense industries moved to the city. These industries are still important in the city's economy, with Rolls-Royce, Airbus, and Boeing all operating joint ventures for civilian aircraft manufacturing at the Xi'an Aviation Corporation and the Xi'an Aero-engine Corporation. This shift of key strategic heavy industries deeper inland into China became known as the Third Front; it accompanied the downturn of relations with the Soviet Union from the late 1950s onward. The shift was predicated on the belief that Xi'an, Chengdu, and other hinterland cities would be harder to attack.

EDUCATION AND DEVELOPMENT

This period also saw the establishment in Xi'an of new universities, such as the Shanghai Jiaotong University. Xi'an is now served by some forty public and thirty-five private universities. In addition to these, the city has around 700 scientific research institutes. Xi'an's human capital and well-educated population is one of its main strengths, although it has suffered from the traditional problems of most of China's western cities: little experience in management, poor infrastructure, a politically backward leadership, and its location in a generally less developed province.

The completion in 2000 of a major new airport, the Xianyang Airport, and the establishment of direct air links to Japan, Germany, Hong Kong, and South Korea, helped greatly to open Xi'an to the world. The airport is quarter-owned by Frankfurt Airport, making it one of the first of China's airports to sanction foreign stakeholders. The opening of the airport was accompanied by the construction of good-quality highways to Beijing and Shanghai. Xi'an is also one of the main rail hubs of central China.

Since China's reform process started in 1978, Xi'an has developed as a manufacturing center, and has attempted to exploit its well-educated workforce to become one of China's major software and technology centers. Two high-tech zones have been set up: the Xi'an Economic Development Zone and the Xi'an High-Tech Industry Development Zone. The latter encompassed a total of 8,681 companies in 2006, with 813 foreign investors, among them NEC, Brother, and Fujitsu from Japan. As of 2005, Xi'an had 2,258 foreign-invested enterprises, with 3.12 billion U.S. dollars of utilized investment, more than a fivefold increase over the amount in 2000. Such companies as HSBC, BP, IBM, and ABB were all present in the city. Xi'an's major foreign investors were Japan, Taiwan, and South Korea, but there were significant enclaves of American and European investment. Some of the investors hoped to exploit Xi'an's role as one of the major hubs of the Great Western Development Scheme, launched under former President Jiang Zemin in 1999 and 2000. A Xi'an-based fertilizer company listed on the London Stock Exchange secondary market in early 2006, raising almost 100 million pounds.

CHALLENGES

The fact remains, however, that economically Xi'an still ranks low among Chinese cities, with a per capita annual gross domestic product of 19,560 Chinese yuan ($2,600) in 2006. Despite an 85 percent increase over the figure of five years earlier, Xi'an still ranks far behind Beijing, Shanghai, Guangzhou, and other coastal cities. Xi'an has also suffered from a brain-drain problem, with the well educated and returnees from overseas universities opting to seek work in the coastal provinces.

Despite banning the use of coal in the city in 2002 and replacing it with gas, and improving the energy supply through the construction of a major power station, Xi'an's air quality is among the worst in China. And, according to the Shaanxi Provincial Environmental Bureau, 77 percent of the water taken from the Wei River was not fit for human use in 2004. Massive construction projects throughout the city only add to the environmental problems, meaning that Xi'an, like much of the rest of China, is trying to balance economic performance against the preservation of its natural and historical environment.

SEE ALSO *Architecture, History of: Architecture, 1949– 1979; Shaanxi; Tourism; Urban China: Cities and Urbanization, 1800–1949; Urban China: Organizing Principles of Cities; Urban China: Urban Planning since 1978.*

BIBLIOGRAPHY

Lewis, Mark Edward. *The Early Chinese Empires: Qin and Han.* Cambridge, MA: Belknap Press, 2007.

Mooney, Paul, Catherine Maudsley, and Gerald Hatherly. *Xi'an, Shaanxi, and the Terracotta Army.* Hong Kong: Odyssey, 2005.

Portal, Jane. *The First Emperor: China's Terracotta Army.* London: British Museum Press, 2007.

Wu Dianwei (Tien-Wei Wu). *Sian Incident: A Pivotal Point in Modern Chinese History.* Ann Arbor: Center for Chinese Studies, University of Michigan, 1976.

Xi'an Municipality, official government Web site. http://www.xa .gov.cn/structure/index.htm.

Kerry Brown

XIAFANG

Xiafang, meaning "sending down," was a feature of Maoist society from the early days of the revolution in Yan'an to the last years of the Cultural Revolution (1966–1969). In Yan'an, *xiafang* meant sending cadres (officials) down to the villages to work and live. After 1949 it involved sending cadres and managers to do manual labor on the shop floor or in the villages. In these cases, the cadres' stay was limited, although it could be as long as a few months or a year. In 1956 Liu Shaoqi initiated a new *xiafang* movement, sending urban cadres to the countryside to combat bureaucratic ossification. At the same time, to ease youth unemployment, many school-leavers were sent to work in the countryside or to border regions for the rest of their lives instead of being allocated jobs in the city.

Xiafang for young people was presented as a glorious revolutionary choice, but as political exile it could also be a punishment. In the 1957 "anti-rightist" movement, thousands of disgraced intellectuals were sent to reform themselves through labor in the countryside, including the sociologist Fei Xiaotong and famous writers such as Ding Ling and Liu Binyan.

Investigative work teams of urban cadres and students were "sent down" to the countryside in the course of the Socialist Education campaign (1962–1965) to restore collectivization and root out corruption among village cadres. Liu Shaoqi and Deng Xiaoping worked on policy documents for this movement, and Liu and his wife both went to the villages. Mao Zedong later accused them of having worked against socialism, using the work teams in an authoritarian way to decide where abuses had arisen and refusing to allow the local people a democratic role in the movement.

All these forms of *xiafang* were eclipsed by the "up to the mountains and down to the countryside" movement (*shangshan xiaxiang*) starting in 1968 when Mao called educated youth to receive reeducation from the poor and lower-middle peasants. At the same time, millions of cadres were sent for ideological training in May 7 cadre schools in the countryside.

RATIONALE FOR *XIAFANG*

The populist idea that the corrupting influence of the cities had to be removed through contact with the revolutionary peasant masses has a long history in Chinese Marxist thought. As early as 1918, Li Dazhao, later a founder member of the Communist Party, called on his students to leave the corrupting life of the cities and universities to take up hoes and plows in the villages (Meisner 1971, p. 17).

The idea that urbanites should learn from the peasants was not the only rationale for *xiafang*. It was also hoped that if educated young people used their skills for rural development, the gap between the city and the countryside would be narrowed. The rustication of young urbanites could solve high rates of urban unemployment and supply labor to frontier areas or remote, underdeveloped, and sparsely populated places. Political heretics could be both punished and reformed through *xiafang*. Finally, from 1968, millions of urban Red Guards, who posed both an unemployment and a law-and-order problem to the cities, were absorbed into the rural areas.

Xiafang exiled people far from their homes, split up families, and caused immense human suffering. Even before Mao's death in 1976, urban families were allowed to choose one child to bring back from the countryside. In the reform era, cadre schools were closed and the ideal of *xiafang* was rejected. Millions returned with or without permission, but others who had made their lives in the rural areas remained there.

The *xiafang* movements gave rise to a rich memoir literature. For example, Yang Jiang, a professor of literature from Beijing, wrote an eloquent chronicle of cadre school life, and Yang Rae, an "educated youth" sent to China's Great Northern Waste, produced a moving record of her experience as a seventeen year old working on a pig farm.

SEE ALSO *Cadre System; Chinese Marxism: Mao Zedong Thought; Communist Party; Sent-down Educated Youth.*

BIBLIOGRAPHY

Bernstein, Thomas P. *Up to the Mountains and Down to the Villages: The Transfer of Youth from Urban to Rural China.* New Haven, CT: Yale University Press, 1977.

Meisner, Maurice. Leninism and Maoism: Some Populist Perspectives on Marxism Leninism in China. *China Quarterly* 45 (1971): 2–36.

Yang Jiang. *A Cadre School Life: Six Chapters.* Trans. Geremie Barmé with Bennett Lee. Hong Kong: Joint Publishing, 1982.

Yang Rae. *Spider Eaters: A Memoir.* Berkeley: University of California Press, 1997.

Delia Davin

XIAMEN (AMOY)

Xiamen is a subtropical coastal city and the commercial hub of southern Fujian Province. It consists of Xiamen Island, Gulangyu Island, numerous lesser islands, and the coastal areas of the Jiulong River estuary, encompassing 973 square miles of land and 186 square miles of sea. Xiamen's excellent deepwater harbor is naturally flushed by the sea and ice-free year round. Of its 5 million residents, about 1.5 million live in the urban districts. Many speak Min dialect, which is also widely spoken in Taiwan and in overseas Chinese communities in Southeast Asia.

The name *Xiamen* translates as "mansion gate," but can be understood as "gate to China," reflecting the city's large role in China's international trade, transnational migration, and importation of modernity. Its rise to prominence started in the sixteenth century. The silting of the harbor of nearby Quanzhou (Cathay), previously the region's international trade center, shifted commerce to Xiamen. As trade with Europe grew, the Qing dynasty (1644–1912) established a customs house there in 1684, and Xiamen became a treaty port after the Opium War (1839–1842). Primary exports consisted of tea, porcelain, and foodstuffs, while opium and textiles were imported. By 1936 Xiamen's international trade was 5 percent of the national total and the city had a modern economy that included shipbuilding, banking, and textiles.

During the nineteenth century, a large migration of southern Fujianese to work the tin and rubber plantations of British Malaya occurred, giving rise to Xiamen's nickname as the "overseas Chinese ancestral homeland." This transnational movement helped make Xiamen a key site for a Chinese modernity based on imported Western concepts. The translator Lin Yutang (1895–1976), the reformist Buddhist monk Taixu (1890–1947), and the overseas Chinese philanthropist Chen Jiageng (Tan Kah Kee, 1874–1961) all resided in Xiamen.

After the founding of the People's Republic of China, the state built a causeway connecting Xiamen to the mainland and established a chemical industry during the 1950s. But development was derailed by national politics and Xiamen's status as the front line in the hostilities with the Nationalist Party on Taiwan. The city fell into a decadeslong period of decline and neglect. Xiamen's fortunes rebounded in 1980 upon its designation as one of China's four special economic zones, established to attract investment from overseas Chinese and foreign businesses. Control over key economic decisions, such as authority to approve investments of less than thirty million renminbi, devolved from the central state to the city government. New specialized zones were established for Taiwanese investment, high-tech, free trade, and export processing. A new downtown business district and a bridge linking Xiamen Island to the mainland were built, and the harbor was upgraded to handle container ships.

Since the 1980s, the local economy has especially benefited from investment from Hong Kong, Macau, and Taiwan. By 2000 Xiamen had 4,991 foreign direct investment projects, with a contracted amount of $17.527 billion (U.S. dollars) and an actual amount of $11.452 billion. Further economic reforms boosted foreign trade to $32.8 billion in imports and $20.5 billion in exports (2006 statistics). The city's economic activities include fishing, shipbuilding, food processing, textiles, machine-tool manufacturing, chemical industries, telecommunications, financial services, and tourism. Its urban economy has consistently ranked among China's most economically dynamic. In 2006 Xiamen's gross domestic product (GDP) was 116.2 billion

renminbi, an increase of 16.7 percent over the previous year, and per capita GDP was $6,546. Rapid development also led to corruption, as seen in the city's massive smuggling scandal uncovered in 1999, which involved the entrepreneur Lai Changxing and hundreds of local officials.

Xiamen's wealth has given it one of China's highest standards of living, with a per capita income of $7,172 that ranked fourth of all cities (2005 statistics). Careful attention to environmentally sound urban planning has garnered Xiamen numerous national awards, including designation as a "garden city" and as a United Nations "National Habitat." The city is also known as a creative center, especially in fashion design and Western classical music, and has many institutions of higher learning, most notably Xiamen University, founded by overseas Chinese in 1921. Additionally, Nanputuo Temple and other Buddhist temples, as well as churches, mosques, and Daoist shrines, make up a lively religious scene. These various aspects have led to Xiamen's ranking as one of China's most-livable cities.

Xiamen has also played a pivotal role in cross-strait communication with Taiwan and in dialogue with the Nationalist Party. For years, tourists came to Xiamen to gaze at the Nationalist-held Jinmen Islands, easily visible just off the coast. More recently, Xiamen was one of five cities selected to send and receive direct flights between China and Taiwan beginning July 4, 2008.

SEE ALSO *Chinese Overseas: Tan Kah Kee; Fujian; Treaty Ports; Urban China.*

BIBLIOGRAPHY

Chen Zhiming (Tan Chee-beng), ed. *Southern Fujian: Reproduction of Traditions in Post-Mao China.* Hong Kong: Chinese University of Hong Kong, 2006.

Cook, James A. Reimagining China: Xiamen, Overseas Chinese, and Transnational Modernity. In *Everyday Modernity in China,* eds. Madeleine Yue Dong and Joshua L. Goldstein, 156–194. Seattle: University of Washington Press, 2006.

Howell, Jude. *China Opens its Doors: The Politics of Economic Transition.* Boulder, CO: Lynne Rienner, 1993.

Wank, David L. *Commodifying Communism: Business, Trust, and Politics in a Chinese City.* New York: Cambridge University Press, 1999.

David L. Wank

XIAO QIAN (XIAO BINGQIAN)
1910–1999

Xiao Qian was a journalist, editor, essayist, and, prior to the Communist revolution, writer of imagistic, well-crafted fiction of social manners. He struggled after 1949 to adapt his near-native English-language skills, perfected during wartime residence in Britain, to the needs of the Maoist era as an editor and translator. Condemned as a rightist in 1957 and ostracized for the duration of Mao Zedong's rule, he reconstituted his literary career in the 1980s as a memoirist, essayist, and translator.

RISING LITERARY STAR

Born Xiao Bingqian in Beijing, the author was orphaned at age seven and raised in poverty by an aunt. His father, who died before his birth, was an assimilated Mongol guardsman, Xiao Qian disclosed in 1956. Christian relatives helped him enter a work-study program at a Presbyterian boarding school, Chongshi Xiaoxue (Truth Hall). A stint as trainee and proofreader at the Beixin Bookstore (publisher of Lu Xun and the *Yusi* or *Threads of Talk* literary journal) introduced Xiao to world literature and socialist ideas. During the anti-imperialist May Thirtieth movement (1925), the fifteen-year-old helped the Communist Youth League organize student protests and was briefly imprisoned in 1926, until his school bailed him out. Xiao lacked fixed ideological commitments for the rest of his life, but enjoyed career assists from leftist Chinese in England and China.

Xiao Qian taught Mandarin, took college courses, and was a part-time editor-translator (in English) of modern Chinese literature for small magazines (1928–1932), until settling on a degree in journalism at Yanjing University in Beijing (1933–1935). He collaborated with journalism professor Edgar Snow in translating contemporary Chinese fiction. Xiao also wrote his own short stories, first published in 1933 by his literary inspiration and mentor Shen Congwen in the *Dagongbao* (L'Impartial) literature column. Xiao Qian's fiction, collected in *Li xia ji* (Under the eaves of others, 1936), *Lizi* (Chestnuts, 1936), *Xiao shu ye* (Little leaf, 1937), *Luo ri* (Setting sun, 1937), and *Huijin* (Ashes, 1939), is lyric and bucolic in style, often depicting both the misery and colorful folkways of the downtrodden from the innocent perspective of a poor orphan or country lad. Xiao's *Meng zhi gu* (Valley of dream, 1938) is an avantgarde novel.

JOURNALIST AND MAN OF THE WORLD

Xiao Qian published his first journalism in 1933. After graduation in 1935, he joined the *Dagongbao* at its headquarters in Tianjin and gained fame for firsthand reporting of social problems and natural disasters, notably floods, famines, and the onset of the Sino-Japanese War (1937–1945), in a direct and engaging literary style. His desk job was editing the *Xiao gongyuan* (Little public garden) column, a public forum for brief literary essays and opinion pieces. Xiao helped Shen Congwen edit the paper's more formal literature column in 1935 and took over its Sunday

editions in 1936, moving to Shanghai when the paper established a branch there. He published articles from across the political spectrum, as well as his own literary criticism. As Japan advanced, the paper sent Xiao to edit the literature and entertainment columns for its new Hong Kong edition.

Xiao Qian's sojourn in England, where he was a war correspondent for the *Dagongbao* and a major cultural interlocutor between wartime China and Britain, began in 1939 with a job teaching Chinese at the School of Oriental and African Studies. He wrote back to China about the Blitz and interpreted the Chinese war effort and culture to the British in books such as *China but Not Cathay* (1942) and at the British PEN Club. At the China Campaign Committee, a lobbying and relief group of socialist and progressive opinion makers, he worked with Victor Gollancz, Kingsley Martin, Dorothy Woodman, Margery Fry, and Harold Laski. Xiao also did BBC radio broadcasts. He entered King's College, Cambridge (1942–1944), assisted Chinese classics translator Arthur Waley, and studied the works of Virginia Woolf and then E. M. Forster, who became a good friend; Xiao's English memoirs do not dispel the possibility of mutual homoerotic attraction.

Xiao Qian became a full-time journalist (1944–1946), opening a London office for the *Dagongbao* and traveling to newly liberated and postwar Europe and America to continue his social- and human-interest travelogue reporting. Reassigned to China (1946–1948), then Hong Kong, he wrote editorials about international affairs and anonymously satirized Chinese society in the voice of a foreigner, in *Hongmao changtan* (Platitudes from a red-haired barbarian, 1948). His views were generally "neutral," anti–civil war and anti-Guomindang but independent of domestic Communism and wary of the USSR. Declining offers to become a Guomindang official or a tenured Chinese professor at Cambridge, he returned to the mainland in 1949 to help build New China.

VICISSITUDES UNDER COMMUNISM

Xiao Qian edited propaganda magazines and wrote upbeat feature articles about the revolution for what became the Foreign Languages Press. Though warned in 1950 that his background would bar him from foreign travel, he became deputy editor of the English-language magazine *People's China* that year, and in 1954 began a lasting and happy marriage (his fourth) with Wen Jieruo, a literary translator.

Invited by Feng Xuefeng, Xiao joined the Chinese Writers' Association staff (1951–1961). In 1955 he became a salaried creative writer and in 1956 a deputy editor of *Wenyibao* (Literature and arts gazette), only to be named a rightist in the 1957 campaign, on bogus charges that he seized power at *Wenyibao*, joined a dissident magazine with alleged head rightist Zhang Bojun, and committed other political betrayals. After penal reformation on a state farm (1958–1961), Xiao translated foreign literature for the People's Literature Press. Persecuted again in the Cultural Revolution (1966–1969), he attempted suicide in 1966. His mother-in-law hanged herself, but Wen Jieruo survived and the family lived together at a rural reformatory May Seventh cadre school (1969–1973). Their translation skills in demand again, the Xiaos won transfers back to Beijing in 1973.

After Mao died, Xiao Qian's rightist designation was removed in 1979. He traveled abroad and his frozen individuality gradually "thawed," as he put it. Active again as an essayist and translator (of, for example, James Joyce's *Ulysses*, done with Wen Jieruo), he wrote revealing memoirs, gathered in English in *Traveller without a Map*, detailing not only his vacillations and lost opportunities, but also the discomfiture of non-Communist intellectuals like him from the very start of the People's Republic.

SEE ALSO *Journalism.*

BIBLIOGRAPHY
Xiao Qian. *The Spinners of Silk*. London: Allen and Unwin, 1944.
Xiao Qian. *Semolina and Others*. Hong Kong: Joint Publishing, 1984.
Xiao Qian. *Traveller without a Map*. Trans. by Jeffrey C. Kinkley. London: Hutchinson, 1990. English revised by the author; content varies from Chinese editions.
Xiao Qian. *Xiao Qian quan ji* [Complete works of Xiao Qian]. 5 vols. Wuhan, PRC: Hubei Renmin Chubanshe, 2005.

Jeffrey C. Kinkley

XIE JIN
1923–2008

Xie Jin was one of the most prominent film directors of the early decades of the People's Republic of China (PRC), and after the Cultural Revolution (1966–1969) he enjoyed a revived career. Born in Zhejiang Province, Xie Jin began studying drama in 1939. During World War II (1937–1945), he enrolled in the Jiang'an National Drama School in Shanghai, where he studied under such famous playwrights as Cao Yu (1910–1996) and Hong Shen (1894–1955). Xie Jin remained involved in dramatic activities until 1948, when he entered the Datong Film Corporation and became an assistant director.

After the establishment of the PRC, Xie Jin became a director at the Changjiang Film Studio and the Shanghai Film Studio. His first film, *Yichang fengbo* (A crisis), made in 1954, successfully combined the techniques of socialist realism with Hollywood melodrama, but he only came to critical attention in 1957 with *Nülan wuhao* (Woman basketball player number five), which established his reputation as a "feminist director." His next major success was the filmed version of *Hongse niangzijun* (Red detachment of women), completed in 1961. He presented a more subtle treatment of feminist themes in *Wutai jiemei* (Two stage sisters, 1965), often regarded as his finest film, despite the fact that to ensure its completion he was forced to make many editorial adjustments, which were called for by Jiang Qing, because Xie had incorporated a number of suggestions by Xia Jan, Jiang Qing's bitter enemy, in his original script. Despite the changes, the film was not released until after the Cultural Revolution.

During the Cultural Revolution, Xie Jin was incarcerated in a labor camp for a time, although he was released to direct three films during this period. One was a ballet version of his earlier *Hongse niangzijun*, released in 1970. With the revival of the cinematic industry after the Cultural Revolution, Xie Jin released two films that proved popular in China and abroad: *Tianyun Shan chuanqi* (Tianyun Mountain legend, 1980) and *Furong zhen* (Hibiscus town, 1986). The latter was especially popular. Adapted from the novel by Gu Hua, this harrowing tale of the suffering inflicted on ordinary people and artists by Maoist politics starred the actress Liu Xiaoqing, as well as Jiang Wen, who would later rise to prominence as a director. The film and its actors won many awards in China. However, in the 1980s the career of Xie Jin was already being eclipsed by the Fifth Generation of Chinese filmmakers, of whom Zhang Yimou became internationally acclaimed.

Zuihou de guizu (The last aristocrat), made in 1989, based on a novel by Bai Xianyong, the prominent writer from Taiwan, received little attention from critics. Xie Jin continued to produce films and television dramas in the 1990s. *Da Shanghai wuyan xia* (Under the eaves of greater Shanghai), a television series that he made in 1994, and not to be confused with the similarly titled stage play by Xia Yan, was banned for a time, but his 1997 epic *Yapian zhanzheng* (The Opium War), the release of which coincided with the British restoration to China of sovereignty over Hong Kong, was feted by the authorities. Despite its political timeliness, the film presents a balanced view of the events that led to Britain wresting the colony from China by the Treaty of Nanjing (1842). At a cost of the equivalent of $15 million, *Yapian zhanzheng* was one of the most expensive films made in China at that time. Xie Jin had the distinction of being a member of both the Academy of Motion Picture Arts and Sciences and the Directors Guild of America.

SEE ALSO *Film Industry: Overview.*

BIBLIOGRAPHY

Bergan, Robert. Chinese Film Director Who Survived the Cultural Revolution. *The Guardian*, October 20, 2008.

Leyda, Jay. *Dianying: An Account of Films and the Film Audience in China*. Cambridge, MA: MIT Press, 1972.

Lösel, Jörg. *Die Politische Funktion des Spielfilms der Volksrepublik China Zwischen 1949 und 1965*. Munich: Minerva, 1980.

Rayns, Tony, and Scott Meek. *Electric Shadows: 45 Years of Chinese Cinema*. London: British Film Institute, 1980.

Bruce G. Doar

XINJIANG

When in the late 1750s the armies of Qianlong (r. 1736–1796) defeated the Zunghar Mongol confederacy and pushed south across the Tianshan Range ousting the Turkic Muslim *khwāja* leaders of the Zunghar dependency in Altishahr, they took control of a vast and geographically diverse region. Nearly three times the size of France, the region extended from Mongolia and the Altai Mountains in the north, down through the fertile Zungharian Plateau, across the Tianshan Range and south to the oasis cities of the Tarim Basin bordered by the Kunlun Mountains. To the west of the so-called New Territories (*Xinjiang*) lay the Central Asian steppe of present-day Kazakhstan, Kyrgyzstan, and Tajikistan, to the south the Indian Subcontinent, while to the east stretched the Gobi Desert and the transit zone to the Chinese heartland. Not surprisingly, then as now, geopolitics played a critical role in shaping the fate of the region and its ethnically diverse inhabitants: sedentary Turkic Muslims (Uygurs), Kazakhs, Kyrgyz, Tajiks, Mongols, Uzbeks, Manchus (Xibo), Sino-Muslims (Hui), and Han Chinese.

THE QING CONQUEST

For the Qing dynasty (1644–1912), the driving force behind the conquest of the Mongols had been security. Now with victory secured, stability of the region became paramount. The approach was twofold: strong military control with garrisons in every major city, coupled with a laissez-faire approach to the day-to-day administration. In the south, local Turkic administrators, *beg*s, were integrated into the Qing official system but continued to carry out their traditional functions, while to the north, the remnant Mongols retained their tribal organizational structure under the control of native chiefs, *jasak*s. Even in Ürümqi and the eastern oasis cities of Qumul (Hami) and Turpan, where a degree of Qing civilian administrative rule was employed, native elites and Muslim clerics continued to function alongside the new rulers.

But despite a superficially light touch, Qing colonial rule inevitably left its mark on the fabric of local society. In

---

XINJIANG

Capital city: Ürümqi

Largest cities (population): Ürümqi (2,020,000 [2006]), Turfan, Kashgar

Area: 1,660,001 sq. km. (640,930 sq. mi.)

Population: 20,500,000 (2006)

Demographics: Uygur, 45%; Han, 41%; Kazakh, 7%; Hui, 5%; Kyrgyz, 0.9%; Mongol, 0.8%; Dongxiang, 0.3%; Tajik, 0.2%; Xibo, 0.2%

GDP: CNY 304.5 billion (2006)

Famous sites: Gaochang Ruins, Tianshan mountain range, Jiaohe Ruins

---

the north, where long years of war and the scourge of smallpox epidemics had left the Mongol population decimated, there was an influx of Han and Sino-Muslim Chinese migrants: the families of soldiers who settled in the military-agricultural colonies, convicts, and migrant farmers from the drought-worn impoverished northwest. Slowly but surely, merchants, too, were attracted by the new markets. Conversely, in the south, pressure on land remained acute. Continuing a practice initiated under the Mongols, thousands of families were relocated to the Yili (Ili) Valley in the northwest, while in an effort to avert competition for scarce resources, not until the 1830s were Chinese from the interior officially allowed to settle in Altishahr.

For almost fifty years, the region remained relatively stable, but by the nineteenth century, economic decline, corruption, and the social upheaval resulting from repeated attacks by the *khwājas* and their sponsors in the Central Asian khanate of Khokand, had all served to undermine Qing rule. In the 1860s, the Khokandi Yaqqūb Beg (Yakub Beg, 1820–1877), backed by one of the *khwāja* descendants, finally drove the Qing from Xinjiang, and for some ten to twelve years much of the region was administered under Yaqqūb Beg's independent and autocratic rule.

In Beijing, the merits of reoccupation were virulently debated, and only in 1878 did the Qing armies of General Zuo Zongtang (1812–1885) finally retake the region. But with hesitation had come the loss of the vast northwestern region of Yili, which Russia had annexed in 1871. The new Chinese administration now broke with the laissez-faire policies of earlier Qing rule. It abolished the authority of the local *beg*s, and native people who sought office within the administration were encouraged to master Chinese and Confucian mores. Further steps were taken

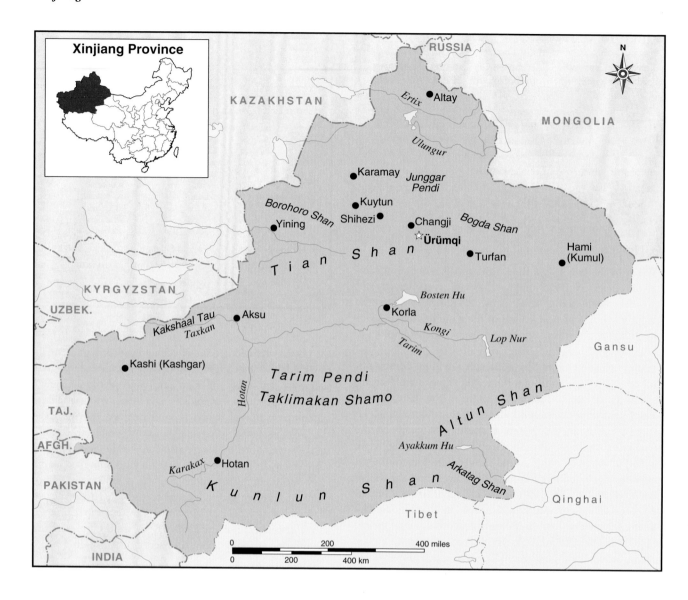

to bind the economy to that of the interior, while land opening and resettlement plans were reinvigorated. In 1881, after lengthy negotiations, Russia returned the Yili territories, and three years later Xinjiang was finally incorporated into the provincial system.

THE REPUBLICAN ERA

Provincial status did not mean that the fate of Xinjiang was sealed. In January 1912, the last Qing governor, Yuan Dahua (1851–1935), was overthrown, and Yang Zengxin (1863–1928) seized control as provincial governor. The brutality with which Yang and his successors dealt with opposition, their autocratic style of government, and the extent of Soviet economic and political influence all underline their tenuous and ambivalent relationships with the central government. In fact, Russian and Soviet influence in the region was to remain stronger than that of the central government until the 1940s.

After Yang's assassination in 1928, the rule of his successor, Jin Shuren (1879–1941), coincided with the rise of *jadidism* and Turkic nationalism. With Soviet assistance in suppressing rebellion, Jin was able to maintain an uneasy stability until 1933, but under his successor, Sheng Shicai (1897–1970), unrest grew to new levels. Soviet support was instrumental in quashing the short-lived Eastern Turkestan Republic (1933–1934) in Kashgar and again in 1937 in ousting the Sino-Muslims who had continued to hold power in Khotan. But there was a price to be paid: Soviet access to oil and other minerals. In 1941, fearing that the Soviets would fall to the German advance, Sheng publicly proclaimed his allegiance to the Nationalist center, and having cut off Soviet trade, requested that all military and technical advisers withdraw from the province. A Guomindang (GMD) provincial party headquarters was established in Ürümqi, with party branches throughout the province. Two years later, when the Soviet position appeared secure,

Sheng attempted to switch allegiance back to the Soviet Union, but now he had lost credibility with both the Soviet Union and the GMD, and in 1944 the central government appointed a new governor, Wu Zhongxin (1884–1959), to replace him.

Under Sheng, significant attempts had been made to modernize the region. Schools had been opened, roads built, and natural resources and industry developed. But as pastureland was enclosed, the nomadic way of life became harder to sustain. Between 1938 and 1941, seven thousand Kazakh nomads migrated from the steppes of northern Xinjiang. Further demographic changes resulted in 1942 when the GMD government launched a land-settlement project, moving more than ten thousand refugees, ex-soldiers, and unemployed workers from Henan, Shanxi, and Shaanxi provinces to eastern Xinjiang to undertake construction, irrigation, forestry, and reclamation projects. The reinforcement of Nationalist influence through development projects, coupled with Han (and Sino-Muslim) migration, initiated a pattern that would reverberate into the Communist era as more and more expertise was brought into the region to develop its rich oil and mineral resources.

By the early 1940s, a new generation of Turkic nationalists, many of whom were trained in the Soviet Union, had emerged. As inflation spiraled out of control in autumn 1944, a rebellion against Nationalist rule resulted in the establishment of a second Eastern Turkestan Republic centered on Yili; once again, a large expanse of northwestern Xinjiang was lost to central government control. Suspected Soviet involvement led to the suspension of trade between Xinjiang and Soviet Russia, and although after less than a year a negotiated settlement resulted in a coalition government, GMD influence never reasserted itself in the three districts of the Yili region.

THE XINJIANG UYGUR AUTONOMOUS REGION

As the People's Liberation Army (PLA) approached Xinjiang in summer 1949, Zhang Zhizhong (1890–1969), who had stepped down as leader of the coalition government in favor of the first non-Han governor, Masqūd Sabrī (1888–1952), negotiated the surrender of the GMD forces. The leadership of the Eastern Turkestan Republic was also cooperating with the Chinese Communist Party (CCP), but in August many of their number reportedly died in a plane crash while traveling to Beijing. By mid-October 1949, with the north secured, units of the PLA moved into southern Xinjiang. Five years later, in 1955, when all opposition had been put down, the CCP announced the establishment of the Xinjiang Uygur Autonomous Region, covering some 1.6 million square kilometers and constituting one-sixth of China's total territory.

Initially, land reform progressed slowly; the pastoral nomadic economy was ill-suited to the policies of collectivization, and the expropriating of *waqf* lands was vigorously opposed. From the late 1950s, however, as collectivization was pushed forward, the party adopted a less tolerant approach to Islam and "minority" cultures, culminating in the destructive and assimilative policies of the Cultural Revolution (1966–1969). Despite attempts to train local people as cadres, power had remained largely in the hands of Han Chinese, and the ethnic mix in the region was undergoing significant shifts. The Xinjiang Production and Construction Corps, established to serve both as a militia and to promote economic development, was absorbing thousands of Han immigrants. By 1966 the corps had grown from its original 100,000 demobilized soldiers to 600,000, and was augmented daily by hundreds of Red Guards arriving from Shanghai and other cities in the interior. Conversely, in 1962, economic hardship fueled by the Great Leap Forward had caused some 60,000 people, predominantly Kazakhs, to cross the border into the Soviet Union.

In the post-reform period, and notably since the launch of the Great Western Development Strategy (Xibu Da Kaifa) in 1999, China's prodigious economic development has transformed the landscape of Xinjiang, and for many the quality of their lives. In the rural areas, agriculture still plays a major role, with the raising of fruit, cotton, wheat, and sheep predominating, but oil and petrochemicals now constitute 60 percent of the region's economy. Health care and, more controversially, education have been extended, and while improved communications have allowed a deeper penetration of the state into local affairs, the opening of links to the Central Asian Republics, the interior of China, and the West have expanded freedom of movement and aspirational horizons. On the one hand, this has led to a more stable society focused on economic goals; on the other, opposition to Han rule and the influx of Han migrants who by 2009 constituted 40 percent of the population (as opposed to 6 percent in 1949) continues. Periodic crackdowns and arrests deal swiftly with those termed separatists, religious extremists, or terrorists, while autonomy remains elusive.

SEE ALSO *Central Asian States, Relations with; Muslim Uprisings; Zuo Zongtang.*

BIBLIOGRAPHY

Benson, Linda. *The Ili Rebellion: The Moslem Challenge to Chinese Authority in Xinjiang, 1944–1949.* Armonk, NY: Sharpe, 1990.

Dillon, Michael. *Xinjiang: China's Muslim Far Northwest.* London: RoutledgeCurzon, 2004.

Forbes, Andrew. *Warlords and Muslims in Chinese Central Asia: A Political History of Republican Sinkiang, 1911–1949.* Cambridge, U.K.: Cambridge University Press, 1986.

Kim Hodong. *Holy War in China*: *The Muslim Rebellion and State in Chinese Central Asia, 1864–1877*. Stanford, CA: Stanford University Press, 2004.

Millward, James. *Beyond the Pass*: *Economy, Ethnicity, and Empire in Qing Central Asia, 1759–1864*. Stanford, CA: Stanford University Press, 1998.

Millward, James. *Eurasian Crossroads*: *A History of Xinjiang*. London: Hurst, 2007.

L. J. Newby

XU BEIHONG

1895–1953

The painter and art educator Xu Beihong was one of the most significant figures in reformist efforts to modernize Chinese art in the first half of the twentieth century. He was himself skilled in both Chinese ink painting and Western oil painting, and he expected his students to paint naturalistically in both mediums.

He was born into a painter's family in Qitingqiao, a village in Yixing County, Jiangsu Province. His father, Xu Dazhang (1874–1914), was a self-taught painter known locally for his expertise in figure painting and calligraphy. When Xu Beihong was nine years old, his father began to transmit to him his own painting skills. As many aspiring artists did in the early twentieth century, Xu practiced by copying popular illustrations, including the figural narratives Wu Youru (d. 1893) published in the *Dianshizhai Pictorial Magazine*, as well as animals printed on cigarette boxes produced in foreign-run Shanghai factories, which were rendered in Western styles. These early experiences laid the foundations for Xu's interest in realistic art. By the time Xu Beihong was a teenager, he was well versed in different genres of painting, and in these years he and his father supported the family by working as itinerant painters. As his father's health declined, they returned to their hometown and Xu Beihong began to provide for his family by teaching art at local schools, including the Pengcheng Secondary School, Yixing Girls' Normal Secondary School, and Shiqi Primary Girls' School in nearby Heqiao.

EDUCATION OF THE ARTIST

After his father's death, Xu Beihong left home in 1915 to seek his fortune in Shanghai. Although Xu experienced many hardships in this period, he also made critical social and artistic connections in Shanghai. He became friends with the Gao brothers, Gao Jianfu (1879–1951) and Gao Qifeng (1889–1933), the founders of the reformist Lingnan school. The Gaos had close ties to anti-Manchu revolutionary leaders and members of the early Guomindang.

They commissioned figure paintings by Xu Beihong to sell in their shop, Shenmei shuguan (the Aesthetics Bookshop). In Shanghai Xu also enrolled at the Université Aurore (Zhendan University) to learn French, and briefly studied at the newly formed Shanghai Art Academy, cofounded in late 1912 by Liu Haisu and several others. As a result of professional and artistic differences, Xu later denied Liu Haisu's claims of having been his teacher, but school archives document his registration there.

During this first Shanghai period Xu Beihong also was drawn into the circle of the real estate tycoon and philanthropist Silas A. Hardoon (1851–1931) by winning a competition sponsored by Mrs. Hardoon to depict the legendary inventor of Chinese writing, Cang Jie (c. 2650 BCE). The Hardoons often held gatherings of Chinese artists and connoisseurs at their huge garden estate, the Ailiyuan, and it was there that Xu met his important early mentor, Kang Youwei. The connection with Kang was important not only intellectually but also because it gave Xu Beihong access to Kang's private art collection. Xu particularly admired Kang's ideas of integrating Western and Chinese art as a potential way of creating a new Chinese painting for their own era. With Kang's encouragement, Xu began to study the calligraphy and paintings in his collection. Kang also introduced him to other important friends such as Shen Zengzhi (1850–1922), Wang Guowei, Zou An (1864–1940), Chen Shanyuan (1853–1937), and Shen Meishu.

In May 1917 Xu Beihong eloped to Tokyo with his second wife, Jiang Biwei (1899–1978). In their brief sojourn in Japan, Xu spent his time in museums, art galleries, and art bookshops, studying Western painting and the new forms of art developed in Japan since the Meiji restoration. However, their funds were rapidly depleted, and the young couple was forced to return to Shanghai by December, after only half a year abroad. On Kang Youwei's recommendation, Cai Yuanpei (1868–1940) appointed Xu Beihong as a teacher in the Painting Methods Research Society that he established at Beijing University. In the midst of the university's revolutionary ferment of the late 1910s, Xu formulated his famous axiom for a rejuvenation of Chinese painting. He argued that Chinese ink painting should be modernized through the preservation of those traditional methods that were good, the revival of those good methods that were moribund, the reform of those that were bad, the strengthening of those that were weak, and the integration of Western painting elements that could be adopted.

In March 1919, through the assistance of Cai Yuanpei and with a small stipend from the government, Xu Beihong traveled to France to begin his studies in art. Initially, he enrolled at the private Académie Julian, but the following year he was admitted to the prestigious École nationale supérieure des beaux-arts, where he received a firm academic

Galloping *by Xu Beihong, 1944. While initially trained in China, Xu Beihong continued his art education abroad, studying in Japan, France, and Germany and blending these influences in his work. Xu remains best known, however, for his expressive horse figures, combining traditional Chinese techniques with Western elements of realism.* XU BEIHONG/COLPHOTO/FOTOE

training in drawing and oil painting. Beyond the studios, Xu was a frequent visitor to the Louvre and the Luxembourg, where he diligently sketched and copied the works of masters in the Western canon such as Delacroix, Velázquez, Rembrandt, Prud'hon, and Rubens. In winter 1920 Xu also became the student of the French naturalist and academic painter Pascal Dagnan-Bouveret (1852–1929), who taught

him the importance of *dessin* (drawing) as the foundation of painting, an idea that Xu firmly promoted in his subsequent career as an art educator.

When his scholarship was interrupted by political turbulence in China, the Xus moved from Paris to Berlin for about twenty months to take advantage of Germany's lower cost of living in that period. There Xu worked under

Arthur Kampf (1864–1950), the head of the Hochschole für Bildende Künste in Charlottenburg, and spent much time in the Berlin zoo sketching animals, especially lions. In 1923, his scholarship restored, he returned to Paris to resume his studies with Dagnan-Bouveret. He achieved much success, exhibiting nine paintings in the official salon exhibitions of that year. Two years later, in 1925, Xu Beihong returned home via Singapore, where he established lifelong friendships with significant local art collectors and patrons, and procured lucrative portrait commissions to fund his travels. Upon his arrival in Shanghai, he held a successful large one-man show that firmly established his reputation in Chinese art circles.

THE ARTIST AS EDUCATOR

In 1926 and 1927, Xu traveled again to Paris and embarked on an art study tour to Italy, Switzerland, and Belgium. When he finally returned to China, he was invited by the writer Tian Han (1898–1968) to join his short-lived Académie du Midi (Nanguo yishu xueyuan) as head of its art department. By the end of 1927, Cai Yuanpei had appointed Xu to head the art department of the newly established National Central University in Nanjing, which remained the base of his influence in the art world for the next decade. During those years, he assembled a group of faculty members, including the venerable reformist Gao Jianfu, who implemented his vision of a new Chinese art based on synthesis of Chinese art with Western realism. In 1933 and 1934 Xu Beihong organized a series of solo and group exhibitions in Europe, beginning with a group show in Paris that received a warm reception from the public, press, and critics. The French government purchased twelve contemporary Chinese ink paintings from the show, of which Xu's *Ancient Cypress* (*Gubo*) is particularly notable. The exhibition subsequently traveled to Brussels, Berlin, Milan, Frankfurt, Moscow, and Leningrad with success, resulting in the establishment of galleries to display the paintings purchased by and presented to the respective governments. Besides Xu Beihong's works, the paintings featured in the exhibition included works by Qi Baishi (1864–1957), Zhang Daqian, Chen Shuren (1883–1948), and Wang Zhen (Wang Yiting).

When the Sino-Japanese War broke out in 1937, Xu Beihong organized fund-raising exhibitions throughout Southeast Asia, including Singapore, Malaysia, and India, and donated the proceeds to the resistance movement in China. Invited by Rabindranath Tagore (1861–1941) to Santiniketan, the site of the university he had founded in Bengal, Xu spent most of 1940 exhibiting and lecturing in India. It was there that he created one of his most ambitious allegorical paintings in ink, *Yu Gong Removes the Mountains* (*Yugong yishan*, 1940), a Chinese subject for which he used Indian models. In 1946 he was hired as principal of the Beijing Art College. After the liberation of

Beijing in 1949, the school was renamed and reorganized, and he was appointed the first principal of the newly named Central Academy of Fine Arts, as well as the chairman of the Chinese Artists Association. In early autumn 1953 Xu Beihong suffered a brain hemorrhage during a meeting of the Second National Congress of Literature and Art Workers, and passed away on September 26, a respected patriot and revered teacher.

XU'S LEGACY

Xu's art and art theory were based on a belief that Chinese painting had declined in the Ming and Qing periods as artists neglected realism, whereas modern Western art had begun to deteriorate when it rejected the classical canon. Consequently, Xu admired and promoted masters of realistic painting in both traditions, and in his teaching and artwork Xu advocated drawing or sketching as the basis of technique in both oils and Chinese ink. Xu Beihong was an exceptionally skilled draftsman, and some of his best works are the innumerable sketches he made during his student days in Europe, as well as studies made before embarking on his large oil paintings such as his well-known *Tian Heng and His Five Hundred Retainers* (*Tian Heng wubaishi*, 1930) and *Awaiting the Deliverer* (*Xi Wo Hou*, 1933). In traditional Chinese ink media, Xu Beihong also attempted to create similarly large historical paintings that were based on heroic Chinese themes and an amalgamation of traditional Chinese brush techniques and realistic renderings of the human figure. Famous examples include *Jiu Fang Gao* (1931), and *Yugong Removes the Mountains*. Nevertheless, Xu Beihong is most famous today for his horse paintings, in which he successfully integrated the Chinese line and his Western realist training in drawing. These were the most numerous paintings he sold in his lifetime, especially during his wartime fund-raising exhibitions, and with the martial spirit of the horse read as symbolic of China's own determination, Xu embedded his deep patriotic feelings in them and thus left an indelible mark on the public's memory.

After his death in 1953, Xu Beihong was lionized for his contributions to Chinese realism, particularly in the context of the Communist government's embrace of socialist-realism as the official style. However, when China reopened its doors to the West in the late 1980s, Xu was equally criticized for this antimodernist stance; some critics asserted that he had set back the development of Chinese painting by forty years. Although it may be true that the only art school faculties readily capable of undertaking the shift to socialist realism were those nurtured in Xu Beihong's academic realism, blaming him alone for forty years of Communist art policies is unjustifiable. Nevertheless, Xu Beihong's belief in the virtues of European academic realism and in the necessity of merging Chinese painting with Western naturalism has had a lasting impact on the Chinese art world, and his students were instrumental in constructing the art educational system of the 1950s.

In the twenty-first century Xu Beihong's popularity in Asia is returning, as evinced by a major exhibition of his works at the Singapore Art Museum (April to July 2008), and the record-breaking sales of his works in the auction houses of China and Hong Kong. With his exemplary European education, his talent for attracting the support of influential cultural and political figures, and the loyalty he inspired among his students, Xu Beihong was one of the most influential figures in early twentieth-century Chinese art. His rejection of the abstraction of literati painting and of Western modernism set him apart from fellow art educators Lin Fengmian and Liu Haisu and have had a powerful effect on Chinese art. His legacy remains influential, and the suitability of his approach has continued to stir controversy and debate in the Chinese art world more than half a century after his death.

SEE ALSO *Art Exhibitions Abroad; Chinese Painting (guohua); Kang Youwei; Lin Fengmian; Liu Haisu; Oil Painting (youhua).*

BIBLIOGRAPHY

PRIMARY WORK

Xu Beihong. *Xu Beihong yishu wenji* [Collected writings on art by Xu Beihong]. 2 vols. Taibei: Taiwan Artists Press, 1987.

SECONDARY WORKS

Andrews, Julia F. *A Century in Crisis: Modernity and Tradition in the Art of Twentieth-century China.* New York: Harry N. Abrams and Guggenheim Museum Publications, 1998.

Barnhart, Richard M., Yang Xin, and Nie Chongzheng, et al. *Three Thousand Years of Chinese Painting.* Beijing, New Haven, CT, and London: Foreign Language Press and Yale University Press, 1997.

Sullivan, Michael. *Art and Artists of Twentieth-century China.* Berkeley and Los Angeles: University of California Press, 1996.

Ying Chua

XU BING
1955–

Xu Bing is a leading figure in the post–Cultural Revolution Chinese art world. He was particularly important in the transition from socialist realism to postmodernism and, by virtue of the originality of his artistic vision, in moving contemporary Chinese art into the international mainstream. Born in Chongqing, Sichuan Province, Xu Bing grew up in Beijing. He undertook studies in printmaking at the Central Academy of Fine Arts (CAFA) in Beijing between 1977 and 1981, joined the faculty, and received his master of fine arts degree from CAFA in 1987. Although Xu was trained as a printmaker, he soon turned his attention to crafting installations and performance pieces, working in a wide variety of media. In 1990, at the invitation of the University of Wisconsin, Madison, Xu Bing moved to the United States, eventually establishing his studio in Brooklyn, New York.

Xu Bing's work retains roots in his early training but he continues to challenge the limits of printmaking and has focused on exposing the process of artistic creation. His manipulation of language and potent cultural icons also enables him to create powerful works that confront the semiotic relationship between words and meanings. History, impeccable technical skill, humor, originality, wordplay, and the transgression of boundaries are all elements of Xu Bing's conceptually based art. A recurring theme in his work is the cognitive process of reading, which he violates or problematizes through his use of illegible, semilegible, or newly invented scripts. His works tend to be understood differently by viewers of different linguistic and cultural backgrounds, an openness encouraged by the artist, who considers the ongoing relationship between the work and its viewers, and the interpretive processes that occur after a work is completed, to be an integral part of his art. Many of his exhibitions are interactive.

Xu Bing's first and best-known installation, *Book from the Sky*, first exhibited in 1988 at the Chinese National Art Gallery (now China National Museum of Art) in Beijing and later exhibited in a number of venues in Asia and the West, exemplifies these themes. The installation is comprised of long scrolls of woodblock-printed text draped from the ceiling, boxed sets of books bound in blue paper covers in the Song dynasty (960–1279) manner, and large printed sheets of text that may be mounted on the wall to resemble monumental steles. Through the rearrangement of elements from real Chinese characters, Xu first invented thousands of imaginary characters to approximate the number of Chinese characters in frequent use today, and then hand-carved them in the Song style onto the small wooden blocks from which they are typeset and printed. A product of four years of labor, this extraordinary work first frustrates the Chinese viewers' impulse to read its text and concurrently provides them a mental space without meaning, thereby inviting them to fill it with their reading and interpretation. *Book from the Sky* drew both wide acclaim and sharp criticism from critics and the press in Beijing, who focused on its illegibility, while overseas exhibitions produced new sets of interpretations among viewers who did not expect to be able to read the characters and thus concentrated more on the work's austere beauty and laborious process of creation.

Since Xu Bing's move to the United States in 1990, his works have been exhibited internationally at major biennials and museums. Xu is also the recipient of a number of prestigious awards, including the Artes

Mundi Prize (2004) and a MacArthur Foundation award (1999). His representative works include *Book from the Sky* (1987–1991), *Ghosts Pounding the Wall* (1990), *Square Calligraphy Classroom* (1994), *A Case Study of Transference* (1994), *Book from the Ground* (2003, ongoing), and *Where Does the Dust Itself Collect?* (2004). In 2008 Xu Bing was appointed vice president of the Central Academy of Fine Arts in Beijing. He continues to startle viewers' expectations of the relationship of written language and the visual image in an active exhibition career in the United States and internationally.

SEE ALSO *Art, History of: since 1949.*

BIBLIOGRAPHY

Erickson, Britta. *The Art of Xu Bing: Words without Meaning, Meaning without Words.* Washington, DC: Sackler Gallery; Seattle: University of Washington Press, 2001.

Silbergeld, Jerome, and Dora C. Y. Ching, eds. *Persistence-Transformation: Text as Image in the Art of Xu Bing.* Princeton, NJ: Princeton University Press, 2006.

Xu Bing Studio. http://www.xubing.com

Ying Chua

XU ZHIMO
1897–1931

A poet, essayist, editor, translator, and critic, Xu was one of the most influential men of letters in early-twentieth-century China. His legendary romantic pursuits are an integral part of his enduring allure to readers and scholars alike, and have helped to make him known today mainly for his poetic genius.

LIFE

Xu was born into a prominent merchant family in Xiashi, Zhejiang Province. Endowed from birth with money and intelligence, Xu received the best care and education that his doting father could manage, care that included arranging for his son to be a private student of Liang Qichao, the most prominent intellectual of the time in China. Family fortune played no small part in Xu's interest in poetry, allowing him, throughout most of his adult years, to lead a high-flying social life without worrying about the mundane burden of making a living. Very few writers and artists of the May Fourth generation were blessed with such a lifestyle.

Early on all signs pointed toward Xu becoming a black sheep of the family, a role that he eventually filled. He had a precocious intelligence, an insatiable mind, and an unruly range of interests. In his pursuit of education, it seemed that acquiring knowledge became an end unto itself. After brief stays at Shanghai University and Beiyang University in Tianjin, he read law at Peking University (1914–1917), studied banking and history at Clark University in the United States (1918–1919), earned an MA in political science from Columbia University (1919–1920), and finally ended up at the London School of Economics and Cambridge University, where what was intended to be a study of economics turned into an self-guided initiation into literature (1920–1922). Cambridge was where Xu's formal education ended, without a diploma, but it was also where Xu found himself as a writer. European culture—its past masters and present giants—swept Xu away, English Romantic poetry presented itself as a voice that Xu discovered genuinely his own, and Cambridge became a spiritual shrine that would anchor Xu's dreams and inspirations for the rest of his life. Later Xu would make two more pilgrimages to Europe to rejuvenate himself, but by the end of his first journey, he had already become a poet.

In late 1922 Xu returned to China with a bag full of penned poems, some of which quickly found their way into various literary journals. Coincidentally, one of his earliest published poems was titled "Kangqiao zaihui ba" (Farewell to Cambridge), a farewell that lasted a lifetime for him. As his poetic fame rapidly rose, his flamboyant social life started to fill the society pages of newspapers. Two events helped establish Xu as a central figure in cultural circles. In 1923 he founded Xinyue She (Crescent Moon Society) from his Beijing residence. This small and private literary club quickly became an influential forum for literature, sharing national attention with other two well-known literary societies, Wenxue Yanjiu Hui (Literary Research Association) and Chuangzao She (Creation Society). Many of the Crescent Moon Society's activities—its press, newspaper supplements, and journals, in all of which Xu played a leadership role—promoted poetry, and Xu was invaluable at discovering new talents and offering venues for poetic discussion. In 1924 the Indian poet Rabindranath Tagore (1861–1941), a Nobel laureate, came to visit China, and during his nearly half-year-long nationwide tour, Xu was his guide and chief interpreter, a task that gave Xu a rare opportunity to exhibit his luminous personality and linguistic brilliance. By the end of the tour Xu not only had developed a devout friendship with his guest but had also become one of the most sought-after intellectuals in China.

In the following years Xu continued to live a highly visible and successful public life. He wrote, edited, translated, and taught at an amazing pace, but he never settled on one endeavor or in one place. Traveling was sometimes a necessity, but at other times, it was a desired way of existence. In the meantime, his private life was slowly falling apart. China's incorrigible social ills and political corruption greatly disappointed him, and his father's disapproval of his life choices—his second marriage in particular—added onto his sense of gloom and disillusionment. Then on November 19, 1931, a postal transport airplane fell out of the sky on a routine flight from Nanjing to Beijing, taking down with it two pilots and Xu Zhimo, its only passenger, who was returning to Peking University for a faculty appointment.

ROMANCE

"My life's ups and downs are threaded together by emotions," Xu Zhimo said (Xie Mian 1993, p. 200). This self-description is as true for his tortured educational pathway as for his experiences with love and marriage. Xu's love life had a familiar beginning typical of reform-minded intellectuals of his time, but a tumultuous middle and a spectacular end that bear his individual marks of being free-spirited and flamboyant.

In 1913, while still in high school, Xu was engaged to Zhang Youyi (1900–1989), a thirteen-year-old young woman from a family that matched Xu's in wealth and status, and they were married two years later. This arranged marriage never produced the sparks that Xu needed. Yet Zhang was the only daughter-in-law that Xu's father would accept, and he tried everything to make his son's marriage last, including sending Zhang to Europe to rein in Xu's wandering heart, but to no avail. In early 1922 Xu begged Zhang to "return freedom to one who deserves it" (Han Shishan 2005, p. 27), a plea with which she complied, knowing that Xu was already in love with another woman. Lin Huiyin was a friend's daughter whom Xu met upon his arrival in London. This was love at first sight. Taken by Lin's stunning beauty and literary sensibility, Xu carried on a blissful secret love affair with her that contributed to his decision to become a poet. The love affair ended unexpectedly with Lin's return to China in October 1921, but Xu decided to follow her home after finalizing his divorce with Zhang.

Xu's pursuit of Lin in China did not go anywhere. Lin became unresponsive to his overtures because she was already engaged to the son of his mentor Liang Qichao, a fact that put Xu in a rather awkward position. In fact, Liang intervened by subtly reprimanding Xu's "immoral behavior" as public criticism of his character flew around. Even though Xu and Lin remained friends until his death, this unfulfilled love was a deep wound that never healed. In fact, this frustrated desire often sneaked back into his poems.

Xu was a restless romantic. Before the fallout of his affair with Lin quieted down, he was already involved with the third and last woman in his life. Her name was Lu Xiaoman, a beautiful married woman who was a close match to Lin in terms of artistic talent and modern sensibility, but she also had many qualities of a high-society woman, to which Xu was oblivious in their initial encounters. He saw Lu as a love goddess who personified beauty, passion, and spiritual union, all of which were Xu's lifelong pursuits; that she was a prohibited love goddess only intensified his interest. Against wide negative publicity and his father's stern warnings, Xu and Lu married in 1926 after she obtained a divorce from her husband, but their subsequent life together soon became another tired tale of diminishing married love. Xu started to dislike Lu's hectic and purposeless social life, her taste for extravagance, and particularly her opium addiction. To the public, they remained an ideal couple until separated by death, but inside Xu was a tormented soul, frustrated and disappointed probably less with Lu as an unsatisfactory wife and more with the elusive quest called love.

WRITING

Xu Zhimo was a versatile writer. Readers love his diaries and letters, his travelogues and personal essays, but his literary reputation rests mainly on a corpus of about 200 poems, most of which are collected in the following three volumes: *Zhimo de shi* (Zhimo's Poems, 1925), *Feilengcui de yiye* (A Night in Florence, 1927), and *Meng hu* (Fierce Tiger, 1931). A fourth volume titled *Yunyou* (Wandering among the Clouds) was published posthumously in 1932.

Critics often credit Xu with reintroducing regulation into Chinese poetry as a correction to the artistic anarchy rampant in early vernacular poetry. Indeed, evident in the span of his poetic writings is a transformation from unruly free verse to controlled formal versification. His skillful use of lineation, rhyme scheme, meter, and other controlling devices creates a sense of formal regularity that evokes both classical Chinese poetry and modern English poetry, and that fully explores the potential of the vernacular language as a vehicle for poetry. His contribution to the "new regulated poetry" (*xin gelüshi*) notwithstanding, Xu's unique poetic persona that transcends time and space had a greater influence on modern Chinese poetry.

This poetic persona has a complex and conflicted identity: He is a homebound traveler getting stuck in ancient and foreign places; he is a social critic indignant over a poor man's misery; he is a leisurely rambler appreciating nature's offerings to its minutest details; but above all, he is a romantic idealist who never gives up his pursuit of beauty despite frustration without end. Beauty, for Xu, usually resides in things that draw one toward them despite their mystery and inaccessibility. Sometimes this sense of unattainable beauty gives rise to a namable emotion, such as nostalgia in "Zai bie Kangqiao" (A Second Farewell to Cambridge) or transient sensation in "Shayangnala" (Sayonara), but at other times it is associated with the image of a woman as the object of love who is either unresponsive or is in the process of leaving a relationship, as in "Feilengcui de yiye" (A Night in Florence) or "Yueye tingqin" (Listening to a Chinese Lute on a Moonlit Night). In developing the familiar literary motif of unfulfilled love and thwarted desire into a poetic persona, and in describing this motif with exotic imagination and linguistic exactitude, Xu has no match among modern Chinese poets. In real life, this poetic persona served as an alter ego for Xu. Perhaps it is the blending of Xu's real life and poetic persona that has sustained his enduring popularity among Chinese readers.

SEE ALSO *Literary Societies; May Fourth Movement.*

BIBLIOGRAPHY

Han Shishan. *Beiqing Xu Zhimo* [Xu Zhimo's sad songs]. Beijing: Tongxin Chubanshe, 2005.

Lee, Leo Ou-fan. *The Romantic Generation of Modern Chinese Writers.* Cambridge, MA: Harvard University Press, 1973.

Lee, Leo Ou-fan. Literary Trends: The Road to Revolution, 1927–1949. In *The Cambridge History of China*, vol. 13, *Republican China, 1912–1949*, ed. Denis Twitchett and John K. Fairbank, 421–491. New York: Cambridge University Press, 1983.

Lin, Julia. *Modern Chinese Poetry: An Introduction.* Seattle: University of Washington Press, 1972.

Xie Mian, ed. *Xu Zhimo mingzuo xinshang* [An annotated selection of Xu Zhimo's famous works]. Beijing: Zhongguo Heping Chubanshe, 1993.

Yeh, Michelle. *Modern Chinese Poetry: Theory and Practice since 1917.* New Haven, CT: Yale University Press, 1991.

Dian Li

Y

───────────■───────────

YAN FU
1853–1921

Yan Fu was born in Fuzhou and is remembered today as a reformer and translator, best known for introducing to China the nineteenth-century social application of Charles Darwin's ideas, if not the writings of Darwin himself. Yan's theories about translation are still cited in China today.

While studying navigational sciences in the English-language section at the Fuzhou Navy Yard and Academy, a Self-strengthening movement (1861–1894) institution established in 1866, Yan Fu first encountered Western science and studied arithmetic, geometry, algebra, physics, chemistry, and geology. In 1877 he went to Britain for two years to continue his studies, first at Portsmouth and then at the Royal Naval College at Greenwich. After returning to the Fuzhou Navy Yard and Academy, he was appointed dean in 1880 of the Beiyang Naval Academy in Tianjin newly founded by Li Hongzhang, of which he eventually became the chancellor in 1889.

Yan Fu became increasingly active as a political reformer. After China's defeat in the Sino-Japanese War of 1894 to 1895, he published influential articles in Tianjin's *Zhi Bao* (Zhili times) calling on China to strengthen itself through military modernization and the introduction of political reforms. His articles included *"Lun shibian zhi ji"* (A discussion of the urgent need for change), *"Yuan qiang"* (On strengthening), and *"Jiuwang jue lun"* (A discussion of the remedy for national collapse). There was an implicit call for constitutional monarchy in these pieces. In 1896 he provided funds to Liang Qichao and Wang Kangnian (1860–1911) to set up the reformist newspaper *Shiwu Bao* (Chinese progress) in Shanghai. In 1897 he and several colleagues also set up a reformist newspaper in Tianjin, *Guowen Bao* (National register), and it was in these pages that he first published his translations of the writings of the English biologist T. H. Huxley (1825–1895). Although his daily work required him to supervise technical translations, Yan Fu had already embarked on the series of ground-breaking translations that over the following decade would introduce Western political thought and sociology to Chinese readers: *Evolution and Ethics* by T. H. Huxley, 1898; *The Study of Sociology* by Herbert Spencer, 1902; *The Wealth of Nations* by Adam Smith, 1902; *On Liberty* by John Stuart Mill, 1903; *A History of Politics* by Edward Jenks, 1904; *System of Logic* by John Stuart Mill, 1905; *The Spirit of the Laws* by Montesquieu, 1909; and *Primer of Logic* by W. S. Jevons, 1909. Some of these translations were among the most influential and widely read books of their time, largely because they were part of a reformist political trend, and many of the ideas they contained were taken up and further amplified by the leading reformers of the day, such as Kang Youwei and Liang Qichao. Yan Fu thus came to exert an influence far beyond that of a translator, because of his own active involvement in reform. However, he was not a proponent of revolution, and his advocacy of reform stressed the importance of science and education, including the education of women, in strengthening the nation.

In the prefaces to his translation of Huxley's *Evolution and Ethics*, titled *Tianyan Lun* (On evolution), Yan Fu elaborated on the principles to which he adhered in his translation: faithfulness to the original text (*xin*); the communication of the ideas (*da*); and literary elegance (*ya*). His style was an elegant form of classical Chinese, which resulted in these works being taken seriously by readers. He often slipped Chinese analogies and classical allusions into his texts, yet his tampering with the original texts only enhanced the impact of these works, so that the terms *natural selection* (*tianze*) and *survival of the fittest* (*shizhe shengcun*) were adopted by reformers as concepts that explained how China had failed to compete with other nations in the nineteenth century.

The crushing of the 1898 reform and the arrest of the Guangxu emperor (r. 1875–1908) temporarily brought the Chinese reform movement to an end. Yan Fu was forced to close *Guowen Bao*, but in 1901 he was invited to head the general office of the Kaiping Mining Bureau, signalling a resurgence of the modernizing movement in the wake of the Boxer Rebellion. In 1902 the National University in Beijing set up the Bureau for the Compilation and Translation of Books (Bianyi Shuju), which Yan headed for two years. In 1905 he met Sun Yat-sen in Britain and returned to Shanghai, where he assisted Ma Xiangbo in setting up Fudan University. After the 1911 Revolution Yan Fu was appointed by Yuan Shikai as the first chancellor of the National Peking University, which eventually became Peking University. The political association with Yuan Shikai diminished his influence after Yuan attempted to set up himself up as an emperor, as did his advocacy of Confucianism in the era of the New Culture Movement.

BIBLIOGRAPHY

Schwartz, Benjamin I. *In Search of Wealth and Power: Yen Fu and the West.* Cambridge, MA: Harvard University Press, 1964.

Wright, David. Yan Fu and the Tasks of the Translator. In *New Terms for New Ideas: Western Knowledge and Lexical Change in Late Imperial China*, ed. Michael Lackner, Iwo Amelung, and Joachim Kurtz, 235–256. Leiden, Netherland: Brill, 2001.

Bruce G. Doar

YAN'AN

Located in the northern part of Shaanxi Province, Yan'an was the headquarters of the Chinese Communist Party (CCP) from 1935 to 1947. During these "Yan'an years," the CCP transformed itself from a defeated and demoralized force after the Long March to a unified and formidable rival of the Nationalist government. In official CCP propaganda, Yan'an has become the symbol of the Chinese Communist revolution, with Mao Zedong Thought as its ideological orthodoxy, and the prolonged rectification movement as its organizational mechanism The nonpublicized purpose of the rectification movement was to eliminate non-Maoist elements within the party and the regional governments in areas under CCP control, and to instill revolutionary discipline under the new Mao cult. In

essence, Yan'an was the cradle of the future Communist state, where all the major salient features and policies of Mao's China after 1949 were formed and practiced.

In the summer of 1935, the Chinese Communist forces marching toward Soviet Central Asia were turned eastward after the Comintern and Joseph Stalin (1879–1953) adopted a policy of a worldwide "Popular Front" designed to allow various Communist parties around the world to concentrate on fighting fascism. The CCP-led Red Army forces under several commanders soon converged and settled in the remote and desolated area of Yan'an, strategically located near Japanese-controlled Manchuria, or North China, and the Soviet satellite of the People's Republic of Mongolia.

THE XI'AN INCIDENT

The newly established headquarters of the Chinese Communists might not have been able to survive the Nationalist government's elimination campaigns had there not been an epic event in December 1936 when Chiang Kaishek (Jiang Jieshi), the leader of the Chinese Nationalist government, was kidnapped in the nearby metropolis of Xi'an by the Communist-influenced Nationalist generals Zhang Xueliang (1901–2001) and Yang Hucheng (1893–1949). Chiang's release was only made possible after the Nationalists acceded to the Communists' demand that Chiang abandon elimination campaigns against the CCP and instead join the Communists in a "United Front"— that is, Moscow's Popular Front—in an effort to fight the ever-increasing Japanese occupation in China. The Xi'an Incident was crucial in shielding Yan'an from any major military attacks by Nationalist government troops for the next eleven years.

Although the settlement in the aftermath of the Xi'an Incident stipulated that Yan'an would be, in theory, under the command of the Nationalist government in Nanking (Nanjing), the CCP never yielded command of its armed forces or the operational autonomy of local governments in the "border region." As a result, Yan'an became a de facto capital of a new Communist state, with political independence and its own currency, economy, armed forces, and police.

Another significant impact of the Xi'an Incident amounts to a grand historic irony: In the Xi'an settlement, the Nationalist government insisted, and the CCP leadership agreed, that the CCP would give up the radical and disastrous land-reform policies that Mao and his cohorts had been practicing in the Jiangxi Soviet area. As a result, during much of the Yan'an period, the CCP conducted a relatively moderate land policy of rent reduction rather than the orthodox approach of outright state confiscation of land and mass killing of "landlords" as class enemies, which made the CCP government in Yan'an more popular. But this moderate land-reform policy did not generate nearly as much support among the people of North China as did the CCP's successful organizing and propaganda efforts to expel any Nationalist guerrillas in North China and build the CCP as the leading force of anti-Japanese sentiment. As a whole, the CCP's agrarian reform in Yan'an remained spotty, reluctant, and not thorough because the bulk of its agrarian activities soon amounted to rigorous conscription of peasants into the CCP armed forces to involve them in "military cultivation of land" in places such as Nanniwan. Another agrarian policy of Yan'an was to grow cash crops, the most important of which was opium.

YAN'AN THOUGHT REFORM AND THE BIRTH OF THE MAO ORTHODOXY

The CCP's most significant activities during the Yan'an years were related to the central mission of creating a new Communist orthodoxy with Mao at the center of its leadership cult and Mao Zedong Thought as its revolutionary theology. Mao was able to achieve these objectives during the twelve long years in Yan'an using two main approaches. The first was a complete restructuring of CCP operational and control mechanisms, an effort designed to eliminate organizational factions within the Chinese Communist Party. With tenuous power gained during the Long March in the top echelon of the CCP, Mao was able to consolidate his power by forming a small circle of fiercely loyal deputies who would gradually diminish the influence of the Comintern-returned CCP leaders. In late 1938, Mao allied with a former Moscow favorite, Kang Sheng (1898–1975), to form a Soviet-style internal security organization called the Central Social Affairs Department, which instantly became Mao's instrument of terror in Yan'an. Within a few years after arriving in Yan'an, most of Mao's chief rivals, including Zhang Guotao (1897–1979) and Wang Ming (1904–1974), were rendered disgraced or powerless. By 1941, Mao had become significantly organizationally secure within the power struggle of the CCP.

However, Mao and his loyalists would have to implement a second tactic called the Mass Line to purify the thought of the revolutionary masses. This new tactic made far more indelible the impact of Mao's relentless Yan'an rectification movement upon the Communist revolution. Through mandatory self-criticism and forced confessions, all had to "draw a line" with non-Maoist thoughts and factions, which would be eliminated through intimidation and terror. During the rectification movement, from 1942 to 1945, thousands were executed by the Social Affairs Department as traitors, Trotskyites, antiparty activists, counterrevolutionary elements, or spies.

YAN'AN AND THE OUTSIDE WORLD

Outside the Communist headquarters, Yan'an generated great utopian romanticism. The publication of the American journalist Edgar Snow's *Red Star over China* in 1937 was instrumental in creating global fascination with the incorruptible, noble Communists in areas encircled and blockaded by the reactionary Nationalist government and the Japanese troops. Influenced by various romantic notions of Yan'an, many people living in the Japanese-occupied areas and in Nationalist-controlled parts of China went to Yan'an in search of a revolutionary paradise.

While Yan'an enjoyed a public reputation of being remote, full of proverbial Chinese peasants in straw hats under a rustic agrarian leadership of pastoral virtues, the Yan'an Communists were not purely agrarian reformers trapped in the isolated northern plains. They had extensive international connections. Paramount to Mao Zedong and the CCP leadership was the Yan'an-Moscow tie, maintained through the Narodnyi komissariat vnutrennikh del (NKVD, or People's Commissariat of Internal Affairs) team. The team had a powerful secret radio station headed by Stalin's personal envoy to Mao, Peter Vladimirov (1905–1953), also known as Sun Ping or Song Ping, who from 1941 until the end of the civil war remained the most intimate and powerful foreign presence for Mao. During the same period, Stalin assigned to Mao a personal physician who enjoyed the rank of general in the Soviet Red Army. After 1938, many Asian Communist leaders left Moscow and became long-term residents in Yan'an, including the chiefs of the Japanese Communist Party and the Communist Party of Dutch East India. Ho Chi Minh (1890–1969) briefly transited through Yan'an after he left Moscow. Beginning in 1941, the eccentric left-leaning British aristocrat Michael Lindsay became another long-term foreign fixture in Yan'an as a radio expert.

Intense personal strife and interservice rivalry for turf and operational control also drove some partisan American personalities to Yan'an. To gain political leverage and operational independence from Chiang Kai-shek's Nationalist government, U.S. Army general Joseph Stilwell (1883–1946) initiated the Dixie mission in June 1944. This mission resulted in no significant military accomplishments, and produced strong political ill will between Stilwell and his titular boss, Chiang Kai-shek, which among other things became a reason for Stilwell's recall by U.S. president Franklin D. Roosevelt in October 1944. The American intelligence organization, the Office of Strategic Services (OSS), in late 1944 was prompted by pro-Yan'an army officers and State Department officials to provide illegal and unauthorized arms to Yan'an, bypassing the Nationalist government. When blunted by the new American ambassador Patrick Hurley (1883–1963), Mao offered to meet with President Roosevelt in order to discuss the OSS's grandiose promises of weapons. The meeting did not occur, but Mao's offer has led to countless what-if conjectures among Western historians who consider it a "missed opportunity" by the Americans, a myth that has been debunked by newly available post–Soviet Union archival documents and academic works, such as that by Michael Sheng (1997).

SEE ALSO *Chinese Marxism: Mao Zedong Thought; Communist Party; Mao Zedong; Trotskyism; Wang Shiwei.*

BIBLIOGRAPHY

Chen Yongfa (Chen Yung-fa). *Yan'an di yinying* [The shadow of Yan'an]. Taibei: Academia Sinica, 1990.

Gao Hua. *How Did the Red Sun Rise? The Origins and Development of Yan'an Rectification Movement.* Hong Kong: Chinese University of Hong Kong Press, 2000.

Garver, John. *Chinese-Soviet Relations, 1937–1945: The Diplomacy of Chinese Nationalism.* New York: Oxford University Press, 1988.

Seldon, Mark. *China in Revolution: The Yenan Way Revisited.* Armonk, NY: Sharpe, 1995.

Shi Zhe. *Alongside Historical Giants: A Memoir.* Beijing: CCP Central Committee Historical Documents Press, 1995.

Sheng, Michael M. *Battling Western Imperialism: Mao, Stalin, and the United States.* Princeton, NJ: Princeton University Press: 1997.

Yu Maochun

YAN'AN FORUM

The Yan'an Forum on Literature and Art (Yan'an wenyi zuotanhui) was a major event during the Yan'an rectification campaign (Yan'an zhengfeng yundong) of 1942 to 1944, which saw Mao Zedong's political and ideological preeminence in the Chinese Communist Party and its fledgling regime in northern Shaanxi confirmed and consolidated. The forum comprised meetings held on May 2, 16, and 23, 1942, and Mao Zedong's speeches at two of these meetings formed the basis of the keynote cultural policy document that would later be known as "Talks at the Yan'an Forum on Literature and Art" ("Zai Yan'an wenyi zuotanhui shang de jianghua"), comprising his introductory remarks (Yinyan) of May 2 and his summing up (Jielun). The "Talks" later were revised and published in *Jiefang ribao* (Liberation daily) in Yan'an on October 19, 1943, and later were revised again for inclusion in the second volume of *Mao Zedong xuanji* (*Selected Works of Mao Zedong*), published in 1953.

In his speeches Mao made it clear that he opposed the literature and art of the May Fourth movement, as well as most of the left-wing literature and art produced in China that preceded it. At the same time, he acknowledged its historical contribution. Alarmed by some young Yan'an writers' wish to create a literature independent of Communist Party direction, and arguing against left-wing Yan'an

writers such as Ding Ling, Xiao Jun, and Wang Shiwei, who insisted that writers should address social problems even in revolutionary areas, Mao made it clear that the time had passed for creating exposé literature (*baolu*), feuilleton (*zawen*), and literature examining human nature (*renxing*). Mao placed the literature and art he wanted to see created by Yan'an's "revolutionary" writers squarely within a Leninist revolutionary context, by insisting that proletarian art and literature were part of the proletarian revolution, Lenin's "cogs and screws." Also citing Lenin, Mao argued that writers must wholeheartedly serve the workers, peasants, and soldiers, that literature and art could come only from the people, and that their interests were defined by the party. He enjoined writers to go among the people to gain experience of their struggles, a formulation that recalled the pre-Bolshevik Narodnik movement in Russia.

Mao also made it clear that writers and artists needed to be mindful of different audiences. In Guomindang-controlled areas, such as Shanghai, for example, he argued that the main audience for revolutionary works comprised students, employees, and shopkeepers. Writers and artists in liberated areas should cater to the workers, peasants, and soldiers, and to the revolutionary cadres. To reach the illiterate peasantry, writers and artists needed to work in the forms they appreciated—wall newspapers, village dramas, folk stories, posters, folk songs, and folk music. The new revolutionary literary and art workers that Mao described in "Talks" needed to create "heroes" that the workers, peasants, and soldiers could emulate, and these new heroes needed to come from the ranks of the revolutionary masses. Mao also stressed that the workers were the leading class, then the peasants, soldiers, and urban petty bourgeoisie. He cited A. A. Fadeyev's 1927 novel *The Rout* (Chinese: *Huimie*) as a literary work catering to these classes and worthy of commendation; the only Chinese contemporary writer Mao quoted in "Talks" was Lu Xun, but Mao made it clear that the feuilleton, of which Lu Xun was a master, did not fit his criteria for revolutionary art. The only Chinese folk art form Mao mentioned was *xiaofangniu* (literally, "little herding"), a traditional folk dance drama.

In the decades following the Yan'an Forum a number of novels and works of art were held to embody Mao's principles, but none withstood the literary and artistic critique of the Cultural Revolution, underscoring the basic premise Mao set forth in "Talks"—that literature and art were subservient to politics and that writers and artists must obey the Chinese Communist Party. The political control of artistic and literary development in China was relaxed only in September 1979, when Deng Xiaoping in an address to the Chinese Writers Congress announced that the party would no longer issue directives to writers and artists, and that their service to politics would be limited to specific, short-term "political tasks" (*zhengzhi renwu*).

SEE ALSO *Chinese Marxism: Mao Zedong Thought; Communist Party; Ding Ling; Folk Art; Influences Abroad: Maoism and Art; Literature since 1800; Lu Xun; Mao Zedong; May Fourth Movement; Socialist Realism in Art; Trotskyism; Woodblock Printing (xylography); Zhao Shuli.*

BIBLIOGRAPHY

Goldman, Merle. *Literary Dissent in Communist China.* Cambridge, MA: Harvard University Press, 1967.

McDougall, Bonnie S. *Mao Zedong's "Talks at the Yan'an Conference on Literature and Art": A Translation of the 1943 Text with Commentary.* Ann Arbor: Center for Chinese Studies, University of Michigan Press, 1980.

Bruce G. Doar

YANG MO (YANG CHENGYE)
1914–1996

Yang Mo, born Yang Chengye in Beijing on August 25, 1914, had an unhappy childhood, but found comfort and enlightenment in literature. At the age of sixteen, her father went bankrupt and her mother was going to marry her to a Guomindang officer. The defiant young woman ran away from home and over the next few years made a living as a teacher, bookstore clerk, and tutor. Despite financial difficulty, she stayed in the Beijing area to audit courses at Peking University. It was also during this time that she fell in love with Zhang Zhongxing (1909–2006), a student in the Chinese Department of that university, and they lived together for five years. Eventually they broke up, as they embraced different goals in life: He wanted to be a scholar of Chinese classics, while she identified more and more with the Communist revolution. Yang joined the Communist Party in 1936 and, after the start of the Second Sino-Japanese War, went to the Communist Party base in Northwest China, where she worked as an editor for newspapers. After 1949 she became a writer for Beijing Film Studio and married Ma Jianmin, with whom she had two children. During the decade of the Cultural Revolution (1966–1976), they became estranged and divorced under bitter circumstances. She later married Li Yunchang. Her daughter was killed during this period; her son Ma Bo grew up to be a writer under the pen name Lao Gui, or Old Ghost. In 2005 Ma Bo published a memoir titled *Muqin Yang Mo* (My mother Yang Mo), which gives a candid account of Yang's personal and political life.

In March 1934, Yang Mo published her first work, a piece of reportage about the oppression of peasants in south Rehe Province. She went on to write many stories and prose works under the pen name Little Hui. One of her stories, published in 1937 and titled "Nutao" (Raging tide), depicts a young college student named Meizhen who falls in love and lives together with a young man named Zhao. They have a baby son. But conflict arises between the couple when she becomes socially aware while he considers it a woman's duty to stay home with her husband and children. As a result, Meizhen breaks up with Zhao and devotes herself to helping the peasants and fighting the Japanese invaders. Clearly autobiographic, the protagonist of this story provides the prototype of Lin Daojing in Yang Mo's magnum opus *Qingchun zhi ge* (*The Song of Youth*).

THE SONG OF YOUTH

Lin Daojing's father is a wealthy landlord; her mother is a peasant who is brought into the household by force and then kicked out of the house after giving birth to a baby girl, Lin Daojing. Distraught by the loss of her daughter, she kills herself. Fast forwarding to 1931, Lin is a recent graduate from middle school. Forced to marry Hu, chief of the Education Bureau, by her stepmother, she runs away from home. Failing to find her cousin, she is about to commit suicide but is rescued by Yu Yongze, a student in the Chinese Department at Peking University. Despite opposition from his parents, they fall in love and start living together. Now auditing classes at the university, Lin joins a progressive group and goes south with the students to petition against the Guomindang policy of not resisting Japanese aggression. Under pressure from the authorities, Yu withdraws from the student movement, but Lin remains committed. In 1933 she joins the Youth Revolutionary Salon and familiarizes herself with Communism. On May 31 the Guomindang signs the Tanggu Agreement with Japan, which in essence opens the door to Japanese occupation of Manchuria. Lin participates in the demonstrations, for which her friend Lu Jiachuan is arrested, and she has to flee Beijing. Working at a primary school, she is visited by her friend Jiang Hua, who teaches her how to organize the masses.

Back in Beijing, Lin is arrested and jailed for engaging in leftist activities. In prison, she meets Lin Hong, whose martyrdom inspires her to join the Communist Party. Through her father's connections, she is released and exposes Zheng Juncai, who secretly works for the Guomindang and is responsible for the death of Lu Jiachuan. Yu Yongze, her former lover, has been used by Zheng, and in shame he commits suicide. On December 9, 1935, Lin and Jiang Hua, now lovers, take part in the student movement calling for national resistance against Japan's military expansion in North China.

The Song of Youth, written from 1951 to 1957, is a bildungsroman that delineates the transformation of Lin Daojing from her renunciation of the feudal family system to her full participation in the Communist revolution. Narrated from the third-person omniscient point of view, the story is memorable for its vivid characterization, gripping episodes, and lyrical language. It presents an array of young intellectuals living through a tumultuous time in Chinese history and the choices they make: Yu Yongze is a selfish and cowardly student whose only ambition is to become a famous scholar; Jiang Hua is a dedicated Communist; and Zheng Juncai is a traitor.

Upon its publication, *The Song of Youth* became immensely popular, especially among students. Yang's phenomenal success is demonstrated by the fact that she was invited to join a delegation of Chinese writers visiting the Soviet Union in October 1958. The delegation was headed by Mao Dun, with Ba Jin and Zhou Yang as deputy heads. Only three women writers were included—Xu Guangping, Bing Xin, and the much younger Yang Mo. In 1959 a film based on the novel was made to celebrate the tenth anniversary of the founding of the People's Republic of China; directed by Cui Wei and Chen Huaiai, the movie, of the same title, was also well received.

Despite its popularity, *The Song of Youth* was criticized for its focus on urban intellectuals and its depiction of romantic love. It was even accused of being pornographic. During the decade of the Cultural Revolution, *The Song of Youth* was again singled out for criticism. In response, Yang Mo revised the novel several times to put more emphasis on peasants and workers and to downplay Lin Daojing's "petty bourgeois" tendencies. But her effort did not save her from persecution. It was only after the Cultural Revolution was recanted in the late 1970s that she was "rehabilitated." In the 1980s and 1990s she wrote several novels, such as *Dongfang yu xiao* (Dawning in the east), *Fangfei zhi ge* (The song of flowers), and *Yinghua zhi ge* (The song of blossoms). However, there is no question that *The Song of Youth* remains her most important and enduring work.

SEE ALSO *Bingxin; Literature of National Defense; Literature since 1800.*

BIBLIOGRAPHY

Button, Peter. Aesthetics, Dialectics, and Desire in Yang Mo's *Song of Youth*. Positions 14, 1 (2006): 193–218.

Knight, Sabina. Moral Decision in Mao-Era Fiction. In her *The Heart of Time: Moral Agency in Twentieth-Century Chinese Fiction*, 133–161. Cambridge, MA: Harvard University Asia Center, 2006.

Wang, Ban. Revolutionary Realism and Revolutionary Romanticism: *The Song of Youth*. In *Columbia Companion to Modern East Asian Literature*, ed. Joshua Mostow, 470–475. New York: Columbia University Press, 2003.

Michelle Yeh

YANG ZHENNING
1922–

Yang Zhenning (known abroad as Chen Ning Franklin Yang) is often called the first Chinese Nobel Prize winner. However, he spent most of his working life in the United States, and it was there that he did the investigatory work on parity laws leading to important discoveries regarding elementary particles for which he and a Chinese American colleague were awarded the Nobel Prize for Physics in 1957. Yang returned to live in China in 1999.

Yang Zhenning was born in Hefei, in Anhui Province, in 1922. His father was an American-educated professor of mathematics at Tsinghua (Qinghua) University in Beijing. The family became refugees when Japanese troops occupied Beijing. Yang Zhenning later attended the National Southwest Associated University in Kunming, a wartime establishment set up by academics fleeing Japanese-occupied China. He received his Bachelor of Science in 1942 and his Master of Science from Tsinghua University in 1944. At the end of the war he entered the University of Chicago on a Tsinghua University fellowship. He came under the influence of the distinguished Italian American physicist Enrico Fermi (1901–1954), who had won the Nobel Prize for Physics in 1938 and had been a leading physicist on the Manhattan Project for the development of nuclear energy and the atomic bomb.

After receiving his PhD in 1948, Yang was an instructor at the University of Chicago for a year. He was associated with the Institute for Advanced Study in Princeton, New Jersey, from 1949 and became a professor there in 1955. In 1965 he was appointed Albert Einstein Professor of Physics at the State University of New York at Stony Brook and became the first director of what was later named the C. N. Yang Institute for Theoretical Physics.

Yang worked on various subjects in physics, but his chief interest was in two fields: statistical mechanics and symmetry principles. From his earliest days as a physicist, his work advanced knowledge of weak interactions, the forces once thought to cause elementary particles to disintegrate. With Li Zhengdao (Tsung-Dao Lee, 1926–), another Chinese American scientist, he attempted to solve the mystery of why newly discovered K mesons, contrary to expectation, seemed to exhibit decay modes into configurations of differing parity. Their experiments revealed large parity-violating effects and in addition showed that the symmetry between particle and antiparticle known as charge-conjugation symmetry is also broken by weak decays.

In addition to his work on weak interactions, Yang, in collaboration with Li Zhengdao and others, carried out important work in statistical mechanics (the study of systems with large numbers of particles) and later investigated the nature of elementary-particle reactions at extremely high energies. Yang is also well known for his collaboration with Robert Mills (1927–1999) in developing a gauge theory of a new class. Yang-Mills theories are now a fundamental part of the standard model of particle physics.

Yang published a number of books in both English and Chinese, and his articles have appeared in the *Bulletin of the American Mathematical Society*, the *Physical Review*, the *Review of Modern Physics*, and the *Chinese Journal of Physics*. He has won many prizes for his work and holds numerous honorary degrees.

In 1950 Yang married his former student Du Zhili, by whom he had two sons and a daughter. Her father, Du Yuming, an important Guomindang (Nationalist Party) general, had been captured during the civil war and was imprisoned until 1959, when he was pardoned and awarded a high-ranking position. It was widely believed that his treatment was intended to persuade his son-in-law to return to China.

From 1972 Yang visited China regularly. He was received by Mao Zedong and Zhou Enlai in 1973. He urged that China should give more attention to theoretical work and basic training in science education. Zhou Enlai and later Deng Xiaoping recognized that Yang could give invaluable advice on the revitalization of science in China. When Yang retired from the State University of New York at Stony Brook in 1999, he became one of many distinguished academics of Chinese origin to accept an invitation to a prestigious post in order to strengthen research in China's universities. He returned to his alma mater, Tsinghua University, where he took up the Huang Jibei, Lu Kaiqun chair in physics at the Institute of Advanced Studies.

Yang's first wife died in 2003. In 2005 he married Weng Fan, a twenty-eight-year-old MA student at Guangzhou Foreign Studies University. This marriage to a woman fifty-four years his junior attracted considerable media attention and provoked much debate in China on age difference in marriage.

Yang will be chiefly remembered for his work as a physicist. Yet he is also interesting as an example of a scientist from the Chinese diaspora whose life and work has transcended national boundaries. Though he took U.S. nationality and was to a large extent cut off from China during the Cold War, when U.S.-Chinese relations were at their worst, by the 1970s he was able to establish himself as a respected figure in Beijing. Like other U.S. scientists of Chinese origin, he has worked to improve relations between the two countries.

BIBLIOGRAPHY

Friedman, Edward. Einstein and Mao: Metaphors of Revolution. *China Quarterly*, no. 93 (March 1983): 51–75.

Koehn, Peter H., and Xiao-huang Yin, eds. *The Expanding Roles of Chinese Americans in U.S.-China Relations: Transnational Networks and Trans-Pacific Interactions*. Armonk, NY: Sharpe, 2002.

Nobelprize.org. Chen Ning Yang: The Nobel Prize in Physics 1957. http://nobelprize.org/nobel_prizes/physics/laureates/1957/yang-bio.html.

Yang Zhenning. *Dushu jiaoxue sishi nian* [Forty years of study and teaching]. Hong Kong: Sanlian Shudian, 1985.

Delia Davin

YANGZHOU

Yangzhou, a medium-sized city in Jiangsu Province, lies north of the Yangzi River on the west bank of the Grand Canal, formerly the main transport route between the Yangzi River Valley and Beijing. Like Hangzhou and Suzhou, it holds great appeal for tourists due to its rich historical and cultural legacy. An important difference is that Hangzhou and Suzhou are both within easy distance of Shanghai, and enjoy a high degree of visibility in the foreign tourist market. Yangzhou is less well known, particularly to Westerners. This marks a historical reversal from a time when it was a natural port of call for travelers within the Chinese empire.

Before its occupation by the Taiping rebels in the 1850s, Yangzhou was the premier city in northern Jiangsu, where it combined the roles of prefectural capital and administrative center of the Lianghuai salt monopoly. Until around 1800, it was also one of the richest cities in China. Its position at a crucial node in the long-distance communication network made it an important entrepôt and center of administration. Qing Yangzhou was known for its wealthy salt merchants and magnificent gardens, as well as for its cultural productivity, most notably in painting. Members of the "Yangzhou painting school" (*Yangzhou huapai*), often referred to as the "eight eccentrics of Yangzhou" (*Yangzhou baguai*), are among the most famous painters of the Qing dynasty, their influence evident among Shanghai painters of the nineteenth and early twentieth centuries. The "Yangzhou school of learning" (*Yangzhou xuepai*), epitomized by the scholar official Ruan Yuan, included an eclectic mix of scholars whose diverse outlooks and interests were a sign of the complexity and diversified character of Yangzhou society.

Yangzhou was adversely affected by a number of developments in the middle and later years of the nineteenth century, including the Taiping Uprising (1851–1864), the decline of the Grand Canal, the growth of coastal transport by steamship, and the creation of a rail system that bypassed the city. This left it isolated and out of touch with the forces for modernization, which in the early twentieth century were transforming not only Shanghai but also Nanjing and Zhenjiang, on the other side of the Yangzi River. Visitors to the city in the Republican era found it quaint and old-fashioned. Zhu Ziqing's famous essay, "Wo shi Yangzhouren" (I am a man of Yangzhou; 1941), was essentially a defense of a place widely derided among people from the south of the Yangzi River.

Occupied by the Japanese in 1937, Yangzhou became the site of internment camps, where large numbers of foreigners from Shanghai spent the duration of the Pacific War (1937–1945). Chinese Communist forces controlled much of the terrain to the city's northwest during the war. After 1949 Communist cadres from the greater Yangzhou region moved into positions of responsibility in Shanghai. One of Yangzhou's most famous sons, former president Jiang Zemin, served as mayor of Shanghai from 1985 to 1989 before being promoted to general secretary of the Communist Party during the crisis of 1989.

During the reform era, efforts were made to restore and promote the city's old historical sites, which now constitute its major attraction for domestic visitors. A 2008 report claimed that the city hosted 16 million visitors, predominantly Chinese, in the preceding year. The city does have some built-in attractions for foreigners. The Yangzhou Museum features a monument to Marco Polo, who claimed to have served as governor of the city during the reign of Kublai Khan (1215–1294). The Daming Temple is venerated as the former residence of the Buddhist monk Jian Zhen (688–763), a native of Yangzhou who spent the last ten years of his life teaching in Japan. An old mosque in the city's east holds gravestones engraved in Arabic. Apart from these material reminders of the outside world, the city's most famous sites are old gardens and architectural structures created by salt merchants in the eighteenth and nineteenth centuries. The most striking of these, located by Slender West Lake, are the White Stupa, built in 1784 in imitation of the stupa in Beijing's Beihai Park, and the Five Pavilion Bridge, built in 1757 and now used as the city's tourist insignia.

The municipal and provincial governments have made a number of other initiatives to ensure economic growth in Yangzhou and the surrounding region, which, with the exception of wealth generated by the salt trade, has always lagged behind the southern part of the province. Road, rail, and bridge construction in the 1990s helped reduce the effective distance between the north and south, and also the prosperity gap. A population of around 4.6 million in the municipality supports a mixed economy of heavy and light industry with a diminishing agricultural sector. In 2007 Yangzhou ranked forty-ninth for competitiveness among Chinese cities. Major recent initiatives include the creation of an ecological city to the north of the present urban area, and the development of a river port. The Grand Canal is in the process of renovation. When it is completed, travelers will once again be able to travel by boat from Beijing in the north to Hangzhou in the south, stopping at Yangzhou along the way.

SEE ALSO *Grand Canal; Jiangsu; Ruan Yuan; Salt, 1800– 1949; Urban China: Cities and Urbanization, 1800– 1949; Urban China: Organizing Principles of Cities; Urban China: Urban Planning since 1978; Zhu Ziqing (Zhu Zihua).*

BIBLIOGRAPHY

China Daily. Exquisite Yangzhou: A Vigorous Ancient City. May 26, 2008. Spec. suppl.

Finnane, Antonia. *Speaking of Yangzhou: A Chinese City, 1550– 1850.* Cambridge, MA: Harvard University Asia Center, 2004.

Honig, Emily. *Creating Chinese Ethnicity: Subei People in Shanghai, 1850–1980.* New Haven, CT: Yale University Press, 1992.

Hsü, Ginger Cheng-chi. *A Bushel of Pearls: Painting for Sale in Eighteenth-Century Yangchow.* Stanford, CA: Stanford University Press, 2001.

Meyer-Fong, Tobie. *Building Culture in Early Qing Yangzhou.* Stanford, CA: Stanford University Press, 2003.

Zhu Ziqing. Wo shi Yangzhouren [I am a man of Yangzhou]. In *Zhu Ziqing yanjiu ziliao* [Research materials on Zhu Ziqing], ed. Zhu Jinshun, 305–309. Beijing: Shifandaxue Chubanshe, 1981.

Antonia Finnane

YOUTH

An understanding of youth in China (i.e., those aged fifteen to thirty, see Gold 1991, p. 598) requires an appreciation of the extraordinary strength of the family as an institution in Chinese culture. The Chinese relate normatively to others not as individuals but in terms of their membership in their families. The notion of filial piety, in particular, provides moral guidance and influences social thoughts and interactions. Although expectations of obedience and deference to authority are found in other cultures, "filial piety surpasses all other ethics in its historical continuity, the proportion of humanity under its governance, and the encompassing and imperative nature of its precepts. The attributes of intergenerational relationships governed by filial piety are structural, enduring, and invariable across situations within Chinese culture" (Ho 1996, p. 155). To disregard or violate one's filial obligations is considered the most serious breach of Chinese moral norms. Filial piety also constitutes the framework against which authority in all generalities is understood and observed, and the Chinese have always regarded the family as a microscopic state. In a society where the media and other sources of information are controlled by the party-state, youth is expected to be a time during which submission to official teachings is inculcated, rather than a time to search for self-identity.

Nevertheless, using a sociological life course approach, Thomas Gold (1991) finds that while the party has sought to exert control over youth directly and through state- and party-led organizations since 1949, its efforts have not been

CHILD PROTECTION

China's transition to a market economy has fostered rapid social stratification and a growing socioeconomic divide, and the country's child-protection system reveals important challenges and gaps. Although China ratified the United Nations (UN) Convention on the Rights of the Child in 1991, and consequently drew up National Plans of Action for Children (*Zhongguo ertong fazhan gangyao*) in the 1990s and for the 2001–2010 decade, there was no comprehensive child-protection system in place in 2008. Despite a growing economy, overall spending on education and health care remains comparatively low, well beneath that of Organization for Economic Cooperation and Development countries and 50 percent below the UN-recommended level.

Imbalances in socioeconomic development have resulted in uneven capacities in situation analysis, targeting, funding, and monitoring actions at the local level. Child mortality rates are still two to five times higher in rural areas and among migrant populations, whereas obesity and moral and psychological development are new concerns in cities. The financial difficulties of parents, underpaid and undermotivated teachers, an unequal distribution of resources for education, and miscellaneous fees contribute to high dropout rates in schools, especially in rural schools, pushing children to enter into child labor.

Using a narrow legal definition of *trafficking*—that is, for the purpose of selling—only a few thousand cases of child trafficking have been reported. However, a broader definition that include forced labor reveals that child trafficking is dramatically increasing in China, especially among the country's twenty million "migrant" children. The fragile status of China's 150 million surplus rural workers looking for jobs, mainly in coastal cities, affects migrant children in terms of access to adequate housing, heath care, and education. Besides, some 23 million "left-behind" children remain in the villages while one or both parents have migrated to other provinces to find work. Among these children, 30 percent are cared for by grandparents or other relatives, and some even have no adult in charge. They emotionally suffer from loneliness and perform poorly in school.

Official estimates of the number of street children in China vary from 1 million to 1.5 million, although in reality there are far more. Beyond the classic causes, such as poverty and family breakdown, the phenomenon is also linked to marginalization of nonresident and nonregistered children, a consequence of the birth-limitation policy, which imposes penalties on parents who have out-of-plan babies. Meanwhile, pilot projects of the Ministry of Civil Affairs, with the support of UNICEF-China and some international nongovernmental organizations, have adopted a more progressive approach to assisting children in street situations, with intervention combining protection, service provisions, and participation. Coordination among nineteen ministries for the protection of street minors started in 2005.

BIBLIOGRAPHY

Committee on the Rights of the Child: *Concluding Observations: China (Including Hong-Kong and Macau Special Administrative Regions)*. CRC/C/OSPC/CHN/CO/ 2, United Nations, Geneva, November 24, 2005.

Goodkind, Daniel. *China's Missing Children: The 2000 Census Underreporting Surprise*. Population Studies, Vol. 58, No. 3, 2004, 281–295.

Stoecklin, Daniel. *Enfants des rues en Chine* [Street children in China]. Paris: Karthala, 2000.

Ye, Jingzhong; James Murray, and Yihuan Wang. *Left-Behind Children in Rural China. Impact Study of Rural Labor Migration on Left-Behind Children in Mid-West China.* Beijing: Social Sciences Academic Press (China), 2005.

Daniel Stoecklin

consistent and have resulted in huge disparities in outlook and behavior among different age cohorts and generations. Gold points to the Cultural Revolution as a watershed event that "influenced not only the life course of Chinese people . . . but also the very construction of the Chinese life course" (1991, p. 594; see also Zhou and Hou 1999).

Since China opened to more outside influences in the 1980s, Chinese youth have become increasingly discontented with their lives, which they compare with their counterparts in other countries as well as Hong Kong and Taiwan. Market and attendant educational reforms have resulted in a more competitive job market and educational system, as well as increased endorsement of the notions of autonomy and choice, with young graduates "facing selection dilemmas instead of reluctantly submitting to national needs" (Cheng 1994, p. 68). Kai-Ming Cheng finds that changes among Chinese youth include a shift from a collective toward an individualistic outlook, which indicates their recognition that while national needs continue to be important, individual needs and values also ought to be taken into account in one's decision making. In addition, Cheng notes the development of pluralistic beliefs and ideologies among Chinese youth, as well as a movement away from idealistic life objectives (namely, joining the party) toward accumulations of wealth (Cheng 1994, p. 69). Ian Weber discerns that "once exposed to the values of materialism, freedom, change, and progress, the once constrictive boundaries of appropriate behaviour were suddenly and irreversibly stretched" (2002, p. 354).

In order to curb population growth, China introduced the one-child policy in 1979, under which second and subsequent children are denied state benefits and their parents are penalized, with certain exceptions. At the same time, various rural economic reforms were introduced under which it would be economically advantageous to have more children. Resistance by rural families to the one-child policy resulted in a de facto two-child policy in rural China that was officially endorsed by the state in 1989 (Cooney and Li 1994; Davin 1985; Deutsch 2006). Acceptance of the one-child policy was much greater in the cities (Kane 1985). As a result of the one-child policy, the long-standing preference among the Chinese for sons to continue the family line has intensified in rural areas, as have sex-selective abortion, abandonment, and adoption or infanticide of female children (Coale and Banister 1994; Croll 1994).

The one-child policy, however, has led to a child-centered approach in parenting, with many resources devoted to the only child's needs and desires, including those for consumption. The policy has also led to a generation of children without siblings and who receive a level of parental attention and support vastly exceeding that found in Western countries. Francine Deutsch (2006) finds that this has led to a closer parent-child relationship than was traditionally the case and has paradoxically increased gender equality in China. While legal protection has been accorded youth as an area of social vulnerability alongside old age and gender, Michael Palmer states that the legal protection accorded youth in the 1991 Law on the Protection of Minors is "a strongly controlling framework of rules and policies, seemingly directed at creating the model Chinese socialist citizen" (2007, p. 152).

BIBLIOGRAPHY

Cheng, Kai-Ming. Young Adults in a Changing Socialist Society: Post-Compulsory Education in China. *Comparative Education* 30 (1994): 63–73.

Coale, Ansley J., and Judith Banister. Five Decades of Missing Females in China. *Demography* 31 (1994): 459–479.

Cooney, Rosemary Santana, and Jiali Li. Household Registration Type and Compliance with the "One Child" Policy in China, 1979–1988. *Demography* 31 (1994): 21–32.

Croll, Elisabeth. *From Heaven to Earth: Images and Experiences of Development in China.* London: Routledge, 1994.

Davin, Delia. The Single-Child Family Policy in the Countryside. In *China's One-Child Family Policy*, ed. Elisabeth Croll, Delia Davin, and Penny Kane, 37–82. New York: St. Martin's, 1985.

Deutsch, Francine M. Filial Piety, Patrilineality, and China's One-Child Policy. *Journal of Family Issues* 27 (2006): 366–389.

Gold, Thomas B. Youth and the State. *China Quarterly* 127 (1991): 594–612.

Ho, David Y. F. Filial Piety and Its Psychological Consequences. In *The Handbook of Chinese Psychology*, ed. Michael Harris Bond, 155–165. Hong Kong: Oxford University Press, 1996.

Kane, Penny. The Single-Child Family Policy in the Cities. In *China's One-Child Family Policy*, ed. Elisabeth Croll, Delia Davin, and Penny Kane, 83–113. New York: St. Martin's, 1985.

Palmer, Michael. On China's Slow Boat to Women's Rights: Revisions to the Women's Protection Law, 2005. *International Journal of Human Rights* 11 (2007): 151–177.

Weber, Ian. *Shanghai Baby*: Negotiating Youth Self-Identity in Urban China. *Social Identities* 8 (2002): 347–368.

Zhou, Xueguang, and Liren Hou. Children of the Cultural Revolution: The State and the Life Course in the People's Republic of China. *American Sociological Review* 64 (1999): 12–36.

Phil C. W. Chan

YU DAFU
1896–1945

Yu Dafu is a key literary figure from the May Fourth period. He was one of the founding members of the Creation Society, one of the two leading literary societies (the other being the Literary Association) of the 1920s and 1930s. Yu is best known for his short fiction, though he was considered by many to be especially talented in writing classical-style poetry. His short-story collection, *Sinking* (*Chenlun*; 1921), next to Lu Xun's *Call to Arms* (*Nahan*; 1923), is possibly the earliest such collection in modern Chinese literary history. The eponymous story, "Sinking," is widely studied as a classic personal and national allegory that explores the relationship between self, sexuality, and nationalism. It is also representative of a body of "student immigrant literature" (*liuxuesheng wenxue*) that began to emerge in the late nineteenth century with the Qing government's policy of sponsoring Chinese students to study abroad in an effort to modernize. Their experience abroad shaped many May Fourth intellectuals' understanding of other nations, especially Japan, and instilled, in turn, their sense of the pressing urgency for China to establish its own sovereignty in the modern world. Yu's early fiction, as well as that of his contemporary and close friend Guo Moruo, often takes the "East Ocean" as the setting where the Chinese male protagonist undergoes a tormented spiritual journey that ends with a symbolic return of the prodigal son to the place of his roots and identity.

Contrary to the nationalistic milieu in which he established his literary voice, Yu is widely known, not always approvingly, for his sentimentality and decadent aesthetics. His often brash portrayals of male sexuality and unfulfilled desires, coupled with his penchant for public confessions about his personal life, made him a controversial figure in an atmosphere dominated by the ideology of rising socialism and national salvation. His emphasis on individual desires singled him out as a writer whose aesthetics was perhaps more heavily colored by European romanticism than any of his contemporaries. Yu often found himself having to defend his artistic choices against accusations of debauchery and lack of political and social engagement.

This earlier view of the romanticist Yu Dafu, however, must be contrasted to the last years of his life. In 1938 Yu moved to Southeast Asia, first to Singapore then eventually to northern Bukit Tinggit on the Indonesian island of Sumatra. He produced no fiction during this period and primarily edited and contributed essays to newspaper columns while in Singapore, which has prompted interesting debates concerning the legacy of mainland Chinese literature in places geographically peripheral to its nationalist vision. Yu later joined the underground resistance movement against the Japanese occupation. During this period, Yu Dafu posed as a wine merchant and changed his name to Zhao Lian, or Moustache Zhao, as he was known among friends and the Japanese military commanders he befriended. He built relations with the Japanese, while secretly helping the resistance by providing intelligence. He also married a Malay woman who bore him two children, but who did not learn of his true identity until after his death in 1945.

The circumstances surrounding Yu's death have been a subject of considerable speculation. Even after the Japanese archives were made available to the public years later, little could be gleaned from the documents. Witnesses present at Yu's house on the night of August 29, 1945, recalled a young local man knocking on his door. He apparently came to ask for Yu's assistance, and Yu hastily left with him, wearing only his undershirt and slippers. Another witness claimed to have seen him get into a car, and others speculated that he was executed as part of the Japanese cleanup process. Some of the Japanese military commanders had suspected that Yu was working for the resistance movement, but kept only a close watch because they knew of his local influence. Yu Dafu specialists in Japan, however, believe that his death was the result of a local vendetta on the part of a lower-ranking member of the Japanese military who feared that

Yu would testify to his wrongdoings. The order for Yu's execution, in this view, did not come from the top.

Whatever the circumstance, Yu's body was never found. His legacy, however, left an extraordinary imprint on the literary imagination of contemporary Malaysian-Chinese writers such as Huang Jinshu, who saw in Yu's martyr presence an allegory for the still contentious literary heritage of mainland Chinese writers in exile or sojourn in Southeast Asia. Yu's enigmatic death in the South, in many ways, speaks to his chameleonlike literary personality as a whole, wherein he donned many versions of a self that, in the end, eludes both the historiography of modern Chinese literature and the ideological grasp of nationalism.

SEE ALSO *Anti-Japanese War, 1937–1945; Guo Moruo; League of Left-Wing Writers; Literary Societies; Lu Xun; Poetry: Classical Poetry.*

BIBLIOGRAPHY
Lee, Leo Ou-fan. *The Romantic Generation of Modern Chinese Writers.* Cambridge, MA: Harvard University Press, 1973.
Suzuki Masao. *Sumatora nuo Iku Tatsufu:* Taiheiyō Sensō to Chūgoku sakka (Yu Dafu in Sumatra: The Pacific War and Chinese writers). Tokyo: Toho Shoten, 1995.
Wong Yoon Wah. Yu Dafu in Exile: His Last Days in Sumatra. *Renditions* 23 (1985): 71–83.

Jing Tsu

YU HUA
1960–

Yu Hua was born on April 3, 1960, to two medical doctors in Hangzhou, Zhejiang Province. He grew up in Haiyan, a small town near Hangzhou. After high school he studied dentistry and practiced for five years, but gave it up to pursue a writing career in 1983. Yu Hua first came to the attention of the literary world with the publication in 1984 of his story "On the Road at Eighteen," a parable of his generation's idealism and disappointment. Since then he has published six collections of stories, four collections of essays, and four novels. His works have been translated into many languages and received important international awards, including Italy's Premio Grinzane Cavour (1998) and the James Joyce Foundation Award (2002).

Yu Hua was early identified with the movement of experimental or "avant-garde" writers, which began around 1987 and ended in the early 1990s. But unlike many of the others in this group, he has gone far beyond formalistic experimentation. He moves easily from one fiction genre to another, from premodern tales of "scholars and beauties" (*caizi jiaren*) to martial arts fiction, from ghost stories and detective fiction to historical novels and epics, from political parables to pop fiction. Yu Hua writes in a brisk style that stresses dialogue and action. Because of his rare combination of accessibility and depth, he has achieved a popular success that has escaped most of the other avant-garde writers. Two of his novels, *To Live* (1992) and *Chronicle of a Blood Merchant* (1995), were selected by a national panel of one hundred Chinese literary critics as among the ten most influential novels of the decade in China. *To Live* was made into a film directed by Zhang Yimou, which won the Grand Jury Prize at the Cannes Film Festival in 1994.

After almost ten years during which he traveled widely and wrote mainly essays, Yu Hua published the two volumes of his latest novel, *Brothers* (*Xiongdi*), in 2005 and 2006. *Brothers* tells of two stepbrothers growing up together during the decade of the Cultural Revolution (1966–1976) and growing apart after the economic reforms of the 1980s. Their history covers the span of Yu's own life, and mirrors the current troubles of the nation: the eager pursuit of wealth after years of dire poverty, the moral confusion of breakneck social change, the tragic separation that is the new inequality, and inconsolable regrets. Full of black humor, absurdity, and violence, *Brothers* has nevertheless touched a deep chord with readers, and is widely regarded as a profound psychological portrait of a difficult time.

Yu Hua's writing faces the reality of brutal physical damage with a directness and even humor that can be disconcerting, especially in his early work. For instance, his story "One Kind of Reality" (1988) narrates with calm detachment how an accident escalated into a series of murders within a family, ending in a bloody dissection. Yu Hua's interest in writing was stimulated in his childhood by the "big character posters" of the Cultural Revolution, a kind of writing open to anyone, in which people would post complaints against their neighbors, often in lurid detail and often resulting in public violence. At the same time, as a child of two doctors, he was familiar with human bodies as objects of medical attention and had no fear of corpses. He reports having been glad to take refuge from hot summer days by napping on the cool cement floor of the nearby morgue.

Yu Hua's dagger-style narrative and his critical insight into the psychological drama of a culture in transition are reminiscent of Lu Xun (1881–1936). Both writers first pursued a medical career, and both came from Zhejiang Province. Yu Hua plays with the comparison in the story "Classical Love" (1988), turning the symbolic cannibalism of Lu Xun's "Diary of a Madman" into fictional reality by presenting people as dinner entrées to be selected by the quality of their flesh. However, there is at least one important difference. Lu Xun characterized his literary work as an effort to treat what he saw as a national spiritual illness. But Yu Hua has said that for him, the turn to literature was an escape from the rules of medical practice into the world of human imagination. He has described his writing as a form of personal liberation, enabling him to explore the irrational, the obscure, the fantastic, and the ambiguous.

SEE ALSO *Avant-garde Fiction; Lu Xun; Zhang Yimou.*

BIBLIOGRAPHY

WORKS BY YU HUA

The Noon of Howling Wind. 1987. Trans. Denis C. Mair. In *China's Avant-garde Fiction*, ed. Jing Wang, 69–73. Durham, NC: Duke University Press, 1998.

"1986." 1987. Trans. Andrew F. Jones. In *China's Avant-garde Fiction*, ed. Jing Wang, 74–113. Durham, NC: Duke University Press, 1998.

One Kind of Reality. 1988. Trans. Jeanne Tai. In *Running Wild: New Chinese Writers*, ed. David Der-wei Wang, 21–68. New York: Columbia University Press, 1994.

This Story Is for Willow. 1989. Trans. Denis C. Mair. In *China's Avant-garde Fiction*, ed. Jing Wang, 114–146. Durham, NC: Duke University Press, 1998.

Cries in the Drizzle. 1991. Trans. Allan H. Barr. New York: Anchor, 2007.

To Live. 1992. Trans. Michael Berry. New York: Anchor, 2003.

Chronicle of a Blood Merchant. 1995. Trans. Andrew F. Jones. New York: Pantheon, 2003.

The Past and the Punishment. Trans. Andrew F. Jones. Honolulu: University of Hawai'i Press, 1996. This volume contains the following stories: "On the Road at Eighteen," "Classical Love," "World Like Mist," "The Past and the Punishment," "1986," "Blood and Plum Blossoms," "The Death of a Landlord," and "Predestination."

Yu Hua zuopin xilie [Works by Yu Hua]. 12 vols. Shanghai: Shanghai Wenyi Chubanshe, 2004.

Xiongdi [Brothers], Vol. 1. Shanghai: Shanghai Wenyi Chubanshe, 2005.

Xiongdi [Brothers], Vol. 2. Shanghai: Shanghai Wenyi Chubanshe, 2006.

Brothers. Trans. Eileen Cheng-Yin Chow and Carlos Rojas. New York: Pantheon, 2009.

Jingyuan Zhang

YUAN SHIKAI
1859–1916

Yuan Shikai was the military strongman of the late Qing and the early Republic. He is one of the most universally reviled characters in modern Chinese history, a man who seems to embody the antithesis of what modern-minded Chinese hoped for as the imperial system ended and the new Republic was born: unity, strength, and progress. Yuan's authoritarian militarism stood as a powerful enemy of democratic republicanism. He has remained a symbol of all that moderate Chinese most dislike.

Yuan's outstanding characteristic, in popular accounts, was his capacity for betrayal. In 1898 he betrayed the Guangxu emperor (1871–1908), forcing the abandonment of the wide-ranging reforms that the emperor had introduced. In 1911 Yuan betrayed the Qing dynasty (1644–1912), by turning against the last emperor when it became clear that the revolutionaries would succeed. In 1912 he betrayed the first president of the new republic, Sun Yatsen (Sun Yixian or Sun Zhongshan), and succeeded him as president.

All the negatives about Yuan are true, but the condemnations neglect to put him in context; he was very much a man of his times, making his way in a complex, shifting world, in which the military was coming to dominate the civilian world, in China as in Europe and Japan. The development of new weapons, especially automatic ones, and the construction of capital warships, led to a global arms race, while competition between nations led to the rapid expansion of armies. These twin processes culminated in World War I (1914–1918). China was not immune to militarization, which was, in fact, one of the first stages of its modernization.

Yuan was the first major modern military figure in China. He loved the military way of life. The discipline of the army appealed to his authoritarian character, and military decisiveness seemed to him exactly what the country needed as imperial China slid into decline under the combined assaults of internal rebellions and external pressure. Yuan also loved the trappings of the military. His appearance alone was a complete break with the tradition of elegant, silk-gowned mandarins. He always wore Westernstyle uniforms, which became more elaborate as he aged but did nothing to improve his squat, corpulent physique.

EARLY CAREER: THE SOLDIER

Yuan's early life foretold what was to come. He was a tough, aggressive boy from a prosperous family in Henan, one of the poorest provinces in North China. His family put him through the traditional examinations, based on the Confucian classics, but he failed twice, and was sent instead into the army, as what was seen then as a poor substitute for a mandarin career. In fact, it was a good choice; the military was on the threshold of replacing the mandarinate, and it suited Yuan's toughness and his natural bent for fighting.

Yuan was a very capable soldier. He rose quickly through the ranks, and then was sent, in his formative years, to Korea as a military liaison officer. Korea was coming increasingly under Japanese influence, and Yuan learned a great deal there about the modern military. Japan was at the time leading the way to military modernization in Asia. Yuan also showed his uncanny ability to be in the right place at the right time. He was recalled to China just before the Sino-Japanese War (1894–1895) broke out. Japan's victory was the seminal event in the history of both countries. Those directly involved on the Chinese side were disgraced. Yuan escaped their fate.

Yuan went on instead to play a major role in the creation of a new and effective armed force, designed to protect China from further foreign attacks. In 1895 he became the head of the New Army. He was given an immense budget and *carte blanche* to do whatever he wanted to produce an efficient army. He set about doing this with great zeal, only to be faced with quite a different challenge. China's defeat by Japan, and the devastating "scramble for the concessions" that followed, triggered demands for political reform; the most eloquent came from highly educated young men who were in direct touch with the young Guangxu emperor. In 1898 Yuan was asked by one of the reformers, Tan Sitong (1865–1898), to join in the reform movement. This was the first of Yuan's betrayals. He informed men close to the Empress Dowager Cixi (1835–1908), the redoubtable aunt of the emperor and a diehard authoritarian. She came out of retirement to destroy her nephew's plan and to root out reform. Her nephew was imprisoned for the rest of his life. Several of the reformers, including Tan, were executed; others, including Kang Youwei (1858–1927) and Liang Qichao (1873–1929), went into exile.

The next year, Yuan was in a new position, governor of the strategic province of Shandong. One of his first acts was to evict the bands of rambunctious peasants roaming the province, the Boxers. He thus avoided the debacle that followed, when the Boxers precipitated a crisis between China and the Western powers, including Britain, France, Russia, and Germany. The outcome was disgrace for many leading Chinese, though Yuan again escaped personal trouble. In the early 1900s, Yuan devoted himself to the evolution of what became the most important unit of the new armies, the Beiyang Army. He brought together numbers of capable men, many of whom later became warlords. He went to pains to secure their loyalty, a recognition of the importance of personal connections. Ironically, in the process of building up the new armies, Yuan created a tool that would bring down the Qing dynasty. Some of the young officers were inspired by the revolutionary ideas of Sun Yat-sen and others.

THE REPUBLICAN REVOLUTION

Yuan stayed close to the empress dowager when she returned to power after the Boxer Uprising, so close that in 1908 he had to withdraw from active service when she died (immediately after the death of the emperor). He remained in retirement, but not in seclusion, until late 1911. His ability to command personal loyalty meant that he was still effectively in command of the Beiyang Army during this period. After the Wuchang Uprising in October 1911, the court turned to him in desperation, knowing that he was the only man who could save the dynasty. In another betrayal, Yuan turned against the dynasty and negotiated the abdication of the child Xuantong emperor (1906–1967). Another betrayal followed immediately, when Yuan forced Sun Yat-sen to retire as president of the new Republic, after less than six weeks in office. Yuan

Chinese President Yuan Shikai, May 6, 1915. *Most Chinese remember Yuan Shikai for his series of betrayals, first against the Guangxu emperor, then against the last Qing emperor, and finally against Sun Yat-sen to become president of China. Uninterested in a republican form of government, Yuan attempted to establish himself as head of a new imperial empire, an effort thwarted by regional warlords unwilling to cede power.* © **BETTMANN/CORBIS**

became the second president. One of his first decisions was to keep the capital of China in Beijing, rather than in the southern capital, Nanjing, which had been chosen by Sun as the capital of the Republic.

YUAN AS PRESIDENT

As president, Yuan moved to block any progress toward political revolution. He maintained tight military control, and opposed all nascent movements toward democracy. He also attacked Sun Yat-sen's party and closed down China's first parliament. As the influence of the Western powers waned with the start of World War I, Yuan developed close relations with Japan, which included the infamous 1915 agreement (the Twenty-one Demands) that Japan would eventually take over the German concessions in Shandong.

Yuan did not believe in republicanism; his political leaning was toward the imperial system. He wanted to do what military conquerors had always done in China's past: found a new dynasty, with himself as the first emperor. In a reversion to tradition, he started planning in 1914 to make himself emperor. He built a new palace for himself in Beijing, to the southwest of the Forbidden City. This compound, entered through the Zhonghuamen, is now the official residence of the Chinese leadership. Within a year, all the preparations for his installation as the Hongxian emperor, including the design of new imperial robes (in purple), were complete. But the effort was doomed. By the start of 1916, it was clear that the provinces, under new military rulers, had turned against him. The imperial system really had ended. Yuan fell into despondency and died, many people believed of a broken heart.

YUAN'S LEGACY

Despite his betrayal of republicanism, Yuan did at least give China a unified government, and he staved off the country's decline into complete regional devolution for five years. After his death, disseminated military rule, commonly known as warlordism, dominated China for the next decade. Ironically, given the legacy of his rule, one image of Yuan stood out as a symbol of security for two decades: his face on the silver dollar, which was one of the most secure currencies in China's chaotic fiscal world.

SEE ALSO *Army and Politics; Beiyang Clique; Revolution of 1911; Sun Yat-sen (Sun Yixian); Wars and the Military, 1800–1912.*

BIBLIOGRAPHY
Chen Zhirang (Jerome Ch'en). *Yuan Shih-k'ai.* 2nd ed. Stanford, CA: Stanford University Press, 1972.

van de Ven, Hans, ed. *Warfare in Chinese History.* Leiden, Netherlands: Brill, 2000.

Young, Ernest. *The Presidency of Yuan Shih-k'ai: Liberalism and Dictatorship in Early Republican China.* Ann Arbor: University of Michigan Press, 1977.

Diana Lary

YUNNAN

Yunnan is a mountainous province of 394,000 square kilometers occupying the western part of the Yunnan-Guizhou Plateau. To the east, Yunnan borders Guangxi and Guizhou, and to the north, Sichuan. To the west, Yunnan borders Tibet, from the higher lands of which four of Asia's main rivers flow into Yunnan: the Dulong (Irrawaddy), Nu (Salween), Lancang (Mekong), and Jinsha (Yangzi). All except the Yangzi (Chang) River then flow southward into Myanmar, with the Mekong forming Myanmar's border with Laos. Yunnan also borders Laos and Vietnam. The Red River (Honghe) rises in Yunnan, flowing into Vietnam. Yunnan is thus a border province with important international rivers. The capital, Kunming, is located in the central plain.

HISTORY

Chinese control over northern Yunnan dates from the fourth century BCE. In 1382 the Ming took Yunnan from the Mongols, and Chinese control increased over the following centuries. A rebellion led by the Muslim Du Wenxiu (1823–1872) lasted from 1855 to 1873. The British and French, both involved in the suppression of the rebellion, gained influence and economic power in the province. In 1910 the French completed a trade-facilitating railway linking Kunming to Haiphong in Vietnam.

Warlord rule characterized the early Republic in China. Conditions improved during the war against Japan (1937–1945), as financial and educational resources were moved from the coastal and Yangzi regions to the interior. Even government became more stable and effective. In the 1950s and 1960s, the establishment of eight autonomous prefectures and fifteen autonomous counties among ethnic minorities helped integrate Yunnan's minority groups. The Cultural Revolution (1966–1969) attempted to uproot traditional values, but the anthropologist Margaret Swain sees the reform period "as a reinvented Confucian civilizing project emphasizing family values and solidarity" (Fitzgerald 2002, pp. 190–191) by restoring the household's production and consumption functions.

POPULATION AND ETHNICITY

Yunnan's population fell between 1855 and 1884 due to Du Wenxiu's rebellion. The province's population under

---

YUNNAN

∎

Capital city: Kunming
Largest cities (population): Kunming (5,140,000 [2006])
Area: 394,000 sq. km. (152,124 sq. mi.)
Population: 44,830,000 (2006)
Demographics: Han, 67%; Yi, 11%; Bai, 3.6%; Hani, 3.4%; Zhuang, 2.7%; Dai, 2.7%; Miao, 2.5%; Hui, 1.5% (2000)
GDP: CNY 400.6 billion (2006)
Famous sites: Shangri-La County (Zhongdian); Kunming Stone Forest; Lijiang (Naxi Area); Dali (Bai area); Xishuang Banna (Dai area); Yuanyang Rice Terraces; Songtsesling Monastery

---

the Republic was unstable, with years of famine, rebellion, and war, but Yunnan saw overall growth and extensive immigration during the war against Japan. Generally, the PRC has seen population expansion, apart from the 1959–1961 famine, due to factors like economic growth and improved health delivery. However, Yunnan is China's most severely HIV/AIDS-affected province, largely because of narcotics smuggling and trafficking in women within the opium-rich Golden Triangle of Vietnam, Laos, and Myanmar. Life expectancy in Yunnan was 63.49 in 1990, rising to 65.49 in 2000. In 2006 the province's urban population made up 30.5 percent of the total, the largest city, Kunming, having 5.14 million people.

There are some twenty-four state-recognized ethnic groups in Yunnan, the largest number of any Chinese province. Han immigration into Yunnan intensified from the thirteenth century, many families being sent for farming, exile, or even imprisonment. The Han tended to take over Yunnan, especially the cities and plains, with minority populations driven into the hills. In 1946 minorities made up one-quarter of Yunnan's population. The 1964 census showed the same proportion, but better registration and more flexible birth-control regulations for minorities pushed their population up to 31.7 percent by 1982. In both 1990 and 2000, about one in three people in Yunnan belonged to a minority group.

All the figures in Table 2, except those for 1946, are from the five national censuses. The four minority groups listed in the table were chosen for their importance in the province.

The Yi, still strong in ethnic consciousness, live over much of north and central Yunnan, especially in the areas adjoining Sichuan. The greatest Bai concentration is found

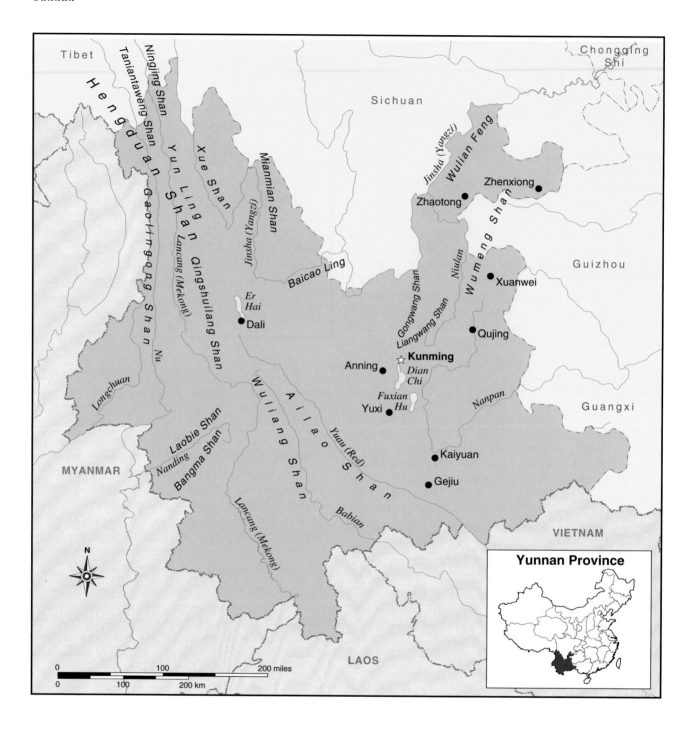

Yunnan Province

in the Dali Bai Autonomous Prefecture in northwestern Yunnan. The Hani, who live mostly in the south, claim to be the originators of the terraced rice paddy fields so important over much of Southeast Asia. The Dai are kin to the Thai of Thailand and the Shan of Myanmar. Apart from the Bai, there are significant populations of these ethnic groups living in Southeast Asian countries. Though a frontier province with many ethnic minorities, Yunnan now has firm central control.

ECONOMY

Under the Qing (1644–1912), Yunnan became a leading province for its government and private mines, which provided material for the copper cash that constituted the main currency in everyday use. As the traditional village unit, the household held common property, the clan organization being "stronger in Yunnan than in other parts of China" (Fei Xiaotong and Zhang Zhiyi 1945, p. 11). Based on field research carried out from 1939 to 1943, Fei Xiaotong and

Yunnan population, 1806–2006

Year	Population (millions)	Year	Population (millions)
1806	5.033	1953 (census)	17.473
1855	7.522	1964 (census)	20.510
1884	2.983	1982 (census)	32.554
1912	9.468	1990 (census)	36.973
1938	12.390	2000 (census)	42.880
1949	15.95	2006	44.830

Table 1

Population of ethnic minorities in Yunnan, 1946–2000

Year	1946	1953	1964	1982	1990	2000
Yi	733,120	1,838,652	2,136,113	3,354,951	4,054,177	4,705,658
Bai	304,745	592,085	704,012	1,101,251	1,339,056	1,505,644
Hani	162,499	494,480	624,175	1,058,416	1,248,106	1,424,990
Dai	262,935	501,517	534,282	836,089	1,014,318	1,142,139

SOURCE: All figures, except those of 1946, are from the five national censuses.

Table 2

Zhang Zhiyi (1945, pp. 299–300) found that, while rice cultivation was crucial to Yunnan peasants, they depended for survival also on other crops and on rural industrial production of such products as baskets and silk. The "Burma Road," completed in 1938, linked Kunming with Lashio in Myanmar and was important for the transport of war materials during the war against Japan.

The economy has modernized and industrialized since the 1950s. In 1970 the Kunming-Chengdu railway opened to traffic, followed by the Kunming-Nanning line in 1997. Total road-length more than quadrupled from 46,000 kilometers in 1982 to 198,496 in 2006.

Yunnan has become important for China as a link to Southeast Asia. It is China's main gateway to the rapidly growing Greater Mekong Subregion and a beneficiary of significant investment loans through the Asian Development Bank's Economic Cooperation Program, established in 1992. The Kunming-Bangkok Expressway is the first international expressway from China. Linking the Yunnan and Thai capitals through Laos, it is nearly 2,000 kilometers long and was partly funded by the Asian Development Bank.

Though the cities are now modernizing, in 2002 Yunnan still had the largest population of absolute poor of any Chinese province, with poverty concentrated among rural minorities. Numerous government and international projects have tried to alleviate this poverty, but despite achievements, the problem remains serious. In 1994 there were some 7 million people below a poverty line of 300 yuan per person annually, but by the end of 2002, the number had fallen to 2.86 million, the borderline in that year being 625 yuan.

Ethnic and other tourism is a major area of development. The number of international tourists totaled 596,900 in 1995, bringing in $165 million. By 2006 the figure had more than trebled to 1.81 million, with income rising to $658 million. In May 2002 the government successfully encouraged tourism by changing the name of the Tibetan region Zhongdian to Shangri-La, a name associated in many minds with paradise.

BIBLIOGRAPHY

Fei Xiaotong (Fei Hsiao-tung) and Zhang Zhiyi (Chang Chih-I). *Earthbound China: A Study of the Rural Economy in Yunnan.* Rev. English ed. in collaboration with Paul Cooper and Margaret Park Redfield. Chicago: University of Chicago Press, 1945.

Fitzgerald, John, ed. *Rethinking China's Provinces.* London and New York: Routledge, 2002.

Goodman, David S. G., and Gerald Segal, eds. *China Deconstructs: Politics, Trade, and Regionalism.* London and New York: Routledge, 1994.

Harrell, Stevan, ed. *Perspectives on the Yi of Southwest China.* Berkeley: University of California Press, 2001.

Harrell, Stevan. *Ways of Being Ethnic in Southwest China.* Seattle: University of Washington Press, 2001.

Kolås, Åshild. *Tourism and Tibetan Culture in Transition: A Place Called Shangrila.* London and New York: Routledge, 2007.

Colin Mackerras

Z

ZENG GUOFAN

1811–1872

Zeng Guofan was a scholar, official, statesman, and architect of the Qing victory over the Taiping Uprising (1851–1864), as well as a leading member of the Qing restoration. Zeng came from a landlord family in Xiangxiang, Hunan Province, but the family did not gain gentry status until his father earned his *xiucai* degree in 1832, barely a year ahead of his son. Zeng Guofan won his *jinshi* degree five years later, in 1838. Though his performance at these examinations was less than sterling, it was good enough for him to enter the Hanlin Academy. During his seven years as a Hanlin scholar, Zeng was much influenced by Tang Jian (1778–1861), a master of Song Confucianism. This gave Zeng a moral compass and inner strength in both his private and public life later on. Yet, on a regular basis, his studies were primarily concerned with practical statecraft, which he subsequently put to good use as administrator, military commander, and judge of men.

Zeng pursued his studies tenaciously at the academy. Success at the periodic examinations led to rapid promotions. By 1849 he was already a junior vice president of the Board of Ceremonies. He gained knowledge of a broad range of state affairs serving in similar capacities on several other boards until he was dispatched to Jiangxi as the provincial examiner in 1852. News of his mother's death, however, redirected his journey to his native Hunan for an extended mourning according to Confucian tradition.

THE HUNAN ARMY THAT ZENG BUILT

When Zeng arrived home in Xiangxiang on October 6, he found the province wrecked by the Taipings; the provincial capital, Changsha, a mere 80 kilometers away, was under siege. Though the rebels were repelled, they quickly swept down the Xiang River, capturing Yuezhou on Lake Dongting and seizing a huge cache of weapons and 5,000 boats. They were poised to take control of the Yangzi on the way to Nanjing. By year's end, they had taken Hankou.

In desperation, the court ordered Zeng to work with Hunan's governor, Zhang Liangji (1807–1871), to manage the province's militia (*tuanlian*), a position that soon evolved into that of *tuanlian dachen* (commissioner). In early 1853, Zeng began to put together several existing militia into what became the Hunan Army (Xiangjun). Raised initially for purposes of local defense, the Hunan Army derived its strength from its small-unit training and discipline, as well as a network of personal loyalties. Prior to engagement in battles, troops were given experience in bandit suppression. Zeng's methods were deliberate; he was hesitant to send troops against rebels outside Hunan. For this he was roundly criticized, even by the throne, and ridiculed by some as well. Meanwhile, he doggedly tried to build up a river naval force to dislodge the Taipings from the Yangzi.

Having settled at Nanjing in March 1853, the Taipings conducted a major campaign to the north, and a second campaign westward toward Anhui, Jiangxi, and Hubei. Under pressure, Zeng finally dispatched his Hunan Army to Jiangxi, but he could not meet the requests from Hubei. His nascent flotilla, made up of 240 boats and 5,000 marines, suffered two defeats at Yuezhou and Jinggang (April 28, 1854). Despondent, he attempted suicide. Only the timely recapture of Yuezhou and victories elsewhere by his land forces lifted his spirits.

After regrouping, Zeng planned a three-pronged campaign down the Yangzi in July 1854. A major naval victory in early December gave his flotilla a much-needed morale boost, and by the end of the month, Hubei was cleared of rebels and Zeng's troops were poised to attack Jiujiang, the Yangzi port in Jiangxi. He now moved his headquarters to Nanchang, Jiangxi's capital, 120 kilometers to the south. But setbacks in Hubei resulted in the loss yet again of Hankou, Hanyang, and Wuchang in early 1855, while local rebels surged north from Guangdong and Guangxi. Zeng was isolated, a virtual "prisoner at Nanchang" (Hail 1927, pp. 183–184), and he became a laughingstock among Jiangxi's officials and gentry.

The bloody power struggle among the Taiping leaders in Nanjing gave Zeng a much-needed reprieve. At the same time, the commanders he had chosen—Hu Linyi, Li Xubin, Li Xuyi, Peng Yulin, Yang Yuebin, and Yang Zaifu—were proving their mettle, even though he had recently lost Taqibu and Luo Zenan. Thus when Zeng retired once more to mourn his father's passing in early 1857, his generals were able to hold their own, pushing the rebels toward Anhui and Zhejiang.

FINAL PHASES OF THE TAIPING WAR

Zeng's services could not be missed for long. In July 1858 the throne once again ordered him to shorten his mourning and resume his command. But as the Taipings and their splinter group under Shi Dakai (1831–1863) began attacking in various directions, the throne in quick succession ordered Zeng to campaign in several provinces without allowing him time enough to reach any of the destinations. Finally, in September 1859, he was sent to fight the rebels in Anhui.

The dynasty's fortunes in mid-1860 were bleak. While the Anglo-French forces were raging up the coast toward Beijing, the imperial forces outside Nanjing collapsed. Once more, the throne turned to Zeng, this time giving him the real power and territorial control he needed. A series of appointments culminated in him becoming governor-general of the three Liang-Jiang provinces (Jiangsu, Jiangxi, and Anhui) and concurrently imperial commissioner in charge of military affairs of the same three provinces, plus Zhejiang. All civil and military authorities in these provinces were placed under his authority. No Qing official had been given so much power since the 1670s.

Zeng plotted the final phase of the anti-Taiping campaign methodically. But he encountered an unexpected resurgence of the Taipings under two able generals, Li Xiucheng (1823–1864) and Li Shixian (1834–1865). By now he had encamped at Qimen, from whence he hoped to retake Anqing, the key Anhui city guarding the approaches to Nanjing. Qimen was strategically a bad location, and it nearly cost him his campaign but for the timely arrival of Zuo Zongtang (1812–1885) and his forces. Eventually, his younger brother, Zeng Guoquan (1824–1890), took Anqing in September 1861, allowing him to move his base for the final assault on Nanjing. In the remaining two years and ten months, Zeng divided the war theater into three zones, with Anhui under his own command, Jiangsu under Li Hongzhang (1823–1901), who was to raise a separate army from his native Anhui after the Hunan Army model, and Zhejiang under Zuo Zongtang, with his own Hunanese troops. The final assault on Nanjing was placed in the hands of Guoquan, while Zeng's protégé, Shen Baozhen (1820–1879), was to turn the resources of Jiangxi Province into his commissariat.

The plan worked well, but Zeng was careful not to accept the offers of foreign military aid for fear of losing control of the situation. It has been suggested too that he wanted to save the honor of defeating the Taipings for his brother. Be that as it may, the end came in July 1864, when Guoquan's forces took Nanjing. For his twelve years in the war and for his final success, Zeng was made a marquis of the first class with the designation Yiyong, the first civil official to be so honored.

ZENG'S MILITARY LEADERSHIP

Throughout the Taiping war, Zeng demonstrated perseverance and unswerving loyalty to the throne. Twice he cut short his mourning in order to carry out his duty. He went where he was ordered and executed his responsibilities under trying circumstances. When the Taipings were defeated, he lost little time in demobilizing the bulk of his army, underscoring the total absence of any personal ambition or aggrandizement. He saw the war against the Taipings in ideological terms, identifying the challenge for what it really was—a threat to the Confucian polity. His 1854 proclamation accused the Taipings of having caused "the most extraordinary crisis of all time for Confucian teachings, the reason why our Confucius and Mencius are weeping in the nether world" (adapted from Cheng and Lestz 1999, pp. 147–148). Zeng was not the perfect commander. His army sustained its worse defeats, as at the battle at Jinggang, when he was personally in command. His military success came mainly from his ability to select men who combined character and principles with leadership qualities. Since many of them were essentially men of learning, they continued to play vital roles in the Qing restoration.

Zeng had high moral standards, and he demanded more of himself than of others, fully recognizing that in extraordinary times rules had to be bent in order to accommodate men who had what it took to get the most urgent tasks done. If he was unyielding in his devotion to Confucian principles, he was flexible enough to recognize the needs of changing times. Even as he was fighting the

Taipings, he did not lose sight of the external threat to the dynasty and saw the need for Western technology to shore up the Confucian order. Among the many advisers he retained, which numbered about a hundred, there were specialists in mathematics, astronomy, machinery, and law. In 1863 he interviewed Rong Hong (Yung Wing, 1828–1912), China's first graduate from Yale University, and dispatched him to Fitchburg, Massachusetts, to purchase the machinery that formed the core equipment of the future Jiangnan Arsenal (Jiangnan Zhizao Zongju).

ZENG AND THE QING RESTORATION

In the period of recovery and reconstruction known as the Qing restoration, Zeng, as governor-general of the Liang-Jiang provinces, played a leading role. Believing that official corruption and negligence were the source of the midcentury disorders, he led the way in rebuilding the civil administration and economy as territories were wrested from the rebels. Refugees were encouraged to return to their land with tax breaks and officially sponsored irrigation projects. In the late 1850s, taxes were reduced in the lower Yangzi provinces to win back support for the dynasty, to make taxes more realistic in the wake of wartime destruction, and to ensure a more reliable though reduced revenue for military campaigns and postwar reconstruction. Suspended civil service examinations were resumed to raise the morale of scholars and restore their faith in the dynasty. Zeng also established official printing offices to promote knowledge in the classics and histories and to revivify a trade damaged by war.

As Zeng helped found the Jiangnan Arsenal, he made sure that its capabilities included shipbuilding as well, mindful that the latest foreign threat had come from the sea. The Jiangnan Arsenal also housed a school for the study of related technical subjects, and a translation bureau that rendered Western knowledge accessible in China. In 1872 Zeng worked with Li Hongzhang in sending 120 students to study in the United States. His restoration efforts were thus closely tied to those of "self-strengthening." As a Confucian scholar of repute, his engagement in bringing Western knowledge to China and in establishing its first modern arsenal greatly helped legitimize such activities in a conservative milieu.

In 1865 Zeng was summoned to Shandong to suppress the Nian Uprising (1851–1868), because the Qing commander, Prince Senggelinqin (Senggerinchin, 1811–1865), had fallen. But after more than a year trying to hem in these extremely mobile rebels, Zeng, dissatisfied with the results, recommended Li Hongzhang for the task. He returned to his Liang-Jiang position in December 1866, and continued his effort in developing the Jiangnan Arsenal.

ZENG'S FINAL YEARS

Zeng was made a grand secretary in 1867 and governor-general of the metropolitan province of Zhili later that year. There, in the vein of a statecraft scholar-official, he improved administrative efficiency and cleared up a huge backlog of legal cases. But his tenure was marred by his handling of the 1870 Tianjin massacre, in which a number of French Catholic nuns and several foreigners were killed in an antimissionary outrage. Zeng had been rather open-minded about China's relations with the West. In 1867, for example, he had suggested that Western diplomats need not kowtow before the emperor, as the Russians never did before the Kangxi emperor (r. 1662–1722). Blaming antimissionary outbreaks on vicious rumors about Christian practices, which Chinese officials should have actively suppressed, and weary of potential armed conflicts with the West, Zeng took a conciliatory approach, thus incurring the wrath of many at court. Following the assassination of Liang-Jiang governor-general Ma Xinyi (1821–1870), Zeng was transferred back to Nanjing, leaving Li Hongzhang to close the case. Zeng died in office in 1872.

Throughout his official life, Zeng kept in close touch with his family through "family letters" (*jiashu*) and "exhortations and admonitions for the family" (*jiaxun*). Filled with advice and moral exhortations, they reveal his sincere belief in Confucian morality and its practical applications. As a scholar and an official, he inspired many, yet few managed to follow his moral examples. His own brother Guoquan ignored his advice about the negative consequences of power, while his protégé Li Hongzhang went on to great accomplishments but sometimes with questionable methods or motives. Still, Zeng's famous sayings have been collected and published repeatedly by people like Chiang Kai-shek (Jiang Jieshi) for the purpose of instilling discipline in his troops as well as the citizens of the Republic. Since the 1980s, in the China of the reform era, there has been a strong revival of interest in Zeng, for much the same reasons. Twice in history, his role in suppressing the Taipings has been vilified: first in the era of feverish anti-Manchuism at the turn of the last century for his killing of fellow Han people, and again in the Maoist era for his suppression of a popular uprising.

Zeng was officially married once, and had two sons and five daughters. Zeng Jize (1839–1890), his eldest son, inherited his rank of marquis and become a noted diplomat in the late Qing period.

SEE ALSO *Qing Restoration.*

BIBLIOGRAPHY
Cheng Pei-kai (Zheng Peikai) and Michael Lestz, eds. *The Search for Modern China: A Documentary Collection.* New York: Norton, 1999.

Hail, William J. *Tseng Kuo-fan and the Taiping Rebellion: With a Short Sketch of His Later Career.* New Haven, CT: Yale University Press, 1927.

Kuhn, Philip A. *Rebellion and Its Enemies in Late Imperial China: Militarization and Social Structure, 1796–1864.* Cambridge, MA: Harvard University Press, 1970.

Li Shuchang. *Zeng Guofan nianpu.* Changsha: 岳麓书社 yuelu shushe, 1986.

Pong, David. The Income and Military Expenditure of Kiangsi Province in the Last Years (1860–1864) of the Taiping Rebellion. *Journal of Asian Studies* 26, 1 (1966): 49–66.

Porter, Jonathan. *Tseng Kuo-fan's Private Bureaucracy.* Berkeley: Center for Chinese Studies, University of California, 1972.

Shen Chen Han-yin. Tseng Kuo-fan in Peking, 1840–1852: His Ideas on Statecraft and Reform. *Journal of Asian Studies* 27, 1 (1967): 61–80.

Su Tongbing. *Zhongguo jindai shishang de guanjian renwu* [Key personages in the history of modern China]. Tianjin: Baihua Wenyi Chubanshe, 2007.

David Pong

ZHANG, AILING

SEE *Chang, Eileen (Zhang Ailing).*

ZHANG DAQIAN (CHANG DAI-CHIEN)
1899–1983

Zhang Daqian (Chang Dai-chien) was one of the preeminent Chinese painters of the modern era. He was also one of the twentieth century's leading connoisseurs and collectors of ancient Chinese painting and calligraphy. In addition to achieving an international reputation as a creative artist, Zhang was notorious for being a gifted forger who was able to create convincing imitations based on the artistic styles of a wide range of ancient Chinese masters. According to the scholar Fu Shen, "Chang Dai-chien was surely one of the most versatile, prolific, best-trained, and well-traveled artists in the history of Chinese painting. More than anyone else, Chang transformed traditional Chinese painting into a contemporary idiom. He was both the last great traditionalist of literati painting and an internationally acclaimed modernist, the most avant-garde of his generation" (Fu and Stuart 1991, p. 15).

EARLY EDUCATION

Zhang was born in Neijiang County, Sichuan Province. His given name was Zhengquan, and he also was called Zhang Yuan ("Gibbon Zhang") and a variety of other names. The name *Daqian,* by which he is most commonly known, was bestowed upon him by a Buddhist abbot in 1919. Daqian took an interest in art from an early age. His mother, Zeng Youzhen (1860–1936), was a noted painter of animals and flowers, and Zhang learned painting from her and his older siblings, especially his elder brother Zhang Shanzi (1882–1940), who was famous for his paintings of tigers. In 1917 Shanzi brought his younger brother to Japan, where Daqian enrolled in a Kyoto commercial art school to study textile manufacture. This practical training in producing and dyeing cloth provided useful technical knowledge about fabrics and pigments that later benefited him both as an artist and a forger.

In 1919 Zhang Daqian moved to the cosmopolitan city of Shanghai, where he studied calligraphy with two of the leading scholars of the time, Zeng Xi (1861–1930), who was skilled at both landscape painting and calligraphy, and Li Ruiqing (1867–1920), known primarily as a calligrapher. The talented young artist quickly mastered a wide range of ancient and modern script forms, and he developed his own eclectic style of writing. In addition to teaching him calligraphy, these two lofty scholars also shared with the youthful Daqian their deep knowledge of history, literature, and painting. They encouraged him to study the works of the old masters, particularly the great individualist painter Shitao (1642–1707), whose paintings and calligraphy were an important early artistic influence. Zhang learned Shitao's methods thoroughly and he took pride in the fact that his own imitations of the master's style were convincing enough to fool even the most knowledgeable experts of Shitao's oeuvre. Although he doubtless benefited financially from the sale of his forgeries of Shitao and other old masters, Zhang defended the practice of creating new works of art in the spirit of past masters as a kind of intellectual game in which he pitted his understanding of art history against that of the scholars and collectors who, believing them to be authentic ancient paintings, acquired the works. In the cultural environment in which Zhang was raised, participants in the elite practice of art collecting adhered to the principle of *caveat emptor* ("buyer beware") and it was primarily the responsibility of the collector to judge the authenticity and quality of the artwork he was acquiring. Museum directors in the West, however, who sometimes mistook Zhang's imitations for original works, were accustomed to doing business under a different set of ethical and legal imperatives, by which sellers of art were held responsible for the authenticity of the works they handled and the creation of forgeries was seen as a criminal act. Zhang's practice of making forgeries therefore has tarnished his reputation among museum curators in the West.

MIDDLE CAREER

Zhang Daqian was both a serious scholar and skilled practitioner of Chinese painting. He dedicated his life to exploring all aspects of Chinese culture and art. In the 1940s he spent more than two years at Dunhuang, a remote desert outpost in Gansu Province that was a repository of Buddhist cave paintings dating back to the Tang dynasty (618–907). With help from a group of assistants that included family members, students, and Tibetan monks from Qinghai Province, Zhang created large-scale copies of hundreds of ancient mural paintings, many of which depicted Buddhist deities. These paintings helped to further establish Zhang's reputation as an important artist when they were exhibited in Chongqing, Sichuan in 1944. At Dunhuang Zhang perfected the art of figure painting, a genre of Chinese painting that had been somewhat neglected because literati artists of the Yuan, Ming, and Qing dynasties tended to favor landscape and flower-and-bird painting.

Fearing that the impending Communist takeover would put an abrupt end to his extravagant lifestyle, in 1949 Zhang Daqian left China for good. He lived briefly in India and Hong Kong before settling down in South America, first in Argentina and then, beginning in 1953, in São Paolo, Brazil. In 1972 Zhang Daqian moved to Carmel, California, and in 1978 he returned to Asia, establishing his final residence in a suburb outside of Taibei, Taiwan. He remained in Taiwan until his death in 1983 and never returned to mainland China.

No matter where Zhang resided, he always created an environment that reflected a traditional Chinese scholar's aesthetic and lifestyle. Zhang himself supervised both the landscaping of the fanciful gardens that surrounded his elaborate residences and the preparation of sumptuous Chinese meals for his family, students, and the constant flow of guests. He always wore a traditional Chinese robe of the type associated with the Song dynasty scholars, and from the age of twenty-six he sported a long beard, which gave him an older and more distinguished appearance. Zhang's youngest daughter, Sing (Zhang Xinsheng), recalled that while growing up in Brazil the local children, upon seeing this bearded gentleman wearing a long robe and tall hat, came running over to greet them because they thought that he might be Santa Claus.

Even if he were not a great artist, Zhang Daqian's abilities as a connoisseur and his success as a collector of ancient masterpieces would establish him an important figure in Chinese art history. Many great works that are now the prized property of Western and Chinese museum collections at one time passed through Zhang's hands. For example, most of the works in the John M. Crawford Collection, which was bequeathed to the Metropolitan Museum of Art in New York, originally came from Zhang's personal collection. The four-volume illustrated catalog *Dafengtang mingji,* published from 1955 to 1956, reproduced a small portion of his collection, which at its height is reported to have included several thousand

works of painting and calligraphy dating from the Tang through Qing dynasties. Like generations of Chinese scholar-painters before him, Zhang believed that preserving the high technical achievement and aesthetic standards of the great masters of the past was the responsibility of every Chinese artist. Surrounding oneself with ancient works imbued the artist with a sense of history and reminded him of this responsibility. Furthermore, it was only through the intense study and copying of high quality original artworks that an artist was able to hone his technique and train his eye. For Zhang Daqian, collecting, connoisseurship, and the practice of writing and painting were all integral parts of a single process designed to understand, preserve, and develop the traditional art forms of painting and calligraphy.

Zhang Daqian was an extremely versatile artist. He mastered virtually every style of classical Chinese painting, from the *gongbi* (fine-line) technique to the expressive, broad-brushed *xieyi* (literally "idea-writing") manner. He painted figures, landscapes, flowers-and-birds (*huaniao*), and animals with equal skill. He could emulate the painting and calligraphic styles of artists from any period of Chinese history, he had an encyclopedic knowledge of Chinese art history, and he possessed a near-photographic visual memory. He was also a diligent student of Chinese philosophy, history, religion, and literature, and an accomplished poet.

LATER CAREER AND LEGACY

Beginning in the 1960s Zhang Daqian's painting style moved away from the detailed, fine-line rendering that characterized much of his early paintings toward a more boldly expressive manner that became increasingly abstract during the later years of his life. One reason for this stylistic evolution was the fact that, beginning in 1957, the artist's vision became impaired and, even with the aid of thick glasses, he was unable to see clearly enough to do very fine work. Zhang was undeterred by this physical handicap, and some would argue that it served as a catalyst for a major stylistic breakthrough that successfully modernized and internationalized traditional Chinese painting. He began painting monumental works, and was particularly fond of depicting huge windswept lotuses using broad ink washes vigorously applied with large brushes.

Zhang also began to develop completely new landscape painting techniques that included splashing and pouring ink and color directly onto the painting ground and meticulously working these random configurations into dramatic compositions, gradually adding details, such as trees or houses, with a smaller brush until they became recognizable as landscapes. These semi-abstract paintings, often employing brilliant blue and green mineral pigments, resonated with the international art movements of the time, especially abstract expressionism. Although Zhang was adamant about citing precedents within Chinese art history for his breakthrough style—mentioning, for example, an eighth-century artist named Wang Xia who is recorded to have used a similar splashed-ink style, though none of his paintings are extant—there is no doubt that Zhang was influenced by the modern and contemporary art that he saw in art museums and galleries in the West. He met Pablo Picasso in France in 1956, and in that same year the Musée d'Art Moderne held simultaneous exhibitions of Henri Matisse and Zhang Daqian. Although one should be cautioned not to imply a causal relationship between modern Western art and Zhang Daqian's later style, it would be equally wrong to completely deny any Western influence. Zhang was able to find aesthetic common ground between the modern formalist and kinesthetic approaches to painting and the traditional Chinese scholar-artist's cultivation of spontaneity and self-expression through brushwork.

In addition to his prodigious talents as a visual artist, Zhang Daqian was also a master of self-promotion. His meeting with Picasso, recorded by photographs and widely circulated press accounts, was a calculated publicity effort by Zhang to raise his international stature through his association with one of the greatest living Western masters. Zhang Daqian made friends with influential people from all walks of life, including politicians, opera stars, chefs and restaurant owners, businessmen, bankers, and journalists, in addition to scholars, dealers, scroll mounters, and museum curators. Zhang was very generous with his paintings, which he often gave away as gifts to friends and even casual acquaintances. It is estimated that Zhang Daqian produced roughly 30,000 paintings in his lifetime, but many of these were hastily produced, trivial sketches that were given away to fulfill social obligations. This tremendous output, however, ensured that his works would be widely distributed and that his fame would extend far and wide. Fully embracing the role of the ancient Chinese scholar-artist, Zhang Daqian was a charismatic, amiable figure and a master showman, whose fame reached near-legendary proportions both in China and abroad.

More than any other Chinese artist of the twentieth century, Zhang Daqian was able to reconcile the seemingly contradictory goals of preserving traditional artistic values while modernizing a classical art form. His stylistic innovations bridged the gap between East and West, ancient and modern. Relying on a unique combination of skill, knowledge, and originality, coupled with the sheer force of his personality, Zhang Daqian led Chinese painting into the modern era.

SEE ALSO *Chinese Painting* (guohua); *Collections and Collecting.*

BIBLIOGRAPHY

Andrews, Julia F., and Kuiyi Shen. *A Century in Crisis: Modernity and Tradition in the Art of Twentieth-century China.* New York: Guggenheim Foundation, 1998.

Chang Dai-chien, ed. *Dafeng Tang mingji* [Illustrated catalogue of masterpieces of Chinese painting from the Dafeng Tang collection]. 4 vols. Reprint. Taibei: Lianjing Chubanshe, 1987.

D'Argencé, René-Yvon Lefebvre. *Chang Dai-chien: A Retrospective Exhibition.* San Francisco: Center of Asian Art and Culture, 1972.

Exhibition of Paintings by Chang Dai-chien. Intro. by James Cahill. New York: Hirschl and Adler Gallery, 1963.

Fong, Wen C. *Between Two Cultures: Late Nineteenth- and Twentieth-century Chinese Paintings from the Robert H. Ellsworth Collection in the Metropolitan Museum of Art.* New York: Metropolitan Museum of Art; New Haven, CT: Yale University Press, 2001.

Fu, Shen C. Y., and Jan Stuart. *Challenging the Past: The Paintings of Chang Dai-chien.* Seattle: Smithsonian Institution and University of Washington Press, 1991.

Kao, Mayching, ed. *Twentieth-century Chinese Painting.* New York: Oxford University Press, 1988.

Kao, Mayching, ed. *The Mei Yun Tang Collection of Paintings by Chang Dai-chien.* Hong Kong: Mei Yun Tang and Chinese University of Hong Kong, 1993.

Li, Chu-tsing. *Trends in Modern Chinese Painting: The C. A. Drenowatz Collection.* Ascona, Switzerland: Artibus Asiae, 1979.

Modern Chinese Art: The Khoan and Michael Sullivan Collection. Oxford, U.K.: Ashmolean Museum, 2001.

Sullivan, Michael. *Art and Artists of Twentieth-century China.* Berkeley and Los Angeles: University of California Press, 1996.

Arnold Chang

ZHANG JIAN
1853–1926

Zhang Jian was a scholar, industrialist, modernizer, and key figure in China's transition from the late Qing empire (1644–1912) to the Republic (1912–1949). His versatile career and patriotic reputation reflect in many ways the fundamental political, economic, and social changes that accompanied the transformation from Chinese empire to nation-state and led to modernization efforts in the state, society, and economy.

Zhang Jian was born in Haimen County, close to the northern bank of the Yangzi River in Jiangsu Province northeast of Shanghai, into a well-off farming family who provided him with the opportunity to study and prepare for the imperial examinations. Although Zhang Jian soon acquired fame as a gifted scholar, he failed to pass the examinations several times and earned his livelihood as tutor in private academies and as a personal assistant to high-ranking officials for many years. When he finally achieved a first-place ranking in the metropolitan examination in 1894, the year he returned from the capital to Jiangsu Province to mourn the death of his father, Zhang Jian decided against pursuing a prestigious career in government service. His transformation from scholar to industrialist was directly linked to the events of 1895, when China lost the war with Japan: In response to the defeat, the Chinese government started to promote the founding of domestic industrial enterprises to strengthen the nation's economy and military.

A typical example of an official-turned-businessman at the time, Zhang Jian used his personal connections from his previous career to help with his entrepreneurial initiatives. He also used educational and welfare projects to enhance his social capital in Tongzhou County, where he founded the first Dasheng Cotton Mill in 1895. Located in the countryside close to Nantong city and conveniently connected to the Yangzi River through the canal system, the Dasheng Cotton Mill became China's first large-scale cotton-spinning mill in a rural setting with a predominantly female workforce that commuted to the mill from the surrounding villages. Set up originally as a "joint government-merchant enterprise," the Dasheng mill experienced a difficult launch after the government backed out of its promised financial sponsorship. In the end, local investors, many of them with a connection to the cotton cloth trade, as well as Shanghai investors provided the capital for the mill. Dasheng registered as one of the first domestic incorporated companies with limited liability under China's 1904 Company Law.

As an industrialist and reformer, Zhang Jian introduced modern factory work and discipline to his spinning mill, which was equipped with state-of-the-art machinery imported from England and the United States. Controlling his mills in a highly paternalistic and autocratic fashion as founder and managing director, Zhang Jian was aided by local business associates and by his brother Zhang Cha (1851–1939), who headed the No. 2 branch mill founded on Chongming Island in 1907. Zhang Jian actively pursued a strategy of local business expansion, which led to the founding of four cotton-spinning mills in the Nantong area and a large conglomerate of subsidiary companies, which were tied into the cotton-related manufacturing process through their products or services.

Zhang Jian's most prominent initiative, which combined his business interests with aspirations for local and regional development, was the founding of several large land-reclamation companies along the northern Jiangsu coastline. By turning land previously used for salt-production into agricultural land for the growing of cotton, he hoped to increase the local cotton supply for the Dasheng mills and create new settlements and farming opportunities for

landless peasants and unemployed salt workers. However, the transformation of saline coastal land into agricultural fields was a costly and risky undertaking plagued by setbacks due to natural disasters like typhoons. The land-reclamation companies also exemplified serious problems with Zhang Jian's financial management, such as their practice of capitalization through fund transfer from the Dasheng mills without approval from shareholders. This was possible because the headquarters in Shanghai, the Shanghai accounts office, took care of all business accounts together with Zhang Jian's personal and family accounts. As an accounting practice rooted in Chinese family business, moving funds between private and business accounts was not unusual at the time. The lack of auditing procedures and corporate transparency enabled Zhang Jian to engage in risky financial transactions and hide Dasheng's debt accumulation with dire consequences for the company's financial sustainability.

The city of Nantong became the focus of Zhang Jian's reform projects in the early twentieth century, when improvement and modernization of education, industry, and welfare became suitable pursuits for local elites throughout the country. As a modernizer in Nantong, Zhang Jian founded the first Western-style museum, a hospital, a modern prison, a theater, libraries, and orphanages. Zhang Jian was not involved actively in national politics, but he played a dominant role in organizations like the chamber of commerce and in various associations of local self-government. Although his charitable projects did not extend to the rural areas and the workforce of his factories but centered on Nantong's urban citizens, his involvement in these institutions and activities added to his reputation as a patriotic reformer nationwide and allowed him to exert financial and political clout for business purposes.

By the late 1910s, the Dasheng mills had achieved great financial success within the domestic textile industry and planned further business and product expansion. However, unsound accounting strategies, overextension through bank loans, and the collapse of the raw cotton market in the early 1920s jeopardized the health of the company. Threatened by bankruptcy, the Dasheng mills came under the financial and managerial control of a Shanghai bank consortium in 1924. As a result, Zhang Jian retired from active business management but remained in Nantong until his death in 1926. His company struggled to survive the period of Japanese occupation and the civil war from 1945 to 1949, before it was transformed into a state-owned enterprise under the new socialist government in 1953. In the wake of China's economic reforms since the 1990s, Zhang Jian's image is again promoted as an example of productive Chinese entrepreneurship and enlightened patriotism.

SEE ALSO *Industrialization, 1860–1949; Textiles.*

BIBLIOGRAPHY

Bastid, Marianne. *Educational Reform in Early Twentieth-century China*. Trans. Paul J. Bailey. Ann Arbor: University of Michigan, Center for Chinese Studies, 1988.

Köll, Elisabeth. *From Cotton Mill to Business Empire: The Emergence of Regional Enterprises in Modern China*. Cambridge, MA: Harvard University East Asia Center, 2003.

Shao Qin. *Culturing Modernity: The Nantong Model, 1890–1930*. Stanford, CA: Stanford University Press, 2003.

Zhu Changling (Samuel C. Chu). *Reformer in Modern China: Chang Chien, 1853–1926*. New York: Columbia University Press, 1965.

Elisabeth Köll

ZHANG JUNMAI (CARSUN CHANG)
1887–1969

Zhang Junmai (also known as Carsun Chang and Zhang Jiasen) was well known in Republican China for his constitution-drafting, his founding and leading of two minor political parties, his establishment of a series of private schools, and his defense of a Confucian tradition under attack since the May Fourth movement. Many of his political activities in the first half of the twentieth century could be described as third-force efforts, from his opposition to the Qing and the revolutionaries before 1911 to his resistance to the Guomindang (GMD; Nationalist Party) and the Chinese Communist Party (CCP) from the 1920s to 1949 and beyond. Following the Communist victory in 1949, he joined other exiled politicians and military men in an abortive effort to launch a third-force movement outside China. His last years were spent writing books and articles on contemporary Chinese politics and Neo-Confucianism. His key work in English was his quasi memoir, *The Third Force in China* (1952).

EARLY YEARS

Zhang came from a prominent family in the Shanghai area. His father was a doctor and his grandfather a graduate of the civil-service examination and a Qing official. His older brother, Zhang Jiaao (Chang Kia-ngau; 1889–1979), served as head of the Bank of China from 1929 to 1935. While Zhang Junmai opposed Chiang Kai-shek's (Jiang Jieshi) rule, Zhang Jiaao later served in Chiang's government as minister of railways and then minister of communications. Zhang's sister, Zhang Youyi (1900–1989), also won a degree of fame as the abandoned wife of the famous poet Xu Zhimo. In addition, she was a pioneer businesswoman, having operated the Shanghai Women's Savings Bank in the 1930s.

After a mixed Chinese-Western education in Shanghai, Zhang studied at Waseda University in Tokyo from 1906 to 1910. There, he met and became a follower of the constitutional reformer, Liang Qichao. After the revolution, Zhang briefly participated in Liang's political party. In 1913 Zhang went to Germany, where he studied at the University of Berlin until moving to England for several months in 1915 and 1916. From 1916 to 1918, he threw himself into politics, arguing for China's entry into World War I (1914–1918) on the side of the democracies. When Liang left, in late 1918, for the Paris Peace Conference, Zhang was in his entourage. After the failure at the conference to recover Shandong from the Japanese, Zhang turned much of his attention to philosophy and socialism. Thus, he studied the works of German philosophers Rudolf Eucken (1846–1926) and Hans Driesch (1867–1941), French thinker Henri Bergson (1859–1941), and German political theorist Karl Korsch (1886–1961). He also paid close attention to the rise of Soviet and German communism.

POLITICS AND EDUCATION IN THE 1920s

Following his return to China in 1922, he won a modicum of fame in the 1923 debate over science versus metaphysics. In the same year, he founded the Institute of Self-Government (Guoli Zizhi Xueyuan)—later the National Political University (Guoli Zhengzhi Daxue)—in his native province of Jiangsu.

Having benefited from the support and protection of warlord Sun Chuanfang (1885–1935) for his school and belonging to Liang Qichao's political group, it was not surprising that when the Northern Expedition reached Shanghai in March 1927, the GMD closed his university and issued a warrant for his arrest. In writings in 1928 published in the magazine *Xinlu* (New way), he made matters worse for himself by criticizing the GMD's one-party dictatorship. Fearful for his safety in Shanghai, he fled to Germany, where he taught at Jena University from 1929 to 1931. When he returned to China, he took up a post teaching in the philosophy department at Yenching University in Beijing.

THE CHINESE NATIONAL SOCIALIST PARTY, 1932–1937

In April 1932, Zhang joined a hundred or so others to establish the Chinese National Socialist Party (Zhongguo guojia shehui dang, NSP) in Beijing. It was a third-force organization, opposed to both the GMD and CCP. The party stood for parliamentary democracy and a mixed economy. Considered illegal by the GMD dictatorship, Zhang and his party functioned underground. When the Fujian Rebellion occurred in late 1933 and early 1934, Zhang

146

traveled to that province to investigate it. When it failed, he fled, with Zhang Jiaao's help, to Guangzhou (Canton).

After journeying to Tianjin for the first congress of the NSP, Zhang returned to Guangzhou and founded the Xuehai Institute (Xuehai shuyuan) with the support of Chen Jitang (1890–1954). Like the National Political University, this school sought to function outside GMD or CCP control. Because of his opposition to the GMD and CCP, in the 1930s he investigated various provincial reconstruction movements, such as Yan Xishan's (1883–1960) in Shanxi, the Guangxi clique's, and Chen Jitang's in Guangdong.

THE WAR OF RESISTANCE

When the Second Sino-Japanese War broke out in 1937, Zhang and his party members promptly shelved their third-force opposition to the GMD and CCP and entered the anti-Japanese united front. Forced to take refuge in southwest China by the war, Zhang founded yet another school, the Institute of National Culture (Minzu wenhua shuyuan), which once again attempted to stand outside of GMD and CCP control. However, after the December 1941 attack on Pearl Harbor brought the United States into the war on China's side, Chiang Kai-shek restricted Zhang to Chongqing and, in the spring of 1942, closed his school. With the entrance of the United States into the war, Chiang and the GMD were free to crack down on the opposition to their dictatorship.

During the war, Zhang participated in attempts to form a stronger third force. In 1941 he joined with other leaders of small political parties and groups to found the League of Chinese Democratic Political Groups (Zhongguo minzhu zhengtuan datongmeng). In 1944 the group was reorganized as the China Democratic League (Zhongguo minzhu tongmeng).

THE CIVIL WAR

After a sojourn in the United States from December 1944 until January 1946, Zhang returned to Chongqing as a Democratic League member of the Political Consultative Conference called in an attempt to avert a GMD-CCP civil war. Subsequently, he drafted the 1946 constitution. At the same time, he presided over the merger of his party with the Democratic Constitutional Party (Minzhu xianzheng dang) to create the Chinese Democratic Socialist Party (Zhongguo minzhu shehui dang). Unfortunately, it almost immediately split and thus sank into political impotence. Seeing the handwriting on the wall and having already declared he could not live under a Communist dictatorship (his name appeared on a Communist list of "war criminals"), in April 1949 he fled to Macau on his way to India to lecture.

EXILE

After two years in India, in which he participated in the abortive third force—awkwardly called the Fighting League for Chinese Freedom and Democracy (Zhongguo ziyou minzhu zhandou tongmeng)—along with Zhang Fakui (1896–1980), Gu Mengyu (1888–1973), and others, Zhang left for the United States. There, he spent the remainder of his days penning articles on politics in China and Taiwan, writing books and articles on Neo-Confucianism, dabbling in émigré politics, and traveling to Europe and Asia. He never relinquished his belief in democracy and socialism.

Following 1949, he emerged as a participant in the New Confucian movement (*xin ruxue yundong*) and a member of the "third generation of Confucians" (*dangdai xin ruxue*), a group that appeared as a result of the Western challenge to traditional Chinese civilization. Among his colleagues, Zhang knew the most about Western politics and philosophy and also was the most heavily involved in party politics. He managed to combine liberalism, democracy, socialism, and Confucianism in his political thought. In 1958 he joined with several other New Confucianists to issue "A Manifesto for a Reappraisal of Sinology and Reconstruction of Chinese Culture." In this document, he and his colleagues called for including democracy in a revival of Confucianism. He would have been pleased with the contemporary revival of interest in Confucianism in China.

SEE ALSO *Classical Scholarship and Intellectual Debates: Debates, 1900–1949; Confucianism; Constitutionalism; Liberalism; Political Parties, 1905–1949.*

BIBLIOGRAPHY

Fung, Edmund S. K. (Feng Zhaoji). *In Search of Chinese Democracy: Civil Opposition in Nationalist China, 1929–1949.* Cambridge, U.K.: Cambridge University Press, 2000.

Fung, Edmund S. K. (Feng Zhaoji). New Confucianism and Chinese Democratization: The Thought and Predicament of Zhang Junmai. *Twentieth Century China* 28, 2 (2003): 41–71.

Jeans, Roger B. *Democracy and Socialism in Republican China: The Politics of Zhang Junmai (Carsun Chang), 1906–1941.* Lanham, MD: Rowman & Littlefield, 1997.

Peterson, Kent McLean. A Political Biography of Zhang Junmai, 1887–1949. Ph.D. diss., Princeton University, 1999.

Waldman, Phyliss. Chang Kia-ngau (Zhang Jiaao) and the Bank of China: The Politics of Money. Ph.D. diss., University of Virginia, Charlottesville, 1984.

Zhang, Bangmei (Pang-Mei Natasha Chang). *Bound Feet and Western Dress.* New York: Doubleday, 1996. Zhang Youyi's own story.

Zheng Dahua. *Zhang Junmai zhuan* [A biography of Zhang Junmai]. Beijing: Zhonghua Shuju, 1997.

Roger B. Jeans

ZHANG YIMOU
1950–

As the most prominent film director to emerge in the People's Republic of China (PRC) after the Cultural Revolution (1966–1969), Zhang Yimou has been responsible not only for reinventing Chinese film language but also for introducing Chinese cinema to overseas audiences, establishing patterns of transnational production, and promoting a domestic commercial film industry competitive in the global economy.

Born in 1950 and raised in Xi'an, Zhang graduated from the Photography Department of the Beijing Film Academy in 1982. Zhang and his classmates, soon dubbed the "Fifth Generation" of Chinese filmmakers, responded to Zhang Nuanxin (1940–1995) and Li Tuo's call for "the modernization of film language" and broke away from socialist realism by adapting principles and practices used in Italian neorealism, the French new wave, and contemporary Hollywood. Zhang first implemented his vision as

director of cinematography for films by his classmates, most notably *Yi ge he ba ge* (*One and Eight*, 1983), *Huang tu di* (*Yellow Earth*, 1984), and *Da yuebing* (*The Big Parade*, 1985), and then as a director, beginning with *Hong gaoliang* (*Red Sorghum*, 1987). In these films, Zhang introduced saturated colors and dramatically unbalanced compositions. Drawing on his and his cohort's previous experiences as sent-down youth, Zhang depicts the remote countryside as teeming with raw desires. In his subsequent films of the late 1980s and early 1990s—*Ju Dou* (1989), *Da hong denglong gaogao gua* (*Raise the Red Lantern*, 1991), and *Qiu Ju da guan si* (*The Story of Qiu Ju*, 1992)—Zhang developed his signature style and focused on women defiant in the face of injustice. Critics such as Dai Jinhua and Chen Xihe praised Zhang's criticism of patriarchal ideology in both premodern and modern society. Rey Chow sees the foregrounding of "primitive passions" as Zhang's strategy to situate his films within Third World discourses. These films also catapulted the lead actress, Gong Li (b. 1965), to international stardom.

Chinese gymnast Li Ning lighting the Olympic torch at the Beijing Olympics, August 8, 2008. *A highly regarded member of the Fifth Generation of Chinese filmmakers, Zhang Yimou directed the opening ceremonies of the 2008 Summer Olympics, hosted by the city of Beijing.* **MICHAEL KAPPELER/AFP/GETTY IMAGES**

Zhang's early films marked a novel approach to production and distribution. The films received top awards at prestigious international film festivals and turned a profit at art-house theaters in Europe and the United States. Zhang came to rely on the international film market, which served him in good stead when PRC authorities banned the distribution of *Ju Dou* and *Raise the Red Lantern*. The international success, and the prospect of replicating *Red Sorghum's* high domestic revenue, allowed Zhang to attract foreign investment, especially from other East Asian countries.

Beginning in the mid-1990s, Zhang's productions appealed to increasingly larger audiences, turning away from gut-wrenching narratives based on the experimental literature of the 1980s and becoming associated with commercial genres. The shift may owe to Zhang's recognition of the official bans' damage to his career, as well as to changes in the Chinese film industry, which could survive integration with the global market only by competing on Hollywood's terms. *Wode fuqin muqin* (*The Road Home*, 1999) followed the formula of nostalgia and romance that made *Titanic* (1997) a blockbuster in China; *Xingfu shiguang* (*Happy Times*, 2000) may be understood in the context of Feng Xiaogang's contemporary lucrative urban comedies; *Yingxiong* (*Hero*, 2002), *Shi mian mai fu* (*House of Flying Daggers*, 2004), and *Mancheng jindai huangjinjia* (*Curse of the Golden Flower*, 2006) cashed in on the renewed interest in martial arts movies after Ang Lee's *Wohu canglong* (*Crouching Tiger, Hidden Dragon*, 2000). These films produced record box-office revenue but met with critical disapproval for what some perceived as simplistic storylines and superficial grandeur: Evans Chan even cited *Hero* as a fascistic endorsement of totalitarian rule. It may be useful, however, to bear in mind that prominent intellectuals consistently have accused Zhang of compromising content for visual extravagance. With the release of *Red Sorghum*, Zheng Dongtian rebuked Zhang for relinquishing the Fifth Generation's mission of "bearing the cross"; Dai Qing censured *Raise the Red Lantern* for the use of inauthentic cultural symbols. In hindsight, such reactions may have ignored Zhang's innovative manipulation of cultural symbols.

Zhang Yimou's reputation has gone beyond that of an accomplished film director. He has branched into choreographing spectacles such as the opera *Turandot*, staged in the Forbidden City of Beijing in 1999; the ballet *Raise the Red Lantern*, adapted from his own film, produced in 2003; the touristy light-and-sound extravaganza in Guilin, *Impressions of Third Sister Liu* (2005); and the production *The First Emperor* at the New York Metropolitan Opera in 2007. These endeavors culminated in Zhang's central role in producing the opening ceremonies of the Beijing Olympic Games in 2008. From an experimental director with a dissident aura in his early years, Zhang has become an icon of the PRC's growing economic and political power.

SEE ALSO *Film Industry: Fifth Generation Filmmakers.*

BIBLIOGRAPHY

Chen Mo. *Qingchun de huhan: Zhang Yimou de dianying shijie* [The Call of youth: Zhang Yimou's film world]. Taipei: Fengyun Shidai Chubanshe, 2006.

Chow, Rey. *Primitive Passions: Visuality, Sexuality, Ethnography, and Contemporary Chinese Cinema.* New York: Columbia University Press, 1995.

Ni Zhen. *Memoirs from the Beijing Film Academy: The Genesis of China's Fifth Generation.* Trans. Chris Berry. Durham, NC: Duke University Press, 2002.

Zhang Jiuying. *Fanpai Zhang Yimou* [Reproducing Zhang Yimou]. Beijing: Zhongguo Mangwen Chubanshe, 2001.

Yomi Braester

ZHANG ZHIDONG
1837–1909

Zhang Zhidong was an eminent statesmen of the late Qing dynasty (1644–1912). He was the promoter of China's national railway network, the first builder of China's modern heavy industry and school system, and an advocate as well as the architect of China's political transformation into a constitutional monarchy. Buttressed by his early military experience and extensive travel through the deep inland in times of insurgency, Zhang's classical scholarship and literary skills turned him into a major exponent of modern Chinese nationalism.

NATIONALIST SCHOLAR

Although Zhang's family of middle-ranking officials was native to Nanpi in Zhili (present-day Hebei Province), he was born in Xingyi in Guizhou Province, where his father was serving as prefect. During his youth, he learned the rigorous principles of thrift and devotion to studies, and he was exposed to whatever books and young literary talents were available in that remote area. Among them was Hu Linyi (1812–1861), a brilliant Hanlin scholar, well-versed in practical studies (*shixue*) and later a great leader in the victory over the Taiping rebels.

In 1850 Zhang Zhidong traveled to Nanpi to earn a bachelor's degree (*shengyuan*). Two years later, at age fifteen, he passed the provincial graduate degree (*juren*). He ranked first in the Beijing provincial examinations, an exceptional success, due to the style of his essays, which won him early fame among the official literati.

Back in Guizhou, Zhang fought rebels alongside his father. In 1856, after Zhang qualified in Beijing to be an instructor in the official schools of the imperial clan, his father died, postponing Zhang's plans for employment and further examinations. While in mourning in Nanpi,

Zhang led a local militia against British and French foreigners waging war in Zhili. In 1860, after witnessing the plight in Beijing brought about by the Anglo-French victory in the Second Opium War (1856–1860), he voiced for the first time his distress at the threat to China posed by foreigners in a poem that expressed his strong feelings for the Chinese land, people, and way of government. This nationalist concern colored by his literary devotion to the Han and Song dynasties was a deep, career-long commitment for Zhang. His basic thoughts on the issue were boldly stated in the essay that won him the third rank at the palace examination for the metropolitan degree in 1863: "Today, the greatest evil in the empire is poverty. The officials are poor and therefore greedy. The people are poor and therefore become bandits. The army is poor and therefore unable to fight." (*Zhang Wenxiang gong quanji*, 222/3b). Although some examiners found the paper too critical and "contrary to tradition," a Manchu examiner recommended it, and Cixi (1835–1908) gave it a top rank, a decision that instilled in Zhang a lifelong personal loyalty to the empress dowager.

For twenty years, Zhang's nationalist agenda remained within the conservative limits of the so-called *qingyi*, the "disinterested counsel" offered by supposedly upright middle-ranking officials, whose criticism of policies and ministers Cixi encouraged in order to increase her control over high-ranking officials. Zhang's remedies for financial difficulties were austerity, military colonies, and repair of dikes. He also argued that the bureaucracy could be improved by recommending truly able men for office instead of relying on the purely literary criterion of examinations. In addition, he believed that foreign demands should be rejected, eventually by warfare. In his various posts as provincial examiner and director of education in Zhejiang, Hubei, and Sichuan, then as Hanlin academician, he worked to police the unruly ranks of the literati elite, who were impoverished and inflated by rebellions. To improve their living and learning, he called a halt to permanent increases in examination quotas in return for wartime contributions, he opened new academies, and he provided awards, books, and study aids, such as his own famous critical bibliography of ancient works, *Shumu dawen* (Answers and questions on book catalogues, 1875). He further ingratiated himself with Cixi in 1879 by refuting attacks against her decision on imperial succession after her son's death. In January 1882, after Zhang's recommended position against Russia in the Yili crisis resulted in some success, he was promoted to the post of governor of Shanxi.

PROVINCIAL MODERNIZER

In Shanxi, faced with an isolated province devastated by the horrendous 1876–1879 famine, Zhang converted to a policy of Western-style modernization based on indus-

trial, commercial, and scientific development. He based his policy on programs he found in the local archives, suggested by the British missionary Timothy Richard (1845–1919) when he led relief work in Taiyuan in 1878. Zhang built a new road linking Shanxi and Zhili. He invited experts from all over China to join an Office of Foreign Affairs in Taiyuan established for the purpose of gathering knowledge of Western sciences, techniques, law, languages, and literature. These experts helped Zhang to revise the old land survey for more efficient taxation, to run silk- and cotton-weaving mills and a gunpowder factory, to start mining projects, and to train troops with Western arms and drill. Some of these experts followed Zhang in his postings as governor-general of Guangdong and Guangxi (1884–1889), then of Hubei and Hunan (1889–1907), where he greatly expanded his modernizing programs.

Arriving in Guangzhou in 1884, Zhang's primary concern was to strengthen the region's defenses in the war with France. The cosmopolitan life of the treaty port and nearby Hong Kong sharpened his views on "self-strengthening," which had been shaped until then by reading memorials on foreign issues and programs (*yangwu*) by Zuo Zongtang and other officials. Zhang initiated the use of the press and the practice of boycotts for the sake of Chinese national salvation. Such actions failed to bring Britain and Germany to China's side, but they stirred local Chinese opinion and helped Zhang to collect large supplies and to impose cooperation among disordered troops and their commanders. He thus was able to put a halt to encroachments on the Sino-Vietnamese border with a victory at Langson that led to the downfall of the French premier Jules Ferry (1832–1893) (the only record of such Chinese sway over Western cabinets) and eventually to some territorial extensions. While Zhang condemned the peace settlement as an unwarranted surrender by the conciliatory faction headed by Li Hongzhang, Zhang's war efforts earned him further imperial trust and literati backing, which he relied upon to expand reforms designed to provide China with the skills and power to sustain its claims against foreign demands.

Zhang's reforms were aimed at transforming the Chinese polity. He believed that changing the ruling elite was a basic requirement before China could build a new structure of state power wielding efficient authority. For Zhang, learning was the source of strength; government should therefore belong to literati, but to those who would combine a thorough knowledge of foreign sciences with a true understanding of human nature and Chinese society gained through the study of Chinese classical practical learning.

Zhang understood that because the examinations provided a living to so many people, the system could not be changed rapidly. He thus promoted and expanded subsidiary systems. He reformed old academies and founded new ones that espoused modern curricula and teaching methods and were organized as Western schools. He also established special schools for training military officers, engineers, and civil servants, instilling them with foreign competence. Those students and the new-style literati he attracted were recommended to the throne for appointment or kept on his own staff, which from the old-type private secretariat (*mufu*) grew into the core of a highly specialized provincial administration of several hundred individuals.

In Guangzhou, Zhang trained new military forces and promoted industrial development with an arsenal, the first modern mint in China, a cotton mill, and an ironworks. He also initiated the diplomatic protection and official courtship of overseas Chinese. In 1889, anxious to strengthen national communications, Zhang designed the blueprint for China's railroad network, with a trunk line linking Beijing to Hankou; he was transferred to Wuchang to serve as Huguang governor-general and oversee construction. The line opened to traffic in 1906, during Zhang's long tenure there, while his earlier educational, economic, and military projects were expanded with the founding of modern schools, textile factories, and coal mines, as well as the Hanyang steelworks, which began production in 1894.

Zhang's undertakings sparked the beginnings of modern industrialization in Central China. Unlike efforts by Li Hongzhang, Zhang's projects, though provincially based, aimed to benefit the entire country and strove to rapidly reach the highest world standards with the best equipment and foreign expertise, and to promote comprehensive, interconnected development in all sectors. Zhang's leadership and Hubei's success highlighted the province as a cornerstone of China's reform and modernization.

NATIONAL REFORMER

In 1894 Zhang advocated war against Japan and went to great lengths to supply resources for national resistance. While the defeat undermined Li Hongzhang's power, Zhang emerged as a central figure of the reform movement in the war aftermath, with extensive connections to all reform-minded groups. He had early on employed Kang Youwei to revitalize an academy in Guangzhou. Riding the tide of patriotism among local elites, Zhang accelerated his projects in all fields and provided support for new programs in Hunan.

A temporary transfer to Nanjing to serve as acting governor-general of Liangjiang (from November 1894 to February 1896) allowed Zhang to usher in an interregional program for national development in the Yangzi area, where he initiated a coordinated allocation of resources and personnel, and provided support to the organizations

and efforts of young reformers. Zhang sponsored their Strength Study Society (Qiangxuehui) and their *Journal of Current Affairs* (*Shiwu bao*) in Shanghai. In April 1898, in response to mounting attacks on reform activities both from outside circles and within the court, he urged acceleration of real reforms in a pamphlet, *Exhortation to Learning* (*Quanxuepian*), which met with enormous and lasting success. In July, after the Hundred Days' Reform began, the emperor ordered the distribution of Zhang's pamphlet to all officials and students. Zhang advocated following a middle road, arguing against "clinging to the old," while also advising against making hasty commitments to foreign patterns and catchwords. Though he never used the slogan "Chinese learning for essence, Western learning for functioning" (*Zhongxue wei ti xixue wei yong*), he endorsed the basic essence/functioning (*tiyong*) dualism in his quest to establish Western knowledge and institutions in the service of Chinese genius through thoroughgoing acculturation.

During the Hundred Days' Reform, Zhang recommended to the throne bold young reformers and he strove to implement the flood of imperial decrees. Many of these men carried on or matched Zhang's own proposals to the throne on military and educational reform. Still, Zhang's efforts met with impatient admonition more often than recognition from the inexperienced Guangxu emperor (1871–1908). With no close allies at court, Zhang failed to save his protégés from execution among the "six martyrs" of Cixi's coup. His own vulnerability as the patron of the reformers, along with his suspicion of Kang Youwei's dogmatic distortion of Confucianism, led Zhang to voice condemnation of the political exiles and issue a subdued protest against Guangxu's removal. Zhang then became a scapegoat and the object of the reformist and revolutionary press slanders that culminated when Zhang cracked down on his disciple Tang Caichang's (1867–1900) aborted uprising of secret societies in August 1900. The slanders left an enduring imprint on his image in historiography, long based mainly on such writings. In fact, Zhang continued to enlarge the scope of his regional reform, sending many students to Japan, and attracting domestic and foreign capital and expertise, with the goal of turning Wuhan into a major economic hub, opened to the world. "Whatever the mood in Beijing," he told his friends, "China needs more competent people and more wealth, that is what I work for" (*Zhang Jian riji* [Zhang Jian's diary], 16 June 1901).

All along, albeit ingrained with Confucian commitment to his duty to the ruler and to the emperorship's legitimacy as a fundamental principle of unity, Zhang was more concerned with China's fate than with the Manchu dynasty, whose many political practices he aimed to discard. As he wrote in a private letter in 1889: "My rule of conduct in life and towards the dynasty is to respect and support those men and actions that benefit the nation [*guojia*], and to loathe and attack those that prey upon the nation and injure her." (*Zhang Wenxiang gong quanji*, 214/19a–b). Following this line of thinking, Zhang ignored imperial orders during the Boxer Uprising, and induced other top officials of Central and South China to conclude a pact with the foreign consuls in Shanghai to preserve peace and the safety of foreigners in the area, under their own responsibility. Outraged by the disastrous blow to national resources and sovereignty caused by a discretionary central power, and stirred by the growing resentment and even subversive radicalization among wider elite circles, with secret society collaboration that would lead to foreign intervention and partition of the country, Zhang resolved in autumn 1900 to force constitutional government on the court. While working to limit foreign demands in the peace negotiations, he pressed the throne for elimination of the worst reactionary councilors and for resumption of reform. The January 29, 1901, imperial edict promising reform gave him an opportunity to lead a new comprehensive national policy.

In 1898, frustrated by the negative response from Guangdong and Hubei gentry and merchants when he called on them to support modernization projects, Zhang warned that "people's rights" (*minquan*) in the form of elected assemblies overruling the bureaucracy, as discussed by a few reformers, would result only in the selfish assertion of local gentry interests with no regard for the public good. He now advocated a parliamentary system. Election of a lower house had to be postponed, Zhang argued, because modern education was not yet sufficiently widespread. But an upper house made up of responsible high officials could be convened immediately, and appointments should be made through an elective process among officialdom, with local elites participating at the lowest level. This proposal failed to enlist the support of other higher-ranking provincial officials.

Zhang then drafted three memorials, which he submitted with Liu Kunyi (1830–1902) in July 1901. They stressed the need to restore the Chinese people's faith in their own government, and advocated transformation of the civil service examinations, establishment of a national school system, and military and administrative reform by a change of law and institutions along Western lines. Though imperial edicts soon initiated such changes, Zhang wished to hasten the pace of reform to pacify growing anti-Manchu opposition. Becoming a spokesperson for progressive southern elites, Zhang won improved foreign-loan agreements for national railways, authored the 1904 regulations that standardized the national school system, promoted the teaching of a unified language, and opened official careers for graduates. He had the old examination system finally abolished in 1905, and a mission sent abroad to investigate suitable constitutional changes.

In 1907, beset with factional feuding at court, student unrest, and many intractable foreign and domestic issues, Cixi summoned Zhang to Beijing to provide leadership, and he became grand secretary and councilor alongside Yuan Shikai. Zhang urged the accelerated establishment of constitutional government and the election of a parliament. Though unable to overrule Prince Qing, who supported a nine-year preparatory program, Zhang was successful in integrating returned students and graduates of modern schools into the state service and in suppressing Manchu ethnic privileges.

Under Zhang's supervision, the Education Ministry upgraded facilities both in specialized training and primary education, with strong centralized control of textbooks. The Ministry also encouraged various provinces to open a school to preserve Confucian classical learning. Entrusted with the Guangzhou-Hankou railway and its extension to Sichuan, Zhang managed to find, and impose upon reluctant local opinion, adequate financing by a three-power consortium loan, which was soon toppled by American demands for a share. Despondent about his failure and the reckless reliance on Manchus by the regent, for whom he had secured a smooth transition to power after Cixi's death in November 1908, Zhang died convinced that the dynasty was doomed. He had married three times. His wives died early. He left six sons, four daughters, and no personal fortune.

SEE ALSO *Cixi, Empress Dowager; Hundred Days' Reform.*

BIBLIOGRAPHY

Ayers, William. *Chang Chih-tung and Educational Reform in China.* Cambridge, MA: Harvard University Press, 1971.

Bays, Daniel H. *China Enters the Twentieth Century: Chang Chih-tung and the Issues of a New Age, 1895–1909.* Ann Arbor: University of Michigan Press, 1978.

Li Renkai and Zhong Kangmo. *Zhang Zhidong yu jindai Zhongguo* [Zhang Zhidong and modern China]. Baoding, PRC: Hebei Daxue Chubanshe, 1999.

Zhang Zhidong. *Zhang Wenxiang gong quanji* [Complete works of Zhang Zhidong]. Ed. Wang Shunan. Beiping, PRC: Wang Shunan, 1928. Reprint, Taibei: Wenhai Chubanshe, 1963.

Zhang Zhidong. *Zhang Zhidong quanji* [Complete works of Zhang Zhidong]. Eds. Yuan Shuyi, Sun Huafeng, and Li Bingxin. Shijiazhuang, PRC: Hebei Renmin Chubanshe, 1998.

Marianne Bastid-Bruguière

ZHAO DAN
1915–1980

A major actor and an artist of integrity, Zhao Dan devoted his life to studying acting skills and defending artistic independence. For these, he duly received the title of "People's Artist."

Growing up in Nantong, Jiangsu Province, a center for famous opera singers and dramatic actors, Zhao developed an early interest in acting. After brief training in traditional Chinese painting at Shanghai Art Academy (1931–1932), Zhao returned to acting, joining Zhongguo zuoyi xijujia lianmeng (Chinese Leftist Dramatists' League) in 1933. He also established himself as a screen actor in Star Film Studio, one of Shanghai's major film companies. Zhao's acting career, which began in 1932, suffered from two major setbacks: While working with an anti-Japanese traveling drama troupe in 1939, he was imprisoned by a warlord in Xinjiang until 1945, and he was imprisoned again, for five years, during the Cultural Revolution (1966–1969). Despite these periods of incarceration, Zhao acted in forty films, most of which were made before 1949.

Zhao's best known early films are *Shizi jietou* (Crossroads, 1937), *Malu tianshi* (Street Angel, 1937), and *Wuya yu maque* (Crows and Sparrows, 1949). *Crossroads* and *Street Angel* were canonized as key leftist films. *Crows and Sparrows* is a progressive social exposé whose narrative closely echoes and allegorizes the historical threshold moment when the Communist Party was dramatically displacing the Guomingdang regime. In these films Zhao enlivens his realistic portrayals of downtrodden urban residents with wit, sarcasm, and sympathy.

Zhao actively participated in the politics and new film culture of the People's Republic of China (PRC). He joined the Communist Party in 1957. From 1950 to 1965 he starred in ten films, most of which are biopics about well known Chinese historical figures. The only exception is *Wu Xun zhuan* (The story of Wu Xun, 1950), which chronicles a peasant's lifelong devotion to building schools for poor children with money he had obtained through begging. Conceived in 1944 and finished in 1950, the film initially received positive reviews from the PRC's high officials, but soon was condemned by Mao Zedong as petty-bourgeois "poisonous weed." This denunciation led to the persecution of Zhao Dan and the film's director, Sun Yu (1900–1990).

Despite this, Zhao's unwavering artistic integrity persisted till the end of his life. In 1979 he published two books about his life and acting career, *Yinmu xingxiang chuangzao* (The creation of screen images) and *Diyu zhi men* (The gate to Hell). He also made a major contribution to defending artistic independence with his article "Guan de tai juti, wenyi mei xiwang" (Too much surveillance kills the art), published in *Renmin Ribao* (People's daily) on October 8, 1980, just two days before his death. Zhao's article revived some artist-intellectuals long silenced by the Cultural Revolution, and brought artistic creation back into the picture.

In 1995 the China Film Century Best Actor award was conferred posthumously on Zhao. A television drama titled *Zhao Dan* was in production in 2008 with China's Central TV (CCTV).

SEE ALSO *Film Industry: Overview.*

BIBLIOGRAPHY

Xiang Jidong. Chongdu Zhao Dan de yiyan: Zhao Dan shishi er'shi zhounian ji [Rereading Zhao Dan's *Last Words*: commemorating the twentieth anniversary of Zhao Dan's death]. *Shu Wu* [Book house] 4 (2001). http://www.housebook.com.cn/200104/17.htm.

Xu Xun. Wu Xun Zhuan paishe neimu [The backstage story of *The Story of Wu Xun*]. *Renmin zhengxie bao* [People's political consultative committee newspaper]. April 2001. http://www.gmw.cn/content/2004-12/31/content_156213.htm.

Zhao Dan file. *Shanghai nianhua* [Shanghai memory] Web site. http://memoire.digilib.sh.cn/SHNH/star/star_index.jsp?starId=011.

Yiman Wang

ZHAO SHULI
1906–1970

Zhao Shuli was born into a poor farming family in Yuchi village, Qinshui County, Shanxi Province. He succeeded in attending teachers college in Changzhi, where he developed an interest in new literature and left-wing literature in the mid-1920s and began writing fiction in 1930. In 1926 he was expelled from the teachers college because of his involvement in protests against the corruption of the college principal, for which he was imprisoned later in that year by the Yan Xishan government. In 1927 he joined the Chinese Communist Party and is reported in some sources to have been subsequently imprisoned again. In 1933 he began publishing literary pieces in *Shanxi Dangxun Fukan* (Shanxi party newsletter supplement). In 1937 he threw himself into the resistance to the Japanese invasion and engaged in patriotic cultural and propaganda work, preparing small plays and longer dramas, as well as ballads, in the local vernaculars. In 1941, Zhao was editing *Kangzhan Shenghuo* (War of resistance life) and *Zhongguoren* (The Chinese), for which publications he prepared works in many genres of *quyi*, a collective term for the extensive variety of dramatic folk literary forms that can feature various combinations of recitative, rhyme, dramatization, singing, musical accompaniment, and even elements of dance. In 1943 Zhao was transferred to the North China School of the Central Committee.

His novel *Xiao Erhei Jiehun* (The marriage of Xiao Erhei), published in 1943, eulogized the new marital freedom introduced by the Communists in the Yan'an base area. In the novel Zhao set out to emulate the principles of a literature of the workers, peasants, and soldiers called for by Mao Zedong in 1942, and the novel won the praise of Yan'an's cultural commissar, Zhou

Yang. Zhao Shuli's *Li Youcai Banhua* (The rhymes of Li Youcai, 1943), regarded as a more representative work embodying these principles, is set in a fictional village that the Communist Party is gradually taking over. Li Youcai is a local itinerant entertainer whose earthy ditties expose the corruption of the incumbent politicians and encourage the peasants to support the Communists. These two novels, *Xiao Erhei Jiehun* and *Li Youcai Banhua*, represented a departure in Chinese Communist literature because of their dissociation from the dominant urban leftist tradition. Following the success of these two novels, in 1946 Zhao Shuli published *Lijiazhuang de bianqian* (The changes in Li village), which is described by many critics as the most readable of his fictional works.

Zhao went to Beijing in 1949 and took part in organizing the Beijing Municipality Masses Literature and Art Creation Research Society (Beijing-shi Dazhong Wenyi Chuangzuo Yanjiu Hui), then became the organization's chairman. Together with Li Bozhao, Zhao edited the monthly *Shuoshuo Changchang* (Reciting and singing), a journal devoted to traditional folk recitative literature. The journal published many influential recitative works and articles establishing a theoretical base for creative work and research on folk literary forms. In 1953 Zhao returned to his hometown in Shanxi Province and devoted himself to writing. There he produced his long novel *Sanliwan*, the short stories included in the collection *Xiaxiang Ji* (Going down to the countryside), and various dramatic works.

His works inspired a number of other writers, and by the latter half of the 1950s Zhao's fiction about rural life became the centerpiece of what was called the "mountain yam school" (*shanyaodan pai*), characterized by strong folk and regional linguistic features. Other Shanxi writers who produced fiction in the same vein included Ma Feng (b. 1922), Xi Rong (1922–2001), Sun Qian (1920–1996), Hu Zheng (b. 1924), Han Wenzhou (b. 1926), and Li Yimin (b. 1929), but scholars have debated whether they constituted an organized "school." Nevertheless, it is reported that Zhou Yang traveled to Shanxi in July 1956 and proposed that a characteristic literary school be established there. The literary journal of Shanxi, *Huohua* (Spark), and the national newspaper *Wenyi Bao* (Literary gazette), organized a symposium of this "school" of writing in May 1958.

Despite his exemplary class background, Communist credentials, and long-term involvement with peasant life, Zhao Shuli suffered a particularly terrible fate in the Cultural Revolution. His persecution began in July 1966 and continued intermittently until, after an exceptionally savage beating in 1970, he died aged sixty-four.

SEE ALSO *Literary Societies; Literature since 1800; Zhou Yang.*

BIBLIOGRAPHY
Zhao Shuli. *Zhao Shuli wenji* [Anthology of Zhao Shuli's writings]. 4 vols. Beijing: Gongren Chubanshe, 1980.
Zhao Shuli. *Zhao Shuli quanji* [The complete works of Zhao Shuli]. 5 vols. Taiyuan, China: Beiyue Wenyi Chubanshe, 1986–1994.
Zhongguo Wenxuejia Cidian Bianweihui [Editorial committee of the Dictionary of Chinese Writers], ed. *Zhongguo wenxuejia cidian (Xiandai diyi fence)* [Dictionary of Chinese writers: Modern period, volume one]. Hong Kong: Wenhua Ziliao Gongying She, 1979. See pp. 367–370.

Bruce Doar

ZHAO ZIYANG
1919–2005

Zhao Ziyang, premier of the People's Republic of China from 1980 to 1987 and general secretary of the Chinese Communist Party (CCP) from 1987 to 1989, was a major architect of China's post-Mao economic reform and a pioneer of political reform. Zhao's political career of five decades brought him to the nominal number-one position of the nation, but his career came to an abrupt end after he expressed sympathy for the prodemocracy movement of 1989. He died in 2005 under house arrest in Beijing.

Born in October 1919 in Henan to the family of a rich farmer, Zhao joined the CCP in 1938 during the war against the invading Japanese, and later led guerrilla and local base-area governments through the civil war between the CCP and Guomindang (Nationalist Party) that followed the end of World War II (1939–1945). When the CCP took power in 1949, Zhao marched with his army south to Guangdong, where he worked as a provincial leader of the party and government until the early years of the Cultural Revolution of the 1960s. During this period, he became known by national leaders, including Mao Zedong and Zhou Enlai, as an expert on agricultural development.

In 1966, when Tao Zhu (1908–1969) was appointed the number-four official of the reshuffled national leadership, Zhao, as Tao's deputy in Guangdong, replaced him as the first secretary of the party's provincial committee, becoming one of the youngest at the rank at that time. Zhao soon lost power, however, as the Cultural Revolution swept away party secretaries and governors. When he was rehabilitated years later, he found himself in Inner Mongolia supervising livestock production and agriculture for the Inner Mongolia Autonomous Region.

When Deng Xiaoping returned to power in 1975 after his ouster during the Cultural Revolution, he implemented "rectifications" of industry, agriculture, transportation, and education. These programs gained powerful support from Zhao, who now held the leadership position in Sichuan, a

A candlelight vigil mourning the death of Zhao Ziyang, Hong Kong, China, January 21, 2005. *A former Chinese premier and Communist Party general secretary, Zhao Ziyang looked to reform China's political system in ways similar to the liberalization of the economic system. After expressing support with pro-democracy demonstrators at Tiananmen Square in 1989, Zhao was removed from all party posts and placed under house arrest, where he died in 2005.* © **BOBBY YIP/REUTERS/CORBIS**

significant agricultural region and the most populous province at the time. Zhao began experimenting in industrial and agricultural reforms by introducing individual incentives into production and income allocation. This effort was interrupted after Deng's second ouster from Beijing politics in 1976, and resumed with even greater momentum when Deng returned to power in 1977, after Mao's death the previous year. Zhao's tolerance and support for farmers' initiatives as part of the "household responsibility system" greatly improved agricultural output, earning him a positive reputation among farmers, who spoke of "seeking Ziyang when one needs grain."

Zhao was promoted to the national leadership in 1979 and was appointed premier of China's cabinet, the State Council, the following year. Thereafter, he became the main force behind China's economic reform, which laid the foundations for the rise of Chinese economic power in the twenty-first century. Zhao was also a leading advocate of the open-door policy that integrated China with the

world economy. He championed the designation of special economic zones and open coastal cities as centers for foreign trade and investment. Zhao also initiated China's bid for a seat in the World Trade Organization. The economic success of Guangdong and other coastal provinces in the 1980s, the transformation of Hainan Island into a province and special economic zone with a high degree of economic autonomy, and the "coastal development strategy" in which China's maritime provinces took part in the international division of labor that helped spur national development, all owed much to Zhao.

Although Zhao never finished high school, he was well known for his lifelong zeal for the acquisition of new knowledge. He became a pioneer in China in the early 1980s when he emphasized the revolutionary significance of new technologies, including information technology, to the human progress with which China had struggled to keep pace. He created space for policy input from experts, think tanks, and, to a lesser degree, popular opinion, inaugurating a transition from the Maoist dictatorship of policy making. Zhao's grasp of economic issues was admired by leading economists, including a Nobel laureate of economics, Milton Friedman (1912–2006).

A milestone of his political career was the Thirteenth CCP National Congress, held in October 1987. On that occasion, Zhao was formally elected general secretary of the party. He had been serving as acting secretary since January 1987, after his fellow reformer, Hu Yaobang, was forced by party elders to resign from the position. More importantly, Zhao proposed to the Congress a systematic plan for political reform, the first and only such plan presented during the rule of the CCP. Zhao suggested "building up socialist democracy" as the goal of China's political transition from Maoist institutions, defining *democracy* against the existing political system, which offered few civic rights and little opportunity for popular participation. Various measures were outlined and, to a lesser degree, implemented for downgrading the role of the party in political, economic, and social arenas. Zhao also proposed establishing a modern system of civil service, enhancing the rule of law, introducing competitive (though still limited) elections to various levels of party and state organizations, promoting individual rights and civil organizations, and enlarging the participation of Chinese citizens in politics.

Zhao faced tremendous ideological, political, and bureaucratic resistance to his reform proposals, a difficulty compounded by new problems, such as inflation, income disparity, and governmental corruption, that were fueled by the transitional economy. In spring of 1989, when the student-led mass protests calling for political reform and democratization arose in Beijing, Zhao disagreed with his Politburo colleagues on how to deal with the protestors' demands: Zhao regarded substantive political reform toward democracy and rule of law as the answer, while premier Li Peng (1928–), backed by Deng Xiaoping, insisted on a hard-line response. This split became public when the leadership decided to send troops to Tiananmen Square, a move Zhao opposed. Zhao had lost his leadership positions and personal freedom by the time the People's Liberation Army opened fire on protesters on June 4.

Zhao spent his final years under house arrest at 6 Fuqiang Alley in Beijing. Even his name had become taboo in China. He refused to confess his alleged "serious mistakes of supporting the turmoil and splitting the party." After his death in January 2005, the authorities did not allow citizens to express their feelings about him.

SEE ALSO *Communist Party; Cultural Revolution, 1966–1969; Deng Xiaoping; Hu Yaobang.*

BIBLIOGRAPHY

Boda chubanshe. *Ta zhongyu ziyou le: Zhao Ziyang shishi fengyun lu* [He eventually is in freedom: Events around the funeral of Zhao Ziyang]. Hong Kong: Author, 2005.

Fewsmith, Joseph. *Dilemmas of Reform in China: Political Conflict and Economic Debate.* Armonk, NY: Sharpe, 1994.

Goldman, Merle. *Sowing the Seeds of Democracy in China: Political Reform in the Deng Xiaoping Era.* Cambridge, MA: Harvard University Press, 1994.

Hutchings, Graham. *Modern China: A Guide to a Century of Change.* Cambridge, MA: Harvard University Press, 2000.

Keyser, Catherine. *Professionalizing Research in Post-Mao China: The System Reform Institute and Policy Making.* Armonk, NY: Sharpe, 2002.

Liu Shousen. *Nianqing shi de Zhao Ziyang* [Early years of Zhao Ziyang]. Hong Kong: Pacific Century Press, 2005.

MacFarquhar, Roderick, ed. *The Politics of China: The Eras of Mao and Deng.* 2nd ed. New York: Cambridge University Press, 1997.

Nathan, Andrew J., and Perry Link, eds., and Zhang Liang, comp. *The Tiananmen Papers.* New York: Public Affairs, 2001.

Naughton, Barry. *Growing Out of the Plan: Chinese Economic Reform, 1978–1993.* New York: Cambridge University Press, 1995.

Shambaugh, David. *The Making of a Premier: Zhao Ziyang's Provincial Career.* Boulder, CO: Westview, 1984.

Wu Guoguang. *Zhao Ziyang yu zhengzhi gaige* [Zhao Ziyang and political reform]. Hong Kong: Pacific Century Press, 1997.

Wu Guoguang, and Helen Lansdowne, eds. *Zhao Ziyang and China's Political Future.* London: Routledge, 2008.

Zhao Ziyang. *Yanzhe you Zhongguo tese de shehuizhuyi daolu qianjin* [Marching along with the road of socialism with Chinese characteristics]. Report to the Thirteenth CCP National Congress. Beijing: Renmin Chubanshe, 1987.

Zong Fengming. *Zhao Ziyang ruanjin zhong de tanhua* [Zhao Ziyang: Captive conversations]. Hong Kong: Open Press, 2007.

Guoguang Wu

ZHEJIANG

Zhejiang province, with an area of roughly 100,000 square kilometers (40,000 square miles), is named after the Zhe River, better known locally as the Qiantang River, which flows through the heart of the province and issues into Hangzhou Bay. Mountains and hills dominate the areas of the province south and east of the Qiantang, and in its upper reaches, while the prefectures north and west of the river—Hangzhou, Jiaxing, and Huzhou (Hang-Jia-Hu)—occupy a flat alluvial plain that is interlaced by small waterways and canals, part of the fabled *yu mi zhi xiang* (land of rice and fish). These two areas have been conventionally characterized, respectively, as Zhedong (eastern Zhejiang) and Zhexi (western Zhejiang), capturing a fundamental distinction in the natural ecology of the political unit of the province. Zhexi more closely resembles the areas of the lower Yangzi (Chang) River Delta in southern Jiangsu, while Zhedong resembles more mountainous areas in the surrounding provinces of Fujian, Jiangxi, and Anhui.

ZHEJIANG

Capital city: Hangzhou

Largest cities (population): Hangzhou (6,660,000 [2006]), Ningbo (5,600,000 [2006]), Haining

Area: 101,800 sq. km. (39,300 sq. mi.)

Population: 46,770,000 (2000)

Demographics: Han, 99.2%; She, 0.4%

GDP: CNY 1,574.2 billion (2006)

Famous sites: Baoguo Temple, Mount Putuo, Qita (Seven Pagoda) Temple, Mount Tiantai, Xi Hu (West Lake); Mount Yandang, Qiandao Lake; Guoqing Temple

QING-ERA PROSPERITY

Ecological variation encouraged development of at least four distinct socioeconomic patterns across the province during the late Qing dynasty (1644–1912). In the north, Ningbo and Shaoxing prefectures could be added to the Zhexi core area of Hang-Jia-Hu to form a single socioeconomic unit. These areas fell mostly within the lower Yangzi regional core, as delineated by anthropologist and historian G. William Skinner, and had fertile agricultural land. But just as important to this area during the late imperial period was the development of premodern industry and commerce. Hang-Jia-Hu was part of the preeminent silk-producing region of the empire during the nineteenth century, operating mostly on a cottage-industry basis. As much as a quarter to a third of all arable land in some rural areas of Zhexi (including, according to Lillian Li [1981], Wuxing, Deqing, Tongxiang, Haiyan, and Shimen counties) was given over to mulberry trees, and silk production became the primary economic focus of these areas well into the twentieth century. Trade was equally developed and sophisticated. The capital of Hangzhou was the southern terminus of the Grand Canal, connecting the province to the major north-south axis of the empire-wide trading system. A thriving coastal and regional export trade centered on the port city of Ningbo.

Commercial vibrancy along with agricultural and industrial productivity provided a foundation for academic and political success. Overall, Zhejiang, with roughly 7 percent of the empire's population, provided 8 to 10 percent of the Qing empire's local officials from the Kangxi (1662–1722) through the Guangxu (1875–1908) periods, as calculated by Li Guoqi (1982), demonstrating consistent achievement in the competitive civil service examination system. Schools established by lineages, gentry families, or merchant associations, which were supported by commer-

cial or agricultural wealth, cultivated talented young men, providing the basis for long-term examination success. Shaoxing prefecture was extremely successful at training fine scholars, producing 977 *jinshi* (metropolitan examination degree holders) during the Ming dynasty. Shaoxing men filled the Qing imperial bureaucracy, with even unsuccessful candidates in the upper-level examinations in demand to serve as clerks and secretaries, dominating provincial secretarial posts and staff positions in many of the central government boards.

Areas outside of Zhejiang's northernmost prefectures exhibited three distinct socioeconomic patterns. The basin of the Qiantang River valley formed in the prefectures of Yanzhou, Jinhua, and Quzhou. Towns along the river, especially Lanxi at the confluence of Qiantang tributaries, were centers for trade in agricultural and mountain products. Goods were gathered from river- and road-based trading networks extending into surrounding provinces of Fujian, Jiangxi, and Anhui and funneled downriver into the empire-wide trading system. Areas farther inland, including portions of Chuzhou, Quzhou, and Yanzhou prefectures, were highly mountainous, limiting development of agriculture and trade. Along the coast, Taizhou and Wenzhou prefectures participated in the coastal trade but were overshadowed by Ningbo in long-distance trade and had limited access to inland commercial networks, in contrast to cities and towns along the Qiantang. The ecology of these coastal trading areas, composed of maritime-oriented communities with limited agricultural hinterlands, made them resemble areas farther south on the Fujian coast more than the northern Zhejiang areas of Hang-Jia-Hu and Ning-Shao. The dialects of Taizhou and Wenzhou also differed from those in northern Zhejiang, contributing to cultural separation.

FROM THE TAIPING TO THE REPUBLIC

Zhejiang thrived for much of the Qing, as witnessed by healthy population growth between the late eighteenth and mid-nineteenth centuries. In 1786 the province had a population of roughly 21.5 million, which had grown to more than 30 million by the 1850s, according to Li Guoqi. Soon thereafter the Taiping Uprising (1850–1864) set in motion depopulation and devastation that conditioned the province's development during the late nineteenth and early twentieth centuries. Battles between Taiping and Qing troops raged throughout the years 1862 to 1864, affecting Hang-Jia-Hu and southwestern areas most dramatically. The resulting depopulation was striking. By 1873 the population had fallen to 18 million, recovering somewhat to 25.3 million by 1957 (Rankin, 1986)—but still below its mid-nineteenth-century level of 30 million. There were parallel drops in amount of arable land under cultivation during the post-Taiping decades.

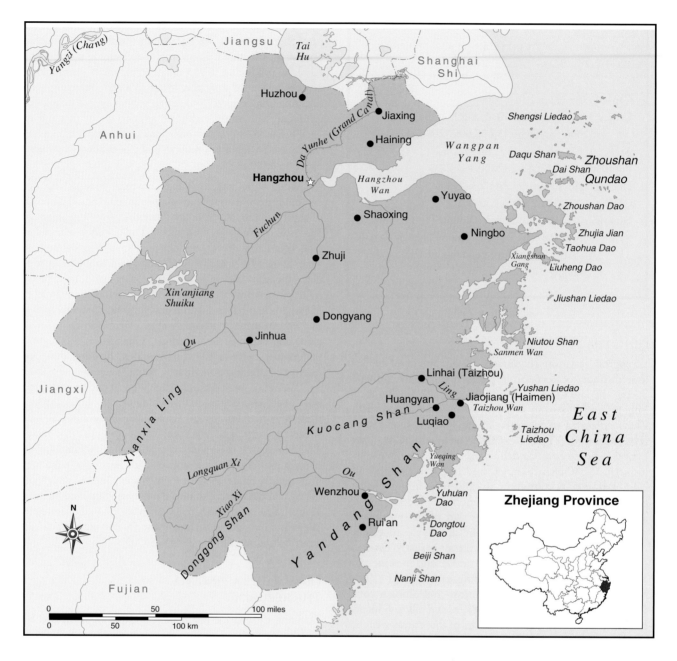

Distinctions among Zhejiang's socioeconomic areas were accentuated by the fast-paced economic activity centered in Shanghai, which transformed the lower Yangzi region during the late nineteenth and early twentieth centuries. Infrastructural development drew northern Zhejiang inexorably into Shanghai's orbit. Telegraph lines linked Shanghai to Hangzhou and Ningbo by 1884; and the rail link between Shanghai and Hangzhou opened in 1909. Hang-Jia-Hu consequently became part of Shanghai's hinterland, as it has remained, with a high-speed train ride of only a little over an hour now separating Hangzhou and Shanghai. Ningbo's trade and banking shifted almost entirely to Shanghai during the second half of the nineteenth century. Ningbo bankers and entrepreneurs were one of the dominant *bang* (financial cliques) in Shanghai commerce and industry, and they organized the powerful *siming gongsuo* (Ningbo commercial guild). Northern prosperity and enhanced commercial integration contrasted with growing isolation and consequent economic stagnation in the Zhedong interior. New trade patterns based on modern communication and finance systems drew trade and industry away from the cities and towns in the Qiantang basin, which had depended on late imperial infrastructural networks. Instead of serving as thriving nodes for the export of native manufactured goods, these towns now became conduits for cheap Western imports and manufactured products from Shanghai to the interior.

Zhejiang's prosperity and flourishing culture put it in the forefront of social and political changes in the last decades of the nineteenth century. After the fall of the Taiping, Zhejiang's wealthy and educated elite organized various relief and reconstruction efforts. Elites provided grain, built orphanages and foundling homes, and rebuilt academies. These activities were often coordinated by *tongshan tang* (united welfare agencies) that became a prototype for new kinds of elite parapolitical organization. The post-Taiping reconstruction fostered an ethos of elite civic engagement that was formalized when the Qing government mandated new local civic and political organizations with the introduction of the so-called New Policies in the first years after 1900. Chambers of commerce, education associations, agricultural associations, and then provincial and county assemblies provided new contexts for elite social and political activity. These organizations allowed elites to assert various forms of political influence after establishment of the Republic in 1912, despite a succession of dominant military governors. Emergent forms of elite-led civic action were suppressed or co-opted with the incorporation of Zhejiang as a core area of Nationalist Party rule during the Nanjing decade (1927–1937). During the period of the Second Sino-Japanese War (1937–1945), large areas of northern and coastal Zhejiang were occupied by Japanese and collaborationist forces.

NEW CYCLE OF DEVELOPMENT

Centralized national economic policies during the Maoist period (1949–1978) worked against the province's trajectory of late imperial and modern development, which had focused on consumer-oriented light industry and trade. Maoist emphasis on heavy industrial development and provincial self-sufficiency hurt resource-poor Zhejiang. Prioritizing grain production contradicted centuries of agricultural specialization and reliance on the national market. Coastal areas suffered disproportionately from low levels of state investment because they were viewed as front-line areas in any potential conflict related to Taiwan. Coastal cities were also hobbled by restrictive trade policies. Historically prosperous Zhejiang became economically disadvantaged, with per capita income standing at only 81 percent of the national average by 1976, as noted by Keith Forster (1998).

Hangzhou Bay Bridge, Jiaxing, Zhejiang province, April 28, 2008. *Reducing the travel time from Shanghai to Zhejiang's port city of Ningbo, the Hangzhou Bay Bridge opened to the public in 2008. Spanning twenty-two miles over the sea, the crossing was the world's largest trans-oceanic bridge upon completion.* © **LARRY LEUNG/EPA/CORBIS**

Decades of limited opportunity and stagnation meant that, by 1978, local communities and officials were primed to take advantage of the new era of *gaige kaifeng* (Reform and Opening). Starting in the mid-1970s, households and individuals in resource-poor and underdeveloped Wenzhou, which was also culturally, logistically, and politically separate from the rest of the province, began experimenting with private industry and trade. To ensure protection in an uncertain political environment, these individual entrepreneurs often partnered with local officials in a variety of guises so that they became, in name if not in essence, "collective" businesses, paying fees to local governments in exchange for affiliation. During the 1980s increasingly aggressive forms of private enterprise, focused in light manufacturing, trade, and private banking, characterized the so-called *Wenzhou moshi* (Wenzhou model). As growth progressed, Wenzhou became the focus of national debate about the pace and mode of economic reform in the post-Mao era.

Light industrial development, in both private and collective forms, fueled extremely rapid growth rates in Zhejiang beginning in the late 1970s, outpacing even the impressive growth numbers in China nationally. For instance, according to Forster, between 1978 and 1995 provincial GDP grew by nine times versus a national increase of just over four times. As of the 2000 census, the province's population had grown to 46.77 million. With renewed market-driven growth, regional differences in infrastructural integration have again exacerbated economic imbalances between northern and coastal Zhejiang and mountainous, interior areas. By the mid-1990s, Forster notes, per capita GDP was already 80 percent higher in Zhejiang's northern counties than it was in the province's south. Northern Zhejiang's infrastructural advantage is now symbolized by the Hangzhou Bay Bridge, which covers approximately 35 kilometers (22 miles) of open water to cut the travel time from Shanghai to Ningbo to about two hours. From the late 1990s to the late 2000s, formation of economic development and technology zones in historically advantaged Hangzhou and Ningbo, combined with the magnetic pull of Shanghai as a global financial and industrial center, led to resumed regional and national dominance for the Hang-Jia-Hu and Ning-Shao areas. In 2006 Hangzhou was considered by the World Bank to have the best investment environment in China, with Shaoxing ranked third. Wealth was accompanied by the growth of an increasingly cosmopolitan global culture to rival that of neighboring Shanghai. As during the late imperial period, Zhejiang in the twenty-first century is a single political unit encompassing two distinct socioeconomic communities.

SEE ALSO *Hangzhou; Ningbo (Ningpo); Wenzhou.*

BIBLIOGRAPHY

Forster, Keith. *Zhejiang in Reform.* Sydney, Australia: Wild Peony, distributed by Honolulu: University of Hawaii Press, 1998.

Li Guoqi. *Zhongguo xiandaihua de quyu yanjiu: Min Zhe Tai diqu, 1860–1916* (Regional research in China's modernization: The Fujian, Zhejiang, Taiwan region, 1860–1916). Taibei: Zhongyang Yanjiu Yuan Jindaishi Yanjiusuo, 1982.

Li, Lillian M. *China's Silk Trade: Traditional Industry in the Modern World, 1842–1937.* Cambridge, MA: Council on East Asian Studies, Harvard University Press, 1981.

Parris, Kristen. Local Initiative and National Reform: The Wenzhou Model of Development. *China Quarterly*, no. 134 (June 1993): 242–263.

Rankin, Mary Backus. *Elite Activism and Political Transformation in China: Zhejiang Province, 1865–1911.* Stanford, CA: Stanford University Press, 1986.

Schoppa, R. Keith. *Chinese Elites and Political Change: Zhejiang Province in the Early Twentieth Century.* Cambridge, MA: Harvard University Press, 1982.

Yeh, Wen-hsin. *Provincial Passages: Culture, Space, and the Origins of Chinese Communism.* Berkeley: University of California Press, 1996.

Robert Culp

ZHONGGUO

Use of the term *Zhongguo* can be traced back to the Zhou dynasty (1046–256 BCE). *Zhongguo*, literally "middle kingdom" or "central kingdom," signified differentiation from other communities in terms of geography, race, and culture. Zhongguo was where the ruler lived, governing his people under the mandate of heaven. This kingdom was initially located along the Yellow River, and was extended to incorporate the area around the Yangzi River and subsequently also the Pearl River, all with a predominantly Han population. The word *guo* here carried the idea of a culturally homogenous kingdom under a central governing body providing military and economic control.

China exercised influence over its neighbors through the tributary system. This system evolved over many centuries, and reached its most mature form during the Ming (1368–1644) and the first half of the Qing (1644–1912) dynasties. The meaning and use of the term *Zhongguo* changed along with shifts in China's relations with outsiders. For example, around the time of the Song dynasty (960–1279), when the Han people had a more equal relationship with other ethnic communities, which at that time were not necessarily weaker than the Song, *Zhongguo* denoted an awareness of territorial boundaries. As Chinese history progressed, the word *guo* gradually assumed more than a cultural and racial meaning, although it was never precisely the same as the modern Western concept of *nation-state*. During the nineteenth century, as China was forced by the Western powers and Japan to cede territories and shed its tributary states, often as a consequence of lost wars, *Zhongguo* acquired a more precise geographical meaning. *Zhongguo* had become a territory that must be defended. In consequence, the Chinese began to negotiate international agreements in an attempt to define the nation's boundaries.

This terminological quality of *Zhongguo* became even more important in the discourse of nationalism that emerged in the second half of the nineteenth century. After a long period of prosperity under Qing rule, China was forced to reconsider its position. As its territories were attacked, and its historic political, economic, and cultural privileges were abruptly challenged, the term *Zhongguo* was reexamined and reinterpreted with the acknowledgement of the existence of other, much stronger, powers.

With the arrival of foreigners in increasing numbers since the nineteenth century, China and its people's characteristics, including their flaws, were widely discussed around the world in books, journals, and newspapers. The image of an ancient prosperous empire, a source of precious silk, porcelain, and fine art, was replaced with one of a poor backward nation living on past glories.

In China, revolutionaries and intellectuals thought that what their country urgently needed was an awakening. In order to allow China's objective situation to emerge from the fantasy of the ancient Sinocentric worldview still held by the vast majority of Chinese people, the truth had to be told. Those who sought to rebuild the country believed that the way to achieve their goal was to rouse people's feelings of shame. By transforming these feelings into passion for change, the old, decaying Middle Kingdom would be transformed into a modern state, with its subjects transformed into citizens.

The negative feelings associated with the condition of China contributed to the rise of modern nationalism and a new understanding of the term *Zhongguo*. At the higher level of society, *Zhongguo* became part of the discourse of intellectuals who were pressing for a new kind of China, and embracing modernization, self-strengthening, and even a completely new political structure, such as a republic or a constitutional monarchy. At a lower level, common people increasingly experienced feelings of national shame after many defeats at the hands of foreign countries in the late nineteenth century. Anger toward foreigners and disappointment about the lack of strength shown by the Qing government were finally expressed through the Boxer Uprising of 1900 and the 1911 revolution.

A new China, with the official name *Zhonghua Minguo* (Republic of China) finally arrived after the success of the revolution in 1911. This official name, although communicating the new political form, did not dispense with the central claim expressed by the word *Zhongguo* in terms of culture, language, and philosophy. Under the new regime, the concept of China embraced a multi-ethnic approach, and *Zhongguo* was settled as a term that went beyond a political signifier of a homogenous han territory.

SEE ALSO *Nationalism.*

BIBLIOGRAPHY

Cohen, Paul A. *History in Three Keys: The Boxers as Event, Experience, and Myth.* New York: Columbia University Press, 1997.

Fitzgerald, John. *Awakening China: Politics, Culture, and Class in the Nationalist Revolution.* Stanford, CA: Stanford University Press, 1996.

Liu, Lydia H. (Liu He). *Translingual Practice: Literature, National Culture, and Translated Modernity—China, 1900–1937.* Stanford, CA: Stanford University Press, 1995.

Rossabi, Morris, ed. *China among Equals: The Middle Kingdom and Its Neighbors, 10th–14th Centuries.* Berkeley: University of California Press, 1983.

Saari, Jon L. *Legacies of Childhood: Growing Up Chinese in a Time of Crisis, 1890–1920.* Cambridge, MA: Council on East Asian Studies, Harvard University, 1990.

Tsai Weipin

ZHOU ENLAI
1898–1976

Zhou Enlai was born March 5, 1898, in Huaian County, Jiangsu Province. Upon graduating from Tianjin Middle School, he studied at Waseda and Nippon universities in Japan (1917–1918), before enrolling in Nankai University in Tianjin. He rarely attended classes, however, becoming immersed in student mobilization as one of the organizers of the Tianjin Students' Union and editor of the union's newspaper, *Tianjin Student*. Hence he also became involved in the May Fourth movement, for which he (with twenty-eight others) was arrested and briefly imprisoned.

EDUCATION ABROAD

In 1920 Zhou was selected to go to France on a work-study program (where he actually did little of either, dedicating himself rather to political organization in France and Germany). For the next four years he was chair of the Chinese Socialist Youth League (in which capacity he worked closely with Deng Xiaoping, who edited the league newspaper, *Red Light*, and succeeded him to the chairmanship). Zhou also joined the Chinese Communist Party (CCP) when a branch was formed in 1922. There were then two thousand Chinese students in France, some two hundred each in Belgium and England and between three hundred and four hundred in Germany, and he helped organize their recruitment and later departure for study in Moscow.

Upon his return to China, Zhou also joined the Guomindang (Nationalist Party or GMD), which included the Chinese Communist Party (CCP) as a "bloc within" a United Front that was collaborating to overcome warlordism and restore national unity and order. Though that coalition fell apart upon the achievement of unity in the Northern Expedition in 1927, Zhou was elected to both the CCP Central Committee and the Politburo in 1927; he was to remain a member of both bodies until his death in 1976, completing an amazingly uninterrupted leadership tenure of nearly half a century. He was concurrently also premier of the Central People's Government from 1949 to 1976 and China's first foreign minister from 1949 to 1958, as well as vice chair and later chair of the Chinese People's Political Consultative Conference (CPPCC) from 1949 to 1976.

Born a member of China's traditional elite, scion of a déclassé scholar-gentry family, Zhou bore with him the gracious manners and quiet self-assurance of his class. As a student activist in Japan and later in China he learned how to use his considerable interpersonal charm and rhetorical skills to persuade and mobilize his peers. He married Deng Yingchao (1904–1992), his revolutionary collaborator at Nankai, in 1925 and remained faithful to her until his death in 1976; though the couple remained childless, they adopted many orphaned children of "revolutionary martyrs," including the future premier Li Peng. During his bachelor days in Germany, Zhou reportedly also sired a child who was killed in the Wehrmacht during the Nazi offensive against the Soviet Union at the time of the second United Front.

Zhou returned to China in 1924, a seasoned Party organizer. He showed a prescient early interest in military affairs becoming director of the CCP Guangdong Military Affairs Department, director of training at the National Revolutionary Army Political Training Department, and acting director of the Whampoa Military Academy's Political Department in 1924. Chiang Kai-shek (Jiang Jieshi) then named Zhou political commissar of the First Division, First Corps during the successful Eastern campaign of 1925. Though the United Front was dissolved and Zhou was relieved of those positions on the eve of the Northern Expedition (1926–1927), he pioneered thereafter in building the Red Army during the 1927–1931 urban uprisings, demonstrating considerable organizational skill but little strategic sense.

During the ensuing Jiangxi period, as GMD armies launched five "encirclement and annihilation campaigns" against the Jiangxi Soviet, Zhou found himself contending with Mao Zedong for military leadership. In December 1931, he replaced Mao as secretary of the First Front Army with Xiang Ying (c. 1898–1941), and as political commissar of the Red Army. Although Zhou managed in this capacity to fend off the first four GMD attacks, the Red Army's defeat and subsequent Long March (1934–1935) resolved the strategic issue in Mao's favor. Yet by gracefully yielding control of the CCP Military Affairs Commission to Mao Zedong at the watershed Zunyi Conference (1935), Zhou retained his place within the elite and became Mao's always useful collaborator and facilitator—though Mao sometimes pointedly reminded him of his previous opposition.

Zhou Enlai was ever the consummate representative of the CCP in negotiations with outside forces. Thus he was the CCP's chief contact with the dissident GMD commander Zhang Xueliang (c. 1901–2001) when the latter placed Chiang Kai-shek (Zhou's former commander at Whampoa) under house arrest in Xi'an in 1936. Coining the slogan, "Chinese should not fight Chinese but a common enemy: the invader," Zhou managed (with Soviet support) to avert Chiang's execution (which Mao had favored) and broker a deal that would eventuate in formation of the second United Front in 1937.

During much of the ensuing War of Resistance against Japan, Zhou remained in the wartime capital of Chongqing (Chungking) as the highest CCP official in the National United Front government, not only negotiating CCP-GMD relations but also establishing broad contacts among leaders of the small bourgeois democratic parties. He also retained close contact with Wang Ming and the Returned Student grouping, much to Mao's ire, but he used self-criticism to survive attack in the 1942–1944 Yanan Rectification Movement [Zhengfeng]. Zhou also set up a major Communist news and propaganda center, later to be institutionalized as the New China News Agency (Xinhua She). After the Japanese defeat, the CCP and GMD alliance disintegrated despite Zhou's efforts to hold it together, giving rise to renewed civil war. Yet for myriad economic and political reasons, the Communist victory over corrupt and overextended GMD forces proved unexpectedly swift.

When the CCP formed its "new democratic" government in 1949, Zhou played a leading role in assembling representatives of the minority parties into a showpiece parliamentary body, the CPPCC, the main instrument of governance in what was called "New Democracy." As first chair of that body, he took charge of planning the economy and implementing the new regime's domestic-policy program. Though the CPPCC was superseded by the National People's Congress in 1954 (on which Zhou also took the leading executive position), Zhou ensured its survival as a symbol of the United Front and an advisory body to the new parliament.

Chinese politician Zhou Enlai, September 1, 1973. Born to a privileged family, Zhou Enlai joined other young students studying in Europe during the 1920s, eventually returning to China with a greater understanding of communism and political activism. After fighting alongside Mao Zedong during China's civil war, Zhou became premier and the first foreign minister of the People's Republic of China. **KEYSTONE/GETTY IMAGES**

Although he was a highly articulate communicator who wrote a series of documents posthumously compiled into two volumes of collected works, Zhou made no distinctive theoretical contribution to Marxism-Leninism, due either to innate modesty or to prudential considerations (i.e., to avoid challenging Mao). Yet his philosophy has emerged operationally in the form of an ever-nimble balancing act, making core strategic choices based on realistic balance-of-power considerations but then moderating or extenuating those positions tactically to the degree he deemed expedient and feasible.

CHINESE FOREIGN POLICY

As the PRC's first foreign minister, Zhou Enlai continued to exercise dominant influence over the foreign policy process, even after selecting Marshal Chen Yi (1901–1972) to succeed him in this post in 1958. Zhou's cosmopolitan background, ingratiating manners, and negotiating skill enabled him to parlay a large and populous but still

weak and underdeveloped nation into a major role on the world stage. He is credited with intense but futile efforts to avert a direct Sino-American confrontation in Korea, and upon Joseph Stalin's (1879–1953) death was able to negotiate a conclusion to the Korean conflict in July 1953.

Zhou then participated in the Geneva Conference in April 1954, helping to work out a settlement of the Indochinese conflict following the French defeat at Dien Bien Phu. On June 23, 1954, French Premier Pierre Mendès-France (1907–1982) and Zhou Enlai drew up a framework of the basic agreement to be signed by representatives of France and the Viet Minh, establishing communist rule in North Vietnam.

During the temporary adjournment of the Geneva Conference in June and July 1954, Zhou returned to Asia to hold talks with the prime ministers of India and Burma (Myanmar), two countries that had expressed interest in freeing themselves from tight commitments to the emerging bipolar international structure and taking a more neutral position in world affairs. On June 28, Zhou joined with Prime Minister Jawaharlal Nehru (1889–1964) of India in issuing the Panch Sila ("five principles"), setting forth guidelines for relations between the two states, specifically with regard to Tibet. These included mutual respect for each other's territorial integrity and sovereignty, nonaggression, noninterference in each other's internal affairs, equality and mutual benefit, and peaceful coexistence. It was agreed during Zhou's visits to New Delhi and Rangoon (Yangon), and the reciprocal visits of Nehru and the Burmese prime minister U Nu (1907–1995) to Beijing, that India and Burma would maintain neutrality in the Cold War and friendly relations with China, while China, in turn, agreed to refrain from aggression or the export of revolution along the Indian or Burmese borderlands. These principles and policies represented a sharp departure from the confrontational policies of international class struggle and violent revolution typically associated with the Maoist era, yet they have survived bouts of revolutionary rhetoric to remain near the heart of Chinese foreign policy ever since.

Zhou's meetings with Nehru and U Nu paved the way for Chinese participation in an Afro-Asian Conference held in Bandung, Indonesia, in April 1955. During the Bandung meetings, Zhou added further elements to the Panch Sila affirmations: recognition of racial equality and respect for the rights of people of all nations to choose their own way of life and their own political and economic systems. Zhou made use of his increasing contacts to conduct several extended goodwill tours in the third world in the 1950s and 1960s, as the informal standard-bearer of the moderate face of a sometimes more militant Chinese foreign policy. An unexpected result of the Afro-Asian Conference was the initiation of an extended diplomatic engagement between China and the United States. Zhou made a public offer at Bandung to enter into negotiations with the United States, which was accepted, initiating ambassadorial-level talks at Geneva in 1955. It was through this channel that Sino-American rapprochement was to begin in earnest in the 1970s, after a decade in which China had, on ideological grounds, taken issue not only with the United States but also with the Soviet Union and most other socialist countries. Though he generously credited Mao with the pathbreaking visit of Richard Nixon (1913–1994) to China in February 1972, Zhou negotiated an enduring compromise over the Taiwan issue that was to facilitate the February 27 Shanghai Communiqué and the eventual normalization of Sino-American diplomatic relations in 1979.

THE ART OF COMPROMISE

But undoubtedly Zhou played his most indispensable mediatory role during the Cultural Revolution (1966–1969), which he almost alone among the party's pragmatic faction was able to survive, thanks to his unconditional alliance with Mao Zedong. Though that alliance entailed his endorsement of a movement that had devastating political-economic consequences, earning him an enduring reputation for unprincipled opportunism among many of those he sacrificed to the Red Guards (e.g., harsh inner-Party criticism in a 1977 expanded Politburo meeting), Zhou apparently decided he could do more to contain the chaos as an unprincipled survivor than as a principled victim. In tireless negotiations with feuding radical and moderate factions during the 1966–1976 decade, he was able to assuage internecine violence somewhat, often later rehabilitating many of the bureaucratic victims of radical "mass criticism." He shifted coalition partners shrewdly, sometimes seeming to encourage the radicals, more frequently defending establishment forces, but always maintaining a loyal demeanor toward Mao.

Toward the end of his life, Zhou seemed finally to depart from his characteristic prudence to leave his own imprint on succession arrangements in two acts: by selecting Deng Xiaoping to succeed him as premier, and by supporting the program of "Four Modernizations" he introduced at the Fourth National People's Congress in 1975, around which he and Deng Xiaoping proceeded to build a strong bureaucratic coalition for the next year. Deng Xiaoping's succession was derailed by the Gang of Four acting with Mao's implicit support shortly after Zhou Enlai died of bladder cancer on January 8, 1976, but the Four Modernizations (agriculture, industry, science and technology, and national defense) were to survive him, first under Mao's designated successor, Hua

Guofeng, and then as transmuted into the "reform and opening" policy inaugurated at the Third Plenum of the Eleventh Party Congress in December 1978. The Four Modernizations represented the first official consensus, albeit implicit, that the Cultural Revolution was theoretically and politically bankrupt, and that China had to depart from revolutionary redistribution and refocus on rapid economic and cultural modernization, all of which became far more explicit during Deng's reform policy. Although Deng Xiaoping was never to succeed Zhou as premier, he succeeded in redefining the course of Chinese politics from the more modest nominal position of (first) vice premier.

Zhou Enlai was so deeply mourned upon his death that it seemed to excite Mao's jealousy, with short-run adverse political consequences. Because Zhou's body was cremated, mourners chose on Qing Ming (April 5, Chinese Memorial Day) to express their grief at the Monument to the People's Heroes at Tiananmen Square, and they did so in such profusion and righteous indignation that the Maoist leadership arranged to have the many wreaths that had been displayed in Zhou's honor surreptitiously removed, resulting in a spontaneous protest movement, which was then brutally (though not lethally) suppressed by the People's Militia. Deng Xiaoping, who had been under house arrest since delivering the eulogy at Zhou's funeral, was accused of having inspired this demonstration and purged once again of all leadership positions (though not evicted from the party). After Mao died, however, the Gang of Four were deposed and arrested for having allegedly conspired to launch a coup d'état, and Deng Xiaoping was soon rehabilitated, after making further self-criticism. A Tianjin Zhou Enlai–Deng Yingchao Memorial Hall was dedicated to the couple after their deaths, and a statue was also erected in Nanjing, where he had worked with the GMD in the mid-1940s.

BIBLIOGRAPHY

Barnouin, Barbara, and Yu Changgen. *Zhou Enlai: A Political Life.* Hong Kong: Chinese University Press, 2006.

Gao Wenqian. *Wan nian Zhou Enlai.* Hong Kong: Ming Jing Chubanshe, 2003.

Lee Chae-Jin. *Zhou Enlai: The Early Years.* Stanford, CA: Stanford University Press, 1994.

Zhonggong zhongyang wenxian yanjiushi, ed. *Zhou Enlai nianpu (1898–1949)* [Chronicle of Zhou Enlai (1898–1949)]. Beijing: Renmin Chubanshe, 1990.

Zhonggong zhongyang wenxian yanjiushi, ed. *Zhou Enlai nianpu (1949–1976)* [Chronicle of Zhou Enlai, 1949–1976]. Beijing: Zhongyang Wenxian Chubanshe, 1997.

Zhonggong zhongyang wenxian yanjiushi, ed. *Zhou Enlai zhuan* [Biography of Zhou Enlai]. Beijing: Zhongyang Wenxian Chubanshe, 1998.

Zhou Enlai. *Selected Works of Zhou Enlai*. Beijing: Foreign Language Press, 1981 (Vol. 1), 1989 (Vol. 2).

Lowell Dittmer

ZHOU XUAN
1918–1957

Nicknamed "Golden Throat" (*jin sangzi*), Zhou Xuan had an illustrious career as a singer-actress from the 1930s to the 1940s, yet her tumultuous personal life and schizophrenia led to an untimely death.

Brought up by foster parents, Zhou entered show business in Shanghai at a tender age when she joined Li Jinhui's (1891–1967) Bright Moon Song and Dance Troupe, and emerged as first runner-up in the 1934 Top Three Broadcasting Stars contest. In 1935 she was recruited by Yihua Film Studio and launched a film acting career.

Riding on the crest of talkies, Zhou benefited from her musical talent and took full advantage of new technologies in the film and recording industries. Her breakthrough came in 1937, when she was loaned to Star Film Studio for *Malu tianshi* (Street angel, 1937), which later was canonized as a leftist masterpiece that skillfully interweaves comedy, romance, melodrama, and social critique. Its instant popularity made Zhou Xuan a household name. Her "Song of Four Seasons" (Siji ge), based on southeast Chinese folk ditties, was featured in the film and became ingrained in collective memory. Zhou's *shidai qu* (contemporary pop songs) and film song numbers were popularized through radio play and the wide dissemination of gramophone records, and the interactions between the Shanghai film industry and the Southeast Asian market made song-and-dance films the most sought-after film genre.

Shortly after the outbreak of the Second Sino-Japanese War (1937–1945) Zhou joined Guohua Film Studio and starred in a series of period and contemporary films embellished with musical numbers. Between 1939 and 1942 Zhou acted in seventeen films and performed thirty-six songs by famous musicians including Chen Gexin (1914–1961) and Chen Dieyi (1907–2007). Her drawing power in Southeast Asia far surpassed that of Hollywood stars.

By 1943 Zhou had become a major star at Zhonghua diaying lianhe gufen youxian gongsi (United China Film), a conglomerate formed by Wang Jingwei's government with the explicit agenda of supporting Japan's cultural battle in East Asia. Zhou's acting in this period continued to emphasize singing; representative films include *Yujia nu* (The fisher girl, 1943), *Honglou meng* (Dream of the red chamber, 1944), and *Fenghuang yu fei* (Away flies the phoenix, 1945), in which she performed all eleven of the featured songs.

After the war, Zhou joined many other film workers in shuttling between Shanghai and Hong Kong. Her Hong Kong debut was *Chang xiangsi* (Everlasting longing, 1947), which included the song "Huayang nianhua" (The blooming time) that later was immortalized in Wong Kar-wai's film *Fa yeung nin wa* (*In the Mood for Love*, 2000). Another important film that Zhou made in Hong Kong was *Qinggong mishi* (Sorrows of the forbidden city, 1948).

Zhou acted in more than forty films during her short life. Many of her songs, including "He'ri jun zai lai" (When will you return), "Ye Lai Xiang" (Night fragrance), and "Ye Shanghai" (Night Shanghai), were revived by later actresses (such as Li Xianglan, b. 1920) and singers (such as Teresa Teng, 1953–1995). In 1995 the Chinese Film Century award was posthumously conferred on Zhou Xuan. In 2007, half a century after her death, a Beijing film retrospective commemorated her contribution to early Chinese cinema.

SEE ALSO *Film Industry: Overview.*

BIBLIOGRAPHY
Wei Qiren. *Zhou Xuan, Li Xianglan, Bai Guang: Shiji ying ge xing sanjiao ding* [The tripod of the twentieth century's singer-actress-stars: Zhou Xuan, Li Xianglan, Bai Guang]. Taibei: Nantian Shuju Youxian Gongsi, 2002.
Zhou Min, ed. *Zhou Xuan riji* [Zhou Xuan diary]. Wuhan, China: Changjiang Wenyi Chubanshe, 2003.

Yiman Wang

ZHOU YANG
1908–1989

Zhou Yang was one of the most important Marxist theorists and literary critics of twentieth-century China, as well as the chief guardian of Mao Zedong's literary policy until the Cultural Revolution (1966–1969). Originally named Zhou Yunyi and self-styled Zhou Qiying, he was born in Yiyang, Hunan Province. He went to Shanghai for college after attending high school in Changsha, and graduated from Daxia University in Shanghai in 1928. He joined the Chinese Communist Party (CCP) in 1927 shortly after the start of the "white terror" and went to Japan in 1928.

THE SHANGHAI AND YAN'AN YEARS
Upon his return to Shanghai in 1930 Zhou Yang began his career as a Marxist theorist by participating in the League of Left-Wing Writers. Between 1931 and 1932 he joined Lu Xun, Qu Qiubai (1899–1935), and Feng Xuefeng (1906–1976) in writing a series of articles defending the

movement for creating proletariat art and literature, and in 1932 he became editor in chief of the league's magazine, *Wenxue yuebao* (Literary monthly). When Ding Ling was arrested by the Nationalist (GMD) government in 1933, Zhou Yang assumed a major leadership position in the league until it was dissolved in 1936. During these years Zhou Yang debated with other left-wing writers and critics about what constituted revolutionary or proletarian literature and why. He was particularly interested in realism. In identifying the "positive" and "negative" aspects of nineteenth-century European "critical realism," Zhou Yang argued for the need to develop a different kind of realism that was combined with romanticism. With his article "Guanyu shehui zhuyi xianshi zhuyi he geming langman zhuyi" (On socialist realism and revolutionary romanticism, 1933), Zhou Yang was among the earliest left-wing writers to introduce this Soviet literary theory into China.

During the same period, Zhou Yang promoted what he termed the "literature of national defense" (*guofang wenxue*). He put forward the concept in an article in 1934, but the concept did not become part of the "two slogan debate" until 1936, when Lu Xun and his supporters raised the competing slogan "national revolutionary literature for the masses" (*minzu geming yundong zhong de dazhong wenxue*). The bitter debate concerned two not particularly dissimilar left-wing views on literature, but its impact was palpable.

Zhou Yang further honed his theory of socialist realism and socialist romanticism after he arrived in 1937 in Yan'an, where he continued to argue for the need to create literature of "positive" (*leguan de*) realism that reflected the lives of ordinary people. Between 1940 and 1945 he headed the Lu Xun College of Arts (Lu Xun yishu xueyuan). Zhou Yang was particularly interested in developing the "proletarian revolutionary art and literature," and was critical of Ding Ling and others for leaning toward "negative" realism (*xiaoji de xianshi zhuyi*), which tended to expose the dark side of the society. He wrote many articles on the May Fourth literary movement, on Lu Xun and other May Fourth writers, and on aesthetics. After the Yan'an Forum in 1942, Zhou presided over the movement to create new art forms that represented the masses. One of the art forms was the reformed *yangge*, a type of musical drama that combined local music and dance.

AFTER 1949

After 1949 Zhou Yang assumed a number of high-ranking positions in charge of propaganda and cultural matters in the first seventeen years of the People's Republic of China. In that period he was involved in political campaigns against his former colleagues Ding Ling, Hu Feng, and Feng Xuefeng, among others. During the Cultural Revolution Zhou himself was persecuted and imprisoned for nine years, and

that experience seems to have changed his views on a range of issues, especially with regard to how to rethink Marxism. Shortly after the Cultural Revolution, when he was "rehabilitated," Zhou Yang was joined by Wang Ruoshui (1926–2002) and others in voicing the need for a "third thought liberation" (*di sanci sixiang jiefang*) and in initiating debates on "alienation" and "humanism." Zhou Yang's health deteriorated in the mid-1980s and he died on July 31, 1989, leaving behind a range of unanswered questions with regard to his thinking on his own Marxist theory of art and literature.

Zhou Yang remains a controversial figure, particularly because of his role in the persecution and mistreatment of well-known revolutionary figures. As a historical figure, however, he is remembered as a Chinese Marxist who contributed significantly to the development of a Marxist theory on art and literature. His contribution was marked by a mixture of dogmatic views and partisan positions demonstrated in various debates in the 1930s in Shanghai and in the 1940s in Yan'an, by his genuine attempts at theorizing the basis for "revolutionary literature" and "proletariat literature," by a strong conviction derived from his acceptance of Mao Zedong's understanding and analysis of China's social and political conditions, and by his willingness to rethink all of this after the Cultural Revolution and to call for another "thought liberation" initiating debates on "alienation" and "humanism." His writings, collected in the five-volume *Zhou Yang Wenji* (Collection of Zhou Yang's writings) the two-volume *Zhou Yang Jiwaiji* (Zhou Yang's uncollected writings), represent the long history of his life's work.

SEE ALSO *Ding Ling; Hu Feng; League of Left-Wing Writers; Literature of National Defense; Lu Xun.*

BIBLIOGRAPHY

Goldman, Merle. *Literary Dissent in Communist China.* Cambridge, MA: Harvard University Press, 1967.

MacFarquhar, Roderick. *The Origins of the Cultural Revolution: Contradictions among the People, 1956–1957.* New York: Columbia University Press, 1974.

Xueping Zhong

ZHU DE
1886–1976

Zhu De was a founder of the Chinese Red Army and a leader of the Chinese Communist Party (CCP) and the People's Republic of China (PRC). Hailing from a farming family in Sichuan Province, Zhu De studied at the Yunnan Military Academy in 1909. The patriotic education that

Zhu acquired there influenced his future emphasis on the political indoctrination of the "people's army." In 1911 Zhu was involved in the Yunnan Uprising against the Manchu. From 1913 to 1915, his military operations against bandits at the Yunnan-Vietnam-Laos border helped him develop mobile guerrilla tactics. From 1915 to 1921, Zhu participated in the anti-Yuan Shikai National Protection movement and fought enemy warlord troops in Sichuan and Yunnan.

Having lost power, Zhu left for Shanghai in June 1922. There he applied for CCP membership, but was rejected due to his former warlord status. In September 1922, he went to Germany to study military science. In Berlin, he met Zhou Enlai, who sponsored his membership in the CCP. After Zhu's expulsion from Germany for left-wing political activities in 1925, he traveled to Russia to study military affairs. He returned to China in 1926. In January 1927, Zhu began serving as director of the Public Security Bureau and head of an officer-training regiment in Nanchang, Jiangxi.

NANCHANG UPRISING, AUGUST 1, 1927

According to CCP historiography, Zhu was the second-ranking leader (after Zhou Enlai) in the Nanchang Uprising, which commenced the CCP's strategy of armed struggle, and resulted in the creation of the Chinese Red Army. Zhu's main contributions were his development of military-political cadres for the CCP and his deployment of loyal troops to fight the enemy.

After the uprising failed, Zhu convinced his comrades to continue the struggle by "fighting a guerrilla war in the mountains, preserving power, and launching uprisings again" (Zhu Minyan 1993, p. 54). Like Mao Zedong, Zhu stressed a rural strategy and an "up to the mountains" approach. From August to November 1927, Zhu reorganized his regiment three times. His efforts in establishing party influence within the army were as important as Mao's reorganization among his Autumn Harvest Uprising veterans in Sanwan, Jiangxi, in September 1927. Zhu pioneered the methodology of combining ideological education, army reorganization, and military training. This approach contributed to the strengthening of the nascent "people's army," and Zhu's reorganizations provided the first Communist experience in army and party building.

In January 1928, Zhu directed the Southern Hunan Uprising, which focused on the union of armed struggle and village mobilization, and the establishment of a revolutionary base. Like Mao, Zhu contributed to the theory of "an armed independent regime of workers and peasants."

THE ZHU–MAO RELATIONSHIP, 1928–1976

Zhu's lifelong association with Mao began in April 1928, when Mao's 1,600-man regiment joined Zhu's better-equipped 10,000 troops (including 9,000 peasant volunteers) in Jinggangshan, where they established the Fourth Red Army. On May 25, 1928, the CCP Center issued a "Military Work Outline" that praised Zhu's and Mao's guerrilla tactics and their experience in using land reform to win over farmers and other villagers. The CCP Center ordered other armies to follow their model of organization and operation. Zhu and Mao made Jinggangshan the cradle of the Communist military and rural revolution.

Because of their close working relationship, local people called them "Zhu Mao," which came to symbolize the Red Army. Zhu served as military commander and Mao as the supreme political commissar. Zhu engaged in fighting, but Mao rarely did, although he loved to critique military strategy. In 1929 Mao published the operational principles of guerrilla warfare, summarized in the quatrain: "When the enemy advances, we retreat. When the enemy encamps, we harass them. When the enemy is tired, we attack. When the enemy retreats, we pursue." Today, historians argue over whether this quatrain was, in fact, Zhu's unique contribution to military science or a Zhu–Mao composition.

In 1929 the Zhu–Mao army moved to the borderland straddling southern Jiangxi and western Fujian, which later became the site of the Chinese Soviet Republic (1931–1934). In 1930 Zhu and Mao opposed Li Lisan's (1899–1967) attempt to seize large cities. During the Jiangxi Soviet period, Zhu and Mao, as heads of the Red Army, further developed guerrilla warfare, but were opposed by the "Internationalists" who descended upon them in 1932, forcing a shift in military tactics that cost them their base.

In October 1932, Mao was replaced by Zhou Enlai as general political commissar, and for a time he lost influence in the Red Army. Dominated by the Internationalists and their Comintern adviser (Otto Braun [1900–1974]), the Red Army was transformed into a conventional fighting force that became engaged in positional warfare during Chiang Kai-shek's (Jiang Jieshi's) Fourth Encirclement and Extermination campaign (1932–1933). The CCP Center abandoned the previously successful Zhu–Mao military strategy of "luring the enemy deep" into the base area in favor of an offensive strategy of attacking the enemy outside the area. However, Zhu's Red Army was able to fend off the Guomindang (GMD) forces in the Fourth campaign.

In January 1934, Zhu was elected to the CCP Politburo, and the following month he was reelected chairman of the Military Commission. By then, his party status equaled Mao's, while the latter had been eclipsed in military power. However, the Red Army was so severely beaten in Chiang's Fifth campaign (1933–1934) that the

Zhu De, right, with Mao Zedong, 1938. *In his fight against the right-wing faction of the Guomindang during the Nanchang Uprising, Zhu De organized what would become the Chinese Red Army. Losing the battle, Zhu retreated to the mountains and retrained his peasant soldiers in guerilla combat, a technique that would prove useful during both the Japanese invasion of 1937 and the Chinese Civil War.* **MICHAEL OCHS ARCHIVE / CORBIS**

Communists decided to abandon the Jiangxi Soviet and launch the Long March (October 1934–October 1935).

During the march, Zhu supported Mao's criticism of the Internationalists at the pivotal Zunyi Conference in January 1935. Afterward, Zhu remained in his posts as chairman of the Military Commission and Red Army commander in chief. But real military power was vested in a new three-person CCP Central Military Leadership Group consisting of Mao, Zhou Enlai, and Wang Jiaxiang (1906–1974), established in March 1935. Taking advantage of Zhou's illness, Wang's assistance, and Zhu's cooperation, Mao, the de facto head of the group, became the military strongman of the CCP.

The reunion of Mao's and Zhang Guotao's (1897–1979) Long Marchers in June 1935 proved to be problematic in policy disputes and power rivalries. Zhang was a CCP Politburo member and leader of the Hebei-Henan-Anhui Soviet. A dispute arose over the future site

of the revolutionary base: Mao favored Shaanxi while Zhang favored the richer Sichuan, one of China's "rice bowls." The two agreed to reorganize their combined forces, then separate: Zhu's Red Army headquarters and a portion of Mao's First Front Army joined Zhang's Fourth Front Army and headed for Sichuan. According to CCP historiography, Zhu's action and his "hostage" status within Zhang's army were the result of Zhu's concern for party unity and his desire to influence Zhang to rectify his erroneous military-political stand. In September 1935, Mao broke with Zhang Guotao and traveled northward on the pretext that the militarily stronger Zhang was plotting against the CCP Center.

In October 1935, Zhang established a new party center in Sichuan. Zhu was named a Politburo member and head of the Central Secretariat. He turned down both appointments and emphasized that the "Zhu Mao" duo was so well-known that "Zhu" would be unable to oppose "Mao."

It remains unclear whether Zhu disagreed with Mao or whether Zhang detained Zhu in 1935. Some scholars surmise that Zhu, a Sichuan native who had served as Red Army commander in chief under Zhang, may have endorsed Zhang's preference of establishing a new base in Sichuan. Badly beaten by GMD troops in 1936, Zhang abolished his own party center. By December 1936, he and Zhu reunited with Mao in Shaanxi; Zhang later escaped to GMD areas in 1938. Mao seemed to ignore Zhu's association with Zhang, however. Zhu continued to serve as Red Army commander in chief under Mao, while Peng Dehuai directed the reconstruction of the Red Army.

In August 1937, the CCP established a Mao-led Central Revolutionary Military Council, with Zhu and Zhou Enlai as deputies. During the Sino-Japanese War (1937–1945), Zhu became commander of the Eighth Route Army, a reorganized Red Army. He led this army into battles throughout northern China and helped create anti-Japanese base areas behind enemy lines. Zhu was largely responsible for the Communist guerrilla campaign against the Japanese. In early 1938, he published portions of a seminal work, *The Anti-Japanese Guerrilla War,* which elaborated Mao's theory of "protracted war."

In 1940, without support from Mao, Zhu and Peng Dehuai launched the Hundred Regiments campaign to show that the CCP was a champion of anti-Japanese national resistance. The Red Army suffered heavy losses and their territories shrank, but the campaign did not seem to damage the Zhu-Mao working relationship. During the Rectification campaign (1942–1944) in Yan'an, Zhu criticized Wang Ming (1904–1974), leader of the Internationalists. The rectification was a political triumph for Mao in defeating the Internationalists and paving the way for his party preeminence in 1945.

In August 1945, the Central Revolutionary Military Council was reorganized as a Mao-led five-person Central Military Council. After the Japanese surrender, Zhu ordered the Communist forces to disarm Japanese troops and consolidate and expand CCP territories. Zhu became commander in chief of the People's Liberation Army (PLA) in March 1947, during the GMD-CCP civil war. Under Zhu's supervision, the Battle of Shijiazhuang of November 1947 became a turning point in the PLA's shift from mobile warfare to positional warfare. In 1948 Zhu announced a strategic offensive and new military strategies and tactics for various PLA armies.

After the establishment of the PRC in October 1949, Zhu's political and military influence began to decline, even though he was revered as the fourth-ranking leader (after Mao, Liu Shaoqi, and Zhou Enlai) until the outbreak of the Cultural Revolution in 1966. Zhu oversaw the Korean War (1950–1953), but it was Peng Dehuai who was in charge of prosecuting the military campaigns. After the armistice brought large-scale warfare to an end, Zhu declared that the PLA would begin to reorganize its overstaffed command system and reduce the number of troops. He also supported the modernization, professionalism, and Soviet-type reform of the PLA under Peng's direction.

In September 1954, Peng became the first minister of defense, while Zhu was elected vice chairman of the PRC. In the same month, the military forces were put under the control of a new Mao-led twelve-person Central Military Council. In 1955 Zhu was the first military commander to be awarded the rank of marshal by Mao. In 1956 Zhu was reelected vice chairman of the CCP, but he enjoyed little authority in policy making. He was later elected chairman of the Standing Committee of the National People's Congress, a ceremonial position he occupied until 1976. During the Cultural Revolution, Zhu was accused by Lin Biao and Jiang Qing's radical groups of being an antiparty warlord general who had infiltrated the CCP. Thanks to Mao's "protection," Zhu was spared persecution. He was allowed to retain his seat on the Politburo until he died.

LEGACY

Zhu's revolutionary career has been identified with the Red Army. His leadership in the Nanchang Uprising entitles him to the sobriquet, "father of the Chinese Red Army," though no such honor has been given in CCP historiography. Zhu was well loved in the PLA, and was affectionately addressed as Zhu Lao Zong (Zhu the Old Commander in Chief). Though he parted ways with Mao on occasion, he was ultimately willing to accept Mao's

political authority, allowing Mao to take practically all of the credit for Communist military victories and to incorporate Zhu's writings into his own.

Still, Mao acknowledged Zhu's indispensability to his success. In 1973 Mao clarified that Zhu was the "red commander," not the "black commander" condemned by Lin Biao and Jiang Qing. Above all, Mao admitted that, "without Zhu, there would be no Mao" (Wu Dianyao 2006, vol. 3, p. 1982). Zhu De was literally Mao Zedong's closest comrade-in-arms. Coincidentally, Zhu died only two months before Mao in 1976.

SEE ALSO *Communist Party; Long March; Mao Zedong; People's Liberation Army.*

BIBLIOGRAPHY

Averill, Stephen C. *Revolution in the Highlands: China's Jinggangshan Base Area.* Lanham, MD: Rowman & Littlefield, 2006.

Graff, David A., and Robin Higham, eds. *A Military History of China.* Boulder, CO: Westview, 2002.

Li Xiaobing. *A History of the Modern Chinese Army.* Lexington: University of Kentucky Press, 2007.

Lu Xinggou, ed. *Zhu De he tade shiye: Yanjiu xuancui* [Zhu De and his career: Research collection]. Beijing: Zhonggong Dangshi Chubanshe, 1993.

Wang Jianying. *Zhongguo hongjun renwu zhi* [A biographical sketch of the Chinese Red Army]. Zhanjiang, Guangdong, PRC: Guangdong Renmin Chubanshe, 2000.

Wu Dianyao, ed. *Zhu De nianpu (1886–1976)* [The chronology of Zhu De (1886–1976)]. 3 vols. Beijing: Zhonggong Zhongyang Wenxie Yanjiushi, 2006.

Zhou Yurui. *Hongchao renwu zhi* [A biographical sketch in the red dynasty]. New York: Shijie Ribao, 1976.

Zhu De. *Zhu De xuanji* [Selected works of Zhu De]. Beijing: Renmin Chubanshe, 1983.

Zhu Minyan, ed. *Zhonggong dangshi renwu yanjiu huicui* [Research on personalities in CCP history]. Shanghai: Fudan Daxue Chubanshe, 1993.

Joseph K. S. Yick

ZHU RONGJI
1928–

Zhu Rongji, born 1928 in Changsha in central Hunan Province, was China's economic czar from 1993 to 2003—the first five years as executive vice premier in charge of the economy and the last five years as premier. An engineering graduate of prestigious Tsinghua (Qinghua) University in the early 1950s, Zhu is recognized as arguably the most brilliant economic policy maker in Communist Chinese history.

MARGINALIZATION AND REHABILITATION

Zhu is also a maverick. After graduation in 1952, he started work in the State Planning Commission (SPC), at the time one of the most powerful units in the Chinese Communist Party (CCP) and government. Yet the well-read cadre was declared a "rightist" at the start of the anti-intellectual anti-rightist movement (1957–1959) largely for singing the praises of the pro-market economic reforms being implemented in Hungary and Yugoslavia in the mid-1950s. This resulted in the rising star being marginalized in the SPC: Zhu was demoted to doing clerical work—and from 1970 to 1975, he was "rusticated," that is, dispatched to the villages to "learn from the peasants." Zhu never retracted his earlier statements about the importance of heeding market forces and curtailing party and state bureaucracy.

It was not until the start of Deng Xiaoping's reform and open-door policy in 1979 that Zhu was fully rehabilitated; he was given a fast-track job in the State Economic Commission (SEC). Zhu's talent, vigor, and zeal were so obvious that he became SEC vice minister in 1983. His big break came in 1987 when the still-energetic fifty-five-year-old was appointed mayor of Shanghai. It was Zhu who paved the way for the leap forward that the east China metropolis took in the mid-1990s. For example, "One Chop Zhu" vastly simplified the daunting bureaucratic red tape that overseas investors had to tackle while setting up shop in Shanghai: The mayor's office made sure that multinationals could launch their operations in the city after going through a minimum of paperwork. Mayor Zhu, who speaks good English, set up the first council of foreign business advisers in a major city. Most significantly, Zhu, together with the much more conservative party secretary of the time, Jiang Zemin, began the arduous task of persuading the Beijing leadership to open up Pudong for capitalist-style development. Much of the modern infrastructure of Shanghai and Pudong—as well as plans for developing high-tech industries and financial markets—was laid down during Zhu's watch.

INTERNATIONALIZING THE ECONOMY

Zhu's ardor caught the eye of Deng, who became his principal patron. At the Fourteenth Party Congress in 1992, Zhu, then nothing more than an alternate member of the CCP Central Committee, got a three-rung promotion when he was made a member of the Politburo Standing Committee (PBSC). He became executive vice premier in charge of the economy, and concurrently governor of the People's Bank of China, in 1993. As both vice premier, and later, premier (1998–2003), Zhu successfully defused huge bubbles in the property sector and other sectors in the mid-1990s, in the process bringing about a soft landing of the economy. "Boss Zhu" also devised a largely successful "dual-tax system" that divided the country's taxes and levies, with some going to central coffers, others to the localities, and the rest shared between the two. This measure reversed the trend of Beijing's diminishing share of national revenue. The technocrat par excellence was so proud of his track record that he told intimates in the late 1990s that he should be awarded the Nobel Prize for Economics.

Zhu, who was almost universally admired in the West, played a key role in China's successful accession to the World Trade Organization (WTO) in 2001. He and President Jiang brushed aside opposition from the ministries, as well as regional administrations, and granted foreign countries access to numerous sectors of the Chinese market. Americans in particular liked his frankness and acerbic wit. During overseas tours, Zhu often gave off-the-cuff public addresses about the realities of China. As befitting such an unconventional politician, Zhu's legacy is clouded by controversy. For example, he was widely accused by "nationalistic" officials and intellectuals for "selling out to the Americans" through making too many trade concessions to Washington in the two years prior to China's WTO accession.

DOMESTIC AFFAIRS

Irrespective of his global fame, Zhu was hardly popular back home. Owing to his penchant for reprimanding underlings who failed to pass muster, Zhu was feared but not loved. While he was never in charge of corruption (which in the Chinese context, is the responsibility of the secretary of the Central Commission on Disciplinary Inspection, usually a PBSC member), Zhu was the mastermind behind campaigns for cracking major graft cases, such as the one involving Lai Changxing (1958–), the ringleader of the smuggling ring centered on the Fujian city of Xiamen. One of Zhu's most memorable sayings was: "Get me one hundred coffins [for corrupt officials]—but be sure to reserve one for myself." The message was that he would not mind risking his life to nab the villains, many of whom were protected by senior officials, including Zhu's Politburo colleagues.

Owing to the imperative of rejuvenation, Zhu had to step down from the premier's job in 2003 at the ripe old age of seventy-five. Apart from achievements in the economic and anticorruption fields, Zhu deserves credit for having trained a large number of technocrats, many of whom have since occupied ministerial-level positions or above. These have included Premier Wen Jiabao, Vice Premier Wang Qishan (1948–), former vice premier Wu Yi (1938–), bankers Zhou Xiaochuan (1948–) and Liu Mingkang (1946–), and chairman of the China Investment Corporation, Lou Jiwei (1950–). And despite his never

Chinese Premier Zhu Rongji (left) seated with German Chancellor Gerhard Schroeder, Shanghai, China, December 31, 2002. *While serving as mayor of Shanghai, Zhu Rongji earned a reputation as a reformer, eliminating bureaucratic obstacles to foreign investment. A committed subscriber to free-market principles, Premier Zhu guided China's expanding economy at the turn of the twenty-first century, winning the nation membership in the World Trade Organization in 2001.* © MARTIN ATHENSTAEDT/POOL/REUTERS/CORBIS

having handled portfolios including ideology and propaganda, Zhu is known as a liberal. He never once criticized the student demonstrators of 1989, saying merely at the time that "history would deliver a correct verdict" on the Tiananmen Square incident. And while visiting media units, he always encouraged editors and reporters to be true to their professions and to expose "the dark side of society."

After retirement in 2003, Zhu set an example for other senior statesmen by totally disappearing from the limelight. Some of Zhu's friends said he was unhappy about how Premier Wen had indirectly criticized his predecessor for neglecting the development—and welfare—of central and western China. Yet the usually outspoken Zhu never once tried to defend himself, believing, perhaps, that his achievements would stand the test of time.

SEE ALSO *Corruption; Jiang Zemin; Wen Jiabao.*

BIBLIOGRAPHY

Brahm, Laurence J. *Zhu Rongji and the Transformation of Modern China.* Singapore: Wiley, 2003.

Eckholm, Erik, with Seth Faison. China's New Premier: Fast Riser Who Tamed Economy in Chaos. *New York Times,* March 16, 1998.

Hanes, Kathryn, and Dave Lindorff. Can Zhu Rongji Save China's Banks? BNET: Global Finance, May 1998. http://findarticles.com/p/articles/mi_qa3715/is_199805/ai_n8797998.

Zhu Rongji. Premier Zhu Rongji Takes Questions about China's Focal Issues. March 15, 2000. http://www.gov.cn/english/official/2005-07/25/content_17144.htm.

Zhu Rongji. Government Work Report. Delivered at the First Session of the Tenth National People's Congress on March 5, 2003. http://english.peopledaily.com.cn/200303/19/eng20030319_113573.shtml.

Zweig, David. China's Stalled "Fifth Wave": Zhu Rongji's Reform Package of 1998–2000. *Asian Survey* 41, 2 (2001): 231–247.

Willy Wo-Lap Lam

ZHU ZIQING (ZHU ZIHUA)
1899?–1948

Zhu Ziqing (born Zhu Zihua), essayist, poet, and scholar, created a distinctive persona as a modern Chinese intellectual immersed in the lifestyle and institutions of the twentieth century, yet writing in the new vernacular style in a way that showed concern for features of the cultural heritage. His early poetry, collected under the title *Huimie*

(Destruction, 1924), adapts elements of the ancient elegies of Chu (*Chu ci*) to his philosophical reflections on maturing. Many of the familiar essays, for which he is chiefly known, Zhu anchored in encounters with past culture. Often these essays have a mildly erotic quality. For instance, a landscape may be feminized after the manner of earlier poets; a scroll painting evokes a sense of intimacy and longing; a trip along a river leads to an encounter with prostitutes still maintaining a traditional form of their trade. Even a stroll by a lotus pond in a Beijing courtyard house to calm unsettled nerves inspires recollections of age-old depictions of flirting girls and boys in "He tang yuese" ("The Lotus Pond by Moonlight"). Although read often in reference to political turmoil of 1927, when it was written, the essay offers itself as a quiet demonstration of the capacity of the vernacular language to assimilate classical emblems and motifs and imaginatively pursue them in a psychologically reassuring appreciation of a garden in a modern city. The tensions exist largely between the moon as a traditional emblem of a pure heart set against a corrupt world and the erotic associations of gathering lotuses.

By contrast, romantic or erotic atmosphere disappears in essays such as "Ze ou ji" (Choosing a wife, 1934), which describes the various preoccupations and priorities of matrons in arranging a wife for him when he was a boy at the end of the Qing dynasty. Zhu struck the most sympathetic chord with his readers in the essay "Bei ying" (1927, translated as "The View from the Rear"), which transposes the classic poetic theme of parting from someone close, with his father seeing him off at a railroad station when the author was returning from his home in Jiangsu to university. As the scholar Leo Ou-Fan Lee has noted, here Zhu departed from the typically negative depictions of fathers in the literature of the 1920s to portray a sympathetic father who evokes love from his son. The warmth of this essay made it one of the most anthologized pieces in school texts of the twentieth century.

Yet Zhu's essays also departed from thematic ties to the poetic tradition, as in his reflections on racial tensions in "Baizhongren: Shangdi de jiaozi" (White people: God's favored sons), in which a young white boy on a tram at first evokes the essayist's appreciation of his appearance and placidity, then his resentment at the boy's sudden rude gesture, after which the essayist reflects that the boy, for all his arrogance, still offers a fearless confidence toward the world that commends itself to the writer. Here, as elsewhere in his essays, Zhu resolves his ambivalence in favor of an apparently constructive outlook.

Zhu's style of Mandarin vernacular prose, as well as the presentation of feeling in them, also made his essays a model for schoolchildren. His vocabulary avoids heavy use of foreign loanwords, then flooding the media, and makes only occasional use of Europeanized grammar for local rhetorical

effect. Hence, his essays give the impression of a plain style. This is reinforced by composition that typically begins with visually coherent descriptions of ordinary detail in anecdotal fashion and only gradually introduces stronger emotions to bring description and narration to a climax.

Zhu wrote and collaborated on several books on prose style and textbooks. From the mid-1920s he was a pioneer of modern literary criticism, teaching the first course on modern Chinese literature at Tsinghua (Qinghua) University, publishing reviews, and editing the volume of new poetry for the historical collection *Zhongguo xin wenxue da xi* (Compendium of Chinese new literature, 1917–1927, 1935). His reviews of new literary works, collected in *Ni wo* (You and I, 1936), have had a wide influence on later critics, and his writing on classical literature in *Jingdian changtan* (Lectures on the classics, 1946) is still often cited.

Zhu graduated from Peking University in 1920, studied in England, and chaired the Chinese Department of Tsinghua University from 1932 until 1937. To avoid the Japanese occupation, he moved to Kunming and taught at Southwest United University from 1937 to 1945, when he resumed chairing the Chinese Department at Tsinghua. By 1948 he was seriously ill and unable to support his extended family of twelve. He nevertheless signed a petition against the Nationalist receipt of U.S. aid. Mao Zedong cited this fact in a well-known note: "Although gravely ill, Zhu Ziqing would rather starve than accept American aid rations."

BIBLIOGRAPHY

Haft, Lloyd, ed. *A Selective Guide to Chinese Literature, 1900–1949*. Vol. 3, *The Poem*. Leiden, Netherlands: E. J. Brill, 1989.

Lau, Joseph S. M., and Howard Goldblatt, eds. *The Columbia Anthology of Modern Chinese Literature*. New York: Columbia University Press, 1995.

Mao Zedong. Biele, Situleideng [Farewell, Stuart Leighton (Ambassador John Leighton Stuart)] (1949). In *Mao Zedong xuanji* [Selected works of Mao Zedong], vol. 4. Beijing: Renmin Chubanshe, 1966, 1991.

Pollard, David. *The Chinese Essay*. New York: Columbia University Press, 2003. Contains "The Lotus Pond by Moonlight" and "The View from the Rear."

Edward Mansfield Gunn Jr.

ZUO ZONGTANG
1812–1885

Farmer, scholar, soldier, industrialist, and patriot, Zuo Zongtang decisively strengthened the Qing empire in the late nineteenth century.

EARLY LIFE AND CAREER

Born into a poor scholarly family in Xiangyin, Hunan Province, Zuo learned the classical texts but liked practical information about world geography more than philosophy. His intelligence impressed the Hunanese statecraft scholars, who used classical teachings to address contemporary affairs. He obtained the second-rank *juren* examination degree, but failed three times to get the highest degree of *jinshi*. With no chance for an official post, he supported himself as a scholar-farmer until the age of forty, reading agricultural manuals and experimenting with new techniques of cultivation. He planted mulberry trees and new strains of rice, tea, sweet potato, and bamboo, while poring over geography books and preparing maps. Zuo admired military strategists like Sun Zi and Zhuge Liang (181–234). Zuo's refusal to practice writing eight-legged essays kept him from getting a higher degree, but his brilliant iconoclasm earned him respect from leading officials, connecting him with major Hunanese scholars like Hu Linyi (1812–1861). When Lin Zexu (1785–1850), the imperial commissioner sent to stamp out the opium trade, heard of Zuo's talents, Hu Linyi recommended that Zuo join Lin's personal staff, but Zuo refused. Still, Lin and Zuo shared their interests in practical statecraft, and Lin's actions in exile in Xinjiang aroused Zuo's lifelong dedication to the frontier.

In the 1850s, major mass uprisings challenged Qing authority all over the empire. The Taiping, a Christian-inspired mass movement, the Nian, a dispersed collection of local bands of smugglers and peasant militia, and Muslim Chinese in the southwest and northwest fought Qing troops for two decades. Zuo joined the Hunanese who responded vigorously to this challenge with new military forces, new financing, and new attitudes toward foreign powers.

In 1852 Zuo left his rural retreat when the Taiping mass movement threatened Hunan. He organized the military defense of Changsha and rose to become the head of Hunan's military affairs. He advocated the use of Western weaponry, and built his first factory to produce ships and guns. The provincial leaders Zeng Guofan and Li Hongzhang, realizing that the conventional Chinese and Manchu forces could not suppress the locally based, rapidly moving rebel bands, created regional forces of "braves," conscripts led by local gentry who volunteered to defend their home areas. As Zeng's Hunanese army and Li's Anhui army moved against the Taiping, Zuo imitated Zeng's success by raising and training his own Hunanese army of five thousand braves. After achieving stunning victories in Hunan, Zuo led them farther afield into Anhui, Zhejiang, and Fujian. Zuo, Li, and Zeng realized that local connections and regional defense motivated men more strongly than distant, ineffective orders from Beijing. But they aimed to preserve the Manchu court's authority by mobilizing regional networks. Even though they were Han Chinese, they firmly endorsed Manchu imperial rule.

DEFEAT OF THE MUSLIM REBELLION

Impressed by Zuo's success, in September 1866 the court appointed Zuo governor-general of Shaanxi and Gansu provinces in the northwest, where a Muslim uprising had destroyed Qing authority. But in 1867, fearing that the Nian would threaten the northwest and link up with the Muslims, the court ordered him to suppress the Nian. After doing so, he turned against the Muslims in 1868.

Since 1862, Han and Muslim Chinese in Shaanxi, Gansu, and Ningxia had fought each other with paramilitary forces. Small incidents in villages blew up into major attacks by armed bands on the Shaanxi provincial capital of Xi'an. Qing forces barely held them off, but the Muslims retreated to Gansu, raising mass support by claiming that Qing armies would exterminate all Muslims in the northwest. Qing armies, helpless to confront the rebels, faced starvation, while soldiers deserted the front.

As a military leader, Zuo stood out not by heroic battlefield exploits, but by careful, diligent planning. He had studied the geography of the Northwest since his youth, but he also investigated the region carefully by consulting with local scholars. Wang Boxin, an old friend of Zuo, for example, had kept a detailed diary of his travels in Shaanxi. He advised Zuo to accumulate large food supplies and take three years to plan his campaign. Then he should hit hard at the main Muslim leader, Ma Hualong (d. 1871). Severe punishment of Ma Hualong would frighten his followers into surrender. But he should be lenient with these "coerced followers," by moving them to other regions and providing them with land and seed, separating them strictly from non-Muslim Chinese. He should select capable Muslim leaders and let them rule themselves. Instead of lashing out blindly at all the Muslims, Wang realized that the Qing could use knowledge about local conditions to divide the rebel movement.

Zuo followed his advice carefully. He besieged Ma Hualong for sixteen months in southern Ningxia, forcing him to surrender in March 1871. Zuo executed him with death by slicing, killed eighty of his top officials, and transported thousands of followers far away. Two years later, after assaulting Suzhou in Gansu, he had eliminated nearly all of the rebels. Zuo firmly rejected returning the Muslims to their homelands, but he promoted measures to improve Muslim livelihoods. He pardoned those who surrendered, but he ruthlessly executed anyone suspected of giving support to rebels.

INNOVATIONS IN MILITARY FUNDING AND LOGISTICS

The defeat of the Muslim rebellion from 1868 to 1873 was Zuo's greatest military achievement. His innovations were not in strategy itself, but in personnel, finance, logistics, and the restoration of damaged society. He extended precedents set by the great Qing emperors of the eighteenth century to meet the new demands of the nineteenth century. When he found out how well his own Hunan braves fought, he sent 20,000 of them to fight in the distant northwest. To support his armies, he demanded subventions from the wealthy coastal provinces. The barren lands of the Northwest had never been able to support even their own populations from their tax revenue in normal times, but Zuo greatly expanded the scale of subventions. He also induced the court to direct customs revenue from the rich ports of Shanghai, Fuzhou, Hankou, Guangzhou (Canton), and Zhejiang. By 1869, his military budget had risen to three million *taels* per year. Resistance from provincial officials reduced his funds by half, despite his pleas for support. Zuo believed that smaller, well-supplied military forces fought much better than those supported by the bloated payrolls of the traditional Qing forces. By constantly hectoring the other provincial officials, he obtained a total of thirty-two million *taels* for the years 1866 to 1874.

Since provincial subventions arrived too little and too late, Zuo also relied on loans from domestic and foreign merchants. The prosperous Hangzhou merchant Hu Guangyong (c. 1825–1885) provided critical support for Zuo. Hu arranged a loan of 1.2 million *taels* from foreign merchants in Shanghai, secured on future deliveries of provincial subsidies and endorsed by the foreign commissioner of Maritime Customs. Later, Zuo borrowed several million *taels* more, paying up to 10.5 percent interest per year. Zuo made Hu Guangyong his purchasing agent for all military supplies, and even obtained for him the high honor of the Yellow Riding Jacket, reserved only for those who achieved great military victories. Hu sent most funds in bulk silver from the customs ports on the coast, channeled through Shanghai to the northwest. He also purchased foreign arms and ammunition from British and German dealers. Undoubtedly, Hu personally profited from this military contracting; he had a personal fortune of twenty million *taels* in 1872. Zuo's aggressive fund-raising aroused strong opposition even from the most ardent reformers. Zeng Jize (1839–1890), the son of Zeng Guofan, attacked Zuo for paying too high interest to European lenders, and for delivering high profits to Hu Guangyong. He privately thought that Hu's property should be confiscated and that he should be indicted as a traitor.

RECOVERY OF XINJIANG

After subduing the Muslims in Gansu, Zuo actively promoted the recovery of Xinjiang. The Muslims of Xinjiang, mainly a Turkic people now known as Uygurs, had rebelled in 1864, taking the capital of Ürümqi (Urumchi) and Yili (Ili) and putting the Manchu army to flight. In 1870 a military adventurer from Khokand named Yakub Beg (1820–1877) declared an independent kingdom, while Russian troops moved into the fertile Yili Valley. Since all Qing power had vanished, Li Hongzhang felt that it was useless to struggle for Xinjiang's recovery. Instead, Li and other officials from the coastal provinces wanted more funds for maritime defense.

Zuo, however, strongly argued for the strategic importance of Xinjiang: The European powers on the coast only sought trade relations, while the Russians wanted territory. The loss of Xinjiang to Yakub Beg exposed northwest China, Mongolia, and ultimately the core of the empire to strategic danger. He bluntly rejected Li's claim for the priority of coastal defense, correctly noting that China had always faced greater threats from the northwest than from the coast.

Zuo convinced the court to appoint him imperial commissioner in charge of military affairs in Xinjiang in 1875. Zuo began amassing food supplies for an extended campaign, but Yakub Beg's kingdom collapsed without a fight when he died in 1877. Zuo took the credit anyway, and then promoted his last aggressive campaign: to make Xinjiang a regular province of the empire. He first proposed this idea in 1880, and succeeded in getting it adopted in 1884. The proposal fulfilled the dream of the early nineteenth-century statecraft writers, who saw Xinjiang as the "new frontier" that would relieve population pressure in the poor Northwest and reinvigorate Han Chinese exposed to the bracing environment of deserts and oases in Central Eurasia.

In 1881 Zuo clashed again with his allies when he demanded the removal of Russian troops from Yili. The Russians, who had occupied the valley in 1871, promising to leave when order was restored, dragged their feet after the end of hostilities, demanding heavy indemnities, territorial concessions, and access to trade in Xinjiang. In addition, the Russians demanded consular rights in Xinjiang and Mongolia, and commercial rights in major cities like Tianjin, Xi'an, and Hankou. The first Manchu negotiator gave in to nearly all Russian demands, but on his return he faced angry demands for his execution from court officials. Li Hongzhang once again was ready to give in, but Zuo defiantly proposed to drive the Russians out. Zuo's firm line, combined with British intervention and Russia's domestic difficulties, gained China one of its few diplomatic victories of the nineteenth century: the renegotiation of the treaty in St. Petersburg, leading to the recovery of nearly all of the Yili Valley, a reduction in the indemnity to nine million rubles, and only limited access to China's frontier cities. The truculent Zuo Zongtang had faced down a foreign power and won.

MODERNIZATION EFFORTS
AND LEGACY

Zuo knew that China needed industrial strength as well as military modernization. From the 1850s on, he acquired Western arms and planned to have China produce its own modern weaponry. After using steamships in his Taiping campaigns, he founded a dockyard in Fuzhou, hiring French advisers to build a modern navy and instruct students in military and industrial technology. Chinese steamships would not only support the navy, but compete for trade with foreign merchants. The managers of the dockyard built fifteen major ships from 1869 to 1874. In the northwest, at Lanzhou, Zuo founded a woolen mill using German experts and power-driven machinery. Unlike the other enterprises of officials, of the self-strengthening movement, located near the coast, Zuo focused his efforts on the economic development of poorer regions. Zuo's mill in the remote interior did not last, but it was a pioneering effort to develop China's northwest.

Zuo Zongtang's forceful personality and sharp positions left an ambivalent legacy. Against opposition from top Han officials, he loyally supported the ambitious goals of the Manchu rulers to restore Qing power in Central Eurasia. Later, radical nationalists condemned Zuo's loyalty to the barbarian Manchus, but they admired his commitment to military and territorial expansion and industrial development. Communist historians accused him of "great historical crimes" for suppressing the Taiping revolutionary movement, but they too endorsed his expansionism. Now, most Chinese historians view him as a model patriot, but Muslims despise him for his massacres in the Northwest. Zuo was a controversial figure in his own time, too. He vigorously criticized his friends and enemies alike. His military campaigns succeeded sometimes by careful planning, sometimes by force of personality, and sometimes by luck. His industrial enterprises did not fare well, and he was not popular among the cautious circles at the court. He had no interest in democracy, although he did take a paternalist interest in the welfare of the empire's subjects. Zuo's authoritarian, militarist, expansionist ideology fits with one kind of Chinese nationalism, but it only represents one side of China's modernization.

SEE ALSO *Li Hongzhang; Muslim Uprisings; Qing Restoration.*

BIBLIOGRAPHY

Bales, William Leslie. *Tso Tsungt'ang: Soldier and Statesman of Old China.* Shanghai: Kelly and Walsh, 1937.

Chen Qitian (Gideon Chen). *Tso Tsung Táng: Pioneer Promoter of the Modern Dockyard and the Woolen Mill in China.* New York: Paragon, 1961.

Xu Zhongyue (Immanuel Chung-yueh Hsü). *The Ili Crisis: A Study of Sino-Russian Diplomacy, 1871–1881.* Oxford, U.K.: Clarendon Press, 1965.

Zhu Wenzhang (Chu Wen-djang). *The Moslem Rebellion in Northwest China, 1862–1878: A Study of Government Minority Policy.* The Hague, Netherlands: Mouton, 1966.

Zuo Zongtang. *Zuo Zongtang quanji* [Complete works of of Zuo Zongtang]. 20 vols. Shanghai: Shanghai Shu Dian, 1986.

Peter C. Perdue

Appendixes

Table 1: Major international treaties of the People's Republic of China, 1949–2007

Treaty	Signing date	Remarks
Treaty of Friendship, Alliance, and Mutual Assistance between the USSR and the People's Republic of China	02/14/1950	Set out the foundations for Sino-Soviet alliance against external aggression and common threats, on the principles of equality, mutual interests, state sovereignty, territorial integrity, and noninterference. The contracting parties were to consult each other on important issues. Expired in 1980.
Sino-(East) German Treaty of Friendship and Cooperation	12/25/1955	Stipulated that the contracting parties develop friendship and cooperation, in accordance with the principles of sovereignty and equality, noninterference, and territorial integrity. The parties affirmed their respect of each other's culture, and were willing to consult each other on important issues and strengthen mutually beneficial economic and technical cooperation. Expired in 1990 (upon the reunification of Germany).
Sino-Czechoslovak Treaty of Friendship and Cooperation	03/27/1957	Cemented friendship and cooperation between the contracting parties, in accordance with the principles of sovereignty and equality, noninterference, and territorial integrity. The parties were to consult each other on important issues. Expired in 1967.
China-Yemen Friendship Treaty	01/13/1958	Stipulated that the contracting parties develop friendship and cooperation, in accordance with the principles of sovereignty and equality, noninterference, and territorial integrity. The parties were to resolve interstate disputes peacefully. Valid until 1964.
Treaty of Friendship and Co-operation between the People's Republic of China and the People's Republic of Hungary	05/06/1959	Stipulated that the contracting parties develop friendship and cooperation, in accordance with the principles of sovereignty and equality, noninterference, and territorial integrity. The parties were to consult each other on important issues.
Treaty of Friendship and Mutual Non-Aggression between the People's Republic of China and the Union of Burma	01/28/1960	Stipulated nonaggression obligations and peaceful resolution of disputes between the contracting parties.
Sino-Nepalese Treaty of Peace and Friendship	04/28/1960	Stipulated nonaggression obligations and peaceful resolution between the contracting parties.
Sino-Mongolian Treaty of Friendship and Mutual Assistance	05/31/1960	Set out the principles for Sino-Mongolian relations in the spheres of Asian security, mutually beneficial cooperation, economic aid, and peaceful conflict resolution.
Treaty of Friendship and Mutual Non-Aggression between Afghanistan and China	08/26/1960	Set out principles of equality, mutual benefit, nonaggression, and nonalignment with third countries against a contracting party, for developing peaceful and friendly relations.
Treaty of Friendship between the People's Republic of China and the Republic of Guinea	09/13/1960	Set out principles of equality, mutual benefit, and friendship in political, economic, and cultural relations. The parties were to develop mutually beneficial economic and cultural cooperation.
Boundary Treaty between the People's Republic of China and the Union of Burma	10/01/1960	A formal delimitation of the entire Chinese-Burmese boundary, setting out the boundary line and border regulation rules.
Sino-Cambodian Treaty of Friendship and Mutual Non-Aggression	12/19/1960	Stipulated nonaggression obligations and peaceful resolution of disputes between the contracting parties. The parties were to develop mutually beneficial economic and cultural cooperation.
Treaty of Friendship between the People's Republic of China and the Republic of Indonesia	06/14/1961	Stipulated nonaggression obligations and peaceful resolution of disputes between the contracting parties. The parties were to develop mutually beneficial economic and cultural cooperation.
Boundary Treaty between the People's Republic of China and the Kingdom of Nepal	10/05/1961	A formal delimitation of the entire China-Nepalese boundary, setting out the boundary line and border regulation rules.
The Treaty of Friendship, Cooperation, and Mutual Assistance between the People's Republic of China and the Democratic People's Republic of Korea	07/11/1961	Set out the principles of political and military alliance between China and the DPRK. The contracting parties intended to strengthen their cooperative relationship for the purpose of socialist reconstruction.
Treaty of Friendship between the People's Republic of China and the Republic of Ghana	08/18/1961	Stipulated nonaggression obligations and peaceful resolution of disputes between the contracting parties. The parties were to develop mutually beneficial economic and cultural cooperation.
Treaty of Friendship between the People's Republic of China and the Arab Republic of Yemen	06/09/1964	Formulated the principles of amicable relations between China and the Arab Republic of Yemen. The parties were to conform to principles of nonaggression and peaceful resolution of disputes. The parties intended to develop mutually beneficial economic and cultural cooperation.
Treaty of Friendship between the People's Republic of China and the Republic of Congo (Brazzaville)	10/02/1961	Stipulated nonaggression obligations and peaceful resolution of disputes between the contracting parties. The parties were to develop mutually beneficial economic and cultural cooperation.
Boundary Agreement between the People's Republic of China and the Government of Pakistan	03/02/1963	A formal delimitation of the entire Chinese-Pakistani boundary, setting out the boundary line and border regulation rules.

continued

Table 1: Major international treaties of the People's Republic of China, 1949–2007 [CONTINUED]

Treaty	Signing date	Remarks
Boundary Treaty between the People's Republic of China and the People's Republic of Mongolia	03/26/1963	A formal delimitation of the entire Chinese-Mongolian boundary, setting out the boundary line and border regulation rules.
Boundary Treaty between the People's Republic of China and the Kingdom of Afghanistan	11/22/1963	A formal delimitation of the entire Chinese-Afghan boundary, setting out the boundary line and border regulation rules.
Treaty of Friendship between the People's Republic of China and the Republic of Mali	04/20/1965	Stipulated nonaggression obligations and peaceful resolution of disputes between the contracting parties. The parties were to develop mutually beneficial economic and cultural cooperation.
Treaty of Friendship between the People's Republic of China and the United Republic of Tanzania	02/20/1965	Stipulated nonaggression obligations and peaceful resolution of disputes between the contracting parties. The parties were to develop mutually beneficial economic and cultural cooperation.
Shanghai Communiqué between the People's Republic of China and the United States	02/27/1972	Began the process of normalization of China-U.S. relations. It called for Sino-American joint effort to maintain peace in Asia, and formulated the rationale for this. The parties refused from seeking hegemony in Asia and clarified their position on reducing tensions in Indochina, the Korean Peninsula, and South Asia. The parties agreed over the gradual withdrawal of US military from Taiwan, on the basis of the "One China" formula.
Treaty of Peace and Friendship between the People's Republic of China and Japan	08/12/1978	The Treaty confirmed the five principles of peaceful coexistence as the foundation for Sino-Japanese relations. Though the Treaty is not directed against third countries, the parties oppose any country's hegemony in Asia-Pacific. The Treaty makes provisions for enhanced Sino-Japanese economic ties.
Joint Communiqué on the Establishment of Diplomatic Relations between the People's Republic of China and the United States of America	01/01/1979	The statement of Sino-U.S. mutual recognition and the establishment of diplomatic relations between the parties on January 1, 1979. The parties affirmed their antihegemonic posture and reiterated their adherence to the "One China" principle.
Sino-U.S. Joint Communiqué	08/17/1982	The statement of respect for each other's sovereignty and territorial integrity and noninterference each other's internal affairs. It formulated the two parties' position regarding the Taiwan issue and the U.S. arms sales to Taiwan.
Sino-Soviet Border Agreement on the Eastern Section of the Boundary	05/16/1991	Accomplished the delimitation of the 4,200-km boundary line between China and Russia, except for a few disputed areas. Determined the border as the center of the main river channel. Set out peaceful principles of border dispute resolution.
Boundary Agreement between the People's Republic of China and the People's Democratic Republic of Laos	12/03/1993	Finalized the demarcation of the 700-km boundary line between the two countries.
Sino-Indian Agreement on the Maintenance of Peace and Tranquility Along the Line of Actual Control in the Sino-Indian Border Areas	09/07/1993	Set out principles of peaceful settlement of the boundary questions.
Border Junction Agreement between China, Laos, and Myanmar	04/08/1994	Demarcated the border junction between the three countries located in the middle of the Mekong River.
Sino-Kazakhstan Boundary Agreement	04/26/1994	Identified the Sino-Kazakhstan boundary line except a few disputed border areas.
Treaty on Friendly Relations and Cooperation between the People's Republic of China and Mongolia	04/29/1994	Reaffirmed the principle of sovereignty and noninterference in bilateral relations, and precluded either party's alignment with third countries targeted against the other.
Agreement on the Western Section of the Boundary between China and Russia	09/03/1994	Delimited the 53-km boundary between China and Russia to the west of Mongolia.
Sino-Kyrgyzstan Boundary Agreement	07/04/1996	Accomplished the delimitation process of the 858-km-long Sino-Kyrgyzstan border.
Agreement on Confidence Building Measures in the Military Field along the Line of Actual Control in the China-India Border Areas	11/29/1996	Further developed confidence-building measures at the disputed Sino-Indian border areas.
Complimentary Sino-Kazakhstan Boundary Agreement	07/04/1998	Comprehensive settlement of the 1,700-km Sino-Kazakh border.
Treaty of Land Border between China and Vietnam	12/31/1999	Resolved the outstanding disputed border issues between the two countries.
Treaty of Good Neighborliness, Friendship and Cooperation between the People's Republic of China and the Russian Federation	07/16/2001	Set out the fundamentals of Sino-Russian strategic partnership, based on the principles of the international law, and mutual respect of sovereignty, territorial integrity, and national characteristics. Determined the fields of mutually beneficial cooperation and reaffirmed the absence of territorial claims toward each other.

continued

Tabel 1: Major international treaties of the People's Republic of China, 1949–2007 [CONTINUED]

Treaty	Signing date	Remarks
Treaty of Friendship between the People's Republic of China and the United Republic of Tanzania	04/25/2002	The Treaty stipulated nonaggression obligations and peaceful resolution of disputes between the contracting parties. The parties were to develop mutually beneficial economic and cultural cooperation.
Complementary Agreement on China-Tajikistan Boundary	05/17/2002	The agreement marked the complete solution of the Sino-Tajikistan 430-km boundary issues.
Treaty of Good Neighborliness, Friendship and Cooperation between the People's Republic of China and the Kyrgyz Republic	06/24/2002	Set up a framework for bilateral cooperation between the two countries, including the issues of international and regional security, trade, separatism, and economic cooperation.
Supplementary Agreement on the Eastern Section of the China-Russia Boundary Line	10/14/2004	Finalizes the delimitation of the Chinese-Russian border to the east of Mongolia, resolving the last two disputed parcels of land in the eastern section of Sino-Russian border—Bolshoy Ussuriyski (Heihaizi) Island and Tarabarov (Yinlong) Island at the confluence of the Amur (Heilongjiang) and Ussuri Rivers.
China-Pakistan Treaty of Friendship, Cooperation and Good-Neighborly Relations	04/05/2005	Provides a legal foundation for Sino-Pakistani friendship and strategic cooperation, neutralizing the other great powers' influence in South and Central Asia.
China-Uzbek Treaty of Friendship and Cooperation	05/25/2005	Stipulates that the PRC and Uzbekistan develop friendly cooperation based on equality and mutual trust. The contracting parties refrain from any kind of relationships with third parties or support any activities detrimental to the parties' sovereignty and territorial integrity.
China-Afghanistan Treaty on Friendly Cooperation	06/19/2006	Develops bilateral comprehensive and cooperative partnership, with a special emphasis on nontraditional security threats (terrorism and separatism), trade and economy. Sets up the foundation for coordination of the two countries' policies in multilateral organizations. China pledges to participate in the process of Afghanistan reconstruction.
Agreement on Border Regime between Russia and China	11/09/2006	Cements border delimitation agreements of 1991–2004, setting border inspection, signing, resource division rules, and cross-border regulations.
Agreement on Border Regime between Kazakhstan and China	12/20/2006	Cements border delimitation agreements of 1994, 1997, 1998, 1999, setting border inspection, signing, resource division rules, and cross-border regulations.
Good-Neighborly Treaty of Friendship and Cooperation between China and Tajikistan	01/15/2007	Covers the issues of cooperation, separatism, terrorism, and "One-China" policy, and calls for stability secured bilaterally and within the SCO.

SOURCE: China International Laws and Treaties with Foreign Countries Handbook. Washington, DC: International Business Publications, 2008; Ministry of Foreign Affairs of the People's Republic of China. http://www.fmprc.gov.cn/eng/default.htm; Online Collection of the Treaties of the People's Republic of China. Beijing University. http://www.fsou.com/Html/mulu/eag/2.html; Rhode, Grant F., and Reid E. Whitlock. *Treaties of the People's Republic of China, 1949–1978: An Annotated Compilation*. Boulder, CO: Westview Press, 1980.

Table 2: China's membership in the international arms control and nonproliferation treaties

Treaty	Signing/ accession date
Geneva Protocol (Protocol for the Prohibition of the Use in War of Asphyxiating, Poisonous, or Other Gases, and of Bacteriological Methods of Warfare)	August 1952
Treaty of Tlatelolco (Treaty for the Prohibition of Nuclear Weapons in Latin America and the Caribbean)	August 1973
Convention on the Physical Protection of Nuclear Material	June 1974
Inhuman Weapons Convention (IWC)	September 1981
The Antarctic Treaty	June 1983
Treaty on Principles Concerning the Activities of States in the Exploration and Use of Outer Space Including the Moon and Other Celestial Bodies (Outer Space Treaty)	December 1983
Convention on the Prohibition of the Development, Production, and Stockpiling of Bacteriological (Biological) Weapons and on Their Destruction	November 1984
Treaty of Rarotonga (South Pacific Nuclear-Free-Zone Treaty)	February 1987
Agreement between the People's Republic of China and the International Atomic Agency for the Application of Safeguards in China	September 1988
Convention on Registration of Objects Launched into Outer Space	December 1988
Convention on the Physical Protection of Nuclear Material	February 1989
Treaty on the Prohibition of the Emplacement of Nuclear Weapons and Other Weapons of Mass Destruction on the Sea-Bed and the Ocean Floor and in the Subsoil Thereof (Seabed Arms Control Treaty)	February 1991
Treaty of Non-Proliferation of Nuclear Weapons (Non-Proliferation Treaty, NPT)	March 1992
Convention on the Prohibition of the Development, Production, Stockpiling and Use of Chemical Weapons and on their Destruction	January 1993
Treaty of Pelindaba (African Nuclear-Weapon-Free Zone Treaty)	April 1996
Comprehensive Nuclear Test Ban Treaty	September 1996
Convention on the Prohibition of Military or Any Other Hostile Use of Environmental Modification Techniques	June 2005

SOURCE: Ministry of Foreign Affairs of the People's Republic of China. List of Arms Control, Disarmament and Non-Proliferation Treaties that China has Joined, http://www .fmprc.gov.cn/eng/wjb/zzjg/jks/tyylb/t141338.htm; Nuclear Threat Initiative, www.nti.org; Online Collection of the Treaties of the People's Republic of China. Beijing University, http://www.fsou.com/Html/mulu/eag/2.html.

Table 3: China as a state party to international human rights treaties

Treaty	Signing/ accession date
Geneva Convention Relative to the Protection of Civilian Persons in Times of War	July 1952
Geneva Convention Relative to the Treatment of Prisoners of War	July 1952
Convention on the Elimination of All Forms of Discrimination Against Women (CEDAW)	July 1980
International Convention on the Elimination of All Forms of Racial Discrimination (ICERD)	December 1981
Convention Relating to the Status of Refugees	September 1982
Convention on the Prevention and Punishment of the Crime of Genocide	April 1983
Convention Against Torture and Other Cruel, Inhuman or Degrading Treatment or Punishment (CAT)	December 1986
Convention on the Rights of the Child (CRC)	August 1990
International Covenant on Economic, Social and Cultural Rights (ICESCR)	October 1997
International Covenant on Civil and Political Rights (ICCPR)	October 1998

SOURCE: Ministry of Foreign Affairs of the People's Republic of China, http://www.fmprc.gov.cn/eng/default.htm; United Nations Office of High Commissioner for Human Rights, http://www .ohchr.org; Wan, Ming. Human Rights Lawmaking in China: Domestic Politics, International Law, and International Politics. *Human Rights Quarterly* 29 (2007): 727–753.

Table 4: Countries recognizing the People's Republic of China and dates of establishment of diplomatic ties

Country	Date	Remarks
Soviet Union	10/03/1949	Succeeded by the Russian Federation in 1991
Republic of Bulgaria	10/04/1949	
Romania	10/05/1949	
Republic of Hungary	10/06/1949	
Democratic People's Republic of Korea (DPRK, North Korea)	10/06/1949	
Czechoslovakia (former Czechoslovak Socialist Republic)	10/06/1949	Succeeded by the Czech Republic in 1993
Republic of Poland	10/07/1949	
Republic of Mongolia	10/16/1949	
German Democratic Republic	10/27/1949	Succeeded by Federal Republic of Germany in 1990
Republic of Albania	11/23/1949	
Socialist Republic of Vietnam (formerly Democratic Republic of Vietnam-North Vietnam)	01/18/1950	
Republic of India	04/01/1950	
Republic of Indonesia	04/13/1950	
Kingdom of Sweden	05/09/1950	
Kingdom of Denmark	05/11/1950	
Union of Burma	06/08/1950	Renamed Union of Myanmar 06/18/1989
Switzerland (Swiss Confederation)	09/14/1950	
Principality of Liechtenstein	09/14/1950	
Republic of Finland	10/28/1950	
Islamic Republic of Pakistan	05/21/1951	
Kingdom of Norway	10/05/1954	
Socialist Federal Republic of Yugoslavia	01/02/1955	Succeeded by Serbia in 2003
Islamic Republic of Afghanistan	01/20/1955	
Federal Democratic Republic of Nepal	08/01/1955	
Arab Republic of Egypt	05/30/1956	
Syria (Syrian Arab Republic)	08/01/1956	
Yemen Arab Republic (North Yemen)	09/24/1956	Succeeded by the Republic of Yemen in 1990
Democratic Socialist Republic of Sri Lanka	02/07/1957	
Kingdom of Cambodia	07/19/1958	
Republic of Iraq	08/25/1958	
Kingdom of Morocco	11/01/1958	
People's Democratic Republic of Algeria	12/20/1958	
Republic of the Sudan	02/04/1959	
Republic of Guinea	10/04/1959	
Republic of Ghana	07/05/1960	
Republic of Cuba	09/28/1960	
Republic of Mali	10/25/1960	
Somalia	12/14/1960	
Laos (Lao People's Democratic Republic)	04/25/1961	
Republic of Uganda	10/18/1962	
Republic of Kenya	12/14/1963	
Republic of Burundi	12/21/1963	Relations were disrupted 1965–1971
Tunisia (Tunisian Republic)	01/10/1964	
France (French Republic)	01/27/1964	
Republic of Congo	02/22/1964	
United Republic of Tanzania	04/26/1964	Successor of Tanganyika and Zanzibar (relations established in 1961 and 1963, respectively)
Central African Republic	09/29/1964	From 07/1991 to 01/1998 maintained diplomatic relations with the Republic of China
Republic of Zambia	10/29/1964	
Republic of Benin	11/12/1964	From 04/1966 to 12/1972 maintained diplomatic relations with the Republic of China
Islamic Republic of Mauritania	07/19/1965	
People's Democratic Republic of Yemen (South Yemen)	01/31/1968	Succeeded by the Republic of Yemen in 1990
Canada	10/13/1970	
Republic of Equatorial Guinea	10/15/1970	
Italy (Italian Republic)	11/06/1970	
Federal Democratic Republic of Ethiopia	11/24/1970	
Republic of Chile	12/15/1970	
Federal Republic of Nigeria	02/10/1971	
State of Kuwait	03/22/1971	
Republic of Cameroon	03/26/1971	
Republic of San Marino	05/06/1971	
Republic of Austria	05/28/1971	
Republic of Sierra Leone	07/29/1971	
Republic of Turkey	08/04/1971	

continued

Table 4: Countries recognizing the People's Republic of China and dates of establishment of diplomatic ties [CONTINUED]

Country	Date	Remarks
Islamic Republic of Iran	08/16/1971	
Kingdom of Belgium	10/25/1971	
Republic of Peru	11/02/1971	
Lebanon (Lebanese Republic)	11/09/1971	
Republic of Rwanda	11/12/1971	
Republic of Senegal	12/07/1971	From 01/1996 to 10/2005 maintained diplomatic relations with the Republic of China
Republic of Iceland	12/08/1971	
Republic of Cyprus	12/14/1972	
Republic of Malta	01/31/1972	
Mexico (United Mexican States)	02/14/1972	
Argentina (Argentine Republic)	02/19/1972	
United Kingdom	03/13/1972	Chargé d'affaires level since 06/1954
Republic of Mauritius	04/15/1972	
Kingdom of the Netherlands	05/18/1972	Chargé d'affaires level since 11/1954
Greece (Hellenic Republic)	06/05/1972	
Cooperative Republic of Guyana	06/27/1972	
Togo (Togolese Republic)	09/19/1972	
Japan	09/29/1972	
Federal Republic of Germany	10/11/1972	
Republic of Maldives	10/14/1972	
Zaire	11/19/1972	Currently Democratic Republic of the Congo
Republic of Madagascar	11/06/1972	
Luxembourg (Grand Duchy of Luxembourg)	11/16/1972	
Republic of Jamaica	11/21/1972	
Republic of Chad	11/28/1972	From 08/1997 to 08/2006 maintained diplomatic relations with the Republic of China
Commonwealth of Australia	12/21/1972	
New Zealand	12/22/1972	
Kingdom of Spain	03/09/1973	
Burkina Faso	09/15/1973	In 02/1994 resumed diplomatic relations with the Republic of China
Republic of Guinea Bissau	03/15/1974	From 05/1990 to 04/1998 maintained diplomatic relations with the Republic of China
Gabon (Gabonese Republic)	04/20/1974	
Malaysia	05/31/1974	
Republic of Trinidad and Tobago	06/20/1974	
Bolivarian Republic of Venezuela	06/28/1974	
Republic of Niger	07/20/1974	From 06/1992 to 08/1996 maintained diplomatic relations with the Republic of China
Federative Republic of Brazil	08/15/1974	
Republic of The Gambia	12/14/1974	In 07/1995 resumed diplomatic relations with the Republic of China
Republic of Botswana	01/06/1975	
Republic of the Philippines	06/09/1975	
Republic of Mozambique	06/25/1975	
Kingdom of Thailand	07/01/1975	
Democratic Republic of São Tomé and Príncipe	07/12/1975	In 05/1997 resumed diplomatic relations with the Republic of China
People's Republic of Bangladesh	10/04/1975	
Republic of the Fiji Islands	11/05/1975	
Independent State of Samoa	11/06/1975	
Union of the Comoros	11/13/1975	
Republic of Cape Verde	04/25/1976	
Republic of Suriname	05/28/1976	
Republic of Seychelles	06/30/1976	
Independent State of Papua New Guinea	10/12/1976	
Republic of Liberia	02/17/1977	From 10/1989 to 08/1993 maintained diplomatic relations with the Republic of China. From 09/1997 to 10/2003 diplomatic relations were frozen.
Hashemite Kingdom of Jordan	04/07/1977	
Barbados	05/30/1977	
Sultanate of Oman	05/25/1978	
Libya (Great Socialist People's Libyan Arab Jamahiriya)	08/09/1978	
United States of America	01/01/1979	
Republic of Djibouti	01/08/1979	
Portugal (Portuguese Republic)	02/08/1979	
Ireland	06/22/1979	

continued

Table 4: Countries recognizing the People's Republic of China and dates of establishment of diplomatic ties [CONTINUED]

Country	Date	Remarks
Republic of Ecuador	01/02/1980	
Republic of Colombia	02/07/1980	
Republic of Zimbabwe	04/18/1980	
Republic of Kiribati	06/25/1980	In 11/2003 established diplomatic relations with the Republic of China
Republic of Vanuatu	03/26/1982	
Antigua and Barbuda	01/01/1983	
Republic of Angola	01/12/1983	
Republic of Côte d'Ivoire	03/02/1983	
Kingdom of Lesotho	04/30/1983	From 04/1990 to 01/1994 maintained diplomatic relations with the Republic of China
United Arab Emirates	11/01/1984	
Republic of Bolivia	07/09/1985	
Grenada	10/01/1985	From 07/1989 to 01/2005 maintained diplomatic relations with the Republic of China
Republic of Nicaragua	12/07/1985	In 11/1990 resumed diplomatic relations with the Republic of China
Belize	02/06/1987	In 10/1989 established diplomatic relations with the Republic of China
Oriental Republic of Uruguay	02/03/1988	
State of Qatar	07/09/1988	
Palestine	11/20/1988	
Kingdom of Bahrain	04/18/1989	
Federated States of Micronesia	09/11/1989	
Republic of Namibia	03/22/1990	
Kingdom of Saudi Arabia	07/21/1990	
Republic of Singapore	10/03/1990	
Republic of the Marshall Islands	11/16/1990	In 11/1998 established diplomatic relations with the Republic of China
Republic of Estonia	09/11/1991	
Republic of Latvia	09/12/1991	
Republic of Lithuania	09/14/1991	
Brunei (Brunei Darussalam)	09/30/1991	
Republic of Uzbekistan	01/02/1992	
Republic of Kazakhstan	01/03/1992	
Republic of Tajikistan	01/04/1992	
Ukraine	01/04/1992	
Kyrgyzstan (Kyrgyz Republic)	01/05/1992	
Turkmenistan	01/06/1992	
Republic of Belarus	01/20/1992	
State of Israel	01/24/1992	
Republic of Moldova	01/30/1992	
Republic of Azerbaijan	04/02/1992	
Republic of Armenia	04/06/1992	
Republic of Georgia	06/09/1992	
Republic of Slovenia	05/12/1992	
Republic of Croatia	05/13/1992	
Republic of Korea (South Korea)	08/24/1992	
Slovakia (Slovak Republic)	01/01/1993	Successor state of former Czechoslovakia
State of Eritrea	05/24/1993	
Republic of Macedonia	10/12/1993	
Principality of Andorra	06/29/1994	
Principality of Monaco	01/16/1995	
Bosnia and Herzegovina	04/03/1995	
Commonwealth of The Bahamas	05/23/1997	
Cook Islands	07/25/1997	
Saint Lucia	09/01/1997	In 04/2007 resumed diplomatic relations with the Republic of China
Republic of South Africa	01/01/1998	
Kingdom of Tonga	11/02/1998	
Democratic Republic of Timor-Leste (East Timor)	05/20/2002	
Republic of Nauru	07/21/2002	In 05/2005 resumed diplomatic relations with the Republic of China

continued

Table 4: Countries recognizing the People's Republic of China and dates of establishment of diplomatic ties [CONTINUED]

Country	Date	Remarks
Commonwealth of Dominica	03/31/2004	
Montenegro	07/06/2006	
Republic of Costa Rica	06/01/2007	
Niue	12/12/2007	
Republic of Malawi	12/28/2007	

SOURCE: Ministry of Foreign Affairs of the People's Republic of China, http://www.fmprc.gov.cn/eng/default.htm; Online Collection of the Treaties of the People's Republic of China. Beijing University, http://www.fsou.com/Html/mulu/eag/2.html.

Table 5: Countries maintaining diplomatic relations with the Republic of China (Taiwan)

Country	Year of establishment/ resuming of diplomatic relations
Vatican City (The Holy See)	1942
Republic of Panama	1954
Republic of Haiti	1956
Dominican Republic	1957
Republic of Paraguay	1957
Republic of Guatemala	1960
Republic of El Salvador	1961
Republic of Honduras	1965
Kingdom of Swaziland	1968
Tuvalu	1979
Republic of Nauru	1980–2002; 2005
Saint Vincent and the Grenadines	1981
Solomon Islands	1983
Federation of Saint Kitts and Nevis	1983
Saint Lucia	1984–1997; 2007
Belize	1989
Republic of Nicaragua	1990
Burkina Faso	1994
Republic of The Gambia	1995
Democratic Republic of São Tomé and Príncipe	1997
Republic of the Marshall Islands	1998
Republic of Palau	1999
Republic of Kiribati	2003

SOURCE: Ministry of Foreign Affairs, Republic of China (Taiwan), http://www.mofa.gov.tw.

Table 6: Major unequal treaties

Treaty	Year	Imperialist powers
Treaty of Nanking	1842	United Kingdom
Treaty of the Bogue	1843	United Kingdom
Treaty of Wanghs'ia	1844	United States
Treaty of Whampoa	1844	France
Treaty of Aigun	1858	Russia
Treaty of Tientsin	1858	France, United Kingdom, Russia, United States
Convention of Peking	1860	United Kingdom, France, Russia
Treaty of Tientsin	1861	Prussia, German Customs Union
Chefoo Convention	1876	United Kingdom
Treaty of Tientsin	1885	France
Sino-Portuguese Treaty of Peking	1887	Portugal
Treaty of Shimonoseki	1895	Japan
Li-Lobanov Treaty	1896	Russia
Convention for the Extension of Hong Kong Territory	1898	United Kingdom
Boxer Protocol	1901	United Kingdom, United States, Japan, Russia, France, Germany, Italy, Austria-Hungary, Belgium, Spain, Netherlands

Primary Sources

LETTER OF ADVICE TO QUEEN VICTORIA

SOURCE *Lin Tse-Hsu (Lin Zexu). Letter to the English Ruler. In Sources of Chinese Tradition, Volume II: From 1600 through the Twentieth Century, 2nd edition, ed. William Theodore de Bary and Richard Lufrano, 202–205. New York: Columbia University Press, 2000.*

INTRODUCTION *This famous 1839 letter prepared by Lin Zexu, an imperial commissioner, for the emperor to send to Queen Victoria, vividly reflects the cultural gap between the Confucian order of China and the thrusting mercantilism of Britain. Neither Lin s moral reasoning against the opium trade nor his condescending tone was likely to persuade the British to change course.*

A communication: Magnificently our great emperor soothes and pacifies China and the foreign countries, regarding all with the same kindness. If there is profit then he shares it with the peoples of the world; if there is harm, then he removes it on behalf of the world. This is because he takes the mind of Heaven-and-earth as his mind.

The kings of your honorable country by a tradition handed down from generation to generation have always been noted for their politeness and submissiveness. We have read your successive tributary memorials saying: "In general our countrymen who go to trade in China have always received His Majesty the Emperor's gracious treatment and equal justice," and so on. Privately we are delighted with the way in which the honorable rulers of your country deeply understand the grand principles and are grateful for the Celestial grace. For this reason the Celestial Court in soothing those from afar has redoubled its polite and kind treatment. The profit from trade has been enjoyed by them continuously for two hundred years. This is the source from which your country has become known for its wealth.

But after a long period of commercial intercourse, there appear among the crowd of barbarians both good persons and bad, unevenly. Consequently there are those who smuggle opium to seduce the Chinese people and so cause the spread of the poison to all provinces. Such persons who only care to profit themselves, and disregard their harm to others, are not tolerated by the laws of Heaven and are unanimously hated by human beings. His Majesty the Emperor, upon hearing of this, is in a towering rage. He has specially sent me, his commissioner, to come to Guangdong, and together with the governor-general and governor jointly to investigate and settle this matter. . . .

We find that your country is sixty or seventy thousand *li* [one *li* is roughly a third of a mile] from China. Yet there are barbarian ships that strive to come here for trade for the purpose of making a great profit. The wealth of China is used to profit the barbarians. That is to say, the great profit made by barbarians is all taken from the rightful share of China. By what right do they then in return use the poisonous drug to injure the Chinese people? Even though the barbarians may not necessarily intend to do us harm, yet in coveting profit to an extreme, they have no regard for injuring others. Let us ask, where is your conscience? I have heard that the smoking of opium is very strictly forbidden by your country; that is because the harm caused by opium is clearly understood. Since it is not permitted to do harm to your own country, even less should you let the harm be passed on to other countries—much less to China! Of all that China exports to foreign countries, there is not a single thing that is not beneficial to people; they are of benefit when eaten, or of benefit when used, or of benefit when resold; all are beneficial. Is there a single article from China that has done any harm to foreign countries? Take tea and rhubarb, for example; the foreign countries cannot get along for a single day without them. If China cuts off these benefits with no sympathy for those who are to suffer, then what can the barbarians rely upon to keep themselves alive? Moreover the woolens, camlets, and longells [i.e., textiles] of foreign countries cannot be woven unless they obtain

Chinese silk. If China again cuts off this beneficial export, what profit can the barbarians expect to make? As for other foodstuffs, beginning with candy, ginger, cinnamon, and so forth, and articles for use, beginning with silk, satin, chinaware, and so on, all the things that must be had by foreign countries are innumerable. On the other hand, articles coming from the outside to China can only be used as toys. We can take them or get along without them. Since they are not needed by China, what difficulty would there be if we closed the frontier and stopped the trade? Nevertheless, our Celestial Court lets tea, silk, and other goods be shipped without limit and circulated everywhere without begrudging it in the slightest. This is for no other reason but to share the benefit with the people of the whole world.

The goods from China carried away by your country not only supply your own consumption and use but also can be divided up and sold to other countries, producing a triple profit. Even if you do not sell opium, you still have this threefold profit. How can you bear to go further, selling products injurious to others in order to fulfill your insatiable desire?...

We have further learned that in London, the capital of your honorable rule, and in Scotland, Ireland, and other places originally no opium has been produced. Only in several places of India under your control, such as Bengal, Madras, Bombay, Patna, Benares, and Malwa, has opium been planted from hill to hill and ponds have been opened for its manufacture. For months and years work is continued in order to accumulate the poison. The obnoxious odor ascends, irritating Heaven and frightening the spirits. Indeed you, O King, can eradicate the opium plant in these places, hoe over the fields entirely, and sow in its stead the five grains [i.e., millet, barley, wheat, and so on]. Anyone who dares again attempt to plant and manufacture opium should be severely punished. This would really be a great, benevolent government policy that will increase the commonweal and get rid of evil. For this, Heaven must support you and the spirits must bring you good fortune, prolonging your old age and extending your descendants. All will depend on this act....

Now we have set up regulations governing the Chinese people. He who sells opium shall receive the death penalty and he who smokes it also the death penalty. Now consider this: If the barbarians do not bring opium, then how can the Chinese people resell it, and how can they smoke it? The fact is that the wicked barbarians beguile the Chinese people into a death trap. How then can we grant life only to these barbarians? He who takes the life of even one person still has to atone for it with his own life; yet is the harm done by opium limited to the taking of one life only? Therefore in the new regulations, in regard to those barbarians who bring opium to China,

the penalty is fixed at decapitation or strangulation. This is what is called getting rid of a harmful thing on behalf of mankind....

Our Celestial Dynasty rules over and supervises the myriad states and surely possesses unfathomable spiritual dignity. Yet the emperor cannot bear to execute people without having first tried to reform them by instruction.... May you, O King, check your wicked and sift out your vicious people before they come to China, in order to guarantee the peace of your nation, to show further the sincerity of your politeness and submissiveness, and to let the two countries enjoy together the blessings of peace. How fortunate, how fortunate indeed! After receiving this dispatch will you immediately give us a prompt reply regarding the details and circumstances of your cutting off the opium traffic. Be sure not to put this off. The above is what has to be communicated. [Vermilion endorsement of the emperor:] This is appropriately worded and quite comprehensive.

TREATY OF NANKING

SOURCE *William Frederick Mayers, ed.* Treaties between the Empire of China and Foreign Powers, *1–3. Shanghai and London, 1877. Reprint. Taipei: Ch'eng-Wen, 1966.*

INTRODUCTION *This treaty signed at the conclusion of the first Opium War (1839–1842) was the first in a long series of unequal treaties subsequently imposed on China by eighteen foreign powers. It granted Britain the island of Hong Kong in perpetuity, promised a fair and regular tariff, opened the ports of Guangzhou (Canton in the document below), Xiamen (Amoy below), Fuzhou (Fuchau-fu), Ningbo (Ningpo) and Shanghai to British residence and trade, and promised an indemnity to pay for the opium confiscated by the Chinese and for the cost of the war.*

TREATY OF PEACE, FRIENDSHIP, AND COMMERCE BETWEEN HER MAJESTY THE QUEEN OF GREAT BRITAIN AND IRELAND AND THE EMPEROR OF CHINA

Signed, in the English and Chinese Languages, at Nanking, 29th August, 1842. Ratifications exchanged at Hongkong, 26th June, 1843.

Her Majesty, the Queen of the United Kingdom of Great Britain and Ireland, and His Majesty the Emperor of China, being desirous of putting an end to the misunderstandings and consequent hostilities which have arisen between the two countries, have resolved to conclude a treaty for that purpose, and have therefore named as their Plenipotentiaries, that is to say: Her Majesty the

Queen of Great Britain and Ireland, Sir Henry Pottinger Bart., a Major-General in the service of the East India Company, &c., &c.; and His Imperial Majesty the Emperor of China, the High Commissioners Ke-ying, a Member of the Imperial House, a Guardian of the Crown Prince, and General of the Garrison of Canton: and Iløpú, of the Imperial Kindred, graciously permitted to wear the insignia of the first rank, and the distinction of a peacock's feather, lately Minister and Governor-General, &c., and now Lieut.-General commanding at Chápú:—Who, after having communicated to each other their respective full powers, and found them to be in good and due form, have agreed upon and concluded the following Articles:—

Article I.

There shall henceforward be peace and friendship between Her Majesty the Queen of the United Kingdom of Great Britain and Ireland, and His Majesty the Emperor of China, and between their respective subjects, who shall enjoy full security and protection for their persons and property within the dominions of the other.

Article II.

His Majesty the Emperor of China agrees, that British subjects, with their families and establishments, shall be allowed to reside, for the purpose of carrying on their mercantile pursuits, without molestation or restraint, at the cities and towns of Canton, Amoy, Fuchau-fu, Ningpo, and Shanghai; and Her Majesty the Queen of Great Britain, &c., will appoint Superintendents, or Consular Officers to reside at each of the above-named cities or towns, to be the medium of communication between the Chinese authorities and the said merchants, and to see that the just duties and other dues of the Chinese Government, as hereafter provided for, are duly discharged by Her Britannic Majesty's subjects.

Article III.

It being obviously necessary and desirable that British subjects should have some port whereat they may careen and refit their ships when required, and keep stores for that purpose, His Majesty the Emperor of China cedes to Her Majesty the Queen of Great Britain, &c., the Island of Hongkong, to be possessed in perpetuity by Her Britannic Majesty, her heirs and successors, and to be governed by such laws and regulations as Her Majesty the Queen of Great Britain, &c., shall see fit to direct.

Article IV.

The Emperor of China agrees to pay the sum of Six Millions of Dollars, as the value of the Opium which was delivered up at Canton in the month of March, 1839, as a ransom for the lives of Her Britannic Majesty's Superintendent and

Subjects, who had been imprisoned and threatened with death by the Chinese high officers.

Article V.

The Government of China having compelled the British merchants trading at Canton to deal exclusively with certain Chinese merchants, called Hong-merchants (or Co-hong), who had been licensed by the Chinese Government for that purpose, the Emperor of China agrees to abolish that practice in future at all ports where British merchants may reside, and to permit them to carry on their mercantile transactions with whatever persons they please; and His Imperial Majesty further agrees to pay to the British Government the sum of Three Millions of Dollars, on account of debts due to British subjects by some of the said Hong-merchants, or Co-hong, who have become insolvent, and who owe very large sums of money to subjects of Her Britannic Majesty.

Article VI.

The Government of Her Britannic Majesty having been obliged to send out an expedition to demand and obtain redress for the violent and unjust proceedings of the Chinese high authorities towards Her Britannic Majesty's Officer and Subjects, the Emperor of China agrees to pay the sum of Twelve Millions of Dollars, on account of the expenses incurred; and Her Britannic Majesty's Plenipotentiary voluntarily agrees, on behalf of Her Majesty, to deduct from the said amount of Twelve Millions of Dollars, any sums which may have been received by Her Majesty's combined forces, as ransom for cities, and towns in China, subsequent to the 1st day of August, 1841.

Article VII.

It is agreed, that the total amount of Twenty-one Millions of Dollars, described in the three preceding Articles, shall be paid as follows:—

- Six millions immediately. Six millions in 1843; that is, three millions on or before the 30th of the month of June, and three millions on or before the 31st of December. Five millions in 1844; that is, two millions and a-half on or before the 30th of June, and two millions and a-half on or before the 31st December. Four millions in 1845; that is, two millions on or before the 30th of June, and two millions on or before the 31st of December.

- And it is further stipulated, that interest, at the rate of 5 per cent. per annum, shall be paid by the Government of China on any portion of the above sums that are not punctually discharged at the periods fixed.

Article VIII.

The Emperor of China agrees to release, unconditionally, all subjects of Her Britannic Majesty (whether natives of Europe or India), who may be in confinement at this moment in any part of the Chinese Empire.

Article IX.

The Emperor of China agrees to publish and promulgate, under His Imperial Sign Manual and Seal, a full and entire amnesty and act of indemnity to all subjects of China, on account of their having resided under, or having had dealings and intercourse with, or having entered the service of Her Britannic Majesty, or of Her Majesty's officers; and His Imperial Majesty further engages to release all Chinese subjects who may be at this moment in confinement for similar reasons.

Article X.

His Majesty the Emperor of China agrees to establish at all the ports which are, by the second Article of this Treaty, to be thrown open for the resort of British merchants, a fair and regular Tariff of Export and Import Customs and other dues, which Tariff shall be publicly notified and promulgated for general information; and the Emperor further engages that, when British merchandise shall have once paid at any of the said ports the regulated customs and dues, agreeable to the Tariff to be hereafter fixed, such merchandise may be conveyed by Chinese merchants to any province or city in the interior of the Empire of China, on paying a further amount as Transit duties, which shall not exceed — per cent. on the Tariff value of such goods.

Article XI.

It is agreed that Her Britannic Majesty's Chief High Officer in China shall correspond with the Chinese High Officers, both at the Capital and in the Provinces, under the term 照會 "communication": the subordinate British Officers and Chinese High Officers in the Provinces under the term 申陈 "statement," on the part of the former, and on the part of the latter, 扎 "declaration," and the subordinates of both countries on a footing of perfect equality; merchants and others not holding official situations, and therefore not included in the above, on both sides to use the term 禀 "representation" in all papers addressed to, or intended for the notice of the respective governments.

Article XII.

On the assent of the Emperor of China to this Treaty being received, and the discharge of the first instalment of money, Her Britannic Majesty's forces will retire from

Nanking and the Grand Canal, and will no longer molest or stop the trade of China. The military post at Chinhai will also be withdrawn; but the islands of Kúlang-sú, and that of Chusan, will continue to be held by Her Majesty's forces until the money payments, and the arrangements for opening the ports to British merchants, be completed.

Article XIII.

The ratification of this Treaty by Her Majesty the Queen of Great Britain, &c., and His Majesty the Emperor of China, shall be exchanged as soon as the great distance which separates England from China will admit; but, in the meantime, counterpart copies of it, signed and sealed by the Plenipotentiaries on behalf of their respective Sovereigns, shall be mutually delivered, and all its provisions and arrangements shall take effect.

Done at Nanking, and signed and sealed by the Plenipotentiaries on board H.B.M.'s ship *Cornwallis*, this 29th day of August, 1842; corresponding with the Chinese date, 24th day of the 7th month, in the 22nd year of Taou-Kwang.

Approved and ratified by the Emperor on the 24th day of the 9th month, in the 22nd year of his reign (27th October, 1842.)

THE LAND SYSTEM OF THE HEAVENLY KINGDOM

SOURCE Sources of Chinese Tradition, Volume II: From 1600 through the Twentieth Century, *2nd edition, ed. William Theodore de Bary and Richard Lufrano, 224–226. New York: Columbia University Press, 2000.*

INTRODUCTION *The Taiping Uprising (1851–1864) attracted millions of followers, affected much of China, and posed a serious threat to the Qing dynasty. Taiping ideology was based on the idea that, being born of the same Father, men and women were all brothers and sisters under Heaven and should be equal. Egalitarianism was reflected in their laws though not always in their practice. The Land System of the Heavenly Kingdom, excerpted below, proposed that land should be equally divided among families on the basis of the number of family members over sixteen. It also made provision for the support of those who were unable to work.*

All officials who have rendered meritorious service are to receive hereditary stipends from the court. For the later adherents to the Taiping cause, every family in each military district (*jun*) is to provide one man to serve as a militia man. During an emergency they are to fight under the command of their officers to destroy the enemy and to suppress bandits. In peacetime they are to engage in agriculture under the direction of their officers, tilling the land and providing support for their superiors.

All land [in the country] is to be classified into nine grades....

The distribution of all land is to be based on the number of persons in each family, regardless of sex. A large family is entitled to more land, a small one to less. The land distributed should not be all of one grade but mixed. Thus for a family of six, for instance, three are to have fertile land and three barren land—half and half of each.

All the land in the country is to be cultivated by the whole population together. If there is an insufficiency [of land] in this place, move some of the people to another place. If there is an insufficiency in another place, move them to this one. All lands in the country are also to be mutually supporting with respect to abundance and scarcity. If this place has a drought, then draw upon the abundant harvest elsewhere in order to relieve the distress here. If there is a drought there, draw upon the abundant harvest here in order to relieve the distress there. Thus all the people of the country may enjoy the great blessings of the Heavenly Father, Supreme Ruler and Lord God-on-High. The land is for all to till, the food for all to eat, the clothes for all to wear, and money for all to spend. Inequality shall exist nowhere; none shall suffer from hunger or cold....

Mulberry trees are to be planted along the walls [of villages] throughout the country. All women are required to grow silkworms, to do weaving, and to make clothes. Every family of the country is required to raise five hens and two hogs, in keeping with the proper breeding seasons.

During the harvest season, the Group Officer should direct [the grain collection by] the sergeants. Deducting the amount needed to feed the twenty-five families until next harvest season, he should collect the rest of the produce for storage in state granaries. The same method of collection is applicable to other kinds of products, such as barley, beans, ramie fiber, cotton clothes, silk, domestic animals, silver and copper cash, and so on, for all people under Heaven are of one family belonging to the Heavenly Father, the Supreme Ruler, the Lord God-on-High. Nobody should keep private property. All things should be presented to the Supreme Ruler, so that He will be enabled to make use of them and distribute them equally to all members of his great world-family. Thus all will be sufficiently fed and clothed....

The Group Officer must keep a record of the amount of grain and cash he has collected and report them to the Treasurers and Receiving and Disbursing Tellers. A state treasury and a church are to be established among every twenty-five families, under the direct administration of the Group Officer. All expenditures of the twenty-five families for weddings, births, or other festival occasions are to be paid for out of the state treasury. But there is to be a fixed limit; not a penny is to be spent beyond that.... Thus, throughout the land in the contracting of marriages, wealth need be no consideration.

In the twenty-five family units pottery-making, metalworking, carpentry, masonry, and other such skilled work should be performed by the sergeants and militiamen in the off-seasons from farming and military service.

In conducting the different kinds of festival ceremonies for the twenty-five families under his administration, the Group Officer should hold religious services to pray to the Heavenly Father, the Supreme Ruler and Lord God-on-High. All the bad customs of the past must be completely abolished.

A PROCLAMATION AGAINST THE BANDITS OF GUANGDONG AND GUANGXI

SOURCE *Zeng Guofan. A Proclamation against the Bandits of Guangdong and Guangxi, 1854. In* The Search for Modern China: A Documentary Collection, *ed. Pei-Kai Cheng and Michael Lestz with Jonathan D. Spence, 146–149. New York: Norton, 1999.*

INTRODUCTION *By 1854 the Taiping Uprising, which had originated in Guangxi Province, established its capital in Nanjing, controlled much of the central and lower Yangzi (Yangtze) area, and threatened North China. The Qing official Zeng Guofan was one of the major figures in the suppression of the rebellion. This proclamation reflects Zeng's deeply Confucian outlook as he attacks the Christianity of the Yue (Yüeh) bandits (the Taipings).*

It has been five years since the rebels Hung Hsiu-ch'üan and Yang Hsiu-ch'ing started their rebellion. They have inflicted bitter sorrow upon millions people and devastated more than 5,000 *li* of *chou* [regions] and *hsien* [counties]. Wherever they pass, boats of all sizes, and people rich and poor alike, have all been plundered and stripped bare; not one inch of grass has been left standing. The clothing has been stripped from the bodies of those captured by these bandits, and their money has been seized. Anyone with five taels or more of silver who does not contribute it to the bandits is forthwith decapitated. Men are given one *ho* [1/10th pint] of rice per day, and forced to march in the forefront in battle, to construct city walls, and dredge moats. Women are also given one *ho* of rice per day, and forced to stand guard on the parapets at night, and to haul rice and carry coal. The feet of women who refuse to unbind them are cut off and shown to other women as a warning. The corpses of boatmen who secretly conspired to fell were hung upside down to show other boatmen as a warning. The Yüeh [Guangdong and Guangxi] bandits indulge themselves in luxury and high position, while the people in our own Yangtze provinces living under their coercion are treated worse than animals. This cruelty and brutality appalls anyone with blood in his veins.

Ever since the times of Yao, Shun, and the Three Dynasties, sages, generation after generation, have upheld the Confucian teachings, stressing proper human relationships, between ruler and minister, father and son, superiors and subordinates, the high and the low, all in their proper place, just as hats and shoes are not interchangeable. The Yüeh bandits have stolen a few scraps from the foreign barbarians and worship the Christian religion. From their bogus ruler and bogus chief ministers down to their soldiers and menial underlings, all are called brothers. They say that only heaven can be called father; aside from him, all fathers among the people are called brothers, and all mothers are called sisters. Peasants are not allowed to till the land for themselves and pay taxes, for they say that the fields all belong to the T'ien Wang [Heavenly King]. Merchants are not allowed to trade for profit, for they say that all goods belong to the T'ien Wang. Scholars may not read the Confucian classics, for they have their so-called teachings of Jesus and the New Testament. In a single day several thousand years of Chinese ethical principles and proper human relationships, classical books, social institutions and statutes have all been completely swept away. This is not just a crisis for our Ch'ing dynasty, but the most extraordinary crisis of all time for the Confucian teachings, which is why our Confucius and Mencius are weeping bitterly in the nether world. How can any educated person sit idly by without thinking of doing something?

Since ancient times, those with meritorious accomplishments during their lifetimes have become spirits after death; the Kingly Way governs the living and the Way of the Spirits governs among the dead. Even rebellious ministers and wicked sons of the most vicious and vile sort show respect and awe toward the spirits. When Li Tzu-ch'eng reached Ch'ü-fu [Confucius' birthplace in Shandong Province], he did not molest the Temple of the Sage. When Chang Hsien-chung reached Tzu-t'ung, he sacrificed to Wen Ch'ang [the patron spirit of literature]. But the Yüeh bandits burned the school at Shen-chou, destroyed the wooden tablet of Confucius, and wildly scattered the tablets of the Ten Paragons in the two corridors all over the ground. Afterwards, wherever they have passed, in every district, the first thing they have done is to burn down the temples, defiling the shrines and maiming the statues even of loyal ministers and righteous heroes such as the awesome Kuan Yü and Yüen Fei. Even Buddhist and Taoist temples, shrines of

guardian deities and altars to local gods have all been burned, and every statue destroyed. The ghosts and spirits in the world of darkness are enraged at this, and want to avenge their resentment.

I, the Governor-General, having received His Imperial Majesty's command leading 20,000 men advancing together on land and water, vow that I shall sleep on nettles and ship gall [to strengthen my determination] to exterminate these vicious traitors, to rescue our captured boats, and to deliver the persecuted people, not only in order to relieve the Emperor of his strenuous and conscientious labors from dawn to dusk, but also to comfort Confucius and Mencius for their silent sufferings over the proper human relationships; and only to avenge the millions who have died unjust deaths, but also to avenge the insults to all the spirits.

Therefore, let this proclamation be disseminated far and near so that all may know the following: Any red-blooded hero who assembles a company of righteous troops to assist in our extermination campaign will be taken in as my personal friend, and the troops given rations. Any Confucian gentleman who cherishes the Way, is pained at Christianity running rampant over the land, and who, in a towering rage, wants to defend our Way, will be made a member of the Governor-General's personal staff and treated as a guest teacher. Any benevolent person, stirred by moral indignation, who contributes silver or assists with provisions, will be given a treasury receipt and a commission from the Board of Civil Appointments for a donation of 1,000 *chin* [1 *chin* = 1 1/5 lb.] or less, and a special memorial will be composed requesting a liberal reward for a donation of over 1,000 *chin*. If anyone voluntarily returns after a long stay among the bandits, and kills one of their leaders or leads a city to surrender, he will be taken into the army of the Governor-General to the Emperor, will be given an official title. Anyone who has lived under the bandits' coercion for some years, whose hair has grown several inches long, but who discards his weapon when the fighting is about to commence and returns to the fold barehanded, will receive an amnesty from the death sentence, and will be given travel expenses to return home.

In the past, at the end of the Han, T'ang, Yuan, and Ming, bands of rebels were innumerable, all because of foolish rulers and misgovernment, so that none of these rebellions could be stamped out. But today the Son of Heaven is deeply concerned and examines his character in order to reform himself, worships Heaven, and is sympathetic to the people. He has not increased the land tax, nor has he conscripted soldiers from households. With the profound benevolence of the sages, he is suppressing the cruel and worthless bandits. It does not require any great wisdom to see that sooner or later they will all be destroyed.

Those of you who have been coerced into joining the rebels, or who willingly follow the traitors, and oppose the Imperial Crusade [are warned that] when the Imperial forces sweep down it will no longer be possible to discriminate between the good and evil—every person will be crushed.

I, the Governor-General, am scant in virtue and of meager ability. I rely solely on two words, trust and loyalty, as the foundation for running the army. Above are the sun and the moon, below the ghosts and spirits; in this world, the vast waters of the Yangtze, and in the other world, the souls of loyal ministers and stalwart heroes who gave their lives in battle against previous rebellions. Let all peer into my heart and listen to my words.

Upon arrival, this proclamation immediately has the force of law. Do not disregard it!

TREATY OF TIANJIN

INTRODUCTION *The Anglo-Chinese Treaty of Tianjin (1858), excerpted below, was a building block in the treaty port system. Originally intended to end the Second Opium War, the treaty included provisions whereby the Chinese government accepted western norms of diplomatic representation. In addition to reaffirming concessions made in the 1842 Treaty of Nanjing, the Treaty of Tianjin gave the British the right of diplomatic residence at Beijing (Peking), the right to travel in the interior, a revised tariff rate and an indemnity. Hostilities broke out again soon after the treaty was signed but its provisions were confirmed in the 1860 Treaty of Beijing ("The Convention of Peking").*

II.

For the better preservation of harmony in future, Her Majesty the Queen of Great Britain and His Majesty the Emperor of China mutually agree that, in accordance with the universal practice of great and friendly nations, Her Majesty the Queen, may, if she see fit, appoint ambassadors, ministers, or other diplomatic agents to the Court of Peking; and His Majesty the Emperor of China may, in like manner, if he see fit, appoint ambassadors, ministers, or other diplomatic agents to the Court of St. James.

III.

His Majesty the Emperor of China hereby agrees that the ambassador, minister, or other diplomatic agent, so appointed by Her Majesty the Queen of Great Britain, may reside, with his family and establishment, permanently at the capital, or may visit it occasionally, at the option of the British Government. He shall not be called upon to perform any ceremony derogatory to him as representing the Sovereign of an independent nation on a footing of equality with that of China. On the other hand, he shall use the same forms of ceremony and respect to His Majesty the Emperor as are employed by the ambassadors, ministers, or diplomatic agents of Her Majesty towards the Sovereigns of independent and equal European nations.

It is further agreed, that Her Majesty's Government may acquire at Peking a site for building, or may hire houses for the accommodation of Her Majesty's Mission, and that the Chinese Government will assist it in so doing.

Her Majesty's Representative shall be at liberty to choose his own servants and attendants, who shall not be subjected to any kind of molestation whatever.

Any person guilty of disrespect or violence to Her Majesty's Representative, or to any member of his family or establishment, in deed or word, shall be severely punished.

VIII.

The Christian religion, as professed by Protestants or Roman Catholics, inculcates the practice of virtue, and teaches man to do as he would be done by. Persons teaching or professing it, therefore, shall alike be entitled to the protection of the Chinese authorities, nor shall any such, peaceably pursuing their calling, and not offending against the law, be persecuted or interfered with.

XI.

In addition to the cities and towns of Canton, Amoy, Fuchow, Ningpo, and Shanghai, opened by the Treaty of Nanking, it is agreed that British subjects may frequent the cities and ports of New Chwang, Tang-Chow, Tai-Wan (Formosa), Chau-Chow (Swatow), and Kiung-Chow (Hainan).

They are permitted to carry on trade with whomsoever they please, and to proceed to and fro at pleasure with their vessels and merchandise.

They shall enjoy the same privileges, advantages, and immunities, at the said towns and ports, as they enjoy at the ports already opened to trade, including the right of residence, of buying or renting houses, of leasing land therein, and of building churches, hospitals, and cemeteries.

LI.

It is agreed, that henceforward the character "I" ("barbarian") shall not be applied to the Government or subjects of Her Britannic Majesty, in any Chinese official document issued by the Chinese authorities, either in the capital or in the provinces.

LIV.

The British Government and its subjects are hereby confirmed in all privileges, immunities, and advantages conferred on them by previous Treaties; and it is hereby expressly stipulated, that the British Government and its subjects will be allowed free and equal participation in all privileges, immunities, and advantages that may have been, or may be hereafter, granted by His Majesty the Emperor of China to the Government or subjects of any other nation.

ON THE MANUFACTURE OF FOREIGN WEAPONS AND ON THE ADOPTION OF WESTERN LEARNING

SOURCE *Feng Guifen. On the Manufacture of Foreign Weapons; On the Adoption of Western Learning. In Sources of Chinese Tradition, Volume II: From 1600 through the Twentieth Century, 2nd edition, ed. William Theodore de Bary and Richard Lufrano, 235–238. New York: Columbia University Press, 2000.*

INTRODUCTION *China's repeated military defeats by foreigners persuaded some high Qing officials that the Chinese needed to study the military sciences from other countries. What became known as the Self-strengthening movement of the 1860s–1890s in which Chinese provincial officials set up language schools, arsenals, shipyards, coal mines and iron and steel works was to a large extent based on the ideas of the scholar-official Feng Guifen written in 1861.*

ON THE MANUFACTURE OF FOREIGN WEAPONS

According to a general geography compiled by an Englishman, the territory of China is eight times that of Russia, ten times that of the United States, one hundred times that of France, and two hundred times that of Great Britain.... Yet we are shamefully humiliated by the four nations, not because our climate, soil, or resources are inferior to theirs, but because our people are inferior.... Now, our inferiority is not due to our allotment [i.e., our inherent nature] from Heaven, but is rather due to ourselves. If it were allotted us by Heaven, it would be a shame but not something we could do anything about. Since the inferiority is due to ourselves, it is a still greater shame but something we can do something about. And if we feel ashamed, there is nothing better than self-strengthening.

Why are the Western nations small and yet strong? Why are we large and yet weak? We must search for the means to become their equal, and that depends solely upon human effort. With regard to the present situation, several observations may be made: in not wasting human talents, we are inferior to the barbarians; in not wasting natural resources, we are inferior to the barbarians; in allowing no barrier to come between the ruler and the people, we are inferior to the barbarians; and in the matching of words with deeds, we are also inferior to the barbarians. The remedy for these four points is to seek the causes in ourselves. They can be changed at once if only the emperor would set us in the right direction. There is no need to learn from the barbarians in these matters....

We have only one thing to learn from the barbarians, and that is strong ships and effective guns.... Funds should be allotted to establish a shipyard and arsenal in each trading port. A few barbarians should be employed, and Chinese who are good in using their minds should be selected to receive instruction so that in turn they may teach many craftsmen. When a piece of work is finished and is as good as that made by the barbarians, the makers should be rewarded with an official *juren* degree and be permitted to participate in the metropolitan examinations on the same basis as other scholars. Those whose products are of superior quality should be rewarded with the *jinshi* degree [ordinarily conferred in the metropolitan examinations] and be permitted to participate in the palace examinations like others. The workers should be paid double so that they will not quit their jobs.

Our nation's emphasis on civil service examinations has sunk deep into people's minds for a long time. Intelligent and brilliant scholars have exhausted their time and energy in such useless things as the stereotyped examination essays, examination papers, and formal calligraphy.... We should now order one-half of them to apply themselves to the manufacturing of instruments and weapons and to the promotion of physical studies.... The intelligence and ingenuity of the Chinese are certainly superior to those of the various barbarians; it is only that hitherto we have not made use of them. When the government above takes delight in something, the people below will pursue it further their response will be like an echo carried by the wind. There ought to be some people of extraordinary intelligence who can have new ideas and improve on Western methods. At first they may take the foreigners as their teachers and models; then they may come to the same level and be their equals; finally they may move ahead and surpass them. Herein lies the way to self-strengthening....

It may be argued: "Guan Zhong repelled the barbarians and Confucius acclaimed his virtue; the state of Chu adopted barbarian ways and [Confucius in] the *Spring and Autumn Annals* condemned them. Is not what you are proposing contrary to the Way of the sages?" No, it is not. When we speak of repelling the barbarians, we must have the actual means to repel them, and not just empty bravado. If we live in the present day and speak of repelling the barbarians we should ask with what instruments we are to repel them.... [The answer is that] we should use the instruments of the barbarians but not adopt the ways of the barbarians. We should use them so that we can repel them.

Some have asked why we should not just purchase the ships and man them with [foreign] hirelings, but the answer is that this will not do. If we can manufacture, repair, and use them, then they are our weapons. If we cannot manufacture, repair, and use them, then they are still the weapons of others.... In the end the way to avoid trouble is to manufacture, repair, and use weapons by ourselves. Only thus can we pacify the empire; only thus can we become the leading power in the world; only thus can we restore our original strength, redeem ourselves from former humiliations, and maintain the integrity of our vast territory so as to remain the greatest country on earth....

ON THE ADOPTION OF WESTERN LEARNING

Western books on mathematics, mechanics, optics, light, and chemistry contain the best principles of the natural sciences. In the books on geography, the mountains, rivers, strategic points, customs, and native products of the hundred countries are fully listed. Most of this information is beyond the reach of the Chinese people....

If we wish to use Western knowledge, we should establish official translation bureaus in Guangzhou and Shanghai. Brilliant students not over fifteen years of age should be selected from those areas to live and study in these schools on double allowances. Westerners should be appointed to teach them the spoken and written languages of the various nations, and famous Chinese teachers should be engaged to teach them classics, history, and other subjects. At the same time they should learn mathematics. (Note: All Western knowledge is derived from mathematics.... If we wish to adopt Western knowledge, it is but natural that we should learn mathematics.)... China has many brilliant people. There must be some who can learn from the barbarians and surpass them....

It is from learning that the principles of government are derived. In discussing good government, the great historian Sima Qian said (following Xunzi), "Take the latter-day kings as your models." This was because they were nearer in time; their customs had changed from the past and were more similar to the present; and their ideas were not so lofty as to be impracticable. It is my opinion that today we should also take the foreign nations as our examples. They live at the same time and in the same world with us; they have attained prosperity and power by their own efforts. Is it not fully clear that they are similar to us and that their methods can easily be put into practice? If we let Chinese ethics and Confucian teachings serve as the foundation, and let them be supplemented by the methods used by the various nations for the attainment of prosperity and power, would it not be the best of all solutions?

Moreover, during the past twenty years since the opening of trade, a great number of foreign chiefs have learned our written and spoken language, and the best of them can even read our classics and histories. They are generally able to speak on our dynastic regulations and civil administration, on our geography and the condition of our people. On the other hand, our officials from the governors down are completely ignorant of foreign countries. In comparison, should we not feel ashamed? The Chinese officials have to rely upon stupid and preposterous interpreters as their eyes and ears. The mildness or severity of the original statement, its sense of urgency or lack of insistence, may be lost through their tortuous interpretations. Thus frequently a small grudge may develop into a grave hostility. At present the most important political problem of the empire is to control the barbarians, yet the pivotal function is entrusted to such people. No wonder that we understand neither the foreigners nor ourselves and cannot distinguish fact from untruth. Whether in peace negotiations or in deliberating for war, we are unable to grasp the essentials. This is indeed the underlying trouble of our nation.

LETTERS OF A CHINAMAN TO ENGLISH READERS

SOURCE *Foote, G. W. Letters of a Chinaman to English Readers. In* Letters of a Chinaman to English Readers on English and Chinese Superstitions and the Mischief of Missionaries, *1–16. London: Pioneer Press, 1903.*

INTRODUCTION *These letters are selected from a volume of letters purporting to be written by a Chinese named Ah Sin. The letters present a reasoned attack on the activities of foreign missionaries in China, apparently from a Chinese antisuperstitious perspective. They had first appeared in the* Freethinker, *an atheist periodical founded by G. W. Foote in 1881. Foote provided the introduction to the collected volume and it is possible that he was the author of the letters. Certainly Ah Sin is now recognized as having been a pseudonym. Whatever the provenance of these letters, they offer a unique perspective on the missionary enterprise.*

LETTER I

On Priests and Prayer

I have always been much interested in the efficacy of prayers, and have always regretted that there were not more definite and reliable data at hand in regard to this subject. We have no exact data as to which form of prayer is the most efficacious. Then, again, we are completely in the dark as to the relative efficiency of prayers, whether addressed to the Trinity, to the individual members of the Trinity, or any of the saints.

Many years ago, when Mr. Tyndall took this important subject up, I had great hopes that we might arrive at some definite and reliable knowledge on this great subject. Mr. Tyndall suggested that experiments should be conducted in a London hospital with a view of ascertaining how much prayer was equal to an ounce of quinine; this was referred to as "Tyndall's prayer-gauge." Had the experiments been carried out as he suggested, they could not have failed to have been of great value to the whole world. As to the formulae of prayers, I think we may reasonably conclude, from all the knowledge at hand in England, that the Lord's Prayer would have the highest efficiency. I should say that mathematically we might consider this as unity, and that all other prayers should be multiplied by some co-efficient less than unity. But who is to establish the co-efficient of the numerous forms of prayer that we find in use among the clergymen of the Church of England?

After long and careful observation of this subject, I am led to the belief that prayer is not so efficient as has been supposed; I think that nearly all prayers have a very low co-efficient—in other words, in order to make them efficacious, we should employ a great number of them. If we look at the matter from a practical standpoint, I do not see that it is possible for there to be any misunderstanding on the subject; it matters not how low the co-efficient of prayer may be, provided that the number of prayers is great enough. The question of prayer has been the subject of careful study for the last 6,000 years, and, as we know, the Chinese have probably given more attention to this subject than any other people in the world. I think that the conclusions that we Chinese have arrived at after long years of careful experiment and observation cannot fail to be of great value and interest to the religious world in England. We very soon learned that prayers were not very effective—*i.e.*, when considered individually; to have any appreciable effect a great number of them was required. We, however, found by experiment that if a prayer was written on a piece of paper and put into a teacup and turned round once that it was just as effective as if it had been repeated orally. If we put ten prayers into a teacup and rotated the cup ten times, it recorded a hundred prayers, each one of which was just as effective as any other prayer; this was a great

and important discovery. Careful study and investigation also showed most conclusively that this system might be enlarged to any extent; so now we print a million prayers on thin, light paper, we place these in a large cylinder which rotates easily on a fine pivot, and by gearing it up and attaching it to a crank we are able to rotate it ten times by turning the crank round once. Suppose, now, that one wishes to pray; the only thing to be done is to give the crank one turn on its axis in order to register ten millions of prayers, each one of which is just as effective as any other prayer. By grinding away at the handle for a few minutes, as many prayers may be recorded by one person as could be prayed by a whole nation orally in a week. This system has other advantages; as we are completely in the dark as to the comparative efficiency of prayers, it may be possible, if one prays orally, that one may repeat over and over again a prayer that has only a very low efficiency; but, with the Chinese system, a good many different kinds may be included, some of which, according to the laws of chance, may be relatively efficient; therefore, there is a greater degree of certainty in the Chinese praying-machines than is possible in England, where the relative efficiency of prayer is unknown, and only a few can be repeated.

May I, therefore, recommend to your clergymen that they should employ a Chinese praying-machine, which is easily made out of a tin can and a bit of wire? I feel certain that if this system is given a fair trial it will be found quite as effective, prayer for prayer, as any other system; moreover, it will save a lot of time.

AH SIN

LETTER II

English and Chinese Superstition

I thank you very much indeed for publishing my letter in the *Freethinker*. I have thought that my experiences might not be uninteresting to some of your thoughtful readers.

When I had passed my examination in China, I took up the study of the English language, and when I had obtained a grasp of what appeared to me at that time a most difficult tongue, I made a study of English literature, making myself fairly well acquainted with the writings of Darwin, Spencer, Huxley, and many others.

I was delighted with the great learning of your wise men. It appeared to me that if one understood the English language a totally new field of thought was open. I was surprised at the great skill of your leading scientific men; I was charmed with their system of reasoning. Quite true, nearly everything that I found in the writings of these men had been foreshadowed by Confucius and some of our great Chinese sages. But the completeness of the English system of reasoning and thought delighted me. However, as I progressed in English learning, I was constantly running across questions that greatly puzzled me.

There were at that time in China a considerable number of English and American missionaries, representing a great variety of different kinds of religion.

In order to get practice in speaking English I used to seek out these gentlemen and converse with them. Just imagine my surprise at their foolish twaddle, after having read Huxley, Darwin, and Spencer! Evidently there must be two totally different kinds of men in England—the scientific, who thinks and writes the works which I had so much admired—and the foolish, who never thinks and who seems to be completely without the power of reasoning. To say the least, I was greatly puzzled.

I then went to America, and finally came to England and made a study of English literature and laws, and I flatter myself that after about six years of study. I was fairly proficient in the subjects I had taken up. The more I studied your literature, your laws and your religion, the more I became convinced that the people of Europe and America were divided into two distinct classes—the logical and the illogical—those who could think, and those who seemed absolutely bereft of all power of reasoning—the extremes in both directions.

I was greatly amused on meeting and conversing with your priests and parsons—euphoniously dubbed "Devil-Dodgers" by many. I found that these gentlemen were quite unable to give any logical reasons why they believed such impossible doctrines and absurd superstitions. For instance, I was at a complete loss to understand how it was possible for intelligent men to believe in the remarkable fish, snake, and devil stories in the Bible, It then occurred to me that these gentlemen connected with the Church only *pretended to believe because their living depended upon doing so.* In speaking to non-clerical people on the subject I found that only a very small number of the intelligent men I met believed anything at all; they generally said in an off-hand sort of way: "Oh, it does well enough for the wife and the kids." Then again, I found that in good society it was considered very indelicate indeed to even refer to religious subjects. I very soon learnt that the so-called believers regarded their religion as a species of very delicate theological fungus, growing in a dark and dismal cavern, so delicate indeed that the least ray of the sunlight of reason would at once prove fatal to it. In some cases I attempted to discuss the relative merits of the Chinese and English systems of religion, and was met with the knock-down argument: "You can reason on anything, on any mortal thing in this world, except Christianity. Christianity is above reason; one is not permitted to reason on anything that relates to the Christian Faith." This was said by people who pretended to believe in Christian mythology.

It never occurred to these gentlemen for one moment that any religion could be made unassailable if its adherents assumed the same position. Suppose, for instance, that the religious beliefs of the Fiji Islanders as they originally existed should be above reason, then of course it would be quite impossible for anyone to show the absurdity of their system of belief.

In England I often see articles in the papers ridiculing Chinese superstitious and religion, and I have often attempted to reply to these articles. However, upon taking my attempt to the editor. I generally received the stereotyped reply: "Oh! yes, this is very good indeed. I like it immensely. It is very witty, and at the same time very logical, but we publish a newspaper to sell, and people would not take it into their families if we should publish your letters." The fact is your people wish to hear but one side of the story. They cannot stand having the truth told to them by the other side.

I think that I have made myself fairly familiar with all the leading superstitions of China and England, and I am quite willing to admit the truth, that in China we have a very large class who are extremely ignorant and unreasoning. They have ancient superstitions which have come down through countless ages, and unfortunately they believe implicitly in them. These ignorant people fancy that there are certain powers in the air and in the earth, that have to be dealt with through the agency of necromancers and geomancers, and they pay these charlatans a considerable amount of money to act as intermediaries between themselves and these imaginary air and earth dragons. This kind of superstition, which, however, only exists among our ignorant classes, is generally known as the Fung Shui. Certainly it is a bothersome and expensive form of superstition, and my countrymen would be much better off without it. Of this there can be no question. There is not a learned man in China to-day, or, in fact, a high official of any kind who would not be pleased to have our ignorant people relieved of all their superstitious fears and of all their belief in supernatural agencies. I have no hesitation in saying that if the very best men that one could find in Europe and America should go to China, and take with them a fair amount of physical apparatus, and deliver scientific lectures, that they would be very well received. If some clever European could thoroughly master our language and come to China and lecture on the system of Darwin and the theory of Herbert Spencer, it would do away with much of our superstition, and would do our people an immense amount of good. I am sure the Government and the wealthy and intelligent classes would do all in their power to help the matter on. But, unfortunately, these are not the kind of men that Europe and America send out to China. They do not send their best men, and they do not go to our country to ask us to do away with superstitions altogether, but rather to swap off our present Fung Shui and take on one which is still more expensive and bothersome.

China is a very thickly populated country. The people, according to French philosophers, are able to get about twice as much out of the soil as the French are able to do, and the French are the cleverest agriculturists outside of China. The art of getting the most out of the land which will enable the greatest possible number to live off a given territory, has been greatly intensified in China, and even with this intensification of production, the population is so vast that it is necessary for the agriculturist to work unceasingly, or starve.

Suppose, now, that our people should exchange their Fung Shui for the English system; suppose that they should take over the English Sunday Fung Shui, it would then require one entire day in every week to propitiate and make peace with these dragons and devils. It would also be necessary for them to say over certain formulae several times in the day to pacify other imaginary phantoms of the air. All this would take time. They would simply starve. It would therefore be evident that our people could not possibly exchange their present Fung Shui for one which would require at least ten times as much to propitiate. It would take too much time. Then, again, the English geomancers and necromancers demand much more to act as intermediaries between the people and the air phantoms than the Chinese necromancers, who perform the same imaginary service for the ignorant Chinese.

All this might be considered very interesting from a purely philosophical standpoint, providing that it did not do any harm, but unfortunately there is a tragic side also. Your necromancers insist upon forcing their particular Fung Shui upon us, while our ignorant classes are equally determined to stick to their old Fung Shui and to reject the new one, which, according to our way of thinking, is at least a hundredfold as foolish and impossible as our own. We have learnt to till the soil to a greater degree of perfection than any other people that have ever lived in the world. Consequently, more of us are able to live in comfort off the land than is possible in any other country. But although we are very proficient in supporting human life off the products of the earth, we are extremely deficient in all systems and machinery intended for the purpose of destroying human life.

In Europe and America, however, clever scientific men, having long made a study of destroying human life, have reduced their machinery and their system to a very high degree of perfection. In fact, incredible as it may seem, I have seen in England an automatic man-killer, which works by itself by simply touching a button. This is truly marvellous. It is also horrible. It therefore follows that, with your trained fighting-man and your automatic man-killers, you are able to invade our country and attempt to thrust your Fung Shui upon us, and this has resulted in the death of many millions of Chinese during the last sixty years.

We do not want your Fung Shui, we do not wish for any system of religion in which devils and miracles have any place whatsoever. We do not like supernaturalism. To every thinking man in the world supernaturalism is simply superstition, and we do not like superstition: we have too much of it already. We therefore pray you to treat us as you would like to be treated yourselves, and withdraw your Devil-Dodgers, necromancers, geomancers, and your foolish and degrading superstitions from our country, and allow us to work out our own salvation, and to gradually do away with our own Fung Shui as best we can. Both are bothersome and foolish. If, however, you will attend to your own Fung Shui, we will attend to ours.

I have never yet seen an Englishman, or, in fact, any Christian who is able to hold an argument on religious subjects with a Chinese. I never have found the man that can show what advantage would accrue to us by abandoning our own superstitions and taking over the superstitions of the English. If there is such a man, I hereby challenge him to a fair discussion in his own language.

AH SIN

LETTER III

Who Made the World?

I thank you very much for publishing my two letters. With your leave I shall translate some of your publications and send them to my friends in China.

A few weeks ago I heard some English gentlemen discussing the merits of Sir Robert Ball's late work, entitled *The World's Beginning*. They all seemed to agree that it was a remarkable work, "so simple and direct that anyone could understand it."

I was told that Sir Robert was the leading astronomer in England, and that his late work had been written expressly for beginners. Evidently it was just what I wanted, and I lost no time in purchasing a copy and reading it. I was pleased—I was more than pleased—I was delighted. The language was simple and easy to understand, the reasoning good, and the logic sound. It appears to me that there cannot be the least doubt about the absolute truth of the theory laid down and reasoned out. It must be so; and what is more, everyone that I have spoken to on the subject agrees with me. Nobody seems to question it. It appears to be accepted by everyone as a matter of course. This being so, let us see now what Sir Robert Ball teaches, and what is admitted to be quite true in England and America.

He says that this world came into its present form by being condensed from a white hot cloud of gas, or matter so very hot and attenuated that it appeared in space as a nebula, or disorganised cloud of white-hot earthy substances such as lime, clay, sand, iron, etc. He says that this hot cloud very slowly condensed and formed our sun and all the planets, including this earth. He says that other worlds than ours are being formed at the present moment, and that we can actually see them with a large telescope in the process of forming in the great spiral nebula, all of which appears very wonderful indeed. I have read this remarkable work with great interest, and, strange as it may seem, I find that Sir Robert Ball does not once mention the name of the Jewish Jehovah or the Christian God as having had anything to do with the making of the world. Why is this? It is either true or false that Jehovah made the world in six days and rested on the seventh. If it is true, why did Sir Robert write this book, and why does everyone accept his theory as being true? If neither the Jehovah of the Jews nor the Christian God made this world, why do you spend good money to teach such a foolish falsehood to our people? Why do you in England accept Sir Robert Ball's account of the Creation, and teach the old Jewish account to us in China? The Chinese philosophers have always taught us that the world has always existed, and therefore it was not created. They say, "It has always been so" and "will always remain so"; that "everything came about in an ordinary manner and according to natural law; that there never was a special creation or a miracle, and never can be one." This is not far off what Sir Robert tells us now; it is certainly very near the truth as it is understood by all the learned men of today.

Let us see now what the missionaries are attempting to teach in China. They tell us that this world, including the sun, moon, and stars, was snapped into existence out of nothing by the Jewish Jehovah in a few hours. That is something like taking a snapshot photograph. Then another snap, and all the animals and plants were made. Then a third snap, and man and woman made their appearance, full-grown, and able to walk and talk and eat. All was done inside of six days, and about six thousand years ago. Then the God that did all this rested on the seventh day. This is certainly why Sunday is observed, there is no question about it; and this is what your missionaries are attempting to make our people believe to-day. This is what you are paying hundreds of thousands of pounds a year to teach to my countrymen. True, it is not good enough for grown-up people in England, so you attempt to force it upon us. I wish it to be distinctly understood that this account of the so-called Creation appears to us to be foolish and absurd in the extreme. We could not believe such a grotesque fable if we tried to. Many of our people resent the attempt to force such stupid falsehoods upon us, and trouble and bloodshed result. I have no hesitation in saying that if you should send Sir Robert Ball to us, to teach the theories that he teaches so successfully in England, that he would be well received, his

doctrines would be accepted as they have been here, and there would be no trouble or bloodshed.

You would find our people sensible enough to understand and accept his theory. There could be no trouble or opposition, because Sir Robert's theory *is true*, and he has the reasoning power to make others see that *it is true*. I would even say more—he leaves no door open to enable one to escape conviction. His theory *is true*, and *in China we love and admire the truth*. Once more allow me to contrast this with what the paid missionaries are now attempting to teach in China. The story they tell is foolish in the extreme, and has every appearance of being a fable; and the more they attempt to prove it the worse they make it appear. It is even too absurd for our children; really we are not such fools as you take us to be. We therefore pray you to withdraw your ignorant and misguided missionaries, and their stupid falsehoods, from our country, and send us your best scientific men; then all will go well. Peace and missionaries cannot both abide in China, and we prefer peace.

AH SIN

LETTER IV

The Way Out of the Trouble

Some few days ago I had the good fortune to meet a very pious English gentleman who had for years given large sums to keep up the Missionary Propaganda in China. I asked him what his object was in attempting to force his religion upon us. I called his attention to the fact that we had been a civilised nation for many thousands of years, and that before our country was invaded by missionaries we were a law-abiding people. Many European writers had shown that there was less crime amongst us than amongst any other people. Moreover, twice as many of us could live in comfort off a square mile of land as was possible in Europe or America.

As our morality and conduct was of the highest order, and as we were contented and happy, what did he wish to change? What could be changed that would make it better for us? He admitted all this, but said our religion was all wrong. The missionaries that he was helping to support wished us to become a Christian people. They wished us to believe in the Lord Jesus and be saved. But I said countless millions of good and virtuous Chinamen have lived blameless lives and died thousands of years before Christ is said to have been born, and many millions have died since that never even heard of him. Certainly they got on very well for a long time without being saved. He said we were heathens, and the Bible held out no hope for us. "Jesus Christ was the only name given under heaven whereby one could be saved." But certainly no one would believe for a moment that all the good people of the greatest empire on earth would be lost or burnt in fire and brimstone to all eternity because they did not believe something that they had never heard of. He could only say: "God's will be done." Why should we accept Christianity? We have three fairly good religions already, which will compare favorably with any three kinds of Christianity. If we changed our religion it would not put better coats on our backs. It certainly would not give us more to eat. Where could one find a Christian that could get as much out of soil as we do? Would our morals be improved? If so, where could we find an example of a higher morality amongst Christians than that possessed by us before we had ever seen a missionary. Would we be made happier? If so, where could we find a nation where peace and happiness would be more secure than in China before our country was invaded by foreigners? No. What then was the advantage to be gained? Why do you send missionaries to our country to stir up strife and cause an infinite amount of bloodshed and suffering if there is nothing to be gained by it?

We certainly do not want them, we will never accept their religion, that is absolutely impossible. We would not have it at any price, and all attempts to force it upon us are vain and hopeless. Therefore why not keep the missionaries at home and save your own money and our lives?

But, says he, our Lord has commanded and we must obey, *"Go thou and preach the Gospel to every living thing."*

This to my mind is a wicked and mischievous doctrine, and I have no hesitation in saying it ought to be abandoned at once, and before another life is added to the long list that have already perished. This supposed command contains ten words, every one of which has cost the Chinese nation a million and a half of human lives. I think it will be admitted by all, that it would be a good thing for all parties concerned if this doctrine could be disregarded or abandoned. There is plenty of precedent for doing so. Other mischievous doctrines have been abandoned with good results. Why not this, the worst of all? For instance, less than 300 years ago, innocent old women were hunted all over Europe and burnt at the stake for the impossible crime of witchcraft, a crime which every child knows to be impossible at the present moment. It was believed in those dreadful days that these old women had supernatural powers. Some of them were burnt for causing storms at sea by stirring up soap-suds with their stockings. The Pope of Rome, who is infallible, commanded his priests to use more vigilance in searching out witches and putting them to death, especially those that caused the bad weather; while the Protestants, not to be outdone by the Catholics, pursued and burnt supposed witches by the thousand because they found these words in their Bible: *"Thou shall not suffer a witch to live."* It is admitted by Christian historians that some hundreds of thousands of poor old women suffered a painful and ignominious death because the teachers of

a debased theology found in their so-called Holy Book this dreadful command. But the number of lives which has been lost by this mischievous doctrine is nothing to be compared with the still more terrible doctrine, *"Go thou and preach the Gospel to every living creature."* For instance, it has been estimated that about two hundred thousand innocent people lost their lives in Europe in 200 years on account of supposed witchcraft before this villainous doctrine was abandoned. But in China during the last sixty years rather more than fifteen millions of our people have lost their lives on account of the attempt to force Christianity upon us; or, say, about seventy-five times as many of my countrymen have perished on account of having the Gospel preached to them during the last sixty years as perished in Europe in 200 years on account of the twin doctrine of witchcraft. Confucius, in fact all our great sages, have taught us over and over again to have nothing whatsoever to do with anyone who pretends to have dealings with the supernatural. They have told us if we allow supernaturalism to enter our country it can only result in the most awful calamity. Add having all the horrors of the Middle Ages in Europe before us, we naturally believe that our great philosophers were quite right, and we have been attempting to keep all kinds of foreign superstition out of the country, while Christian nations have been equally determined to force their own particular kind of superstition upon us. We do not believe any of the supernatural doctrines brought to our country. They all appear extremely foolish and absurd to us, and I feel sure that no new form of supernaturalism can ever hope to find a foothold in our country.

May I, therefore, pray you to abandon the wicked doctrine of the ten mischievous words, and withdraw your missionaries and "Devil-Dodgers" from our country? We do not want them.

AH SIN

TREATY OF SHIMONOSEKI, 1895

INTRODUCTION *Defeat in the Sino-Japanese War of 1894–1895 came as an appalling shock to the Chinese. Japan, a much smaller country that had been regarded as a sort of disciple to China, had been more successful with its modernization efforts than China. The significant territorial and commercial concessions made by China to Japan in this treaty and the huge indemnity exacted caused great unrest among the Chinese scholar gentry and accelerated demands for reform.*

ARTICLE 1

China recognises definitively the full and complete independence and autonomy of Korea, and, in consequence, the payment of tribute and the performance of ceremonies and formalities by Korea to China, in derogation of such independence and autonomy, shall wholly cease for the future.

ARTICLE 2

China cedes to Japan in perpetuity and full sovereignty the following territories, together with all fortifications, arsenals, and public property thereon:

(a) The southern portion of the province of Fêngtien [Fengtian] within the following boundaries [the Liao-dong agreement in November 1895 deleted this and replaced it with an indemnity of 30 million taels of silver to be paid Japan]:

The line of demarcation begins at the mouth of the River Yalu and ascends that stream to the mouth of the River An-ping [Anping], from thence the line runs to Fêng-huang [Fenghuang], from thence to Hai-cheng [Haizheng?], from thence to Ying-kow [Yinzhou?], forming a line which describes the southern portion of the territory. The places above named are included in the ceded territory. When the line reaches the River Liao at Ying-kow, it follows the course of the stream to its mouth, where it terminates. The mid-channel of the River Liao shall be taken as the line of demarcation.

This cession also includes all islands appertaining or belonging to the province of Fêngtien situated in the eastern portion of the Bay of Liao-tung and the northern portion of the Yellow Sea.

(b) The island of Formosa, together with all islands appertaining or belonging to the said island of Formosa.

(c) The Pescadores Group, that is to say, all islands lying between the 119th and 120th degrees of longitude east of Greenwich and the 23rd and 24th degrees of north latitude....

ARTICLE 4

China agrees to pay to Japan as a war indemnity the sum of 200,000,000 Kuping [Gubing] taels; the said sum to be paid in eight instalments. The first instalment of 50,000,000 taels to be paid within six months, and the second instalment of 50,000,000 to be paid within twelve months, after the exchange of the ratifications of this Act. The remaining sum to be paid in six equal instalments as follows: the first of such equal annual instalments to be paid within two years, the second within three years, the third within four years, the fourth within five years, the fifth within six years, and the the sixth within seven years, after the exchange of the ratifications of this Act. Interest at the rate of 5 per centum per annum shall begin to run on all unpaid portions of the said indemnity from the date the first instalment falls due.

China shall, however, have the right to pay by anticipation at any time any or all of the said instalments. In case the whole amount of the said indemnity is paid within three years after the exchange of the ratifications of the present Act all interest shall be waived, and the interest for two years and a half or for any less period, if any already paid, shall be included as part of the principal amount of the indemnity....

ARTICLE 6

All Treaties between Japan and China having come to an end as a consequence of war, China engages, immediately upon the exchange of the ratifications of this Act, to appoint Plenipotentiaries to conclude with the Japanese Plenipotentiaries, a Treaty of Commerce and Navigation and a Convention to regulate Frontier Intercourse and Trade. The Treaties, Conventions, and Regulations now subsisting between China and the European Powers shall serve as a basis for the said Treaty and Convention between Japan and China. From the date of the exchange of ratifications of this Act until the said Treaty and Convention are brought into actual operation, the Japanese Governments, its officials, commerce, navigation, frontier intercourse and trade, industries, ships, and subjects, shall in every respect be accorded by China most favoured nation treatment.

China makes, in addition, the following concessions, to take effect six months after the date of the present Act:

First.—The following cities, towns, and ports, in addition to those already opened, shall be opened to the trade, residence, industries, and manufactures of Japanese subjects, under the same conditions and with the same privileges and facilities as exist at the present open cities, towns, and ports of China:

- Shashih [Shashi], in the province of Hupeh [Hubei].

- Chungking [Chongqing], in the province of Szechwan [Sichuan].

- Suchow [Suzhou], in the province of Kiangsu [Jiangsu].

- Hangchow [Hangzhou], in the province of Chekiang [Zhejiang].

The Japanese Government shall have the right to station consuls at any or all of the above named places.

Second.—Steam navigation for vessels under the Japanese flag, for the conveyance of passengers and cargo, shall be extended to the following places:

- On the Upper Yangtze [Yangzi] River, from Ichang [Yichang] to Chungking [Chongqing].

- On the Woosung [Wusong] River and the Canal, from Shanghai to Suchow [Suzhou] and Hangchow [Hangzhou].

The rules and regulations that now govern the navigation of the inland waters of China by Foreign vessels shall, so far as applicable, be enforced, in respect to the above named routes, until new rules and regulations are conjointly agreed to.

Third.—Japanese subjects purchasing goods or produce in the interior of China, or transporting imported merchandise into the interior of China, shall have the right temporarily to rent or hire warehouses for the storage of the articles so purchased or transported without the payment of any taxes or extractions whatever.

Fourth.—Japanese subjects shall be free to engage in all kinds of manufacturing industries in all the open cities, towns, and ports of China, and shall be at liberty to import into China all kinds of machinery, paying only the stipulated import duties thereon.

All articles manufactured by Japanese subjects in China shall, in respect of inland transit and internal taxes, duties, charges, and exactions of all kinds, and also in respect of warehousing and storage facilities in the interior of China, stand upon the same footing and enjoy the same privileges and exemptions as merchandise imported by Japanese subjects into China.

In the event additional rules and regulations are necessary in connection with these concessions, they shall be embodied in the Treaty of Commerce and Navigation provided for by this Article....

ARTICLE 8

As a guarantee of the faithful performance of the stipulations of this Act, China consents to the temporary occupation by the military forces of Japan of Weihaiwei, in the province of Shantung [Shandong]. [Later in the same day, Japan and China agreed to the terms of the occupation.]

Upon payment of the first two installments of the war indemnity herein stipulated for and the exchange of the ratifications of the Treaty of Commerce and navigation, the said place shall be evacuated by the Japanese forces, provided the Chinese Government consents to pledge, under suitable and sufficient arrangements, the Customs revenue of China as security for the payment of the principal and interest of the remaining instalments of the said indemnity. In the event that no such arrangements are concluded, such evacuation shall only take place upon the payment of the final instalment of said indemnity.

It is, however, expressly understood that no such evacuation shall take place until after the exchange of the ratifications of the Treaty of Commerce and Navigation....

A BOXER DOGGEREL

SOURCE *Esherick, Joseph W. The Origins of the Boxer Uprising. Berkeley: University of California Press, 1987.*

INTRODUCTION *The following rhyme reflects the antiforeign sentiments of the Boxer movement. It attacks missionaries —devils—and their heretical beliefs, blaming them for the drought of that period and promising the use of magic powers to destroy all that was foreign in China. Although the movement was originally anti-Qing as well as antiforeign, by the time of the Boxer insurgence (1899–1900), which did indeed kill foreigners and destroy their property, it had pledged loyalty to the dynasty.*

Divinely aided Boxers,
United-in-Righteousness Corps
Arose because the Devils
Messed up the Empire of yore.

They proselytize their sect,
And believe in only one God,
The spirits and their own ancestors
Are not even given a nod.

Their men are all immoral;
Their women truly vile.
For the Devils it's mother-son sex
That serves as the breeding style.

And if you don't believe me,
Then have a careful view:
You'll see the Devils' eyes
Are all a shining blue.

No rain comes from Heaven.
The earth is parched and dry.
And all because the churches
Have bottled up the sky.

The god are very angry.
The spirits seek revenge.
En masse they come from Heaven
To teach the Way to men.

The Way is not a heresy;
It's not the White Lotus Sect.
The chants and spells we utter,
Follow mantras, true and correct.

Raise up the yellow charm,
Bow to the incense glow.
Invite the gods and spirits
Down from the mountain grotto.

Spirits emerge from the grottos;
Gods come down from the hills,
Possessing the bodies of men,
Transmitting their boxing skills.

When their martial and magic techniques
Are all learned by each one of you,
Suppressing the Foreign Devils
Will not be a tough thing to do.

Rip up the railroad tracks!
Pull down the telegraph lines!
Quickly! Hurry up! Smash them—
The boats and the steamship combines.

The mighty nation of France
Quivers in abject fear,
While from England, America, Russia
And from Germany nought do we hear.

When at last all the Foreign Devils
Are expelled to the very last man,
The Great Qing, united, together,
Will bring peace to this our land.

A BOXER EDICT, "ISSUED BY THE LORD OF WEALTH AND HAPPINESS"

SOURCE *Boxer handbill, issued by the "Lord of Wealth and Happiness." In O'Connor, Richard.* The Spirit Soldiers: A Historical Narrative of the Boxer Rebellion, *15–16. New York: G.P. Putnam's Sons, 1973.*

INTRODUCTION *The rapid spread of the Boxer movement in North China (1898–1900) can largely be attributed to antiforeign feeling inspired both by foreign military and political pressure on China and by the activities of missionaries in North China. The edict reprinted below outlines an undertaking to cleanse China of foreigners (thus restoring normal weather) and the promise of rewards for those who support for the Boxer movement.*

The Catholic and Protestant religions being insolent to the gods, and extinguishing sanctity, rendering no obedience to Buddha, and enraging Heaven and Earth, the rain clouds no longer visit us; but eight million Spirit Soldiers will descend from Heaven and sweep the Empire clean of all foreigners. Then will the gentle showers once more water our lands; and when the tread of soldiers and the clash of steel are heard heralding woes to all our people, then the Buddhist Patriotic League of Boxers will be able to protect the Empire and to bring peace to all its people. Hasten, then, to spread this doctrine far and wide, for if you gain one adherent to the faith your own person will be absolved from all future misfortunes. If you gain five adherents your whole family will be absolved from all future misfortunes, and if you gain ten adherents your whole village will be absolved from all calamities. Those who gain no adherents to the cause shall be decapitated, for until all foreigners have been exterminated the rain can never visit us.

"REVOLUTIONARY ARMY" TRACT

SOURCE *Tsou Jung (Zou Rong).* The Revolutionary Army: A Chinese Nationalist Tract of 1903. *Trans. John Lust. The Hague and Paris: Mouton, 1968.*

INTRODUCTION *Zou Rong was only eighteen when he wrote this widely distributed revolutionary tract in 1903. He died in prison just two years later. Zou advocated the establishment of a parliament, equal rights for women, freedom of speech and freedom of the press, but seems to have had little idea how all of this was to be achieved. The tract was characteristic of the revolutionary writing of the time in its passion and its anti-Manchu racism—rather shocking to modern sensibilities. The tract was taken up by Sun Yat-sen who distributed it in overseas Chinese communities.*

Revolution is the universal principle of evolution. Revolution is a universal principle of the world. Revolution is the essence of the struggle for survival or destruction in a time of transition. Revolution submits to heaven and responds to men's needs. Revolution rejects what is corrupt and keeps the good. Revolution is the advance from barbarism to civilization. Revolution turns slaves into masters. A man may have his own thoughts, ten men may have the thoughts of ten men, a thousand million men may have the thoughts of a thousand million men, a myriad of men may have the thoughts of a myriad of men. Nevertheless, even if each man has his own thoughts, there is not one who does not share these thoughts in common with the others. Dwellings, food, clothing, or utensils, whether good or bad, beautiful or ugly, are one and all buried deeply, and shift secretly, stir about in the bosom, clash in the brain, and lead to debate on what is good, what bad, what beautiful, what ugly. What is good is kept, what is not good is rejected, what is beautiful is kept, what is not beautiful is rejected, and the ultimate kernel of what should be kept and what rejected is precisely what emerges from revolution. Let us go a step further. If we take a panoramic view of things, above and below, ancient and modern, religion and ethics, politics and learning, we see on close examination that there is none which had not undergone weeding out by the process of evolution, and in the course of time appears as it is now. Since this is the case, revolution is an everyday thing. However, there are extraordinary ones, too. We have heard of the English revolution of 1688, the American revolution of 1775 and the French revolution of 1870, revolutions which submitted to heaven and responded to men's need, which removed the corrupt and kept what was good, which advanced from barbarism to civilization, and which turned slaves into masters. They sacrificed the individual to benefit the community, and they sacrificed the nobility to benefit the common people, so that everybody could enjoy equality and freedom. . . .

When I read the *Diary of Ten Days at Yangchow* and *Account of the Chiating Massacre*, my tears came spontaneously before I finished reading them. I speak out to proclaim to my fellowcountrymen: Were not the *Diary of Ten Days at Yangchow* and *Account of the Chiating Massacre* typical of the slaughter of Han which the Manchus perpetrated in every chou and hsien? These two books are merely one or two cases treated very briefly. If you think of those days, when troops were let loose, burning and plundering, when strict orders were issued to shave heads, and wherever the cavalry of the Manchu scoundrels reached there was murder and pillage (you can imagine that), what really took place must have amounted to ten times more than the two episodes of which accounts exist. For these two incidents which are known to everyone, there are a hundred thousand Yangchows and Chiatings. When I think of them, the iron enters my soul and I cannot hold back, I am impelled to proclaim this to my fellowcountrymen:

The *Diary of Ten Days at Yangchow* says: "On the second day of the month, we heard that officials were already functioning in *fu, tao, chou* and *hsien*, having with them pacification notices, and distributing everywhere edicts enjoining the population not to panic. Again, orders went out to temples and monasteries to cremate the heaped corpses. Moreover, women had hidden themselves there and some had died of fright or from starvation. From the registers of burned corpses it can be estimated that in not less that eight days over 800,000 were disposed of in this way, and the figure does not include those who threw themselves into wells or rivers, or locked their doors and (died by) fire or hanging."

I also say to my fellowcountrymen: When the Manchu scoundrels entered the Passes, were not those butchered by them the great great grandfathers of your great great grandfathers? Were they not the uncles of the great great grandfathers of your great great grandfathers? Were not those debauched by the Manchu scoundrels the wives, daughters or sisters of the great great grandfathers of your great great grandfathers? The *Book of Rites* says: "A (filial) son cannot live under the same sky with the murderer of his father and elder uncles." Even a child understands this. Hence, if as a son, you cannot revenge

your father and his elder brothers, you entrust this duty to your own sons, and your sons must entrust it to your grandchildren, and they to your great grandchildren and so to the fifth and seventh generations. Now, this feud of your great great grandfathers (*sic*) is now the feud of your fathers and their brothers today. If it is not avenged and yet you continue to speak of filial piety, I cannot see what you mean by piety. If the spirits of your great great grandfathers are still living, they surely will be unable to close their eyes in peace in the Nine Springs. . . .

If you want thoroughgoing construction, you must first have destruction. If you want thoroughgoing destruction, you must first have construction. This axiom has not changed since time immemorial. The revolution we are carrying out today is a revolution which will destroy in order to construct. However, if you wish to destroy you must first possess the means to construct. The great Italian leader Mazzini, founder of his country, once said finely: "Revolution and education go hand-in-hand together." I cry out in front of my fellowcountrymen: Revolutionary education, and I explain it further as follows: Before revolution there must be education, after revolution there must be education. . . .

Tseng Kuo-fan, Tso Tsung-t'ang and Li Hung-chang were granted posthumous titles of Wen-cheng, Wen-hsiang and Wen-chung by emperors of the Great Ch'ing dynasty. They were distinguished officials, honoured as the Three Statesmen of the T'ung-chih Revival, whom the man in the street respects as marquises and ministers of state, and about whom examination candidates and young people speculate and whom they revere. But I have heard that the German prime minister Bismarck upbraided Li Hung-chang with the words: "We Europeans regard it as a triumph to conquer foreign races. I have never heard that it is an achievement to butcher one's compatriots." If only I could bring back Tseng and Tso to listen to this. If only I could bring back the Tsengs and Tsos who lived before Tseng and Tso to listen to this. If only I could raise up the Tsengs and Tsos to come, those with full responsibility for affairs, and the mass of underlings who are not worth bothering about, so that they could all listen to this together. Tseng, Tso and Li flattered themselves over their scholarly attainments, and they saw themselves as the equal of sages and philosophers. But they were still inhumane and unscrupulous; they butchered their fellowcountrymen and they were the loyal and submissive slaves of the Manchus. It is not worth while continuing with this. I cannot find a comparison for them. I might compare them with Li Tzu-ch'eng and Chang Hsien-chung, but I despise them for being even worse. Li and Chang may have slaughtered their fellowcountrymen and led to the Manchus entering China as masters, but they were illiterate and ill-educated, and they were driven to it by the corrupt government of the Ming. There was nothing else they could do. For these reasons I can excuse them. Now Tseng, Tso and Li knew very well that they were members of the Han race, but to get hereditary rank for their families, they butchered their fellowcountrymen, and they begged the Manchus to rule again over China. I have tried over and over again to see their point of view, but I cannot find any excuses for them....

[I] am young, ignorant and brutish, not equal to speaking for the fundamental principles of revolutionary independence. Wary and fearful, I have carefully modelled (my proposals) on the principles of American revolutionary independence. I have summarized them under a number of headings, and with the utmost deference I offer to my most revered and beloved 400 million fellowcountrymen of the great Han people, to prepare them for the path they are to take:

- China is the China of the Chinese. Fellowcountrymen, you must all recognize the China of the Chinese of the Han race.

- Not to allow any alien race to lay their hands on the least rights of our China.

- Any obligations subordinating people to the Manchus are one and all annulled.

- First, to overthrow the barbaric government set up by the Manchus in Peking.

- To expel the Manchus settled in China or kill them in order to revenge ourselves.

- To kill the emperor set up by the Manchus as a warning to the myriad generations that despotic government is not to be revived.

- To oppose any intervention directed either by Chinese nationals or from foreign soil against Chinese revolutionary independence.

- To set up a central government, which will act as a general body to run affairs.

- In each area and province, a deputy to a general assembly is to be elected by vote in public elections. From these deputies, one is to be elected by vote to serve as provisional president to represent the whole country.

- A vice-president also is to be elected, and all *chou* and *hsien* are to elect a number of deputies.

- The whole population, whether male or female, are citizens.

- All men have the duty to serve as citizen soldiers.

- Everybody has the duty of bearing the burden of taxation.

- The whole country has the duty to show loyalty to the newly established state.

- Everybody in the country, whether male or female, is equal. There is no distinction between upper and lower, base or noble.

- All inalienable rights are bestowed by nature.

- The freedom to live and all other privileges are natural rights.

- Freedoms, such as that of speech, thought, the press, etc. cannot be infringed on.

- All rights must be defended. The government which must be set up by public agreement, must employ all the powers granted it purely to defend popular rights.

- If, at any time, the actions of a government lead to an infraction of people's rights, they have the right to carry out a revolution, and overthrow the old government to retrieve their peace and contentment.

Once these have been obtained, the question of rights must be publicly discussed and a new government set up. This also is to be a right of the people.

Once a government is set up, certain matters may arise which conflict with people's wishes and consequently they may wish to carry out a revolution, and there are continual changes as in an uncertain situation in chess. This is not the way to run a new state. The country cannot be entirely free from evils, but if one values above all things peace and tranquillity, and does not allow these evils to do great harm to the people, then rather than overthrow the existing government and attempt to extend their rights, (the maintenance of) tranquillity would be the best policy. But if elements in the government were to act continuously in a corrupt and tyrannical manner, and place the whole country under a despotic system, the people will rise and overthrow the government and establish a new one with the aim of keeping their rights intact. Surely this is the greatest right of a people, and the duty on which they place the greatest importance. We Chinese have undergone such hardships that we have come to the end of our tether. Today we are to obtain our revolutionary independence, yet we are still suffering under a despotic system, hence we should not be on any account be willing to resign ourselves to it. These are the reasons which make inevitable a change in the old regime.

- To settle the name of the country as the Republic of China.

- The Republic of China is a free and independent country.

- A free and independent state has full rights and equality with other great states in the matter of war and peace, treaties and trade, and all other matters pertaining to an independent state.

- The law of the constitution shall be modelled on American constitutional law, having regard to Chinese conditions.

- The law of self-government shall be modelled on the American law of self-government.

- Likewise in all matters of a national character, negotiations, the establishment of official departments and the determination of official duties in the state. American practice will remain a criterion.

TWENTY-ONE DEMANDS

SOURCE *King, Wunsz, comp.* V. K. Wellington Koo's Foreign Policy: Some Selected Documents, *87–90. Shanghai: Kelly and Walsh, 1931.*

INTRODUCTION *In this communication issued to China by the Japanese government in January 1915, Japan demanded extensive concessions such as wide-ranging economic rights in northeast China and Mongolia, the joint administration of the greatest iron, steel and coal enterprises in central China, new commercial rights in Fujian Province, and the right to station Japanese police and political advisers in North China. Yuan Shikai, China's president, felt that China was too weak to resist the demands. The furious anti-Japanese movement triggered by Yuan's acquiescence contributed ultimately to his downfall.*

I

The Japanese Government and the Chinese Government being desirous of maintaining the general peace in Eastern Asia and further strengthening the friendly relations and good neighbourhood existing between the two nations agree to the following articles:

ART. 1.—The Chinese Government engages to give full assent to all matters upon which the Japanese Government may hereafter agree with the German Government relating to the disposition, of all rights, interests and concessions which Germany, by virtue of treaties or otherwise, possesses in relation to the Province of Shantung.

ART. 2.—The Chinese Government engages that within the Province of Shantung and along its coast, no territory or island will be ceded or leased to a third Power under any pretext.

ART. 3.—The Chinese Government consents to Japan's building a railway from Chefoo or Lungkow to join the Kiaochow-Chinanfu Railway.

ART. 4.—The Chinese Government engages, in interest of trade and for the residence of foreigners, to open by herself as soon as possible certain important cities and towns in the Province of Shantung as Commercial Ports. What places shall be opened are to be jointly decided upon in a separate agreement.

II

The Japanese Government and the Chinese Government, since the Chinese Government has always acknowledged the special position enjoyed by Japan in South Manchuria and Eastern Inner Mongolia, agree to the following articles:

ART. 1.—The two Contracting Parties mutually agree that the term of lease of Port Arthur and Dalny and the term of lease of the South Manchurian Railway and the Antung-Mukden Railway shall be extended to the period of 99 years.

ART. 2.—Japanese subjects in South Manchuria and Eastern Inner Mongolia shall have the right to lease or own land required either for erecting suitable buildings for trade and manufacture or for farming.

ART. 3.—Japanese subjects shall be free to reside and travel in South Manchuria and Eastern Inner Mongolia and to engage in business and in manufacture of any kind whatsoever.

ART. 4.—The Chinese Government agrees to grant to Japanese subjects the right of opening the mines in South Manchuria and Eastern Inner Mongolia. As regards what mines are to be opened, they shall be decided upon jointly.

ART. 5.—The Chinese Government agrees that in respect of the (two) cases mentioned herein below the Japanese Government's consent shall be first obtained before action is taken:

1. Whenever permission is granted to the subject of a third Power to build a railway or to make a loan with a third Power for the purpose of building a railway in South Manchuria and Eastern Inner Mongolia.

2. Whenever a loan is to be made with a third Power pledging the local taxes of South Manchuria and Eastern Inner Mongolia as security.

ART. 6.—The Chinese Government agrees that if the Chinese Government employs political, financial or military advisers or instructors in South Manchuria or Eastern Inner Mongolia, the Japanese Government shall first be consulted.

ART. 7.—The Chinese Government agrees that the control and management of the Kirin-Changchun Railway shall be handed over to the Japanese Government for a term of 99 years dating from the signing of this agreement.

III

The Japanese Government and the Chinese Government, seeing that Japanese financiers and the Hanyehping Co. have close relations with each other at present and desiring that the common interests of the two nations shall be advanced, agree to the following articles:

ART. 1.—The two Contracting Parties mutually agree that when the opportune moment arrives the Hanyehping Company shall be made a joint concern of the two nations and they further agree that without the previous consent of Japan China shall not by her own act dispose of the rights and property of whatsoever nature of the said Company nor cause the said Company to dispose freely of the same.

ART. 2.—The Chinese Government agrees that all mines in the neighbourhood of those owned by the Hanyehping Company shall not be permitted, without the consent of the said Company, to be worked by other persons outside of the said Company; and further agrees that if it is desired to carry out any undertaking which, it is apprehended, may directly or indirectly affect the interests of the said Company, the consent of the said Company shall first be obtained.

IV

The Japanese Government and the Chinese Government with the object of effectively preserving the territorial integrity of China agree to the following special article:

The Chinese Government engages not to cede or lease to a third Power any harbour or bay or island along the coast of China.

V

ART. 1.—The Chinese Central Government shall employ influential Japanese as advisers in political, financial and military affairs.

ART. 2.—Japanese hospitals, churches and schools in the interior of China shall be granted the right of owning land.

ART. 3.—Inasmuch as the Japanese Government and the Chinese Government have had many cases of dispute between Japanese and Chinese police which caused no little misunderstanding, it is for this reason necessary that the police departments of important places (in China) shall be jointly administered by Japanese and Chinese or that the police departments of these places shall employ numerous Japanese, so that they may at the same time help to plan for the improvement of the Chinese Police Service.

ART. 4.—China shall purchase from Japan a fixed amount of munitions of war (say 50% or more of what is needed by the Chinese Government) or that there shall be established in China a Sino-Japanese jointly worked arsenal. Japanese technical experts are to be employed and Japanese material to be purchased.

ART. 5.—China agrees to grant to Japan the right of constructing a railway connecting Wuchang with Kiukiang and Nanchang, another line between Nanchang and Hangchow, and another between Nanchang and Chaochow.

ART. 6.—If China needs foreign capital to work mines, build railways and construct harbor-works (including dockyards) in the Province of Fukien, Japan shall be first consulted.

ART. 7.—China agrees that Japanese subjects shall have the right of missionary propaganda in China.

THE THREE PEOPLE'S PRINCIPLES

SOURCE *Sun Yat-sen. The Three People's Principles. In Sources of Chinese Tradition, Volume II: From 1600 through the Twentieth Century, 2nd edition, ed. William Theodore de Bary and Richard Lufrano, 321–323. New York: Columbia University Press, 2000.*

INTRODUCTION *Sun Yat-sen's Three People's Principles— Nationalism, People's Democracy and People's Livelihood—have long been claimed as guiding principles both by the Guomindang and by the Communist Party and had an important influence on political thought in twentieth-century China. Conceived around 1906 as part of the revolutionary ideology of the Tongmenghui (Revolutionary Alliance), the ideas were developed by Sun in a series of lectures in 1924. The notes taken from these lectures became the basis for subsequent understanding (and interpretations) of the Principles.*

[*China as a Heap of Loose Sand.*] For the most part the four hundred million people of China can be spoken of as completely Han Chinese. With common customs and habits, we are completely of one race. But in the world today what position do we occupy? Compared to the other peoples of the world we have the greatest population and our civilization is four thousand years old; we should therefore be advancing in the front rank with the nations of Europe and America. But the Chinese people have only family and clan solidarity; they do not have national spirit. Therefore, even though we have four hundred million people gathered together in one China, in reality they are just a heap of loose sand. Today we are the poorest and weakest nation in the world and occupy the lowest position in international affairs. Other men are the carving knife and serving dish; we are the fish and the meat. Our position at this time is most perilous. If we do not earnestly espouse nationalism and weld together our four hundred million people into a strong nation, there is danger of China's being lost and our people being destroyed. If we wish to avert this catastrophe, we must espouse nationalism and bring this national spirit to the salvation of the country....

[*China as a "Hypo-colony."*] Since the Chinese Revolution, the foreign powers have found that it was much less easy to use political force in carving up China. A people who had experienced Manchu oppression and learned to overthrow it would now, if the powers used political force to oppress it, be certain to resist, and thus make things difficult for them. For this reason they are letting up in their efforts to control China by political force and instead are using economic pressure to keep us down.... As regards political oppression, people are readily aware of their suffering, but when it comes to economic oppression, most often they are hardly conscious of it. China had already experienced several decades of economic oppression by the foreign powers, and so far the nation had for the most part shown no sense of irritation. As a consequence China is being transformed everywhere into a colony of the foreign powers.

Our people keep thinking that China is only a "semi-colony"—a term by which they seek to comfort themselves. Yet in reality the economic oppression we have endured is not just that of a "semi-colony" but greater even than that of a full colony.... Of what nation then is China a colony? It is the colony of every nation with which it has concluded treaties; each of them is China's master. Therefore China is not just the colony of one country; it is the colony of many countries. We are not just the slaves of one country, but the slaves of many countries. In the event of natural disasters like flood and drought, a nation that is sole master appropriates funds for relief and distributes them, thinking this its own duty; and the people who are its slaves regard this relief work as something to which their masters are obligated. But when North China suffered drought several years ago, the foreign powers did not regard it as their responsibility to appropriate funds and distribute relief; only those foreigners resident in China raised funds for the drought victims, whereupon Chinese observers remarked on the great generosity of the foreigners who bore no responsibility to help....

From this we can see that China is not so well off as Annam [under the French] and Korea [under the Japanese]. Being the slaves of one country represents a far higher status than being the slaves of many, and is far more advantageous. Therefore, to call China a "semi-colony" is quite incorrect. If I may coin a phrase, we should be called a "hypo-colony." This is a term that comes from chemistry, as in "hypo-phosphite." Among chemicals there are some belonging to the class of

phosphorous compounds but of lower grade, which are called phosphites. Still another grade lower, and they are called hypo-phosphites.... The Chinese people, believing they were a semi-colony, thought it shame enough; they did not realize that they were lower even than Annam or Korea. Therefore we cannot call ourselves a "semi-colony" but only a "hypo-colony"....

[*Nationalism and Cosmopolitanism.*] A new idea is emerging in England and Russia, proposed by the intellectuals, which opposes nationalism on the ground that it is narrow and illiberal. This is simply a doctrine of cosmopolitanism. England now and formerly Germany and Russia, together with the Chinese youth of today who preach the new civilization, support this doctrine and oppose nationalism. Often I hear young people say, "The Three Principles of the People do not fit in with the present world's new tendencies; the latest and best doctrine in the world is cosmopolitanism." But is cosmopolitanism really good or not?... Theoretically, we cannot say it is no good. Yet it is because formerly the Chinese intellectual class had cosmopolitan ideas that, when the Manchus crossed China's frontier, the whole country was lost to them....

[*Nationalism and Traditional Morality.*] If today we want to restore the standing of our people, we must first restore our national spirit.... If in the past our people have survived despite the fall of the state [to foreign conquerors], and not only survived themselves but been able to assimilate these foreign conquerors, it is because of the high level of our traditional morality. Therefore, if we go to the root of the matter, besides arousing a sense of national solidarity uniting all our people, we must recover and restore our characteristic, traditional morality. Only thus can we hope to attain again the distinctive position of our people.

This characteristic morality the Chinese people today have still not forgotten. First comes loyalty and filial piety, then humanity and love, faithfulness and duty, harmony and peace. Of these traditional virtues, the Chinese people still speak, but now, under foreign oppression, we have been invaded by a new culture, the force of which is felt all across the nation. Men wholly intoxicated by this new culture have thus begun to attack the traditional morality, saying that with the adoption of the new culture, we no longer have need of the old morality.... They say that when we formerly spoke of loyalty, it was loyalty to princes, but now in our democracy there are no princes, so loyalty is unnecessary and can be dispensed with. This kind of reasoning is certainly mistaken. In our country princes can be dispensed with, but not loyalty.... If indeed we can no longer speak of loyalty to princes, can we not, however, speak of loyalty to our people?

210

THE RESPONSIBILITIES OF CHINA'S YOUTH

SOURCE *Chiang Kai-shek. The Responsibilities of China's Youth. The Collected Wartime Messages of Generalissimo Chiang Kai-Shek, 1937–1945: Volume One, 1937–1940, compiled by Chinese Ministry of Information, 63–70. New York: Kraus Reprint Co., 1969.*

INTRODUCTION *The Guomindang or Three People's Principles Youth Corps was created in 1938 in the spirit of nationalist fervor generated by Japanese aggression. Chiang Kai-shek hoped that the Youth Corps would reinvigorate the Guomindang, which he felt was increasingly corrupt and ineffective. At the suggestion of Chiang's son, Jiang Jingguo, a Youth Corps leader, members were given equal status with Guomindang members. Chiang's ideology as reflected in this speech, mixed Sun Yat-sen–inspired nationalism in the political sphere with the Confucian revivalism of the New Life movement.*

An address to the youth of the whole nation on the occasion of the organization of the San Min Chu I *Youth Corps, June 16, 1938.*

The constitution of the *San Min Chu I* (Three Principles of the People) Youth Corps has already been drawn up, and the process of organization has now begun. As leader of the Party and State to whom, at this time of grave difficulty and peril, solemn responsibilities have been entrusted, I consider the launching of this new movement to be one of the most significant events in our long struggle for national survival. At the beginning, therefore, of its organization I wish to state clearly the meaning and the mission of the Youth Corps and what I expect from the beloved youth of our nation.

Youth are the vanguard of the Revolution; they are the new life of the nation. In every great social advance and in every important revolution youth have provided the driving power and have set the forces of change in motion. For example, in our own recent history, the chief participants in such movements as the Revolution of 1911 (which brought about the downfall of the Manchu dynasty) and the overthrow of the warlords in 1926–1927 were the nation's youth. The glorious history of their struggle and self-sacrifice will be a fragrant memory so long as there is a Republic of China. Today, when a ruthless enemy is invading and ravaging our country, when we have already resisted for a whole year and a new and momentous epoch is dawning in our history, we must look even more to the youth of the nation to unite and press forward as one body if we are to complete the stupendous task of Resistance and Reconstruction.

I am firmly convinced that China, with her long history, her vast territory, and her great population, will

most certainly win the victory and complete the task of reconstruction if she can concentrate her resources and continue the struggle without flinching. Resistance and Reconstruction is a necessary stage in the Revolution, and the Revolution will most certainly in the end be brought to a successful consummation. But how soon the consummation will take place depends entirely on the scale of our efforts, and on the spirit of those who carry on the fight.

As for me, I have given myself completely to the Party and the State, and long ago put all thoughts of personal success or failure out of my mind. I have always regarded the National Revolution as our permanent task, a task of stupendous importance and difficulty. Our youth, full of revolutionary spirit, who are now carrying on the tasks of the Revolution are precious as jewels to me. They are my very life. The countless number of revolutionary youths in our nation must join together to form one mighty body, and as one falls another must step up fearlessly and unwaveringly to take his place. Then we shall be able to carry our principles into effect; then we shall be able to protect the State, to revive the nation, and to reach the ultimate goal of our Revolution. Because of my intense hopes for the youth of China, I feel very keenly my responsibility for their future success or failure. The fate of China lies in their hands. The responsibility for organizing and training them to become worthy citizens of China, able to undertake the tasks of Resistance and Reconstruction, is mine; I cannot evade it. The Youth Corps has now been organized to fulfill this responsibility and to meet the urgent needs of our nation and society at the present time.

First, I want to state briefly the main reasons for the organization of the Youth Corps:

1. To complete the task of Resistance and Reconstruction. If we want to win the war and complete our reconstruction, we must develop the "vast resources of the nation" as a foundation on which to build. By developing the vast resources of the nation I mean awakening and uniting the youth of the whole nation. In the past the number of China's youth who fought and struggled sacrificially for the Revolution was by no means small. But now, because of disorganized education, the lack of habits of discipline, and the absence of training in group living, many youths, although patriotic in spirit, have not known how to express their patriotism in action. So a radical change is necessary. By strict teaching and discipline we must correct the bad habits of the past. We must give the young men and women of the nation training through the Youth Corps that will make them into modern citizens. We must eliminate the old ways of thinking and behavior, and in their place

cultivate the new independent spirit of a modern state, and a strong, self-reliant type of life. Within the Youth Corps there will naturally be different officers, some of higher rank than others, but it is essential that discipline be the same for everyone. Only thus will it be possible to bring about a real change in the daily living habits of our youth, and to direct their thoughts and actions toward a single goal. With a new national and racial consciousness they will be able to give vital expression to their patriotism and loyalty. Their work and influence will be powerfully effective, and they will lay strong foundations for our reviving national life.

2. To secure a concentration of fresh strength for the National Revolution. The strength of the Revolution has always lain in its emphasis upon unity. The forces latent in our youth, who have always been a dynamic source of revolutionary action, must now be united into one solid mass. The Youth Corps must give the nation's youth a single purpose and a thorough physical and mental training; it must develop their character through instruction in the Three Principles of the People, and guide their thoughts and actions, so that they may become the new blood continuing the Revolution. Now when the very existence of our nation is hanging by a thread, if we allow our youth to remain scattered and disorganized, each going his own way, they will have many conflicting purposes, their strength will be reduced and, when the crisis comes, they will all perish together. China's youth, therefore, in the difficult circumstances of this war and reconstruction period, must on no account follow the example of certain other nations and permit the existence and propagation of all sorts of different political beliefs and practices. We shall teach our youth fundamental political ideas—one philosophy of the State, one set of principles, and one direction of our efforts. There is but one road for the young men and women of China who would spend and be spent for their country, and that is the road of devoted loyalty and complete unity. This applies not merely to youths themselves but also to all educated leaders of youth. No matter what their party or group affiliation, they must, if they have at heart the welfare of the nation, lovingly lead our young men and women to unite under the banner of the Youth Movement. Let them do all they can to train our youth, and through them bring the Revolution to completion. Our fresh revolutionary strength will then be powerfully and continuously focused upon a single objective, and the great force thus created—by the fusing of many purposes into one—will not only drive out the Japanese invader and save our country, but will

prove to all future generations the spiritual unity of our nation.

3. To give concrete expression to the Three Principles of the People. The Three Principles, first enunciated by Dr. Sun Yat-sen, are the basis of our Revolution and National Reconstruction. They form the common faith of the whole nation during this War of Resistance. The reason why they are highly regarded is because they are practicable and meet China's real needs. But those who believe in the Three Principles must not be satisfied with mere belief; they must also feel it their responsibility to put the Principles into practice. Dr. Sun Yat-sen's philosophy was: "Knowing is difficult, but doing is easy." Therefore, he first taught the people new principles, and then spurred them on to action. This was just what was needed to correct the bad tendency of our people to fear difficulties and seek ease.

This Youth Corps must, by its own practice of the Three Principles, inspire all the nation's youth. Through its organization and training it must arouse courage and determination to overcome all obstacles and to carry out the Three Principles unswervingly to the end. No matter how difficult or dangerous the circumstances under which they live, no matter how dark their future may be, they must not for one moment despair or give up what has been committed to their charge. The young men and women of the Corps who believe in and practice the Three Principles must become new life-cells of the nation; they must be pioneers in the building of the new China; and worthy examples to all the people. This must go on until we see among the youth of the nation, organized and trained in the ideology and system of the Three Principles, an outburst of tremendously vital energy. If our revolutionary youth all believed in and practiced the Three Principles, we could be absolutely confident of their realization.

The purpose behind the creation of the Youth Corps has been stated. China today must complete her task of Resistance and Reconstruction; even more must she develop revolutionary strength to carry on the tasks that lie ahead. The great mission which the Youth Corps has undertaken on behalf of the State is twofold: the mobilization of the nation's youth for Resistance and Reconstruction, and the union of all the best revolutionary elements to increase the power of our Revolution. If we can fulfill these two missions, then the Three Principles can certainly be realized, the insults of the foreign invader can be blotted out, and a new, free, and independent China can be brought into being. On the one hand, we should meet the urgent needs of wartime mobilization; on the other hand, we should train a staff of workers that will be able in the near future to direct our national and social reconstruction. If we are to carry out this great and hard task, we must expect all the youth who join the Corps to be orderly, dignified, sincere, and single-minded, and to take upon themselves the following special responsibilities:

Wartime Mobilization

In accordance with the plans for total mobilization, our youth must take an active part according to their individual abilities in national defense, production, communications, propaganda, or educational work. They must be public spirited and obedient to law; they must carry out their duties with the utmost loyalty; they must be willing to undergo toil and hardship without seeking ease or rest. They must look upon struggle as their heaven sent lot and accept sacrifice a matter of course. If our youth all have this spirit, then our War of Resistance will unquestionably end in victory.

Military Training

While the war is on, all our youth should receive strict military training. Every member of the Youth Corps will then have the necessary skills to help in the defense of his country. This military training should include training in morale, devotion to country and loyalty to Party, physical training so as to make them strong and healthy, training for life that will enable them to undergo toil and hardship, and training in action that will teach them to do things quickly and accurately. When our youth have had this kind of education, they will get rid of the decadent idea and custom that a scholar must be weak in body; they will go on to influence society; and they will be able, because of the spirit inspired by this military discipline, to carry all our reconstruction forward to completion.

Political Training

All our youth should receive political training, so that they may have some basic knowledge of how to set up the government of a state based on the Three Principles of the People. They should know how the "four powers of government" (executive, legislative, judicial, and the power of impeachment) are to be exercised, how local autonomy works, and other important points. They should know the first steps in training for self-government, and understand the fundamental methods of controlling, organizing, and leading the masses. If our youths are to have in the realm of thought real faith in the Three Principles, and in the realm of action are to make wise use of the rights of citizens in a modern democratic state, such knowledge is essential. Upon it we can build the new China "of, by, and for the people."

Cultural Reconstruction

The strength of a nation is dependent on the cultural standard of the mass of the people. Now the degree of knowledge possessed by the bulk of our people is far inferior to that of the people of the Great Powers. Our educated youth must, therefore, take the initiative, and participate in the task of eliminating illiteracy, and of making popular education a reality. They should also help in wartime propaganda. We must, in as short a time as possible, improve the political knowledge of the ordinary people, and raise their cultural standard, so that our nation may be able to advance along the road to liberty and equality in the modern world.

Hard Work and Service

Our youth must grasp the significance of Dr. Sun's final message that "the purpose of life lies in service." Each week everyone should participate in at least ten hours of some form of productive social service. On the one hand, they will help to increase production and improve the nation's financial position, and on the other, they will, through such service, win their way into the hearts of the people and appreciate fully their sufferings. By mixing with the people, and by their actual work and accomplishments, they will win the confidence of all their fellow-countrymen.

Production

Our young people must pay special attention to scientific training, and make their knowledge and actions scientific. In this way a new type of national character—systematic and methodical, accurate and practical—will be developed. It is even more necessary for youth to make every effort to secure technical training, and so acquire productive skills and the habit of hard work. Then a large number will be available for service in agriculture, commerce, communications, mining, electrical work, and all kinds of light and heavy industries. This will hasten the completion of our great program of national reconstruction.

These are the responsibilities which the Youth Corps must energetically take up now and in the future. They may also be regarded as a covenant to which all the youth of our Revolution should subscribe. But if we want to accomplish this task, our youth must get rid of their old habits, and stir themselves to new action; they must show fresh vitality, and radically reform their mode of life. They must not merely limit their enjoyments and adopt a Spartan regime but they must also cultivate habits of orderliness, cleanliness, simplicity, frankness, quickness, and accuracy. They must eliminate such bad habits as disorderly behavior, uncleanliness, diffuse activity, extravagance, dilatoriness, and superficiality, and through their new life of hard work and real economy help to reform the customs of society. Then all the people of China, inspired by the discipline, obedience, and corporate spirit of our youth, will march together to become a modern nation.

To sum up, the Youth Corps aims to bring together the best youths of the whole nation, whether soldiers, laborers, farmers, merchants, or students, and to give them systematic training. It aims also to unite these youths in one organization, and to subject them to the rules of the New Life Movement, so that as they come to understand the four great virtues—propriety, justice, integrity, and conscientiousness—which are the fundamentals of a modern state, they may combine their strength and wisdom, and with one heart and one mind shoulder responsibility, observe the rules of discipline, and lay the foundation of a new modern state based on the *San Min Chu I*. The Youth Corps was established not to solve the livelihood problems of individuals, but to solve our national problems through the offering by youth of their life, strength and freedom to the service of the State. It was set up, not to enable our youth to live lives of ease and pleasure, but in order that they might share their joys and sorrows, their difficulties and dangers, and accomplish together our task of Resistance and Reconstruction, thus making the Three Principles a living reality.

China's humiliation and danger have now reached the extreme limit. Our vast territory with its rivers and its mountains, its valleys and its steppes, has everywhere been overrun by our enemy. Our nation, with its long history stretching back through five thousand years, today faces a crisis that will decide its survival or its destruction. The sacrifice of countless revolutionary heroes and of the soldiers who are dying today for their country—their red blood and bleached bones—cries out to the youth of the nation to continue the struggle and complete their task. We must courageously face our past failure to lead and train our youth, and earnestly strive now to create a practical revolutionary organization for them all. To meet the immediate pressing needs of our State and people, we must make this an organization that will include the flower of our youth, the keenest and best young revolutionists in the nation. I am confident that our great host of young men and women, filled with the spirit of the Revolution and recognizing clearly their responsibility for the future of the nation, will rouse themselves to vigorous action. Let our youth unite in the Youth Corps, obey its discipline and commands, receive its training and guidance. Thus they will enhance the value of the Youth Corps to the State and enable it to complete its great and sacred mission. I, who have been entrusted with heavy responsibilities by the Party and the State, say again to my young friends throughout the nation that they must unite. They must be willing to live and suffer and, if need be, die together. This is the only way to attain our goal of a new and glorious China. Descendants of Hwang Ti, Youth of China, arise!

HOW TO BE A GOOD COMMUNIST

SOURCE *Liu Shaoqi. How to Be a Good Communist. In* Sources of Chinese Tradition, Volume II: From 1600 through the Twentieth Century, *2nd edition, ed. William Theodore de Bary and Richard Lufrano, 427–432. New York: Columbia University Press, 2000.*

INTRODUCTION *Liu Shaoqi, a veteran Communist who joined the party in 1921, wrote "How to Be a Good Communist" as a series of lectures delivered in Yan'an in July 1939. The essay was widely read among Communist cadres in the 1940s and 1950s. A revised text was reprinted as material for political study in 1962 but was heavily criticized when Liu came under attack during the Cultural Revolution. He died in prison in 1969. How to Be a Good Communist emphasizes the idea of self-cultivation (a concept drawn partly from Confucian tradition) but also focuses on the use of criticism and self-criticism and on submission to party discipline.*

Comrades! In order to become the most faithful and best pupils of Marx, Engels, Lenin, and Stalin, we need to carry on cultivation in all aspects in the masses of the people. We need to carry on cultivation in the theories of Marxism-Leninism and in applying such theories in practice; cultivation in revolutionary strategy and tactics; cultivation in studying and dealing with various problems according to the standpoint and methods of Marxism-Leninism; cultivation in ideology and moral character; cultivation in party unity, inner-party struggle, and discipline; cultivation in hard work and in the style of work; cultivation in being skillful in dealing with different kinds of people and in associating with the masses of the people; and cultivation in various kinds of scientific knowledge, and so on. We are all Communist Party members, and so we have a general cultivation in common. But there exists a wide discrepancy today among our party members. Wide discrepancy exists among us in the level of political consciousness, in work, in position, in cultural level, in experience of struggle, and in social origin. Therefore, in addition to cultivation in general, we also need special cultivation for different groups and for individual comrades.

Accordingly, there should be different kinds of methods and forms of cultivation. For example, many of our comrades keep a diary in order to have a daily check on their work and thoughts, or they write down on small posters their personal defects and what they hope to achieve and put them up where they work or live, together with the photographs of persons they look up to, and ask comrades for criticism and supervision. In ancient China, there were many methods of cultivation. There was Zengzi, who said,

"I reflect on myself three times a day." The *Book of Odes* has it that one should cultivate oneself "as a lapidary cuts and files, carves and polishes." Another method was "to examine oneself by self-reflection" and to "write down some mottoes on the right-hand side of one's desk" or "on one's girdle" as daily reminders of rules of personal conduct. The Chinese scholars of the Confucian school had a number of methods for the cultivation of their body and mind. Every religion has various methods and forms of cultivation of its own. The "investigation of things, the extension of knowledge, sincerity of thought, the rectification of the heart, the cultivation of the person, the regulation of the family, the ordering well of the state and the making tranquil of the whole kingdom" as set forth in the *Great Learning* also means the same. All this shows that in achieving one's progress one must make serious and energetic efforts to carry on self-cultivation and study. However, many of these methods and forms cannot be adopted by us because most of them are idealistic, formalistic, abstract, and divorced from social practice. These scholars and religious believers exaggerate the function of subjective initiative, thinking that so long as they keep their general "good intentions" and are devoted to silent prayer they will be able to change the existing state of affairs, change society, and change themselves under conditions separated from social and revolutionary practice. This is, of course, absurd. We cannot cultivate ourselves in this way. We are materialists, and our cultivation cannot be separated from practice.

What is important to us is that we must not under any circumstances isolate ourselves from the revolutionary struggles of different kinds of people and in different forms at a given moment and that we must, moreover, sum up historical revolutionary experience and learn humbly from this and put it into practice. That is to say, we must undertake self-cultivation and steel ourselves in the course of our own practice, basing ourselves on the experiences of past revolutionary practice, on the present concrete situation, and on new experiences. Our self-cultivation and steeling are for no other purpose than that of revolutionary practice. That is to say, we must modestly try to understand the standpoint, the method, and the spirit of Marxism-Leninism, and understand how Marx, Engels, Lenin, and Stalin dealt with people. And having understood these, we should immediately apply them to our own practice, i.e., in our own lives, words, deeds, and work. Moreover, we should stick to them and unreservedly correct and purge everything in our ideology that runs counter to them, thereby strengthening our own proletarian and Communist ideology and qualities.... At the same time, we must find out in what respects specific conclusions of Marxism-Leninism need to be supplemented, enriched, and developed on the basis of well-digested new experiences. That is to say, we must combine the universal truth of Marxism-Leninism with the concrete practice of the revolution....

First of all, we must oppose and resolutely eliminate one of the biggest evils bequeathed to us by the education and learning in the old society—the separation of theory from practice.... Despite the fact that many people read over and over again books by ancient sages, they did things the sages would have been loath to do. Despite the fact that in everything they wrote or said they preached righteousness and morality, they acted like out-and-out robbers and harlots in everything they did. Some "high-ranking officials" issued orders for the reading of the Four Books and the Five Classics, yet in their everyday administrative work they ruthlessly extorted exorbitant requisitions, ran amuck with corruption and killing, and did everything against righteousness and morality. Some people read the *Three People's Principles* over and over again and could recite the *Will of Dr. Sun Yat-sen*, yet they oppressed the people, opposed the nations who treated us on an equal footing, and went so far as to compromise with or surrender to the national enemy. Once a scholar of the old school told me himself that the only maxim of Confucius that he could observe was "To him food can never be too dainty; minced meat can never be too fine," adding that all the rest of the teachings of Confucius he could not observe and had never proposed to observe. Then why did they still want to carry on educational work and study the teachings of the sages? Apart from utilizing them for window-dressing purposes, their objects were (1) to make use of these teachings to oppress the exploited and make use of righteousness and morality for the purpose of hoodwinking and suppressing the culturally backward people; (2) to attempt thereby to secure better government jobs, make money and achieve fame, and reflect credit on their parents. Apart from these objects, their actions were not restricted by the sages teachings. This was the attitude of the "men of letters" and "scholars" of the old society to the sages they "worshiped." Of course we Communist Party members cannot adopt such an attitude in studying Marxism-Leninism and the excellent and useful teachings bequeathed to us by our ancient sages. We must live up to what we say. We are honest and pure and we cannot deceive ourselves, the people, or our forefathers. This is an outstanding characteristic as well as a great merit of us Communist Party members....

What is the most fundamental and common duty of us Communist Party members? As everybody knows, it is to establish communism, to transform the present world into a Communist world. Is a Communist world good or not? We all know that it is very good. In such a world there will be no exploiters, oppressors, landlords, capitalists, imperialists, or fascists. There will be no oppressed and exploited people, no darkness, ignorance, backwardness, and so on. In such a society, all human beings will become unselfish and intelligent Communists with a high level of culture and technique. The spirit of mutual assistance and mutual love will prevail among mankind. There will be no such irrational things as mutual deception, mutual antagonism, mutual slaughter and war, and so on. Such a society will, of course, be the best, the most beautiful, and the most advanced society in the history of mankind.... Here the question arises: Can Communist society be brought about? Our answer is "yes." About this, the whole theory of Marxism-Leninism offers a scientific explanation that leaves no room for doubt.... The victory of socialism in the USSR has also given us factual proof. Our duty is, therefore, to bring about at an early date this Communist society, the realization of which is inevitable in the history of mankind....

At all times and on all questions, a Communist Party member should take into account the interests of the party as a whole and place the party's interests above his personal problems and interests. It is the highest principle of our party members that the Party's interests are supreme....

If a party member has only the interests and aims of the Party and communism in his ideology, if he has no personal aims and considerations independent of the Party's interests, and if he is really unbiased and unselfish, then he will be capable of the following:

1. He will be capable of possessing very good Communist ethics. Because he has a firm outlook, he "can both love and hate people." He can show loyalty to and ardent love for all his comrades, revolutionaries, and working people, help them unconditionally, treat them with equality, and never harm any one of them for the sake of his own interest. He can deal with them in a "faithful and forgiving" spirit and "put himself in the position of others." He can consider others' problems from their points of view and be considerate to them. "He will never do to others anything he would not like others to do to him." He can deal with the most vicious enemies of mankind in a most resolute manner and conduct a persistent struggle against the enemy for the purpose of defending the interests of the party, the class, and the emancipation of mankind. As the Chinese saying goes, "He will worry long before the rest of the world begins to worry, and he will rejoice only after the rest of the world has rejoiced." Both in the Party and among the people he will be the first to suffer hardship and the last to enjoy himself. He never minds whether his conditions are better or worse than others', but he does mind as to whether he has done more revolutionary work than others or whether he has fought harder. In times of adversity, he will stand out courageously and unflinchingly,

and in the face of difficulties he will demonstrate the greatest sense of responsibility. Therefore, he is capable of possessing the greatest firmness and moral courage to resist corruption by riches or honors, to resist tendencies to vacillate in spite of poverty and lowly status, and to refuse to yield in spite of threats or force.

2. He will also be capable of possessing the greatest courage. Since he is free from any selfishness whatever and has never done "anything against his conscience," he can expose his mistakes and shortcomings and boldly correct them in the same way as the sun and the moon emerge bright and full following a brief eclipse. He is "courageous because his is a just cause." He is never afraid of truth. He courageously upholds truth, expounds truth to others, and fights for truth....

3. He will be best capable of acquiring the theory and method of Marxism-Leninism, viewing problems, and perceiving the real nature of the situation keenly and aptly. Because he has a firm and clear-cut class standpoint, he is free from personal worries and personal desires that may blur or distort his observation of things and understanding of truth.

4. He will also be capable of being the most sincere, most candid, and happiest of men. Since he has no selfish desires and since he has nothing to conceal from the Party, "there is nothing that he is afraid of telling others," as the Chinese saying goes. Apart from the interests of the Party and of the revolution, he has no personal losses or gains or other things to worry about.... His work will be found in no way incompatible with the Party's interests no matter how many years later it is reviewed. He does not fear criticism from others, and he can courageously and sincerely criticize others. That is why he can be sincere, candid, and happy.

5. He will be capable of possessing the highest self-respect and self-esteem. For the interests of the Party and of the revolution, he can also be the most lenient, most tolerant, and most ready to compromise, and he will even endure, if necessary, various forms of humiliation and injustice without feeling hurt or bearing grudges.... But if for the sake of certain important aims of the Party and of the revolution he is required to endure insults, shoulder heavy burdens, and do work that he is reluctant to do, he will take up the most difficult and important work without the slightest hesitation and will not pass the buck.

A Communist Party member should possess all the greatest and noblest virtues of mankind.... Such ethics are not built upon the backward basis of safeguarding the interests of individuals or a small number of exploiters. They are built, on the contrary, upon the progressive basis of the interest of the proletariat, of the ultimate emancipation of mankind as a whole, of saving the world from destruction and of building a happy and beautiful Communist world.

ON ART AND LITERATURE

SOURCE *Mao Zedong. On Art and Literature. In* Sources of Chinese Tradition, Volume II: From 1600 through the Twentieth Century, *2nd edition, ed. William Theodore de Bary and Richard Lufrano, 441–444. New York: Columbia University Press, 2000.*

INTRODUCTION *Mao's 1942 speech, later published in his* Selected Works *as "Talks at the Yan'an Forum on Literature and Art," was for many years used as the ideological guide to what was correct in the arts and as a basis for criticizing writers and artists. Although conceding that art should be more than mere propaganda, Mao insisted that it must have as its purpose to serve the revolution and to awaken and arouse the masses.*

Comrades! We have met three times during this month. In the pursuit of truth, heated debates have taken place and scores of Party and non-Party comrades have spoken, laying bare the issues and making them concrete. I think this is very profitable to the whole artistic and literary movement.

In discussing any problem we should start from actual facts and not from definitions. We shall be following the wrong method if we first look up definitions of art and literature in the textbooks and then use them as criteria in determining the direction of the present artistic and literary movement or in judging the views and controversies that arise today.

What, then, is the crux of our problems? I think our problems are basically those of working for the masses and of how to work for them. If these two problems are not solved, or [are] solved inadequately, our artists and writers will be ill-adapted to their circumstances and unfit for their tasks and will come up against a series of problems from within and without. My conclusion will center round these two problems, while touching upon some other problems related to them.

I

The first problem is: For whom are our art and literature intended?

This problem has, as a matter of fact, been solved long ago by Marxists, and our art and literature should "serve the millions upon millions of working people". . . .

II

The question of "whom to serve" having been solved, the question of "how to serve" comes up. To put it in the words of our comrades: Should we devote ourselves to elevation or to popularization? . . .

Though man's social life constitutes the only source for art and literature, and is incomparably more vivid and richer than art and literature as such, the people are not satisfied with the former alone and demand the latter. Why? Because although both are beautiful, life as reflected in artistic works can and ought to be on a higher level and of a greater power and better focused, more typical, nearer the ideal, and therefore more universal than actual everyday life. Revolutionary art and literature should create all kinds of characters on the basis of actual life and help the masses to push history forward. For example, on the one hand there are people suffering from hunger, cold, and oppression, and on the other hand there are men exploiting and oppressing men—a contrast that exists everywhere and seems quite commonplace to people; artists and writers, however, can create art and literature out of such daily occurrences by organizing them, bringing them to a focal point, and making the contradictions and struggles in them typical—create art and literature that can awaken and arouse the masses and impel them to unite and struggle to change their environment. If there were no such art and literature, this task could not be fulfilled or at least not effectively and speedily fulfilled.

What are popularization and elevation in art and literature? What is the relation between the two? Works of popularization are simpler and plainer and therefore more readily accepted by the broad masses of the people of today. Works of a higher level are more polished and therefore more difficult to produce and less likely to win the ready acceptance of the broad masses of people of today. The problem facing the workers, peasants, and soldiers today is this: engaged in a ruthless and sanguinary struggle against the enemy, they remain illiterate and uncultured as a result of the prolonged rule of the feudal and bourgeois classes, and consequently they badly need a widespread campaign of enlightenment, and they eagerly wish to have culture, knowledge, art, and literature that meet their immediate need and are readily acceptable to them so as to heighten their passion for struggle and their confidence in victory, to strengthen their solidarity, and thus to enable them to fight the enemy with one heart and one mind.

But popularization and elevation cannot be sharply separated. . . . The people need popularization, but along with it they need elevation too, elevation month by month and year by year. Popularization is popularization for the people, and elevation is elevation of the people. Such elevation does not take place in midair, nor behind closed doors, but on the basis of popularization. It is at once determined by popularization and gives direction to it. . . .

Besides the elevation that directly meets the need of the masses, there is the elevation that meets their need indirectly, namely, the elevation needed by the cadres. Being advanced members of the masses, the cadres are generally better educated than the masses, and art and literature of a higher level are entirely necessary to them; and it would be a mistake to ignore this. Anything done for the cadres is also entirely done for the masses, because it is only through the cadres that we can give education and guidance to the masses. . . .

III

One of the principal methods of struggle in the artistic and literary sphere is art and literary criticism. . . .

There are two criteria in art and literary criticism: political and artistic. According to the political criterion, all works are good that facilitate unity and resistance to Japan, that encourage the masses to be of one heart and one mind, and that oppose retrogression and promote progress; on the other hand, all works are bad that undermine unity and resistance to Japan, that sow dissension and discord among the masses, and that oppose progress and drag the people back. And how can we tell the good from the bad here — by the motive (subjective intention) or by the effect (social practice)? Idealists stress motive and ignore effect, while mechanical materialists stress effect and ignore motive; in contradistinction from either, we dialectical materialists insist on the unity of motive and effect of winning their approval, and we must unite the two. . . . In examining the subjective intention of an artist, i.e., whether his motive is correct and good, we do not look at his declaration but at the effect his activities (mainly his works) produce on society and the masses. Social practice and its effect are the criteria for examining the subjective intention or the motive. . . . According to the artistic criterion, all works are good or comparatively good that are relatively high in artistic quality and bad or comparatively bad that are relatively low in artistic quality. Of course, this distinction also depends on social effect. As there is hardly an artist who does not consider his own work excellent, our criticism ought to permit the free competition of all varieties of artistic works, but it is entirely necessary for us to pass correct judgments on them according to the criteria of the science of art, so that we can gradually raise the art of a lower level to a higher level, and to change the art that does not meet the requirements of the struggle of the broad masses into art that does meet them.

There is thus the political criterion as well as the artistic criterion. . . . But criterion second. The bourgeoisie always reject proletarian artistic and literary works, no matter how great their artistic achievement. As for the proletariat, they must treat the art and literature of the past

according to their attitude toward the people and whether they are progressive in the light of history. Some things that are basically reactionary from the political point of view may yet be artistically good. But the more artistic such a work may be, the greater harm will it do to the people, and the more reason for us to reject it. The contradiction between reactionary political content and artistic form is a common characteristic of the art and literature of all exploiting classes in their decline. What we demand is unity of politics and art, of content and form and of revolutionary political content and the highest possible degree of perfection in artistic form. Works of art, however politically progressive, are powerless if they lack artistic quality. Therefore we are equally opposed to works with wrong political approaches and to the tendency toward so-called poster and slogan style that is correct only in political approach but lacks artistic power. We must carry on a two-front struggle in art and literature.

CHINA'S DESTINY

SOURCE *Chiang Kai-shek. China's Destiny. Trans. Wang Chung-hui. In* Sources of Chinese Tradition, Volume II: From 1600 through the Twentieth Century, *2nd edition, ed. William Theodore de Bary and Richard Lufrano, 344–347. New York: Columbia University Press, 2000.*

INTRODUCTION *This nationalistic anti-imperialist treatise by Chiang Kai-shek blamed all China's ills on the unequal treaties. Issued during the war (March 1943) when morale was low, its authoritarian tone and advocacy of the revival of ancient Confucian virtues did not meet with much welcome. It was, however, made required reading in schools and Guomindang circles.*

SOCIAL EFFECTS [OF THE UNEQUAL TREATIES]

During the last hundred years, under the oppression of unequal treaties, the life of the Chinese people became more and more degenerate. Everyone took self-interest as the standard of right and wrong, and personal desires as the criterion of good and evil; a thing was considered right if it conformed to one's self-interest or good if it conformed to one's personal desires. Rascals became influential in the villages, rogues were active in the cities, sacrificing public safety and the welfare of others to satisfy their own interest and desires. In the meantime, extravagant and irresponsible ideologies and political doctrines were freely advanced, either to rationalize self-interest and personal desires or to exploit them for ulterior motives. The rationalizers idolized them as an expression of the self, and the exploiters utilized them as a means of fomenting disturbances in the community, in order to fish in troubled waters. The practice of following in the footsteps of the sages or emulating the heroes and being "friends with the ancients" not only tended to disappear but was even considered mean and despicable. . . .

MORAL EFFECTS

For five thousand years China had always stressed the importance of honest work and frugality. Her people were noted for their simplicity in food and clothing; women occupied themselves with their looms and men with their plows. These good habits, however, were swept away by the prevalence in the [foreign] concessions of the vices of opium smoking, gambling, prostitution, and robbery.

China's ancient ethical teachings and philosophies contained detailed and carefully worked out principles and rules for the regulation and maintenance of the social life of man. The structure of our society underwent many changes, but our social life never deviated from the principles governing the relationship between parent and child, husband and wife, brother and brother, friend and friend, superior and inferior, man and woman, old and young, as well as principles enjoining mutual help among neighbors and care of the sick and weak.

During the past hundred years, wherever the influence of the foreign concessions was felt, these principles were not only neglected but also despised. Between parent and child, husband and wife, brothers and friends, superiors and inferiors, old and young, and among neighbors the old sentiments of respect and affection and the spirit of mutual help and cooperation were disappearing. Only material interests were taken into consideration, and everywhere there was a general lack of moral standards by which to judge oneself. Whenever duty called, people tried to shirk it; whenever there was material profit to be gained, they struggled for it. . . . A country that had hitherto attached the greatest importance to decorum and rightness was now in danger of losing its sense of integrity and honor. What harm these unequal treaties had caused!

The deterioration of national morality also tended to affect the physique of our people. The physical strength of the numberless unemployed in the cities as easily impaired. The health of those merchants who abandoned themselves to a life of extravagance and dissoluteness could not but break down. The most serious thing, however, was the effect upon the health of the youth in the schools. Physical training was not popularized in most of the schools; moral education was also neglected by school masters and teachers. In the meantime, the extravagant and dissolute life outside the school attracted the students caused them to indulge in evil habits, and resulted in the deterioration of their moral character. Infectious and venereal diseases, too, which were rampant in the cities, further undermined their physical constitution. How could these young men, who were unsound in body and mind, help to advance learning reform social customs, render service to the state, and promote enterprise after their graduation? The inevitable result of such a state of affairs was the steady disintegration of our country and the further demoralization of the Chinese nation. . . .

PSYCHOLOGICAL EFFECTS

After the Student Movement of May 4, 1919, two currents of thought, ultra individualistic liberalism and class-struggle communism, found their way into Chinese academic circles and later became widespread in the country. On the whole, Chinese academic circles desired to effect a change in our culture, forgetting that it had certain elements that are immutable. With respect to different Western theories they imitated only their superficial aspects and never sought to understand their true significance in order to improve China's national life. The result was that a large number of our scholars and students adopted the superficialities and nonessentials of Western culture and lost the respect for and confidence in our own culture. . . .

THE DECISIVE FACTOR IN CHINA'S DESTINY

The work of reforming social life and carrying out the program of national reconstruction is one of paramount importance in the process of national survival—a task that requires persistent effort. Individuals, striving singly, will not achieve great results nor lasting accomplishments. Consequently, all adult citizens and promising youths, whether in a town, a district, a province, or in the country at large, should have a common organization, with a systematic plan for binding the members together and headquarters to promote joint record reconstruction activities and also personal accomplishments. . . .

In the past our adult citizens have been unable to unite on a large scale or for a long period. They have been derisively compared to "a heap of loose sand" or spoken of as having "only five minutes' enthusiasm." Now, incapacity to unite is a result of selfishness, and the best antidote for selfishness is public spirit. That unity does not last is due to hypocrisy and the best antidote for hypocrisy is sincerity. With a public spirit, one can take "all men as one's kin and all things as one's company." With sincerity, one can persevere and success in the end. . . .

The principal fault of our youth today and the cause of their failure and ineffectual living lie essentially in the unsound education they have received.

Since they do not follow the guidance of their teachers or realize the importance of organization as a factor in the success or failure of their life, and since they do not understand what freedom and discipline mean, they are irresponsible in their conduct and unrealistic in their thinking. As soon as they enter society, they feel the lack of ability and confidence to take up any practical work, let done the task of social and national reconstruction....

To avoid the mistake of living a misguided and regrettable life, they should never again allow themselves to be led astray by blind and impulsive following of others in the past. We must realize that the Three Principles represent not only the crystallization of China's time-honored civilization and of her people's highest virtues but also the inevitable trend of world affairs in this modern age. The San Min Zhu Yi Youth Corps is the central organization of all Chinese youths who are faithful adherents of the Three Principles. All young men and women must therefore place themselves under the guidance of the Corps in order to keep their aims true and to avoid doing harm to themselves and to the nation. It is only by working within the framework of the Corps' program that they can make decisions about their life work in the right direction.... It will be their mission to save the country from decline and disorganization, to wipe out national humiliation, to restore national strength, and to show loyalty to the state and filial devotion to the nation. They should emulate the sages and heroes of history and be the lifeblood of the people and the backbone of the nation.

To sum up, the Nationalist Party and the San Min Zhu Yi Youth Corps are organic parts of the nation.... Considering the state as an organism as far as its life is concerned, we may say that the Three Principles constitute the soul of our nation, because without these principles our national reconstruction should be deprived of its guiding spirit.... Without the Nationalist Party, China should be deprived of its pivot. If all the revolutionary elements and promising youths in the country really want to throw in their lot with the fate of the country, if they regard national undertakings as their own undertakings and the national life as their own life—then they should all enlist in the party or the Youth Corps. By so doing, they can discharge the highest duties of citizenship and attain the highest ideal in life. Then and only then can our great mission of national reconstruction be completed.

CAIRO DECLARATION, 1943

INTRODUCTION *The Cairo Declaration, signed on November 27, 1943, by President Franklin Roosevelt for the United States, Prime Minister Winston Churchill for the United Kingdom, and Generalissimo Chiang Kai-shek for the Republic of China, stated the Allies' intentions to continue deploying military force until Japan surrendered unconditionally and gave up all the territory that it had occupied by force. The declaration reflected China's acceptance as one of the "Big Four" Allied powers.*

PLEASE SAFEGUARD AGAINST PREMATURE RELEASE OR PUBLICATION.

The following communique is for automatic release at 7:30 P.M., E.W.T., on Wednesday, December 1, 1945.

Extraordinary precautions must be taken to hold this communication absolutely confidential and secret until the hour set for automatic release.

No intimation can be given its contents nor shall its contents be the subject of speculation or discussion on the part of anybody receiving it, prior to the hour of release.

Radio commentators and news broadcasters are particularly cautioned not to make the communication the subject of speculation before the hour of release of publication.

STEPHEN EARLY
Secretary to the President

President Roosevelt, Generalissimo Chiang Kai-Shek and Prime Minister Churchill, together with their respective military and diplomatic advisers, have completed a conference in North Africa.

The following general statement was issued:

The several military missions have agreed upon future military operations against Japan. The Three Great Allies expressed their resolve to bring unrelenting pressure against their brutal enemies by sea, land and air. This pressure is already rising.

The Three Great Allies are fighting this war to restrain and punish the aggression of Japan. They covet no gain for themselves and have no thought of territorial expansion. It is their purpose that Japan shall be stripped of all the islands in the Pacific which she has seized or occupied since the beginning of the First World War in 1914, and that all the territories Japan has stolen from the Chinese, such as Manchuria, Formosa, and the Pescadores, shall be restored to the Republic of China. Japan will also be expelled from all other territories which she has taken by violence and greed. The aforesaid Three Great Powers, mindful of the enslavement of the people of Korea, are determined that in due course Korea shall become free and independent.

With these objects in view the Three Allies, in harmony with those of the United Nations at war with Japan, will continue to persevere in the serious and prolonged operation necessary to procure the unconditional surrender of Japan.

THE COMMON PROGRAM OF THE CHINESE PEOPLE'S POLITICAL CONSULTATIVE CONFERENCE

SOURCE The Important Documents of the First Plenary Session of the Chinese People's Political Consultative Conference. *Peking: Foreign Languages Press, 1949.*

INTRODUCTION *The Common Program was adopted in September 1949 by the Chinese People's Consultative Congress (CPCC), a United Front body that represented a broad range of interests. The program was in effect a constitution of the new People's Republic of China guaranteeing a range of political and civil rights and outlining a plan for economic reform.*

PREAMBLE

The Chinese People's Political Consultative Conference, representing the will of the people of the whole country, proclaims the establishment of the People's Republic of China and is organizing the people's own central government. The Chinese People's Political Consultative Conference unanimously agrees that New Democracy, or the People's Democracy, shall be the political foundation for the national construction of the People's Republic of China. It has also adopted the following Common Program which should be jointly observed by all units participating in the Conference, by the people's government of all levels, and by the people of the whole country.

Article 1.

The People's Republic of China is a New Democratic or a People's Democratic state. It carries out the people's democratic dictatorship led by the working class, based on the alliance of workers and peasants, and uniting all democratic classes and all nationalities in China. It opposes imperialism, feudalism and bureaucratic capitalism and strives for independence, democracy, peace, unity, prosperity and strength of China.

Article 2.

The Central People's Government of the People's Republic of China must undertake to wage the people's war of liberation to the very end, to liberate all the territory of China, and to achieve the unification of China.

Article 3.

The People's Republic of China must abolish all the prerogatives of imperialist countries in China. It must confiscate bureaucratic capital and put it into the possession of the people's state. It must systematically transform the feudal and semi-feudal land ownership system into a system of peasant land ownership; it must protect the public property of the state and of the cooperatives and must protect the economic interests and private property of workers, peasants, the petty [*sic*] bourgeoisie and the national bourgeoisie. It must develop the people's economy of New Democracy and steadily transform the country from an agricultural into an industrial one.

Article 4.

The people of the People's Republic of China shall have the right to elect and to be elected according to law.

Article 5.

The people of the People's Republic of China shall have freedom of thought, speech, publication, assembly, association, correspondence, person, domicile, change of domicile, religious belief and the freedom of holding processions and demonstrations.

Article 6.

The People's Republic of China shall abolish the feudal system which holds women in bondage. Women shall enjoy equal rights with men in political, economic, cultural, educational and social life. Freedom of marriage for men and women shall be put into effect.

Article 7.

The People's Republic of China shall suppress all counter-revolutionary activities, severely punish all Kuomintang counter-revolutionary war criminals and other leading incorrigible counter-revolutionary, elements who collaborate with imperialism, commit treason against the fatherland and oppose the cause of people's democracy. Feudal landlords, bureaucratic capitalists and reactionary elements in general, after they have been disarmed and have had their special powers abolished, shall, in addition, be deprived of their political rights in accordance with law for a necessary period. But, at the same time, they shall be given some means of livelihood and shall be compelled to reform themselves through labour so as to become new men. If they continue their counter-revolutionary activities, they will be severely punished.

Article 8.

It is the duty of every national of the People's Republic of China to defend the fatherland, to abide by the law, to observe labour discipline, to protect public property, to perform public and military service, and to pay taxes.

Article 9.

All nationalities in the People's Republic of China shall have equal rights and duties.

Article 10.

The armed forces of the People's Republic of China, namely, the People's Liberation Army, the people's public security forces and the people's police belong to the people. It is the task of these armed forces to defend the independence, territorial integrity and sovereignty of China, and to defend the revolutionary gains and all legitimate rights and interests of the Chinese people. The Central People's Government of the People's Republic of China shall endeavour to consolidate and strengthen the people's armed forces, so as to enable them to accomplish their tasks effectively.

Article 11.

The People's Republic of China shall unite with all peace-loving and freedom-loving countries and peoples throughout the world, first of all, with the USSR, all Peoples' Democracies and all oppressed nations. It shall take its stand in the camp of international peace and democracy, to oppose imperialist aggression to defend lasting world peace....

Article 27.

Agrarian reform is the necessary condition for the development of the nation's productive power and for its industrialization. In all areas where agrarian reform has been carried out, the ownership of the land acquired by the peasants shall be protected. In areas where agrarian reform has not been carried out, the peasant masses must be set in motion to establish peasant organisations and to put into effect the policy of "land to the tiller" through such measures as the elimination of local bandits and despots, the reduction of rent and interest and the distribution of land.

Article 28.

State-owned economy is of a Socialist nature. All enterprises relating to the economic life of the country and exercising a dominant influence over the people's livelihood shall be under the unified operation of the state. All state-owned resources and enterprises are the public property of all the people and are the main material basis on which the People's Republic will develop production and bring about a prosperous economy. They are the leading force of the entire social economy.

Article 29.

Co-operative economy is of a semi-Socialist nature and is an important component of the people's economy as a whole. The People's Government shall foster its development and accord it preferential treatment.

Article 30.

The People's Government shall encourage the active operation of all private economic enterprises beneficial to the national welfare and to the people's livelihood and shall assist in their development.

Article 31.

The economy, jointly operated by state and private capital, is of a state-capitalist nature. Whenever necessary and possible, private capital shall be encouraged to develop in the direction of state-capitalism, in such ways as processing for state-owned enterprises and exploiting state-owned resources in the form of concessions.

Article 32.

The system of worker's participation in the administration of production shall, for the present period, be established in state-owned enterprises. This means that factory administrative committees shall be set up under the leadership of the factory managers. In privately-owned enterprises, in order to carry out the principle of benefitting both labour and capital, collective contracts shall be signed by the trade union, representing the workers and employees, and the employer. For the present period, an eight to ten-hour day should in general be enforced in publicly and privately operated enterprises, but under special circumstances this matter may be dealt with at discretion. The people's governments shall fix minimum wages according to the conditions prevailing in various localities and trades. Labour insurance shall be gradually established. The special interests of juvenile and women workers shall be safeguarded. Inspection of industries and mines shall be carried out in order to improve their safety devices and sanitary facilities....

Article 37.

Commerce: All legitimate public and private trade shall be protected. Control shall be exercised over foreign trade and the policy of protecting trade shall be adopted. Freedom of domestic trade shall be established under a unified economic state plan, but commercial speculation disturbing the market shall be strictly prohibited. State-owned trading organizations shall assume the responsibility of adjusting supply and demand, stabilizing commodity prices and assisting the people's co-operatives. The people's government shall adopt the measures necessary to encourage the people in saving, to facilitate remittances from overseas Chinese, and to channel into industry and other productive enterprises, all socially idle capital and commercial capital which is not beneficial to the national welfare and/or to the people's livelihood.

Article 38.

Co-operatives: The broad masses of working people shall be encouraged and assisted to develop co-operatives according to the principle of willingness. Supply and marketing co-operatives, as well as consumers', credit, producers', and transport co-operatives shall be organized in towns and villages. Consumers' co-operatives shall first be organised in factories, institutions and schools....

Article 41.

The culture and education of the People's Republic of China shall be New Democratic-national, scientific and popular. The main tasks of the People's Government in cultural and educational work shall be the raising of the cultural level of the people, the training of personnel for national construction work, the eradicating of feudal, compradore [*note: A compradore—the word is Portuguese, was a Chinese agent of a foreign business in China*] and fascist ideology and the developing of the ideology of service to the people....

Article 49.

Freedom of reporting truthful news shall be safeguarded. The utilization of the press for slander, for undermining the interests of the state and the people and for provoking world war shall be prohibited. The people's radio and publication work shall be developed. Attention shall be paid to publishing popular books and journals beneficial to the people.

Article 50.

All nationalities within the boundaries of the People's Republic of China are equal. They shall establish unity and mutual aid among themselves, and shall oppose imperialism and their own public enemies, so that the People's Republic of China will become a big fraternal and co-operative family composed of all its nationalities. Greater Nationalism and chauvinism shall be opposed. Acts involving discrimination, oppression and splitting of the unity of the various nationalities shall be prohibited.

Article 51.

Regional autonomy shall be exercised in areas where national minorities are concentrated and various kinds of autonomy organizations of the different nationalities shall be set up according to the size of the respective populations and regions. In places where different nationalities live together and in the autonomous areas of the national minorities, the different nationalities shall each have an appropriate number of representatives in the local organs of political power....

Article 53.

All national minorities shall have freedom to develop their dialects and languages, to preserve or reform their traditions, customs and religious beliefs. The People's Government shall assist the masses of the people of all national minorities to develop their political, economic, cultural and educational construction work.

Article 54.

The principle of the foreign policy of the People's Republic of China is protection of the independence, freedom, integrity of territory and sovereignty of the country, upholding of lasting international peace and friendly co-operation between the peoples of all countries, and opposition to the imperialist policy of aggression and war.

Article 55.

The Central People's Government of the People's Republic of China shall examine the treaties and agreements concluded between the Kuomintang and foreign governments, and shall recognize, abrogate, revise, or re-negotiate them according to their respective contents.

Article 56.

The Central People's Government of the People's Republic of China may, on the basis of equality, mutual benefit and mutual respect for territory and sovereignty, negotiate with foreign governments which have severed relations with the Kuomintang reactionary clique and which adopt a friendly attitude towards the People's Republic of China, and may establish diplomatic relations with them.

Article 57.

The People's Republic of China may restore and develop commercial relations with foreign governments and peoples on a basis of equality and mutual benefit.

Article 58.

The Central People's Government of the People's Republic of China shall do its utmost to protect the proper rights and interests of Chinese residing abroad.

Article 59.

The People's Government of the People's Republic of China protects law-abiding foreign nationals in China.

Article 60.

The People's Republic of China shall accord the right of asylum to foreign nationals who seek refuge in China because they have been oppressed by their own governments for supporting the people's interests and taking part in the struggle for peace and democracy.

THE CHINESE PEOPLE HAVE STOOD UP

SOURCE *Mao Zedong (Mao Tse-tung). The Chinese People Have Stood Up. The Selected Works of Mao Tse-tung, Volume V. Peking: Foreign Languages Press, 1977.*

INTRODUCTION *Mao Zedong delivered this opening address at the Chinese People's Political Consultative Conference in Peking (Beijing) in September 1949, just before he proclaimed the establishment of the People's Republic of China from the rostrum in Tiananmen Square on October 1.*

Fellow Delegates,

The Political Consultative Conference so eagerly awaited by the whole nation is herewith inaugurated.

Our conference is composed of more than six hundred delegates, representing all the democratic parties and people's organizations of China, the People's Liberation Army, the various regions and nationalities of the country and the overseas Chinese. This shows that ours is a conference embodying the great unity of the people of the whole country.

It is because we have defeated the reactionary Kuomintang government backed by U.S. imperialism that this great unity of the whole people has been achieved. In a little more than three years the heroic Chinese People's Liberation Army, an army such as the world has seldom seen, crushed all the offensives launched by the several million troops of the U.S.-supported reactionary Kuomintang government and turned to the counter-offensive and the offensive. At present the field armies of the People's Liberation Army, several million strong, have pushed the war to areas near Taiwan, Kwangtung, Kwangsi, Kweichow, Szechuan and Sinkiang, and the great majority of the Chinese people have won liberation. In a little more than three years the people of the whole country have closed their ranks, rallied to support the People's Liberation Army, fought the enemy and won basic victory. And it is on this foundation that the present People's Political Consultative Conference is convened.

Our conference is called the Political Consultative Conference because some three years ago we held a Political Consultative Conference with Chiang Kai-shek's Kuomintang. The results of that conference were sabotaged by Chiang Kai-shek's Kuomintang and its accomplices; nevertheless the conference left an indelible impression on the people. It showed that nothing in the interest of the people could be accomplished together with Chiang Kai-shek's Kuomintang, the running dog of imperialism, and its accomplices. Even when resolutions were reluctantly adopted, it was of no avail, for as soon as the time was ripe, they tore them up and started a ruthless war against the people. The only gain from that conference was the profound lesson it taught the people that there is absolutely no room for compromise with Chiang Kai-shek's Kuomintang, the running dog of imperialism, and its accomplices—overthrow these enemies or be oppressed and slaughtered by them, either one or the other, there is no other choice. In a little more than three years the Chinese people, led by the Chinese Communist Party, have quickly awakened and organized themselves into a nation-wide united front against imperialism, feudalism, bureaucrat-capitalism and their general representative, the reactionary Kuomintang government, supported the People's War of Liberation, basically defeated the reactionary Kuomintang government, overthrown the rule of imperialism in China and restored the Political Consultative Conference.

The present Chinese People's Political Consultative Conference is convened on an entirely new foundation; it is representative of the people of the whole country and enjoys their trust and support. Therefore, the conference proclaims that it will exercise the functions and powers of a National People's Congress. In accordance with its agenda, the conference will enact the Organic Law of the Chinese People's Political Consultative Conference, the Organic Law of the Central People's Government of the People's Republic of China and the Common Programme of the Chinese People's Political Consultative Conference; it will elect the National Committee of the Chinese People's Political Consultative Conference and the Central People's Government Council of the People's Republic of China; it will adopt the national flag and national emblem of the People's Republic of China; and it will decide on the seat of the capital of the People's Republic of China and adopt the chronological system in use in most countries of the world.

Fellow Delegates, we are all convinced that our work will go down in the history of mankind, demonstrating that the Chinese people, comprising one quarter of humanity, have now stood up. The Chinese have always been a great, courageous and industrious nation; it is only in modern times that they have fallen behind. And that was due entirely to oppression and exploitation by foreign imperialism and domestic reactionary governments. For over a century our forefathers never stopped waging unyielding struggles against domestic and foreign oppressors, including the Revolution of 1911 led by Dr. Sun Yat-sen, our great forerunner in the Chinese revolution. Our forefathers enjoined us to carry out their unfulfilled will. And we have acted accordingly. We have closed our ranks and defeated both domestic and foreign oppressors through the People's War of Liberation and the great people's revolution, and now we are proclaiming the founding of the People's Republic of China. From now on our nation will belong to the community of the peace-loving and freedom-loving nations of the world and work courageously and industriously to foster its own civilization and well-being and at the same time to promote world peace and freedom. Ours will no longer be a nation subject to insult and humiliation. We have stood up. Our revolution has won the sympathy and acclaim of the people of all countries. We have friends all over the world.

Our revolutionary work is not completed, the People's War of Liberation and the people's revolutionary movement are still forging ahead and we must keep up our efforts. The imperialists and the domestic reactionaries will certainly not take their defeat lying down; they will fight to the last ditch. After there is peace and order throughout the country, they are sure to engage in sabotage and create disturbances by one means or another and every day and every minute they will try to stage a comeback. This is inevitable and beyond all doubt, and under no circumstances must we relax our vigilance.

Our state system, the people's democratic dictatorship, is a powerful weapon for safeguarding the fruits of victory of the people's revolution and for thwarting the plots of domestic and foreign enemies for restoration, and this weapon we must firmly grasp. Internationally, we must unite with all peace-loving and freedom-loving countries and peoples, and first of all with the Soviet Union and the New Democracies, so that we shall not stand alone in our struggle to safeguard these fruits of victory and to thwart the plots of domestic and foreign enemies for restoration. As long as we persist in the people's democratic dictatorship and unite with our foreign friends, we shall always be victorious.

The people's democratic dictatorship and solidarity with our foreign friends will enable us to accomplish our work of construction rapidly. We are already confronted with the task of nation-wide economic construction. We have very favourable conditions: a population of 475 million people and a territory of 9,600,000 square kilometres. There are indeed difficulties ahead, and a great many too. But we firmly believe that by heroic struggle the people of the country will surmount them all. The Chinese people have rich experience in overcoming difficulties. If our forefathers, and we also, could weather long years of extreme difficulty and defeat powerful domestic and foreign reactionaries, why can't we now, after victory, build a prosperous and flourishing country? As long as we keep to our style of plain living and hard struggle, as long as we stand united and as long as we persist in the people's democratic dictatorship and unite with our foreign friends, we shall be able to win speedy victory on the economic front.

An upsurge in economic construction is bound to be followed by an upsurge of construction in the cultural sphere. The era in which the Chinese people were regarded as uncivilized is now ended. We shall emerge in the world as a nation with an advanced culture.

Our national defence will be consolidated and no imperialists will ever again be allowed to invade our land. Our people's armed forces must be maintained and developed with the heroic and steeled People's Liberation Army as the foundation. We will have not only a powerful army but also a powerful air force and a powerful navy.

Let the domestic and foreign reactionaries tremble before us! Let them say we are no good at this and no good at that. By our own indomitable efforts we the Chinese people will unswervingly reach our goal.

The heroes of the people who laid down their lives in the People's War of Liberation and the people's revolution shall live for ever in our memory!

Hail the victory of the People's War of Liberation and the people's revolution!

Hail the founding of the People's Republic of China!

Hail the triumph of the Chinese People's Political Consultative Conference!

SAN FRANCISCO PEACE TREATY, 1951

INTRODUCTION *The treaty excerpted below was signed by the Allied powers and Japan in order to settle questions still outstanding from World War II. Japan recognized the sovereignty of Asian nations that it had previously occupied and renounced various territorial claims and rights it had previously demanded in China. Because there was no international agreement as to which government should represent China, neither the Republic of China nor the People's Republic of China was invited to the San Francisco Peace Conference, and neither was a party to the San Francisco treaty.*

ARTICLE 10

Japan renounces all special rights and interests in China, including all benefits and privileges resulting from the provisions of the final Protocol signed at Peking on 7 September 1901, and all annexes, notes and documents supplementary thereto, and agrees to the abrogation in respect to Japan of the said protocol, annexes, notes and documents....

ARTICLE 14

(a) It is recognized that Japan should pay reparations to the Allied Powers for the damage and suffering caused by it during the war. Nevertheless it is also recognized that the resources of Japan are not presently sufficient, if it is to maintain a viable economy, to make complete reparation for all such damage and suffering and at the same time meet its other obligations.

Therefore,

1. Japan will promptly enter into negotiations with Allied Powers so desiring, whose present territories were occupied by Japanese forces and damaged by Japan, with a view to assisting to compensate those countries for the cost of repairing the damage done, by making available the services of the Japanese people in production, salvaging and other work for the Allied Powers in question. Such arrangements shall avoid the imposition of additional liabilities on other Allied Powers, and, where the manufacturing of raw materials is called for, they shall be supplied by the Allied Powers in question, so as not to throw any foreign exchange burden upon Japan.

2. I. Subject to the provisions of subparagraph II below, each of the Allied Powers shall have the right to seize, retain, liquidate or otherwise dispose of all property, rights and interests of

a. Japan and Japanese nationals,

b. persons acting for or on behalf of Japan or Japanese nationals, and

c. entities owned or controlled by Japan or Japanese nationals,

which on the first coming into force of the present Treaty were subject to its jurisdiction. The property, rights and interests specified in this subparagraph shall include those now blocked, vested or in the possession or under the control of enemy property authorities of Allied Powers, which belong to, or were held or managed on behalf of, any of the persons or entities mentioned in (a), (b) or (c) above at the time such assets came under the controls of such authorities.

II. The following shall be excepted from the right specified in subparagraph (I) above:

i. property of Japanese natural persons who during the war resided with the permission of the Government concerned in the territory of one of the Allied Powers, other than territory occupied by Japan, except property subjected to restrictions during the war and not released from such restrictions as of the date of the first coming into force of the present Treaty;

ii. all real property, furniture and fixtures owned by the Government of Japan and used for diplomatic or consular purposes, and all personal furniture and furnishings and other private property not of an investment nature which was normally necessary for the carrying out of diplomatic and consular functions, owned by Japanese diplomatic and consular personnel;

iii. property belonging to religious bodies or private charitable institutions and used exclusively for religious or charitable purposes;

iv. property, rights and interests which have come within its jurisdiction in consequence of the resumption of trade and financial relations subsequent to 2 September 1945, between the country concerned and Japan, except such as have resulted from transactions contrary to the laws of the Allied Power concerned;

v. obligations of Japan or Japanese nationals, any right, title or interest in tangible property located in Japan, interests in enterprises organized under the laws of Japan, or any paper evidence thereof; provided that this exception shall only apply to obligations of Japan and its nationals expressed in Japanese currency.

III. Property referred to in exceptions (i) through (v) above shall be returned subject to reasonable expenses for its preservation and administration. If any such property has been liquidated the proceeds shall be returned instead.

IV. The right to seize, retain, liquidate or otherwise dispose of property as provided in subparagraph (I) above shall be exercised in accordance with the laws of the Allied Power concerned, and the owner shall have only such rights as may be given him by those laws.

V. The Allied Powers agree to deal with Japanese trademarks and literary and artistic property rights on a basis as favorable to Japan as circumstances ruling in each country will permit.

(b) Except as otherwise provided in the present Treaty, the Allied Powers waive all reparations claims of the Allied Powers, other claims of the Allied Powers and their nationals arising out of any actions taken by Japan and its nationals in the course of the prosecution of the war, and claims of the Allied Powers for direct military costs of occupation.

TREATY OF TAIPEI

INTRODUCTION *The 1951 Treaty of San Francisco between the Allied powers and Japan settled many territorial and political problems left from World War II. Under the Treaty, Japan agreed to give up various rights and interests in China. However, as there was no agreement as to which government should represent China, neither the Republic of China nor the People's Republic of China was invited to sign. The Treaty of Taipei was concluded separately between the Republic of China and Japan in 1952 covering many of the same issues.*

TREATY OF PEACE

The Republic of China and Japan,

Considering their mutual desire for good neighbourliness in view of their historical and cultural ties and geographical proximity; Realising the importance of their close cooperation to the promotion of their common welfare and to the maintenance of international peace and security; Recognising the need for a settlement of problems that have arisen as a result of the existence of a state of war between them; Have resolved to conclude a Treaty of Peace and have accordingly appointed as their Plenipotentiaries,

His Excellency the President of the Republic of China:
Mr. Yeh Kung-Chao;
The Government of Japan: Mr. Isao Kawada

Who, having communicated to each other their full powers found to be in good and due form, have agreed upon the following Articles:—

Article 1

The state of war between the Republic of China and Japan is terminated as from the date on which the present Treaty enters into force.

Article 2

It is recognised that under Article 2 of the Treaty of Peace which Japan signed at the city of San Francisco on 8 September 1951 (hereinafter referred to as the San Francisco Treaty), Japan has renounced all right, title, and claim to Taiwan (Formosa) and Penghu (the Pescadores) as well as the Spratley Islands and the Paracel Islands.

Article 3

The disposition of property of Japan and its nationals in Taiwan (Formosa) and Penghu (the Pescadores), and their claims, including debts, against the authorities of the Republic of China in Taiwan (Formosa) and Penghu (the Pescadores) and the residents thereof, and the disposition in Japan of property of such authorities and residents and their claims, including debts, against Japan and its nationals, shall be the subject of special arrangements between the Government of the Republic of China and the Government of Japan. The terms *nationals* and *residents* include juridical persons.

Article 4

It is recognised that all treaties, conventions, and agreements concluded before 9 December 1941 between Japan and China have become null and void as a consequence of the war.

Article 5

It is recognised that under the provisions of Article 10 of the San Francisco Treaty, Japan has renounced all special rights and its interests in China, including all benefits and privileges resulting from the provisions of the final Protocol signed at Peking on 7 September 1901, and all annexes, notes, and documents supplementary thereto, and has agreed to the abrogation in respect to Japan of the said protocol, annexes, notes, and documents.

Article 6

a. The Republic of China and Japan will be guided by the principles of Article 2 of the Charter of the United Nations in their mutual relations.

b. The Republic of China and Japan will cooperate in accordance with the principles of the Charter of the United Nations and, in particular, will promote their common welfare through friendly cooperation in the economic field.

Article 7

The Republic of China and Japan will endeavour to conclude, as soon as possible, a treaty or agreement to place their trading, maritime, and other commercial relations, on a stable and friendly basis.

Article 8

The Republic of China and Japan will endeavour to conclude, as soon as possible, an agreement relating to civil air transport.

Article 9

The Republic of China and Japan will endeavour to conclude, as soon as possible, an agreement providing for the regulation or limitation of fishing and the conservation and development of fisheries on the high seas.

Article 10

For the purposes of the present Treaty, nationals of the Republic of China shall be deemed to include all the inhabitants and former inhabitants of Taiwan (Formosa) and Penghu (the Pescadores) and their descendents who are of the Chinese nationality in accordance with the laws and regulations which have been or may hereafter be enforced by the Republic of China in Taiwan (Formosa) and Penghu (the Pescadores); and juridical persons of the Republic of China shall be deemed to include all those registered under the laws and regulations which have been or may hereafter be enforced by the Republic of China in Taiwan (Formosa) and Penghu (the Pescadores).

Article 11

Unless otherwise provided for in the present Treaty and the documents supplementary thereto, any problem arising between the Republic of China and Japan as a result of the existence of a state of war shall be settled in accordance with the relevant provisions of the San Francisco Treaty.

Article 12

Any dispute that may arise out of the interpretation or application of the present Treaty shall be settled by negotiation or other pacific means.

Article 13

The present Treaty shall be ratified and the instruments of ratification shall be exchanged at Taipei as soon as possible. The present Treaty shall enter into force as from the date on which such instruments of ratification are exchanged.

Article 14

The present Treaty shall be in the Chinese, Japanese, and English languages. In case of any divergence of interpretation, the English text shall prevail.

In witness whereof the respective Plenipotentiaries have signed the present Treaty and have affixed thereto their seals.

Done in duplicate at Taipei, this Twenty Eighth day of the Fourth month of the Forty First year of the Republic of China, corresponding to the Twenty Eighth day of the Fourth month of the Twenty Seventh year of SHOWA of Japan and to the Twenty Eighth day of April in the year One Thousand Nine Hundred and Fifty Two.

Yeh Kung-Chao, [L.S.]
Minister of Foreign Affairs and Plenipotentiary of the Republic of China
Isao Kawada, [L.S.]
Minister of Foreign Affairs and Plenipotentiary of Japan

ON THE CORRECT HANDLING OF CONTRADICTIONS AMONG THE PEOPLE

SOURCE *Mao Zedong. On the Correct Handling of Contradictions among the People. In* Sources of Chinese Tradition, Volume II: From 1600 through the Twentieth Century, *2nd edition, ed. William Theodore de Bary and Richard Lufrano, 459–464. New York: Columbia University Press, 2000.*

INTRODUCTION *The speech by Mao Zedong that is excerpted below launched the Hundred Flowers (1957), a new movement in which the non-party public was encouraged to criticize the Communist Party. We do not have the original version of the speech. Even in this doctored text published after the movement was brought to an abrupt end and critics of the Communist Party were being punished, Mao appears to wrestle with the problem of distinguishing friendly and hostile criticisms.*

TWO DIFFERENT TYPES OF CONTRADICTIONS

Never has our country been as united as it is today. The victories of the bourgeois-democratic revolution and the socialist revolution, coupled with our achievements in socialist construction, have rapidly changed the face of old China. Now we see before us an even brighter future.... Unification of the country, unity of the people, and unity among our various nationalities—these are the basic guarantees for the sure triumph of our cause. However, this does not mean that there are no longer any contradictions in our society.... We are confronted by two types of social contradictions—contradictions between ourselves and the enemy and contradictions among the people. These two types of contradictions are totally different in nature....

The contradictions between ourselves and our enemies are antagonistic ones. Within the ranks of the people, contradictions among the working people are nonantagonistic, while those between the exploiters and the exploited classes have, apart from their antagonistic aspect, a nonantagonistic aspect. Contradictions among the people have always existed, but their content differs in each period of the revolution and during the building of socialism.

In the conditions existing in China today, what we call contradictions among the people include the following:

Contradictions within the working class, contradictions within the peasantry, contradictions within the intelligentsia, contradictions between the working class and the peasantry, contradictions between the working class and peasantry on the one hand and the intelligentsia on the other, contradictions between and the national bourgeoisie on the other, contradictions within the national bourgeoisie, and so forth. Our People's Government is a government that truly represents the interests of the people and serves the people, yet certain contradictions do exist between the government and the masses. These include contradictions between the interests of the state, collective interests, and individual interests; between democracy and centralism; between those in positions of leadership and the led; and contradictions arising from the bureaucratic practices of certain state functionaries in their relations with the masses. All these are contradictions among the people; generally speaking, underlying the contradictions among the people is the basic identity of the interests of the people.

In our country, the contradiction between the working class and the national bourgeoisie is a contradiction among the people.... The contradiction between exploiter and exploited that exists between the national bourgeoisie and the working class is an antagonistic one. But, in the concrete conditions existing in China, such an antagonistic contradiction, if properly handled, can be transformed into a nonantagonistic one and resolved in a peaceful way. But if it is not properly handled—if, say, we do not follow a policy of unity, criticizing and educating the national bourgeoisie, or if the national bourgeoisie does not accept this policy—then the contradictions between the working class and the national bourgeoisie can turn into an antagonistic contradiction between ourselves and the enemy....

There were other people in our country who took a wavering attitude toward the Hungarian events because they were ignorant about the actual world situation. They felt that there was too little freedom under our people's democracy and that there was more freedom under Western parliamentary democracy. They ask for the adoption of the two-party system of the West, where one party is in office and the other out of office. But this so-called two-party system is nothing but a means of maintaining the dictatorship of the bourgeoisie; under no circumstances can it safeguard the freedom of the working people.

Those who demand freedom and democracy in the abstract regard democracy as an end and not a means. Democracy sometimes seems to be an end, but it is in fact only a means. Marxism teaches us that democracy is part of the superstructure and belongs to the category of politics. That is to say, in the last analysis it serves the economic base. The same is true of freedom. Both democracy and freedom are relative, not absolute, and they come into being and develop under specific historical circumstances.

Within the ranks of the people, democracy stands in relation to centralism, and freedom to discipline. They are two conflicting aspects of a single entity, contradictory as well as united, and we should not one-sidedly emphasize one to the denial of the other. Within the ranks of the people, we cannot do without democracy, nor can we do without centralism. Our democratic centralism means the unity of democracy and centralism and the unity of freedom and discipline but at the same time they have to keep themselves within the bounds of socialist discipline. All this is well understood by the people....

Marxist philosophy holds that the law of the unity of opposites is a fundamental law of the universe. This law operates everywhere—in the natural world, in human society, and in human thinking. Opposites in contradiction unite as well as struggle with each other, and thus impel all things to move and change. Contradictions exist everywhere, but as things differ in nature so do contradictions in any given phenomenon or thing; the unity of opposites is conditional, temporary and transitory, and hence relative, whereas struggle between opposites is absolute. Lenin gave a very clear exposition of this law. In our country, a growing number of people have come to understand it. For many people, however, acceptance of this law is one thing and its application, examining and dealing with problems, is quite another.... Many people refuse to admit that contradictions still exist in a socialist society, with the result that when confronted with social contradictions they become timid and helpless. They do not understand that socialist society grows more united and consolidated precisely through the ceaseless process of correctly dealing with and resolving contradictions....

ON "LETTING A HUNDRED FLOWERS BLOSSOM" AND "LETTING A HUNDRED SCHOOLS OF THOUGHT CONTEND"

The policy of letting a hundred flowers blossom and a hundred schools of thought contend is designed to promote the flourishing of the arts and the progress of science; it is designed to enable a socialist culture to thrive in our land. Different forms and styles in art can develop freely, and different schools in science can contend freely. We think that it is harmful to the growth of art and science if administrative measures are used to impose one particular style of art or school of thought and to ban another.... In the past, new and correct things often failed at the outset to win recognition from the majority of people and had to develop by twists and turns in struggle. Correct and good things have often at first been looked upon not as fragrant flowers but as poisonous weeds; Copernicus's theory of the solar system and Darwin's theory of evolution were once dismissed as erroneous and had to win out over bitter opposition. Chinese history offers many similar examples....

Marxism has also developed through struggle.... It is true that in China socialist transformation, insofar as a change in the system of ownership is concerned, has in the main been completed, and the turbulent, large-scale, mass class struggles characteristic of the revolutionary periods have in the main concluded. But remnants of the overthrown landlord and comprador classes still exist, the bourgeoisie still exists, and the petty [*sic*] bourgeoisie has only just begun to remold itself. Class struggle is not yet over.... In this respect, the question are still a minority of the entire population as well as of the intellectuals. Marxism therefore must still develop through struggle.... As humankind in general rejects an untruth and accepts a truth, a new truth will begin struggling with new erroneous ideas. Such struggles will never end. This is the law of the development of truth, and it is certainly also the law of development in Marxism....

People may ask: Since Marxism is accepted by the majority of the people in our country as the guiding ideology, can it be criticized? Certainly it can. As a scientific truth, Marxism fears no criticism. If it did and could be defeated in argument, it would be worthless. In fact, are not the idealists criticizing Marxism every day and in all sorts of ways?... Fighting against wrong ideas is like being vaccinated—a man develops greater immunity from disease after the vaccine takes effect. Plants raised in hothouses are not likely to be robust. Carrying out the policy of letting a hundred flowers bloom and a hundred schools of thought contend will not weaken but strengthen the leading position of Marxism in the ideological field.

What should our policy be toward non-Marxist ideas? As far as unmistakable counterrevolutionaries and wreckers of the socialist cause are concerned, the matter is easy; we simply deprive them of their freedom of speech. But it is quite a different matter when we are faced with incorrect ideas among the people. Will it do to ban such ideas and give them no opportunity to express themselves? Certainly not.... That is why it is only by employing methods of discussion, criticism, and reasoning that we can really foster correct ideas, overcome wrong ideas, and really settle issues....

So what, from the point of view of the broad masses of the people, should be a criterion today for distinguishing between fragrant flowers and poisonous weeds?...

Basing ourselves on the principles of our constitution, the will of the overwhelming majority of our people, and the political programs jointly proclaimed on various occasions by our political parties and groups, we believe that, broadly speaking, words and actions can be judged right if they:

1. Help to unite the people of our various nationalities and do not divide them

2. Are beneficial, not harmful, to socialist transformation and socialist construction

3. Help to consolidate, not undermine or weaken, the people's democratic dictatorship

4. Help to consolidate, not undermine or weaken, democratic centralism

5. Tend to strengthen, not to cast off or weaken, the leadership of the Communist Party

6. Are beneficial, not harmful, to international socialist solidarity and the and the solidarity of the peace-loving people of the world.

Of these six criteria, the most important are the socialist path and the leadership of the Party.... When the majority of the people have clear-cut criteria to go by, criticism and self-criticism can be conducted along proper lines, and these criteria can be applied to people's words and actions to determine whether they are fragrant flowers or poisonous weeds. These are political criteria. Naturally, in judging the truthfulness of scientific theories or assessing the aesthetic value of works of art, other pertinent criteria are needed, but these six political criteria are also applicable to all activities in the arts or sciences. In a socialist country like ours, can there possibly be any useful scientific or artistic activity that runs counter to these political criteria?

A NEW POPULATION THEORY

SOURCE *Ma Yinchu. Xinrenkoulun.* Renmin ribao *[People's daily], July 5, 1957, 175–196.*

INTRODUCTION *Concern at the huge population reported by China's 1953 census sparked the beginning of family planning education in China's big cities and a debate on the implications of rapid population growth. In June 1957, Ma Yinchu, a well-known economist, presented his* New Population Theory—*advocating state-sponsored population control—at the First National People's Congress. In 1958 the climate changed. The Great Leap Forward was based on a positive evaluation of China's huge population and Ma came under attack for "propagating Malthusianism." Disgraced and dismissed from his post as president of Peking University in 1960, he was not rehabilitated until 1979, long after the Chinese government had accepted the necessity of birth planning. He died at the age of 100 in 1982. To our knowledge, we offer below the first full English translation of the document (translated by Alan Thwaits). Note that the term* contradiction, *in Chinese* maodun, *is a core term in Chinese Marxist discourse, which refers to a dialectical, dynamic relationship between opposing interests or opposing conditions (compare Mao Zedong's famous work* On Contradiction).

As a result of the Party's and Chairman Mao's wise and correct leadership, it is now possible to control the population. Article 29, item 3, of the revised draft of *An Outline of the Development of Agriculture in China from 1956 to 1967 (1956 dao 1967 nian quanguo nongye fazhan gangyao)* stipulates, "Except in regions dominated by minorities, in all densely populated areas, the government will promote reduction in childbirth and advocate family planning so that families can avoid excessive burdens, their children can receive better education, and they can have ample employment opportunities." I firmly believe that this measure will quickly turn the 500 million farmers around from their desire for more sons and grandsons.

In rural China class contradictions [矛盾, *maodun*] perennially existed between landowners and farmers. These contradictions have been resolved as a result of liberation and land reform. After land reform, new contradictions appeared: whether individual farmers would align themselves with capitalism or with socialism. By 1956, after years of struggle and hard work, agriculture around the country had essentially been collectivized; farmers were basically won over and affirmatively aligned themselves with the path of socialism, and these contradictions were resolved. Are there other contradictions? Yes. In addition to the major contradictions among the people mentioned by Chairman Mao, I believe that there are also important contradictions between excess population and limited capital. Past contradictions were those between social classes; present contradictions are mainly contradictions in production.

1. CHINA'S POPULATION IS GROWING TOO FAST

The 1953 census was China's first population census. The census showed that on July 30, 1953, China had a population of 601,938,035, a static record of a moment in time. If we had population statistics for every year after 1953, then we would have a dynamic record of population growth as well. Unfortunately, such figures do not exist today. Going forward, we must create a system of vital statistics, recording the number of births, deaths, marriages, divorces, as well as in-migration and out-migration in each area. Only with such data will we have precise population figures. Current estimates indicate that the population grows by between 12 and 13 million per year, a rate of 2.0 percent. If we extrapolate, we may find that small inaccuracies produce large errors in comparison with the real population size thirty years from now. How has the growth rate of 2.0 percent been derived? In 1953 the government carried out a census in 29 large and medium-size cites, the whole of Ningxia Province, and 10 counties in each of the other provinces, as well as specific areas in 35 other counties, 2 towns, 58 townships, and 9 villages, which together had a population of 30.18 million, a birth rate of 3.7 percent, and a death rate of 1.7 percent. From these figures we can calculate a growth rate of 2.0 percent. Moreover, the growth rate was higher in the cities than in the countryside. The growth rate was 3.9 percent in a section of Shanghai, while it was an average of 2.0 percent per year over all urban and rural areas. But I doubt that the growth rate has remained at 2.0 percent over these past four years. The census figures were accurate in 1953, but if we use the growth rate of 2.0 percent to explain the situation over the following four years (from 1953 to 1957), inaccuracies creep in.

For the following seven reasons, I believe that the growth rate exceeds 2.0 percent:

1. The number of married individuals has increased. Prior to liberation, young people, when they graduated, became unemployed. Now after graduating, young people are allocated jobs. The economic situation has improved to the point where young people now have the means to establish families. Also, full employment lessens reliance on relatives and friends and lightens their financial burdens, and this too increases the number of married individuals. Moreover, the government provides for each married couple, seeking in principle to allocate them both jobs in the same city—increasing the opportunities to bear children.

2. The government also provides benefits to pregnant women, new mothers, and infants. Women have fifty-six days of maternity leave before and after giving birth. This benefit did not exist prior to liberation. With the development of hygiene, rural midwives have now been replaced with proper delivery facilities, and consequently the infant mortality rate has declined. Daycare facilities have been set up everywhere and can take over from families some of the responsibilities of raising children, and children enjoy publicly funded education.

3. The death rate among the elderly has declined. In the past it was rare for a person to live to age seventy, whereas now living beyond seventy is common. The government provides for orphans, widows, and the elderly. After retirement, there are old-age pensions. Widowers, widows, and orphans are all cared for.

4. In the past the nation was plagued with civil wars almost annually. People suffered from military destruction, floods, and droughts. Many were displaced, and large numbers died. Now the nation enjoys stability unknown in the past: Civil war has disappeared, banditry has vanished, and homicide has diminished. As a result, fewer people die of unnatural causes.

5. With the changes in the social order, most nuns and monks have returned to secular life and have married, and in the future the number of monks and nuns will not increase. We have thoroughly solved the problem of prostitution, which is intractable in capitalist countries; as everyone knows, prostitutes, having too many men in their lives, cannot give birth.

6. Even after agricultural collectivization improved people's lives, the elderly still held onto their old ways of thinking. They desire abundant happiness and long life. Widely circulated are such old adages as "prosperity with five living generations and a household full of sons and grandsons" and "of the three most unfilial manifestations, the failure to continue the family line is the gravest." As long as family finances permit it, parents set about arranging a marriage for a son, establishing a household for him, and setting him up in business.

7. The government not only gives prizes to families with twins, triplets, and so on, but also provides them with economic assistance. These factors all increase the birth rate or decrease the death rate. Therefore, I believe that the population growth rate over these past four years is most likely to have exceeded 2.0 percent.

2. CHINA'S ACCUMULATION OF CAPITAL IS TOO SLOW

The greatest contradiction in our nation is that the population is growing too fast and the accumulation of capital seems too slow. Premier Zhou Enlai, in *Report on Suggestions for the Second Five-Year Plan for Development of the National Economy* (*Guanyu fazhan guomin jingji de dier ge wunian jihua de jianyi de baogao*), said,

> The scale of national development depends mainly on how much capital can be accumulated and how the funds are distributed. If we accumulate much capital and distribute it appropriately, we can then achieve relatively rapid extended social reproduction, and each sector of the national economy can then develop proportionately.

National income is the material wealth newly created by the laboring people of the country in the course of production. In a socialist country, the entire national income belongs to the laboring people. The laboring people use a portion of the national income to support and improve their livelihoods and use the other for extended social reproduction, that is, use it for accumulation. In distributing and redistributing the national income, it is necessary to maintain a proper balance between consumption and accumulations. If the proportion allocated to consumption is too small, this can impede the improvement of the people's livelihoods. If the proportion allocated to accumulation is too small, this can slow the extended social reproduction. Both of these conditions are detrimental to the people.

To improve the people's livelihoods, it is necessary to expand both production and the means of production. To expand production and the means of production, it is necessary to increase accumulation. To increase accumulation, it is necessary to raise the national income. China's

national income in 1956 was nearly RMB 90 billion, of which consumption accounted for 79 percent and accumulation 21 percent. Because the population is large, consumption is high, and accumulation is low. And because accumulation has to be allocated to many sectors of production, it seems even smaller. What I wish to investigate here is how to control the population so as to reduce the portion of consumption and simultaneously increase accumulation.

3. I ADVOCATED CONTROLLING THE POPULATION TWO YEARS AGO

I have made three inspection tours of Zhejiang. In former times [prior to liberation] Zhejiang was divided into eleven prefectures (*fu*), and I visited ten. This area has a strikingly high number of children, and this caught my attention. Whenever I visited a village, I would ask local administrative officials and old farmers how many births the village had, how many deaths, and what the net increase was after subtracting deaths from births. Though the increase in population of each area was different, my impression was that it was at least 2.2 percent, and when I visited Shanghai, I sensed that it was even higher. In 1955, after I finished the tour and returned to Beijing, I assembled the materials I gained on the inspection tour to prepare a speech on the population problem, the content being controlling the population and scientific research. I wanted to present this speech at the 1955 National People's Congress. Before presenting this speech, I discussed the issues with the Zhejiang delegation to the congress. Other than a few delegates, many delegates either expressed no opinion at all or disagreed with me. Some of them even thought that I was espousing Malthus's theories. Others thought that though I was saying something different from Malthus, I was still operating within a Malthusian framework. Though I could not accept their opinions, I thought that they all harbored good intentions. Hence, I put away my speech and decided to wait until the time was ripe to present it to the congress. In February of this year Chairman Mao, in a meeting of the Supreme State Conference, clearly brought up the population issue. I thought that his doing so was most timely and necessary. I thus got out the speech and presented it in summary form before the expanded Supreme State Conference. Here I present this essay in revised form and ask readers to make criticism.

4. THE ERRORS AND FAILURE OF MALTHUS'S POPULATION THEORY

Malthus's population theory, as everyone knows, is reactionary. Malthus said that population increases exponentially, that is, according to the series 1, 2, 4, 8, 16, 32, 64, . . . , but that the food supply increases linearly, or like the series 1, 2, 3, 4, 5, 6, 7, . . . After several generations, the population has greatly increased, while there is not enough grain. This leads to disease, epidemics, and even wars. People die off in large numbers, and the population declines sharply. Only thus can the population achieve equilibrium with the grain supply. Hence, the world is often caught up in a vicious cycle, and the outlook for humankind is bleak. Malthus's *Essay on the Principle of Population* was published in 1798, just after the start of the Industrial Revolution. The socioeconomic system underwent fundamental transformations: Workers became unemployed in large numbers; poverty was widespread; on occasion there were riots. The people were greatly dissatisfied with the capitalist government. Malthus wrote his essay to defend capitalism and capitalist government theoretically and to cover up the mistaken policies of the British government. His population theory amounts to saying to workers that widespread poverty among workers was not the government's fault; rather, it was primarily because the population increases too rapidly and the grain supply increases too slowly. This is the starting point of his essay, and in this he was fundamentally mistaken. At the time, the French general Napoleon stirred up a great war in Europe, and many people died. As a result, the grain situation took a turn for the better, and many people thought that Malthus's essay was accurate. But if one applied Malthus's theory to the situation in Germany after the Napoleonic Wars, it did not fit reality. Because of progress, at that time, in German scientific research, which led grain supplies to increase exponentially, even faster than the growth in the population, Malthus's theory that the food supply increases linearly thus collapses. Malthus failed to anticipate that scientific research would develop by leaps and bounds and cause the grain supply to increase exponentially, even faster than the population. One needs to understand that natural factors like land and labor, though they are the most basic components of agricultural production, have a limited effect on the development of production, but that scientific development knows no bounds. The more science advances, the higher the level of culture enjoyed by the people. Increases in knowledge cause labor productivity to rise and fertility to lower. For example, the upper classes and white-collar workers [literally, brain workers or mental workers, as distinguished from physical laborers] had a variety of recreation available to them—such as playing ball games, rowing, horseback riding, and hunting—and this lowered their sexual appetites. In France, the reproduction rate of the upper classes was stable, and they regarded raising children as a burden. Again, as John Rae (1796–1872) pointed out, the soil in the Hawaiian Islands is very fertile, and food grows in abundance, but the population did not increase accordingly. The primary reason for this is that Hawaiians did not like lots of children and grandchildren. This case too strongly refutes Malthus's essay on population; his theory that the population increases exponentially also fails.

5. THE DIFFERENCES BETWEEN MY POPULATION THEORY AND MALTHUS'S THEORY

Malthus's starting point was to cover up the mistaken policies of the British capitalist government. My starting point is to raise the productivity of farmers, to raise the level of the cultural and material life of farmers. Let me use conditions in China to explain the differences of my starting point.

China's first mechanized grain-storage facility built with Soviet aid recently began storing grain. The facility has a 60-meter-high operations tower. The grain arrives by train and is mechanically unloaded, conveyed, dusted, sifted, weighed, and measured for temperature using the machines of the operations tower. The automatic power shovel uses only a few minutes to unload a whole container of grain. Each granary has a resistance thermometer, enabling the inspector to ascertain the temperature of each granary from the instrument panel in the underground operations room. If he discovers that the temperature is high, with the flick of a switch he can air out 70,000 metric tons of grain in six days. If done manually, this amount of grain would take 300 individuals 1.5 years to dry in the sun. This grain-storage facility was built for Shijiazhuang Food Processing Industries to store ingredients and has greatly helped in maintaining product quality (*Dagongbao* [*L'impartial*], May 10, 1957). I once discussed the grain-storage problem with a member of the government's Grain Department and found out that the grain under government control (including the agricultural tax [paid in kind] and requisitions) amounts to about 50 billion kilograms. We must also add in the amount left over from last year, which was 10 billion kilograms, for a total of about 60 billion kilograms, or 60 million metric tons. If all of this grain were to be stored in mechanized grain-storage facilities, we would need to build 857 facilities, at a cost of about RMB 3 million per facility, or RMB 2.55 billion in total. But each granary is actually used at only 60 to 70 percent of capacity, owing to differences in crop yields from year to year. During a bumper-crop year, the harvest may fill up the granaries, but during poor-harvest years, only 60 to 70 percent of the granaries are used. Consequently, for a total storage capacity of 100 million metric tons, we need to build 1,428 grain-storage facilities and invest a total of RMB 4.28 billion. Where, I ask, is the money going to come from? Even if we could raise that kind of money, from where would we get the steel, concrete, and wood to build that many grain-storage facilities?

If we suppose that each old-style storage facility needs a staff of 300 laborers (a manager at an old-style storage facility manages only 250,000 kilograms of grain), crop storage would require a labor force of 428,400 individuals. Moreover, they would take 1.5 years to finish drying the grain out in the sun. But now a new-style storage facility requires only 15 technicians to completely air out 70 metric tons of grain in 6 days. Hence, a modern facility requires a workforce only one-twentieth of that of an old-style facility. The other nineteen-twentieths are redundant. Because the productivity of these 15 technicians is high, their average monthly salary is RMB 80. Because their salaries are high, their purchasing power is high. In this way we can improve the material and cultural life of workers and achieve the goal of socialism. But how can we improve the material and cultural life of workers in the redundant nineteen-twentieths portion? Under the pressure of the present population of 640 million people, we find it hard to improve the material and cultural life of these workers. If an additional 13 million individuals are born every year, this problem will become greater with the passage of time, and we do not know how grave it will become.

According to a factory and mine survey by Mr. Lou Baohua, of the No. 2 Shanghai National Cotton Mill (*Renmin ribao* [People's daily], October 9, 1957), between 1953 and 1957 the female workers of the No. 2 Shanghai State Cotton Mill gave birth to 3,049 babies, nearly equal to the present number of women workers in the mill. The birthrate of 1956 was nearly threefold that of 1946, before liberation. On the one hand, the birthrate of female workers rose, and on the other hand, the infant death rate declined. Prior to liberation, many children died of measles, diphtheria, smallpox, dysentery, and whooping cough, but today few children die of these diseases. This excessively high birthrate among women workers has led to the following unfortunate circumstances in this factory:

1. It has given rise to insufficient housing and difficulties in daily life, or has at least made it difficult to improve the quality of life. To mention just the workers' crowded housing conditions, on average five people live in one room. At present, 40 to 50 percent of the applications for housing give large families as the reason for the application.

2. From January to June 1957, 414 workers of the factory required supplemental assistance because of large families, accounting for about one-third of those requiring supplemental assistance.

3. In 1956 women workers missed 6,842 days of work owing to gynecological problems, the main medical reason for worker absences.

4. Because they have excessive births, are overburdened with housework, lead poor-quality lives and have poor nutrition, their health is affected.

5. Some women workers, because they have many children, are unable to get a proper education.

6. Some young women workers, after they give birth and become busy with housework, lose their enthusiasm for politics.

I firmly believe that as our enterprises become more developed, mechanization and automation will inevitably expand. Jobs requiring 1,000 workers in the past will require only 50 workers (assuming the ratio of one-twentieth across the board). What will the other 950 workers do? From this problem I conclude that with a large population we cannot proceed too quickly with mechanization and automation. At present we cannot create many large industries but rather have to develop small and medium-size industries. One reason is that small and medium-size enterprises can employ many workers. But to build a socialist country, China should create large enterprises. Lenin once said that without large enterprises, there can be no socialism (*Liening wenji* [The collected works of Lenin], vol. 7, p. 151). But our excessively large population prevents us from industrializing at a fast pace and from moving forward in large strides. Some people call me a Malthusian; I call them dogmatists and anti-Leninists.

Of the 13 million people added to the workforce this year, only 1 million can be placed in industry (according to Vice Premier Li Fuchun's explanation in the second five-year plan). The other 12 million will have to work in the countryside. However, the average farmer today annually creates wealth of no more than about RMB 80 for the nation, while the average factory worker, with modern technical equipment, annually produces wealth of more than RMB 4,000 for the nation. The productivity of these two sectors of the population compare at a ratio of 1 to 50. The reason for this great disparity in productivity lies primarily in the fact that industrial workers can use modern technical equipment (some of which is of the newest type), whereas farmers can use only animal power, to which one must add that recently draft animals in some provinces have died in large numbers with the result that human labor is used to pull the plow when tilling the fields, further diminishing agricultural productivity. To increase agricultural productivity, two factors are necessary: water and fertilizer, and without water, spreading fertilizer is useless. Without irrigation equipment, if there is a drought or a flood, no amount of fertilizer will increase productivity. Farmers in the North lack the custom of storing up fertilizer, and this is due to the lack of sufficient water resources in this region. China's technological programs are underdeveloped, and so it has yet to control flooding and droughts. Its industry is also underdeveloped, and so it still lacks the capacity to supply large quantities of chemical fertilizer. These are the main reasons for the labor-productivity gap between industry and agriculture. Saying these things, I no doubt lead some workers mistakenly to believe that they create more wealth for the country, that their contribution is greater, and consequently that they deserve higher salaries. Yet they do not realize that many input materials for industrial production come from the agricultural sector, that the accumulation of value is created in other sectors, and only because the last manufacturing phase is in their sector do the end results become manifest there.

If we follow this line of thought and group together the 1 million workers and 12 million farmers mentioned above, then the average labor productivity per person is pitifully low. The problem is how to raise the labor productivity of these 12 million farmers. Doing so requires electrifying agriculture, mechanizing agriculture, and greatly increasing the production of chemical fertilizers. But where is the capital for all this? Where is the fund accumulation? Even with capital accumulation, where are the materials, such as steel and concrete? As in the past, floods continue to plague China, and now are more violent than ever, as the 1954 flood shows. In light of this, I think that to eliminate farmers' loss of property and life to floods, it would be best to build a reservoir in the Three Gorges area capable of averting a once-in-a-millennium flood so that farmers would be high and dry. Clearly, the investment is considerable, the project vast, and a considerable area on the upper reaches of the Yangzi River would be flooded, but from the perspective of the long-term benefits to the country and farmers, such a project is worth undertaking. According to estimates by Mr. Lu Qinkan, chief engineer at the Waterpower Bureau of the Ministry of Electric Power, the cost of the Three Gorges project would be more than RMB 10 billion. It is also desirable to build industrial enterprises capable of using such electrical capacity. With this added on, the total cost would range from RMB 50 billion to RMB 100 billion. Where would such a large sum of money come from? Even if we had the money, where would such a large amount of steel and concrete come from? Moreover, because the project is so vast, it would take more than twenty years to complete. Even after the project is completed, it is not known how much benefit farmers would reap. Not only would the construction of waterworks and power plants completely transform farm villages; machines, fertilizer, transportation, fuel, and building materials would be brought into the area to service agriculture, with the result that farming villages would be transformed into important markets for heavy industry. But for now we have to wait for a while as far as the great Three Gorges project is concerned. After the socialist transformation of agriculture, that is, after the relations of production have changed and while the forces of production are vigorously moving forward, we must rapidly and positively prepare for the small-scale mechanization of agriculture. At present, a critical problem in the countryside is the seasonality of slack and peak periods. For example, in

the South, where they plant two crops of rice, farmers are exceedingly busy during the fifteen days when they harvest the first crop and plant the second. Hence, the key to increasing agriculture production is to provide machines to help farmers during this exceedingly busy period. The machines that farmers need most are rice harvesters, rice transplanters, and water pumps.

As I mentioned above, our weakness is that consumption is high and fund accumulation is low. In 1956 China's national income was RMB 90 billion, of which consumption accounted for 79 percent and fund accumulation accounted for 21 percent, or more than RMB 18 billion. This capital has to be divided among many enterprises in heavy industry, light industry, agriculture (including forestry, livestock farming, and fisheries), transportation, construction, and business (including foreign trade), and thus the amount of capital allocated to each enterprise is miniscule, so of course none can make rapid strides forward. When capital accumulates this slowly and the population increases this rapidly, is it not nearly impossible to resolve the contradiction of having little capital and a large population? We are disinclined to borrow money from the United States. We cannot imperialistically exploit a colonial people to extract capital from them. Nor can we follow the example of Japan and use the indemnity of the First Sino-Japanese War to finance industrialization. We have to renew ourselves using our own resources and accumulate capital by ourselves. But the ratio of our accumulation to our consumption is 21 percent to 79 percent. Can we decrease consumption and increase capital accumulation? A glance at our national circumstances shows that we are in a precarious situation.

Our national income is divided into capital accumulation and consumption. If accumulation increases, then consumption declines and the people endure a meager quality of life. If, in contrast, consumption increases, then accumulation declines and we have to defer completing our industrialization. Hence we have to seek a balance between the two. To determine how we should balance the two, we need to look at our actual situation. In the Soviet Union, consumption accounts for 75 percent of national income and capital accumulation for 25 percent, or one-quarter. In China, because the standard of living is low and the population is large, the weight of consumption is somewhat higher: we have a ratio of 79 percent to 21 percent. We cannot follow the Soviet Union and increase accumulation to 25 percent and reduce consumption to 75 percent. That would amount to coddling industrialization and ignoring the people, and could lead to political instability. At present we place the population growth of 12 million individuals in the countryside. Though this is the only course open to us, it is difficult to avoid side effects. For example, farmers of today want to keep more of the grain that they produce, and they look to urban residents for their standard of the necessities of life. They want to cook with oil, and as a result, oil is scarcer than grain. They want to wear new clothes, and consequently there is insufficient cloth available. This situation is already serious, yet every year we have to provide for a population increase of 13 million individuals, of whom 1 million are placed in the industrial sector and the remaining 12 million are placed in the countryside. Over the short term, we cannot increase the productivity of those in the countryside, but they have the same expectations as those in the cities. Over the long term, how can we manage? Thus, if we do not plan on how to deal with the population problem early on, farmers will convert all their gratitude into disappointment and dissatisfaction, and this will create difficulties for the government. For this reason, to raise the productivity of farmers, I advocate increasing the accumulation of funds and controlling the population. Otherwise, our nation will labor in vain.

By saying that the farmers will convert all their gratitude into disappointment and dissatisfaction, I refer to the following: With land reform, 300 million farmers with no land or little land acquired 47 million hectares of land and no longer had to deliver 30 billion kilograms of grain annually as rent in kind to landowners and escaped all sorts of exploitation falling outside their obligations. In the seven years after land reform, from 1950 to 1956, the nation spent RMB 3.07 billion on basic waterworks, RMB 1.31 billion on disaster relief, and RMB 1.28 billion on distributing improved varieties of grain, introducing new farm implements, raising the level of agricultural-production technology, and carrying out pest control. These three items total more than RMB 5.66 billion. In addition, farmers during these seven years received low-interest loans of RMB 800 million from the government and no longer had to pay usurious interest rates. Even the poorest farmers no longer sell their children, starve or suffer the cold, are homeless, or beg in the streets. Farmers can live quite well in the agricultural cooperatives. Moreover, the government instituted a system of five guarantees in the countryside, thus giving the elderly something to rely on. What I want to say is that unless the government institutes some means of controlling the population, this gratitude could turn into disappointment and dissatisfaction.

6. WE NEED NOT ONLY TO ACCUMULATE FUNDS BUT ALSO TO SPEED UP ACCUMULATION

The more five-year plans that a socialist country carries out, the higher its productivity and the more advanced its technological requirements. For the fifth year of the Soviet Union's first five-year plan, the fixed capital allocated for technology per worker was 10,000 rubles, and

the liquid funds amounted to 3,000 rubles, for a total of 13,000 rubles. For the fifth year of the third five-year plan, the amount allocated per worker was six times that of the fifth year of the first five-year plan, and for the fifth year of the fifth five-year plan, the amount was twelve times. The reason that Soviet production capacity continued to grow was that technological equipment grew several fold every year. China's future situation should be the same. Hence, to increase industrial labor productivity, we have to greatly increase fund accumulation, increase our technology allocations per worker, and also control the population, because if the population is allowed to grow freely, it is difficult to increase capital accumulation rapidly. The quickest way to increase accumulation is to raise labor productivity. With an increase in labor productivity, workers' incomes will naturally be higher, but if agricultural labor productivity cannot proportionally keep up with industrial labor productivity, the gap between farmers' and workers' incomes will be greater and greater, and this will affect the unity of farmers and workers. Hence, controlling the population is an urgent matter. The longer we put it off, the thornier and more difficult the problem becomes.

Above I said that for the fifth year of the first Soviet five-year plan, the fixed-capital installation per worker was 10,000 rubles and the liquid funds 3,000 rubles. In China from 1953 to 1955, the fixed assets allocated for production equipment per worker in state enterprises, local state enterprises, and public-private partnership enterprises was RMB 5,273 in 1953, RMB 6,072 in 1954, and RMB 6,835 in 1955. One ruble is worth about RMB 0.5. Hence, China and the Soviet Union, in their first five-year plans, allocated roughly the same amount for industrial technology.

7. WE MUST CONTROL THE POPULATION TO HAVE SUFFICIENT INDUSTRIAL RAW MATERIALS

We would do best to invest accumulated capital in light industry, because light industry requires small investments, its construction projects are easier, and the return on investment is greater and quicker. In this way we can more effectively accumulate capital to develop heavy industry more extensively and more quickly. Presently, it costs RMB 35 million to build a cotton textile mill with 100,000 spindles and 3,500 looms. After the start of production, only one year is needed to recoup the complete investment (including the industrial profit, commercial profit, and taxes). The recoupment period is even shorter for printing and dyeing mills and wool textile mills. The expansion of light industry not only does not affect the construction of heavy industry; it aids in the development of heavy industry.

But expanding light industry must be done under conditions of sufficient capital and raw materials. For this reason, I need to discuss the relation between light industry and agriculture. Most of the raw materials for light industry come from agriculture. If we want to build a cotton textile mill, we need cotton from agriculture; if we want to develop a silk textile mill, we need silkworm cocoons from agriculture; if we want to develop an oil mill, we need soybeans, peanuts, sesame seeds, rapeseeds, and so on; if we want to develop a sugar refinery, we need sugarcane and sugar beets; if we want to develop a wool textile mill, we need raw wool. At present, supplies of oil, sugar, and cloth are far from meeting people's ever growing demand for these products; they are scarcer than grain. If we want to increase the supply of these products, we need to expand the area for cultivating such cash crops as cotton, mulberry leaves, soybeans, peanuts, sesame seeds, sugarcane, and sugar beets. This will unavoidably reduce the area for cultivating grain and thus will affect the size of the grain crop. Hence, these various cash crops compete with grain for the available land. We need to find a suitable balance among these competing products. If the population grows without limit, this suitable balance will increasingly be destroyed: The increase in population will necessitate an increase in the production of grain. This will decrease the amount of land available to cash crops, affecting light industry directly and heavy industry indirectly. Thus, increases in the population act to reduce the accumulation of capital and delay industrialization. Hence, we must control the population.

At present sugar is extraordinarily scarce, just like edible oil. If we expand the area for cultivating sugar beets, beets will compete for land with grain and other crops. Xin Zhongguo Sugar Refinery and Fanjia Sugar Refinery, in Jilin Province, rely primarily on the interior counties of Yushu, Huaide, Jiutai, and Dehui for their supply of sugar beets. But these counties are also the province's greatest producers of grain and soybeans. If we greatly expand the production of sugar beets in these areas, we will reduce the area for cultivating grain and soybeans. Also, because the land [area] is limited, it is not possible to carry out crop rotation, which affects the quantity and quality of a sugar beet crop. For example, in 1953 a hectare produced 12,000 kilograms of sugar beets, with an average sugar content of 14.3 percent. In 1955 a hectare produced only 9,000 kilograms of sugar beets, with an average sugar content of just 11.4 percent. Such trends will cause the sugar-refining industry to shrink rather than expand.

From the discussion above, one can draw the following conclusion. Heavy industry and light industry are not yet as closely connected as light industry and agriculture. China is an agricultural country. If agriculture cannot develop rapidly, then it is difficult to expect that heavy industry will make great strides forward. Easing scarcity this year relies on hopes for a big harvest in the fall.

In China's development, heavy-industry projects are given first priority. Much of the turnkey equipment and important goods and materials must be imported from abroad, but how many heavy-industry goods and materials we can import from abroad depends on how many agricultural and light-industry goods and materials we can export, and light-industry goods and materials are made from agricultural goods and materials. Because China's chemical industry, especially its organic-chemical industry, is not yet developed, about 90 percent of the raw materials for light industry come from agriculture. Hence, expansions and contractions of agriculture, that is, good and bad harvests, have a decisive impact on heavy industry and industrialization. If the population is left to expand naturally and is not controlled, it will affect industrialization.

According to a speech given by Foreign Trade Minister Ye Jizhuang at the fourth session of the National People's Congress, in 1957 planned trade amounted to RMB 9.955 billion, a decline of 8.4 percent from the year before. Of this amount, imports accounted for RMB 4.7 billion, a decline of 10.2 percent from the year before, and exports accounted for RMB 5.2 billion, a decline of 6.6 percent from the year before. These declines were due to lower agricultural output as a result of disasters in some areas, which made exporting to meet demand difficult. But the main reason is that over the past several years, agricultural products and processed agricultural products made up about 75 percent of China's exports, while minerals and industrial products such as machines made up about 25 percent. At present, because the pace of increasing agricultural output has been affected by limited arable land and natural disasters, and because Chinese demand for light-industrial products has gradually increased, several types of commercial products have been exported less in order to meet the ever increasing demand in the domestic market. Yet with increases in exports of mineral products, industrial products, handicrafts, and small local products, China this year has maintained a respectable level of exports and can meet its needs and import equipment important for its development. In any case, because international trade has declined, progress in industrialization has been affected.

8. WE MUST CONTROL THE POPULATION TO PROMOTE SCIENTIFIC RESEARCH

The fundamental social transformations, and outstanding achievements in science and technology, of the twentieth century are not just a confluence of circumstances, but rather have an internal, necessary connection in that both are based on developments in material production. The discovery of aviation, radiotelegraphy, remote control, and especially nuclear power would not be possible without formidable present-day industry. These other technologies aside, we cannot even manufacture stainless steel, neither can the Soviet Union produce much stainless steel, and purchasing it from other countries is difficult. The newly built chemical-fertilizer plant in Sichuan still cannot acquire needed stainless steel. To build a chemical-fertilizer plant—from design, construction, and installation to the start of operations—generally takes about five to six years. In most cases, a large-scale chemical-fertilizer plant should be built in a country with an industrial base, or even an advanced industrial base, because advanced technology and materials are required. Such increases in the productive forces form the material basis for far-reaching scientific development, which in turn promotes further development of the productive forces. If theory and practice become well integrated, such development can raise the level of our research. Practice leads to advances in theory, which in turn guides practice. For those working in science, this cycle is a benchmark and the only procedure for pursuing scientific truth. The draft report of the Chinese Academy of Sciences revealed to the nation areas where it had a strong foundation and areas where its foundation was insufficient. For instance, publications that received awards belong mainly to fields that have a good foundation in China, yet in some new fields, especially fields urgently needed for economic and defense construction, few publications received awards. This state of affairs reflects past historical reality, calling out for notice in scientific circles, namely, "that efforts must be correctly directed to urgent areas where we are weak." Yet if economic and defense construction continue to advance, this will naturally promote research within these fields, lead to increased establishment of new institutions, and expand our research capacity. Let me discuss the matter in terms of engineering science. The work of engineering science is to seek theoretical solutions to practical problems and then to test them in practice. At present, in many parts of the country state farms and agricultural cooperatives have raised technical problems related to agricultural production and seek solutions from agricultural-science research institutes. We have to provide those solutions, and researchers, in providing solutions to the continuously appearing technical problems in agriculture, discover new data. Within this data lies the richest source of new theories. It is impossible even to imagine discussing the research of engineering science divorced from practice. If Chinese science is to catch up to the level of the rest of the world, it must do so in tandem with the development of production. We cannot divide scientific research into theoretical and practical research, because this so-called theory is theory in the service of developing solutions to practical problems. The two go hand in hand. In the past the Soviet Academy of Sciences made such a division, but later realized that this division was not appropriate, and did away with it. In addition,

only when there is the pressure of demands related to production can scientific research be hastened along. If our productive sector cannot catch up to the level of the world's advanced countries within twelve years and we insist on driving our research sector forward, this would be like rolling a boulder up a mountain. Premier Zhou Enlai, in a section on promoting science in *Report on the Work of the Government* (*Zhengfu gongzuo baogao*, 1957), said, "A distinguishing feature of science in the new China is the close connection between science and production. Production is the driving force behind science. During the Republican period, because industrial and agricultural production was on the decline, even though scientists carried out research, they could not affect production. In the eight years since liberation, with the development of production, the productive sector has made many demands on the scientific-research sector, our scientists have had ample opportunity to display their talents, and they have already achieved much." From this perspective, we must first equip industry with the technology it needs and raise labor productivity as quickly as possible. Only then can we firm up the material base of scientific research. Although the conditions for doing science have greatly improved, because of the limited level of industry and national budgetary constraints, we still cannot fully meet all the demands for research. If we wish to promote scientific research, we must rapidly accumulate capital and also strive to control the population to keep population growth from restraining the advance of scientific research.

In the future most of China's scientific research capacity will be placed in academies of science, 227 institutions of higher education, and many industrial sectors located throughout the country. The fact that they bring together large groups of research talent, cover so many research areas, and are dispersed to all areas of China is of advantage to the development of the scientific enterprise. To support the establishment of scientific culture in newly established industrial districts and some minority regions, we must build new institutions of higher education and new academies of science in these areas and will need some scientists to "leave their original research environments" and go there to work. In new research environments, these scientists may find that their research is affected, but over the long term, such placement will greatly benefit the development of science in China. Because developments in every field of science do not arise in isolation, the more advanced a field of science is, the more it requires coordination with related fields of science. (A characteristic of modern science is that various fields are closely connected and mutually influencing. Important problems in national construction are often solved only through research that spans many fields. For this reason we are carrying out research in many important areas.) An example of such coordination is building and launching a satellite, a complicated project requiring cross-disciplinary coordination in the areas of rocketry, metallurgy, mechanics, astronomy, mathematics, physics, chemistry, meteorology, geophysics, geodesic surveying, and wireless electronics. Another example is the international geophysical year. Why would scientists of the nations of the world carry out an international geophysical year from July 1 of this year (1957)? One reason is that after World War II, science and engineering made rapid technological progress. Progress in radio physics and rocket technology gave scientists good tools for measuring high-altitude values, and scientists could use these results to measure the earth. From these facts, one can see that without coordination of scientific research in the fields of radio physics and rocket technology, it would be impossible to make observations of the earth. Hence, we should want all sectors related to production to advance in equilibrium. But this state of affairs requires a greater accumulation of capital and stricter control of the population.

9. WE MUST CONTROL THE POPULATION TO HAVE SUFFICIENT GRAIN

For reasons of space, I will limit my discussion here of the relationship between population and food. I plan to devote another essay exclusively to this topic. Here I will just note that China has little land and a large population. The nation has a population of 640 million people and less than 2,000 square meters of land per individual. Some people point out that China has 100 million hectares of wasteland, but some of this consists of craggy mountains, some of arid land, and some of grasslands on which minorities practice nomadic pastoralism and which cannot be developed into farmland. Even today we have no accurate statistics on how much wasteland can be brought under cultivation. In addition, China's industry is backward, and its financial resources are limited; we still cannot quickly open up vast tracts of wasteland to cultivation. From 1953 to 1956 China annually brought 930,000 hectares of wasteland under cultivation, but because the population grew, the average amount of arable land per person fell from 1,867 square meters in 1953 to 1,800 square meters in 1955. Furthermore, natural disasters affect agricultural output and cause farmers' income to vary greatly. For example, in Jiangsu Province in 1955, the average farm household had an income of RMB 306 (this survey data is not representative of all of Jiangsu Province), and if we assume that a household has four individuals, this average income works out to RMB 76.50 per person. In 1956 the province suffered disaster, and the average income per farm individual fell to RMB 49.90. Because farmers' incomes are so variable, to stabilize their incomes, we need to prevent natural disasters from happening by undertaking large water-conservancy projects, like that at Sanmenxia,

but this requires developing and applying the appropriate science and technology and especially requires the accumulation of much capital. Hence, for sufficient grain as well, we must control the population.

In *On the Correct Handling of Contradictions among the People* (*Guanyu zhengque chuli renmin neibu maodun de wenti*), Chairman Mao said, "To help agriculture develop and the cooperatives to consolidate, we are planning to stabilize the total annual amount of the grain tax plus the grain purchased by the state at somewhat more than 40 billion kilograms within a few years. In this way, the small number of grain-deficient households still found in the countryside will no longer be short, all peasant households, except some raising industrial crops, will have grain reserves or at least become self-sufficient, there will no longer be poor peasants in the countryside, and the standard of living of the farmers will reach or surpass the middle peasants' level." These words of the chairman's came from his heart and brings good tidings to the people. If we can control the population, this high aspiration can be realized.

10. A FEW SUGGESTIONS

First, the first national census, taken in 1953, enabled us to get a clear picture of the population and understand its distribution on gender, age, ethnic group, and urban or rural place of residence. This is good, but to effect wise and healthy population policies and to help scientists carry out research, we need to carry out dynamic population surveys, including the statistical distribution of births, deaths, marriages, divorces, and changes of residence. Hence, I suggest that in 1958, or at the latest in 1963 during the general election, we carry out another census to enable us to know the actual growth of the population during these past five or ten years, that we compile dynamic population statistics, that we decide on population policies on this foundation, and that we include population growth in the second or third five-year plan to make these later plans gradually more accurate.

Second, above I discussed how the population of the Hawaiian Islands does not increase with an increase in the food supply. The main reason is that Hawaiians are not fond of having many children and grandchildren. But circumstances are the opposite in China. Here the notion of carrying on the family line is rooted too deeply. If a person's quality of life is good, he thinks of marrying, worries about not having descendents, fears traveling far from home, and loves his native place. In addition, people's actions are still dominated by many feudal ways of thinking, captured in such adages as "Give birth to a precious son early on," "A house full of sons and grandsons," "Five generations under one roof," "Oh, the prosperity of five generations still alive," "More sons means more happiness and longer life." Hence, women regard giving birth to a son as their natural duty and not raising children as a shame, and parents insist that should their daughter-in-law fail to have children, their son should have no qualms about taking a second wife or a concubine. But if we want to limit childbearing and control the population, as a first step we must widely disseminate among farmers the importance of limiting childbearing and ensure that they have the means to practice contraception. We must also widely inform people about the disadvantages of early marriage and the benefits of late marriage, the appropriate age for marriage being about 25 for men and 23 for women. But for the time being, we should not contemplate changing the Marriage Law. The reason is this: Though we should raise the age of marriage, we have not sufficiently instilled the notion of limiting childbearing. Hence, rural men and women, young and old alike, have not yet universally grasped the reasons and need for restricting childbearing. Thus, changing the law may have unintended consequences. For instance, young rural men and women, thinking that changes to the Marriage Law will raise the age of marriage and cause them to delay marriage, may marry early. It is not too late to change the Marriage Law after the education campaign. After we change the Marriage Law, if we find that it does not sufficiently control the population, we can, of course, supplement the law with stricter, more effective administrative measures. According to present calculations, the state spends about RMB 10,000 for each child's education and employment equipment. Ordinary people often do not sufficiently understand that household expenses for a child are less than the state's expenses. Hence, the state ought to have the right to interfere in childbearing and to control the population. In any case, controlling the population has as its purpose to increase the productivity of the people, especially farmers, in order to raise the level of their material and cultural quality of life so that they can live happier, more enriched lives.

Third, the best and most effective way to control the population is family planning. What is important is that we promote contraception and avoid induced abortion. For one, abortion is the taking of life. At the stage of abortion, the child has already formed in the mother's body. It has a right to life. Except in cases where the mother's health is at risk, one should not resort to abortion. For another, abortion can damage the mother's health and cause her to suffer illnesses. Some of my relatives, who originally were in good health, after having their uteruses scraped, suffered one illness after another. A third reason is that abortion can reduce the need to practice contraception. Young women may not concern themselves with contraception and instead rely on abortion. According to several well-known Beijing doctors, some women, just after having an abortion, get pregnant again, run to the hospital, and make a fuss. The main reason for this behavior is that couples rely on abortion

and do not conscientiously practice contraception. Some men especially do not take responsibility for contraception, seek only a moment's pleasure, and do not concern themselves with the long-term suffering of women. This situation is really unfair. A fourth reason is that abortion may increase the burden on physicians. The Soviet Union has a population of only 200 million, but it has more than 350,000 physicians, and its hospitals have 1.354 million beds. China has more than three times the population of the Soviet Union, but it has only 60,000 surgeons who can perform abortion. The situation in China's hospitals is already tight. If we foist upon physicians the additional burden of performing abortions, this will no doubt impede their treating of other illnesses. Hence, I earnestly request the Ministry of Health to consider these matters in formulating policy.

—Translated by Alan Thwaits

ON KHRUSHCHOV'S [KHRUSHCHEV'S] PHONY COMMUNISM AND ITS HISTORICAL LESSONS FOR THE WORLD

SOURCE *Mao Zedong.* On Khrushchov's Phony Communism and Its Historical Lessons for the World: Comment on the Open Letter of the Central Committee of the CPSU (IX). *Peking: Foreign Languages Press, 1964.*

INTRODUCTION *The Sino-Soviet disagreements that split the international communist movement first became public in the early 1960s. The polemic between the Soviet and Chinese parties was expressed in the* Letter of the Central Committee of the Communist Party of the Soviet Union [CPSU] to the Central Committee of the Chinese Communist Party *(March 1963) and in a reply and nine responses issued by the Chinese Central Committee between June 1963 and July 1964. These documents set out Mao's views on Soviet revisionism—its origins, development, and impact—and were read in obligatory political study meetings all over China. The text below is taken from the ninth comment.*

The theories of the proletarian revolution and the dictatorship of the proletariat are the quintessence of Marxism-Leninism. The questions of whether revolution should be upheld or opposed and whether the dictatorship of the proletariat should be upheld or opposed have always been the focus of struggle between Marxism-Leninism and all brands of revisionism and are now the focus of struggle between Marxist-Leninists the world over and the revisionist Khrushchov clique.

At the 22nd Congress of the CPSU, the revisionist Khrushchov clique developed their revisionism into a complete system not only by rounding off their anti-revolutionary theories of "peaceful coexistence" and "peaceful transition" but also by declaring that the dictatorship of the proletariat is no longer necessary in the Soviet Union and advancing the absurd theories of the "state of the whole people" and the "party of the entire people."

The Programme put forward by the revisionist Khrushchov clique at the 22nd Congress of the CPSU is a programme of phoney communism, a revisionist programme against proletarian revolution and for the abolition of the dictatorship of the proletariat and the proletarian party.

The revisionist Khrushchov clique abolish the dictatorship of the proletariat behind the camouflage of the "state of the whole people," change the proletarian character of the Communist Party of the Soviet Union behind the camouflage of the "party of the entire people" and pave the way for the restoration of capitalism behind that of "full-scale communist construction."

In its Proposal concerning the General Line of the International Communist Movement dated June 14, 1963, the Central Committee of the Communist Party of China pointed out that it is most absurd in theory and extremely harmful in practice to substitute the "state of the whole people" for the state of the dictatorship of the proletariat and the "party of the entire people" for the vanguard party of the proletariat. This substitution is a great historical retrogression which makes any transition to communism impossible and helps only to restore capitalism.

The Open Letter of the Central Committee of the CPSU and the press of the Soviet Union resort to sophistry in self-justification and charge that our criticisms of the "state of the whole people" and the "party of the entire people" are allegations "far removed from Marxism," betray "isolation from the life of the Soviet people" and are a demand that they "return to the past."

Well, let us ascertain who is actually far removed from Marxism-Leninism, what Soviet life is actually like and who actually wants the Soviet Union to return to the past....

Khrushchov has abolished the dictatorship of the proletariat in the Soviet Union and established a dictatorship of the revisionist clique headed by himself, that is, a dictatorship of the privileged stratum of the Soviet bourgeoisie. Actually his "state of the whole people" is not a state of the dictatorship of the proletariat but a state in which his small revisionist clique wield their dictatorship over the masses of the workers, the peasants and the revolutionary intellectuals.

Under the rule of the Khrushchov clique, there is no democracy for the Soviet working people, there is democracy only for the handful of people belonging to the revisionist Khrushchov clique, for the privileged stratum and for the bourgeois elements, old and new. Khrushchov's "democracy for the whole people" is nothing but out-and-out bourgeois democracy, i.e., a despotic dictatorship of the Khrushchov clique over the Soviet people.

In the Soviet Union today, anyone who persists in the proletarian stand, upholds Marxism-Leninism and has the courage to speak out, to resist or to fight is watched, followed, summoned, and even arrested, imprisoned or diagnosed as "mentally ill" and sent to "mental hospitals."

Recently the Soviet press has declared that it is necessary to "fight" against those who show even the slightest dissatisfaction, and called for "relentless battle" against the "rotten jokers" who are so bold as to make sarcastic remarks about Khrushchov's agricultural policy....

It is not particularly astonishing that the revisionist Khrushchov clique should have on more than one occasion bloodily suppressed striking workers and the masses who put up resistance.

The formula of abolishing the dictatorship of the proletariat while keeping a state of the whole people reveals the secret of the revisionist Khrushchov clique; that is, they are firmly opposed to the dictatorship of the proletariat but will not give up state power till their doom.

The revisionist Khrushchov clique know the paramount importance of controlling state power. They need it for clearing the way for the restoration of capitalism in the Soviet Union. These are Khrushchov's real aims in raising the banners of the "state of the whole people" and "democracy for the whole people."

THE TWENTY-THREE ARTICLES

SOURCE *Central Committee of the Chinese Communist Party. The Twenty-three Articles. In Baum, Richard, and Frederick C. Teiwes. Ssu-Ch'ing: The Socialist Education Movement of 1962–1966, appendix F, 118–126. Berkeley: University of California Press, 1968.*

INTRODUCTION *The socialist education movement of 1963–1965, which was initially focused on the rural areas, brought to the fore various differences within the Communist Party leadership on agricultural collectivization. The Twenty-three Articles, a summary of discussions on the movement at a national work conference convened in January 1965, reflect Mao's increasing unease that "capitalist roaders" had infiltrated the Communist Party even at the highest levels. The document contains implied criticisms of Liu Shaoqi and is important to an understanding of the origins of the Cultural Revolution.*

**Chinese Communist Party
Central Committee Document No. (65) 026**

Printed by the Fukien Provincial Party Committee General Office, January 18, 1965.
Fu No. 001

(Confidential)

SOME PROBLEMS CURRENTLY ARISING IN THE COURSE OF THE RURAL SOCIALIST EDUCATION MOVEMENT

NOTICE: To regional bureaus of the Central Committee; province, municipality, and autonomous region Party committees; Party member groups of the various central ministries and commissions; and the General Political Department of the Military Affairs Committee.

The Politburo of the Central Committee convened a National Work Conference, discussed some problems currently arising in the course of the rural Socialist Education Movement, and wrote a summary of the discussions. We now send you this document. If this document should contradict previous Central Committee documents concerning the Socialist Education Movement then this document shall uniformly be taken as the standard.

This document should be issued to Party committees at and above the hsien and regiment levels, and to the Party committees of work brigades and teams.

The Central Committee, January 14, 1965

A Summary of the Discussions of the National Work Conference Convened by the Politburo of the Central Committee, January 14, 1965

I. The Situation

Since the tenth plenum of the eighth Central Committee in September 1962, through the development of socialist education in urban areas as well as the countryside, the execution of a series of Central Committee policies by the whole Party, the active efforts of the masses, the broad number of Party members, and cadres, a very good situation has come into being on the political, economic, ideological and cultural, and military fronts in our country. In the past few months, in the entire country more than one million cadres went deeply into the basic level units in the cities and countryside, and the socialist revolutionary movement manifested a new high tide.

All the great accomplishments which our country obtained so quickly during the past few years prove the Party's general line of building socialism is correct, and at the same time prove further that the Chinese Communist Party led by Comrade Mao Tse-tung is a glorious, great and correct party. Our Party will not betray the trust and hopes of the people of the whole nation and of the people of the world.

In our cities and villages alike, there exists serious, acute class struggle. After the socialist reform of the ownership system was basically completed, the class enemies who oppose socialism attempted to use the form of "peaceful evolution" to restore capitalism. This situation of class struggle is necessarily reflected within the Party. The leadership of certain communes, brigades, enterprises and units has either been corrupted or usurped.

In our work, in the process of moving forward, there exist a great many problems. Practice proves that as long as the whole Party penetratingly and correctly continues to execute the Central Committee's various decisions concerning the Socialist Education Movement, continues to grasp the principles of class struggle, continues to rely on the working class, the poor and lower-middle peasants, the revolutionary cadres, the revolutionary intellectuals and other revolutionary elements, and continues to pay close attention to uniting more than 95 percent of our people and 95 percent of our cadres, then the many problems which exist in the cities and in the villages will not only be easy to discover, but will also be easy to resolve.

We must resolutely continue the Socialist Education Movement of the past two years and more, and carry it through to the end; we absolutely must not falter.

The present problem is to sum up the past experience of this movement, assess our achievements, and overcome the shortcomings in our work in order to facilitate an even greater victory.

II. The Nature of the Movement

Several ways of presentation:

1. The contradiction between the Four Cleans and the Four Uncleans;

2. The overlapping of contradictions within the Party and contradictions outside of the Party, or the overlapping of contradictions between the enemy and us and contradictions within the people;

3. The contradiction between socialism and capitalism.

The former two ways do not clarify the fundamental characteristics of the Socialist Education Movement. These two approaches do not refer to what society the contradiction of the Four Cleans and Four Uncleans arises in. Nor do they indicate what the nature is of the overlapping of contradictions within the Party and contradictions outside of the Party. They also do not indicate in what historical period the overlapping of contradictions between the enemy and us and contradictions within the people arises nor the class content of this overlapping. If we take a literal point of view, the so-called Four Cleans and Four Uncleans could be applied to any society in past history and the so-called overlapping of contradictions within the Party and contradictions outside the Party could be applied to any party. The so-called overlapping of contradictions between the enemy and us and contradictions within the people could be applied to any historical period. These approaches do not explain the nature of today's contradictions; therefore they are not Marxist-Leninist methods of looking at things.

The last way of presenting the nature of the movement comprehends the essence of the question, and is Marxist-Leninist. It is decidedly in accord with the scientific theories of Comrade Mao Tse-tung, and with the policies adopted by the Central Committee at various times since the second plenum of the Seventh Central Committee in 1949, concerning the continued existence, during the entire transitional period, of class contradictions, class struggle between the proletariat and the bourgeoisie, and struggle between the two roads of socialism and capitalism.

If we forget the basic theory and basic practice of our Party during the past decade and a half, we will go astray.

The key point of this movement is to rectify those people in positions of authority within the Party who take the capitalist road, and to progressively consolidate and develop the socialist battlefront in the urban and rural areas.

Of those people in positions of authority who take the capitalist road, some are out in the open and some are concealed. Of the people who support them, some are at lower levels and some are at higher levels. Among those lower down, some have already been classified as landlords, rich peasants, counter-revolutionaries and bad elements, while others have been overlooked. Among those at higher levels, there are some people in the communes, districts, hsien, special districts, and even in the work of provincial and Central Committee departments, who oppose socialism. Among them some were originally alien class elements; some are degenerate elements who have shed their original skin and changed their nature; and some have received bribes, banded together for seditious purposes, violated the law, and violated discipline.

Certain people do not distinguish the boundary between the enemy and ourselves; they have lost their class standpoint; and they harbor, within their own families and among their own friends and fellow workers, those people who engage in capitalist activities.

The great majority of our cadres want to take the socialist road, but there are some among them who have but a hazy knowledge of the socialist revolution, who employ personnel improperly, who are haphazard about checking up on work, and who commit the mistake of bureaucratism.

III. A Unified Way of Presentation

The Socialist Education Movement in the cities and countryside will from now on be uniformly simplified as the Four Cleans Movement—clean politics, clean economics, clean organization, and clean ideology.

In the past, the Socialist Education Movement in the cities was called the "Five Anti" movement. From now on we will call it the Four Cleans Movement and will abolish the "Five Anti."

IV. Setting Good Standards for the Movement

At the June 1964 meeting of the Standing Committee of the Politburo of the Central Committee attended by the first secretaries of the regional bureaus of the Central Committee, Comrade Mao Tse-tung said:

> What are good standards for evaluation of the Socialist Education Movement?

1. We must see whether the poor and lower-middle peasants have been truly aroused.

2. Has the problem of the Four Uncleans among the cadres been resolved?

3. Have the cadres participated in physical labor?

4. Has a good leadership nucleus been established?

5. When landlords, rich peasants, counter-revolutionaries and bad elements who engage in destructive activities are discovered, is this contradiction merely turned over to the higher levels, or are the masses mobilized to strictly supervise, criticize, and even appropriately struggle against these elements, and moreover retain them for reform on the spot?

6. We must see whether production is increasing or decreasing.

At that time, the Standing Committee of the Politburo held that these standards for assessing whether the Socialist Education Movement was being carried out properly were fully appropriate.

V. Work Methods

1. Within the movement as a whole, provincial, special district, and hsien level party committees and work teams, relying on the great majority of the masses

and cadres (including cadres who have cast aside their misgivings and doubts), must gradually carry out the "3 unifications" with respect to the masses, cadres, and work teams.

2. Once the movement has begun, we must immediately explain its meaning to the cadres and masses, and we must inform them of our policies. We must clearly declare that, no matter what commune or brigade, and no matter whether during or after the movement, the use of pretexts for opposing the masses of commune members will not be permitted.

3. The work teams must, during the movement and during the process of struggle, arouse the poor and lower-middle peasants, organize class ranks, discover activist elements and train them to form a leadership nucleus, and work together with them. We must not be quiet; we must not be mysterious; and we must not confine our activities to a small minority of the people.

4. In the course of the movement, from start to finish we must grasp production. At the same time, we must pay attention to grasping each year's distribution (the question of livelihood). If we do not grasp the questions of production and distribution, we will become divorced from the masses and will bring grievous harm to our cause.

5. We must proceed on the basis of local conditions. Reality demands this. Whatever problems the masses require to be solved must be solved. Whatever imbalances occur in our work must be rectified.

6. In the movement, we must boldly unleash the masses; we must not be like women with bound feet—we must not bind our hands and feet. At the same time, we must make a deep and fine penetration, and must not make a big fuss over nothing. We must set the facts in order, explain principles, eliminate simple, crude work methods, severely prohibit beating people and other forms of physical punishment, and prevent forced confessions.

7. To sum up: in the course of the movement as a whole, we must make use of contradictions to win over the majority, oppose the minority, and attack and defeat all who persist in taking the capitalist road—always a very small minority. Some people have committed mistakes which can still be rectified. With regard to those people who are the target of the Four Cleans movement, we must be good at discriminating among them and treating them differentially, taking the worst people and isolating them or narrowly confining them.

VI. Concentrate Our Forces, Fight a War of Annihilation

In leading the movement, we must have an overall, balanced point of view and an overall, balanced deployment. We must, through preliminary investigation and study, carry out a preliminary ordering of our ranks. We must suitably concentrate our forces to fight a war of annihilation. Starting in those key areas where the greatest number of problems exist, and where the influence [of those problems] is great, we must first make a breakthrough at a [single] point and then have an all-around thrust.

Point work does not refer merely to our working within production brigades, for we must also appropriately unite upper and lower level bodies as well as different bodies at the same level.

The movement should develop group by group and phase by phase like the motion of a wave—first resolving problems at one place and then moving on to resolve problems elsewhere.

The various provinces and cities should have the right to allocate their forces, and when necessary they may concentrate their cadres for training purposes during the course of the movement.

We should not rely on human sea tactics. We must not concentrate excessively large work teams within a single hsien, commune, or brigade. In this way, more points can be dealt with at the same time. This will also help us to follow the mass line.

The main thing is to go all out to prepare a nucleus of cadres who are able to grasp the Party's policy and who are able to understand and follow the mass line.

VII. Squatting at Points

"If one has not investigated, then one has no right of expression."

This teaching of Comrade Mao Tse-tung must be observed in our work. The effective investigation and research methods used by our Party in the past, such as that of holding investigation meetings, should continue to be utilized. Squatting at a point and dissecting a sparrow [i.e., making a thorough and careful analysis—transl.] is a very important method of leadership. Leading cadres must in a selective and planned manner continue to squat at points, going down to the basic levels and penetrating into the masses and, in the course of the movement and struggle, gaining relatively systematic experience.

There can be different methods of squatting at points. There should be a group of people who, for a relatively long period of time, go down into a brigade to guide the movement to its completion from beginning to end.

The leading personnel of Party organizations at the Central Committee regional bureau, provincial, special district, and hsien levels must implement the leadership methods which combine the general and individual aspects. Besides selecting a locality for squatting, they can convene meetings in places where they are squatting themselves or in other places, and carry out investigation, research and guidance of work in other points, and of production and other kinds of work in whole regions, provinces, special districts and hsien on the plane.

They can also go on inspection tours of other places, or organize small-scale roving inspection groups in order to facilitate their grasping of an active attitude, the mutual communication of information, and the exchange of experience.

VIII. Grasping Work on the Plane

We must look after both points and the plane.

At present the plane, outside of the key points which are carrying out the Four Cleans movement, constitutes the great majority of the country. The main task in these areas is production and construction. This task must conscientiously be well done.

The Central Committee bureaus, provincial committees, and special district committees must grasp the work of entire regions, provinces, and special districts.

With regard to work on the plane, these committees must also appropriately carry on the work of socialist education, of raising the political consciousness of the cadres, and of stimulating the latter to self-awaredly cleanse their hands and bodies. We should clearly declare to them that if their problems are not great, or if their problems are many but they confess and make restitution, and as long as they perform their work and make up for their errors with achievements, then we will not go into these things that are past.

Some hsien on the plane, if they have the proper conditions and the approval of the provincial committee, can also carry out Four Cleans point testing work.

The training of cadres in some localities can be used as reference for effective methods in developing from point to plane.

IX. The Cadre Question

1) In dealing with the cadre question, we must use the method of "one divides into two." We should adopt a serious, positive, and affectionate attitude toward them.

2) The situation will gradually become clarified. There are four possible types of cadres: good, relatively good, those with many problems, and those whose mistakes are of a serious nature. Under general conditions, cadres of the first two types are in the majority.

3) Comrade Mao Tse-tung long ago said: "We must adopt the policy of 'warn a man first so he may afterwards exert himself to goodness' and 'treating the illness to save the man' in dealing with people who make mistakes." He also said, "We must make a distinction between those party members and cadres who have committed mistakes, but who can still be educated, and those who cannot be saved. No matter what their backgrounds, we must step up their education and must not discard them." At the present time, we must continue to heed these instructions of Comrade Mao Tse-tung.

The policy we ought to adopt toward those cadres who have committed mistakes is "to persuade them to accept education, cleanse their hands and bodies, go to battle unencumbered, and unite against the enemy." It is a policy which arises from a profound hope for unity; one which, through criticism or struggle, brings about the resolution of contradictions; and which then attains a new unity on a new foundation.

4) Toward those cadres who have committed minor Four Unclean mistakes or who, though they have had many problems, have freely confessed their past histories, we ought to do our utmost to quickly liberate them. Toward those cadres whose mistakes are of a nature which is presently unclear, and who may therefore have been unsuitably retained at their original work posts, we may change their work or give them concentrated training, and carry on investigation of their cases.

5) Economic indemnities must not be randomly or unsystematically imposed. At the same time, such indemnities must accord with the actual conditions and with reason. In cases where the problems are not serious, and where examination and criticism has been relatively good, if the masses so agree, such indemnities may be reduced, delayed, or even cancelled.

6) We must adopt necessary and suitable disciplinary measures toward those cadres who have committed mistakes. This is for the purpose of educating and transforming them. As long as they are willing to take the socialist road, the Party will unite with them, and the masses will unite with them.

Of those incompetent cadres, some can be regulated and some can be transformed. Those Party members who do not fulfill the conditions of membership can be exhorted to leave the Party. These cases can all be dealt with in the latter stage of the movement.

7) Where the nature of the mistakes is serious—where leadership authority has been taken over by alien class elements or by degenerate elements who have shed their skin and changed their nature—authority must be seized, first by struggle and then by removing these elements from their positions. In general, the question of their membership in the Party should be resolved later. In cases which are especially serious, these elements can be fired from their posts on the spot, their Party membership cards taken away, and they may even, if need be, be

forcibly detained. Counter-revolutionaries, landlords, rich peasants and bad elements who have wormed their way into the Party must all be expelled from the Party.

In places where authority must be seized, or under conditions where the peoples' militia organization is critically impure, we should adopt the method of turning over the weapons and ammunition of the peoples' militia to reliable elements among the poor and lower-middle peasants.

8) When necessary, individual counter-revolutionaries or bad elements who have severely coerced the masses may be placed temporarily under guard or sent to do physical labor in the countryside until their cases are judged. In the most serious cases, such as murder, arson, or other serious crimes where the culprit is actually caught in the act, they may be arrested and their cases dealt with by legal channels.

9) Some bad cadres may have formed cliques. We must guard against classifying too many groups as cliques, or classifying the membership of the cliques too broadly.

X. Establishing Poor and Lower-Middle Peasants' Associations

Poor and Lower-Middle Peasants' Associations are revolutionary class organizations of a mass nature voluntarily organized by the poor and lower-middle peasants under the leadership of the Communist Party. These organizations supervise and assist cadres of various levels within the people's communes in carrying out work. This type of organization will fully develop its functions in the consolidation of the dictatorship of the proletariat, the consolidation of the collective economy, and the development of collective production.

The poor and lower-middle peasants, and their labor power in production, make up 60 to 70 percent of the total population and labor power in the countryside. They constitute the great majority. Poor peasants' associations, once they have been organized, may attract prosperous middle peasants and other people who have ambitions of self-advancement. These latter elements will try to ally with those people whose attitude toward socialism is normally wavering.

During the course of the Socialist Education Movement, in those places where basic-level organizations have atrophied or become paralyzed, and before a new leadership nucleus has been formed, we may implement [the policy of] all power to the poor and lower-middle peasants' associations.

XI. The Question of Time

For a brigade, about half a year; for a hsien, a year or more. Estimating from the fall and winter of 1964, about three years will be needed to complete the movement

throughout one-third of our country. Within six or seven years, the movement will be completed throughout the whole country. So long as our policies and work methods are correct, the pace of the movement may be accelerated somewhat.

XII. Declaration of Policies concerning Concealed Lands

After free and open discussion by the masses, the state will refrain for a period of about five years from increasing burdens on, and will not make further procurements from, those lands which have been concealed.

XIII. The Work of Finance and Trade Departments Must Be Adjusted to Fit the Four Cleans Movement

Increasing burdens or the repayment of loans will not be permitted simply because a certain place has already carried out the Four Cleans movement. Finance and trade organs, with respect to investment and loans, ought suitably to support production and construction in those areas which are carrying out the Four Cleans movement.

XIV. The Composition of Work Teams

It is not necessary to be fully and completely "clean." Those who have committed mistakes may also participate, on the one hand to facilitate their education and transformation, and on the other hand so that some of them can gain an all-around view of the movement and thus become useful workers. The work teams must continually summarize experiences and fix times for readjustment.

XV. Providing a Way Out

With regard to landlords, rich peasants, counter-revolutionaries, bad elements, and elements who have shed their skin and changed their nature, under the supervision of the masses they must undergo reform through labor in order to help them turn over a new leaf. Among those persons who have committed serious Four Unclean mistakes, some are no longer cadres or party members. These persons may still, however, be allowed to serve as commune members, to work diligently. Of the landlords, rich peasants, counter-revolutionaries and other bad elements who have labored honestly and have not done bad deeds for the past decade or more, there are some who have already been labelled. Can these labels be removed? Others have not yet been labelled; can they be excused from again being labelled? These questions should be judged and decided by the masses.

XVI. The Four Cleans Movement Must Rest Firmly on Construction

Speaking of a single hsien, both during and after the Four Cleans movement the work of training a party leadership nucleus must be gradually done. All instruments of the proletarian dictatorship must gradually be grasped in the hands of reliable people. A socialist hsien must gradually be solidly built up in order to enable the work of production, construction, science, culture, education, health and sanitation, public safety and the peoples' militia to make progress.

Production and construction in each commune and brigade throughout the country will be like a great fortress through upholding the policy of relying on one's own efforts.

XVII. The Size of Production Teams

During the process of the Four Cleans movement, after thorough discussion by the poor and lower-middle peasants, and after having been decided by the masses, production teams may carry out adjustment or organizational reform. Is a figure of about thirty households per team reasonable? If people live in relatively tight concentrations, the figure of thirty households may be exceeded. If people are relatively widely dispersed, less than thirty may be appropriate. These matters should not be decided from above.

XVIII. The Tenure of Office of Basic-Level Cadres

In accordance with the "60 articles," we should set a time to carry out democratic elections. Terms of office for reelection, or reappointment should in general be limited to four years. Cadres who are corrupt, who have committed serious mistakes, or who are unable to perform their duties well, may be recalled at any time.

XIX. The Question of Supervision

Cadres must be supervised both from above and from below. The most important supervision is that which comes from the masses. During the Four Cleans movement, cadres and masses should explore effective supervisory and political work systems. The authority of supervisory organs must be greater than that of the administrative organs of the same level.

XX. Four Great Democracies

All communes and brigades must learn from the People's Liberation Army and carry out political democracy, democracy in production, democracy in financial affairs, and military democracy.

XXI. Work Attitudes

All talk—good, bad, correct, and incorrect—must be listened to. It is particularly dissent that we must patiently listen to. We must let people fully express themselves.

XXII. Methods of Thought

We must strive to avoid one-sidedness and partialness. Everything must be analyzed, no matter what it is.

To view everything as absolute, motionless, isolated and unchanging is metaphysical. To spend one's time cataloguing great piles of superficial phenomena, or compiling great quantities of rules and regulations is scholasticism, which renders people unable to receive the necessary leadership. We must be proponents of dialectical materialism; we must oppose metaphysics and scholasticism.

XXIII. Scope

The various points raised above should, in principle, be applied also to the Four Cleans movement in the cities.

DECISION OF THE CENTRAL COMMITTEE OF THE CHINESE COMMUNIST PARTY CONCERNING THE GREAT PROLETARIAN CULTURAL REVOLUTION

INTRODUCTION *The Sixteen Points was a Maoist document adopted on August 8, 1966 by a somewhat irregular meeting of the Central Committee packed with Mao's supporters. It set out what the goals of the Cultural Revolution should be and identified the enemy as the "representatives of the bourgeoisie who had wormed their way into the Party and were taking the capitalist road." The document suggested that there were "capitalist roaders" at the highest levels of the party—and was thus to become the basis for the later persecution of top leaders such as Liu Shaoqi and Deng Xiaoping. The Sixteen Points urged the "free mobilization of the masses" to weed such people out and to destroy "the four olds" (old ideas, culture, customs and habits) which the "exploiting classes used to corrupt the masses." Read in political study classes all over China, the document became a charter for the Cultural Revolution. It was recited by the Red Guards when they damaged temples, destroyed statues or raided private houses in their crusade against "old" things.*

1. A NEW STAGE IN THE SOCIALIST REVOLUTION

The Great Proletarian Cultural Revolution now unfolding is a great revolution that touches people to their very souls and constitutes a new stage in the development of the socialist revolution in our country, a stage which is both broader and deeper.

At the Tenth Plenary Session of the Eighth Central Committee of the Party, Comrade Mao Tse-tung said: to overthrow a political power, it is always necessary first of all to create public opinion, to do work in the ideological sphere. This is true for the revolutionary class as well as for the counter-revolutionary class. This thesis of Comrade Mao Tse-tung's has been proved entirely correct in practice.

Although the bourgeoisie has been overthrown, it is still trying to use the old ideas, culture, customs and habits of the exploiting classes to corrupt the masses, capture their minds and endeavour to stage a comeback. The proletariat must do the exact opposite: it must meet head-on every challenge of the bourgeoisie in the ideological field and use the new ideas, culture, customs and habits of the proletariat to change the mental outlook of the whole of society. At present, our objective is to struggle against and overthrow those persons in authority who are taking the capitalist road, to criticize and repudiate the reactionary bourgeois academic "authorities" and the ideology of the bourgeoisie and all other exploiting classes and to transform education, literature and art and all other parts of the superstructure not in correspondence with the socialist economic base, so as to facilitate the consolidation and development of the socialist system.

2. THE MAIN CURRENT AND THE ZIGZAGS

The masses of the workers, peasants, soldiers, revolutionary intellectuals, and revolutionary cadres form the main force in this Great Cultural Revolution. Large numbers of revolutionary young people, previously unknown, have become courageous and daring pathbreakers. They are vigorous in action and intelligent. Through the media of big-character posters and great debates, they argue things out, expose and criticize thoroughly, and launch resolute attacks on the open and hidden representatives of the bourgeoisie. In such a great revolutionary movement, it is hardly avoidable that they should show shortcomings of one kind or another; however, their general revolutionary orientation has been correct from the beginning. This is the main current in the Great Proletarian Cultural Revolution. It is the general direction along which this revolution continues to advance.

Since the Cultural Revolution is a revolution, it inevitably meets with resistance. This resistance comes chiefly from those in authority who have wormed their way into the Party and are taking the capitalist road. It also comes from the force of habits from the old society. At present, this resistance is still fairly strong and stubborn. But after all, the Great Proletarian Cultural Revolution is an irresistible general trend. There is abundant evidence that such resistance will be quickly broken down once the masses become fully aroused.

Because the resistance is fairly strong, there will be reversals and even repeated reversals in this struggle. There is no harm in this. It tempers the proletariat and other working people, and especially the younger generation, teaches them lessons and gives them experience, and helps them to understand that the revolutionary road zigzags and does not run smoothly.

3. PUT DARING ABOVE EVERYTHING ELSE AND BOLDLY AROUSE THE MASSES

The outcome of this Great Cultural Revolution will be determined by whether or not the Party leadership dares boldly to arouse the masses.

Currently, there are four different situations with regard to the leadership being given to the movement of Cultural Revolution by Party organizations at various levels:

1. There is the situation in which the persons in charge of Party organizations stand in the van of the movement and dare to arouse the masses boldly. They put daring above everything else, they are dauntless communist fighters and good pupils of Chairman Mao. They advocate the big-character posters and great debates. They encourage the masses to expose every kind of ghost and monster and also to criticize the shortcomings and errors in the work of the persons in charge. This correct kind of leadership is the result of putting proletarian politics in the forefront and Mao Tse-tung's thought in the lead.

2. In many units, the persons in charge have a very poor understanding of the task of leadership in this great struggle, their leadership is far from being conscientious and effective, and they accordingly find themselves incompetent and in a weak position. They put fear above everything else, stick to outmoded ways and regulations, and are unwilling to break away from conventional practices and move ahead. They have been taken unaware by the new order of things, the revolutionary order of the masses, with the result that their leadership lags behind the situation, lags behind the masses.

3. In some units, the persons in charge, who made mistakes of one kind or another in the past, are even more prone to put fear above everything else, being afraid that the masses will catch them out. Actually, if they make serious self-criticism and accept the criticism of the masses, the Party and the masses will make allowances for their mistakes. But if the persons in charge don't, they will continue to make mistakes and become obstacles to the mass movement.

4. Some units are controlled by those who have wormed their way into the Party and are taking the capitalist road. Such persons in authority are extremely afraid of being exposed by the masses and therefore seek every possible pretext to suppress the mass movement. They resort to such tactics as shifting the targets for attack and turning black into white in an attempt to lead the movement astray. When they find themselves very isolated and no longer able to carry on as before, they resort still more to intrigues, stabbing people in the back, spreading rumours, and blurring the distinction between revolution and counter-revolution as much as they can, all for the purpose of attacking the revolutionaries.

What the Central Committee of the Party demands of the Party committees at all levels is that they persevere in giving correct leadership, put daring above everything else, boldly arouse the masses, change the state of weakness and incompetence where it exists, encourage those comrades who have made mistakes but are willing to correct them to cast off their mental burdens and join in the struggle, and dismiss from their leading posts all those in authority who are taking the capitalist road and so make possible the recapture of the leadership for the proletarian revolution.

4. LET THE MASSES EDUCATE THEMSELVES IN THE MOVEMENT

In the Great Proletarian Cultural Revolution, the only method is for the masses to liberate themselves, and any method of doing things in their stead must not be used.

Trust the masses, rely on them and respect their initiative. Cast out fear. Don't be afraid of disturbances. Chairman Mao has often told us that revolution cannot be so very refined, so gentle, so temperate, kind, courteous, restrained and magnanimous. Let the masses educate themselves in this great revolutionary movement and learn to distinguish between right and wrong and between correct and incorrect ways of doing things.

Make the fullest use of big-character posters and great debates to argue matters out, so that the masses can clarify the correct views, criticize the wrong views and expose all the ghosts and monsters. In this way the masses will be able to raise their political consciousness in the course of the struggle, enhance their abilities and talents, distinguish right from wrong and draw a clear line between ourselves and the enemy.

5. FIRMLY APPLY THE CLASS LINE OF THE PARTY

Who are our enemies? Who are our friends? This is a question of the first importance for the revolution and it is likewise a question of the first importance for the Great Cultural Revolution.

Party leadership should be good at discovering the left and developing and strengthening the ranks of the left; it should firmly rely on the revolutionary left. During the movement this is the only way to isolate the most reactionary rightists thoroughly, win over the middle and unite with the great majority so that by the end of the movement we shall achieve the unity of more than 95 per cent of the cadres and more than 95 per cent of the masses.

Concentrate all forces to strike at the handful of ultra-reactionary bourgeois rightists and counter-revolutionary revisionists, and expose and criticize to the full their crimes against the Party, against socialism and against Mao Tsetung's thought so as to isolate them to the maximum.

The main target of the present movement is those within the Party who are in authority and are taking the capitalist road.

Care should be taken to distinguish strictly between the anti-Party, anti-socialist rightists and those who support the Party and socialism but have said or done something wrong or have written some bad articles or other works.

Care should be taken to distinguish strictly between the reactionary bourgeois scholar despots and "authorities" on the one hand and people who have the ordinary bourgeois academic ideas on the other.

6. CORRECT HANDLING OF CONTRADICTIONS AMONG THE PEOPLE

A strict distinction must be made between the two different types of contradictions: those among the people and those between ourselves and the enemy. Contradictions among the people must not be made into contradictions between ourselves and the enemy; nor must contradictions between ourselves and the enemy be regarded as contradictions among the people.

It is normal for the masses to hold different views. Contention between different views is unavoidable, necessary and beneficial. In the course of normal and full debate, the masses will affirm what is right, correct what is wrong and gradually reach unanimity.

The method to be used in debates is to present the facts, reason things out, and persuade through reasoning. Any method of forcing a minority holding different views to submit is impermissible. The minority should be protected, because sometimes the truth is with the minority. Even if the minority is wrong, they should still be allowed to argue their case and reserve their views.

When there is a debate, it should be conducted by reasoning, not by coercion or force.

In the course of debate, every revolutionary should be good at thinking things out for himself and should develop the communist spirit of daring to think, daring to speak and daring to act. On the premise that they have the same general orientation, revolutionary comrades should, for the sake of strengthening unity, avoid endless debate over side issues.

7. BE ON GUARD AGAINST THOSE WHO BRAND THE REVOLUTIONARY MASSES AS "COUNTER-REVOLUTIONARIES"

In certain schools, units, and work teams of the Cultural Revolution, some of the persons in charge have organized counter-attacks against the masses who put up big-character posters criticizing them. These people have even advanced such slogans as: opposition to the leaders of a unit or a work team means opposition to the Central Committee of the Party, means opposition to the Party and socialism, means counter-revolution. In this way it is inevitable that their blows will fall on some really revolutionary activists. This is an error on matters of orientation, an error of line, and is absolutely impermissible.

A number of persons who suffer from serious ideological errors, and particularly some of the anti-Party and anti-socialist rightists, are taking advantage of certain shortcomings and mistakes in the mass movement to spread rumours and gossip, and engage in agitation, deliberately branding some of the masses as "counter-revolutionaries." It is necessary to beware of such "pick-pockets" and expose their tricks in good time.

In the course of the movement, with the exception of cases of active counter-revolutionaries where there is clear evidence of crimes such as murder, arson, poisoning, sabotage or theft of state secrets, which should be handled in accordance with the law, no measures should be taken against students at universities, colleges, middle schools and primary schools because of problems that arise in the movement. To prevent the struggle from being diverted from its main target, it is not allowed, under whatever pretext, to incite the masses or the students to struggle against each other. Even proven rightists should be dealt with on the merits of each case at a later stage of the movement.

8. THE QUESTION OF CADRES

The cadres fall roughly into the following four categories:

1. good;

2. comparatively good;

3. those who have made serious mistakes but have not become anti-Party, anti-socialist rightists;

4. the small number of anti-Party, anti-socialist rightists.

In ordinary situations, the first two categories (good and comparatively good) are the great majority.

The anti-Party, anti-socialist rightists must be fully exposed, refuted, overthrown and completely discredited and their influence eliminated. At the same time, they should be given a chance to turn over a new leaf.

9. CULTURAL REVOLUTION GROUPS, COMMITTEES AND CONGRESSES

Many new things have begun to emerge in the Great Proletarian Cultural Revolution. The Cultural Revolutionary groups, committees and other organizational forms created by the masses in many schools and units are something new and of great historic importance.

These Cultural Revolutionary groups, committees and congresses are excellent new forms of organization whereby the masses educate themselves under the leadership of the Communist Party. They are an excellent bridge to keep our Party in close contact with the masses. They are organs of power of the proletarian Cultural Revolution.

The struggle of the proletariat against the old ideas, culture, customs and habits left over by all the exploiting classes over thousands of years will necessarily take a very, very long time. Therefore, the Cultural Revolutionary groups, committees and congresses should not be temporary organizations but permanent, standing mass organizations. They are suitable not only for colleges, schools and government and other organizations, but generally also for factories, mines, other enterprises, urban districts and villages.

It is necessary to institute a system of general elections, like that of the Paris Commune, for electing members to the Cultural Revolutionary groups and committees and delegates to the Cultural Revolutionary congresses. The lists of candidates should be put forward by the revolutionary masses after full discussion, and the elections should be held after the masses have discussed the lists over and over again.

The masses are entitled at any time to criticize members of the Cultural Revolutionary groups and committees and delegates elected to the Cultural Revolutionary congresses. If these members or delegates prove incompetent, they can be replaced through election or recalled by the masses after discussion.

The Cultural Revolutionary groups, committees and congresses in colleges and schools should consist mainly of representatives of the revolutionary students. At the same time, they should have a certain number of representatives of the revolutionary teaching and administrative staff and workers.

10. EDUCATIONAL REFORM

In the Great Proletarian Cultural Revolution a most important task is to transform the old educational system and the old principles and methods of teaching.

In this Great Cultural Revolution, the phenomenon of our schools being dominated by bourgeois intellectuals must be completely changed.

In every kind of school we must apply thoroughly the policy advanced by Comrade Mao Tse-tung of education serving proletarian politics and education being combined with productive labour, so as to enable those receiving an education to develop morally, intellectually and physically and to become labourers with socialist consciousness and culture.

The period of schooling should be shortened. Courses should be fewer and better. The teaching material should be thoroughly transformed, in some cases beginning with simplifying complicated material. While their main task is to study, students should also learn other things. That is to say, in addition to their studies they should also learn industrial work, farming and military affairs, and take part in the struggles of the Cultural Revolution to criticize the bourgeoisie as these struggles occur.

11. THE QUESTION OF CRITICIZING BY NAME IN THE PRESS

In the course of the mass movement of the Cultural Revolution, the criticism of bourgeois and feudal ideology should be well combined with the dissemination of the proletarian world outlook and of Marxism-Leninism, Mao Tse-tung's thought.

Criticism should be organized of typical bourgeois representatives who have wormed their way into the Party and typical reactionary bourgeois academic "authorities," and this should include criticism of various kinds of reactionary views in philosophy, history, political economy and education, in works and theories of literature and art, in theories of natural science, and in other fields.

Criticism of anyone by name in the press should be decided after discussion by the Party committee at the same level, and in some cases submitted to the Party committee at a higher level for approval.

12. POLICY TOWARDS SCIENTISTS, TECHNICIANS AND ORDINARY MEMBERS OF WORKING STAFFS

As regards scientists, technicians and ordinary members of working staffs, as long as they are patriotic, work energetically, are not against the Party and socialism, and maintain no illicit relations with any foreign country, we should in the present movement continue to apply the policy of "unity, criticism, unity." Special care should be taken of those scientists and scientific and technical personnel who have made contributions. Efforts should be made to help them gradually transform their world outlook and their style of work.

13. THE QUESTION OF ARRANGEMENTS FOR INTEGRATION WITH THE SOCIALIST EDUCATION MOVEMENT IN CITY AND COUNTRYSIDE

The cultural and educational units and leading organs of the Party and government in the large and medium cities are the points of concentration of the present proletarian Cultural Revolution.

The Great Cultural Revolution has enriched the socialist education movement in both city and countryside and raised it to a higher level. Efforts should be made to conduct these two movements in close combination. Arrangements to this effect may be made by various regions and departments in the light of the specific conditions.

The socialist education movement now going on in the countryside and in enterprises in the cities should not be upset where the original arrangements are appropriate and the movement is going well, but should continue in accordance with the original arrangements. However, the questions that are arising in the present Great Proletarian Cultural Revolution should be put to the masses for discussion at the proper time, so as to further foster vigorously proletarian ideology and eradicate bourgeois ideology.

In some places, the Great Proletarian Cultural Revolution is being used as the focus in order to add momentum to the socialist education movement and clean things up in the fields of politics, ideology, organization and economy. This may be done where the local Party committee thinks it appropriate.

14. TAKE FIRM HOLD OF THE REVOLUTION AND STIMULATE PRODUCTION

The aim of the Great Proletarian Cultural Revolution is to revolutionize people's ideology and as a consequence to achieve greater, faster, better and more economical results in all fields of work. If the masses are fully aroused and proper arrangements are made, it is possible to carry on both the Cultural Revolution and production without one hampering the other, while guaranteeing high quality in all our work.

The Great Proletarian Cultural Revolution is a powerful motive force for the development of the social productive forces in our country. Any idea of counterposing the Great Cultural Revolution to the development of production is incorrect.

15. THE ARMED FORCES

In the armed forces, the cultural revolution and the socialist education movement should be carried out in accordance with the instructions of the Military Commission of the Central Committee of the Party and the General Political Department of the People's Liberation Army.

16. MAO TSE-TUNG'S THOUGHT IS THE GUIDE FOR ACTION IN THE GREAT PROLETARIAN CULTURAL REVOLUTION

In the Great Proletarian Cultural Revolution, it is imperative to hold aloft the great red banner of Mao Tse-tung's thought and put proletarian politics in command. The movement for the creative study and application of Chairman Mao Tse-tung's works should be carried forward among the masses of the workers, peasants and soldiers, the cadres and the intellectuals, and Mao Tse-tung's thought should be taken as the guide to action in the Cultural Revolution.

In this complex Great Cultural Revolution, Party committees at all levels must study and apply Chairman Mao's works all the more conscientiously and in a creative way. In particular, they must study over and over again Chairman Mao's writings on the Cultural Revolution and on the Party's methods of leadership, such as On New Democracy, Talks at the Yenan Forum on Literature and Art, On the Correct Handling of Contradictions Among the People, Speech at the Chinese Communist Party's National Conference on Propaganda Work, Some Questions Concerning Methods of Leadership and Methods of Work of Party Committees.

Party committees at all levels must abide by the directions given by Chairman Mao over the years, namely that they should thoroughly apply the mass line of "from the masses, to the masses" and that they should be pupils before they become teachers. They should try to avoid being one-sided or narrow. They should foster materialist dialectics and oppose metaphysics and scholasticism.

The Great Proletarian Cultural Revolution is bound to achieve brilliant victory under the leadership of the Central Committee of the Party headed by Comrade Mao Tse-tung.

PREFACE TO QUOTATIONS BY CHAIRMAN MAO

SOURCE *Foreword to the First Chinese Edition; Foreword to the Second Chinese Edition.* Quotations from Chairman Mao Tse-Tung, ed. Stuart R. Schram, xxxi–xxxiv. New York: Frederick A. Praeger, 1967.

INTRODUCTION *The* Little Red Book *or* Quotations from Chairman Mao *was first compiled for use in political education in the People's Liberation Army and then issued in a second edition for more general use in political education in 1966. During the Cultural Revolution almost every citizen carried a copy. Lin Biao (Lin Piao), China's minister of defense and from 1969 Mao's designated successor, supplied obsequious introductions for the later editions (1966 and 1967). After Lin's mysterious death and disgrace in 1971, people were instructed to rip the introduction out of their copies. Subsequent editions carried no introduction. The size and format of the book was designed for portability in the pocket of a "Mao jacket."*

FOREWORD TO THE FIRST CHINESE EDITION

Comrade Mao Tse-tung is the greatest Marxist-Leninist of our era. Mao Tse-tung's thought is the application of the universal truths of Marxism-Leninism in the era in which imperialism is heading for collapse and socialism is advancing to victory, in the concrete practice of the Chinese revolution, in the collective struggles of the party and the people; it is Marxism-Leninism creatively developed. Mao Tse-tung's thought is the guiding principle for the Chinese people's revolution and socialist construction, it is a powerful ideological weapon for opposing imperialism and for opposing revisionism and dogmatism. Comrade Mao Tse-tung has not only established a fixed and immovable political orientation for our army, he has also established the only correct line for the edification of our army. The guiding thought of our party, our party's experience in struggle, and the theories of our party are concentrated in their most general form in Mao Tse-tung's thought. Therefore, the most fundamental task in our army's political and ideological work is at all times to hold high the great red banner of Mao Tse-tung's thought, to arm the minds of all our commanders with it and to persist in using it to command every field of activity. All the comrades in our army should really master Mao Tse-tung's thought; they should all study Chairman Mao's writings, follow his teachings, act according to his instructions and be his good fighters.

Comrade Lin Piao has instructed us that in order really to master Mao Tse-tung's thought, it is essential to study many of Chairman Mao's basic concepts over and over again, and even to memorize important statements and study and apply them repeatedly. Comrade Lin Piao has moreover directed that the *Liberation Army Daily* should regularly carry quotations from Chairman Mao for cadres and soldiers to study. The experience of the various army corps in their creative study and application of Chairman Mao's works in the last few years has proved also that to study selected quotations from Chairman Mao with specific problems in mind is a good way to learn Mao Tse-tung's thought, a method conducive to quick results. We have compiled *Quotations from Chairman Mao Tse-Tung* by gathering together the quotations already published in *Liberation Army Daily* and adding some others, in order to help lower-level cadres and soldiers learn Mao Tse-tung's thought more effectively; we have also endeavored, in accordance with the principle of selecting brief but essential passages, to ensure that the contents we have selected are adapted to the needs and standard of the lower-level cadres and soldiers. In organizing their study, the various army corps should select passages that are relevant to the situation, their tasks, the current thinking of their personnel, and the state of their work. This volume of quotations was published in May 1964. In reprinting it this time, we have made a few additions and deletions and partial changes in arrangement.

In conformity with Comrade Lin Piao's instructions, we must issue *Selected Readings from Chairman Mao* and *Quotations from Chairman Mao Tse-Tung* to every soldier in the whole army, just as we issue weapons. It is our hope that all comrades will learn earnestly, bring about an even greater and broader high tide in the creative study and application of Chairman Mao's works in the whole army, and struggle to speed up the revolutionarization, modernization and edification of our army.

The General Political Department
August 1, 1965

FOREWORD TO THE SECOND CHINESE EDITION

Comrade Mao Tse-tung is the greatest Marxist-Leninist of our era. He has inherited, defended and developed Marxism-Leninism with genius, creatively and comprehensively and has brought it to a higher and completely new stage.

Mao Tse-tung's thought is Marxism-Leninism of the era in which imperialism is heading for total collapse and socialism is advancing to world-wide victory. It is a powerful ideological weapon for opposing imperialism and for opposing revisionism and dogmatism. Mao Tse-tung's thought is the guiding principle for all the work of the Party, the army and the country.

Therefore, the most fundamental task in our Party's political and ideological work is at all times to hold high the great red banner of Mao Tse-tung's thought, to arm the minds of the people throughout the country with it and to persist in using it to command every field of activity. The broad masses of the workers, peasants and soldiers and the broad ranks of the revolutionary cadres and the intellectuals should really master Mao Tse-tung's thought; they should all study Chairman Mao's writings, follow his teachings, act according to his instructions and be his good fighters.

In studying the works of Chairman Mao, one should have specific problems in mind, study and apply his works in a creative way, combine study with application, first study what must be urgently applied so as to get quick results, and strive hard to apply what one is studying. In order really to master Mao Tse-tung's thought, it is essential to study many of Chairman Mao's basic concepts over and over again, and it is best to memorize important statements and study and apply them repeatedly. The newspapers should regularly carry quotations from Chairman Mao relevant to current issues for readers to study and apply. The experience of the broad masses in their creative study and application of Chairman Mao's works in the last few years has proved that to study selected quotations from Chairman Mao with specific problems in mind is a good way to learn Mao Tse-tung's thought, a method conducive to quick results.

We have compiled *Quotations from Chairman Mao Tse-Tung* in order to help the broad masses learn Mao Tse-tung's thought more effectively. In organizing their study, units should select passages that are relevant to the situation, their tasks, the current thinking of their personnel, and the state of their work.

In our great motherland, a new era is emerging in which the workers, peasants and soldiers are grasping Marxism-Leninism, Mao Tse-tung's thought. Once Mao Tse-tung's thought is grasped by the broad masses, it becomes an inexhaustible source of strength and a spiritual atom bomb of infinite power. The large-scale publication of *Quotations from Chairman Mao Tse-Tung* is a vital measure for enabling the broad masses to grasp Mao Tse-tung's thought and for promoting the revolutionization of our people's thinking. It is our hope that all comrades will learn earnestly and diligently, bring about a new nation-wide high tide in the creative study and application of Chairman Mao's works and, under the great red banner of Mao Tse-tung's thought, strive to build our country into a great socialist state with modern agriculture, modern industry, modern science and culture and modern national defence!

Lin Piao
December 16, 1966

SHANGHAI COMMUNIQUÉ (FIRST JOINT COMMUNIQUÉ OF THE UNITED STATES OF AMERICA AND THE PEOPLE'S REPUBLIC OF CHINA)

INTRODUCTION *After the establishment of the People's Republic of China in 1949, the United States continued to recognize the Guomindang government on Taiwan as the true government of China. When*

JOINT COMMUNIQUÉ OF THE UNITED STATES OF AMERICA AND THE PEOPLE'S REPUBLIC OF CHINA

February 28, 1972

1. President Richard Nixon of the United States of America visited the People's Republic of China at the invitation of Premier Chou En-lai of the People's Republic of China from February 21 to February 28, 1972. Accompanying the President were Mrs. Nixon, U.S. Secretary of State William Rogers, Assistant to the President Dr. Henry Kissinger, and other American officials. . . .

5. The leaders of the People's Republic of China and the United States of America found it beneficial to have this opportunity, after so many years without contact, to present candidly to one another their views on a variety of issues. They reviewed the international situation in which important changes and great upheavals are taking place and expounded their respective positions and attitudes.

6. The Chinese side stated: Wherever there is oppression, there is resistance. Countries want independence, nations want liberation and the people want revolution-- this has become the irresistible trend of history. All nations, big or small, should be equal: big nations should not bully the small and strong nations should not bully the weak. China will never be a superpower and it opposes hegemony and power politics of any kind. The Chinese side stated that it firmly supports the struggles of all the oppressed people and nations for freedom and liberation and that the people of all countries have the right to choose their social systems according their own wishes and the right to safeguard the independence, sovereignty and territorial integrity of their own countries and oppose foreign aggression, interference, control and subversion. All foreign troops should be withdrawn to their own countries. The Chinese side expressed its firm support to the peoples of Viet Nam, Laos and Cambodia in their

efforts for the attainment of their goal and its firm support to the seven-point proposal of the Provisional Revolutionary Government of the Republic of South Viet Nam and the elaboration of February this year on the two key problems in the proposal, and to the Joint Declaration of the Summit Conference of the Indochinese Peoples. It firmly supports the eight-point program for the peaceful unification of Korea put forward by the Government of the Democratic People's Republic of Korea on April 12, 1971, and the stand for the abolition of the "U.N. Commission for the Unification and Rehabilitation of Korea". It firmly opposes the revival and outward expansion of Japanese militarism and firmly supports the Japanese people's desire to build an independent, democratic, peaceful and neutral Japan. It firmly maintains that India and Pakistan should, in accordance with the United Nations resolutions on the Indo-Pakistan question, immediately withdraw all their forces to their respective territories and to their own sides of the ceasefire line in Jammu and Kashmir and firmly supports the Pakistan Government and people in their struggle to preserve their independence and sovereignty and the people of Jammu and Kashmir in their struggle for the right of self-determination.

7. The U.S. side stated: Peace in Asia and peace in the world requires efforts both to reduce immediate tensions and to eliminate the basic causes of conflict. The United States will work for a just and secure peace: just, because it fulfills the aspirations of peoples and nations for freedom and progress; secure, because it removes the danger of foreign aggression. The United States supports individual freedom and social progress for all the peoples of the world, free of outside pressure or intervention. The United States believes that the effort to reduce tensions is served by improving communication between countries that have different ideologies so as to lessen the risks of confrontation through accident, miscalculation or misunderstanding. Countries should treat each other with mutual respect and be willing to compete peacefully, letting performance be the ultimate judge. No country should claim infallibility and each country should be prepared to reexamine its own attitudes for the common good. The United States stressed that the peoples of Indochina should be allowed to determine their destiny without outside intervention; its constant primary objective has been a negotiated solution; the eight-point proposal put forward by the Republic of Viet Nam and the United States on January 27, 1972 represents a basis for the attainment of that objective; in the absence of a negotiated settlement the United States envisages the ultimate withdrawal of all U.S. forces from the region consistent with the aim of self-determination for each country of Indochina. The United States will maintain its close ties with and support for the Republic of Korea;

the United States will support efforts of the Republic of Korea to seek a relaxation of tension and increased communication in the Korean peninsula. The United States places the highest value on its friendly relations with Japan; it will continue to develop the existing close bonds. Consistent with the United Nations Security Council Resolution of December 21, 1971, the United States favors the continuation of the ceasefire between India and Pakistan and the withdrawal of all military forces to within their own territories and to their own sides of the ceasefire line in Jammu and Kashmir; the United States supports the right of the peoples of South Asia to shape their own future in peace, free of military threat, and without having the area become the subject of great power rivalry.

8. There are essential differences between China and the United States in their social systems and foreign policies. However, the two sides agreed that countries, regardless of their social systems, should conduct their relations on the principles of respect for the sovereignty and territorial integrity of all states, non-aggression against other states, non-interference in the internal affairs of other states, equality and mutual benefit, and peaceful coexistence. International disputes should be settled on this basis, without resorting to the use or threat of force. The United States and the People's Republic of China are prepared to apply these principles to their mutual relations.

9. With these principles of international relations in mind the two sides stated that:

- progress toward the normalization of relations between China and the United States is in the interests of all countries

- both wish to reduce the danger of international military conflict

- neither should seek hegemony in the Asia-Pacific region and each is opposed to efforts by any other country or group of countries to establish such hegemony

- neither is prepared to negotiate on behalf of any third party or to enter into agreements or understandings with the other directed at other states.

10. Both sides are of the view that it would be against the interests of the peoples of the world for any major country to collude with another against other countries, or for major countries to divide up the world into spheres of interest.

11. The two sides reviewed the long-standing serious disputes between China and the United States. The Chinese side reaffirmed its position: the Taiwan question is the crucial question obstructing the normalization of relations between China and the United States; the Government of the People's Republic of China is the sole legal government of China; Taiwan is a province of China which has long been returned to the motherland; the liberation of Taiwan is China's internal affair in which no other country has the right to interfere; and all U.S. forces and military installations must be withdrawn from Taiwan. The Chinese Government firmly opposes any activities which aim at the creation of "one China, one Taiwan," "one China, two governments," "two Chinas," an "independent Taiwan" or advocate that "the status of Taiwan remains to be determined."

12. The U.S. side declared: The United States acknowledges that all Chinese on either side of the Taiwan Strait maintain there is but one China and that Taiwan is a part of China. The United States Government does not challenge that position. It reaffirms its interest in a peaceful settlement of the Taiwan question by the Chinese themselves. With this prospect in mind, it affirms the ultimate objective of the withdrawal of all U.S. forces and military installations from Taiwan. In the meantime, it will progressively reduce its forces and military installations on Taiwan as the tension in the area diminishes. The two sides agreed that it is desirable to broaden the understanding between the two peoples. To this end, they discussed specific areas in such fields as science, technology, culture, sports and journalism, in which people-to-people contacts and exchanges would be mutually beneficial. Each side undertakes to facilitate the further development of such contacts and exchanges.

13. Both sides view bilateral trade as another area from which mutual benefit can be derived, and agreed that economic relations based on equality and mutual benefit are in the interest of the peoples of the two countries. They agree to facilitate the progressive development of trade between their two countries.

14. The two sides agreed that they will stay in contact through various channels, including the sending of a senior U.S. representative to Peking from time to time for concrete consultations to further the normalization of relations between the two countries and continue to exchange views on issues of common interest.

15. The two sides expressed the hope that the gains achieved during this visit would open up new prospects for the relations between the two countries. They believe that the normalization of relations between the two countries is not only in the interest of the Chinese and American peoples but also contributes to the relaxation of tension in Asia and the world....

President Nixon, Mrs. Nixon and the American party expressed their appreciation for the gracious hospitality shown them by the Government and people of the People's Republic of China.

ON THE SOCIAL BASIS OF THE LIN PIAO [LIN BIAO] ANTI-PARTY CLIQUE

SOURCE *Yao Wenyuan. On the Social Basis of the Lin Piao Anti-Party Clique.* Peking Review, *March 7, 1975.*

INTRODUCTION *The information that Chairman Mao's designated successor and "close comrade in arms" had been killed in a plane crash after organizing a failed attempt to assassinate Mao shocked the Chinese public. Very little explanation was offered at the time of the announcement in late 1971, but from 1972 there were attempts to show that Lin Biao had always been a "political swindler." Yao Wenyuan, the author of this 1975 attack on Lin, himself received a twenty-year prison sentence as a member of the Gang of Four after Mao's death in 1976.*

It is fairly clear that the Lin Piao anti-Party clique represented the interests of the overthrown landlord and capitalist classes and the aspirations of the overthrown reactionaries to topple the dictatorship of the proletariat and restore the dictatorship of the bourgeoisie. The Lin Piao anti-Party clique opposed the Great Proletarian Cultural Revolution and had inveterate hatred for the socialist system under the dictatorship of the proletariat in our country, slandering it as "feudal autocracy" and cursing it as "Chin Shih Huang of the contemporary era." They wanted the landlords, rich peasants, counter-revolutionaries, bad elements and Rightists "to achieve genuine liberation politically and economically," i.e., politically and economically they wanted to turn the dictatorship of the proletariat into a dictatorship of the landlord and comprador-capitalist classes and the socialist system into the capitalist system. As an agent in the Party, an agent of the bourgeoisie working hard for a restoration, the Lin Piao anti-Party clique was wild in its attack on the Party and the dictatorship of the proletariat, so much so that it set up an organization of secret agents and plotted a counter-revolutionary armed coup d'etat. Such frenzy is a reflection of the fact that the reactionaries who have lost political power and the means of production inevitably will resort to every means to recapture the lost positions of the exploiting classes. We have seen how Lin Piao, after his political and ideological bankruptcy, tried to "eat up" the proletariat by staking everything on a single cast as a desperate gambler would do, and how he finally betrayed the country and fled to defect to the enemy; despite the very patient education, waiting and efforts to save him by Chairman Mao and the Party Central Committee, his counter-revolutionary nature did not change in the least. All this reflects the life-and-death struggle between the proletariat and the bourgeoisie, the two major antagonistic classes, under the dictatorship of the proletariat, a struggle that will go on for a long period. As long as the overthrown reactionary classes still exist, the possibility remains for the emergence within the Party (and in society as well) of representatives of the bourgeoisie who will try to turn their hope for restoration into attempt at restoration. Therefore, we must heighten our vigilance and guard against and smash any plot by the reactionaries at home and abroad, and on no account must we slacken our vigilance. . . .

COMMUNIQUÉ OF THE THIRD PLENARY SESSION OF THE 11TH CENTRAL COMMITTEE OF THE COMMUNIST PARTY OF CHINA

INTRODUCTION *The Third Plenary Session of the 11th Central Committee approved the first measures in the program of economic liberalization and opening, which transformed the Chinese economy in the final decades of the twentieth century. The language of the document, dated December 22, 1978, is cautious. It pays tribute to Mao Zedong and claims that the policy decision is that of Hua Guofeng, still the Communist Party Chairman at this juncture, but the Plenum in fact represented a triumph for policies associated with Chen Yun and Deng Xiaoping, proponents of economic reform.*

In the early years after the founding of the People's Republic, especially after the socialist transformation was in the main completed, Comrade Mao Tsetung instructed the whole Party time and again to shift the focus of our work to the field of the economy and technical revolution. Under the leadership of Comrade Mao Tsetung and Comrade Chou En-lai, our Party did a great deal for socialist modernization and scored important achievements. But the work was later interrupted and sabotaged by Lin Piao and the "gang of four." Besides, we had some shortcomings and mistakes in our leading work because we lacked experience in socialist construction, and this also hampered the transition in the focus of our Party's work. Since the nationwide mass movement to expose and criticize Lin Piao and the "gang of four" has fundamentally come to a successful conclusion, though in a small number of places and departments the movement is less developed, still needs some time to catch up and so cannot end simultaneously, on the whole there is every condition needed for that transition. Therefore the plenary session unanimously endorsed the policy decision put forward by Comrade Hua Kuo-feng on behalf of the Political Bureau of the Central Committee that, to meet the developments at home and abroad, now is an appropriate time to take the decision to expose the large-scale nationwide mass movement to expose and criticize Lin Piao and the "gang of four" and to shift the emphasis of our Party's work and the attention of the people of the whole country to socialist modernization. This is of major significance for fulfillment of the three-year and eight-year programmes for the development of the national economy and the outline for 23 years, for the modernization of science and technology and for the consolidation of the dictatorship of the proletariat in our country. The general task put forward by our Party for the new period reflects the demands of history and the people's aspirations and represents their fundamental interests. Whether or not we can carry this general task to completion, speed socialist modernization and on the basis of rapid growth in production improve the people's living standards significantly and strengthen national defence—this is a major issue which is of paramount concern to all our people and of great significance to the cause of world peace and progress. Carrying out the four modernizations requires great growth in the productive forces, which in turn requires diverse changes in those aspects of the relations of production and the superstructure not in harmony with the growth of the productive forces, and requires changes in all methods of management, actions and thinking which stand in the way of such growth. Socialist modernization is therefore a profound and extensive revolution. There is still in our country today a small handful of counter-revolutionary elements and criminals who hate our socialist modernization and try to undermine it. We must not relax our class struggle against them, nor can we weaken the dictatorship of the proletariat. But as Comrade Mao Tsetung pointed out, the large-scale turbulent class struggles of a mass character have come to an end. Class struggle in socialist society should be carried out on the principle of strictly differentiating the two different types of contradictions and correctly handling them in accordance with the procedures prescribed by the Constitution and the law. It is impermissible to confuse the two different types of contradictions and damage the political stability and unity required for socialist modernization. The plenary session calls on the whole Party, the whole army and the people of all our nationalities to work with one heart and one mind, enhance political stability and unity, mobilize themselves immediately to go all out, pool their wisdom and efforts and carry out the new Long March to make China a modern, powerful socialist country before the end of the century.

THE FIFTH MODERNIZATION: DEMOCRACY

SOURCE *Wei Jingsheng. The Fifth Modernization: Democracy. In* The Courage to Stand Alone: Letters from Prison and and Other Writings, *201–212. New York: Viking Press, 1997.*

INTRODUCTION *The four modernizations of agriculture, industry, technology and defense were first promoted by Zhou Enlai but later used by Deng Xiaoping as a slogan for the reform era. The famous article reprinted below first appeared as a signed poster on December 5, 1978, on Democracy Wall, the Beijing wall where activists publicized their ideas and conducted debates. In the article Wei Jingsheng insists that democracy is a fifth modernization, necessary for China's development. The text was subsequently cited at Wei's trial at which he was sentenced to fifteen years imprisonment.*

Newspapers and television no longer assail us with deafening praise for the dictatorship of the proletariat and class struggle. This is in part because these were once the magical incantations of the now-overthrown Gang of Four. But more importantly, it's because the masses have grown absolutely sick of hearing these worn-out phrases and will never be duped by them again.

The laws of history tell us that only when the old is gone can the new take its place. Now that the old is gone, the people have been anxiously waiting to see what the new will bring; gods never betray the faithful, they thought. But what they've long awaited is none other than a grandiose promise called the Four Modernizations. Our wise leader, Chairman Hua Guofeng, along with Vice Chairman Deng Xiaoping, whom many consider even wiser and grander, have finally crushed the Gang of Four. There is now the possibility that those brave souls whose blood flowed over Tiananmen Square might have their dreams of democracy and prosperity realized.

After the arrest of the Gang of Four, the people eagerly hoped that Vice Chairman Deng Xiaoping, who might possibly "restore capitalism," would rise up again like a magnificent banner. Finally, he did regain his position in the central leadership. How excited the people felt! How inspired they were! But alas, the old political system so despised by the people remains unchanged, and the democracy and freedom they longed for has not even been mentioned. Their living conditions remain the same and "increased wages" have far from kept up with the rapid rise in prices. There was talk of "restoring capitalism" and instituting a bonus system, but after careful consideration, it was determined that such measures would simply be "invisible whips" of the type once cursed by our Marxist forefathers as "the greatest form of worker exploitation."

There are reports confirming that "deceptive policies" will no longer be implemented and that the people will no longer follow a "great helmsman." Instead, "wise leaders" will lead them to "catch up with and surpass the most advanced nations of the world" such as Britain, the United States, Japan, and Yugoslavia(!). It's no longer fashionable to take part in the revolution, a college education will take you further in the world. Cries of "class struggle" no longer need fill people's ears, the Four Modernizations will take care of everything. Of course, in order to realize this beautiful dream, we must still follow the guiding central spirit passed down from the "April Fifth Society" as well as the guidance and direction of a unified leadership

There are two ancient Chinese sayings that go: "Sketch cakes to allay your hunger" and "Think of plums to quench your thirst." People of ancient times had such wit and sarcasm, and they've even been said to have progressed since then. So now no one would ever actually consider doing such ridiculous things, would they?

Well, not only did some consider doing such things, they actually did.

For decades, the Chinese people faithfully followed the Great Helmsman while he used "Communist idealism" to sketch cakes and offered up the Great Leap Forward and the Three Red Banners as thirst-quenching plums. People tightened their belts and forged ahead undaunted. Thirty years flew by and the experience taught them one lesson: For three decades we've been acting like monkeys grabbing for the moon's reflection in a lake—no wonder we've come up empty-handed! Therefore, when Vice Chairman Deng called for "practicality," the people's enthusiasm surged forth like a rolling tide and swept him back into power. Everyone expected him to employ the maxim "Seek truth from facts" to review the past and lead the people toward a promising future.

But once again there are people warning us that Marxist-Leninist-Mao Zedong Thought is the foundation of all things, even speech; that Chairman Mao was the "great savior" of the people; and that "without the Communist Party, there would be no new China" actually means "without Chairman Mao, there would be no new China." Official notices will clear things up for anyone who refuses to believe this. There are even those who seek to remind us that Chinese people need a dictator; if he is even more dictatorial than the emperors of old, this only proves his greatness. The Chinese people don't need democracy, they say, for unless it is a "democracy under centralized leadership," it isn't worth a cent. Whether you believe it or not is up to you, but there are plenty of empty prison cells waiting for you if you don't.

But now someone has provided us with a way out: Take the Four Modernizations as your guiding principle; forge ahead with stability and unity; and bravely serve the revolution like a faithful old ox and you will reach your paradise—the prosperity of Communism and the Four Modernizations. And these kind-hearted someones have warned us that if we are confused, we must undertake a serious and thorough study of Marxist-Leninist-Mao Zedong Thought! If you're still confused, it's because you don't understand, and not understanding only reflects

just how profound the theory is! Don't be disobedient or the leadership of your work unit will be uncompromising! And so on and so on.

I urge everyone to stop believing such political swindlers. When we all know that we are going to be tricked, why don't we trust ourselves instead? The Cultural Revolution has tempered us and we are no longer so ignorant. Let us investigate for ourselves what should be done!

I. WHY DEMOCRACY?

People have discussed this question for centuries. And now those who voice their opinions at Democracy Wall have carried out a thorough analysis and shown just how much better democracy is than autocracy.

"People are the masters of history." Is this fact or merely empty talk? It is both fact and empty talk. It is fact that without the effort and participation of the people there can be no history. No "great helmsman" or "wise leader" could exist, let alone any history be created. From this we can see that the slogan should be "Without the new Chinese people, there would be no new China," not "Without Chairman Mao, there would be no new China." It's understandable that Vice Chairman Deng is grateful to Chairman Mao for saving his life, but why is he so ungrateful to all of those whose "outcries" propelled him back into power? Is it reasonable for him to say to them: "You must not criticize Chairman Mao, because he saved my life"? From this we can see that phrases like "people are the masters of history" are nothing but empty talk. Such words become hollow when people are unable to choose their own destiny by majority will, or when their achievements are credited to others, or when their rights are stripped away and woven into the crowns of others. What kind of "masters" are these? It would be more appropriate to call them docile slaves. Our history books tell us that the people are the masters and creators of everything, but in reality they are more like faithful servants standing at attention and waiting to be "led" by leaders who swell like yeasted bread dough.

The people should have democracy. When they call for democracy they are demanding nothing more than that which is inherently theirs. Whoever refuses to return democracy to them is a shameless thief more despicable than any capitalist who robs the workers of the wealth earned with their own sweat and blood.

Do the people have democracy now? No! Don't the people want to be the masters of their own destiny? Of course they do! That is precisely why the Communist Party defeated the Nationalists. But what became of all their promises once victory was achieved? Once they began championing a dictatorship of the proletariat instead of a people's democratic dictatorship, even the "democracy" still enjoyed by a tenth of a millionth of the population was displaced by the individual dictatorship of the "great leader." Even Peng Dehuai was denounced for following the orders of the "great leader" and airing complaints.

A new promise was made: If a leader is great, then blind faith in him will bring greater happiness to the people than democracy. Half forced, half willingly, people have continued to believe in this promise right up until the present. But are they any happier? No. They are more miserable and more backward. Why, then, are things the way they are? This is the first question the people must consider. What should be done now? This is the second. At present, there is absolutely no need to assess the achievements and failures of Mao Zedong. When Mao himself suggested this be done, it was only out of self-defense. Instead, the people should be asking themselves whether without the dictatorship of Mao Zedong China would have fallen into its current state. Are the Chinese people stupid? Are they lazy? Do they not want to live more prosperous lives? Or are they unruly by nature? Quite the opposite. How, then, did things get the way they are? The answer is obvious: The Chinese people should not have followed the path they did. Why, then, did they follow this path? Was it because a self-glorifying dictator led them down it? The truth is, even if people had refused to follow this path, they would still have been crushed by the dictatorship. And when no one could hear any other alternative, the people felt that this was the one and only path to take. Is this not deceit? Is there any merit in this at all?

What path was taken? It's often called the "socialist road." According to the definition formulated by our Marxist forefathers, the premise of socialism is that the masses, or what is called the proletariat, are the masters of everything. But let me ask the Chinese workers and peasants: Aside from the few coins you receive each month to feed yourselves with, what are you the masters of? And what do you master? It's pitiful to say it, but the truth is, you are mastered by others, even down to your own marriages!

Socialism guarantees that the producer will receive the surplus fruits of his labor after he has fulfilled his duty to society. But is there any limit to the amount of this duty? Are you getting anything more than the meager wage necessary to sustain your productive labor? Can socialism guarantee the right of every citizen to receive an education, to make full use of his abilities, and so forth? We can observe none of these things in our daily lives. We see only "the dictatorship of the proletariat" and "a variation of Russian autocracy"—that is, Chinese-style socialist autocracy. Is this the kind of socialist road the people need? Does dictatorship, therefore, amount to the people's happiness? Is this the socialist road Marx described and the people aspired to? Obviously not. Then what is it? As ridiculous as it may sound, it actually resembles the feudal socialism referred to in *The Communist Manifesto* as feudal monarchy under a socialist cloak. It's said that the Soviet Union has been elevated to socialist imperialism from socialist feudalism. Must the Chinese people follow the same path?

People have suggested that we settle all our old accounts by blaming them all on the fascist dictatorship of feudal socialism. I completely agree with this because there is no question of right or wrong. In passing, I would like to point out that the correct name for the notorious German fascism is "national socialism." It too had an autocratic tyrant; it too ordered people to tighten their belts; and it too deceived the people with the words: "You are a great people." Most importantly, it too stamped out even the most rudimentary forms of democracy, for it fully recognized that democracy was its most formidable and irrepressible enemy. On this basis, Stalin and Hitler shook hands and signed the German-Soviet Pact whereby a socialist state and a national-socialist state toasted the partition of Poland while the peoples of both countries suffered slavery and poverty. Must we go on suffering from this kind of slavery and poverty? If not, then democracy is our only choice. In other words, if we want to modernize our economy, sciences, military, and other areas, then we must first modernize our people and our society.

II. THE FIFTH MODERNIZATION: WHAT KIND OF DEMOCRACY DO WE WANT?

I would like to ask everyone: What do we want modernization for? Many might still feel that the times depicted in *Dream of the Red Chamber* were just fine. One could do some reading, dabble in poetry, cavort with women, and be fed and clothed effortlessly. These days such a person might even go to see foreign movies as well— what a godlike existence! It's not bad to live like a god, but such a lifestyle remains irrelevant to ordinary people. They want simply to have the chance to enjoy a happy life, or at least one that is no less than what people enjoy in other countries. A prosperity that all members of society can enjoy equally will only be achieved by raising the level of social productivity. This is quite obvious, but some people have completely overlooked one important point: When social productivity increases, will the people be able to enjoy prosperous lives? The problems of allocation, distribution, and exploitation still remain.

In the decades since Liberation, people have tightened their belts and worked hard to produce a great deal of wealth. But where has it all gone? Some say it's gone to plump up small-scale autocratic regimes like Vietnam, while others say it's been used to fatten the "new bourgeois elements" like Lin Biao and Jiang Qing. Both are correct, but the bottom line is, none of it has trickled down into the hands of the working people of China.

If powerful political swindlers, both big and small, have not squandered the wealth themselves, then they have given it to scoundrels in Vietnam and Albania who cherish ideals similar to their own. Shortly before his death, Mao Zedong got upset when his old lady asked him for several thousand yuan, but did anyone ever know him to feel any pain as he threw away tens of billions of yuan earned with the sweat and blood of the Chinese people? And this was all done while the Chinese people were building socialism by tightening their belts and begging on the streets for food. Why, then, can't all those people who keep running to Democracy Wall to praise Mao Zedong open their eyes and see this? Could it be that they are deliberately blind to it? If they genuinely can't see it, I would ask them all to use the time they spend writing wall posters to go over to Beijing or Yongdingmen Train Station, or to any street in the city, and ask those country folk arriving from the provinces whether begging for food is such a rare occurrence where they come from. I can also bet that they aren't that willing to give away their snow-white rice to aid "friends in the Third World"! But does their opinion matter? The sad thing is that in our people's republic all real power is in the hands of those people who live like gods and have nothing better to do after stuffing their faces than to read novels and write poetry. Are not the people completely justified in seizing power from the hands of such overlords?

What is democracy? True democracy means placing all power in the hands of the working people. Are working people unable to manage state power? Yugoslavia has taken this route and proven to us that people have no need for dictators, whether big or small; they can take care of things much better themselves.

What is true democracy? It is when the people, acting on their own will, have the right to choose representatives to manage affairs on the people's behalf and in accordance with the will and interests of the people. This alone can be called democracy. Furthermore, the people must have the power to replace these representatives at any time in order to keep them from abusing their powers to oppress the people. Is this actually possible? The citizens of Europe and the United States enjoy precisely this kind of democracy and can run people like Nixon, de Gaulle, and Tanaka out of office when they wish and can even reinstate them if they so desire. No one can interfere with their democratic rights. In China, however, if a person even comments on the "great helmsman" or the "Great Man peerless in history," Mao Zedong, who is already dead, the mighty prison gates and all kinds of unimaginable misfortunes await him. If we compare the socialist system of "centralized democracy" with the "exploiting class democracy" of capitalism, the difference is as clear as night and day.

Will the country sink into chaos and anarchy if the people achieve democracy? On the contrary, have not the scandals exposed in the newspapers recently shown that it is precisely due to an absence of democracy that the dictators, large and small, have caused chaos and anarchy? The maintenance of democratic order is an internal problem that the people themselves must solve. It is not something that the privileged overlords need concern themselves with. Besides, they are not really concerned with democracy for the people, but use this as a pretext to deny the people of their democratic rights. Of course, internal problems cannot be solved overnight but must be constantly addressed as part of a long-term process. Mistakes and shortcomings will be inevitable, but these are for us to worry about. This is infinitely better than facing abusive overlords against whom we have no means of redress. Those who worry that democracy will lead to anarchy and chaos are just like those who, following the overthrow of the Qing dynasty, worried that without an emperor, the country would fall into chaos. Their decision was to patiently suffer oppression because they feared that without the weight of oppression, their spines might completely collapse!

To such people, I would like to say, with all due respect: We want to be the masters of our own destiny. We need no gods or emperors and we don't believe in saviors of any kind. We want to be masters of our universe; we do not want to serve as mere tools of dictators with personal ambitions for carrying out modernization. We want to modernize the lives of the people. Democracy, freedom, and happiness for all are our sole objectives in carrying out modernization. Without this "Fifth Modernization," all other modernizations are nothing but a new lie.

Comrades, I appeal to you: Let us rally together under the banner of democracy. Do not be fooled again by dictators who talk of "stability and unity." Fascist totalitarianism can bring us nothing but disaster. Harbor no more illusions; democracy is our only hope. Abandon our democratic rights and we shackle ourselves again. Let us have confidence in our own strength! We are the creators of human history. Banish all self-proclaimed leaders and teachers, for they have already cheated the people of their most valuable rights for decades.

I firmly believe that production will flourish more when controlled by the people themselves because the workers will be producing for their own benefit. Life will improve because the workers' interests will be the primary goal. Society will be more just because all power will be exercised by the people as a whole through democratic means.

I don't believe that all of this will be handed to the people effortlessly by some great savior. I also refuse to believe that China will abandon the goals of democracy, freedom, and happiness because of the many difficulties it will surely encounter along the way. As long as people clearly identify their goal and realistically assess the obstacles before them, then surely they will trample any pests that might try to bar their way.

III. MARCHING TOWARD MODERNIZATION: DEMOCRACY IN PRACTICE

To achieve modernization, the Chinese people must first put democracy into practice and modernize China's social system. Democracy is not merely an inevitable stage of social development as Lenin claimed. In addition to being the result of productive forces and productive relations having developed to a certain stage, democracy is also the very condition that allows for the existence of such development to reach beyond this stage. Without democracy, society will become stagnant and economic growth will face insurmountable obstacles. Judging from history, therefore, a democratic social system is the premise and precondition for all development, or what we can also call modernization. Without this precondition, not only is further development impossible, but even preserving the level of development already attained would be very difficult. The experience of our great nation over the past three decades is the best evidence for this.

Why must human history follow a path toward development, or modernization? It is because humans need all of the tangible advantages that development can provide them. These advantages then enable them to achieve their foremost goal in the pursuit of happiness: freedom. Democracy is the greatest freedom ever known to man. Therefore, isn't it quite apparent why the goal of all recent human struggles has been democracy?

Why have all the reactionaries in modern history united under a common banner against democracy? It is because democracy gives their enemy—the common people—everything, and provides them—the oppressors—no weapons with which to oppose the people. The greatest reactionaries are always the greatest opponents of democracy. The histories of Germany, the Soviet Union, and "New China" make this very clear and show that these reactionaries are also the most formidable and dangerous enemies of social peace and prosperity. The more recent histories of these countries make it apparent that all the struggles of the people for prosperity and of society for development are ultimately directed against the enemies of democracy—the dictatorial fascists. When democracy defeats dictatorship, it always brings with it the most favorable conditions for accelerating social development. The history of the United States offers the most convincing evidence of this.

The success of any struggle by the people for happiness, peace, and prosperity is contingent upon the quest for democracy. The success of all struggles by the people against oppression and exploitation depends upon achieving democracy. Let us throw ourselves completely into the struggle for democracy! Only through democracy can the people obtain everything. All illusions of undemocratic means are hopeless. All forms of dictatorship and totalitarianism are the most immediate and dangerous enemies of the people.

Will our enemies let us implement democracy? Of course not. They will stop at nothing to hinder the progress of democracy. Deception and trickery are the most effective means they have. All dictatorial fascists tell their people: Your situation is truly the best in the entire world.

Does democracy come about naturally when society reaches a certain stage? Absolutely not. A high price is paid for every tiny victory; even coming to a recognition of this fact will cost blood and sacrifice. The enemies of democracy have always deceived their people by saying that just as democracy is inevitable, it is doomed, and, therefore, it is not worth wasting energy to fight for.

But let us look at the real history, not that fabricated by the hired hacks of the "socialist government." Every small branch or twig of true and valuable democracy is stained with the blood of martyrs and tyrants, and every step taken toward democracy has been fiercely attacked by the reactionary forces. The fact that democracy has been able to surmount such obstacles proves that it is precious to the people and that it embodies their aspirations. Therefore the democratic trend cannot be stopped. The Chinese people have never feared anything. They need only recognize the direction to be taken and the forces of tyranny will no longer be invincible.

Is the struggle for democracy what the Chinese people want? The Cultural Revolution was the first time they flexed their muscles, and all the reactionary forces trembled before them. But at that time the people had no clear direction and the force of democracy was not the main thrust of their struggle. As a result, the dictators silenced most of them through bribes, deception, division, slander, or violent suppression. At the time, people also had a blind faith in all kinds of ambitious dictators, so once again they unwittingly became the tools and sacrificial lambs of tyrants and potential tyrants.

Now, twelve years later, the people have finally recognized their goal. They see clearly the real direction of their fight and have found their true leader: the banner of democracy. The Democracy Wall at Xidan has become the first battlefield in the people's fight against the reactionary forces. The struggle will be victorious—this is already a commonly accepted belief; the people will be liberated—this slogan has already taken on new significance. There may be bloodshed and sacrifice, and people may fall prey to even more sinister plots, yet the banner of democracy will never again be obscured by the evil fog of the reactionary forces. Let us unite together under this great and true banner and march toward modernization of society for the sake of the tranquillity, happiness, rights, and freedom of all the people!

EMANCIPATE THE MIND, SEEK TRUTH FROM FACTS AND UNITE AS ONE IN LOOKING TO THE FUTURE

SOURCE *Deng Xiaoping. Emancipate the Mind, Seek Truth from Facts and Unite as One in Looking to the Future. Selected Works of Deng Xiaoping (1975–1982), 151–165. Translated by The Bureau for the Compilation and Translation of Works of Marx, Engels, Lenin and Stalin Under the Central Committee of the Communist Party of China. Beijing: People's Publishing House, 1983.*

INTRODUCTION *The key speech reprinted below was delivered on December 13, 1978, just before the Third Plenary session of the Eleventh Central Committee, the meeting that approved Deng Xiaoping's reform program. Deng is careful to pay tribute to Mao Zedong and his record (indeed "seek truth from facts" is taken from a 1941 speech by Mao), but in urging the "emancipation of the mind" he also criticizes much of the Maoist past and signals commitment to thoroughgoing reform.*

Comrades,

This conference has lasted over a month and will soon end. The Central Committee has put forward the fundamental guiding principle of shifting the focus of all Party work to the four modernizations and has solved a host of important problems inherited from the past. This will surely strengthen the determination, confidence and unity of the Party, the army and the people of all of China's nationalities. Now we can be certain that under the correct leadership of the Central Committee, the Party, army and people will achieve victory after victory in our new Long March.

The present conference has been very successful and will have an important place in our Party's history. We have not held one like it for many years. There has been lively debate here and the Party's democratic tradition has been revived and carried forward. We should spread this style of work to the whole Party, army and people.

At this conference we have discussed and resolved many major issues concerning the destinies of our Party and state. The participants have spoken their minds freely and fully and have boldly aired their honest opinions. They have laid problems on the table and have felt free to criticize things, including the work of the Central Committee. Some comrades have criticized themselves to

varying degrees. All this represents marked progress in our inner-Party life and will give a big impetus to the cause of our Party and people.

Today, I mainly want to discuss one question, namely, how to emancipate our minds, use our heads, seek truth from facts and unite as one in looking to the future.

I. EMANCIPATING THE MIND IS A VITAL POLITICAL TASK

When it comes to emancipating our minds, using our heads, seeking truth from facts and uniting as one in looking to the future, the primary task is to emancipate our minds. Only then can we, guided as we should be by Marxism-Leninism and Mao Zedong Thought, find correct solutions to the emerging as well as inherited problems, fruitfully reform those aspects of the relations of production and of the superstructure that do not correspond with the rapid development of our productive forces, and chart the specific course and formulate the specific policies, methods and measures needed to achieve the four modernizations under our actual conditions.

The emancipation of minds has not been completely achieved among our cadres, particularly our leading cadres. Indeed, many comrades have not yet set their brains going; in other words, their ideas remain rigid or partly so. That isn't because they are not good comrades. It is a result of specific historical conditions.

First, it is because during the past dozen years Lin Biao and the Gang of Four set up ideological taboos or "forbidden zones" and preached blind faith to confine people's minds within the framework of their phoney Marxism. No one was allowed to go beyond the limits they prescribed; anyone who did was tracked down, stigmatized and attacked politically. In this situation, some people found it safer to stop using their heads and thinking questions over.

Second, it is because democratic centralism was undermined and the Party was afflicted with bureaucratism resulting from, among other things, overconcentration of power. This kind of bureaucratism often masquerades as "Party leadership," "Party directives," "Party interests" and "Party discipline," but actually it is designed to control people, hold them in check and oppress them. At that time many important issues were often decided by one or two persons. The others could only do what those few ordered. That being so, there wasn't much point in thinking things out for yourself.

Third, it is because no clear distinction was made between right and wrong or between merit and demerit, and because rewards and penalties were not meted out as deserved. No distinction was made between those who worked well and those who didn't. In some cases, even people who worked well were attacked while those who did nothing or just played it safe weathered every storm. Under those unwritten laws, people were naturally reluctant to use their brains.

Fourth, it is because people are still subject to the force of habit of the small producer, who sticks to old conventions, is content with the status quo and is unwilling to seek progress or accept anything new.

When people's minds aren't yet emancipated and their thinking remains rigid, curious phenomena emerge.

Once people's thinking becomes rigid, they will increasingly act according to fixed notions. To cite some examples, strengthening Party leadership is interpreted as the Party's monopolizing and interfering in everything. Exercising centralized leadership is interpreted as erasing distinctions between the Party and the government, so that the former replaces the latter. And maintaining unified leadership by the Central Committee is interpreted as "doing everything according to unified standards." We are opposed to "home-grown policies" that violate the fundamental principles of those laid down by the Central Committee, but there are also "home-grown policies" that are truly grounded in reality and supported by the masses. Yet such correct policies are still often denounced for their "not conforming to the unified standards."

People whose thinking has become rigid tend to veer with the wind. They are not guided by Party spirit and Party principles, but go along with whatever has the backing of the authorities and adjust their words and actions according to whichever way the wind is blowing. They think that they will thus avoid mistakes. In fact, however, veering with the wind is in itself a grave mistake, a contravention of the Party spirit which all Communists should cherish. It is true that people who think independently and dare to speak out and act can't avoid making mistakes, but their mistakes are out in the open and are therefore more easily rectified.

Once people's thinking becomes rigid, book worship, divorced from reality, becomes a grave malady. Those who suffer from it dare not say a word or take a step that isn't mentioned in books, documents or the speeches of leaders: everything has to be copied. Thus responsibility to the higher authorities is set in opposition to responsibility to the people.

Our drive for the four modernizations will get nowhere unless rigid thinking is broken down and the minds of cadres and of the masses are completely emancipated.

In fact, the current debate about whether practice is the sole criterion for testing truth is also a debate about whether people's minds need to be emancipated. Everybody has recognized that this debate is highly important and necessary. Its importance is becoming clearer all the time. When everything has to be done by the book, when thinking turns rigid and blind faith is the fashion, it is impossible for a party or a nation to make progress. Its life will cease and that party or nation will perish. Comrade Mao Zedong said this time and again during the rectification movements. Only if we emancipate our minds, seek truth from facts, proceed from reality in everything and integrate theory with practice, can we carry out our socialist modernization programme smoothly, and only then can our Party further develop Marxism-Leninism and Mao Zedong Thought. In this sense, the debate about the criterion for testing truth is really a debate about ideological line, about politics, about the future and the destiny of our Party and nation.

Seeking truth from facts is the basis of the proletarian world outlook as well as the ideological basis of Marxism. Just as in the past we achieved all the victories in our revolution by following this principle, so today we must rely on it in our effort to accomplish the four modernizations. Comrades in every factory, government office, school, shop and production team as well as comrades in Party committees at the central, provincial, prefectural, county and commune levels — all should act on this principle, emancipate their minds and use their heads in thinking questions through and taking action on them.

The more Party members and other people there are who use their heads and think things through, the more our cause will benefit. To make revolution and build socialism we need large numbers of pathbreakers who dare to think, explore new ways and generate new ideas. Otherwise, we won't be able to rid our country of poverty and backwardness or to catch up with — still less surpass — the advanced countries. We hope every Party committee and every Party branch will encourage and support people both inside and outside the Party to dare to think, explore new paths and put forward new ideas, and that they will urge the masses to emancipate their minds and use their heads.

II. DEMOCRACY IS A MAJOR CONDITION FOR EMANCIPATING THE MIND

One important condition for getting people to emancipate their minds and use their heads is genuine practice of the proletarian system of democratic centralism. We need unified and centralized leadership, but centralism can be correct only when there is a full measure of democracy.

At present, we must lay particular stress on democracy, because for quite a long time democratic centralism was not genuinely practised: centralism was divorced from democracy and there was too little democracy. Even today, only a few advanced people dare to speak up. There are a good many such people at this conference. But in the Party and the country as a whole, there are still many who hesitate to speak their minds. Even when they have worthwhile opinions, they hesitate to express them, and they are not bold enough in struggling against bad things and bad people. If this doesn't change, how can we persuade everyone to emancipate his mind and use his head? And how can we bring about the four modernizations?

We must create the conditions for the practice of democracy, and for this it is essential to reaffirm the principle of the "three don'ts": don't pick on others for their faults, don't put labels on people, and don't use a big stick. In political life within the Party and among the people we must use democratic means and not resort to coercion or attack. The rights of citizens, Party members and Party committee members are respectively stipulated by the Constitution of the People's Republic and the Constitution of the Communist Party. These rights must be resolutely defended and no infringement of them must be allowed.

The recent reversal of the verdict on the Tiananmen Incident has elated the people of all of China's nationalities and greatly stimulated mass enthusiasm for socialism. The masses should be encouraged to offer criticisms. There is nothing to worry about even if a few malcontents take advantage of democracy to make trouble. We should deal with such situations appropriately, having faith that the overwhelming majority of the people are able to use their own judgement. One thing a revolutionary party does need to worry about is its inability to hear the voice of the people. The thing to be feared most is silence. Today many rumours — some true, some false — circulate through the grapevine inside and outside the Party. This is a kind of punishment for the long-standing lack of political democracy. If we had a political situation with both centralism and democracy, both discipline and freedom, both unity of will and personal ease of mind and liveliness, there wouldn't be so many rumours and anarchism would be easier to overcome. We believe our people are mindful of the overall interests of the country and have a good sense of discipline. Our leading cadres at all levels, and especially those of high rank, should for their part take care to strictly observe Party discipline and keep Party secrets; they should refrain from spreading rumours, circulating handwritten copies of speeches and the like.

As it is only natural that some opinions expressed by the masses should be correct and others not, we should examine them analytically. The Party leadership should be good at synthesizing the correct opinions and explaining why the others are incorrect. In dealing with ideological problems we must never use coercion but should genuinely carry out the policy of "letting a hundred flowers bloom, a hundred schools of thought contend." We must firmly put a stop to bad practices such as attacking and trying to silence people who make critical comments — especially sharp ones — by

ferreting out their political backgrounds, tracing political rumours to them and opening "special case" files on them. Comrade Mao Zedong used to say that such actions were really signs of weakness and lack of courage. No leading comrades at any level must ever place themselves in opposition to the masses. We must never abandon this principle. But of course we must not let down our guard against the handful of counter-revolutionaries who still exist in our country.

Now I want to speak at some length about economic democracy. Under our present system of economic management, power is over-concentrated, so it is necessary to devolve some of it to the lower levels without hesitation but in a planned way. Otherwise it will be difficult to give full scope to the initiative of local as well as national authorities and to the enterprises and workers, and difficult to practise modern economic management and raise the productivity of labour. The various localities, enterprises and production teams should be given greater powers of decision regarding both operation and management. There are many provinces, municipalities and autonomous regions in China, and some of our medium-sized provinces are as big as a large European country. They must be given greater powers of decision in economic planning, finance and foreign trade — always within the framework of a nationwide unity of views, policies, planning, guidance and action.

At present the most pressing need is to expand the decision-making powers of mines, factories and other enterprises and of production teams, so as to give full scope to their initiative and creativity. Once a production team has been empowered to make decisions regarding its own operations, its members and cadres will lie awake at night so long as a single piece of land is left unplanted or a single pond unused for aquatic production, and they will find ways to remedy the situation. Just imagine the additional wealth that could be created if all the people in China's hundreds of thousands of enterprises and millions of production teams put their minds to work. As more wealth is created for the state, personal income and collective benefits should also be increased somewhat. As far as the relatively small number of advanced people is concerned, it won't matter too much if we neglect the principle of more pay for more work and fail to stress individual material benefits. But when it comes to the masses, that approach can only be used for a short time — it won't work in the long run. Revolutionary spirit is a treasure beyond price. Without it there would be no revolutionary action. But revolution takes place on the basis of the need for material benefit. It would be idealism to emphasize the spirit of sacrifice to the neglect of material benefit.

It is also essential to ensure the democratic rights of the workers and peasants, including the rights of democratic election, management and supervision. We must create a situation in which not only every workshop director and production team leader but also every worker and peasant is aware of his responsibility for production and tries to find ways of solving related problems.

To ensure people's democracy, we must strengthen our legal system. Democracy has to be institutionalized and written into law, so as to make sure that institutions and laws do not change whenever the leadership changes, or whenever the leaders change their views or shift the focus of their attention. The trouble now is that our legal system is incomplete, with many laws yet to be enacted. Very often, what leaders say is taken as the law and anyone who disagrees is called a law-breaker. That kind of law changes whenever a leader's views change. So we must concentrate on enacting criminal and civil codes, procedural laws and other necessary laws concerning factories, people's communes, forests, grasslands and environmental protection, as well as labour laws and a law on investment by foreigners. These laws should be discussed and adopted through democratic procedures. Meanwhile, the procuratorial and judicial organs should be strengthened. All this will ensure that there are laws to go by, that they are observed and strictly enforced, and that violators are brought to book. The relations between one enterprise and another, between enterprises and the state, between enterprises and individuals, and so on should also be defined by law, and many of the contradictions between them should be resolved by law. There is a lot of legislative work to do, and we don't have enough trained people. Therefore, legal provisions will have to be less than perfect to start with, then be gradually improved upon. Some laws and statutes can be tried out in particular localities and later enacted nationally after the experience has been evaluated and improvements have been made. Individual legal provisions can be revised or supplemented one at a time, as necessary; there is no need to wait for a comprehensive revision of an entire body of law. In short, it is better to have some laws than none, and better to have them sooner than later. Moreover, we should intensify our study of international law.

Just as the country must have laws, the Party must have rules and regulations. The fundamental ones are embodied in the Party Constitution. Without rules and regulations in the Party it would be hard to ensure that the laws of the state are enforced. The task of the Party's discipline inspection commissions and its organization departments at all levels is not only to deal with particular cases but, more important, to uphold the Party's rules and regulations and make earnest efforts to improve its style of work. Disciplinary measures should be taken against all persons who violate Party discipline, no matter who they are, so that clear differentiation is made between merits and demerits, rewards and penalties are meted out as deserved, and rectitude prevails and bad tendencies are stemmed.

III. SOLVING OLD PROBLEMS WILL HELP PEOPLE LOOK TO THE FUTURE

This conference has solved some problems left over from the past and distinguished clearly between the merits and demerits of some persons, and remedies have been made for a number of major cases in which the charges were false or which were unjustly or incorrectly dealt with. This is essential for emancipating minds and for ensuring political stability and unity. Its purpose is to help us turn our thoughts to the future and smoothly shift the focus of the Party's work.

Our principle is that every wrong should be righted. All wrongs done in the past should be corrected. Some questions that cannot be settled right now should be settled after this conference. But settlement must be prompt and effective, without leaving any loose ends and on the basis of facts. We must solve these problems left over from the past thoroughly. It is not good for them to be left unsolved or for comrades who have made mistakes to refuse to make self-criticisms, or for us to fail to deal with their cases properly. However, we cannot possibly achieve — and should not expect — a perfect settlement of every case. We should have the major aspect of each problem in mind and solve it in broad outline; to go into every detail is neither possible nor necessary.

Stability and unity are of prime importance. To strengthen the unity of people of whatever nationality, we must first strengthen unity throughout the Party, and especially within the central leadership. Our Party's unity is based on Marxism-Leninism and Mao Zedong Thought. Inside the Party we should distinguish right from wrong in terms of theory and of the Party line, conduct criticism and self-criticism and help and supervise each other in correcting wrong ideas.

Comrades who have made mistakes should be urged to sum up their experience and draw the necessary lessons, so that they can recognize those mistakes and correct them. We should give them time to think. Once they improve their understanding of cardinal issues of right and wrong and conduct self-criticism, we should make them welcome again. In dealing with people who have made mistakes, we must weigh each case very carefully. Where there is a choice, it is better to err on the side of leniency, but we should be more severe if the problems recur. We should be somewhat lenient with rank-and-file Party members, but more severe with leading cadres, especially those of high rank.

From now on we must be very careful in the selection of cadres. We must never assign important posts to persons who have engaged in beating, smashing and looting, who have been obsessed by factionalist ideas, who have sold their souls by framing innocent comrades, or who disregard the Party's vital interests. Nor can we lightly trust persons who sail with the wind, curry favour with those in power and ignore the Party's principles. We should be wary of such people and at the same time educate them and urge them to change their world outlook.

People both at home and abroad have been greatly concerned recently about how we would evaluate Comrade Mao Zedong and the "cultural revolution." The great contributions of Comrade Mao in the course of long revolutionary struggles will never fade. If we look back at the years following the failure of the revolution in 1927, it appears very likely that without his outstanding leadership the Chinese revolution would still not have triumphed even today. In that case, the people of all our nationalities would still be suffering under the reactionary rule of imperialism, feudalism and bureaucrat-capitalism, and our Party would still be engaged in bitter struggle in the dark. Therefore, it is no exaggeration to say that were it not for Chairman Mao there would be no New China. Mao Zedong Thought has nurtured our whole generation. All comrades present here may be said to have been nourished by Mao Zedong Thought. Without Mao Zedong Thought, the Communist Party of China would not exist today, and that is no exaggeration either. Mao Zedong Thought will forever remain the greatest intellectual treasure of our Party, our army and our people. We must understand the scientific tenets of Mao Zedong Thought correctly and as an integral whole and develop them under the new historical conditions. Of course Comrade Mao was not infallible or free from shortcomings. To demand that of any revolutionary leader would be inconsistent with Marxism. We must guide and educate the Party members, the army officers and men and the people of all of China's nationalities and help them to see the great services of Comrade Mao Zedong scientifically and in historical perspective.

The Cultural Revolution should also be viewed scientifically and in historical perspective. In initiating it Comrade Mao Zedong was actuated mainly by the desire to oppose and prevent revisionism. As for the shortcomings that appeared during the course of the "cultural revolution" and the mistakes that were made then, at an appropriate time they should be summed up and lessons should be drawn from them — that is essential for achieving unity of understanding throughout the Party. The "cultural revolution" has become a stage in the course of China's socialist development, hence we must evaluate it. However, there is no need to do so hastily. Serious research must be done before we can make a scientific appraisal of this historical stage. It may take a rather long time to fully understand and assess some of the particular issues involved. We will probably be able to make a more correct analysis of this period in history after some time has passed than we can right now.

IV. STUDY THE NEW SITUATION AND TACKLE THE NEW PROBLEMS

In order to look forward, we must study the new situation and tackle the new problems in good time; otherwise, there can be no smooth progress. In three fields especially, the new situation and new problems demand attention: methods of management, structure of management and economic policy.

So far as methods of management are concerned, we should lay particular stress on overcoming bureaucratism.

Our bureaucracy, which is a result of small-scale production, is utterly incompatible with large-scale production. To achieve the four modernizations and shift the technological basis of our entire socialist economy to that of large-scale production, it is essential to overcome the evils of bureaucracy. Our present economic management is marked by overstaffing, organizational overlapping, complicated procedures and extremely low efficiency. Everything is often drowned in empty political talk. This is not the fault of any group of comrades. The fault lies in the fact that we haven't made reforms in time. Our modernization programme and socialist cause will be doomed if we don't make them now.

We must learn to manage the economy by economic means. If we ourselves don't know about advanced methods of management, we should learn from those who do, either at home or abroad. These methods should be applied not only in the operation of enterprises with newly imported technology and equipment, but also in the technical transformation of existing enterprises. Pending the introduction of a unified national programme of modern management, we can begin with limited spheres, say, a particular region or a given trade, and then spread the methods gradually to others. The central government departments concerned should encourage such experiments. Contradictions of all kinds will crop up in the process and we should discover and overcome them in good time. That will speed up our progress.

Henceforth, now that the question of political line has been settled, the quality of leadership given by the Party committee in an economic unit should be judged mainly by the unit's adoption of advanced methods of management, by the progress of its technical innovation, and by the margins of increase of its productivity of labour, its profits, the personal income of its workers and the collective benefits it provides. The quality of leadership by Party committees in all fields should be judged by similar criteria. This will be of major political importance in the years to come. Without these criteria as its key elements, our politics would be empty and divorced from the highest interests of both the Party and the people.

So far as the structure of management is concerned, the most important task at present is to strengthen the work responsibility system.

Right now a big problem in enterprises and institutions across the country and in Party and government organs at various levels is that nobody takes responsibility. In theory, there is collective responsibility. In fact, this means that no one is responsible. When a task is assigned, nobody sees that it is properly fulfilled or cares whether the result is satisfactory. So there is an urgent need to establish a strict responsibility system. Lenin said, "To refer to collegiate methods as an excuse for irresponsibility is a most dangerous evil." He called it "an evil which must be halted at all costs as quickly as possible and by whatever the means."

For every job or construction project it is necessary to specify the work to be done, the personnel required to do it, work quotas, standards of quality, and a time schedule. For example, in introducing foreign technology and equipment we should specify what items are to be imported from where, where they are going, and who is to take charge of the work. Whether it is a question of importing foreign equipment or of operating an existing enterprise, similar specifications should be made. When problems arise, it doesn't help just to blame the planning commissions and Party committees concerned, as we do now — the particular persons responsible must feel the heat. By the same token, rewards also should go to specific collectives and persons. In implementing the system according to which the factory directors assume overall responsibility under the leadership of the Party committees, we must state explicitly who is responsible for each aspect of the work.

To make the best use of the responsibility system, the following measures are essential.

First, we must extend the authority of the managerial personnel. Whoever is given responsibility should be given authority as well. Whoever it is — a factory director, engineer, technician, accountant or cashier — he should have his own area not only of responsibility but of authority, which must not be infringed upon by others. The responsibility system is bound to fail if there is only responsibility without authority.

Second, we must select personnel wisely and assign duties according to ability. We should seek out existing specialists and train new ones, put them in important positions, raise their political status and increase their material benefits. What are the political requirements in selecting someone for a job? The major criterion is whether the person chosen can work for the good of the people and contribute to the development of the productive forces and to the socialist cause as a whole.

Third, we must have a strict system of evaluation and distinguish clearly between a performance that should be rewarded and one that should be penalized. All enterprises, schools, research institutes and government offices should set up systems for evaluating work and conferring academic, technical and honorary titles. Rewards and penalties, promotions and demotions should be based on work performance. And they should be linked to increases or reductions in material benefits.

In short, through strengthening the responsibility system and allotting rewards and penalties fairly, we should create an atmosphere of friendly emulation in which people vie with one another to become advanced elements, working hard and aiming high.

In economic policy, I think we should allow some regions and enterprises and some workers and peasants to earn more and enjoy more benefits sooner than others, in accordance with their hard work and greater contributions to society. If the standard of living of some people is raised first, this will inevitably be an impressive example to their "neighbours," and people in other regions and units will want to learn from them. This will help the whole national economy to advance wave upon wave and help the people of all our nationalities to become prosperous in a comparatively short period.

Of course, there are still difficulties in production in the Northwest, Southwest and some other regions, and the life of the people there is hard. The state should give these places many kinds of help, and in particular strong material support.

These are major policies which can have an effect on the whole national economy and push it forward. I suggest that you study them carefully.

During the drive to realize the four modernizations, we are bound to encounter many new and unexpected situations and problems with which we are unfamiliar. In particular, the reforms in the relations of production and in the superstructure will not be easy to introduce. They touch on a wide range of issues and concern the immediate interests of large numbers of people, so they are bound to give rise to complications and problems and to meet with numerous obstacles. In the reorganization of enterprises, for example, there will be the problem of deciding who will stay on and who will leave, while in that of government departments, a good many people will be transferred to other jobs, and some may complain.

And so on. Since we will have to confront such problems soon, we must be mentally prepared for them. We must teach Party members and the masses to give top priority to the overall situation and the overall interests of the Party and the state. We should be full of confidence. We will be able to solve any problem and surmount any obstacle so long as we have faith in the masses, follow the mass line and explain the situation and problems to them. There can be no doubt that as the economy grows, more and more possibilities will open up and each person will be able to make his contribution to society.

The four modernizations represent a great and profound revolution in which we are moving forward by resolving one new contradiction after another. Therefore, all Party comrades must learn well and always keep on learning.

On the eve of nationwide victory in the Chinese revolution, Comrade Mao Zedong called on the whole Party to start learning afresh. We did that pretty well and consequently, after entering the cities, we were able to rehabilitate the economy very quickly and then to accomplish the socialist transformation. But we must admit that we have not learned well enough in the subsequent years. Expending our main efforts on political campaigns, we did not master the skills needed to build our country. Our socialist construction failed to progress satisfactorily and we experienced grave setbacks politically. Now that our task is to achieve modernization, our lack of the necessary knowledge is even more obvious. So the whole Party must start learning again.

What shall we learn? Basically, we should study Marxism-Leninism and Mao Zedong Thought and try to integrate the universal principles of Marxism with the concrete practice of our modernization drive. At present most of our cadres need also to apply themselves to three subjects: economics, science and technology, and management. Only if we study these well will we be able to carry out socialist modernization rapidly and efficiently. We should learn in different ways — through practice, from books and from the experience, both positive and negative, of others as well as our own. Conservatism and book worship should be overcome. The several hundred members and alternate members of the Central Committee and the thousands of senior cadres at the central and local levels should take the lead in making an in-depth study of modern economic development.

So long as we unite as one, work in concert, emancipate our minds, use our heads and try to learn what we did not know before, there is no doubt that we will be able to quicken the pace of our new Long March. Under the leadership of the Central Committee and the State Council, let us advance courageously to change the backward condition of our country and turn it into a modern and powerful socialist state.

JOINT COMMUNIQUÉ ON THE ESTABLISHMENT OF DIPLOMATIC RELATIONS BETWEEN THE PEOPLE'S REPUBLIC OF CHINA AND THE UNITED STATES OF AMERICA

INTRODUCTION *After the Shanghai Communiqué of 1972, which began the thaw in U.S.-China relations, the status of Taiwan remained a difficult issue. The United States continued its diplomatic recognition of the Republic of China on Taiwan until January 1, 1979, when it recognized the Beijing government as the sole legal government of China. This move accelerated the growing diplomatic isolation of Taiwan.*

The United States of America and the People's Republic of China have agreed to recognize each other and to establish diplomatic relations as of January 1, 1979.

The United States of America recognizes the Government of the People's Republic of China as the sole legal Government of China. Within this context, the people of the United States will maintain cultural, commercial, and other unofficial relations with the people of Taiwan.

The United States of America and the People's Republic of China reaffirm the principles agreed on by the two sides in the Shanghai Communiqué and emphasize once again that:

- Both wish to reduce the danger of international military conflict.

- Neither should seek hegemony in the Asia-Pacific region or in any other region of the world and each is opposed to efforts by any other country or group of countries to establish such hegemony.

- Neither is prepared to negotiate on behalf of any third party or to enter into agreements or understandings with the other directed at other states.

- The Government of the United States of America acknowledges the Chinese position that there is but one China and Taiwan is part of China.

- Both believe that normalization of Sino-American relations is not only in the interest of the Chinese and American peoples but also contributes to the cause of peace in Asia and the world.

The United States of America and the People's Republic of China will exchange Ambassadors and establish Embassies on March 1, 1979.

[Note: This is the English version in which the United States takes precedence.]

A MESSAGE TO COMPATRIOTS IN TAIWAN

INTRODUCTION *The context of this 1979 New Year's message, adopted by the National People's Congress at its Fifth Plenary Session, in effect set out a new line on Taiwan that was adopted by China's reform leadership. The insistence that Taiwan is part of China was preserved, but the message made clear that the Chinese government would consider an arrangement that allowed the people of Taiwan to preserve their way of life. The message announced an end to the bombardment of Taiwanese islands and proposed closer links between Taiwan and the Mainland.*

[The] Chinese nation is a great nation. It accounts for almost a quarter of the world's population and has a long history and brilliant culture, and its outstanding contributions to world civilization and human progress are universally recognized. Since ancient times Taiwan has been an inalienable part of China. The Chinese nation has great vitality and cohesion. Throughout its history, foreign invasions and internal strife have failed to permanently split our nation. Taiwan's separation from the motherland for nearly thirty years has been artificial and against national interests and aspirations, and this state of affairs must not be allowed to continue. Every Chinese, in Taiwan or on the mainland, has a compelling responsibility for the survival, growth and prosperity of the Chinese nation. The important task of reunifying our motherland, on which hinges the future of the whole nation, now lies before us all; it is an issue no one can, or should try to evade. If we do not quickly set about ending this disunity so that our motherland is reunified at an early date, how will we answer to our ancestors and explain it to our descendants? This sentiment is shared by all. Who among the descendants of the Yellow Emperor wishes to go down in history as a traitor?

Radical changes have taken place in China's status in the world over the past thirty years. Our country's international prestige is rising constantly and its international role becomes ever more important. The people and governments of almost all countries place tremendous hope on us in the struggle against hegemonism and in safeguarding peace and stability in Asia and the whole world.

Every Chinese is proud to see the growing strength and prosperity of our motherland. If we can end the present disunity and join forces soon, we will make limitless contributions to the future of mankind. Early reunification of our motherland is not only the common desire of all the people of China, including our compatriots in Taiwan, but the common wish of all peace-loving peoples and countries the world over.

Reunification of China today is consonant with popular sentiment and the unfolding of history. The world by and large recognizes only one China, with the Government of the People's Republic of China as its sole legal Government. The recent conclusion of the China-Japan Treaty of Peace and Friendship and the normalization of relations between China and the United States show still more clearly that no one can stop this trend. The present situation in the motherland, one of stability and unity, is better than ever. The people of all nationalities on the mainland are working hard with one will for the great goal of the four modernizations. It is our fervent hope that Taiwan returns to the embrace of the motherland at an early date so that we can work together for the great cause of national development. Our state leaders have firmly declared that in accomplishing the great cause of reunification they will take present realities into account, respect the status quo on Taiwan and the opinions of Taiwan people in all walks of life, and adopt reasonable policies and measures in settling the question of reunification so as not to cause the people of Taiwan any losses. On the other hand, people in all walks of life in Taiwan have expressed their yearning for their homeland and old friends, stated their desire "to identify themselves with and rejoin their kinsmen," and raised diverse proposals which are expressions of their earnest hope for an early return to the embrace of the motherland. Now that all conditions are favourable and ready for reunification, no one should go against the will of the nation and against the trend of history.

We place our hope on the 17 million people on Taiwan, including the Taiwan authorities. The Taiwan authorities have always firmly stood for one China and opposed an independent Taiwan. We take the same stand and it is the basis for our co-operation. Our position has always been that all patriots belong to one family. The responsibility of reunifying the motherland rests with each of us. We hope the Taiwan authorities will treasure national interests and make valuable contributions to the reunification of the motherland.

The Chinese Government has ordered the People's Liberation Army to stop the bombardment of Jinmen (Quemoy) and other islands as of today. A state of military confrontation between the two sides still exists along the Taiwan Straits. This can only breed tension. We hold first of all that this military confrontation be ended through discussions between the Government of the People's Republic of China and the Taiwan authorities; only in this way can we create the necessary conditions and a secure environment for the two sides to make contact in any and all areas.

Our prolonged separation has led to inadequate mutual understanding between and inconveniences for the compatriots on the mainland and on Taiwan. Since overseas Chinese residing in distant lands can return for visits and reunite with their families, why can't compatriots living so close to each other, on the mainland and on Taiwan, visit each other freely? We hold that there is no reason for such barriers to remain. We hope that at an early date, transportation and postal links will be established, allowing compatriots of both sides to have direct contact, write to each other, visit relatives and friends, exchange tours and visits and carry out academic, cultural, athletic and technological interchanges.

Economically, Taiwan and the mainland of the motherland were originally one entity. Unfortunately, economic ties have been suspended for many years. Construction is going ahead vigorously on the motherland and it is our wish that Taiwan also continues to prosper. There is every reason for us to develop trade and carry out economic exchanges, with each side making up for what the other lacks. This is mutually desired and will benefit both parties without harming either.

Dear compatriots in Taiwan:

The bright future of our great motherland belongs to us and to you. The reunification of the motherland is the sacred mission history has handed to our generation. Times are moving ahead and circumstances are changing. The earlier we fulfil this mission, the sooner we can jointly write an unprecedented, brilliant page in the history of our country, catch up with advanced powers, and work together with them for world peace, prosperity and progress. Let us join hands and work together for this glorious goal!

UPHOLD THE FOUR CARDINAL PRINCIPLES

SOURCE *Deng Xiaoping. Uphold the Four Cardinal Principles. In* Selected Works of Deng Xiaoping (1975–1982), *166–191. Translated by The Bureau for the Compilation and Translation of Works of Marx, Engels, Lenin and Stalin Under the Central Committee of the Communist Party of China. Beijing: People's Publishing House, 1983.*

INTRODUCTION *By his insistence that China must uphold these four very left-sounding political principles, Deng Xiaoping, in this excerpt of a speech delivered on*

March 30, 1979, fends off attacks from leftists who considered his program of reform a betrayal of Marxism-Leninism and Mao Zedong Thought. At the same time he makes it clear that he has no sympathy with those who challenge the leadership of the Communist Party or advocate "bourgeois democracy."

[What] I want to talk about now is ideological and political questions. The Central Committee maintains that, to carry out China's four modernizations, we must uphold the Four Cardinal Principles ideologically and politically. This is the basic prerequisite for achieving modernization. The four principles are:

1. We must keep to the socialist road.

2. We must uphold the dictatorship of the proletariat.

3. We must uphold the leadership of the Communist Party.

4. We must uphold Marxism-Leninism and Mao Zedong Thought.

As we all know, far from being new, these Four Cardinal Principles have long been upheld by our Party. The Central Committee has been adhering to these principles in all its guidelines and policies adopted since the smashing of the Gang of Four, and especially since the Third Plenary Session of the Eleventh Central Committee....

[To] sum up, in order to achieve the four modernizations we must keep to the socialist road, uphold the dictatorship of the proletariat, uphold the leadership of the Communist Party, and uphold Marxism-Leninism and Mao Zedong Thought. The Central Committee considers that we must now repeatedly emphasize the necessity of upholding these four cardinal principles, because certain people (even if only a handful) are attempting to undermine them. In no way can such attempts be tolerated. No Party member and, needless to say, no Party ideological or theoretical worker, must ever waver in the slightest on this basic stand. To undermine any of the four cardinal principles is to undermine the whole cause of socialism in China, the whole cause of modernization.

Is the Central Committee making a mountain out of a molehill when it takes this view of the matter? No, it is not. In the light of current developments the Party has no choice.

In the recent period a small number of persons have provoked incidents in some places. Instead of accepting the guidance, advice, and explanations of leading officials of the Party and government, certain bad elements have raised sundry demands that cannot be met at present or are altogether unreasonable. They have provoked or tricked some of the masses into raiding Party and government organizations, occupying offices, holding sit-down and hunger strikes and obstructing traffic, thereby seriously disrupting production, other work and public order.

Moreover, they have raised such sensational slogans as "Oppose hunger" and "Give us human rights," inciting people to hold demonstrations and deliberately trying to get foreigners to give worldwide publicity to their words and deeds. There is a so-called China Human Rights Group which has gone so far as to put up big-character posters requesting the President of the United States to "show concern" for human rights in China. Can we permit such an open call for intervention in China's internal affairs? There is also a so-called Thaw Society which has issued a declaration openly opposing the dictatorship of the proletariat on the ground that it "divides mankind." Can we tolerate this kind of freedom of speech which flagrantly contravenes the principles of our Constitution?

In Shanghai there is a so-called Democracy Forum. Some of its members have slandered Comrade Mao Zedong and put up big counter-revolutionary posters proclaiming that "proletarian dictatorship is the source of all evils" and that it is necessary to "resolutely and thoroughly criticize the Communist Party of China." They allege that capitalism is better than socialism and that, therefore, instead of carrying out the four modernizations China should introduce what they call "social reform," by which they mean that it should turn to capitalism. They publicly declare that their task is to settle accounts with those whom the Gang of Four called the capitalist roaders but whom it had failed to deal with. Some of them have asked to go abroad to seek political asylum, and some have even made clandestine contact with the Kuomintang secret service, plotting sabotage.

It is obvious that these people are out to use any and all means to disrupt our effort to shift the focus of our work to the achievement of modernization. If we ignored these grave problems, our Party and government organs at various levels would be so harassed that they would find it impossible to function. How, then, could we concentrate on the four modernizations?

It is true that there are very few such incidents and that the overwhelming majority of our people disapprove of them. Nevertheless, they merit our serious attention. First, these trouble-makers generally say they speak in the name of democracy, a claim by which people are easily misled. Second, taking advantage of social problems left over from the time when Lin Biao and the Gang of Four held sway, they may deceive some people who have difficulties which the government cannot help to clear up at the moment. Third, the trouble-makers have begun to form all kinds of secret or semi-

secret organizations which seek to establish contact with each other on a nationwide scale and at the same time to collaborate with political forces in Taiwan and abroad. Fourth, some of these people work hand in glove with gangster organizations and followers of the Gang of Four, trying to expand the scope of their sabotage. Fifth, they do all they can to use as a pretext — or as a shield — indiscreet statements of one sort or another made by some of our comrades. All this shows that the struggle against these individuals is no simple matter that can be settled quickly. We must strive to clearly distinguish between people (many of them innocent young people) and the counter-revolutionaries and bad elements who have hoodwinked them, and whom we must deal with sternly and according to law. At the same time, we must educate comrades throughout the Party about the necessity of sharpening their vigilance, bearing in mind the interests of the country as a whole and uniting as one under the leadership of the Central Committee. We must encourage them to continue the emancipation of their minds and consistently promote democracy so that they can mobilize all positive forces while at the same time endeavouring to clear up the ideological confusion among a small section of the people, especially young people.

We must make a special effort to explain the question of democracy clearly to the people, and to our youth in particular. The socialist road, the dictatorship of the proletariat, the leadership of the Communist Party and Marxism-Leninism and Mao Zedong Thought — all these are tied up with democracy. What kind of democracy do the Chinese people need today? It can only be socialist democracy, people's democracy, and not bourgeois democracy, individualist democracy. . . .

[While] propagating democracy, we must strictly distinguish between socialist democracy on the one hand and bourgeois, individualist democracy on the other. We must link democracy for the people with dictatorship over the enemy, and with centralism, legality, discipline and the leadership by the Communist Party. At present when we are confronted with manifold difficulties in our economic life which can be overcome only by a series of readjustments and by consolidation and reorganization, it is particularly necessary to stress publicly the importance of subordinating personal interests to collective ones, interests of the part to those of the whole, and immediate to long-term interests. Only when everyone — whether inside or outside the Party, in a leading position or among the rank and file — is concerned for the overall interests shall we be able to overcome our difficulties and ensure a bright future for the four modernizations. Conversely, departure from the four cardinal principles and talk about democracy in the abstract will inevitably lead to the unchecked spread of ultra-democracy and anarchism, to the complete disruption of political stability and unity, and to the total failure of our modernization programme. If this happens, the decade of struggle against Lin Biao and the Gang of Four will have been in vain, China will once again be plunged into chaos, division, retrogression and darkness, and the Chinese people will be deprived of all hope. This is a matter of deep concern not only for the Chinese people of whatever nationality but also for all people abroad who wish to see China strong....

ANSWERS TO THE ITALIAN JOURNALIST ORIANA FALLACI

SOURCE *Fallaci, Oriana, with Deng Xiaoping. Answers to the Italian Journalist Oriana Fallaci. Selected Works of Deng Xiaoping (1975–1982), 326–344. Translated by The Bureau for the Compilation and Translation of Works of Marx, Engels, Lenin and Stalin Under the Central Committee of the Communist Party of China. Beijing: People's Publishing House, 1983.*

INTRODUCTION *The well-known Italian journalist Oriana Fallaci, who died in 2006, conducted the interview excerpted below with Deng Xiaoping in 1980. She questioned the reform leader about many sensitive issues such as the historical assessment of Mao Zedong and his mistakes, the Cultural Revolution and the future role of foreign capital in China.*

Oriana Fallaci: Will Chairman Mao's portrait above Tiananmen Gate be kept there?

Deng Xiaoping: It will, forever. In the past there were too many portraits of Chairman Mao. They were hung everywhere. That was not proper and it didn't really show respect for Chairman Mao. It's true that he made mistakes in a certain period, but he was after all a principal founder of the Chinese Communist Party and the People's Republic of China. In evaluating his merits and mistakes, we hold that his mistakes were only secondary. What he did for the Chinese people can never be erased. In our hearts we Chinese will always cherish him as a founder of our Party and our state.

Question: We Westerners find a lot of things hard to understand. The Gang of Four are blamed for all the faults. I'm told that when the Chinese talk about the Gang of Four, many of them hold up five fingers.

Answer: We must make a clear distinction between the nature of Chairman Mao's mistakes and the crimes of Lin Biao and the Gang of Four. For most of his life, Chairman Mao did very good things. Many times he saved the Party and the state from crises. Without him the Chinese people would, at the very least, have spent much more time groping in the dark. Chairman Mao's greatest contribution was that he applied the principles of Marxism-Leninism to the concrete practice of the Chinese revolution, pointing the way to victory. It should be said that before the sixties or the late fifties many of his ideas brought us victories, and the fundamental principles he advanced were quite correct. He creatively applied Marxism-Leninism to every aspect of the Chinese revolution, and he had creative views on philosophy, political science, military science, literature and art, and so on. Unfortunately, in the evening of his life, particularly during the "Cultural Revolution," he made mistakes — and they were not minor ones — which brought many misfortunes upon our Party, our state and our people. As you know, during the Yan'an days our Party summed up Chairman Mao's thinking in various fields as Mao Zedong Thought, and we made it our guiding ideology. We won great victories for the revolution precisely because we adhered to Mao Zedong Thought. Of course, Mao Zedong Thought was not created by Comrade Mao alone — other revolutionaries of the older generation played a part in forming and developing it — but primarily it embodies Comrade Mao's thinking. Nevertheless, victory made him less prudent, so that in his later years some unsound features and unsound ideas, chiefly "Left" ones, began to emerge. In quite a number of instances he went counter to his own ideas, counter to the fine and correct propositions he had previously put forward, and counter to the style of work he himself had advocated. At this time he increasingly lost touch with reality. He didn't maintain a good style of work. He did not consistently practise democratic centralism and the mass line, for instance, and he failed to institutionalize them during his lifetime. This was not the fault of Comrade Mao Zedong alone. Other revolutionaries of the older generation, including me, should also be held responsible. Some abnormalities appeared in the political life of our Party and state — patriarchal ways or styles of work developed, and glorification of the individual was rife; political life in general wasn't too healthy. Eventually these things led to the "Cultural Revolution," which was a mistake.

Question: You mentioned that in his last years, Chairman Mao was in poor health. But at the time of Liu Shaoqi's arrest and his subsequent death in prison Mao's health wasn't so bad. And there are other mistakes to be accounted for. Wasn't the Great Leap Forward a mistake? Wasn't copying the Soviet model a mistake? And what did Chairman Mao really want with the "Cultural Revolution"?

Answer: Mistakes began to occur in the late fifties — the Great Leap Forward, for instance. But that wasn't solely Chairman Mao's fault either. The people around him got carried away too. We acted in direct contravention of objective laws, attempting to boost the economy all at once. As our subjective wishes went against objective laws, losses were inevitable. Still, it is Chairman Mao who should be held primarily responsible for the Great Leap Forward. But it didn't take him long — just a few months — to recognize his mistake, and he did so before the rest of us and proposed corrections. And in 1962, when because of some other factors those corrections had not been fully carried out, he made a self-criticism. But the lessons were not fully drawn, and as a result the "Cultural Revolution" erupted. So far as Chairman Mao's own hopes were concerned, he initiated the "Cultural Revolution" in order to avert the restoration of capitalism, but he had made an erroneous assessment of China's actual situation. In the first place, the targets of the revolution were wrongly defined, which led to the effort to ferret out "capitalist roaders in power in the Party." Blows were dealt at leading cadres at all levels who had made contributions to the revolution and had practical experience, including Comrade Liu Shaoqi. In the last couple of years before Chairman Mao's death he said that the "Cultural Revolution" had been wrong on two counts: one was "overthrowing all," and the other was waging a "full-scale civil war." These two counts alone show that the "Cultural Revolution" cannot be called correct. Chairman Mao's mistake was a political mistake, and not a small one. On the other hand, it was taken advantage of by the two counter-revolutionary cliques headed by Lin Biao and the Gang of Four, who schemed to usurp power. Therefore, we should draw a line between Chairman Mao's mistakes and the crimes of Lin Biao and the Gang of Four.

Question: But we all know that it was Chairman Mao himself who chose Lin Biao1 as his successor, much in the same way as an emperor chooses his heir.

Answer: This is what I've just referred to as an incorrect way of doing things. For a leader to pick his own successor is a feudal practice. It is an illustration of the imperfections in our institutions which I referred to a moment ago.

Question: To what extent will Chairman Mao be involved when you hold your next Party congress?

Answer: We will make an objective assessment of Chairman Mao's contributions and his mistakes. We will reaffirm that his contributions are primary and his mistakes secondary. We will adopt a realistic approach towards the mistakes he made late in life. We will continue to adhere to Mao Zedong Thought, which represents the correct part of Chairman Mao's life. Not only did Mao Zedong Thought lead us to victory in the revolution in the past; it is — and will continue to be — a treasured possession of the Chinese Communist Party and of our country. That is why we will forever keep Chairman Mao's portrait on Tiananmen Gate as a symbol of our country, and we will always remember him as a founder of our Party and state. Moreover, we will adhere to Mao Zedong Thought. We will not do to Chairman Mao what Khrushchov did to Stalin.

Question: Do you mean to say that the name of Chairman Mao will inevitably come up when the Gang of Four is brought to trial as well as when you have your next Party congress?

Answer: His name will be mentioned. Not only at the next Party congress but also on other occasions. But the trial of the Gang of Four will not detract from Chairman Mao's prestige. Of course, he was responsible for putting them in their positions. Nevertheless, the crimes the Gang of Four themselves committed are more than sufficient to justify whatever sentences may be passed on them.

Question: I have heard that Chairman Mao frequently complained that you didn't listen to him enough, and that he didn't like you. Is it true?

Answer: Yes, Chairman Mao did say I didn't listen to him. But this wasn't directed only at me. It happened to other leaders as well. It reflects some unhealthy ideas in his twilight years, that is, patriarchal ways which are feudal in nature. He did not readily listen to differing opinions. We can't say that all his criticisms were wrong. But neither was he ready to listen to many correct opinions put forward not only by me but by other comrades. Democratic centralism was impaired, and so was collective leadership. Otherwise, it would be hard to explain how the "Cultural Revolution" broke out.

Question: There was one personage in China who always went unscathed, and that was Premier Zhou Enlai. How do you explain this fact?

Answer: Premier Zhou was a man who worked hard and uncomplainingly all his life. He worked 12 hours a day, and sometimes 16 hours or more, throughout his life. We got to know each other quite early, that is, when we were in France on a work-study programme during the 1920s. I have always looked upon him as my elder brother. We took the revolutionary road at about the same time. He was much respected by his comrades and all the people. Fortunately he survived during the "Cultural Revolution" when we were knocked down. He was in an extremely difficult position then, and he said and did many things that he would have wished not to. But the people forgave him because, had he not done and said those things, he himself would not have been able to survive and play the neutralizing role he did, which reduced losses. He succeeded in protecting quite a number of people.

Question: I don't see how terrible things like the "Cultural Revolution" can be avoided or prevented from recurring.

Answer: This issue has to be addressed by tackling the problems in our institutions. Some of those we established in the past were, in fact, tainted by feudalism, as manifested in such things as the personality cult, the patriarchal ways or styles of work, and the life tenure of cadres in leading posts. We are now looking into ways to prevent such things from recurring and are preparing to start with the restructuring of our institutions. Our country has a history of thousands of years of feudalism and is still lacking in socialist democracy and socialist legality. We are now working earnestly to cultivate socialist democracy and socialist legality. Only in this way can we solve the problem.

Question: Are you sure that things will proceed more smoothly from now on? Can you attain the goal you have set yourselves? I hear that the so-called Maoists are still around. By "Maoists" I mean those who backed the "Cultural Revolution."

Answer: The influence of the Gang of Four should not be underrated, but it should be noted that 97 or 98 per cent of the population hate them intensely for their crimes. This was shown by the mass movement against the Gang of Four which erupted at Tiananmen Square on April 5, 1976, when the Gang were still riding high, Chairman Mao was critically ill and Premier Zhou had passed away. Since the Gang's overthrow [in 1976], and particularly in the past two years, the will and demands of the people have been given expression in the Third, Fourth and Fifth Plenary Sessions of the Central Committee of the Chinese Communist Party. We are considering ways of resolving our problems by improving our institutions. Many issues have already been raised now. Particular emphasis is being laid on working single-mindedly for the four modernizations, and this is winning the hearts of the people. They want political stability and unity. They are fed up with large-scale movements. Such movements invariably ended up hurting a number — and not a small number — of people. Incessant movements make it practically impossible to concentrate on national construction. Therefore, we can say for sure that given the correctness of our present course, the people will support us and such phenomena as the "Cultural Revolution" will not happen again.

Question: The Gang of Four could only have been arrested after the death of Chairman Mao. Who engineered their arrest? Who initiated the idea?

Answer: It was collective effort. First of all, I think, it had a mass base laid by the April 5th Movement [of 1976]. The term "Gang of Four" was coined by Chairman Mao a couple of years before his death. We waged struggles against the Gang for two years, in 1974 and 1975. By then people clearly saw them for what they were. Although Chairman Mao had designated his successor, the Gang of Four refused to accept this. After Chairman Mao's death, the Gang took the opportunity to try and get all power into their own hands, and the situation demanded action from us. They were rampant at that time, trying to overthrow the new leadership.

Under these circumstances, the great majority of the comrades of the Political Bureau were agreed that measures had to be taken to deal with the Gang. The efforts of one of two individuals would not have sufficed for this purpose.

It should be pointed out that some of the things done after the arrest of the Gang of Four were inconsistent with Chairman Mao's wishes, for instance, the construction of the Chairman Mao Memorial Hall. He had proposed in the fifties that we should all be cremated when we died and that only our ashes be kept, that no remains should be preserved and no tombs built. Chairman Mao was the first to sign his name, and we all followed suit. Nearly all senior cadres at the central level and across the country signed. We still have that book of signatures. What was done in the matter after the smashing of the Gang of Four was prompted by the desire to achieve a relative stability.

Question: Does this mean that the Chairman Mao Memorial Hall will soon be demolished?

Answer: I am not in favour of changing it. Now that it is there, it would not be appropriate to remove it. It wasn't appropriate to build it in the first place, but to change it would give rise to all kinds of talk. Many people are now speculating whether we will demolish the Memorial Hall. We have no such idea.

Question: It is said that you are giving up the post of Vice-Premier.

Answer: I will not be the only one to resign. All other comrades of the older generation are giving up their concurrent posts. Chairman Hua Guofeng will no longer serve concurrently as Premier of the State Council. The Central Committee of the Party has recommended Comrade Zhao Ziyang as candidate for that post. If we old comrades remain at our posts, newcomers will be inhibited in their work. We face the problem of gradually reducing the average age of leaders at all levels. We have to take the lead.

There were previously no relevant rules. In fact, however, there was life tenure in leading posts. This does not facilitate the renewal of leadership or the promotion of younger people. It is an institutional defect which was not evident in the sixties because we were then in the prime of life. This issue involves not just individuals but all the relevant institutions. It has an even greater bearing on our general policy and on whether our four modernizations can be achieved. Therefore, we say it would be better for us old comrades to take an enlightened attitude and set an example in this respect.

Question: I have seen other portraits in China. At Tiananmen I've seen portraits of Marx, Engels and Lenin and particularly of Stalin. Do you intend to keep them there?

Answer: Before the "Cultural Revolution" they were put up only on important holidays. The practice was changed during the "Cultural Revolution," when they were displayed permanently. Now we are going back to the former way.

Question: The four modernizations will bring foreign capital into China, and this will inevitably give rise to private investment. Won't this lead to a miniaturized capitalism?

Answer: In the final analysis, the general principle for our economic development is still that formulated by Chairman Mao, that is, to rely mainly on our own efforts with external assistance subsidiary. No matter to what degree we open up to the outside world and admit foreign capital, its relative magnitude will be small and it can't affect our system of socialist public ownership of the means of production. Absorbing foreign capital and technology and even allowing foreigners to construct plants in China can only play a complementary role to our effort to develop the productive forces in a socialist society. Of course, this will bring some decadent capitalist influences into China. We are aware of this possibility; it's nothing to be afraid of.

Question: Does it mean that not all in capitalism is so bad?

Answer: It depends on how you define capitalism. Any capitalism is superior to feudalism. And we cannot say that everything developed in capitalist countries is of a capitalist nature. For instance, technology, science — even advanced production management is also a sort of science — will be useful in any society or country. We intend to acquire advanced technology, science and management skills to serve our socialist production. And these things as such have no class character.

Question: I remember that several years ago, when talking about private plots in rural areas, you acknowledged that man needs some personal interest to produce. Doesn't this mean to put in discussion communism itself?

Answer: According to Marx, socialism is the first stage of communism and it covers a very long historical period in which we must practise the principle "to each according to his work" and combine the interests of the state, the collective and the individual, for only thus can we arouse people's enthusiasm for labour and develop socialist production. At the higher stage of communism, when the productive forces will be greatly developed and the principle "from each according to his ability, to each according to his needs" will be practised, personal interests will be acknowledged still more and more personal needs will be satisfied.

Question: You mentioned that there are others who made contributions to Mao Zedong Thought. Who were they?

Answer: Other revolutionaries of the older generation, for example Premier Zhou Enlai, Comrades Liu Shaoqi and Zhu De — and many others. Many senior cadres are creative and original in their thinking.

Question: Why did you leave your own name out?

Answer: I am quite insignificant. Of course, I too have done some work. Otherwise, I wouldn't be counted as a revolutionary.

Question: What we did not understand was: If the Gang of Four was, as you said, a minority with all the country against them, how could it happen that they were holding the whole country, including the veteran leaders? Was it because one of the four was the wife of Mao Zedong and the ties between Mao Zedong and her were so profound that no one dared to touch her?

Answer: This was one of the factors. As I've said, Chairman Mao made mistakes, one of which was using the Gang, letting them come to power. Also, the Gang had their own factional set-up and they built a clique of some size — particularly they made use of ignorant young people as a front, so they had a fair-sized base.

Question: Was Mao Zedong blinded by her so that he wouldn't see what she was doing? And was she an adventuress like the Empress Dowager Yehonala?

Answer: Jiang Qing did evil things by flaunting the banner of Chairman Mao. But Chairman Mao and Jiang Qing lived separately for years.

Question: We didn't know that.

Answer: Jiang Qing did what she did by flaunting the banner of Chairman Mao, but he failed to intervene effectively. For this he should be held responsible. Jiang Qing is rotten through and through. Whatever sentence is passed on the Gang of Four won't be excessive. They brought harm to millions upon millions of people.

Question: How would you assess Jiang Qing? What score would you give her?

Answer: Below zero. A thousand points below zero.

Question: How would you assess yourself?

Answer: I would be quite content if I myself could be rated fifty-fifty in merits and demerits. But one thing I can say for myself: I have had a clear conscience all my life. Please mark my words: I have made quite a few mistakes, and I have my own share of responsibility for some of the mistakes made by Comrade Mao Zedong. But it can be said that I made my mistake with good intentions. There is nobody who doesn't make mistakes.

We should not lay all past mistakes on Chairman Mao. So we must be very objective in assessing him. His contributions were primary, his mistakes secondary. We will inherit the many good things in Chairman Mao's thinking while at the same time explaining clearly the mistakes he made.

RESOLUTION ON CERTAIN QUESTIONS IN THE HISTORY OF OUR PARTY SINCE THE FOUNDING OF THE PEOPLE'S REPUBLIC OF CHINA

INTRODUCTION *The post-Mao leadership of China jettisoned many of Mao's policies, condemned the "leftist excesses of his later years," in particular the Cultural Revolution, and rehabilitated many victims of his political campaigns. Yet given that the reform leaders' own records and that of the Communist Party and the revolution were so closely associated with the late leader, the evaluation of Mao Zedong's legacy was a delicate task. The* Resolution on Certain Questions *(adopted by the Sixth Plenary Session of the Eleventh Central Committee of the Communist Party of China on June 27, 1981), the authoritative official verdict that was made required reading for China's 37 million party members, ruled that Mao's contributions to the revolution far outweighed his mistakes and reaffirmed the value of Mao Zedong Thought, redefined as the crystallization of the collective wisdom of the Chinese Communist Party.*

27. Comrade Mao Zedong was a great Marxist and a great proletarian revolutionary, strategist and theorist. It is true that he made gross mistakes during the "cultural revolution," but, if we judge his activities as a whole, his contributions to the Chinese revolution far outweigh his mistakes. His merits are primary and his errors secondary. He rendered indelible meritorious service in founding and building up our Party and the Chinese People's Liberation Army, in winning victory for the cause of liberation of the Chinese people, in founding the People's Republic of China and in advancing our socialist cause. He made major contributions to the liberation of the oppressed nations of the world and to the progress of mankind.

28. The Chinese Communists, with Comrade Mao Zedong as their chief representative, made a theoretical synthesis of China's unique experience in its protracted revolution in accordance with the basic principles of Marxism-Leninism. This synthesis contributed a scientific system of guidelines befitting China's conditions, and it is this synthesis which is Mao Zedong Thought, the product of the integration of the universal principles of Marxism-Leninism with the concrete practice of the Chinese revolution.... [I]t constitutes a correct theory, a body of correct principles and a summary of the experiences that have been confirmed in the practice of the Chinese revolution, a crystallization of the collective wisdom of the Chinese Communist Party. Many outstanding leaders of our Party made important contributions to the formation and development of Mao Zedong Thought, and they are synthesized in the scientific works of Comrade Mao Zedong....

31. Mao Zedong Thought is the valuable spiritual asset of our Party. It will be our guide to action for a long time to come. The Party leaders and the large group of cadres nurtured by Marxism-Leninism and Mao Zedong Thought were the backbone forces in winning great victories for our cause; they are and will remain our treasured mainstay in the cause of socialist modernization. While many of Comrade Mao Zedong's important works were written during the periods of new-democratic revolution and of socialist transformation, we must still constantly study them. This is not only because one cannot cut the past off from the present and failure to understand the past will hamper our understanding of present-day problems, but also because many of the basic theories, principles and scientific approaches set forth in these works are of universal significance and provide us with invaluable guidance now and will continue to do so in the future. Therefore, we must continue to uphold Mao Zedong Thought, study it in earnest and apply its stand, viewpoint and method in studying the new situation and solving the new problems arising in the course of practice. Mao Zedong Thought has added much that is new to the treasure-house of Marxist-Leninist theory. We must combine our study of the scientific works of Comrade Mao Zedong with that of the scientific writings of Marx, Engels, Lenin and Stalin. It is entirely wrong to try to negate the scientific value of Mao Zedong Thought and to deny its guiding role in our revolution and construction just because Comrade Mao Zedong made mistakes in his later years. And it is likewise entirely wrong to adopt a dogmatic attitude towards the sayings of Comrade Mao Zedong, to regard whatever he said as the immutable truth which must be mechanically applied everywhere, and to be unwilling to admit honestly that he made mistakes in his later years, and even try to stick to them in our new activities. Both these attitudes fail to make a distinction between Mao Zedong Thought—a scientific theory formed and tested over a long period of time—and the mistakes Comrade Mao Zedong made in his later years. And it is absolutely necessary that this distinction should be made. We must treasure all the positive experience obtained in the course of integrating

the universal principles of Marxism-Leninism with the concrete practice of China's revolution and construction over fifty years or so, apply and carry forward this experience in our new work and enrich and develop Party theory with new principles and new conclusions corresponding to reality, so as to ensure the continued progress of our cause along the scientific course of Marxism-Leninism and Mao Zedong Thought.

CONSTITUTION OF THE PEOPLE'S REPUBLIC OF CHINA

INTRODUCTION *The first Constitution of the People's Republic of China appeared in 1954, replacing the Common Program [see p. 221] which had played the role of a constitution since 1949. It effectively became irrelevant during the Cultural Revolution when regular political institutions and processes ceased to operate. A second constitution, adopted in 1975 and reflecting the more radical tone of the Cultural Revolution, was replaced by the constitution of 1978, which essentially reasserted the pre-Cultural Revolution norms. The 1982 Constitution which is excerpted here reflected the views of the post-Mao reform leadership by then firmly in power. It attempted to reduce the control of the Communist Party over state organizations and to strengthen the rights of the citizen notably in relation to property and inheritance. It was passed by the National People's Congress December 4, 1982. Minor amendments to it were passed in 1988, 1993, 1999, and 2004.*

PREAMBLE

China is one of the countries with the longest histories in the world. The people of all nationalities in China have jointly created a splendid culture and have a glorious revolutionary tradition. Feudal China was gradually reduced after 1840 to a semi-colonial and semi-feudal country. The Chinese people waged wave upon wave of heroic struggles for national independence and liberation and for democracy and freedom. Great and earth-shaking historical changes have taken place in China in the 20th century. The Revolution of 1911, led by Dr Sun Yat-sen, abolished the feudal monarchy and gave birth to the Republic of China. But the Chinese people had yet to fulfil their historical task of overthrowing imperialism and feudalism. After waging hard, protracted and tortuous struggles, armed and otherwise, the Chinese people of all nationalities led by the Communist Party of China with Chairman Mao Zedong as its leader ultimately, in

1949, overthrew the rule of imperialism, feudalism and bureaucrat capitalism, won the great victory of the new-democratic revolution and founded the People's Republic of China. Thereupon the Chinese people took state power into their own hands and became masters of the country. . . .

CHAPTER II: THE FUNDAMENTAL RIGHTS AND DUTIES OF CITIZENS

Article 33.

All persons holding the nationality of the People's Republic of China are citizens of the People's Republic of China. All citizens of the People's Republic of China are equal before the law. Every citizen enjoys the rights and at the same time must perform the duties prescribed by the Constitution and the law.

Article 34.

All citizens of the People's Republic of China who have reached the age of 18 have the right to vote and stand for election, regardless of nationality, race, sex, occupation, family background, religious belief, education, property status, or length of residence, except persons deprived of political rights according to law.

Article 35.

Citizens of the People's Republic of China enjoy freedom of speech, of the press, of assembly, of association, of procession and of demonstration.

Article 36.

Citizens of the People's Republic of China enjoy freedom of religious belief. No state organ, public organization or individual may compel citizens to believe in, or not to believe in, any religion; nor may they discriminate against citizens who believe in, or do not believe in, any religion. The state protects normal religious activities. No one may make use of religion to engage in activities that disrupt public order, impair the health of citizens or interfere with the educational system of the state. Religious bodies and religious affairs are not subject to any foreign domination.

Article 37.

The freedom of person of citizens of the People's Republic of China is inviolable. No citizen may be arrested except with the approval or by decision of a people's procuratorate or by decision of a people's court, and arrests must be made by a public security organ. Unlawful deprivation or restriction of citizens' freedom of person by detention or other means is prohibited; and unlawful search of the person of citizens is prohibited.

Article 38.

The personal dignity of citizens of the People's Republic of China is inviolable. Insult, libel, false charge or frame-up directed against citizens by any means is prohibited.

Article 39.

The home of citizens of the People's Republic of China is inviolable. Unlawful search of, or intrusion into, a citizen's home is prohibited.

Article 40.

The freedom and privacy of correspondence of citizens of the People's Republic of China are protected by law. No organization or individual may, on any ground, infringe upon the freedom and privacy of citizens' correspondence except in cases where, to meet the needs of state security or of investigation into criminal offences, public security or procuratorial organs are permitted to censor correspondence in accordance with procedures prescribed by law.

Article 41.

Citizens of the People's Republic of China have the right to criticize and make suggestions to any state organ or functionary. Citizens have the right to make to relevant state organs complaints and charges against, or exposures of, violation of the law or dereliction of duty by any state organ or functionary; but fabrication or distortion of facts with the intention of libel or frame-up is prohibited. In case of complaints, charges or exposures made by citizens, the state organ concerned must deal with them in a responsible manner after ascertaining the facts. No one may suppress such complaints, charges and exposures, or retaliate against the citizens making them. Citizens who have suffered losses through infringement of their civil rights by any state organ or functionary have the right to compensation in accordance with the law.

Article 42.

Citizens of the People's Republic of China have the right as well as the duty to work. Using various channels, the state creates conditions for employment, strengthens labour protection, improves working conditions and, on the basis of expanded production, increases remuneration for work and social benefits. Work is the glorious duty of every able-bodied citizen. All working people in state enterprises and in urban and rural economic collectives should perform their tasks with an attitude consonant with their status as masters of the country. The state

promotes socialist labour emulation, and commends and rewards model and advanced workers. The state encourages citizens to take part in voluntary labour. The state provides necessary vocational training to citizens before they are employed.

Article 43.

Working people in the People's Republic of China have the right to rest. The state expands facilities for rest and recuperation of working people, and prescribes working hours and vacations for workers and staff.

Article 44.

The state prescribes by law the system of retirement for workers and staff in enterprises and undertakings and for functionaries of organs of state. The livelihood of retired personnel is ensured by the state and society.

Article 45.

Citizens of the People's Republic of China have the right to material assistance from the state and society when they are old, ill or disabled. The state develops the social insurance, social relief and medical and health services that are required to enable citizens to enjoy this right. The state and society ensure the livelihood of disabled members of the armed forces, provide pensions to the families of martyrs and give preferential treatment to the families of military personnel. The state and society help make arrangements for the work, livelihood and education of the blind, deaf-mute and other handicapped citizens.

Article 46.

Citizens of the People's Republic of China have the duty as well as the right to receive education. The state promotes the all-round moral, intellectual and physical development of children and young people.

Article 47.

Citizens of the People's Republic of China have the freedom to engage in scientific research, literary and artistic creation and other cultural pursuits. The state encourages and assists creative endeavours conducive to the interests of the people made by citizens engaged in education, science, technology, literature, art and other cultural work.

Article 48.

Women in the People's Republic of China enjoy equal rights with men in all spheres of life, political, economic, cultural and social, and family life. The state protects the rights and interests of women, applies the principle of equal pay for equal work for men and women alike and trains and selects cadres from among women.

Article 49.

Marriage, the family, and mother and child are protected by the state. Both husband and wife have the duty to practise family planning. Parents have the duty to rear and educate their minor children, and children who have come of age have the duty to support and assist their parents. Violation of the freedom of marriage is prohibited. Maltreatment of old people, women and children is prohibited.

Article 50.

The People's Republic of China protects the legitimate rights and interests of Chinese nationals residing abroad and protects the lawful rights and interests of returned overseas Chinese and of the family members of Chinese nationals residing abroad.

Article 51.

The exercise by citizens of the People's Republic of China of their freedoms and rights may not infringe upon the interests of the state, of society and of the collective, or upon the lawful freedoms and rights of other citizens.

Article 52.

It is the duty of citizens of the People's Republic of China to safeguard the unity of the country and the unity of all its nationalities.

Article 53.

Citizens of the People's Republic of China must abide by the constitution and the law, keep state secrets, protect public property and observe labour discipline and public order and respect social ethics.

Article 54.

It is the duty of citizens of the People's Republic of China to safeguard the security, honour and interests of the motherland; they must not commit acts detrimental to the security, honour and interests of the motherland.

Article 55.

It is the sacred obligation of every citizen of the People's Republic of China to defend the motherland and resist aggression. It is the honourable duty of citizens of the People's Republic of China to perform military service and join the militia in accordance with the law.

Article 56.

It is the duty of citizens of the People's Republic of China to pay taxes in accordance with the law. . . .

JOINT COMMUNIQUÉ ON ARMS SALES TO TAIWAN

INTRODUCTION *Even as the United States recognized the government of the People's Republic of China as the sole legal government of China on January 1, 1979, U.S. relations with Taiwan continued to be a flashpoint between the two governments. As this communiqué indicates, the Chinese government was particularly annoyed that the U.S. continued to supply arms to Taiwan.*

JOINT COMMUNIQUÉ OF THE UNITED STATES OF AMERICA AND THE PEOPLE'S REPUBLIC OF CHINA

August 17, 1982

1. In the Joint Communiqué on the Establishment of Diplomatic Relations on January 1, 1979, issued by the Government of the United States of America and the People's Republic of China, the United States of America recognized the Government of the People's Republic of China as the sole legal Government of China, and it acknowledged the Chinese position that there is but one China and Taiwan is part of China. Within that context, the two sides agreed that the people of the United States would continue to maintain cultural, commercial, and other unofficial relations with the people of Taiwan. On this basis, relations between the United States and China were normalized.

2. The question of United States arms sales to Taiwan was not settled in the course of negotiations between the two countries on establishing diplomatic relations. The two sides held differing positions, and the Chinese side stated that it would raise the issue again following normalization. Recognizing that this issue would seriously hamper the development of United States - China relations, they have held further discussions on it, during and since the meetings between President Ronald Reagan and Premier Zhao Ziyang and between Secretary of State Alexander M. Haig, Jr. and Vice Premier and Foreign Minister Huang Hua in October 1981.

3. Respect for each other's sovereignty and territorial integrity and non-interference in each other's internal affairs constitute the fundamental principles guiding United States - China relations. These principles were confirmed in the Shanghai Communiqué of February

28, 1972 and reaffirmed in the Joint Communiqué on the Establishment of Diplomatic Relations which came into effect on January 1, 1979. Both sides emphatically state that these principles continue to govern all aspects of their relations.

4. The Chinese Government reiterates that the question of Taiwan is China's internal affair. The Message to Compatriots in Taiwan issued by China on January 1, 1979 promulgated a fundamental policy of striving for peaceful reunification of the motherland. The Nine-Point Proposal put forward by China on September 30, 1981 represented a further major effort under this fundamental policy to strive for a peaceful solution to the Taiwan question.

5. The United States Government attaches great importance to its relations with China, and reiterates that it has no intention of infringing on Chinese sovereignty and territorial integrity, or interfering in China's internal affairs, or pursuing a policy of "two Chinas" or "one China, one Taiwan." The United States Government understands and appreciates the Chinese policy of striving for a peaceful resolution of the Taiwan question as indicated in China's Message to Compatriots in Taiwan issued on January 1, 1979 and the Nine-Point Proposal put forward by China on September 30, 1981. The new situation which has emerged with regard to the Taiwan question also provides favorable conditions for the settlement of United States - China differences over United States arms sales to Taiwan.

Having in mind the foregoing statements of both sides, the United States Government states that it does not seek to carry out a long-term policy of arms sales to Taiwan, that its arms sales to Taiwan will not exceed, either in qualitative or in quantitative terms, the level of those supplied in recent years since the establishment of diplomatic relations between the United States and China, and that it intends gradually to reduce its sale of arms to Taiwan, leading, over a period of time, to a final resolution. In so stating, the United States acknowledges China's consistent position regarding the thorough settlement of this issue.

6. In order to bring about, over a period of time, a final settlement of the question of United States arms sales to Taiwan, which is an issue rooted in history, the two Governments will make every effort to adopt measures and create conditions conducive to the thorough settlement of this issue.

7. The development of United States - China relations is not only in the interests of the two peoples but also conducive to peace and stability in the world. The two sides are determined, on the principle of equality and mutual benefit, to strengthen their ties in the economic, cultural, educational, scientific, technological and other fields and make strong, joint efforts for the continued development of relations between the Governments and peoples of the United States and China.

8. In order to bring about the healthy development of United States - China relations, maintain world peace and oppose aggression and expansion, the two Governments reaffirm the principles agreed on by the two sides in the Shanghai Communiqué and the Joint Communiqué on the Establishment of Diplomatic Relations. The two sides will maintain contact and hold appropriate consultations on bilateral and international issues of common interest.

SINO-BRITISH JOINT DECLARATION

INTRODUCTION *The Chinese leader Deng Xiaoping made it clear to the British government in 1982 that the resumption of Chinese sovereignty over Hong Kong when Britain's 99 year lease on the New Territories came to an end in 1997 was non-negotiable. Under pressure to ensure stability and a smooth handover, Chinese and British officials agreed to the Sino-British Joint Declaration in 1984, promising the territory autonomy under Beijing and a continuation of its laws for 50 years. The Chinese and English language versions of this document were to be accepted as equally valid, sharply distinguishing it from the unequal treaties.*

The Government of the United Kingdom of Great Britain and Northern Ireland and the Government of the People's Republic of China have reviewed with satisfaction the friendly relations existing between the two Governments and peoples in recent years and agreed that a proper negotiated settlement of the question of Hong Kong, which is left over from the past, is conducive to the maintenance of the prosperity and stability of Hong Kong and to the further strengthening and development of the relations between the two countries on a new basis. To this end, they have, after talks between the delegations of the two Governments, agreed to declare as follows:

1. The Government of the People's Republic of China declares that to recover the Hong Kong area (including Hong Kong Island, Kowloon and the New Territories, hereinafter referred to as Hong Kong) is the common aspiration of the entire Chinese people, and that it has decided to resume the exercise of sovereignty over Hong Kong with effect from 1 July 1997.

2. The Government of the United Kingdom declares that it will restore Hong Kong to the People's Republic of China with effect from 1 July 1997.

The Government of the People's Republic of China declares that the basic policies of the People's Republic of China regarding Hong Kong are as follows:

i. Upholding national unity and territorial integrity and taking account of the history of Hong Kong and its realities, the People's Republic of China has decided to establish, in accordance with the provisions of Article 31 of the Constitution of the People's Republic of China, a Hong Kong Special Administrative Region upon resuming the exercise of sovereignty over Hong Kong.

ii. The Hong Kong Special Administrative Region will be directly under the authority of the Central People's Government of the People's Republic of China. The Hong Kong Special Administrative Region will enjoy a high degree of autonomy, except in foreign and defence affairs which are the responsibilities of the Central People's Government.

iii. The Hong Kong Special Administrative Region will be vested with executive, legislative and independent judicial power, including that of final adjudication. The laws currently in force in Hong Kong will remain basically unchanged.

iv. The Government of the Hong Kong Special Administrative Region will be composed of local inhabitants. The chief executive will be appointed by the Central People's Government on the basis of the results of elections or consultations to be held locally. Principal officials will be nominated by the chief executive of the Hong Kong Special Administrative Region for appointment by the Central People's Government. Chinese and foreign nationals previously working in the public and police services in the government departments of Hong Kong may remain in employment. British and other foreign nationals may also be employed to serve as advisers or hold certain public posts in government departments of the Hong Kong Special Administrative Region.

v. The current social and economic systems in Hong Kong will remain unchanged, and so will the lifestyle. Rights and freedoms, including those of the person, of speech, of the press, of assembly, of association, of travel, of movement, of correspondence, of strike, of choice of occupation, of academic research and of religious belief will be ensured by law in the Hong Kong Special Administrative Region. Private property, ownership of enterprises, legitimate right of inheritance and foreign investment will be protected by law.

vi. The Hong Kong Special Administrative Region will retain the status of a free port and a separate customs territory.

vii. The Hong Kong Special Administrative Region will retain the status of an international financial centre, and its markets for foreign exchange, gold, securities and futures will continue. There will be free flow of capital. The Hong Kong dollar will continue to circulate and remain freely convertible.

viii. The Hong Kong Special Administrative Region will have independent finances. The Central People's Government will not levy taxes on the Hong Kong Special Administrative Region.

ix. The Hong Kong Special Administrative Region may establish mutually beneficial economic relations with the United Kingdom and other countries, whose economic interests in Hong Kong will be given due regard.

x. Using the name of 'Hong Kong, China', the Hong Kong Special Administrative Region may on its own maintain and develop economic and cultural relations and conclude relevant agreements with states, regions and relevant international organisations. The Government of the Hong Kong Special Administrative Region may on its own issue travel documents for entry into and exit from Hong Kong.

xi. The maintenance of public order in the Hong Kong Special Administrative Region will be the responsibility of the Government of the Hong Kong Special Administrative Region.

xii. The above-stated basic policies of the People's Republic of China regarding Hong Kong and the elaboration of them in Annex I to this Joint Declaration will be stipulated, in a Basic Law of the Hong Kong Special Administrative Region of the People's Republic of China, by the National People's Congress of the People's Republic of China, and they will remain unchanged for 50 years.

4. The Government of the United Kingdom and the Government of the People's Republic of China declare that, during the transitional period between the date of the entry into force of this Joint Declaration and 30 June 1997, the Government of the United Kingdom will be responsible for the administration of Hong Kong with the object of maintaining and preserving its economic prosperity and social stability; and that the Government of the People's Republic of China will give its cooperation in this connection.

5. The Government of the United Kingdom and the Government of the People's Republic of China declare that, in order to ensure a smooth transfer of government in 1997, and with a view to the effective implementation of this Joint Declaration, a Sino-British Joint Liaison Group will be set up when this Joint Declaration enters into force; and that it will be established and will function in accordance with the provisions of Annex II to this Joint Declaration.

6. The Government of the United Kingdom and the Government of the People's Republic of China declare that land leases in Hong Kong and other related matters will be dealt with in accordance with the provisions of Annex III to this Joint Declaration.

7. The Government of the United Kingdom and the Government of the People's Republic of China agree to implement the preceding declarations and the Annexes to this Joint Declaration.

8. This Joint Declaration is subject to ratification and shall enter into force on the date of the exchange of instruments of ratification, which shall take place in Beijing before 30 June 1985. This Joint Declaration and its Annexes shall be equally binding.

Done in duplicate at Beijing on 19 December 1984 in the English and Chinese languages, both texts being equally authentic.

IMPLEMENTING "THE THREE PEOPLE'S PRINCIPLES"

SOURCE *Jiang Jingguo. Implementing "The Three People's Principles." In* Sources of Chinese Tradition, Volume II: From 1600 through the Twentieth Century, *2nd edition, ed. William Theodore de Bary and Richard Lufrano, 349–350. New York: Columbia University Press, 2000.*

INTRODUCTION *Jiang Jingguo (Chiang Ching-kuo), son of Chiang Kai-shek, was president of the Republic of China on Taiwan from 1978 to his death in 1988. In this exerpt of a December 1985 interview with* Reader's Digest, *he attributes Taiwan's modern economic success to the implementation of Sun Yatsen's Three People's Principles and comments unfavorably on the record of the Communist regime on the mainland.*

Question: How did the Republic of China achieve its remarkable economic development?

Answer: The basic reasons for the success of our nation's economic development are:

1. We advocate freedom and democracy and hold fast to a constitutional system. The government and the people trust one another and are harmoniously united, providing for democracy and a stable political environment.

2. Our policy of a free economy with planned characteristics encourages private enterprise and stimulates the diligence of the people and the creativity of entrepreneurs.

3. The implementation of an excellent, universal educational system with everyone having equal access to education and the promotion of the development of science and technology have raised the productive power of the people.

4. [By] adhering to a policy of [providing] equal [access to] wealth, we have lessened the gap between rich and poor, enhanced social well-being, raised the quality of life, and created an equal and harmonious society.

Question: What specific policies did your government adopt to promote this economic development?

Answer: These can be divided into several stages:

1. In the early 1950s we first carried out currency reform, encouraging saving and successfully stabilizing the value of the currency and the price of commodities. Next, we implemented equitable land reform and adapted the strategy of developing both agriculture and industry equally, [thus] smoothly solving the unemployment problem.

2. At the end of the 1950s we successively reformed foreign exchange, trade, financial administartion, and banking and encouraged light industry, which already had a foundation to open up export markets. [All of these measures] caused industrial production and foreign trade to soar in the 1960s.

3. In the 1970s we methodically developed heavy industry and the chemical industry while improving basic infrastructure such as transportation and electricity, [thus] establishing an excellent foundation for economic growth and development. In addition, successive administrative reform measures such as extending compulsory education to nine years beginning in 1968 and actively encouraging foreign-trained students to return and serve the nation greatly enhanced the human resources needed for economic growth.

4. Now in the 1980s our policy is to emphasize the development of high-tech industry and the implementation of the requisite social and economic systemic reforms. At the same time, we strive to maintain the good quality of the environment to become a truly modern nation.

Question: If the regime on the mainland were not communist, could it reach the same economic level as the Republic of China?

Answer: I must first stress that as long as the Communists occupy the mainland, no matter what economic reforms they carry out they will be unable to become a noncommunist regime. Therefore, if the mainland wants to reach our economic level, it must abandon communism and adopt. "The Three People's Principles." If it can do this, considering the size and great human and material resources of the mainland, it would of course be able to attain the economic level of the Republic of China on Taiwan. This is why we have raised the slogan "Unite China with 'The Three People's Principles.'"

THE STRUGGLE WITH COMMUNISTS IS A STRUGGLE OVER LIFESTYLE

SOURCE *Jiang Jingguo. The Struggle with Communists Is a Struggle over Lifestyle. In* Sources of Chinese Tradition, Volume II: From 1600 through the Twentieth Century, *2nd edition, ed. William Theodore de Bary and Richard Lufrano, 348–349. New York: Columbia University Press, 2000.*

INTRODUCTION *By 1987 martial law had ended on Taiwan and rapid economic growth had begun. Jiang Jingguo, then president of the Republic of China on Taiwan, implies in this excerpt of a 1987 interview that the Guomindang can beat the Communists' development record even if it cannot defeat them militarily.*

Since the founding of the Republic of China [in 1912], implementing democratic, constitutional government has been the goal of our nation. Unfortunately, because of frequent domestic and foreign turmoil, constitutional government could not be realized until 1947. It had not been in force for even two years when the Communists seized the mainland. In order to prevent Communist military invasion and subversion after the government moved to Taiwan in 1949, we declared martial law on Taiwan and [the offshore islands of] Penghu, Jinmen, and Mazu to protect national security and guarantee a secure environment for the constitution. The facts clearly show that the scope of martial law was extremely limited and had little effect on the people's daily life and basic rights. Moreover, the government on Taiwan, Penghu, Jinmen, and Mazu worked steadily and vigorously to promote democratic, constitutional government.

The recent decision by the government to end martial law and lift the ban on political activities seeks to realize policies to promote democracy and the rule of law adopted at the beginning of the republic. With more than thirty years of work [on Taiwan], the political situation is stable, the economy flourishing, and education universal. Consequently, the government, after carefully researching social change and the needs of the people, has decided to end martial law, lift the ban on political activities, and expand democratic, constitutional government in the near future.

ANOTHER DISCUSSION OF ONE-PARTY AUTOCRACY

SOURCE *Minzhu Han, ed.* Cries for Democracy: Writings and Speeches from the 1989 Chinese Democracy Movement, *143–145. Princeton, NJ: Princeton University Press, 1990.*

INTRODUCTION *In the "Beijing Spring" of 1989, the student movement demanded political reforms to match the economic reforms carried out by the Communist Party in the previous decade. The text reprinted below, displayed as a big character poster at the elite Beijing Normal University, is typical of many that demanded democracy, equality and the rule of law. Its insistence on the end of one-party rule was of course unacceptable to the government, which suppressed the movement a month later on June 4.*

"China," it has been said, "is following a capitalist road under the guise of socialism." Indeed, this is "socialism with Chinese characteristics": a handful of people have monopolized the political power of the central government and have been exercising a one-party dictatorship.... In this system, in order to secure their rule in perpetuity, this small group is allowed to manipulate the law as they please and rape the people's will. They can appoint their sons or grandsons to important offices, put the mass media under full control, and adopt an obscurantist policy of lying to the people. Or they may grant a portion of their power to "yes men," making them "agree to be chained, so as to put chains on others." In this system, they are able to ask the people of the whole nation to follow the Four Cardinal Principles [adherence to the socialist path, the leadership of the Communist Party, Marxism–Leninism–Mao Tsetung Thought, and the people's democratic dictatorship]. Now, consider only one of the Four Cardinal Principles, "uphold the leadership of the Chinese Communist Party." It has fooled generations of Chinese people, and has left them with a very deep and strong inertia.

"Do whatever the Party asks you to do." This motto is a precise manifestation of the benightedness of the Chinese. And others such as "one hundred thousand people, all of one mind," or "ten thousand people with only one head" are but fairy tales from the Arabian Nights. A person with any sense of independence should have his own mind and own views, and should not blindly follow someone else's instructions. We may give full support to the correct leadership of the Chinese Communist Party, but we may of course choose not to follow misguided leadership. Changing the first of the Four Cardinal Principles to: "Support the correct leadership of the Chinese Communist Party" would, I feel, make it more appropriate.

The world of the future will be a pluralistic world, a world of coexistence; in that world, "a hundred schools of thought" will be able to contend in cultural and art forums, and many economic systems will be able to exist side by side. Thus, to claim that "unified leadership" [under the Party] is the only type of political system required undoubtedly violates laws of common sense. The Party has coined the euphemism of "the coexistence of pluralism with unified leadership." Such a creature is really hard to understand; "pluralism" in the hand of one-party leadership is like a free man dancing in chains. If we do want democracy, it is necessary that we destroy the one-party autocracy or establish genuine democratic institutions capable of truly representing the interests of all social strata (such as nongovernment-controlled labor unions). And if we want democracy and freedom, the only thing to do is to give legislative power to the people. Only by following the principle of legislation by the people can there be true freedom of press and true freedom of speech.

I believe that the only way to change the current political situation in China is to fight for democracy—to emphasize that all people are equal before the law, and that no one is above the law. Political change requires that the right of legislation truly belong to the people. It means that laws will not be made by a small handful of government officials, and that they shall reflect the common will of the people.

The primary objective of legislation is freedom and equality. Only when people equally abide by laws that reflect their common wishes can there be freedom. Only when genuine rule by law replaces rule by autocracy, which is monarchy in disguise, can there be genuine democracy, and can it be possible for our society to overcome the defects of feudalism. The government is only an administrator of the people's sovereign will, an institution to which the people grant administrative power and entrust law enforcement power. If the National People's Congress is truly to reflect the people's will, the electoral procedures for its representatives must be changed.

In the absence of a genuine people's supervisory organ, a government [with unchecked power to] implement the law will become corrupt.

Let us greet the coming of a genuinely democratic, free spring with our actions!

—By a Non-Revolutionary of Beijing Normal University, May 2, 1989
(big-character poster at Beijing Normal University)

REFLECTIONS ON THE CHINESE COMMUNIST PARTY

SOURCE *Minzhu Han, ed.* Cries for Democracy: Writings and Speeches from the 1989 Chinese Democracy Movement, *145–148. Princeton, NJ: Princeton University Press, 1990.*

INTRODUCTION *The excerpted text reprinted below, appearing in an anonymous big character poster from the student movement in the "Beijing Spring" of 1989, attacks the dominance of the Chinese Communist Party and its lack of answerability. These "reflections" insist that China is not a democracy and suggest that citizens have no obligation to support a political party that has not been chosen by the people. Such ideas alarmed the Communist Party and eventually led it to condemn the movement as counter-revolutionary.*

[Turning] now to its organizational principles and methodology, the Chinese Communist Party has been an excellent carrier of the genes for dictatorship and bureaucracy; the latter is not only a true-to-the-original copy of the former but also its logical extension. Today, after so many years, the Party still maintains the organizational form that existed when our nation had not yet been founded, a structure shaped by security considerations and based on military models. [This structure] stipulates that "the individual obeys the organization, subordinates obey their superiors, the entire Party obeys the Central Committee, and the Central Committee obeys one person (or a few persons)." In short, "to obey orders is a duty." How could this type of closed organization be anything but a breeding ground for dictatorships, patriarchies, and personality cults? Ours is a case of absolute nondemocracy (at times, the dictatorship of a single individual is realized through the tyranny of the majority, such as the Cultural Revolution and the downfall of Hu Yaobang), and all the dictatorships in China originate from within the Party (as in the case of Mao as well as Hua Guofeng). In a country such as ours, it is not at all surprising that, under the lengthy centralized leadership of a single party which founded itself on such principles and methods, dictatorship and bureaucracy should arise again and again. Nowadays, many people are placing their hopes in the possibility that one or two wise and capable individuals might arise from within the Party. The idea is absolutely terrifying; have we not had enough of handing over the lives of a billion people to one or two leaders? So many times has the Party said the simple phrase: "in the end, our great Party always brings order to chaos," but this is nothing but [a justification for] at the cost of several decades of their lives for hundreds of millions of people (half their lives); the cost of the lives of hundreds and thousands of others, and the cost of pushing history back several decades, or several hundreds of years (as did the Cultural Revolution in China, and Stalinist revisionism in the Soviet Union). Now, if a party has been committing unpardonable errors for most of its time, and yet we continue to place the fate of a billion people into its hands instead of their own, how does it differ from gambling? The Communist Party has always loved to drag out in the open a "handful of persons" outside its ranks. Why doesn't it expose the "large handful" within the Party itself? If 80 percent of the [nearly forty-seven million] Party members are good (and the standard for goodness is here measured by the ethical standards ordinary citizens ought to possess), how about the other 20 percent? Can nearly ten million people not be considered a "large handful"?

…When it comes to the political structure of the entire country, the Communist Party holds a rather dubious position. It was announced on October 1, 1949 [upon the founding of the People's Republic], that all the power resides in the people and in the National People's Congress composed of people's representatives, and that daily administrative affairs are the domain of the government. However, up to the present day in China we still have a system of unified leadership under the Party. The Party, instead of establishing its political program through national elections, and instead of having its will expressed through the mechanism of the National People's Congress, has placed itself high above what the Constitution has designated as the supreme organ of state power—the National People's Congress—and the supreme administrative body—the State Council. If the National People's Congress and the State Council are its machines, what's the point of adding the word "supreme" to them? And if the "representative assembly" that the people has elected is only the Party's machine, isn't the phrase "all power resides with the people" superfluous? Better just to get it over with and acknowledge that all power lies in the Party and the "Party's Gestapo." Indeed, when a few statements of a certain individual from the Party, who is neither an organ of state power nor an administrative body, can for a few years determine the directions or policy decisions of a country, does this not alarm us and make us bristle with anger?

…It is not that our nation does not need a nucleus; what is crucial is that this nucleus be chosen by the people. If a party or an organization has the people on its side, the people will elect it to power and make it possible for it to carry out its program. In brief, everything must be chosen by the people.

If, let us say, a citizen who has no right to speak up and express his opinions has no obligation to obey his government, then the people will have no need or obligation to support or heed a political party which, claiming as it may to represent the people, is totally devoid of a conscience and which has not been chosen by the people.

We should recognize that the people and the national government come first and that the Party comes last. It is absolutely not the other way round, where we recognize not the people and the government but a Party which represents nothing at all!

—May 17, 1989
(big-character poster at Beijing University)

HUNGER STRIKE MANIFESTO

SOURCE *Liu Xiaobo, with Zhou Duo, Hou Dejian, and Gao Xin. Hunger Strike Manifesto. In* Cries for Democracy: Writings and Speeches from the 1989 Chinese Democracy Movement, *ed. Han Minzhu, 349–354. Princeton, NJ: Princeton University Press, 1990.*

INTRODUCTION *Students first occupied Tiananmen Square with their demands for political reform and democracy on May 4, 1989. For a month demonstrators came and went, and there were speeches, discussions, teach-ins, and hunger strikes. The "hunger strike manifesto" issued by four well-known figures on June 2 argued that this was not merely a student movement, pleading for a new political culture and advocating only peaceful means to achieve change. Two days later the occupation of Tiananmen was brought to an end with extraordinary violence by the People's Liberation Army.*

We are on a hunger strike! We protest! We appeal! We repent!

Death is not what we seek; we are searching for true life.

In the face of the irrational, high-handed military violence of the Li Peng government, Chinese intellectuals must dispose of their age-old disease, passed down over centuries, of being spineless, of merely speaking and not acting. By means of action, we protest against military control; by means of action, we call for the birth of a new political culture; and by means of action, we express our repentance for the wrongs that have been the doing of our own age-old weakness. The Chinese nation has fallen behind; for this, each one of us bears his share of responsibility.…

Our hunger strike is no longer a petition, but a protest against martial law and military control! We advocate the use of peaceful means to further democratization in China and to oppose any form of violence. Yet we do not fear brute force; through peaceful means, we will demonstrate the resilience of the democratic strength of the people, and smash the undemocratic order held together by bayonets and lies. . . .

The thousands of years of Chinese history have been a story of violence met with violence, of learning to hate and to be hated. Entering the modern era, this "enemy consciousness" [where one separates the enemy from the people] has become the legacy of the Chinese. The post-1949 slogan: "Take class struggle as the key link [to all human struggles and as the motive force of history]" has pushed to the extreme this traditional mentality of hatred, this enemy consciousness, and the practice of meeting violence with violence. This time, the imposition of military control is but another manifestation of the political culture of "class struggle." It is because of this that we are on a hunger strike; we appeal to the Chinese people that from now on they gradually discard and eradicate [our] enemy consciousness and mentality of hatred, and completely forsake [our] "class struggle" form of political culture, for hatred generates only violence and autocracy. We must use a democratic spirit of tolerance and cooperation to begin the construction of democracy in China. For democratic politics is a politics without enemies and without a mentality of hatred, a politics of consultation, discussion, and decision by vote, based on mutual respect, mutual tolerance, and mutual accommodation. Since as Premier, Li Peng has made grave mistakes, he should be made to resign according to democratic processes.

However, Li Peng is not our enemy; even if he steps down, he would still enjoy the rights that citizens should have, even the right to adhere to his mistaken beliefs. We appeal to all Chinese, from those in the government down to every ordinary citizen, to give up the old political culture and begin a new one. We ask that the government end martial law at once. We ask that both the students and the government once again turn to peaceful negotiation and consultative dialogue to resolve their differences.

The present student movement has received an unprecedented amount of sympathy, understanding, and support from all sectors of society. The implementation of martial law has turned a student movement into a national democracy movement. Undeniable, however, is the fact that many of those who have supported the students have acted out of humanitarian sympathy and discontent with the government; they have lacked a citizen's sense of political responsibility. Because of this, we appeal to all [members] of [Chinese] society gradually to drop the attitude of [merely] being onlookers and simply expressing sympathy. We appeal to you to acquire a sense of citizen consciousness. First of all, this citizen consciousness is the awareness that [all citizens] possess

political rights. Every citizen must have the self-confidence that one's own political rights are equal to the rights of the Premier. Next, citizen consciousness is a consciousness of rationalized political involvement—of political responsibility—not just a sense of justice and sympathy. It means that every man or woman cannot only express sympathy and support, but also must become directly involved in the construction of democracy. Finally, citizen consciousness means self-awareness of one's responsibilities and obligations. In the construction of social politics bound by rationality and law, every one of us must contribute his part; likewise, where social politics are irrational and lawless, each bears his share of responsibility. Voluntary participation in the political life of society and voluntary acceptance of one's responsibilities are the inescapable duties of every citizen. The Chinese people must see that, in democratized politics, everyone is first and foremost a citizen, and then a student, a professor, a worker, a cadre, or a soldier.

For thousands of years, Chinese society has followed a vicious cycle of overthrowing an old emperor just to put up a new one. History has shown that the fall of a leader who has lost the people's support or the rise of a leader who has the backing of the people cannot solve China's essential political problem. What we need is not a perfect savior, but a sound democratic system. We thus call for the following: (1) all [sectors of] society should establish lawful, autonomous citizens' organizations, and gradually develop these organizations into citizens' political forces that will act to check government policy making, for the quintessence of democracy is the curbing and balancing of power. We would rather have ten monsters that are mutually restrained than one angel of absolute power; (2) by impeaching leaders who have committed serious errors, [we should] gradually establish a sound system for the impeachment of officials. Whoever rises and whoever falls is not important; what is important is how one ascends to, or falls from, power. An undemocratic procedure of appointment and dismissal can only result in dictatorship.

In the course of the present movement, both the government and the students have made mistakes. The main mistake of the government was that, conditioned by the outmoded political ideology of "class struggle," it has chosen to take a stand in opposition to [the position of] the great majority of students and residents, thus causing continuous intensification of the conflict. The main mistake of the students is that, because the organizing of their own organizations left much to be desired, many undemocratic elements have appeared in the very process of striving for democracy. We therefore call on both the government and students to conduct level-headed self-examination. It is our belief that, on the whole, the greater fault for the present situation lies with the government. Actions such as demonstrations and hunger strikes are democratic ways through which people express their wishes; they are completely legal and reasonable. They are anything but "turmoil." Yet the government ignored the basic rights of the people granted by the Constitution; on the basis of its autocratic political ideology, it labeled the student movement as "turmoil." This stand led to a series of wrong decisions, which then led to the growth of the movement and rising antagonism. The real catalyst for the turmoil is therefore the government's wrong decisions, errors of a gravity no less than [those committed in] the "Cultural Revolution." It was only due to the great restraint shown by the students and people of Beijing and to impassioned appeals from all sectors of society—including the Party, the government, and the military—that wide-scale bloodshed has been avoided. In view of this, the government must admit to and examine these mistakes it has made. We believe that it is not yet too late to correct the mistakes. The government should draw some painful lessons from this major movement. It should learn to become accustomed to listening to the voice of the people, to allowing people to express their desires through the exercise of the constitutionally granted rights, and to governing the country in a democratic way. This nationwide movement for democracy is a lesson for the government in how to govern society by means of democracy and the rule of law.

The students' mistakes are mainly manifested in the internal chaos of their organizations and the lack of efficient and democratic procedures. Although their goal is democracy, their means and procedures for achieving democracy are not democratic. Their theories call for democracy, but their handling of specific problems is not democratic. Their lack of cooperative spirit and the secretarianism that has caused their forces to neutralize each other have resulted in all their policies coming to naught. More faults can be named: financial chaos; material waste; an excess of emotion and a lack of reason; too much of the attitude that they are privileged, and not enough of the belief in equality; and so on. In the last hundred years, the great majority of the Chinese people's struggles for democracy has remained at the level of ideological battles and slogan shouting. Enlightenment is much talked about, but little is said about the actual running of a democracy. Goals are discussed, but not the means, the procedures, or process through which they will be achieved. We believe that the actual realization of a democratic political system lies in the democratization of the process, means, and procedures of operating such a system. For this, we appeal to the Chinese people to forsake this tradition of "empty democracy," a democracy of only ideology, slogans, and [abstract] goals, and begin the construction of the process, means, and procedures for the operation of a democracy. We ask you to

transform a democratic movement focused on ideological enlightenment into a movement of democracy in action; this must be done by starting with each specific matter. We call for the students to begin a self-examination that should focus on the overhaul and reorganization of the student groups in Tiananmen Square.

The government's grave mistakes in its approach were also reflected in its use of the term "a handful of persons" [to refer to participants in pro-democracy protests]. Through our hunger strike, we would like to tell the media, home and abroad, who this so-called "handful of persons" [really] are: they are not [a bunch of] students, but citizens with a sense of political responsibility who have voluntarily participated in the present nationwide democratic movement led by the students. All we have done and all we are doing is lawful and reasonable. In this combat of opposing political cultures, of character cultivation and of moral strength, the hunger strikers intend to use their wisdom and actions to make the government feel shamed, to make it admit and correct its wrongdoings. We also intend to encourage the autonomous student organizations to improve themselves daily in accordance with democratic and legal procedures.

It must be acknowledged that democratic governance of the country is unfamiliar to every Chinese citizen. And every Chinese citizen, including the highest officials in the Party and the government, must learn it from the bottom up. In this learning process, mistakes by both the government and the people are inevitable. The key is to admit mistakes when they become evident and to correct them after they appear; to learn from our mistakes and turn them into positive lessons; and, during the continuous process of rectifying our mistakes, to learn gradually how to govern the country democratically.

We don't have enemies!

Don't let hatred and violence poison wisdom and the process of democratization in China!

We all must carry out a self-examination!

Everyone bears responsibility for the backwardness of China!

We are above all citizens!

We are not seeking death!

We are searching for true life!

—Liu Xiaobo, Ph.D. in Literature, Assistant Professor, Chinese Department, Beijing Normal University.
—Zhou Duo, former Assistant Professor, Sociology Research Institute, Beijing University; Director, Comprehensive Planning Division, Beijing Stone Corporation Group.
—Hou Dejian, well-known composer and song writer.
—Gao Xin, former Chief Editor of Normal University Weekly, *Party member.*

THE TRUTH ABOUT THE BEIJING TURMOIL

SOURCE *The Truth about the Beijing Turmoil. Edited by the Editorial Board of the Truth about the Beijing Turmoil. Beijing Publishing House, 1990. http://www.tsquare.tv/themes/truthturm.html.*

INTRODUCTION *The massacre of students and other demonstrators in and near Tiananmen Square on the night of June 3–4, 1989, provoked horrified and indignant reactions all around the world. The decision to fire was even criticized by some in the Chinese leadership. The Chinese government attempted damage limitation by issuing its own statements and accounts, which always refer to the demonstrations and their suppression as "turmoil," a pejorative term frequently also employed in official descriptions of the Cultural Revolution since the death of Mao.*

In 1989 when spring was passing to summer, a shocking turmoil happened in Beijing, which has attracted the close attention of people at home and abroad. Influenced by foreign media, people have many questions, guesses and misunderstandings. What really happened in China? What is the situation now like in Beijing? This album, with its abundant pictures, will help our readers understand the whole story of and truth about the turmoil and the present situation in Beijing.

This turmoil was not a chance occurrence. It was a political turmoil incited by a very small number of political careerists after a few years of plotting and scheming. It was aimed at subverting the socialist People's Republic. By making use of some failings in the work of the Chinese government and the temporary economic difficulties, they spread far and wide many views against the Constitution, the leadership of the Chinese Communist Party and the People's Government, preparing the ground for the turmoil ideologically, organizationally and in public opinion. The former general secretary of the Central Committee of the Chinese Communist Party Zhao Ziyang supported the turmoil and thus has unshirkable responsibility for its formation and development. The various political forces and reactionary organizations abroad had a hand in the turmoil from the very beginning. Some newspapers, magazines and broadcasting stations, especially the Voice of America, fabricated rumours to mislead people, thus adding fuel to the flames.

When Hu Yaobang suddenly died on April 15, a handful of people, thinking that their time had come, stirred up a student upheaval on the pretext of "mourning" for Hu Yaobang. The student unrest had been taken advantage of by the organizers of the turmoil from the very beginning. In violation of the Constitution, laws and regulations, some people put up big-character posters everywhere on the college campuses, preaching bourgeois liberalization and calling for the overthrow of the Communist Party and the legal government. They held many rallies, made speeches, boycotted classes and organized demonstrations, all without permission; they stormed the seat of the Party Central Committee and the State Council; they forcibly occupied the Tiananmen Square on many occasions and organized various illegal organizations without registration for approval. In Changsha, Xi'an and other cities, some people engaged in grave criminal activities such as beating, smashing, looting and burning stores, and even broke into the compounds of provincial government seats and set fire to the motor vehicles there.

In view of this turmoil, the People's Daily issued, on April 26, an editorial exposing the nature of the turmoil. Even under this circumstance, the Party and the government exercised great restraint towards the students' extremist slogans and actions and had all along given due recognition to the students' patriotic enthusiasm and reasonable demands. At the same time, the Party and the government warned the students not to be made use of by a handful of people and expressed the hope for solving the problems through dialogues and by normal, democratic and legal procedures. However, on May 13, the illegal student organization started a general hunger strike involving over 3,000 people and lasting for seven days. Party and government leaders, on the one hand, went to see the fasting students at Tiananmen Square and met with students' representatives on many occasions, asking them to value their lives and stop the hunger strike, and on the other hand, they lost no time in organizing on-the-spot rescue teams and providing all kinds of materials so as to relieve the suffering of the fasting students. Thanks to efforts of the government and other quarters. not a single student died in the hunger strike. But all this failed to win active response.

On the contrary, some media, taking the cue from a small number of people, wrongly guided the public opinion, escalating the turmoil and throwing Beijing and even the whole country in a serious anarchic situation, something that cannot be tolerated in any other country. In Beijing, demonstrations were held continuously, slogans insulting and attacking leaders and openly calling for overthrowing the government could be heard and seen everywhere. The traffic was seriously congested and difficulties were created for Beijing's production and daily supplies. The police was unable to keep normal social order. Gorbachev's schedules in China were also seriously hampered. The small handful of people attempted to take the chaos as an opportunity to seize political power and threatened to "set up a new government in three days."

288

On May 19, the Party Central Committee held a meeting attended by cadres from the Party, government and military institutions in Beijing, At the meeting, Premier Li Peng and President of the People's Republic of China Yang Shangkun announced the decision to adopt resolute measures to stop the turmoil. But Zhao Ziyang, then general secretary of the Party Central Committee, refused to attend this important meeting.

On May 20, Li Peng signed a martial law order as empowered by Clause 16 of Article 89 of the Constitution of the People's Republic of China. The martial law was to be enforced at 10 a.m. on the same day in parts of Beijing. The small handful of people took fright and coerced those residents who were in the dark about the truth to set up roadblocks at major crossroads to stop the advance of army vehicles and prevent the martial law enforcement troops from getting to designated places according to plan. Besides, they threatened to mobilize 200,000 people to occupy Tiananmen Square and organize a nation-wide general strike. Using the funds provided by reactionary forces at home and abroad, they installed sophisticated communication facilities and illegally purchased weapons. They gathered together hooligans and ruffians to set up terrorist organizations such as the "Dare-to-Die Corps" and the "Flying Tiger Team," and threatened to kidnap or put Party and government leaders under house arrest. They offered high prices in recruiting thugs and fabricated rumours to deceive people.

All the facts proved that, no matter how tolerant and restrained the government was, such people would not give up their wild scheme; on the contrary they threatened to "fight to the end" against the government.

On the evening of June 2, a handful of people bent upon inciting a riot used a traffic accident to spread rumours and mislead people, lighting the fuse of a rebellion. In the small hours of June 3, rioters set up roadblocks at every crossroad, beat up soldiers and armed police, seized weapons, ammunition and other military materials. Mobs also assaulted the Great Hall of the People, the Central Propaganda Department, the Ministry of Public Security, the Ministry of Radio, Film and Television and the west and south gates of Zhongnanhai, the seat of the Party Central Committee and the State Council. At about 5 p.m., the illegal organizations distributed kitchen knives, daggers and iron bars, to the crowd on Tiananmen Square and incited them to "take up weapons and overthrow the government." A group of ruffians banded together about 1,000 people to push down the wall of a construction site near Xidan and seized large quantities of tools, reinforcing bars and bricks, ready for street fighting. They planned to incite people to take to the streets the next day, a Sunday, to stage a violent rebellion in an attempt to overthrow the government and seize power at one stroke.

At this critical juncture, the martial law troops were ordered to move in by force to quell the anti-government rebellion. At 6:30 p.m., on June 3, the Beijing municipal government and the headquarters of the martial law enforcement troops issued an emergency announcement, asking all citizens to keep off the streets and stay at home. The announcement was broadcast over and over again. At about 10 p.m., the martial law troops headed for Beijing proper from various directions. The rioters, taking advantage of the soldiers' restraint, blocked military and other kinds of vehicles before they smashed and burned them. They also seized guns, ammunitions and transceivers. Several rioters seized an armoured car and fired guns as they drove it along the street. Rioters also assaulted civilian installations and public buildings. Several rioters even drove a public bus loaded with gasoline drums towards the Tiananmen gatetower in an attempt to set fire to it. At the same time, rioters savagely beat up, kidnapped and killed soldiers and officers. On the Chang'an Avenue, when a military vehicle suddenly broke down, rioters surrounded it and ferociously crushed the driver with bricks. At Fuchengmen, a soldier's body was hung heel over head on the overpass balustrade after he had been savagely killed. At Chongwenmen, another soldier was thrown down from the flyover and burned alive. Near a cinema, an officer was beaten to death, disembowelled and his eyes gouged out. His body was then strung up on a burning bus.

Over 1,280 vehicles were burned or damaged in the rebellion, including over 1,000 military trucks, more than 60 armoured cars, over 30 police cars, over 120 public buses and trolley buses and over 70 motor vehicles of other kinds. More than 6,000 martial law officers and soldiers were injured and scores of them killed.

Such heavy losses are eloquent testimony to the restraint and tolerance shown by the martial law enforcement troops. For fear of injuring civilians by accident, they would rather endure humiliation and meet their death unflinchingly, although they had weapons in their hands. It can be said that there is no other army in the world that can exercise restraint to such an extent.

The martial law troops, having suffered heavy casualties and been driven beyond forbearance, were forced to fire into the air to clear the way forward. During the counter-attack, some rioters were killed, some onlookers were hit by stray bullets and some wounded or killed by armed ruffians. According to reliable statistics, more than 3,000 civilians were wounded and over 200, including 36 college students, were killed.

At 1:30 a.m. on June 4, the Beijing municipal government and the martial law headquarters issued an emergency notice asking all students and other citizens to leave Tiananmen Square. The notice was broadcast repeatedly for well over three hours over loudspeakers. The students on Tiananmen Square, after discussion among themselves, sent representatives to the troops to express their willingness to withdraw from the square and this was approved by the troops. Then at about 5 a.m., several thousand students left the square in an orderly manner through a wide corridor in the southeastern part of the square vacated by the troops, carrying their own banners and streamers. Those who refused to leave were forced to leave by the soldiers. By 5:30 a.m., the clearing operation of the square had been completed.

During the whole operation not a single person was killed. The allegations that "Tiananmen Square was plunged into a bloodbath" and "thousands of people were killed in the square" are sheer rumours, and the true state of affairs will eventually be clear to the public.

After the decisive victory in quelling the riot, order in the capital was basically restored to normal and the situation throughout China soon became stable. The measures adopted by the Chinese government to stop the turmoil and put down the rebellion have not only won the acclaim and support of the Chinese people, but they have also won the understanding and support of the governments and people of many other countries. The Chinese government has announced that it will unswervingly carry on the policy of reform and opening to the outside world, the policy of developing friendly cooperation with different countries of the world on the basis of the five principles of peaceful coexistence, and the policy towards Hong Kong, Macao and Taiwan. We will continue to strive for the realization of the socialist modernization. We are fully confident of our future.

WHITE PAPER ON HUMAN RIGHTS, PREFACE

INTRODUCTION *The Chinese government is very sensitive to international criticism of its human rights record and has reacted especially strongly to the United States' tabling of critical draft resolutions in the United Nations Commission on Human Rights. Beginning in 1991, often in response to such criticism, the State Council Information Office has published at least 18 white papers on human rights and related subjects emphasizing aspects of China's human rights work such as success in feeding and educating its population, its efforts to guarantee the rights of women and children, and to establish gender and ethnic equality. The major titles were:* Human Rights in China *(1991),* The Progress of Human Rights in China *(1995),* Progress in China's Human Rights Cause in 1996 *(1996),* Fifty Years of Progress in China's Human Rights *(2000), and* Progress in China's Human Rights Cause in 2004 *(2005). The following excerpt is from the Preface to the first White Paper on Human Rights in 1991.*

It has been a long-cherished ideal of mankind to enjoy human rights in the full sense of the term. Since this great term—human rights—was coined centuries ago, people of all nations have achieved great results in their unremitting struggle for human rights. However, on a global scale, modern society has fallen far short of the lofty goal of securing the full range of human rights for people the world over. And this is why numerous people with lofty ideals are still working determinedly for this cause.

Under long years of oppression by the "three big mountains"—imperialism, feudalism and bureaucrat-capitalism—people in old China did not have any human rights to speak of. Suffering bitterly from this, the Chinese people fought for more than a century, defying death and personal sacrifices and advancing wave upon wave, in an arduous struggle to overthrow the "three big mountains" and gain their human rights. The situation in respect to human rights in China took a basic turn for the better after the founding of the People's Republic of China. Greatly treasuring this hard-won achievement, the Chinese government and people have spared no effort to safeguard human rights and steadily improve their human rights situation, and have achieved remarkable results. This has won full confirmation and fair appraisal from all people who have a real understanding of Chinese conditions and who are not prejudiced.

The issue of human rights has become one of great significance and common concern in the world community. The series of declarations and conventions adopted by the United Nations have won the support and respect of many countries. The Chinese government has also highly appraised the Universal Declaration of Human Rights, considering it the first international human rights document that has laid the foundation for the practice of human rights in the world arena. However, the evolution of the situation in regard to human rights is circumscribed by the historical, social, economic and cultural conditions of various nations, and involves a process of historical development. Owing to tremendous differences in historical background, social system, cultural tradition and economic development, countries differ in their understanding and practice of human rights. From their different situations, they have taken different attitudes towards the relevant UN conventions. Despite its international aspect, the issue of human rights falls by and large within the sovereignty of each country. Therefore, a country's human rights situation should not be judged in total disregard of its history and national conditions, nor can it be evaluated according to a preconceived model or the conditions of another country or region. Such is the practical attitude, the attitude of seeking truth from facts.

From their own historical conditions, the realities of their own country and their long practical experience, the Chinese people have derived their own viewpoints on the human rights issue and formulated relevant laws and policies. It is stipulated in the Constitution of the People's Republic of China that all power in the People's Republic of China belongs to the people. Chinese human rights have three salient characteristics. First, extensiveness. It is not a minority of the people or part of a class or social stratum but the entire Chinese citizenry who constitutes the subject enjoying human rights. The human rights enjoyed by the Chinese citizenry encompass an extensive scope, including not only survival, personal and political rights, but also economic, cultural and social rights. The state pays full attention to safeguarding both individual and collective rights. Second, equality. China has adopted the socialist system after abolishing the system of exploitation and eliminating the exploiting classes. The Chinese citizenry enjoys all civic rights equally irrespective of the money and property status as well as of nationality, race, sex, occupation, family background, religion, level of education and duration of residence. Third, authenticity. The state provides guarantees in terms of system, laws and material means for the realization of human rights. The various civic rights prescribed in the Constitution and other state laws are in accord with what people enjoy in real life. China's human rights legislation and policies are endorsed and supported by the people of all nationalities and social strata and by all the political parties, social organizations and all walks of life.

As a developing country, China has suffered from setbacks while safeguarding and developing human rights. Although much has been achieved in this regard, there is still much room for improvement. It remains a long-term historical task for the Chinese people and government to continue to promote human rights and strive for the noble goal of full implementation of human rights as required by China's socialism. . . .

THE TAIWAN QUESTION AND REUNIFICATION OF CHINA

INTRODUCTION *China's reform leadership maintained the position that Taiwan was an inalienable part of China and the country should one day be reunited. The Taiwan Affairs Office, which issued the 1993*

document that is excerpted below, works directly under the State Council and is responsible for all matters connected to Taiwan. The offer of "one country, two systems" meant that in the event of reunification Taiwan would preserve internal autonomy—the arrangement that was made for Hong Kong after its return to Chinese sovereignty in 1997.

FOREWORD

It is the sacred right of each and every sovereign State and a fundamental principle of international law to safeguard national unity and territorial integrity. The Charter of the United Nations specifically stipulates that the United Nations and its Members shall refrain from any action against the territorial integrity or political independence of any of its Members or any State and shall not intervene in matters which are essentially within the domestic jurisdiction of any State. The United Nations Declaration on Principles of International Law Concerning Friendly Relations and Co-operation Among States in Accordance with the Charter of the United Nations points out that any attempt aimed at the partial or total disruption of the national unity, territorial integrity or political independence of a State or country is incompatible with the purposes and principles of the Charter of the United Nations.

The modern history of China was a record of subjection to aggression, dismemberment and humiliation by foreign powers. It was also a chronicle of the Chinese people's valiant struggles for national independence and in defense of their state sovereignty, territorial integrity and national dignity. The origin and evolution of the Taiwan question are closely linked with that period of history. For various reasons Taiwan is still separated from the mainland. Unless and until this state of affairs is brought to an end, the trauma on the Chinese nation will not be healed and the Chinese people's struggle for national reunification and territorial integrity will continue.

What is the present state of the Taiwan question? What is the crux of the problem? What are the position and views of the Chinese Government regarding the settlement of this issue? In order to facilitate a better understanding by the international community, it is necessary to elucidate the following points. . . .

III. THE CHINESE GOVERNMENT'S BASIC POSITION REGARDING SETTLEMENT OF THE TAIWAN QUESTION

To settle the Taiwan question and achieve national reunification—this is a sacrosanct mission of the entire Chinese people. The Chinese Government has persistently worked towards this end since the founding of the People's Republic. Its basic position on this question is: peaceful reunification; one country, two systems.

Peaceful reunification; one country, two systems—how has this position been formulated? The Chinese Government conceived a peaceful settlement of the Taiwan question as early as in the 1950s. In May 1955 the late Premier Zhou Enlai said at an NPC Standing Committee meeting that two alternatives were open to the Chinese people for the solution of the Taiwan question—by resort to war or by peaceful means. The Chinese people would strive for a peaceful solution wherever possible, he affirmed. In April 1956 the late Chairman Mao Zedong put forward thoughts for policymaking such as "peace is the best option," "all patriots are of one family" and "it is never too late to join the ranks of patriots." However, those wishes have not come to fruition for reasons such as interference by foreign forces.

Major changes took place in and outside China in the 1970s. Diplomatic ties were established and relations normalized between China and the United States. The Third Plenary Session of the Eleventh Central Committee of the Communist Party of China decided to shift the focus of the work of the Party and the State to the economic modernization programme. In the meantime, people on both sides of the Taiwan Straits, compatriots of Hong Kong and Macao as well as overseas Chinese and people of Chinese descent all expressed their fervent hope that the two sides of the Straits would join hands to work for a resurgence of China. It was against this historical background that the Chinese Government formulated the position of "peaceful reunification; one country, two systems." The position takes the overall national interests and the future of the country into consideration. It respects history as well as the prevailing situation. It is realistic and takes care of the interests of all. . . .

Basic Contents of "peaceful reunification; one country, two systems."

This position is an important component of the theory and practice of building socialism with Chinese characteristics and a fundamental state policy of the Chinese Government which will not change for a long time to come. Its basic contents are as follows:

1. *Only one China.*

There is only one China in the world, Taiwan is an inalienable part of China and the seat of China's central government is in Beijing. This is a universally recognized fact as well as the premise for a peaceful settlement of the Taiwan question. The Chinese Government is firmly against any words or deeds designed to split China's sovereignty and territorial integrity. It opposes "two Chinas," "one China, one Taiwan," "one country, two governments" or any attempt or act that could

lead to "independence of Taiwan." The Chinese people on both sides of the Straits all believe that there is only one China and espouse national reunification. Taiwan's status as an inalienable part of China has been determined and cannot be changed. "Self-determination" for Taiwan is out of the question.

2. *Coexistence of two systems.*

On the premise of one China, socialism on the mainland and capitalism on Taiwan can coexist and develop side by side for a long time without one swallowing up the other. This concept has largely taken account of the actual situation in Taiwan and practical interests of our compatriots there. It will be a unique feature and important innovation in the state system of a reunified China.

After reunification, Taiwan's current socio-economic system, its way of life as well as economic and cultural ties with foreign countries can remain unchanged. Private property, including houses and land, as well as business ownership, legal inheritance and overseas Chinese and foreign investments on the island will all be protected by law.

3. *A high degree of autonomy.*

After reunification, Taiwan will become a special administrative region. It will be distinguished from the other provinces or regions of China by its high degree of autonomy. It will have its own administrative and legislative powers, an independent judiciary and the right of adjudication on the island. It will run its own party, political, military, economic and financial affairs. It may conclude commercial and cultural agreements with foreign countries and enjoy certain rights in foreign affairs. It may keep its military forces and the mainland will not dispatch troops or administrative personnel to the island. On the other hand, representatives of the government of the special administrative region and those from different circles of Taiwan may be appointed to senior posts in the central government and participate in the running of national affairs.

4. *Peace negotiations.*

It is the common aspiration of the entire Chinese people to achieve reunification of the country by peaceful means through contacts and negotiations. People on both sides of the Straits are all Chinese. It would be a great tragedy for all if China's territorial integrity and sovereignty were to be split and its people were to be drawn into a fratricide. Peaceful reunification will greatly enhance the cohesion of the Chinese nation. It will facilitate Taiwan's socio-economic stability and development and promote the resurgence and prosperity of China as a whole. . . .

CONCLUSION

Reunification of the country embodies the fundamental interest of the Chinese nation.

After national reunification the two sides of the Taiwan Straits can pool their resources and make common cause in economic development and work towards China's resurgence. Numerous problems that have been besetting Taiwan would be judiciously resolved within the framework of one China. Taiwan compatriots will share the pride and glory of a great nation with their kith and kin from the other parts of the motherland.

MARRIAGE LAW OF THE PEOPLE'S REPUBLIC OF CHINA

INTRODUCTION *Marriage law in China is in effect family law. It is interesting because it shows what the Communist Party regards as desirable in family relations and what it sees as undesirable. The first marriage law of the People's Republic of China came into force in 1950. The law was concerned to establish free choice monogamous marriage based on equality between men and women. Minimum ages for marriage at 18 for women and 20 for men were high by international standards because it was believed that this would help young people to avoid being coerced into unwanted matches by their parents. Women could keep their own surnames after marriage and children could take the surname of either their father or their mother. Both this law and subsequent texts expressly forbade infanticide.*

Current marriage law is based on a new and more detailed law adopted in 1980 and amended in 2001. It still reflects the major concerns of the 1950 law but there are some interesting changes and additions based on more contemporary social problems. Minimum age for marriage was raised to 20 for women and 22 for men, as late marriage is thought to contribute to lower birthrate. Married couples were required to practice family planning.

More detail on property regimes in marriage, on inheritance and on the disposition of property after divorce reflected increasing prosperity and a rising divorce rate. Domestic violence is mentioned in the 2001 amendments, probably as a result of the influence of Western feminism. The treatment of cases of the abduction of women is considered. This became a problem in China beginning in the 1990s as in some areas the demand for brides exceeded the supply of women, and weakened social and political control made it easier to get away with such crime. A concern for vandalism can be discerned in the clause that makes parents responsible for any damage to property done by their children.

With an aging population the state has become concerned about the cost of care for the elderly. While the 1950 law mentioned only the obligation of parents to care for their children, the 1980 version made grandparents responsible for grandchildren when parents were dead and made children responsible for parents and grandparents when people of the older generation were unable to care for themselves. Citizens also have an obligation to care for their siblings who are unable to support themselves.

The All-China Women's Federation was involved in the drafting of the law and in publicizing it and promoting its implementation.

Adopted at the Third Session of the Fifth National People's Congress on September 10, 1980, and amended in accordance with Decision Regarding the Amendment (of Marriage Law of the People's Republic of China) passed at the 21st Session of the Standing Committee of the Ninth National People's Congress on April 28, 2001.

CHAPTER I: GENERAL PROVISIONS

Article 1

This Law is the fundamental code governing marriage and family relations.

Article 2

A marriage system based on the free choice of partners, on monogamy and on equality between man and woman shall be applied.

The lawful rights and interests of women, children and old people shall be protected.

Family planning shall be practised.

Article 3

Marriage upon arbitrary decision by any third party, mercenary marriage and any other acts of interference in the freedom of marriage shall be prohibited. The exaction of money or gifts in connection with marriage shall be prohibited.

Bigamy shall be prohibited. Cohabitation of a married person with any third party shall be prohibited. Domestic violence shall be prohibited. Within the family maltreatment and desertion of one family member by another shall be prohibited.

Article 4

Husband and wife shall be faithful to and respect each other. Within the family, family members shall respect the old and cherish the young, help one another, and maintain equal, harmonious and civilized marriage and family relations.

CHAPTER II: MARRIAGE CONTRACT

Article 5

Marriage must be based upon the complete willingness of both man and woman. Neither party may use compulsion on the other party and no third party may interfere.

Article 6

No marriage may be contracted before the man has reached 22 years of age and the woman 20 years of age. Late marriage and late childbirth shall be encouraged.

Article 7

No marriage may be contracted under any of the following circumstances:

1. if the man and the woman are lineal relatives by blood, or collateral relatives by blood up to the third degree of kinship; and

2. if the man or the woman is suffering from any disease, which is regarded by medical science as rendering a person unfit for marriage.

Article 8

Both the man and the woman desiring to contract a marriage shall register in person with the marriage registration office. If the proposed marriage is found to conform with the provisions of this Law, the couple shall be allowed to register and issued marriage certificates. The husband and wife relationship shall be established as soon as they acquire the marriage certificates. In the absence of the marriage registration, the man and the woman shall go through the procedures subsequently.

Article 9

After a marriage has been registered, the woman may become a member of the man's family or vice versa, depending on the agreed wishes of the two parties.

Article 10

Marriage shall be invalid under any of the following circumstances:

1. if one party commits bigamy;

2. if the man and the woman are relatives by blood up to the third degree of kinship;

3. if, before marriage, one party is suffering from a disease which is regarded by medical science as

rendering a person unfit for marriage and, after marriage, a cure is not effected; and

4. if the legally marriageable age is not attained.

Article 11

In the case of a marriage made under coercion, the coerced party may make a request to the marriage registration office or the people's court for the dissolution of the marriage contract. Such a request shall be made within one year as of the marriage registration date. The party concerned whose personal freedom is curbed illegitimately shall make a request for dissolution of the marriage contract within one year as of the date on which his or her personal freedom is restored.

Article 12

Void or dissolved marriage shall be invalid from its inception. Neither party concerned shall have the rights and duties of husband or wife. The property acquired during their cohabitation shall be subject to disposition by mutual agreement. If they fail to reach an agreement, the people's court shall give a ruling on the principle of caring for the no-fault party. The disposition of the property of void marriage caused by bigamy may not be to the detriment of the property rights and interests of the party concerned to the lawful marriage. The provisions of this Law regarding parents and children shall apply to the children born from the parties concerned.

CHAPTER III: FAMILY RELATIONS

Article 13

Husband and wife shall have equal status in the family.

Article 14

Both husband and wife shall have the right to use his or her own surname and given name.

Article 15

Both husband and wife shall have the freedom to engage in production and other work, to study and to participate in social activities; neither party may restrict or interfere with the other party.

Article 16

Both husband and wife shall have the duty to practise family planning.

Article 17

The following items of property acquired by husband and wife during the period in which they are under contract of marriage shall be jointly possessed:

1. pay and bonus;

2. earnings from production and operation;

3. earnings from intellectual property rights;

4. property obtained from inheritance or gift except as provided for in Article 18 (3) of this Law; and

5. any other items of property which shall be jointly possessed. Husband and wife shall enjoy equal rights in the disposition of their jointly possessed property.

Article 18

Any of the following items shall be husband's or wife's separate property:

1. prenuptial property in his or her separate possession;

2. expenses such as medical costs and costs of living of the disabled given to one party for his or her bodily infliction;

3. the property going only to husband or wife, as specified in a will or a gift contract;

4. one party's private articles for daily use; and

5. any other items of property which shall be in his or her separate possession.

Article 19

So far as the property acquired during the period in which they are under contract of marriage and the prenuptial property are concerned, husband and wife may agree as to whether they should be in the separate possession, joint possession or partly separate possession and partly joint possession. The agreement shall be made in writing. The provisions of Articles 17 and 18 of this Law shall apply to the absence of such an agreement or to a vague one.

The agreement reached between the husband and wife on the property acquired during the period in which they are under contract of marriage and on the prenuptial property is binding on both parties.

If husband and wife agree, as is known to the third party, to separately possess their property acquired during their marriage life, the debt owed by the husband or the wife to any other person, shall be paid off out of the property separately possessed by him or her.

Article 20

Husband and wife shall have the duty to maintain each other. If one party fails to perform this duty, the party in need of maintenance shall have the right to demand maintenance payments from the other party.

Article 21

Parents shall have the duty to bring up and educate their children; children shall have the duty to support and assist their parents.

If parents fail to perform their duty, children who are minors or who are incapable of living on their own shall have the right to demand the cost of upbringing from their parents.

If children fail to perform their duty, parents who are unable to work or have difficulties in providing for themselves shall have the right to demand support payments from their children.

Infant drowning, deserting and any other acts causing serious harm to infants and infanticide shall be prohibited.

Article 22

Children may adopt their father's or their mother's surname.

Article 23

Parents shall have the right and duty to subject their children who are minors to discipline and to protect them. If children who are minors cause damage to the State, the collective, or individuals, their parents shall have the duty to bear civil liability.

Article 24

Husband and wife shall have the right to inherit each other's property.

Parents and children shall have the right to inherit each other's property.

Article 25

Children born out of wedlock shall enjoy the same rights as children born in wedlock. No one may harm or discriminate against them.

The natural father or the natural mother who does not rear directly his or her child born out of wedlock shall bear the child's living and educational expenses until the child can support himself or herself.

Article 26

The State shall protect lawful adoption. The relevant provisions of this Law governing the relationship between parents and children shall apply to the rights and duties in the relationship between foster parents and foster children.

The rights and duties in the relationship between a foster child and his or her natural parents shall terminate with the establishment of this adoption.

Article 27

Maltreatment or discrimination shall not be permitted between stepparents and stepchildren.

The relevant provisions in this Law governing the relationship between parents and children shall apply to the rights and duties in the relationship between stepfathers or stepmothers and their stepchildren who receive care and education from them.

Article 28

Grandparents or maternal grandparents who can afford it shall have the duty to bring up their grandchildren or maternal grandchildren who are minors and whose parents are dead or have no capacity of bringing them up. Grandchildren or maternal grandchildren who can afford it shall have the duty to support their grandparents or maternal grandparents whose children are dead or cannot afford it.

Article 29

Elder brothers or elder sisters who can afford it shall have the duty to bring up their younger brothers or sisters who are minors if their parents are dead or have no means to bring them up. Younger brothers or sisters who have been brought up by their elder brothers or elder sisters and have the means of maintenance shall have the duty to support them who are lacking in the capacity to work and in the source of income.

Article 30

Children shall have respect for their parents' matrimonial rights and shall not interfere in their parents' remarriage and post-nuptial life. Children's duty to maintain their parents shall not terminate with the change in their parents' matrimonial relationship.

CHAPTER IV: DIVORCE

Article 31

Divorce shall be granted if husband and wife both desire it. Both parties shall apply to the marriage registration office for divorce. The marriage registration office, after clearly establishing that divorce is desired by both parties and that appropriate arrangements have been made for the care of any children and the disposition of property, shall issue divorce certificates.

Article 32

When one party alone desires a divorce, the organizations concerned may carry out mediation, or the party may appeal directly to a people's court to start divorce proceedings.

In dealing with a divorce case, the people's court should carry out mediation between the parties. Divorce shall be granted if mediation fails because mutual affection no long exists. Divorce shall be granted if mediation fails under any of the following circumstances:

1. bigamy or, cohabitation of a married person with any third party;

2. domestic violence or, maltreatment and desertion of one family member by another;

3. bad habits of gambling or drug addiction which remain incorrigible despite repeated admonition;

4. separation caused by incompatibility, which lasts two full years; and

5. any other circumstances causing alienation of mutual affection.

Divorce shall be granted if one party is declared to be missing and the other party thereby files an action for divorce.

Article 33

If the spouse of a soldier in active military service desires a divorce, the soldier's consent must be obtained, except that the soldier commits a serious fault.

Article 34

A husband may not apply for a divorce when his wife is pregnant or within one year after the birth of a child or within six months after pregnancy suspension. This restriction shall not apply in cases where the wife applies for a divorce, or when the people's court deems it necessary to accept the divorce application made by the husband.

Article 35

If, after divorce, both parties desire to resume their husband-and-wife relationship, they shall register for the remarrying of each other with the marriage registration office.

Article 36

The relationship between parents and children shall not come to an end with the parents' divorce. After divorce, whether the children are put in the custody of the father or the mother, they shall remain the children of both parents.

After divorce, both parents shall still have the right and duty to bring up and educate their children.

In principle the mother shall have the custody of a breast-fed infant after divorce. If a dispute arises between the two parties over the custody of their child who has been weaned and they fail to reach an agreement, the people's court shall make a judgment in accordance with the rights and interests of the child and the actual conditions of both parents.

Article 37

If, after divorce, one party has been given custody of a child, the other parent shall bear part or the whole of the child's necessary living and educational expenses. The two parties shall seek agreement regarding the amount and duration of such payment. If they fail to reach an agreement, the people's court shall make a judgment.

The agreement or the court judgment on a child's living and educational expenses shall not prevent the child from making a reasonable request, when necessary, to either parent for an amount exceeding what was decided upon in the said agreement or judgment.

Article 38

After divorce, the father or the mother who does not rear their children directly shall have the right to visit them, while the other party shall have the duty to give assistance.

The parents shall reach an agreement about how and when to exercise the right of visit. If they fail to reach an agreement, the people's court shall make a judgment.

If the father or the mother visits their children to the detriment of their mental and physical health, a people's court shall suspend the right of visit according to law; and such a right shall be restored after the main content of the suspension disappears.

Article 39

At the time of divorce, the disposition of the property in the joint possession of husband and wife is subject to agreement between the two parties. In cases where an agreement cannot be reached, the people's court shall make a judgment in consideration of the actual circumstance of the property and on the principle of caring for the rights and interests of the wife and the child or children.

The rights and interests enjoyed by husband or wife in the operation of land under a contract based on the household shall be protected according to law.

Article 40

According to a couple's written agreement, the items of property acquired during their marriage are in the separate possession. In this connection, if one party performs more duties in rearing their children, looking after their elders and assisting the other party in work, he or she shall have the right at the time of divorce to request compensation from the other party who shall make the compensation.

Article 41

At the time of divorce, debts incurred by the husband and wife during their marriage shall be paid off out of their jointly possessed property. If such property is insufficient to pay off the debts or, the items of the property are in the separate possession, the two parties shall work out an agreement with regard to the payment. If they fail to reach an agreement, the people's court shall make a judgment.

Article 42

If, at the time of divorce, one party has difficulties supporting himself or herself, the other party shall render appropriate help from her or his personal property such as a dwelling house. Specific arrangements shall be made between both parties through consultation. If they fail to reach an agreement, the people's court shall make a judgment.

CHAPTER V: SUCCOUR MEASURES AND LEGAL LIABILITY

Article 43

In regard to the domestic violence to or maltreatment of family member(s), the victim shall have the right to make a request, and the neighborhood or villager committee as well as the units in which the parties concerned work shall dissuade the wrongdoer, and offer mediation.

In regard to the domestic violence being committed, the victim shall have the right to make a request, the neighborhood or villager committee shall dissuade the wrongdoer, and the public security organ shall stop the violence.

If, in regard to the domestic violence to or maltreatment of family member(s), the victim makes a request, the public security organ shall subject the wrongdoer to administrative penalty in accordance with the relevant provisions of administrative sanctions for public order.

Article 44

In regard to the desertion of one family member by another, the victim shall have the right to make a request, and the neighborhood or villager committee as well as the units in which the parties concerned work shall dissuade the wrongdoer and offer mediation.

If, in regard to the desertion of one family member by another, the victim makes a request, the people's court shall pass a judgment on the effecting of maintenance, upbringing and support payments according to law.

Article 45

If bigamy, domestic violence to or maltreatment and desertion of family member(s) constitute a crime, the criminal responsibility of the wrongdoer shall be investigated according to law. The victim may institute a voluntary prosecution in a people's court in accordance with the relevant provisions of the criminal procedure law. The public security organ shall investigate the case according to law and the people's procuratorate shall initiate a public prosecution according to law.

Article 46

A no-fault party shall have the right to make a request for damage compensation under any of the following circumstances bringing about divorce:

1. bigamy;

2. cohabitation of a married person with any third party;

3. domestic violence; and

4. maltreatment and desertion of one family member by another.

Article 47

When the couple's joint property is divided, the party may get smaller or no share of the property if he or she conceals, transfers, sells off, destroys the couple's joint property, or forges debts in an attempt to convert the other party's property at the time of divorce. After divorce, the other party, on finding the above-mentioned acts, may file an action in a people's court, and make a request for another division of the couple's joint property.

Regarding the acts to the prejudice of the civil litigation that are specified in the preceding paragraph, the people's court shall subject the wrongdoer to the punishment according to the provisions of the civil procedure law.

Article 48

In cases where the person refuses to abide by judgments or rulings on maintenance, upbringing or support payments, or on the division or inheritance of property, or on visits to children, the people's court shall enforce the execution of the judgments or rulings according to law. The individuals and units concerned shall have the duty to assist such executions.

Article 49

Where laws provide otherwise against illegal acts and for legal liability in regard to marriage and family, the provisions in such laws shall apply.

CHAPTER VI: SUPPLEMENTARY PROVISIONS

Article 50

The people's congresses in national autonomous areas shall have the right to formulate certain adaptations in the light of the specific conditions of the local nationalities in regard to marriage and family. Provisions of adaptations formulated by autonomous prefectures and autonomous counties must be submitted to the standing committee of the people's congress of the relevant province or autonomous region or municipality directly under the Central Government for approval. Provisions of adaptations formulated by autonomous regions must be submitted to the Standing Committee of the National People's Congress for the record.

Article 51

This Law shall come into force as of January 1, 1981. The Marriage Law of the People's Republic of China promulgated on May 1, 1950 shall be invalidated as of the day this Law comes into force.

JIANG ZEMIN'S SPEECH AT THE MEETING CELEBRATING THE 80th ANNIVERSARY OF THE FOUNDING OF THE COMMUNIST PARTY OF CHINA

INTRODUCTION *The First Congress of the Chinese Communist Party was held in Shanghai in 1921. The delegates first met in a small store in the French concession and then, fearing a police raid, fled to a houseboat on a lake near Hangzhou, Zhejiang. Scholars dispute the exact date of the founding but in China July 1 is always celebrated as the "Party's birthday." The 80th anniversary of the founding was celebrated with considerable official pomp. Jiang Zemin, general secretary of the Central Committee of the Communist Party of China, delivered a speech (excerpted below) at a grand gathering at the Great Hall of the People in Beijing held on July 1, 2001 to emphasize the Party's achievements and the continuation of its leading role.*

Comrades and Friends,

We gather here today at this grand rally to celebrate the 80th anniversary of the founding of the Communist Party of China together with the people of all ethnic groups across the country, and look to the bright future of the development of China and the rest of the world along with all people on earth who love peace and pursue progress.

The Communist Party of China had only some 50 members at its birth 80 years ago and what it faced was a calamity-ridden old China. But today, 80 years later, our Party has become a big party that has been in power for more than 50 years and has more than 64 million members and what the Chinese people see is a prosperous socialist motherland. This tremendous change is a historic miracle in the development of the Chinese nation.

Reviewing the course of struggle of the Party and the people in the last century, we feel exultant and infinitely proud. Looking into the great journey of the Party and the people ahead in the new century, we are filled with strength and confidence that we are bound to win....

From the Opium War to the founding of the Communist Party of China, and from the founding of the Party to the present, China has experienced two completely different periods of 80 years. In the first 80-year period, the feudal rulers surrendered the country's sovereign rights under humiliating terms, the society was thrown into wars and chaos, the country became impoverished and weak and the people lived in hunger and cold. In the second 80-year period, the Chinese people, under the leadership of the Communist Party of China, have got unprecedentedly united and organized, overcome numerous difficulties and won one victory after another in their revolutionary struggle. Since the founding of New China, the economy and society have developed rapidly; the country has become increasingly prosperous; the people's social status, living standards and cultural and educational level have risen markedly. Through the comparison of the two periods, the Chinese people and all the patriotic forces in China have come to realize that it is precisely the leadership of the Communist Party of China that has enabled the country to materialize the great historical transformation. China has thus come out of the most miserable plight and is now heading for a bright future. Without the Communist Party, there would have been no New China. With the Communist Party, China has put on an entirely new look. This is the fundamental and most important conclusion drawn by the Chinese people from their long years of struggle....

To ensure that our Party forever represent the orientation of the development of China's advanced culture, it is imperative that the Party's theories, line, program, principles, policies and all its work should orient toward modernization, the world and the future, reflect the requirements of developing a national, scientific and popular socialist culture, serve to upgrade the ideological and ethical standards and scientific and cultural levels of the whole nation and provide spiritual and intellectual support for the economic development and social progress.

Socialist society is one of all-round development and progress. The socialist modernization cause features a mutually supplementary and coordinated development of both material and spiritual civilizations. All comrades in the Party must have a comprehensive mastery of the dialectical relationship between the two civilizations and energetically promote socialist spiritual civilization while

advancing material civilization. In contemporary China, to develop an advanced culture means to develop a socialist culture with distinctive Chinese characteristics and build socialist spiritual civilization.

We should have a firm grip on the development trend and requirements of China's advanced culture. We must never deviate from the guidance of Marxism-Leninism, Mao Zedong Thought and Deng Xiaoping Theory. We should base ourselves on the practice of building socialism with Chinese characteristics, have our eyes on the frontline of the world science and culture, and develop a healthy, progressive, rich and colorful socialist culture with Chinese styles and characteristics to meet the growing spiritual and cultural needs of the people, and guide people to arming themselves with correct thinking and ideas so as to improve their mental outlook. That is also the fundamental expression and requirement for our Party to remain in the forefront of the times and maintain its advanced nature....

Marxism is the fundamental guiding principle for the consolidation of the Party and the development of the country. It also constitutes the common theoretical foundation of the concerted efforts of the people of all ethnic groups. The fundamental tenets of Marxism must never be abandoned, otherwise we would get lost or come to failure in the pursuit of our cause due to a lack of a correct theoretical basis and ideological soul. That explains why we must always uphold the basic tenets of Marxism. In terms of theory, Marxism develops with the advance of the times. If we dogmatically cling to some individual theses and specific programs of action formulated for a special situation by authors of Marxist classics under the specific historical conditions in spite of the changes in historical conditions and present realities, we will have difficulty in forging ahead smoothly and we may even make mistakes because our thinking is divorced from reality. That is one reason why we have remained opposed to dogmatism toward the theory of Marxism. Our Party made mistakes and even suffered serious setbacks in some historical periods. The most important cause for that was the fact that the guiding ideology of the Party was divorced from Chinese reality at the time. It was after our Party restored and upheld the ideological line of emancipating the mind and seeking truth from facts that the Party corrected its mistakes, overcame its setbacks and forged ahead triumphantly by relying on the strengths of itself and the people. The experience and lessons our Party has in this regard have been reviewed systematically in its Resolution on Certain Questions in the History of Our Party and Resolution on Certain Questions in the History of Our Party Since the Founding of the People's Republic of China. These are something that we must never forget. All comrades in the Party must uphold the scientific principles and spirit of Marxism, put changes in the right perspective and sum up fresh experience that people have gained from practice, so as to constantly enrich and develop the theory of Marxism....

The main criterion to judge the nature of a political party is its theory and program. If it is Marxist and represents the correct orientation of social development and the fundamental interests of the overwhelming majority of the people, the party is an advanced one and the vanguard of the working class. Our Party is a product of integration of Marxism-Leninism with the Chinese workers' movement. The emergence of the working class is an essential condition for founding the Party. During the period of democratic revolution, given the social conditions then, most of our Party members came from peasants and other laborers, quite a few from intellectuals and some from other revolutionaries of non-laborers' background. But the theory and program of our Party were Marxist and represented the correct orientation of China's social development. Our Party attached great importance to building up the Party ideologically and persisted in educating and arming all Party members with Marxist theory. It required Party members to join the Party not just organizationally, but first of all ideologically. It gave them guidance as to how to achieve the Party's program and tasks. All these enabled the Party to keep its nature of being the vanguard of the working class....

ANTI-SECESSION LAW

INTRODUCTION *For decades, the Beijing government and the Guomindang government in Taiwan agreed that Taiwan was an integral part of China and looked forward to eventual reunification. The defeat of the Guomindang government and the election to the presidency of Chen Shui-bian, leader of the Democratic Progressive Party, in 2000 and again in 2004, caused alarm in Beijing. The fear that pro-independence sentiment was on the rise in Taiwan may have triggered the decision to draft the Anti-Secession Law setting out Beijing's position on the island's status. The law was adopted at the Third Session of the Tenth National People's Congress Monday, March 13, 2005.*

Article 1

This Law is formulated, in accordance with the Constitution, for the purpose of opposing and checking Taiwan's secession from China by secessionists in the name of "Taiwan independence", promoting peaceful national reunification, maintaining peace and stability in the Taiwan Straits, preserving China's sovereignty and territorial integrity, and safeguarding the fundamental interests of the Chinese nation.

Article 2

There is only one China in the world. Both the mainland and Taiwan belong to one China. China's sovereignty and territorial integrity brook no division. Safeguarding China's sovereignty and territorial integrity is the common obligation of all Chinese people, the Taiwan compatriots included.

Taiwan is part of China. The state shall never allow the "Taiwan independence" secessionist forces to make Taiwan secede from China under any name or by any means.

Article 3

The Taiwan question is one that is left over from China's civil war of the late 1940s.

Solving the Taiwan question and achieving national reunification is China's internal affair, which subjects to no interference by any outside forces.

Article 4

Accomplishing the great task of reunifying the motherland is the sacred duty of all Chinese people, the Taiwan compatriots included.

Article 5

Upholding the principle of one China is the basis of peaceful reunification of the country.

To reunify the country through peaceful means best serves the fundamental interests of the compatriots on both sides of the Taiwan Straits. The state shall do its utmost with maximum sincerity to achieve a peaceful reunification.

After the country is reunified peacefully, Taiwan may practice systems different from those on the mainland and enjoy a high degree of autonomy.

Article 6

The state shall take the following measures to maintain peace and stability in the Taiwan Straits and promote cross-Straits relations:

1. to encourage and facilitate personnel exchanges across the Straits for greater mutual understanding and mutual trust;

2. to encourage and facilitate economic exchanges and cooperation, realize direct links of trade, mail and air and shipping services, and bring about closer economic ties between the two sides of the Straits to their mutual benefit;

3. to encourage and facilitate cross-Straits exchanges in education, science, technology, culture, health and sports, and work together to carry forward the proud Chinese cultural traditions;

4. to encourage and facilitate cross-Straits cooperation in combating crimes; and

5. to encourage and facilitate other activities that are conducive to peace and stability in the Taiwan Straits and stronger cross-Straits relations.

The state protects the rights and interests of the Taiwan compatriots in accordance with law.

Article 7

The state stands for the achievement of peaceful reunification through consultations and negotiations on an equal footing between the two sides of the Taiwan Straits. These consultations and negotiations may be conducted in steps and phases and with flexible and varied modalities.

The two sides of the Taiwan Straits may consult and negotiate on the following matters:

1. officially ending the state of hostility between the two sides;

2. mapping out the development of cross-Straits relations;

3. steps and arrangements for peaceful national reunification;

4. the political status of the Taiwan authorities;

5. the Taiwan region's room of international operation that is compatible with its status; and

6. other matters concerning the achievement of peaceful national reunification.

Article 8

In the event that the "Taiwan independence" secessionist forces should act under any name or by any means to cause the fact of Taiwan's secession from China, or that major incidents entailing Taiwan's secession from China should occur, or that possibilities for a peaceful reunification should be completely exhausted, the state shall employ non-peaceful means and other necessary measures to protect China's sovereignty and territorial integrity.

The State Council and the Central Military Commission shall decide on and execute the non-peaceful means and other necessary measures as provided for in the preceding paragraph and shall promptly report to the Standing Committee of the National People's Congress.

Article 9

In the event of employing and executing non-peaceful means and other necessary measures as provided for in this Law, the state shall exert its utmost to protect the lives, property and other legitimate rights and interests of Taiwan civilians and foreign nationals in Taiwan, and to minimize losses. At the same time, the state shall protect the rights and interests of the Taiwan compatriots in other parts of China in accordance with law.

Article 10

This Law shall come into force on the day of its promulgation.

CHARTER 08

SOURCE *Link, Perry, trans. Charter 08.* The New York Review of Books. *http://www.nybooks.com/articles/22210.*

INTRODUCTION *The manifesto, Charter 2008, signed by a group of more than 300 Chinese intellectuals, journalists, and rural activists, provided a blueprint for a free and democratic China where human rights, democracy and the rule of law would be paramount. Charter 08 took its name from Charter 77, the manifesto produced by Czech intellectuals in 1977 which demanded an alternative to Soviet-style communism. Like the signatories of the Czech document, the signatories of Charter 08 have been subjected to monitoring and arrest.*

A hundred years have passed since the writing of China's first constitution. 2008 also marks the sixtieth anniversary of the promulgation of the *Universal Declaration of Human Rights*, the thirtieth anniversary of the appearance of the Democracy Wall in Beijing, and the tenth of China's signing of the International Covenant on Civil and Political Rights. We are approaching the twentieth anniversary of the 1989 Tiananmen massacre of pro-democracy student protesters. The Chinese people, who have endured human rights disasters and uncountable struggles across these same years, now include many who see clearly that freedom, equality, and human rights are universal values of humankind and that democracy and constitutional government are the fundamental framework for protecting these values.

By departing from these values, the Chinese government's approach to "modernization" has proven disastrous. It has stripped people of their rights, destroyed their dignity, and corrupted normal human intercourse. So we ask: Where is China headed in the twenty-first century? Will it continue with "modernization" under authoritarian rule, or will it embrace universal human values, join the mainstream of civilized nations, and build a democratic system? There can be no avoiding these questions....

[The] political reality, which is plain for anyone to see, is that China has many laws but no rule of law; it has a constitution but no constitutional government. The ruling elite continues to cling to its authoritarian power and fights off any move toward political change.

The stultifying results are endemic official corruption, an undermining of the rule of law, weak human rights, decay in public ethics, crony capitalism, growing inequality between the wealthy and the poor, pillage of the natural environment as well as of the human and historical environments, and the exacerbation of a long list of social conflicts, especially, in recent times, a sharpening animosity between officials and ordinary people.

As these conflicts and crises grow ever more intense, and as the ruling elite continues with impunity to crush and to strip away the rights of citizens to freedom, to property, and to the pursuit of happiness, we see the powerless in our society—the vulnerable groups, the people who have been suppressed and monitored, who have suffered cruelty and even torture, and who have had no adequate avenues for their protests, no courts to hear their pleas—becoming more militant and raising the possibility of a violent conflict of disastrous proportions. The decline of the current system has reached the point where change is no longer optional. . . .

[For] China the path that leads out of our current predicament is to divest ourselves of the authoritarian notion of reliance on an "enlightened overlord" or an "honest official" and to turn instead toward a system of liberties, democracy, and the rule of law, and toward fostering the consciousness of modern citizens who see rights as fundamental and participation as a duty. Accordingly, and in a spirit of this duty as responsible and constructive citizens, we offer the following recommendations on national governance, citizens' rights, and social development:

1. *A New Constitution.* We should recast our present constitution, rescinding its provisions that contradict the principle that sovereignty resides with the people and turning it into a document that genuinely guarantees human rights, authorizes the exercise of public power, and serves as the legal underpinning of China's democratization. The constitution must be the highest law in the land, beyond violation by any individual, group, or political party.

2. *Separation of Powers.* We should construct a modern government in which the separation of legislative, judicial, and executive power is guaranteed. We need an Administrative Law that defines the scope of government responsibility and prevents abuse of administrative power. Government should be responsible to taxpayers. Division of power between provincial governments and the central government should adhere to the principle that central powers are only those specifically granted by the constitution and all other powers belong to the local governments.

3. *Legislative Democracy.* Members of legislative bodies at all levels should be chosen by direct election, and legislative democracy should observe just and impartial principles.

4. *An Independent Judiciary.* The rule of law must be above the interests of any particular political party and judges must be independent. We need to establish a constitutional supreme court and institute procedures for constitutional review. As soon as possible, we should abolish all of the Committees on Political and Legal Affairs that now allow Communist Party officials at every level to decide politically sensitive cases in advance and out of court. We should strictly forbid the use of public offices for private purposes.

5. *Public Control of Public Servants.* The military should be made answerable to the national government, not to a political party, and should be made more professional. Military personnel should swear allegiance to the constitution and remain nonpartisan. Political party organizations must be prohibited in the military. All public officials including police should serve as nonpartisans, and the current practice of favoring one political party in the hiring of public servants must end.

6. *Guarantee of Human Rights.* There must be strict guarantees of human rights and respect for human dignity. There should be a Human Rights Committee, responsible to the highest legislative body, that will prevent the government from abusing public power in violation of human rights. A democratic and constitutional China especially must guarantee the personal freedom of citizens. No one should suffer illegal arrest, detention, arraignment, interrogation, or punishment. The system of "Reeducation through Labor" must be abolished.

7. *Election of Public Officials.* There should be a comprehensive system of democratic elections based on "one person, one vote." The direct election of administrative heads at the levels of county, city, province, and nation should be systematically implemented. The rights to hold periodic free elections and to participate in them as a citizen are inalienable.

8. *Rural-Urban Equality.* The two-tier household registry system must be abolished. This system favors urban residents and harms rural residents. We should establish instead a system that gives every

citizen the same constitutional rights and the same freedom to choose where to live.

9. *Freedom to Form Groups.* The right of citizens to form groups must be guaranteed. The current system for registering nongovernment groups, which requires a group to be "approved," should be replaced by a system in which a group simply registers itself. The formation of political parties should be governed by the constitution and the laws, which means that we must abolish the special privilege of one party to monopolize power and must guarantee principles of free and fair competition among political parties.

10. *Freedom to Assemble.* The constitution provides that peaceful assembly, demonstration, protest, and freedom of expression are fundamental rights of a citizen. The ruling party and the government must not be permitted to subject these to illegal interference or unconstitutional obstruction.

11. *Freedom of Expression.* We should make freedom of speech, freedom of the press, and academic freedom universal, thereby guaranteeing that citizens can be informed and can exercise their right of political supervision. These freedoms should be upheld by a Press Law that abolishes political restrictions on the press. The provision in the current Criminal Law that refers to "the crime of incitement to subvert state power" must be abolished. We should end the practice of viewing words as crimes.

12. *Freedom of Religion.* We must guarantee freedom of religion and belief, and institute a separation of religion and state. There must be no governmental interference in peaceful religious activities. We should abolish any laws, regulations, or local rules that limit or suppress the religious freedom of citizens. We should abolish the current system that requires religious groups (and their places of worship) to get official approval in advance and substitute for it a system in which registry is optional and, for those who choose to register, automatic.

13. *Civic Education.* In our schools we should abolish political curriculums and examinations that are designed to indoctrinate students in state ideology and to instill support for the rule of one party. We should replace them with civic education that advances universal values and citizens' rights, fosters civic consciousness, and promotes civic virtues that serve society.

14. *Protection of Private Property.* We should establish and protect the right to private property and promote an economic system of free and fair markets. We should do away with government monopolies in commerce and industry and guarantee the freedom to start new enterprises. We should establish a Committee on State-Owned Property, reporting to the national legislature, that will monitor the transfer of state-owned enterprises to private ownership in a fair, competitive, and orderly manner. We should institute a land reform that promotes private ownership of land, guarantees the right to buy and sell land, and allows the true value of private property to be adequately reflected in the market.

15. *Financial and Tax Reform.* We should establish a democratically regulated and accountable system of public finance that ensures the protection of taxpayer rights and that operates through legal procedures. We need a system by which public revenues that belong to a certain level of government—central, provincial, county or local—are controlled at that level. We need major tax reform that will abolish any unfair taxes, simplify the tax system, and spread the tax burden fairly. Government officials should not be able to raise taxes, or institute new ones, without public deliberation and the approval of a democratic assembly. We should reform the ownership system in order to encourage competition among a wider variety of market participants.

16. *Social Security.* We should establish a fair and adequate social security system that covers all citizens and ensures basic access to education, health care, retirement security, and employment.

17. *Protection of the Environment.* We need to protect the natural environment and to promote development in a way that is sustainable and responsible to our descendants and to the rest of humanity. This means insisting that the state and its officials at all levels not only do what they must do to achieve these goals, but also accept the supervision and participation of nongovernmental organizations.

18. *A Federated Republic.* A democratic China should seek to act as a responsible major power contributing toward peace and development in the Asian Pacific region by approaching others in a spirit of equality and fairness. In Hong Kong and Macao, we should support the freedoms that already exist. With respect to Taiwan, we should declare our commitment to the principles of freedom and democracy and then, negotiating as equals and ready to compromise, seek a formula for peaceful unification. We should approach disputes in the national-minority areas of China with an open mind, seeking ways to find a workable framework within which all ethnic and religious groups can flourish. We should aim ultimately at a federation of democratic communities of China.

19. *Truth in Reconciliation.* We should restore the reputations of all people, including their family members, who suffered political stigma in the political campaigns of the past or who have been labeled as criminals because of their thought, speech, or faith. The state should pay reparations to these people. All political prisoners and prisoners of conscience must be released. There should be a Truth Investigation Commission charged with finding the facts about past injustices and atrocities, determining responsibility for them, upholding justice, and, on these bases, seeking social reconciliation.

China, as a major nation of the world, as one of five permanent members of the United Nations Security Council, and as a member of the UN Council on Human Rights, should be contributing to peace for humankind and progress toward human rights. Unfortunately, we stand today as the only country among the major nations that remains mired in authoritarian politics. Our political system continues to produce human rights disasters and social crises, thereby not only constricting China's own development but also limiting the progress of all of human civilization. This must change, truly it must. The democratization of Chinese politics can be put off no longer.

Bibliography

This annotated bibliography is the product of the efforts of the Board of Editors to identify works that have had a major academic or sociopolitical impact or that represent exceptional creativity and originality. This list may be helpful as a starting point for students and researchers; by no means do the Board of Editors claim that this bibliography encompasses all works of merit on the study of China.

Andrews, Julia F. *Painters and Politics in the People's Republic of China, 1949–1979.* Berkeley: University of California Press, 1994.
> *The definitive English-language work on painting in the early decades of the Communist era.*

Andrews, Julia F. and Kuiyi Shen, eds. *A Century in Crisis: Modernity and Tradition in the Art of Twentieth-Century China.* New York: Guggenheim Museum, 1998.
> *An important collection of essays by leading scholars exploring modern and contemporary Chinese art. Color plates highlight commercial art, calligraphy, woodblock prints, the Shanghai school paintings, socialist realist paintings, and more.*

Banister, Judith. *China's Changing Population.* Stanford, CA: Stanford University Press, 1987.
> *A classic study of China's population issues and a major contribution to the research on China's demographic trends, making full use of the insights of the 1982 Chinese census and critically analyzing issues of fertility.*

Béja, Jean-Philippe. *A la recherche d'une ombre chinoise: Le mouvement pour la démocratie en Chine, 1919–2004* [In search of a Chinese shadow: The movement for democracy in China, 1919–2004]. Paris: Seuil, 2004.
> *An essay on the persistence of the prodemocracy movement from 1919 to 2004 and the way it has influenced political developments in the People's Republic, especially after 1976.*

Benton, Gregor, and Edmund Terence Gomez. *The Chinese in Britain, 1800–Present: Economy,* *Transnationalism, Identity.* Basingstoke, U.K.: Palgrave Macmillan, 2008.
> *Provides a thorough and well-researched case study of Chinese overseas communities, placing them in their historical and political context and understanding them as political and social agents acting in an international arena. Setting a new, high standard for writing on the Chinese diaspora, this work is poised to become a classic.*

Bergère, Marie-Claire. *Sun Yat-sen.* Trans. Janet Lloyd. Stanford, CA: Stanford University Press, 1998.
> *Of a handful of biographies of the "Father of the Republic" available in English, this is arguably the best to date.*

Bianco, Lucien. *Peasants Without the Party: Grass-roots Movements in Twentieth-century China.* Armonk, NY: Sharpe, 2001.
> *A good book on the continuity of peasants' actions against the representatives of the state from the Republican to the reform eras.*

Bramall, Chris. *The Industrialization of Rural China.* Oxford: Oxford University Press, 2007.
> *The most up-to-date and authoritative exploration of China's rural industrialization processes, which became a hallmark of the economic reforms after 1978. This book, critically evaluating the existing literature, brings out new perspectives and juxtaposes earlier debates. It is poised to become a core work on its topic.*

Cahill, James. *The Painter's Practice: How Artists Lived and Worked in Traditional China.* New York: Columbia University Press, 1994.
> *Examines the working conditions of artists in historical China, analyzing social, political, and economic influences on their work since the sixteenth century. Drawing on diaries, letters, and other primary source documents, Cahill details matters of payment and patronage, revealing how artists in China earned their living and providing new perspectives on their art.*

Chan, Anita, Richard Madsen, and Jonathan Unger. *Chen Village under Mao and Deng*. 2nd ed. Berkeley: University of California Press, 1992.

A classic study of a village in revolution under Mao, updated with research on the same village's experience of the reform era under Deng Xiaoping.

Chen Sihe. *Zhongguo dangdai wenxueshi jiaocheng* [Lectures on contemporary Chinese literature]. Shanghai: Fudan Daxue Chubanshe, 2001.

Highly acclaimed as a pioneering critical work that deconstructed Chinese literary discourse informed by the ideology of the party apparatus by reexamining how the history of modern Chinese literature is studied and presented.

Coble, Parks M. *Chinese Capitalists in Japan's New Order: The Occupied Lower Yangzi, 1937–1945*. Berkeley: University of California Press, 2003.

Drawing from extensive sources in Chinese, Japanese, and English, this work is an important addition to still embryonic research on the areas of China occupied by Japan during the Anti-Japanese War (1937–1945). Coble's study focuses on the strategies employed by China's capitalists to survive Japanese occupation.

Cohen, Paul A. *History in Three Keys: The Boxers as Event, Experience, and Myth*. New York: Columbia University Press, 1997.

Cohen scrutinizes the Boxer Rebellion of 1898 to 1900 to demonstrate how a generally accepted explanation of a historical event can be dismantled to expose the connection between the event and the resulting narrative(s) and the role of the historian in conveying an understanding of the past.

Cohen, Paul A. *Speaking to History: The Story of King Goujian in Twentieth-century China*. Berkeley: University of California Press, 2008.

This work explores the connection between past and present through the study of a little-known monarch of the fifth century, King Goujian, whose story has been a source of inspiration to the Chinese throughout their recent "turbulent history."

Cohen, Warren I. *America's Response to China: A History of Sino-American Relations*. 4th ed. New York: Columbia University Press, 2000.

A standard reference on this topic.

Croizier, Ralph C. *Traditional Medicine in Modern China: Science, Nationalism, and the Tensions of Cultural Change*. Cambridge, MA: Harvard University Press, 1968.

A pioneering study that anticipated many of the issues of culture and nationalism taken up by later historians of China.

Croizier, Ralph. *Art and Revolution in Modern China: The Lingnan (Cantonese) School of Painting, 1906–1951*. Berkeley: University of California Press, 1988. New York: Guggenheim Museum, 1998.

Examines the twentieth century art movement initiated by Chinese painters Gao Jianfu and others during the rise of the Nationalist Party in China.

Dittmer, Lowell. *China's Continuous Revolution: The Postliberation Epoch, 1949–1981*. Berkeley: University of California Press, 1987.

Examines the transition from the war years of the 1940s to the People's Republic of China.

Eastman, Lloyd E. *The Abortive Revolution: China under Nationalist Rule, 1927–1937*. Cambridge, MA: Harvard University Press, 1974.

In seven thoroughly researched chapters, Eastman investigates the Guomindang during the Nanjing decade, the heyday of the ruling party. The author exposes the party's failure to inspire unity and commitment among its members.

Eastman, Lloyd E. *Seeds of Destruction: Nationalist China in War and Revolution, 1937–1949*. Stanford, CA: Stanford University Press, 1984.

Eastman explores a difficult period in modern Chinese history (the war against Japan and the civil war) that has generated an ongoing controversy on the reasons behind the failure of the Guomindang to succeed in creating and maintaining a new regime in China.

Economy, Elizabeth, and Michel Oksenberg, eds. *China Joins the World: Progress and Prospects*. New York: Council on Foreign Relations Press, 1999.

A good introduction to the foreign policy of the Chinese Communist Party after Mao's death.

Edmonds, Richard L. *Patterns of China's Lost Harmony: A Survey of the Country's Environmental Degradation and Protection*. London: Routledge, 1994.

In this well-written and data-rich book, a geographer specializing in China explores major environmental problems, their origins, and policy approaches to solve them. Edmonds deals in more depth than Vaclav Smil with the policy-making processes and the social dynamics of environmental issues. This work has become a classic, a must-read for those embarking on research on China's environment. However, due to more recent policy measures, a new understanding of environmental problems, and further developments in the economy, this book can only serve as a starting point for the study of a rapidly evolving theme.

Elvin, Mark. *The Retreat of the Elephants: An Environmental History of China*. New Haven, CT: Yale University Press, 2004.

In this environmental history of China, Elvin, a historian of the large and sweeping trends in China's past, charts millennia of interaction between nature and humans on what was to become Chinese soil, providing a long perspective on the formation of China politically, ecologically, and culturally until the end of the nineteenth century.

Evans, Harriet. *Women and Sexuality in China: Female Sexuality and Gender since 1949*. London: Continuum, 1997.

A key work on an important social issue that was a major concern for government in the People's Republic of China.

Fairbank, John K., and Denis Twitchett, eds. *The Cambridge History of China*. 15 vols. Cambridge, U.K.: Cambridge University Press, 1978–.

A comprehensive and scholarly history.

Faure, David. *China and Capitalism: A History of Business Enterprise in Modern China*. Hong Kong: Hong Kong University Press, 2006.

A brief interpretative history of business in China from late imperial to contemporary times.

Finnane, Antonia. *Changing Clothes in China: Fashion, History, Nation*. London: Hurst, 2007.

An interpretative social history of dress in China from late imperial to contemporary times.

Fitzgerald, John. *Awakening China: Politics, Culture, and Class in the Nationalist Revolution.* Stanford, CA: Stanford University Press, 1996.

This original account of how Chinese revolutionaries and intellectuals awakened China during the Republican revolution provides a detailed analysis of the methods used in such an awakening, with examples in the fields of art and architecture, medicine, literature, political institutions, and popular organization. Fitzgerald also compares Communists and Nationalists, and Sun Yat-sen and Mao Zedong, in their efforts "to awaken China."

Fong, Wen C. *Between Two Cultures: Late-Nineteenth- and Twentieth-Century Chinese Paintings from the Robert H. Ellsworth Collection in the Metropolitan Museum of Art.* New York: Metropolitan Museum of Art, 2001.

Analyzes Chinese paintings from the 1860s to about 1980, tracing the transformation of Chinese art from the last revival of traditionalist expression in the nineteenth century. Special attention is devoted to Xu Beihong, Fu Baoshi, Qi Baishi, Huang Binhong, and Zhang Daqian.

Friedman, Edward, Paul G. Pickowicz, Mark Selden, and Kay Ann Johnson. *Chinese Village, Socialist State.* New Haven, CT: Yale University Press, 1991.

Friedman, Edward, Paul G. Pickowicz, and Mark Selden. *Revolution, Resistance, and Reform in Village China.* New Haven, CT: Yale University Press, 2005.

In Chinese Village, Socialist State and its 2005 follow-up, the authors trace the history of one of Mao's model villages, situated some 200 kilometers south of Beijing, whose mission was to prove that collective work surpassed, in its ethics and results, all that capitalism can achieve. This inside look exposes the hardships faced by villagers (ever-higher production standards, corruption, flooding, family feuds) versus a distant, unaware, and changing central bureaucracy.

Galikowski, Maria. *Art and Politics in China, 1949–1984.* Hong Kong: Chinese University Press, 1998.

Examines the relationship between art and politics in the People's Republic of China, focusing on the Mao years and the start of the reform period.

Gladney, Dru C. *Dislocating China: Reflections on Muslims, Minorities, and Other Subaltern Subjects.* London: Hurst, 2004.

This book, by the most prolific writer in English on China's Muslim populations, is accessible and essayistic in style, covering a wide range of topics. The breadth of topics featured and the dynamics of the writing make it a good starting point for a critical understanding of China's national minorities.

Gold, Thomas, Doug Guthrie, and David Wank, eds. *Social Connections in China: Institutions, Culture, and the Changing Nature of Guanxi.* New York: Cambridge University Press, 2002.

A good sociological presentation of a concept that plays an important role in China's society, economics, and politics: personal connections or guanxi.

Goldman, Merle. *Sowing the Seeds of Democracy in China: Political Reform in the Deng Xiaoping Era.* Cambridge, MA: Harvard University Press, 1994.

An excellent study of the political participation of prodemocracy intellectuals in the early reform era by one of the world's best specialists of the field.

Greenhalgh, Susan. *Just One Child: Science and Policy in Deng's China.* Berkeley: University of California Press, 2008.

Greenhalgh, an anthropologist specializing in China studies, examines China's birth-planning policy, which has been met with great controversy, chiefly in the United States. She analyzes the perceptions of science underpinning the policy and its implementation. This well-written and accessible book goes far beyond the moral debates, and is poised to become a classic that not only deals with population policy, but provides a thorough examination of the political and scientific discourse behind it.

Grieder, Jerome B. *Intellectuals and the State in Modern China: A Narrative History.* New York: Free Press, 1981.

Examines the changing roles and shifting perceptions of intellectuals in relation to the state from the Boxer Rebellion in 1900 to the beginning of the People's Republic.

Hamilton, Gary. *Commerce and Capitalism in Chinese Societies.* London: Routledge, 2006.

A Weberian viewpoint informs this important collection of essays on the logic and organization of commerce and capitalism in China, past and present.

Harrison, Henrietta. *The Making of the Republican Citizen: Political Ceremonies and Symbols in China, 1911–1929.* Oxford: Oxford University Press, 2000.

Explores changes in the political mood, as much as the politics, in the transition from the imperial state to the Chinese republic.

Heberer, Thomas. *China and its National Minorities: Autonomy or Assimilation?* Armonk, NY: Sharpe, 1989.

A favorite starting point for students wanting to understand China's national-minority issues, providing an excellent overview, a thorough examination of core issues, and good pointers for further study.

Hershatter, Gail. *Women in China's Long Twentieth Century.* Berkeley: University of California Press, 2007.

A comprehensive introduction to the history of women in twentieth-century China, including an extensive bibliography of English-language scholarship in the field.

Hinton, William. *Fanshen: A Documentary of Revolution in a Chinese Village.* 1966. Reprint. Berkeley: University of California Press, 1997.

This eyewitness account of social and economic change in a Chinese village from 1949 to 1953 remains one of the most important English-language documents on the Maoist revolution.

Hsia, C. T. (Hsia Chih-tsing). *A History of Modern Chinese Fiction, 1917–1957.* New Haven, CT: Yale University Press, 1961.

Hsia, C. T. (Hsia Chih-tsing). *The Classic Chinese Novel: A Critical Introduction.* New York: Columbia University Press, 1968.

Two groundbreaking works in Chinese literary studies in the West, particularly in the United States. Well known for his critical insights and methodological approaches, Hsia in these two works sheds new light on Chinese literary studies, particularly on the study of modern Chinese literature. However, ideological considerations have also made his works, in particular the one on modern Chinese fiction, highly controversial.

Jacka, Tamara. *Women's Work in Rural China: Change And Continuity in an Era of Reform.* Cambridge, U.K.: Cambridge University Press, 1997.

A study of a significant aspect of China's society and economy in the post-Mao era.

Kennedy, Thomas L. *The Arms of Kiangnan: Modernization in the Chinese Ordnance Industry, 1860–1895.* Boulder, CO: Westview, 1978.

The ordnance industry represents China first efforts at mechanization; this work studies arms production in the Self-strengthening era.

Köll, Elisabeth. *From Cotton Mill to Business Empire: The Emergence of Regional Enterprises in Modern China.* Cambridge, MA: Harvard University Asia Center, 2003.

An interesting case study that draws together changes in business and Chinese society.

Kuhn, Philip A. *Soulstealers: The Chinese Sorcery Scare of 1768.* Cambridge, MA: Harvard University Press, 1990.

Explores eighteenth-century China and the workings of the imperial bureaucracy.

Kuhn, Philip A. *Chinese Among Others: Emigration in Modern Times.* Lanham, MD: Rowan & Littlefield, 2008.

A history of Chinese migration since the sixteenth century, tracing journeys that created diasporas all over the world.

Kwong, Luke S. K. (Kuang Zhaojiang). *A Mosaic of the Hundred Days: Personalities, Politics, and Ideas of 1898.* Cambridge, MA: Council on East Asian Studies, Harvard University, 1984.

A revisionist view of the famous reforms of 1898.

Lansdowne, Helen, and Wu Guoguang, eds. *China Turns to Multilateralism: Foreign Policy and Regional Security.* London and New York: Routledge, 2007.

A kaleidoscopic analysis of China's foreign relations in the twenty-first century by American, European, and Chinese specialists.

Lee, Leo Ou-fan (Li Oufan). *Shanghai Modern: The Flowering of a New Urban Culture in China, 1930–1945.* Cambridge, MA: Harvard University Press, 1999.

A study of cultural change in China's largest city in the pre-Communist era.

Leys, Simon. *The Burning Forest: Essays on Chinese Culture and Politics.* New York: Holt, Rinehart, and Winston, 1986.

A wonderful presentation of Chinese culture and politics by one of the most perspicacious sinologists of the twentieth century.

Li, Lillian M., Alison J. Dray-Novey, and Kong Haili. *Beijing: From Imperial Capital to Olympic City.* London: Palgrave Macmillan, 2007.

An illustrated historical survey of Beijing, based on original research and recent scholarship.

Li Zhisui. *The Private Life of Chairman Mao: The Memoirs of Mao's Personal Physician.* Trans. Tai Hung-chao. New York: Random House, 1994.

An insight by Mao's private doctor into Mao's inner circle from 1949 until his death. This extraordinary account is indispensable to anyone who wants to understand the psychology of the Great Helmsman.

Lieberthal, Kenneth G., and Michel Oksenberg. *Policy Making in China: Leaders, Structures, and Processes.* Princeton, NJ: Princeton University Press, 1988.

This book, which uses the energy sector as a case study, is a major contribution to the understanding of bureaucratic politics in China. This outstanding work remains an inspiration for people researching China's political system, as it provides strong methodological foundations for such research.

Lin Manhong (Man-houng Lin). *China Upside Down: Currency, Society, and Ideologies, 1808–1856.* Cambridge, MA: Harvard University Asia Center, 2006.

Analyzes the time of transition in mid-nineteenth-century China.

Liu Kwang-ching (Liu Guangjing). *Anglo-American Steamship Rivalry in China, 1862–1874.* Cambridge, MA: Harvard University Press, 1962.

Still the best study of business and entrepreneurial rivalry on the China coast.

Lu Xun (Lu Hsun). *Zhongguo xiaoshuo shilüe.* Beijing: Beixin Press, 1925. Published as *A Brief History of Chinese Fiction,* trans. Yang Hsien-yi and Gladys Yang. Beijing: Foreign Language Press, 1959.

Lu Xun is widely regarded as the founder of modern Chinese literature. His Brief History of Chinese Fiction *was based on lecture notes he used while teaching at Peking University and Beijing Normal University. A truly pioneering project, Lu Xun's seminal work is a systematic study of the Chinese literary tradition from antiquity to the late Qing dynasty. Lu's methodology is informed by the approaches of sociological, psychological, and comparative studies, and is enhanced by an insightful historical perspective and meticulous research . A classic study of Chinese literature that was very influential in Lu's time, this work remains an important source for scholars in the field.*

Ma Qiusha. *Non-governmental Organizations in Contemporary China: Paving the Way to Civil Society?* London and New York: Routledge, 2006.

A detailed panorama of the emergence of China's nongovernmental organizations and a good analysis of its "civil society."

MacFarquhar, Roderick. *The Origins of the Cultural Revolution.* 3 vols. New York: Columbia University Press, 1974–1997.

In this seminal work on the history of Chinese politics, MacFarquhar analyzes politics under Mao in detail.

Marks, Robert B. *Tigers, Rice, Silk, and Silt: Environment and Economy in Late Imperial South China.* Cambridge, U.K.: Cambridge University Press, 1998.

Marks's environmental history of Lingnan (roughly Guangdong and Guangxi) is a masterpiece of scholarship that convincingly examines how the society, economy, and politics of South China emerged in conjunction with ecological change. The very existence today of the Pearl River Delta as a motor of economic development can be traced in this remarkable book.

Murphy, Rachel. *How Migrant Labor is Changing Rural China.* Cambridge, U.K.: Cambridge University Press, 2002.

Murphy's contribution to the large body of literature about migrant labor in China during the post-1978 reform period provides excellent case studies and insights into core social dynamics of the time. It also serves as an important entry point for core debates and a broader understanding of the underlying dynamics of labor migration.

Naughton, Barry. *Growing Out of the Plan: Chinese Economic Reform, 1978–1993*. New York: Cambridge University Press, 1995.

A detailed study of the evolution of the Chinese economic system since the launch of the reform.

Naughton, Barry. *The Chinese Economy: Transitions and Growth*. Cambridge, MA: MIT Press, 2007.

An up-to-date, accessible, and comprehensive overview of China's reform economy, written by an economist with longstanding credentials as a major authority on this topic.

Oi, Jean Chun. *State and Peasant in Contemporary China: The Political Economy of Village Government*. Berkeley: University of California Press, 1989.

Jean Oi's classic examination of rural reforms introduces an analysis of clientelism and lays the foundation for future research on the institutional frameworks of rural-urban relations during the post-1978 reform period. It is a foundational work for anybody researching farmers during the reform era.

Ong, Aihwa, and Donald M. Nonini, eds. *Ungrounded Empires: The Cultural Politics of Modern Chinese Transnationalism*. London: Routledge, 1997.

Ong and Nonini's collection of papers includes historical and contemporary cases of Chinese transnationalism, exploring how the Chinese developed communities that spanned continents and maintained innovative forms of global interaction from the beginning to the end of the twentieth century.

Perry, Elizabeth J. *Shanghai on Strike: The Politics of Chinese Labor*. Stanford, CA: Stanford University Press, 1993.

Considered an important contribution to scholarship on labor in China, Perry's study focuses on workers drawn together in Shanghai—their backgrounds, political party affiliations, vocations, and other factors relating to the success of organized labor movements in that city.

Perry, Elizabeth J., and Mark Selden. *Chinese Society: Change, Conflict, and Resistance*. London and New York: Routledge, 2000.

Contrary to what many think, Chinese society is not passive, and this book shows how various social strata have resisted the initiatives of the party.

Peterson, Glen, Ruth Hayhoe, and Lu Yongling. *Education, Culture, and Identity in Twentieth-century China*. Ann Arbor: University of Michigan Press, 2001.

A history of education in China that links developments before and after the watershed of the Communist revolution in 1949.

Polachek, James M. *The Inner Opium War*. Cambridge, MA: Council on East Asian Studies, Harvard University, 1992.

Analyzes the time of transition in mid-nineteenth-century China.

Pong, David. *Shen Pao-chen and China's Modernization in the Nineteenth Century*. Cambridge, U.K.: Cambridge University Press, 1994.

Examines reforms and modernization in the era of Self-strengthening by way of Shen's career: his Confucian upbringing, his success in the Qing bureaucracy, and his role in China's first modern naval dockyard and academy. Available in Chinese as Shen Baozhen pingzhuan: Zhongguo jindaihua de changshi. *Shanghai: Shanghai Guji Chubanshe, 2000.*

Rankin, Mary Backus. *Elite Activism and Political Transformation in China: Zhejiang Province, 1865–1911*. Stanford, CA: Stanford University Press, 1986.

Details the decades leading up to the end of the Qing dynasty.

Rawski, Thomas G. *Economic Growth in Prewar China*. Berkeley: University of California Press, 1989.

A standard work on the subject.

Révo Cul dans la Chine pop: Anthologie de la presse des Gardes Rouges. Paris: Union générale d'éditions, 1974.

An impressive selection of texts published in Red Guard newspapers, including Yang Xiguang's "Whither China."

Rhoads, Edward J. M. *Manchus & Han: Ethnic Relations and Political Power in Late Qing and Early Republican China, 1861–1928*. Seattle: University of Washington Press, 2000.

Details the relations between the Manchu court and Han reformers in the years leading up to and following the revolution of 1911 and the fall of the Qing dynasty. A groundbreaking study that traces the evolution of the Manchus from a hereditary military caste to a privileged and distinct ethnic group.

Riskin, Carl. *China's Political Economy: The Quest for Development since 1949*. Oxford: Oxford University Press, 1987.

A classic on China's economic development since 1949, providing a strong understanding of the planned-economy period and the beginning of the economic reforms in China, written by a major scholar in this field.

Ruan Ming. *Deng Xiaoping: Chronicle of an Empire*. Trans. and ed. Nancy Liu, Peter Rand, and Lawrence R. Sullivan. Boulder, CO: Westview, 1994.

An inside account of the first decade of reforms by an intellectual who worked closely with Hu Yaobang at the party school.

Shirk, Susan L. *The Political Logic of Economic Reform in China*. Berkeley: University of California Press, 1993.

A classic on the Chinese economic reforms, contributing innovative approaches to the analysis of China's political system during the reform process.

Skinner, G. William. *Marketing and Social Structure in Rural China*. Association for Asian Studies, 1964. Reprinted from *Journal of Asian Studies* 24, 1–3 (1964/1965).

Skinner, G. William, ed. *The City in Late Imperial China*. Stanford, CA: Stanford University Press, 1977.

An influential volume of essays, including Skinner's seminal articles on urbanization in late imperial China, among which "Regional Urbanization in Nineteenth-Century China" is the most commonly cited. Skinner's seminal works on local market systems and macroregions are crucial background reading for people doing research on China's geography, economy, political economy, history, and sociology. The understanding of China as regionally structured in terms of trading and production (rather than jurisdictions like provinces) is essential for understanding many dynamics today.

Smil, Vaclav. *China's Environmental Crisis: An Inquiry into the Limits of National Development*. Armonk, NY: Sharpe, 1993.

Smil's polemical yet well-written and substantial work on China's environment has become a classic. It has in many ways been overtaken by events, but can serve as a good starting point for an understanding of the environmental crises facing China and the policies for dealing with them.

Spence, Jonathan D. *The Search for Modern China.* New York: Norton, 1990.

A general and very readable textbook.

Spence, Jonathan D. *God's Chinese Son: The Taiping Heavenly Kingdom of Hong Xiuquan.* New York: Norton, 1997.

A detailed and engaging account of Hong Xiuquan and the Taiping Rebellion, the largest social uprising in history.

Strand, David. *Rickshaw Beijing: City People and Politics in the 1920s.* Berkeley: University of California Press, 1989.

Important study of Beijing society and politics in the 1920s.

Sullivan, Michael. *Art and Artists of Twentieth-Century China.* Berkeley: University of California Press, 1996.

A standard reference on twentieth-century Chinese art, by one of the leading authorities on the subject.

Wachman, Alan. *Taiwan: National Identity and Democratization.* Armonk, NY: Sharpe, 1994.

Wachman's book has become popular because it gives a thorough overview of major events and themes in Taiwan's development, mainly relating to identity, state building, and democratization. This work allows readers to see the broad outlines, well documented with evidence, but spares them the excessive details of bewildering political infighting, the minutiae of electoral processes and political scandals, and the overzealous political analyses marring many works on Taiwan after 1986.

Walder, Andrew G. *Communist Neo-traditionalism: Work and Authority in Chinese Industry.* Berkeley: University of California Press, 1986.

Examines the nature of authority, politics, and social structure in Communist China.

Waldron, Arthur. *From War to Nationalism: China's Turning Point, 1924–1925.* Cambridge, U.K.: Cambridge University Press, 1995.

Traces the development of radical nationalism in China, focusing on events leading up to the May Thirtieth movement in Shanghai.

Wang Gungwu. *China and the Chinese Overseas.* Singapore: Times Academic Press, 1991.

Written by a prominent Chinese diasporic intellectual, this study formed a turning point in research on ethnic Chinese living outside China. In elegant and well-chosen case studies, Wang examined the roles of Chinese in the context of the countries they lived in, mapped their history, and helped synthesize their contributions. The book's publication coincided with a rising global awareness of the Chinese diaspora and the trends toward a patriotic politics in China, contributing a timely reappraisal of overseas Chinese as part of greater China.

Wang Guowei. *Renjian Cihua* [Poetics of Ci lyrics and the human world], 1908. Neimenggu: Neimenggu Renmin Chubanshe, 2003.

As a talented and original scholar, Wang Guowei distinguished himself in a wide range of fields such as literary criticism, philosophy, aesthetics, Chinese history, and epigraphy. He was also an accomplished poet in Ci lyrics, a classical genre of Chinese poetry that flourished in the Song dynasty (960–1279). Renjian Cihua, which was published in 1908, is an intellectual manifestation of Wang Guowei's insightful critique of Chinese Ci poems in terms of the

principles of artistic creation and aesthetic appreciation. Well versed in the German philosophical and aesthetic thinking of Arthur Schopenhauer, Friedrich von Schiller, and particularly Immanuel Kant, Wang formulated his own theory of poetic discourse of Jingjie shuo, which has informed a growing modern Chinese aesthetic thought. The publication of this seminal work was a turning point in the history of Chinese aesthetic thought, marking the beginning of the modern Chinese aesthetic tradition.

Wang Zheng. *Women in the Chinese Enlightenment: Oral and Textual Histories.* Berkeley: University of California Press, 1999.

A pioneering study of women in the May Fourth era, featuring oral histories of five women born around the turn of the twentieth century.

White, Lynn T., III. *Policies of Chaos: The Organizational Causes of Violence in China's Cultural Revolution.* Princeton, NJ: Princeton University Press, 1989.

Argues that the turmoil of the Cultural Revolution resulted mainly from reactions by masses of individuals and small groups to three specific policies: labeling groups, designating party bosses, and institutionalizing violence in political campaigns.

Widor, Claude. *Documents on the Chinese Democratic Movements, 1978–1980.* Vol. 1. Paris: Editions de l'Ecole des hautes études en sciences sociales; Hong Kong: Observer, 1981–1985.

A complete collection (in Chinese) of the underground journals that appeared during the Democracy Wall movement in 1978 and 1979.

Wong, Linda. *Marginalization and Social Welfare in China.* London: Routledge, 1998.

Provides an overview of social welfare in China since the late Qing dynasty. Wong's work forms an important background for any examination of more recent developments, and needs to be used in conjunction with sources that allow an understanding of the huge changes that have taken place since the book was published, in particular after 2003.

Wong, Roy Bin. *China Transformed: Historical Change and the Limits of European Experience.* Ithaca, NY: Cornell University Press, 1997.

A critical comparative history of political and economic change in China.

Wright, Mary Clabaugh. *The Last Stand of Chinese Conservatism: The T'ung-chih Restoration, 1862–1874.* Rev. ed. New York: Atheneum, 1965.

This pioneering work on reform in nineteenth-century China remains a standard reference.

Wright, Tim. *Coal Mining in China's Economy and Society, 1895–1937.* Cambridge, U.K.: Cambridge University Press, 1984.

An insightful analysis of a key modern industry in China's early industrialization.

Wu Yongping. *Political Explanation of Economic Growth: State Survival, Bureaucratic Politics, and Private Enterprises in the Making of Taiwan's Economy, 1950–1985.* Cambridge, MA: Harvard University Asia Center, 2005.

Wu's well-written and accessible analysis of the Republic of China on Taiwan as a "developmental state" challenges many preconceived ideas at the same time that it provides a useful and reliable overview of Taiwan's business history from 1949 onward.

Yang Jisheng. *Mubei* [Funerary stele]. 2 vols. Hong Kong: Cosmos, 2008.

The most comprehensive study of the Great Leap .Forward famine by a retired Xinhua journalist whose adoptive father died of hunger during this period.

Yang Xiguang and Susan McFadden. *Captive Spirits: Prisoners of the Cultural Revolution.* Hong Kong: Oxford University Press, 1997.

This prison memoir of Yang Xiguang, a high school student arrested during the Cultural Revolution, takes the reader into the arcana of life in China in the 1960s and contains some wonderful biographies of dissidents Yang met while serving a ten-year prison sentence.

Yeh Wen-hsin (Ye Wenxin). *Shanghai Splendor: Economic Sentiments and the Making of Modern China, 1843– 1949.* Berkeley: University of California Press, 2007.

Provides a fascinating account of everyday life in Shanghai, arguably China's most colorful city.

Yue Daiyun (Yueh Tai-yun), with Carolyn Wakeman. *To the Storm: The Odyssey of a Revolutionary Chinese Woman.* Berkeley: University of California Press, 1985.

Autobiographical memoir by Yue Daiyun detailing her personal turmoil as a young mother and intellectual during the Maoist years and the period of the Cultural Revolution in China.

Zarrow, Peter Gue. *China in War and Revolution, 1895– 1949.* London: Routledge, 2005.

A history of the rise and fall of the Republic of China with a strong focus on intellectual change.

Zhang Liang, comp. *The Tiananmen Papers.* Eds. Andrew J. Nathan and Perry Link. New York: Public Affairs, 2001.

A fascinating account of the way the Chinese leadership dealt with the 1989 prodemocracy movement.

Zhang, Heather Xiaoquan, Wu Bin, and Richard Sanders, eds. *Marginalisation in China: Perspectives on Transition and Globalisation.* Aldershot, U.K.: Ashgate, 2007.

Provides detailed topical studies of social exclusion in China that allow an understanding of the social and economic dynamics of marginalization and of the institutional and political efforts at play in dealing with marginal groups.

Zhao Jiabi, ed. *Zhongguo xinwen xuedaxi* [Comprehensive anthology of modern Chinese literature]. Shanghai: Liangyou Press, 1935–1936.

Arguably the most authoritative and influential literary guide for the study of Chinese literature from the May Fourth movement to the 1930s, this anthology includes works by well-known literary critics and writers such as Hu Shi, Lu Xun, Mao Dun, Yu Dafu, Zhou Zuoren, Zhu Ziqing, Hong Shen, and Zheng Zhenduo. The anthology consists of ten volumes, collecting more than 200 articles, 153 literary works, 202 essays, 441 poems, and eighteen plays. Each volume opens with a well-written preface discussing literary issues and theories; the prefaces are in a sense more important than the anthology itself.

Zhong Yang. *Local Government and Politics in China: Challenges from Below.* Armonk, NY: Sharpe, 2003.

Local politics in China is an under-researched area, and Zhong's book is probably the most comprehensive and up-to-date overview, well written and accessible in spite of the complexity of the topic.

Zhou, Kate Xiao. *How the Farmers Changed China: Power of the People.* Boulder, CO: Westview, 1996.

This controversial study argues that China's agrarian policy after Mao's death was as much the result of peasant pressure as the decisions of Deng Xiaoping.

Conversion Table of Chinese Romanization: Wade-Giles to Pinyin

Wade-Giles	Pinyin	Wade-Giles	Pinyin	Wade-Giles	Pinyin	Wade-Giles	Pinyin	Wade-Giles	Pinyin	Wade-Giles	Pinyin	Wade-Giles	Pinyin
a	a	chün	jun	k'ang	kang	ming	ming	sen	sen	tse	ze		
ai	ai	ch'ün	qun	kao	gao	miu	miu	seng	seng	ts'e	ce		
an	an	en	en	k'ao	kao	mo	mo	sha	sha	tsei	zei		
ang	ang	erh	er	kei	gei	mou	mou	shai	shai	tsen	zen		
ao	ao	fa	fa	ken	gen	mu	mu	shan	shan	ts'en	cen		
cha	zha	fan	fan	k'en	ken	na	na	shang	shang	tseng	zeng		
ch'a	cha	fang	fang	keng	geng	nai	nai	shao	shao	ts'eng	ceng		
chai	zhai	fei	fei	k'eng	keng	nan	nan	she	she	tso	zuo		
ch'ai	chai	fen	fen	ko	ge	nang	nang	shen	shen	ts'o	cuo		
chan	zhan	feng	feng	k'o	ke	nao	nao	sheng	sheng	tsou	zou		
ch'an	chan	fo	fo	kou	gou	nei	nei	shih	shi	ts'ou	cou		
chang	zhang	fou	fou	k'ou	kou	nen	nen	shou	shou	tsu	zu		
ch'ang	chang	fu	fu	ku	gu	neng	neng	shu	shu	ts'u	cu		
chao	zhao	ha	ha	k'u	ku	ni	ni	shua	shua	tsuan	zuan		
ch'ao	chao	hai	hai	kua	gua	niang	niang	shuai	shuai	ts'uan	cuan		
che	zhe	han	han	k'ua	kua	niao	niao	shuan	shuan	tsui	zui		
ch'e	che	hang	hang	kuai	guai	nieh	nie	shuang	shuang	ts'ui	cui		
chen	zhen	hao	hao	k'uai	kuai	nien	nian	shui	shui	tsun	zun		
ch'en	chen	hei	hei	kuan	guan	nin	nin	shun	shun	ts'un	cun		
cheng	zheng	hen	hen	k'uan	kuan	ning	ning	shuo	shuo	tsung	zong		
ch'eng	cheng	heng	heng	kuang	guang	niu	niu	so	suo	ts'ung	cong		
chi	ji	ho	he	k'uang	kuang	no	nuo	sou	sou	tu	du		
ch'i	qi	hou	hou	kuei	gui	nu	nu	ssu	si	t'u	tu		
chia	jia	hsi	xi	k'uei	kui	nuan	nuan	su	su	tuan	duan		
ch'ia	qia	hsia	xia	kun	gun	nung	nong	suan	suan	t'uan	tuan		
chiang	jiang	hsiang	xiang	k'un	kun	nü	nü	sui	sui	tui	dui		
ch'iang	qiang	hsiao	xiao	kung	gong	nüeh	nüe	sun	sun	t'ui	tui		
chiao	jiao	hsieh	xie	k'ung	kong	o	e	sung	song	tun	dun		
ch'iao	qiao	hsien	xian	kuo	guo	ou	ou	szu	si	t'un	tun		
chieh	jie	hsin	xin	k'uo	kuo	pa	ba	ta	da	tung	dong		
ch'ieh	qie	hsing	xing	la	la	p'a	pa	t'a	ta	t'ung	tong		
chien	jian	hsiu	xiu	lai	lai	pai	bai	tai	dai	tzu	zi		
ch'ien	qian	hsiung	xiong	lan	lan	p'ai	pai	t'ai	tai	tz'u	ci		
chih	zhi	hsü	xu	lang	lang	pan	ban	tan	dan	wa	wa		
ch'ih	chi	hsüan	xuan	lao	lao	p'an	pan	t'an	tan	wai	wai		
chin	jin	hsüeh	xue	le	le	pang	bang	tang	dang	wan	wan		
ch'in	qin	hsün	xun	lei	lei	p'ang	pang	t'ang	tang	wang	wang		
ching	jing	hu	hu	leng	leng	pao	bao	tao	dao	wei	wei		
ch'ing	qing	hua	hua	li	li	p'ao	pao	t'ao	tao	wen	wen		
chiu	jiu	huai	huai	liang	liang	pei	bei	te	de	weng	weng		
ch'iu	qiu	huan	huan	liao	liao	p'ei	pei	t'e	te	wo	wo		
chiung	jiong	huang	huang	lieh	lie	pen	ben	teng	deng	wu	wu		
ch'iung	qiong	hui	hui	lien	lian	p'en	pen	t'eng	teng	ya	ya		
cho	zhuo	hun	hun	lin	lin	peng	beng	ti	di	yai	yai		
ch'o	chuo	hung	hong	ling	ling	p'eng	peng	t'i	ti	yang	yang		
chou	zhou	huo	huo	liu	liu	pi	bi	tiao	diao	yao	yao		
ch'ou	chou	i	yi	lo	luo	p'i	pi	t'iao	tiao	yeh	ye		
chu	zhu	jan	ran	lou	lou	piao	biao	tieh	die	yen	yan		
ch'u	chu	jang	rang	lu	lu	p'iao	piao	t'ieh	tie	yin	yin		
chua	zhua	jao	rao	luan	luan	pieh	bie	tien	dian	ying	ying		
ch'uai	chuai	je	re	lun	lun	p'ieh	pie	t'ien	tian	yo	yo		
ch'uai	chuai	jen	ren	lung	long	pien	bian	ting	ding	yu	you		
ch'uan	chuan	jeng	reng	lü	lü	p'ien	pian	tiu	diu	yung	yong		
chuang	zhuang	jih	ri	lüan	luan	pin	bin	to	duo	yü	yu		
ch'uang	chuang	jo	ruo	lüeh	lüe	p'in	pin	t'o	tuo	yüan	yuan		
chui	zhui	jou	rou	ma	ma	ping	bing	tou	dou	yüeh	yue		
ch'ui	chui	ju	ru	mai	mai	p'ing	ping	t'ou	tou	yün	yun		
chun	zhun	juan	ruan	man	man	po	bo	tsa	za				
ch'un	chun	jui	rui	mang	mang	p'o	po	ts'a	ca				
chung	zhong	jun	run	mao	mao	pou	ou	tsai	zai				
ch'ung	chong	jung	rong	mei	mei	pu	bu	ts'ai	cai				
chü	ju	ka	ga	men	men	p'u	pu	tsan	zan				
ch'ü	qu	k'a	ka	meng	meng	sa	sa	ts'an	can				
chüan	juan	kai	gai	mi	mi	sai	sai	tsang	zang				
ch'üan	quan	k'ai	kai	miao	miao	san	san	ts'ang	cang				
chüeh	jue	kan	gan	mieh	mie	sang	sang	tsao	zao				
ch'üeh	que	k'an	kan	mien	mian	sao	sao	ts'ao	cao				
		kang	gang	min	min	se	se						

Conversion Table of Chinese Romanization: Pinyin to Wade-Giles

Pinyin	Wade-Giles	Pinyin	Wade-Giles	Pinyin	Wade-Giles	Pinyin	Wade-Giles	Pinyin	Wade-Giles	Pinyin	Wade-Giles
a	a	dong	tung	juan	chüan	nao	nao	sao	sao	xiu	hsiu
ai	ai	dou	tou	jue	chüeh	nei	nei	se	se	xu	hsü
an	an	du	tu	jun	chün	nen	nen	sen	sen	xuan	hsüan
ang	ang	duan	tuan	ka	k'a	neng	neng	seng	seng	xue	hsüeh
ao	ao	dui	tui	kai	k'ai	ni	ni	sha	sha	xun	hsün
ba	pa	dun	tun	kan	k'an	nian	nien	shai	shai	ya	ya
bai	pai	duo	to	kang	k'ang	niang	niang	shan	shan	yai	yai
ban	pan	e	o	kao	k'ao	niao	niao	shang	shang	yan	yen
bang	pang	en	en	ke	k'o	nie	nieh	shao	shao	yang	yang
bao	pao	er	erh	ken	k'en	nin	nin	she	she	yao	yao
bei	pei	fa	fa	keng	k'eng	ning	ning	shen	shen	ye	yeh
ben	pen	fan	fan	kong	k'ung	niu	niu	sheng	sheng	yi	i
beng	peng	fang	fang	kou	k'ou	nong	nung	shi	shih	yin	yin
bi	pi	fei	fei	ku	k'u	nu	nu	shou	shou	ying	ying
bian	pien	fen	fen	kua	k'ua	nü	nü	shu	shu	yo	yo
biao	piao	feng	feng	kuai	k'uai	nuan	nuan	shua	shua	yong	yung
bie	pieh	fo	fo	kuan	k'uan	nüe	nüeh	shuai	shuai	you	yu
bin	pin	fou	fou	kuang	k'uang	nuo	no	shuan	shuan	yu	yü
bing	ping	fu	fu	kui	k'uei	ou	ou	shuang	shuang	yuan	yüan
bo	po	ga	ka	kun	k'un	ou	pou	shui	shui	yue	yüeh
bu	pu	gai	kai	kuo	k'uo	pa	p'a	shun	shun	yun	yün
ca	ts'a	gan	kan	la	la	pai	p'ai	shuo	shuo	za	tsa
cai	ts'ai	gang	kang	lai	lai	pan	p'an	si	ssu	zai	tsai
can	ts'an	gao	kao	lan	lan	pang	p'ang	si	szu	zan	tsan
cang	ts'ang	ge	ko	lang	lang	pao	p'ao	song	sung	zang	tsang
cao	ts'ao	gei	kei	lao	lao	pei	p'ei	sou	sou	zao	tsao
ce	ts'e	gen	ken	le	le	pen	p'en	su	su	ze	tse
cen	ts'en	geng	keng	lei	lei	peng	p'eng	suan	suan	zei	tsei
ceng	ts'eng	gong	kung	leng	leng	pi	p'i	sui	sui	zen	tsen
cha	ch'a	gou	kou	li	li	pian	p'ien	sun	sun	zeng	tseng
chai	ch'ai	gu	ku	lian	lien	piao	p'iao	suo	so	zha	cha
chan	ch'an	gua	kua	liang	liang	pie	p'ieh	ta	t'a	zhai	chai
chang	ch'ang	guai	kuai	liao	liao	pin	p'in	tai	t'ai	zhan	chan
chao	ch'ao	guan	kuan	lie	lieh	ping	p'ing	tan	t'an	zhang	chang
che	ch'e	guang	kuang	lin	lin	po	p'o	tang	t'ang	zhao	chao
chen	ch'en	gui	kuei	ling	ling	pu	p'u	tao	t'ao	zhe	che
cheng	ch'eng	gun	kun	liu	liu	qi	ch'i	te	t'e	zhen	chen
chi	ch'ih	guo	kuo	long	lung	qia	ch'ia	teng	t'eng	zheng	cheng
chong	ch'ung	ha	ha	lou	lou	qian	ch'ien	ti	t'i	zhi	chih
chou	ch'ou	hai	hai	lu	lu	qiang	ch'iang	tian	t'ien	zhong	chung
chu	ch'u	han	han	lü	lü	qiao	ch'iao	tiao	t'iao	zhou	chou
chuai	ch'uai	hang	hang	luan	luan	qie	ch'ieh	tie	t'ieh	zhu	chu
chuan	ch'uan	hao	hao	lüe	lüeh	qin	ch'in	ting	t'ing	zhua	chua
chuang	ch'uang	he	ho	lun	lun	qing	ch'ing	tong	t'ung	zhuai	chuai
chui	ch'ui	hei	hei	luo	lo	qiong	ch'iung	tou	t'ou	zhuan	chuan
chun	ch'un	hen	hen	ma	ma	qiu	ch'iu	tu	t'u	zhuang	chuang
chuo	ch'o	heng	heng	mai	mai	qu	ch'ü	tuan	t'uan	zhui	chui
ci	tz'u	hong	hung	man	man	quan	ch'üan	tui	t'ui	zhun	chun
cong	ts'ung	hou	hou	mang	mang	que	ch'üeh	tun	t'un	zhuo	cho
cou	ts'ou	hu	hu	mao	mao	qun	ch'ün	tuo	t'o	zi	tzu
cu	ts'u	hua	hua	mei	mei	ran	jan	wa	wa	zong	tsung
cuan	ts'uan	huai	huai	men	men	rang	jang	wai	wai	zou	tsou
cui	ts'ui	huan	huan	meng	meng	rao	jao	wan	wan	zu	tsu
cun	ts'un	huang	huang	mi	mi	re	je	wang	wang	zuan	tsuan
cuo	ts'o	hui	hui	mian	mien	ren	jen	wei	wei	zui	tsui
da	ta	hun	hun	miao	miao	reng	jeng	wen	wen	zun	tsun
dai	tai	huo	huo	mie	mieh	ri	jih	weng	weng	zuo	tso
dan	tan	ji	chi	min	min	rong	jung	wo	wo		
dang	tang	jia	chia	ming	ming	rou	jou	wu	wu		
dao	tao	jian	chien	miu	miu	ru	ju	xi	hsi		
de	te	jiang	chiang	mo	mo	ruan	juan	xia	hsia		
deng	teng	jiao	chiao	mou	mou	rui	jui	xian	hsien		
di	ti	jie	chieh	mu	mu	run	jun	xiang	hsiang		
dian	tien	jin	chin	na	na	ruo	jo	xiao	hsiao		
diao	tiao	jing	ching	nai	nai	sa	sa	xie	hsieh		
die	tieh	jiong	chiung	nan	nan	sai	sai	xin	hsin		
ding	ting	jiu	chiu	nang	nang	san	san	xing	hsing		
diu	tiu	ju	chü			sang	sang	xiong	hsiung		

Glossary of Chinese Characters

A Cheng 阿城: Ah Cheng

A Fei zhengzhuan 阿飞正传 (阿飛正傳): *Days of Being Wild*

A Ge 阿鸽

a hong 阿洪: imam

A Q zhengzhuan 阿Q正传 (阿Q正傳): *The True Story of Ah Q*

A Ying 阿英

Aba Zangzu Qiangzu Zizhizhou 阿坝藏族羌族自治州: Aba Tibetan and Qiang Autonomous Prefecture

Aerjin Shan 阿尔金山: Altun Mountains

Aertai 阿尔泰: Altai

aha 阿哈: Manchu slaves

Ahei xiaoshi 阿黑小史: The story of Ahei

Ai Qing 艾青

Ai Weiwei 艾未未

Ai Xuan 艾轩 (艾軒)

aiguo 爱国: patriotic

Aiguo Tongyi Zhanxian 爱国统一战线 (愛國統一戰線): Patriotic United Front

aiguozhe 爱国者: patriot

aiguozhuyi jiaoyu jidi 爱国主义教育基地: patriotic educational bases

Aihe 愛河: Love River

Aihun Tiaoyue 瑷珲条约: Treaty of Aigun

Aiqing sanbuqu 爱情三部曲: Love trilogy

Aishanlu mengying 爱山庐梦影 (愛山廬夢影): Dreams from a mountain lover's studio

Aixinjueluo Hongli 爱新觉罗弘历 (弘暦): Qianlong emperor

Aixinjueluo Minning 爱新觉罗旻宁 (旻寧), **later** 绵宁 (綿寧): Daoguang emperor

Aixinjueluo Putong 爱新觉罗溥侗: Aisin Gioro Putong

Aixinjueluo Puyi 爱新觉罗溥仪 (溥儀): Xuantong emperor

Aixinjueluo Yihuan 爱新觉罗奕譞

Aixinjueluo Yixin 爱新觉罗奕欣 (奕訢)

Aixinjueluo Yizhu 爱新觉罗奕詝: Xianfeng emperor

Aixinjueluo Yongyan 爱新觉罗永琰, **later** 顒琰: Jiaqing emperor

Aixinjueluo Zaichun 爱新觉罗载淳: Tongzhi emperor

Aixinjueluo Zaitian 爱新觉罗载湉: Guangxu emperor

aizibing 爱滋病: AIDS

Alibaba 阿里巴巴: Alibaba

Alishan fengyun 阿里山风云 (阿里山風雲): Storm on Mount Ali

anban 安班: Qing imperial resident

anding tuanjie 安定团结: stability and unity

Andō Hiroshige 安藤広重

Anduo 安多: Amdo

Anfu Guohui 安福国会: Anfu Parliament

Anhui 安徽

Anhui Shengli Tushuguan 安徽省立圖書館: Anhui Provincial Library

anjuan 案卷: cases

Ankang 安康

annaqizhuyi 安那其主义: anarchism

"Annaqizhuyi" 安那其主义: On anarchism

Anni Baobei 安妮宝贝

Anqing 安庆

Ansha 3322 暗杀 3322: Assassination 3322

Anshan 鞍山

Anyang 安阳

Anyuan 安源

ao 袄: a long jacket

Aofeng Shuyuan 鳌丰书院: Aofeng Academy

Aoki Masaru 青木正兒

Aomen 澳门: Macau

Ba 巴

Ba Jin 巴金

ba rong ba chi 八荣八耻: Eight Honors and Eight Disgraces

badao 霸道: despotic way

bagongsheng 拔贡生 (拔貢生): senior licentiate of the first class

baguwen 八股文: formal eight-part essays

Bai Chongxi 白崇禧

Bai Guang 白光

Bai Hong 白虹

Bai Hua 白桦

Bai hua qi fang, bai jia zheng ming 百花齐放, 百家争鸣: Let a hundred flowers bloom; let a hundred schools of thought contend

Bai Jingrui 白景瑞: Pai Ching-jui

Bai Ri Weixin 百日维新 (百日維新): Hundred Days' Reform

Bai Shangdi Hui 拜上帝会 (拜上帝會): Society of God Worshippers

Bai Wei 白薇

Bai Xianyong 白先勇

Baidai changci 百代唱词 (百代唱詞): Pathé lyrics

Baidai Changpian Gongsi 百代唱片公司: Pathé Orient

Baidi Tianwang 白帝天王: White Emperor Heavenly Kings

Baidu 百度: Baidu

baihua 白话 (白話): the vernacular language

Baihua bao 白话报: Vernacular journal

baihua shi 白話詩: vernacular poetry

baihua yundong 白话运动 (白話運動): colloquial-language movement

Baihua Yundong 百花运动 (百花運動): Hundred Flowers Campaign

Baijiao 白教: *bka'brgyud* (Kagyu) Tibetan Vajrayāna Buddhism

Bailianhui 白莲会: White Lotus sect

Bailianjiao Qiyi 白莲教起义 (白蓮教起義): White Lotus Rebellion

Bailu Yuan 白鹿原: White Deer Plain

Bailudong Shuyuan 白鹿洞书院: Bailudong Academy

Bailudong Shuyuan jieshi 白鹿洞书院揭示: Guidelines for the Bailudong Academy

Baimahu 白马湖: Lake Baima

Baimao nü 白毛女: *The White-Haired Girl*

Baimao nü jixingqu 白毛女即兴曲: *The White-Haired Girl* impromptu

baimiao 白描: outline technique

bainian guochi 百年国耻: century of humiliation

Baise 百色: Bose, Poseh

Baishe zhuan 白蛇传 (白蛇傳): The story of the white snake

baitang 拜堂: offering food to the ancestors of the groom's family

Baitoushan 白头山: Mt. Baitou

Baiye 白夜: White Nights

Baiyun 白云

Baiyunguan 白云观

"Baizhongren: Shangdi de jiaozi" 白种人: 上帝的骄子: White people: God's favored sons

Baizu 白族: Bai minority

Bajiu Minzhu Yundong 八九民主运动: Tiananmen Incident (1989)

Bajiu Xuesheng Yundong 八九学生运动: Tiananmen Incident (1989)

Bakuning 巴库宁: Bakunin

Balujun 八路军 (八路軍): Eighth Route Army

ban fengjian 半封建: semifeudal

ban maoyi 般贸易: ordinary trade

ban zhimin di 半殖民地: semicolonial

"**Ban zhuren**" 班主任: Class teacher

Banchan Lama 班禅喇嘛: Panchen Lama

bang 帮 (幫): gangs, cliques; specifically, trade coalitions, financial cliques

Banpo 半坡

Banqiao Da Ba 板桥大坝: Banqiao Dam

bao 保: a security group in the *baojia* community self-defense system

bao lu 保路: protect the railways

Bao Pao 包砲

Bao Shichen 包世臣

Bao Tianxiao 包天笑

baochan daohu 包产到户: household responsibility for production, fixing of farm output quotas for each household

Baoding 保定

Baoding Junxiao 保定军校: Baoding Military Academy

baofang 报房: publishing house

baogan daohu 包干到户: household responsibility for all

baogao wenxue 報告文學: reportage

Baohe Dian 保和殿: Preserving Harmony Hall

Baohuang Hui 保皇会 (保皇會): Save the Emperor Society, China Reform Association

Baoji 宝鸡

baojia 保甲: mutual-responsibility system, community self-defense system, neighborhood household registration system for preventing crime

Baoli Keji Youxian Gongsi 保利科技有限公司: China Polytechnologies

Baoliandeng 宝莲灯: Precious lotus lantern

baolu 暴露: exposé

Baoshan Gangtie Chang 宝山钢铁厂: Baoshan Iron and Steel Mill

baoshang zhidu 保商制度: security merchant system

baoshuiqu 保税区: free-trade zone

Baotou 包头

baoyi 包衣: booi, Manchu bondservants

Baoyinghu 宝应湖: Lake Baoying

baozhang 保长 (保長)

baozi 宝子 (寶子): covered dice

Baqi 八旗: Eight Banners

Baqi Jun 八旗军 (八旗軍): Eight Banners Army, Banner forces

Bashidang wenhua 八十垱文化: Bashidang culture

Batang 巴塘

Bawang bie ji 霸王别姬: *Farewell My Concubine* (film and play)

Bawu Meishu Xinchao 八五美术新潮: 1985 Art New Wave

Bawu Meishu yundong 八五美术运动: 1985 New Wave movement

Bayiwu 八佾舞: Confucius Dance

bazhai fengshui 八宅风水: eight-house geomancy

Bazhamiao 八蜡庙 (八蜡廟): Bazha temple

bazi 八字: eight-character form indicating time of birth

bei 碑: stone stele

Bei Cun 北村

Bei Dao 北岛

bei ti 碑体 (碑體): stele script

"**Bei ying**" 背影: "The View from the Rear"

Bei Yuming 贝聿铭: I. M. Pei

Bei Zuyi 贝祖怡: Pei Tsuyee

Beibei 北碚

Beibei nantie lun 北碑南帖论 (北碑南帖論): Northern stelae and Southern copybooks

Beichuan 北川

Beidaihe 北戴河

Beidou 北斗: Big Dipper

Beifa Zhanzheng 北伐战争: Northern Expedition

Beifang Gongye Gongsi 北方工业公司: China North Industries Corporation

Beifang Yishu Qunti 北方艺术群体: Northern Art Group

Beihai 北海: Pakhoi

Beihai Gongyuan 北海公园: Beihai Park

Beijiang 北江: Bei (North) River

Beijing 北京: Peking

Beijing chenbao 北京辰报 (北京辰報): Beijing morning post

Beijing Daxiang Wenhua Youxian Gongsi 北京大象文化有限公司: Beijing Universal Culture Corporation

Beijing Daxue 北京大学 (北京大學): Peking University

Beijing Daxue Huafa Yanjiu Hui 北京大学画法研究会: Peking University Society for the Study of Painting Methods

Beijing Dianying Xueyuan 北京电影学院: Beijing Film Academy

Beijing Dizhi Bowuguan 北京地质博物馆: Beijing Geological Museum

Beijing Dongcun 北京东村: Beijing East Village

Beijing Gongren Wenhuagong 北京工人文化宫: Beijing Workers Cultural Center

Beijing Huayuan 北京畫院: Beijing Painting Academy

Beijing Huochezhan 北京火车站: Beijing Train Station

Beijing Meishujia Xiehui 北京美术家协会 (北京美術家协會): Beijing Artists Association

Beijing Nüxuejie Lianhehui 北京女学界联合会: Beijing Federation of Women Students

Beijing Renmin Yishu Juyuan 北京人民艺术剧院 (北京人民藝術劇院): Beijing People's Art Theater

Beijing Shehui Jingji Kexue Yanjiusuo 北京社会经济科学研究所: Beijing Social and Economic Research Institute

Beijing Shi Da Jianzhu 北京十大建筑: Ten Great Constructions of Beijing

Beijing Shifan Daxue 北京师范大学: Beijing Normal University

Beijing Tiaoyue 北京条约 (北京條約): Beijing Conventions

Beijing Wudao Xueyuan 北京舞蹈学院: Beijing Dance Academy

Beijing Xiehe Yixueyuan 北京协和医学院 (北京協和醫學院): Peking Union Medical College

Beijing zazhong 北京杂种: *Beijing Bastards*

Beijing zhi Chun 北京之春: Beijing Spring

Beijing Zhonggou Huaxue Yanjiu Hui 北京中国画学研究会: Society for Research in Chinese Painting

Beijing Ziran Bowuguan 北京自然博物馆: Beijing Natural History Museum

Beijingren 北京人: *Peking man*

Beijingshi Dazhong Wenyi Chuangzuo Yanjiu Hui 北京市大众文艺创作研究会: Beijing Municipality Masses Literature and Art Creation Research Society

Beijingshi Meishujia Xiehui 北京市美术家协会 (北京市美術家协會): Beijing Municipal Artists Association

beiju mei 悲剧美 (悲劇美): tragic beauty

Beili Wang 被立王: Established King

Beilun 北仑

Beiping 北平

Beiping Guoli yishu zhuanke xuexiao 北平国立艺术专科学校: Beiping National Art College

Beiping jian pu 北平笺谱 (北平箋譜): Beiping Decorated Writing Paper

Beiping Yanjiuyuan 北平研究院: Beiping Research Academy

Beiqing chengshi 悲情城市: *A City of Sadness*

beixue 碑学 (碑學): studies of ancient monuments

Beiyang Jiandui 北洋舰队: Beiyang Fleet

Beiyang jun 北洋军 (北洋軍): Beiyang Army

Beiyang junfa 北洋军阀: Beiyang warlords

Beiyang Shifan Xuetang 北洋师范学堂: Beiyang Normal School

Beiyang Xi Xuetang 北洋西学堂: Tianjin University (Beiyang University)

Beiyang zhengfu 北洋政府: Beiyang (warlord) government

benbao neibu xiaoxi 本报内部消息: this newspaper's confidential news

Bencao gangmu 本草纲目: Compendium of Materia Medica

bendi 本地: local, locals

benshengren 本省人: locals

Benxi 本溪

Benxihu 本溪湖

benzhu 本主: local deity

Bamo 八莫: Bhamo

bi 笔: utilitarian prose

Bi nu 碧奴: Emerald slave

Bi Yihong 毕倚虹

Bi Zhenda 毕振達

Bi'an 彼岸: The other shore

Bian cheng 边城: *Border Town* or *The Frontier City*

Bian Zhilin 卞之琳

Bian zou bian chang 边走边唱: *Life on a String*

Biandan guniang 扁担姑娘: *So Close to Paradise*

Biandi fengliu 遍地风流: Romances of the Landscape

Biandi xiaoxiong 遍地枭雄: Rebels everywhere

bianfa 变法: reform of government

Bianfa tonglun 变法通论 (變法通論): General theory of reform

bianjing jingji hezuoqu 边境经济合作区: border economic-cooperation zone

bianju 变局: unprecedented situation

bianli dian 便利店: convenience store

bianqu 边区: border region

318

bifu 比附: application of law to a case by analogy

biji 笔记: brush jottings

Bijiang 碧江

bijutsu 美術: fine art

bin 嫔 (嬪): concubine

Bing mei guan ji 病梅馆记 (病梅館記): A sanitarium for sick plums

bingmayong 兵马俑: terracotta army, terracotta warriors and horses

Bingxiang baogao 病相报告: Health reports

Bingxin 冰心

Binhai Xinqu 滨海新区: New Coastal District

Binzhou 濱州

Bishu Shanzhuang 避暑山壮: Mountain Resort for Escaping the Heat

"Biye ge" 毕业歌: Graduation song

bizhi zeli 币制则例: currency regulations

Bo Gu 博古

Bo Xilai 薄熙来

Bo Yi 伯夷

Bo Yibo 薄一波

Bo Yun 薄雲

Boan xinbian 驳案新编 (駁案新編): New collection of reversed cases

Bogu tulu 博古圖錄: Illustrated collection of antiquities

Bohai 渤海

bu 不: not (Cantonese, bat)

bu chi 部尺: standard Chinese foot

Bu jian bu san 不见不散: *Be There or Be Square*

Bu Wancang 卜万苍

Buchanzu Hui 不纏足會: Anti-footbinding Society

Budala Gong 布达拉宫: Potala Palace

buge 不隔: transparently

bujiankan de qingxiang 不健康的倾向: unhealthy tendencies

Bujinghua chuanxisuo 布景画传习所

bujun tongling 步军统领: commander of the gendarmerie

bulaji 布拉吉: Russian platye, a frock made of figured cloth

bunjin ga 文人画: literati painting

Bunjinga no fukkō 文人画の復興: The revival of literati painting

bunmei shi 文明史: history of civilization

bupingdeng tiaoyue 不平等条约: unequal treaties

bushou 部首: radicals

Buyi 布衣: Cloth (band)

Buyizu 布依族: Buyi minority, Bouyei

buzhang 部长: minister

Buzhu Jihua 补助计划: Grant-in-Aid Scheme

cai 菜: side dishes

Cai Chang 蔡畅

Cai Chusheng 蔡楚生

Cai Guoqiang 蔡国强: Cai Guo-Qiang

Cai Hong She 彩虹社: Rainbow Club

Cai Mingliang 蔡明亮

Cai Qian 蔡牵

Cai Ruohong 蔡若虹

Cai Weilian 蔡威廉

Cai Yuanpei 蔡元培

caichou wu 彩绸舞: ribbon dance

Caidamu Pengdi 柴达木盆地: Qaidam Basin

Caifeng yundong 采风运动: Folksong collecting movement

caijing shiwu lingdao xiaozu 财经事务领导小组: small group of party leaders concerned with financial and economic matters

caimohua 彩墨画: color and ink painting

caishen 财神: god of wealth

"Caiyuan" 菜园: Vegetable garden

Caizheng Bu 财政部: Ministry of Finance

caizi jiaren 才子佳人: scholars and beauties

Can Xue 残雪

Cang Jie 仓颉

Canglao de fuyun 苍老的浮云: Old floating cloud

Canwu 残雾 (殘霧): Lingering fog

Cao Kun 曹锟 (曹錕)

Cao Menglan 曹夢蘭

Cao Xinzhi 曹辛之

Cao Xueqin 曹雪芹

Cao Yu 曹禺

caohu 漕斛: standard of capacity

caoliang 漕粮: tribute grain

caolishu 草隶书 (草隸書): cursive clerical script

caomi 漕米: tribute grain

caoshu 草书 (草書): cursive script

Caoyuan Fa 草原法: Grasslands Law

Cen Yuying 岑毓英

cha yin 茶引: tea licensing

chadui 插队: inserted into a (production) team

Chaguan 茶馆 (茶館): Teahouse

Chahaer 察哈尔 (察哈爾): Chahar

chaipiao 拆票: promissory notes

Chaishan 柴山: Chai Mountain

chaju 察举

chake 茶课: tea tax

chali 茶礼 (茶禮): wedding tea ceremony

Chang E 嫦娥

Chang hen ge 长恨歌: *Song of Everlasting Sorrow: A Novel of Shanghai*

chang majia 长马甲: long vest

Chang Yu 常玉: Sanyu

Chang'an 长安

Chang'an Jie 长安街: Chang'an Avenue, Avenue of Eternal Peace

Chang'e benyue 嫦娥奔月

Changbaishan 长白山: Changbai Mountains

changben 唱本: songbooks

changbian dang 长编档 (長編檔): long-draft record

Changcheng 长城 (長城): Great Wall

Changchun 长春 (長春)

Changchun Yuan 畅春园 (暢春園): Changchun Garden

Changdu 昌都: Qamdo

changguan 常关 (常關): tax checkpoint, native customs

Changhaixian 长海县: Changhai County

Changhe 长河: Long river

Changjiang 长江 (長江): Yangzi River

Changming yishu zhuanke xuexiao 昌明艺术专科学校: Changming Art College

changpao 长袍 (長袍): man's long gown

changqiang wu 长枪舞: spear dance

Changsha 长沙

Changsha guwu wenjianji 长沙古物闻见记 (長沙古物聞見記): Changsha antiquities news

changshi 常识: basic knowledge

Changshi ji 尝试集: Experiments

Changshuxian 常熟县: Changshu County

changwu fuzhuxi 常务副主席: standing vice chairman

Changxindian 长辛店

Changxing 长兴

Changzheng 长征 (長征): Long March

Changzheng jiaoxiangqu 长征交响曲: Long March symphony

Changzhi 长治

Changzhou 常州

changzhu niangjia hun 长住娘家婚 (長住娘家婚): delayed-transfer marriage

chanhui 忏悔: repentance

chanye hua 产业化: marketization

chaobao 朝报: court gazette

chaoguan 钞关: tax checkpoint

Chaoji nüsheng 超级女声: Super voice girls

"Chaoren" 超人: Superman

chaoshi 超市: supermarket

Chaoxian Zhanzheng 朝鲜战争: Korean War

Chaoxianzu 朝鲜族: Korean Chinese

Chaozhou 潮州: Teochiu

chaxu geju 差序格局: differential mode of association

Chen Baichen 陈白尘

Chen Baoyi 陈抱一 (陳抱一)

Chen Baozhen 陈宝箴

Chen Boda 陈伯达

Chen Boping 陈伯平 (陳伯平)

Chen Cheng 陈诚 (陳誠)

Chen Chongguang 陈崇光

Chen Chuanlin 陈传霖

Chen Da 陈达 (陳達)

Chen Danqing 陈丹青 (陳丹青)

Chen Danxu 陈丹旭 (陳丹旭)

Chen Diexian 陈蝶仙

Chen Duxiu 陈独秀 (陳獨秀)

Chen Fushan 陈福善: Luis Chan

Chen Gang 陈纲

Chen Geng 陈赓

Chen Guofu 陈国夫 (陳國夫)

Chen Hansheng 陈翰笙 (陳翰笙)

Chen Henghe Shulin 陈恒和书林 (陳恒和書林): Chen Henghe Bookshop

Chen Hengke 陈衡恪 (陳衡恪): Chen Hengque

Chen Hengzhe 陈衡哲 (陳衡哲)

Chen Hongshou (1598–1652) 陈洪绶 (陳洪綬)

Chen Hongshou (1768–1822) 陈鸿寿 (陳鴻壽)

Chen Jiageng 陈嘉庚: Tan Kah Kee

Chen Jiageng Gongsi 陈嘉庚公司: Tan Kah Kee & Co.

Chen Jing 陈静

Chen Jinhua 陈锦华

Chen Jinshi 陈谨诗

Chen Jiongming 陈炯明 (陳炯明)

Chen Kunhou 陈坤厚 (陳坤厚)

Chen Li 陈澧 (陳澧)

Chen Liangyu 陈良宇

Chen Lifu 陈立夫 (陳立夫)

Chen Liting 陈鲤庭

Chen Muhua 陈慕华

Chen Ping 陈平

Chen Qigang 陈其钢

Chen Qimei 陈其美

Chen Qiyuan 陈启源

Chen Quan 陈铨

Chen Ruoxi 陈若曦 (陳若曦)

Chen Sanli 陈三立 (陳三立)

Chen Sanyuan 陈散原

Chen Shizeng 陈师曾 (陳師曾)

Chen Shouqi 陈寿祺

Chen Shu 陈书

Chen Shuibian 陈水扁 (陳水扁)

Chen Shuren 陈树人

Chen Tiegeng 陈铁耕

Chen Wanli 陈万里

Chen Xiaocui 陈小翠

Chen Xiaodie 陈小蝶

Chen Xiaoying 陈小滢 (陳小瀅)

Chen Xilian 陈锡联

Chen Xin 陈昕

Chen Xingcan 陈星灿

Chen Xitong 陈希同

Chen Xiying 陈西滢 (陳西瀅)

Chen Yan 陈衍 (陳衍)

Chen Yanning 陈衍宁

Chen Yanqiao 陈烟桥

Chen Yi (1901–1972) 陈毅 (陳毅)

Chen Yi (1883–1950) 陈仪 (陳儀)

Chen Yifei 陈逸飞

Chen Yiming 陈宜明

Chen Yingning 陈樱宁 (陳櫻寧)

Chen Yingshi 陈英士

Chen Yingzhen 陈映真 (陳映真)

Chen Yinke 陈寅恪 (陳寅恪)

Chen Yonggui 陈永贵

Chen Yu 陈瑜

Chen Yuan (1880–1971) 陈垣 (陳垣)

Chen Yuan (1896–1970) 陈源 (陳源)

Chen Yun 陈云 (陳雲)

Chen Zaidao 陈再道

Chen Zhanxiang 陈占祥

Chen Zhaomin 陈肇敏 (陳肇敏)

Chen Zhaozhi 成肇智

Chen Zhifo 陈之佛 (陳之佛)

Chen Zhili 陈至立

Chen Zhongshi 陈忠实

Chen Ziming 陈子明

Chenbao 晨报 (晨報): Morning post

Cheng Conglin 程丛林

Cheng Dan'an 承淡安

Cheng Fangwu 成仿吾

Cheng Jinguan 程金冠

Cheng Jingyi 诚静怡 (誠靜怡)

Cheng Long 成龙 (成龍): Jackie Chan

Cheng Maoyun 程懋筠

Cheng Shewo 成舍我

Cheng Shifa 程十髪

Cheng Yi 程颐 (程頤)

Cheng Zhang 程璋

Chengde 承德

Chengdu 成都

Cheng-Hua Cheng Yishihui 成华城议事会: City Council of Chengdu and Huayang

chenghuang miao 城隍庙 (城隍廟): city-god temples

Cheng-Kun xian 成昆线: Chengdu-Kunming line

Chengnan Xueyuan 城南学院: Chengnan Academy

Chengqinghu 澄清湖: Chengqing Lake

chengshi 城市: city

Chengshi Fangdichan Guanli Fa 城市房地产管理法: Law on Urban Real Estate Administration

Chengshi Guanglang 城市光廊: Urban Spotlight Arcade

Chengshi Guihua Fa 城市规划法: City Planning Act

Chengxiang Guihua Fa 城乡规划法: Urban and Rural Planning Act

chengzhen dengji shiye 城镇登记失业: urban registered unemployment

Cheng-Zhu 程朱

Chengziya 城子崖

Chenlun 沉沦: Sinking

Chezhan 车站: Bus stop

chi 尺: Chinese foot

chi 笞: beating with a light stick

chi 耻: shame

chi butong zhengjian zhe 持不同政见者: dissident

chi huotou 吃伙头: meal rotation

Chi Li 池莉

Chi She 池社: Pond Society

chijiao yisheng 赤脚医生: barefoot doctor

chiku 吃苦: experience bitterness

Chixi 赤溪

Chong Ji Xueyuan 崇基学院 (崇基學院): Chung Chi College

Chongjin 冲进

Chongmingdao 崇明岛: Chongming Island

Chongqing 重庆: Chungking

Chongqing Sanxia Bowuguan 重庆三峡博物馆: Chongqing Three Gorges Museum

Chongqing senlin 重庆森林 (重慶森林): *Chungking Express*

Chongzheng Dian 崇政殿: Hall of Eminent Administration

Chou Yi 醜謬

Chouchu de jijie 踌躇的季节: Season of vacillation

Chouren zhuan 畴人传: Biographies of calendar experts and astronomers

chu 处: division

Chu Anping 储安平

Chu ci 楚辞: elegies of Chu

Chu Ge 楚戈

Chu Minyi 储民宜

Chuan bao 川报: Sichuan newspaper

chuandao 传道

chuangju 创局: unprecedented situation

Chuangzao She 创造社 (創造社): Creation Society

Chuangzao yuekan 创造月刊 (創造月刊): Creation monthly

Chuangzao zhoubao 创造周报 (創造周報): Creation weekly

chuantong 傳統: tradition

chuanye pifa shichang 专业批发市场: special wholesale market

chuban zongshu 出版總署

chuilian tingzheng 垂帘听政 (垂簾聽政): listening from behind screens to reports on governmental affairs

chujia 出家: leaving the family

Chujue Yishu Xiaozu 触觉艺术小组: Tactile Art

chukou jiagong 出口加工: export processing

Chun man Tulufan 春满吐鲁番: Springtime in Turfan

Chun qinwang 醇亲王: Prince Chun

chun wenxue 纯文学: pure literature

"**Chun zhi sheng**" 春之声: Voices of spring

"**Chuncan**" 春蚕: Spring silkworms

Chundi Huahui 春地画会 (春地畫會): Spring Earth Painters Association

Chunguang zhaxie 春光乍泄 (春光乍洩): *Happy Together*

Chū-Nichi Bijutsu Kyōkai 中日美術協会: Association of Sino-Japanese Art

Chunjie 春节 (春節): Spring Festival, Chinese lunar New Year

chunlian 春联: spring festival couplets

Chunqiu 春秋: Spring and autumn annals

Chunshen jun 春申君: Lord Chunshen

Chunshui 春水: Spring water

Chunshui Huayuan 春睡画院: Spring Slumber Studio

Chunü di 处女地: *Virgin Soil*

Chunye yu feifei 春夜雨霏霏: Falling rain on a spring night

chuzhang 处长: section leader

Chuzhou 處州

ci 祠: ancestral alter

ci 詞: song lyric

Ci Qin 刺秦: *The Emperor and the Assassin*

Ci'an 慈安 Empress Dowager Ci'an

cifu lieche 磁浮列车: Maglev (magnetic levitation) train

Cihai 辞海 (辭海): Sea of words

Cishan 磁山

Cishan wenhua 磁山文化: Cishan culture

citang 祠堂: ancestor hall

Cixi taihou 慈禧太后: Empress Dowager Cixi

Ciyuan 辞源 (辭源): Word origins

cizhang 辞章 (辭章): literary works

cizi 刺字: tattooing

"**Cong wenxue geming dao geming wenxue**" 从文学革命到革命文学 (從文學革命到革命文學): From a Literary Revolution to a Revolutionary Literature

Conghua 从化

congshu 丛书 (叢書): reprint series

Congwen zizhuan 从文自传: Congwen's autobiography

Cui Jian 崔建

Cui Zhiyuan 崔之元

Cuiheng 翠亨

cuju 蹴鞠: ancient Chinese football

cun 寸: Chinese inch

cun 村: village

cunmin weiyuanhui 村民委员会: village committee

cunshu 村塾: village school

da 达: communication of ideas

da chuan pai 大船牌: grand chop

da chuanlian 大串联: great networking

Da Han Sichuan Jun Zhengfu 大汉四川军政府: Great Han Military Government

Da hong denglong gaogao gua 大红灯笼高高挂: *Raise the Red Lantern*

da kucha 大裤叉: big shorts

Da Qing Huangjia Haiguan Zong Shuiwu Si 大清皇家海关总税务司 (大清皇家海關總稅務司): Imperial Maritime Customs Service

Da Qing huidian 大清會典: Qing statutes

Da Qing Lüli 大清律例: Qing Code, Qing penal code

Da Qing Men 大清门 (大清門): Great Qing Gate

Da Qing Shanglü 大清商律: Qing commercial code

Da Qing Xianxing Xinglü 大清现行刑律 (大清现行刑律): Qing current criminal code

Da Shanghai wuyan xia 大上海屋檐下: Under the eaves of greater Shanghai

Da wan'r 大腕: *Big Shot's Funeral*

Da Xing'an 大兴安

da xuetang 大学堂: universities

Da Yijin 笪移今

"**Da Youheng xiansheng**" 答有恒先生: In Reply to Mr. Youheng

Da yuebing 大阅兵: *The Big Parade*

Da Yunhe 大运河 (大運河): Grand Canal

Da Zhonghua Baihe Yingpian Gongsi 大中华百合影片公司 (大中華百合影片公司): Da Zhonghua Baihe Film Studio, Great China Lilium Pictures

Da Zhonghua Huochai Gongsi 大中華火柴公司: China Match Company

Dacheng Dian 大成殿: Great Achievement Hall

Dadao xiang guizi toushang kan qu: Kang-Ri gequ zhuanji 大刀向鬼子头上砍去：抗日歌曲专辑: Use the sword to cut off the heads of the foreign invader devils: A special compilation of songs of resistance against Japan

Dadaocheng 大稻埕: Tuatiutia

Dadaohui 大刀会: Big Sword Society

Dadukou Gangtie Chang 大渡口钢铁厂: Dadukou Iron and Steel Works

Dafengtang mingji 大風堂名蹟: an illustrated catalog

Dagong bao 大公报 (大公報): Dagong daily, L'impartial

dagong mei 打工妹: working sisters

"**Dahai hangxing kao duoshou**" 大海航行靠舵手: Sailing the seas depends on the helmsman

Dahua Baoxian Gongsi 大華保險公司: China General Insurance Company

dai hongmaozi 戴红帽子: wearing the red hat

Dai Jitao 戴季陶

Dai Li 戴笠

Dai Qing 戴晴

Dai Tōa Kyōei Ken 大東亜共荣圈 (大東亞共榮圈): Greater East Asia Co-prosperity Sphere

Dai Wangshu 戴望舒

Dai Zhen 戴震

Daibu Juliu Tiaoli 逮捕拘留条例: Regulations on Arrest and Detention

daimyō 大名: Japanese feudal lords

Dairen 大連

daiye qingnian 待业青年: young persons waiting for jobs

daiyezhe 待业者: young persons waiting for jobs

daiyu 带鱼: hairtail

Daiyun Shanmai 戴云山脉: Daiyun mountain range

Daizu 傣族: Dai minority

dajia 大家: great painter

dajun 大军: fronts

Dakulun 大库仑: Ikh Huree

Dalai Lama 达赖喇嘛

Dali 大理

Dali Baizu Zizhi Zhou 大理白族自治州: Dali Bai Autonomous Prefecture

Dali Si 大理寺: Court of Judicial Review

Dali Yuan 大理院: Court of Judicial Review

Dalian 大连

Dalini 达里泥: Dalny

"Dalu ge" 大路歌: Song of the big road

Dalu Shiwu Weiyuanhui 大陆事务委员会: Mainland Affairs Council

Dalu Yinhang 大陆银行: Continental Bank

Daminghu 大明湖: Daming Lake

Damingsi 大明寺: Daming Temple

dan 担 (擔): picul, 145 pounds

dan 旦: female role type in Peking Opera

Dan jian pian 胆剑篇 (膽劍篇): Gall and sword

dang 党: party, faction

dang tianxia 党天下 (黨天下): party empire, all under the party

dang'an 档案 (檔案): personnel dossier

danghua 党化: partify, extend the party's influence into

dangwai 黨外: Taiwanese opposition before 1986

Dangxiangzu 党项族: Tanguts

Dangxiao 党校: Party School

Dangzi 氹仔: Taipa

dangzu 党组: party group

Danmin 蜑民: Dan people, Tanka, boat people

Danshui 淡水: Dan River, also a city on Taiwan, Tamsui

danwei 单位 (單位): work unit, agency

danxian pingtu 单线平涂: single-outline and flat-color technique

dao 道: circuit

Dao 道: the Way

"Dao diren houfang qu" 到敌人后方去: Go to the enemy's rear

Dao Lang 刀郎

Dao ziran qu 到自然去: Return to nature

Daodejing 道德经: Classic of the way and virtue

Daoguang 道光: emperor (r. 1821–1850)

Daojiao 道教: Daoism

Daomazei 盗马贼: *Horse Thief*

daoshi 道士: ordained Daoist priest

daotai 道台 (道臺): viceroy, governor, circuit intendent

Daoxue 道学 (道學): learning of the way

Daoyuan 道院: School of the Way

Daozang 道藏: Daoist canon

Daqing 大庆

Daqing Yinhang 大清银行: Daqing Bank

Daqing Youtian 大庆油田: Daqing Oil Fields

dasao ganjing wuzi zai qingke 打扫干净屋子再请客: cleaning up the house first before receiving guests

Dasheng Shachang 大生纱厂: Dasheng Cotton Mill

Dashou 达受 (達受)

Datang Dianxin Keji Chanye Jituan 大唐电信科技产业集团: Datang Telecom Technology and Industry Group

Datang Guoji Fadian Gufen Youxian Gongsi 大唐国际发电股份有限公司: Datang International Power Generation Co.

datong 大同: place name

datong 大同: great unity, great harmony

Datong shu 大同书 (大同書): Book of great unity

Datong Xuexiao 大同学校: Datong School

daxieyi 大写意 (大寫意): greater free-hand brushwork

Daxin Gongsi 大新公司: Da Sun Department Store

Daxue 大学: *Great Learning*

Daxue Jiaoyu Zizhu Weiyuanhui 大学教育资助委员会: University Grants Committee

Daxue Xingdong Fangan 大学行动方案: University Act

Daxueyuan 大学院: Higher Education Council

Dayan Ta 大雁塔: Big Wild Goose Pagoda

dayang 大洋: dragon dollars

Dayanhe 大堰河: Dayan River

da-Yazhouzhuyi 大亚洲主义: pan-Asianism

Daye Tiekuang 大冶铁矿: Daye Iron Mines

dayi 大义 (大義): great principles

Dayi 大颐 (大頤)

dayuanshuai 大元帅 (大元帥): generalissimo

Dayuejin 大跃进: Great Leap Forward

Dazhai 大寨

Dazhai Shengchandui 大寨生产队: Dazhai Production Team

Dazheng Dian 大政殿: Great Administration Hall

dazhong caipu 大众菜谱: recipes for the working masses

dazhong jiti geyue 大众集体歌乐: collective songs and music for the masses

Dazhong Muke Yanjiuhui 大众木刻研究会: Mass Woodcut Research Society

Dazhong shenghuo 大众生活: Mass life

Dazhong sheying 大众摄影

dazhong shitang caipu 大众食堂菜谱: canteen recipes for the working masses

dazhong yinyue 大众音乐: music of the masses

dazhonghua 大众化: popularize

dazibao 大字报: big-character poster

de 德: morality, virtue

De Wang 德王

De xiansheng 德先生: Mr. Democracy

Demokelaxi xiansheng 德漠克拉西先生: Mr. Democracy

Deng Lijun 邓丽君: Teresa Teng

Deng Shi 邓实

Deng Shu 邓树

Deng Tingzhen 邓廷桢

Deng Tuo 邓拓

Deng Xiaohua 邓小华

Deng Xiaoping 邓小平 (鄧小平)

Deng Xiaoping nanxun 邓小平南巡: Deng Xiaoping's southern tour

Deng Yanda 邓演达 (鄧演達)

Deng Yaping 邓亚萍

Deng Yingchao 邓颖超 (鄧穎超)

Deng Zhongyuan 邓仲元

Deqing 德清

Dezhou 德州

di 邸: liaison hostel

di bao 邸报: Han court gazette

Di Baoxian 狄葆贤

di chao 邸抄: court gazette

Dajia Wenxue Jiang 大家文学奖: Dajia Award

dian 典: conditional land sale, a transfer of possession of immovable property with the option of either redemption or sale at an adjusted price in the future

Dianjiangti Wuli Yanjiusuo 电浆体物理研究所: Institute of Plasma Physics

Dianshizhai huabao 点石斋画报 (點石齋畫報): Dianshi Studio pictorial

Dianying Zhipian, Faxing, Fangying Jingying Zige Zhunru Zanxing Guiding 电影制片、发行、放映经营资格准入暂行规定: Temporary Regulations for Permission of Film Production, Distribution, and Exhibition

Dianzi Gongye Bu 电子工业部: Ministry of Electronics Industry

diao 吊: string of 1, 000 copper coins

diaoke yinshua 雕刻印刷: xylography, woodblock printing

diaolou 碉樓: watchtowers

Diaotonghuan 吊桶环

Diaoyutai 钓鱼台

Diaoyutai Guobing Guan 钓鱼台国宾馆: Diaoyutai State Guest House

dibao 地保: elderly, respected person

didang 帝党 (帝黨): faction of the emperor

diding yin 地丁银: land-poll tax

dier chanye 第二產業: secondary sector

Dier Fangmian Jun 第二方面軍: Second Front Army

Dier Paobing Budui 第二炮兵部队: Second Artillery Corps

Dierci Guo-Gong Hezuo 第二次国共合作 (第二次國共合作): second United Front

dierci sixiang jiefang 第二次思想解放: second liberation of thought

Diershijiujie Oulinpike Yundong Hui Zuzhi Weiyuanhui 第29届奥林匹克运动会组织委员会: Beijing Organizing Committee for the Games of the XXIX Olympiad

difang guanyuan 地方官员: field administration

difang shui 地方税: local taxes

difang xingzheng quyu tiaozheng quan 地方行政区域调整权: local-administrative-region adjustment right

difang zhi 地方志: local gazetteer

diji 地级: regional level

diji shi 地级市: prefectural-level municipalities

Dili Yanjiusuo 地理研究所: Institute of Geography

Ding Cong 丁聪 (丁聰)

Ding En 丁恩: Sir Richard Dane

Ding Guangxun 丁光训: K. H. Ting

Ding Li 丁力

Ding Ling 丁玲

Ding Richang 丁日昌

Ding Ruchang 丁汝昌

Ding Shande 丁善德

Ding Song 丁悚

Ding Wenjiang 丁文江

Ding Wenwei 丁文蔚

Ding Xilin 丁西林

Ding Yanyong 丁衍庸: Ting Yin-yung

dinggou 订购: purchase by order

Dinghai 定海

Dingji Daxue he Yanjiu Zhongxin Xiangmu 顶级大学和研究中心项目: Top Universities and Research Centers Project

Dingwujun 定武军: Pacification Army

Dingxian 定县: Ding County

Dingxian Pingmin Jiaoyu Yundong 定县平民教育运动 (定縣平民教育運動): Mass Education Movement at Dingxian

Dingzhuang meng 丁庄梦 (丁庄夢): Dreams of Ding Village

dingzi 锭子 (錠子): silver ingot

Dinü Hua 帝女花: The flower princess

Diqi Jiandui 第七舰队: Seventh Fleet

Diqiang 氐羌: ancient minority

"Diqiu, wo de muqin" 地球，我的母亲 (地球，我的母親): Earth, my mother

Dilikexue he Ziyuan Yanjiusuo 地理科学和资源研究所: Institute of Geographic Sciences and Natural Resources

diqu 地区: prefecture

diquji 地区级: prefectural level

disan chanye 第三产业: tertiary sector

Disan Dang 第三党 (第三黨): The Third Party

disanzhong ren 第三种人 (第三種人): third category of men

Disi Fangmian Jun 第四方面軍: Fourth Front Army

Ditan 地坛 (地壇): Temple of Earth

Dixiongmen 弟兄们: *Brothers*

diya 地押: loan secured by land

diyi chanye 第一產業: primary sector

Diyi Fangmian Jun 第一方面軍: First Front Army

diyi fuzhuxi 第一副主席: first vice chairman

Diyici Guo-Gong Hezuo 第一次国共合作 (第一次國共合作): first United Front

Dokuritsu Bijutsu Kyōkai 独立美術協会: Independent Art Association

Dong Biwu 董必武

Dong Cunrui 董存瑞

Dong Dayou 董大酉

Dong Hai 东海: East China Sea

Dong Huai 董槐

Dong Jianhua 董建华: Tung Chee Hwa

Dong Qichang 董其昌

Dong Qing Tielu 东清铁路 (東清鐵路): Chinese Eastern Railway

Dong Qizhang 董启章: Dung Kai Cheung

Dong Xi wenhua ji qi zhexue 东西文化及其哲学 (東西文化及其哲學): Eastern and Western cultures and their philosophies

Dong xie xi du 东邪西毒 (東邪西毒): *Ashes of Time*

Dong Xiwen 董希文

Dong Xun 董恂

Dong Yangzi 董陽孜: Grace Tong

Dong Zhongshu 董仲舒

Dong Zuobin 董作宾 (董作賓)

dongba 东巴: Naxi male ritual experts

Dongbei 东北: the Northeast, Manchuria

Dongbei Daxue 东北大学 (東北大學): Northeastern University

Dongbei hua 东北话: Northeast Mandarin

Dongbei ren 东北人: people from the Northeast

Dongbei Tushuguan Dang'an Bu 东北图书馆档案部 (東北圖書館檔案部): Archives Section of the Northeastern Library

Dongcun 东村: East Village (Beijing)

Dongdishi Bashiwu Guoji Guangchang 东帝士85国际广场 (東帝士85國際廣場): Tuntex Sky Tower

Dongfang Baidai 东方百代 (東方百代): Pathé-Orient

Dongfang Binguan 东方宾馆: Dongfang Hotel

Dongfang Shandian 东方闪电 (東方閃電): Eastern Lightning

Dongfang yu xiao 东方欲晓: Dawning in the east

Dongfang zazhi 东方杂志 (東方雜誌): Eastern miscellany

Dongfanghong yinyue wudao shishi 东方红音乐舞蹈史诗: The East is red song and dance epic

Dongfeng Qiche Gongsi 东风汽车公司: Dongfeng (automaker)

Donggong xigong 东宫西宫: *East Palace, West Palace*

Dongguan 东莞

Donghai Daxue 东海大学 (東海大學): Tunghai University

Donghu Xin Jishu Kaifaqu 东湖新技术开发区: Donghu New Technology District

Dongjiang 东江: East River

Dongjing Mei Gongsi 東京煤公司: Hongay Coal Company

Dongling 东陵 (東陵)

dongsansheng 东三省: three eastern provinces

Dongshan 东山

dongshi 懂事: understand matters

Dongtai ribao 东台日报 (東台日報): Dongtai daily

Dongtinghu 洞庭湖: Dongting Lake

Dongwen Xueshe 东文学社 (東文學社): Eastern Language Institute

Dongwu Daxue 东吴大学 (東吳大學): Dongwu University, Soochow University

Dongwu xiongmeng 动物凶猛: Wild beasts

Dongyao 动摇: Vacillation

Dongying 东营

Dongzhi 冬至: Winter Solstice Festival

Dongzhuang 东庄

Dongzu 侗族: Dong minority

douban 餖板: multicolor printing

dougong 斗栱: bracket-arm set

Du Fu 杜甫

Du Fu caotang 杜甫草堂: Du Fu's thatched cottage

du jing 读经: reading the classics

Du Wanxiang 杜晚香

Du Weiming 杜维明: Tu Wei-ming

Du Wenxiu 杜文秀

Du Yuesheng 杜月笙

Duan Fang 端方

Duan Men 端门 (端門): Gate of Uprightness

Duan Qirui 段祺瑞

duanao 短袄: short jacket, jacket-blouse

Duanbishan 断臂山: *Brokeback Mountain*

"**Duanhong lingyan ji**" 断鸿零雁记: The lone swan

Duanmu Hongliang 端木蕻良

duanxian pingheng 短线平衡: equilibrium under constraints

Duchayuan 都察院: Censorate

duijing xiesheng 對景寫生: on-site painting or sketching from nature

"**Duizhang shuji yemao he banjiekuai de gushi**" 队长书记野猫和半截筷的故事: The story of the brigade chief's secretary, the feral cat, and half a chopstick

Dujiangyan 都江堰

dujun 督军: military governor

Dulesi 独乐寺 (獨樂寺): Dule Temple

Duli meishu 獨立美術: Independent art (journal)

duli ren'ge 独立人格: independent personhood

Dumen jilüe 都门纪略 (都門紀略): A glimpse of the capital gates

Dunhuang 敦煌

Dunhuang wu 敦煌舞: Dunhuang Dance

Duoduo 多多

Duoluo tianshi 堕落天使 (墮落天使): *Fallen Angels*

Dushu 读书: Reading

E Qie 莪伽

edu gongji weida lingxiu 恶毒攻击伟大领袖: vicious attacks on the great leader

E'erduosi 鄂尔多斯: Ordos

E'erduosi Shamo 鄂尔多斯沙漠: Ordos Desert

"**Eguo shehui yundong shihua**" 俄国社会运动史话: On the history of Russian social movements

Eqiao Shiwu Ju 俄侨事务局 (俄僑事務局): Bureau for the Affairs of Russian Émigrés

Er Ma 二马 (二馬): *Ma and Son, The Two Ma's*

erchong zhengju fa 二重证据法 (二重證據法): the method of coalescing dual evidence

erhu 二胡: a Chinese two-stringed bowed fiddle

erhuang 二黄: a style of operatic singing

Erhuanlu 二环路: Second Ring Road

erlei shangpin 二类商品: category two goods

2004 Nian Jiaoyu Xiuding Tiaoli 2004 年教育修订条例: Education (Amendment) Ordinance 2004

Erlitou 二里头

Ershinian mudu zhi guai xianzhuang 二十年目睹之怪现状 (二十年目睹之怪現狀): Strange events eyewitnessed in the last twenty years

Ertong Quanli Gongyue 儿童权利公约: Convention on the Rights of the Child

Ertong shidai 儿童时代: Childhood times

Erwu Jianzu 二五减租: Rent Reduction Program

erxian 二線: second border

Erya 尔雅 (爾雅): Near to correctness, an early dictionary

Erzi de da wan'ou 儿子的大玩偶 (兒子的大玩偶): *The Sandwich Man*

Eshi jingwen 俄事警闻 (俄事警聞): Warning of Russian issues

fabi 法币 (法幣): legal tender

faguan 法官: elite Daoist priest

Faguan Fa 法官法: Judges Law

Falü Gongzuo Weiyuanhui 法律工作委员会: Legislative Work Committee

falun dafa 法轮大法: the great way of the dharma wheel

Falun Gong 法轮功: discipline of the revolving dharma wheel

Famensi 法门寺: Famen Temple

fan 饭: rice

Fan Bu Zhengdang Jingzheng Fa 反不正当竞争法: Law against Unfair Competition

Fan Changjiang 范长江 (範長江)

fan cheng feng 返城风: the atmosphere of returning to the cities

Fan Dizhi Zhanzheng 反帝制战争 (反帝制戰爭): Anti-monarchical War

fan Jiang 反蒋: opposition to Chiang Kai-shek

Fan Shi Yizhuang 范氏义庄 (范氏義莊): Fan Clan Charitable Estate

Fan Wenlan 范文澜 (范文瀾)

Fan Xiaomei 樊晓梅

Fan Yanqiao 范烟桥

Fan Zhongyan 范仲淹

fang 房: lineage branch

Fang Dongmei 方东美

Fang Dongshu 方东树 (方東樹)

Fang Fang 方方

Fang Junbi 方君璧

Fang Keli 方克立

Fang Lijun 方力钧

Fang Rending 方人定

Fang Yuping 方育平: Allen Fong

Fang Zengxian 方增先

Fang Zhaoling 方召麟

Fang Zhenzhu 方珍珠

fangbu 方补: rank badge

Fangcun 芳村

fangdan 坊单 (坊單): document of ownership during the Qing

Fangeming Baoluan 反革命暴乱: Tiananmen Incident (1989)

Fangfei zhi ge 芳菲之歌: The song of flowers

fanglüe 方略: general plans, achievements

fangong dalu 反攻大陆: retaking mainland China

Fangqu Zhi 防区制: System of Defense Districts

fangshan fanzhuang 仿膳饭庄: a restaurant imitating imperial cuisine

fangweipai 方位派: directions and positions school

fangzhang 房长 (房長): branch head in a lineage

fanqie 反切: a system of indicating the pronunciation of characters

fansi wenxue 反思文学: reflection literature

fantizi 繁体字: traditional characters

Fanxing 繁星: Myriad stars

fanying lun 反映论 (反映論): theory of reflection

fanyoupai yundong 反右派运动: antirightist movement

fanyou yundong 反右运动: antirightist campaign

fatie 法帖: model writings

Faxiang 法相: a school of Buddhism

fazhan guihua 发展规划: development guidelines

fazhan quan 发展权: right to development

Fazhan Yanjiu Zhongxin 发展研究中心: China Development Center, Development Research Center

fei 费: surtaxes

Fei Danxu 费丹旭

fei Jidujiao yundong 非基督教运动 (非基督教運動): anti-Christian movement

fei liang gai yuan 废两改圆: abolishing silver bullion and introducing the Chinese silver yuan

Fei Ming 废名 (廢名)

Fei Mu 费穆

Fei Xiaotong 费孝通 (費孝通)

Feichang Jianzhu 非常建筑: Atelier Feichang Jianzhu

Feidu 废都: Abandoned capital, Ruined capital

feihuang 飞蝗 (飛蝗): migratory locusts

Feilengcui de yiye 翡冷翠的一夜: A Night in Florence

feiwuzhi wenhua yichan 非物質文化遺產: intangible cultural heritage

feixing fengshui 飞星风水: flying-star geomancy

feixing qi 飞行棋 (飛行棋): Parcheesi

Feixixian 肥西县: Feixi County

Feiyingge huabao 飛影閣畫報: Feiyingge illustrated magazine

Feng 枫: Maple

Feng Boheng 冯伯衡

Feng Guifen 冯桂芬

Feng Guozhang 冯国璋

Feng Jicai 冯骥才 (馮驥才)

Feng Menglong 冯梦龙

Feng Wenbing 冯文炳

Feng Xiaogang 冯小刚

Feng Xuefeng 冯雪峰 (馮雪峰)

Feng Youlan 冯友兰

Feng Yuanjun 冯沅君

Feng Yuxiang 冯玉祥 (馮玉祥)

Feng Zhi 冯至

Feng Zikai 丰子恺 (豐子愷)

Fenggui lai de ren 風櫃來的人: *The Boys of Fengui*

Fenghua 奉化

Fenghuang 凤凰 (鳳凰): Phoenix

Fenghuang Lou 凤凰楼 (鳳凰樓): Phoenix Tower

"Fenghuang niepan" 凤凰涅磐 (鳳凰涅磐): Nirvana of the phoenix

fengjian 封建: feudal

fengjian zhi 封建制: enfeoffment system

fengjianzhuyi 封建主义: feudalism

fengpiao 奉票: Fengtian dollar

Fengru feitun 丰乳肥臀: *Big Breasts and Wide Hips*

fengshui 风水 (風水): geomancy

Fengtian 奉天

Fengxian 奉贤

Fengyangxian 凤阳县: Fengyang County

Feng-Ya-Song 风雅颂: a string quartet

Fengyue 风月: *Temptress Moon*

Fengyun ernü 風雲兒女: Children of troubled times

"Fengzheng piaodai" 风筝飘带: Kite streamers

Fengzi 凤子: Phoenix

Fenhe 汾河: Fen River

fenjia 分家: household division

fenshuizhi 分税制: tax-sharing system

fensi 分司: subcommission

fenzao chifan 分灶吃饭: eating from separate kitchens

Fogongsi 佛宫寺: Fogong Temple

Foguangshansi 佛光山寺: Foguangshan Monastery

Foguangsi 佛光寺: Foguang Temple

Fojiao Xiejin Hui 佛教协进会: Association for the Advancement of Buddhism

Foshan 佛山

Fotiaoqiang 佛跳墙: Buddha jumps over the wall (restaurant)

Fou Lei 傅雷

Foxiang Ge 佛香阁 (佛香閣): Buddha Fragrance Tower

Foxue Yanjiuhui 佛学研究会: Buddhist Research Society

fu 府: prefecture

Fu Baoshi 傅抱石

Fu Hao 婦好

Fu Mingxia 伏明霞

Fu Sinian 傅斯年

Fu yu zi 父与子: *Fathers and Sons*

Fujian 福建: Hokkien

Fujian Bowuguan 福建博物馆: Fujian Museum

Fujian Shifan Daxue 福建师范大学 (福建師範大學): Fujian Normal University

Fujishima Takeji 藤島武二

Fukang'an 福康安

fukua 浮夸: exaggeration

Fukuda Hideko 福田英子

Fukuzawa Yukichi 福沢諭吉 (福澤諭吉)

fulao 父老: elders

Fulian 妇联: All-China Women's Federation

fumu baoban 父母包办: Arranged Marriage

Funanhe 府南河: Funan River

funü jiefang 妇女解放: women's liberation

Funü Lianhehui 妇女联合会: All-China Women's Federation, Women's Association

Funü neng ding banbian tian 妇女能顶半边天: Women hold up half the sky

fupin daikuan 扶贫贷款: poverty loan program

fuqiang 富强: wealth and power

Fuqin 父亲: *Father*

Furen Daxue 辅仁大学 (輔仁大學): Furen University, Fu Jen Catholic University

Furong yuanyang tu 芙蓉鴛鴦圖: *Hibiscus and Mandarin Ducks*

Furong zhen 芙蓉镇: *A Small Town Called Hibiscus*

"Furong zhen" 芙蓉镇: a short story

Fushun 抚顺

fuwu bumen 服务部门: services

Fuxin 阜新

Fuxing Gongyuan 复兴公园: Fuxing Park

Fuzao 浮躁: *Turbulence*

Fuzhou 福州

Fuzhou Chuanzheng Xuetang 福州船政学堂 (福州船政學堂): Fuzhou Naval School

Fuzhou Dudufu 福州都督府: Fuzhou Area Military Command

fuzhuxi 副主席: state vice president (literally, vice chairman)

Gai Qi 改琦

gaige 改革: reform

gaige kaifang 改革开放: reform and opening up, economic reforms

gaige shiyanqu 改革实验区: reform experiment zone

gailiang 改良: reformed or improved

gaizupai 改组派 (改組派): reorganization clique

Gajupai 噶举派: *bka'brgyud* (Kagyu) Tibetan Vajrayāna Buddhism

Gan Shaocheng 甘少城

Gan Yang 甘阳

ganbu 干部: cadre

ganbu zhifu 干部制服: cadre suit

gandalei 干打垒: rammed dry earth

Gandu Yeyu 港都夜雨

gang 纲 (綱): syndicates

Gangdu 港都

Gang-Tai yinyue 港台音乐: a popular music style from Hong Kong and Taiwan

ganhua 感化: moral reform

Ganjiang 赣江: Gan River

Ganjingzi 甘井子

ganqing 感情: feelings of affection, closeness

Gansu 甘肃

ganying 感应 (感應): cosmic resonance

Ganzhou 赣州

Ganzi Zangzu Zizhizhou 甘孜藏族自治州: Ganzi Tibetan Autonomous Prefecture

Gao Gang 高岗

Gao Jianfu 高剑父 (高劍父)

Gao Jianqun 高建群

Gao Qifeng 高奇峰

Gao Xiaohua 高小华

Gao Xiaosheng 高晓声 (高曉聲)

Gao Xingjian 高行健

Gao Xiqing 高西庆

Gao Yaoji 高耀潔

Gao Yong 高邕

Gao Zhisheng 高智晟

gaodeng zhuanye xuetang 高等专业学堂: higher specialty college

gaogan zidi 高干子弟: princeling

gaoji ganbu 高级干部: superior-ranked cadres

gaokao 高考: national college-entrance examinations

Gaolaozhuang 高老庄: Old Gao Village

gaoliang 高粱: sorghum

Gaosheng 高升: Kowshing

Gaoshi zhuan 高士傳: Lives of high-minded men

Gaoxi 高溪

gaoxin jishu kaifaqu 高新技术开发区: high-tech development zone

Gaoxing 高兴: Happiness

Gaoxiong 高雄: Kaohsiung

Gaoxiong Shijian 高雄事件: Gaoxiong Incident

Gaoxiongshili Meishuguan 高雄市立美術館: Kaohsiung Museum of Fine Arts

Gaoyang 高阳

Gaoyouhu 高邮湖: Lake Gaoyou

ge 隔: opaquely

Ge Fei 格非

Ge Gongzhen 戈公振

Ge You 葛优

Ge'ermu 格尔木: Golmud

Gebi Shamo 戈壁沙漠: Gobi Desert

Gebi Tan 戈壁滩: Gobi Desert

"Gechang Wuchan Jieji Wenhua Da Geming" 歌唱无产阶级文化大革命: Ode to the Great Proletarian Cultural Revolution

"Gechang zuguo" 歌唱祖国: Ode to the motherland

gedai hu 隔代户: skipped-generation household

Gedake 噶大克: Gartok

gedimu 格底目，格迪目: Muslim communities based around local mosques

Gegentala 格根塔拉

Gejiu 个旧

Gelaohui 哥老会: Society of Elder Brothers

Gelaozu 仡佬族: Gelao minority

Gelupai 格鲁派: *dge lugs* (Gelug) Tibetan Buddhism

geming gequ 革命歌曲: revolutionary songs

Geming gequ xuanji 革命歌曲选集: Compilation of revolutionary songs

geming langmangzhuyi 革命浪漫主义: revolutionary romanticism

Geming minge ji 革命民歌集: A collection of revolutionary folksongs

Geming Shijian Yanjiuyuan 革命實踐研究院: Revolutionary Practice Institute

geming xiandai jingju 革命现代京剧 (革命现代京劇): modern revolutionary Peking Operas

geming xiandai wuju 革命现代舞剧: revolutionary modern ballet

geming yangbanxi 革命样板戏: revolutionary model theater

Gemingdang 革命黨: Revolutionary Party

geminghua 革命化: revolutionize

Geng Biao 耿飚

Geng Huichang 耿惠昌

Geng Qingguo 耿庆国

Gengzi Peikuan 庚子赔款 (庚子賠款): Boxer Indemnity

Genü Hongmudan 歌女红牡丹 (歌女紅牡丹): Singsong girl Red Peony

gerenhua 个人化: individualization

Geti Laodongzhe Xiehui 个体劳动者协会: Self-Employed Laborers Association

getihu 个体户: individual household businesses, small-scale individual enterprises

Geyao yanjiuhui 歌谣研究会: Folksong Research Society

Geyao zhoukan 歌谣周刊: Folksong weekly

Gezhouba 葛洲坝: Gezhou Dam

go 碁: go (board game)

Guoluo 果洛: Golog

gong 公: public

gong huayuan 公花园: public flower garden

Gong Jin Ou 巩金瓯: To consolidate our country (national anthem)

Gong Li 巩俐

Gong Liu 公刘

Gong qinwang 恭亲王 (恭親王): Prince Gong

Gong Yixin 恭奕欣 (恭奕訢): Prince Gong

Gong Zizhen 龚自珍 (龔自珍)

gong'an 公安: public security

Gong'an Bu 公安部: Ministry of Public Security

gong'an ju 公安局: public security bureau

gongbihua 工笔画 (工筆畫): finely detailed painting, fine line painting

Gongchan Guoji 共产国际 (共產國際): Comintern

Gongchandang 共产党 (共產黨): Communist Party

Gongchandang Daibiao Dahui 共产党代表大会: Communist Party Congress

Gongchandang Zhongyang Weiyuanhui 共产党中央委员会: Communist Party Central Committee

Gongchanzhuyi Qingnian Tuan 共产主义青年团: Communist Youth League

Gongchanzhuyizhe 共产主义者: The communist

Gongche Shangshu 公车上书 (公車上書): a petition of metropolitan candidates opposed to the Treaty of Shimonoseki

Gongchen Qiao 拱宸桥: Gongchen Bridge

Gongcheng zuofa zeli 工程做法则例 (工程做法則例): Construction methods

gongfei sheng 公费生 (公費生): government-sponsored students

gongfei yiliao baoxian 公费医疗保险: public medical insurance

gongfen 工分: work points

gonggong zujie 公共租界: international settlement

gonghang 公行: cohong (authorized foreign traders)

gonghe 共和: republican polity

Gongheguo jiaokeshu 共和国教科书: Republican readers

Gonghui Fa 工会法: Trade Union Law

Gongmin Quanli He Zhengzhi Quanli Guoji Gongyue 公民权利和政治权力国际公约: International Covenant on Civil and Political Rights

gongmin shehui 公民社会: civil society

gongnongbing 工农兵: worker-peasant-soldier

gongpan dahui 公判大会: sentencing rallies

gongren 工人: worker

Gongren Tiyu Chang 工人体育场: Beijing Workers Stadium

gongshe 公社: commune

gongsi 公司: company, corporation

Gongsi Fa 公司法: Company Law

Gongsi Lü 公司律: Company Law

Gongsi Tiaoli 公司条例: 1914 Company Regulation

gongsi zhili 公司治理: corporate governance

gongsuo 公所: professional guild

Gongtong Gangling 共同纲领: Common Program

Gongyang zhuan 公羊传 (公羊傳): Gongyang commentary

gongye 工业: industry

Gongye he Xinxihua Bu 工业和信息化部: Ministry of Industry and Information

gongyijin 公益金: public welfare funds

gongyuan 公园: park, public garden

gongzaishu 公仔书 (公仔書): children's picture book

gongzuo danwei 工作单位: work unit

goujian hexie shehui 构建和谐社会: building a harmonious society

Gu Cheng 顾城

Gu Dexin 顾德新

Gu Gong 顾工

Gu Heqing 顾鹤庆

Gu Hua 古华

Gu Jiegang 顾颉刚 (顧頡剛)

Gu Jizhui Dongwu yu Gu Renlei Yanjiusuo 古脊椎动物与古人类研究所: Institute of Vertebrate Paleontology and Paleoanthropology

Gu Linshi 顾麟士

Gu Qingyao 顾青瑶

Gu Weijun 顾维钧 (顧維鈞): Wellington Koo

Gu Wenda 谷文达 (谷文達)

Gu Yanwu 顾炎武 (顧炎武)

Gu Yishu Baocun Hui 古艺术保存会: Society for Preserving Ancient Art

Gu Yuan 古元

Gu Zhenfu 辜振甫: Koo Chen-fu

guaizi 拐子: knucklebones

guan 官: official, magistrate

guan chi 关尺 (關尺): maritime customs foot

Guan Daosheng 管道升

Guan Hanqing 关汉卿

Guan Liang 关良 (關良)

Guan Moye 管谟业

Guan Shanyue 关山月

Guan Zilan 关紫兰 (關紫蘭)

Guancha 观察 (觀察): The observer

Guanchang xianxing ji 官场现形记 (官場現形記): The bureaucrat: A revelation

guanchao 关钞: internal customs duties

Guandi 关帝 (關帝): Emperor Guan

Guandong 关东

guandu shangban 官督商办 (官督商辦): government supervision and merchant management

Guang chi 广尺 (廣尺): Guangdong foot

Guang Weiran 光未然

Guang yizhou shuangji 广艺舟双楫 (廣藝舟雙楫): Two oars of the boat of art, expanded

Guang'an 广安

Guangbo Dianshi Guanli Tiaoli 广播电视管理条例: Regulatory Measures for Radio and Television

Guangbo Dianying Dianshi Zongju 广播电影电视总局: State Administration of Radio, Film, and Television

Guangbo Yingshi Xinwen Caibian Renyuan Congye Guanli de Shishi Fang'an 广播影视新闻采编人员从业管理的实施方案: Implementation Plan for the Management of Radio and Audiovisual Journalists

Guangchu Si 广储司 (廣儲司): Department of the Privy Purse

Guangdong 广东

Guangdong Nongmin Jiangxi Suo 广东农民讲习所: Guangdong Peasants Lecture Hall

guange ti 馆阁体 (館閣體): examination-hall style

Guangfu Hui 光复会 (光復會): Restoration Society

guanggao 广告 (廣告): advertising

Guangling chao 广陵潮: Tides of Yangzhou

Guangling Shushe 广陵书社 (廣陵書社): Guangling Publishing Company

Guangming ribao 光明日报 (光明日報): Guangming daily

Guangren 广仁

Guangxi 广西

Guangxin 广信

Guangxu 光绪 (光緒): emperor (r. 1875–1908)

Guangya Shuyuan 广雅书院: Guangya Academy

Guangyin de gushi 光阴的故事 (光陰的故事): *In Our Time*

Guangzhou 广州: Canton

Guangzhou hua 广州话: Cantonese

Guangzhou Jingji Jishu Kaifaqu 广州经济技术开发区: Guangzhou Economic and Technological Development Zone

Guangzhou Zhongshan Daxue 广州中山大学 (廣州中山大學): Zhongshan University

Guangzhouwan 广州湾: Guangzhou Bay

guanli danwei 管理单位: management unit

Guanli Jiguan Yingye Guize 管理妓馆营业规则: Regulations Governing the Brothel Business

Guannian 21 Xingwei Huodong 观念21 行为活动: Concept 21 Action Art

guannian sheying 观念摄影: conceptual photography

guanshui 关税: internal customs duties

Guantang 观堂 (觀堂)

Guanwu Shu 关务署 (關務署): Customs Administration

guanxi 关系: personal connections, informal social networks

guanxi mafan 关系麻烦: the bother of connections

guanxiwang 关系网: connection network

guanxixue 关系学: the art of social connections, the art of getting things done

guanxue 管学 (管學): official schools

guanyinhao 官银号: official money shops

"Guanyu lingdao fangfa de ruogan wenti" 关于领导方法的若干问题 (關於領導方法的若干問題): Some questions concerning methods of leadership

Guanyu Zhongguo jin yibu shishi ershiyi richeng de jianyi 关于中国进一步实施二十一日程的建议: Opinions for further implementation of China's Agenda 21

Guanyu Zujin Shijie Heping yu Hezuo de Xuanyan 关于促进世界和平与合作的宣言: Declaration on the Promotion of World Peace and Cooperation

guanzhen 官箴: official handbooks

Guanzhui bian 管锥编: Pipe and awl collection

guapimao 瓜皮帽: man's round cap

guasha 刮痧: to scrape for fever and pain

guci 鼓词: folk literary form accompanied by drum

gudong 古董, 骨董: antiquities

"Guduzhe" 孤独者 (孤獨者): The misanthrope

gufen hehuo 股份合伙: limited partnerships

gufen hezuo qiye 股份合作企业: cooperative shareholding enterprise

gufen lianghe gongsi 股份两合公司: companies with limited- and unlimited-liability shareholders

gufen youxian gongsi 股份有限公司: joint-stock limited-liability company

Gugong Bowuyuan 故宫博物院: Palace Museum

guhua 古画: antique Chinese painting

guifei 贵妃 (貴妃): honored consort

Guifei zuijiu 贵妃醉酒 (貴妃醉酒): An imperial concubine gets tipsy

Guijin 闺瑾

Guilai de ge 归来的歌: Songs of return

Guiliang 桂良

Guilin 桂林

guimao xuezhi 癸卯学制 (癸卯學制): 1903 school system

guiqiao 归侨 (歸僑): returned overseas Chinese

Guiqulai xi 归去来兮 (歸去來兮): Returning

guiren 贵人 (貴人): worthy lady

guishushi 闺塾师 (閨塾師): teachers of the inner chambers

Guixi 桂系

Guiyang Huayuan 贵阳画院 (貴陽畫院): Guiyang Painting Academy

Guizhou 贵州

Guizi lai le 鬼子来了: *Devils on the Doorstep*

Gujing Jingshe 诂经精社: Academy for Glossing the Classics

Gulangyu 鼓浪屿

Guling 牯岭

Guo Fucheng 郭富城: Aaron Kwok Fu-Shing

Guo Jin 郭晋

Guo Jingjing 郭晶晶

Guo Jingming 郭敬明

Guo Kaizhen 郭开贞 (郭開貞)

Guo Le 郭乐 (郭樂): Guo Luo

Guo Lin 郭林

Guo Lusheng 郭路生

Guo Moruo 郭沫若

Guo Pu 郭璞

Guo Quan 郭泉: Guo Chuan

Guo Shixing 过士行

Guo Songdao 郭嵩焘

Guo Wei 郭伟

Guo Wenjing 郭文景

Guobi Tiaoli 国币条例: Legal Tender Act

Guobie Zhanlüe yu Guihua 国别战略与规划: Country Strategy and Program

Guochao huazheng lu 国朝画徵录: Painting annals of the present dynasty

guocui 国粹 (國粹): national essence

Guocui xuebao 国粹学报 (國粹學報): National essence journal

Guocui yuekan 国粹月刊: National essence monthly

Guofang Bu 国防部 (國防部): Ministry of National Defense

Guofang Daxue 国防大学: National Defense University

Guofang Kexue Jishu Gongye Weiyuanhui 国防科学技术工业委员会: Commission of Science, Technology, and Industry for National Defense

guofang wenxue 国防文学 (國防文學): national-defense literature

guofang yinyue 国防音乐: national-defense music

Guofang Zuigao Weiyuanhui 国防最高委员会: Supreme National Defense Council

Guofangbu Zong Zhengzhibu 国防部总政治部 (國防部總政治部): National Defense Political Warfare Department

Guofu 国父 (國父): Father of the Nation

Guo-Gong Hezuo 国共合作 (國共合作): Guomindang–Communist Party Cooperation

Guo-Gong Neizhan 国共内战 (國共內戰): Chinese civil war

Guoguo 虢国: Guo State

Guoguo Mudi Bowuguan 虢国墓地博物馆: Guo State Tomb Museum

guohua 国画 (國畫): traditional Chinese painting

Guohua Jushe 国华剧社: Guohua Drama Society

Guohua Nengyuan Touzi Youxian Gongsi 国华能源投资有限公司: Guohua Energy Investment Co.

Guohua yuekan 国画月刊: Chinese painting monthly

guohuo 国货 (國貨): national products

Guohuo yuekan 国货月刊 (國貨月刊): National products monthly

guohuo yundong 国货运动 (國貨運動): national-products movement

Guoji Fa 国籍法: Nationality Law

Guoji Fuxing Fazhan Yinhang 国际复兴发展银行: International Bank for Reconstruction and Development

"Guoji ge" 国际歌: The Internationale

Guoji Jiaoliu yu Hezuo Chu 国际交流与合作处: International Exchange and Cooperation Office

Guoji Jiaoyu Xueyuan 国际教育学院: School of International Education

Guoji Jinrong Gongsi 国际金融公司: International Finance Corporation

Guoji Kaifa Xiehui 国际开发协会: International Development Association

Guojia Anquan Bu 国家安全部: Ministry of State Security

Guojia Baqi Fupin Gongjian Jihua 国家八七扶贫攻坚计划: Eight-Seven Poverty Reduction Plan

Guojia Bowuguan 国家博物馆: National Museum of China

Guojia Dang'an Ju 国家档案局 (國家檔案局): State Archives Board

Guojia Fazhan he Gaige Weiyuanhui 国家发展和改革委员会: National Development and Reform Commission

Guojia Fazhan Jihua Weiyuanhui 国家发展计划委员会: State Development Planning Commission

guojia fuzhuxi 国家副主席: state vice president

Guojia Gao Jishu Yanjiu Kaifa Jihua (863 Jihua) 国家高技术研究开发计划 (863计划): State High Technology Research and Development Program (863 Program)

Guojia Gongshang Guanli Zongju 国家工商行政管理总局: National Administration of Industry and Commerce

Guojia Hanyu Tuiguang Lingdao Xiaozu Bangongshi 国家汉语推广领导小组办公室: Office of Chinese Language Council International

Guojia Huanjing Baohu Zongju 国家环境保护总局: State Environmental Protection Administration

Guojia Jihua Weiyuanhui 国家计划委员会: State Planning Commission

Guojia Jiliang Ju 国家计量局 (國家計量局): National Institute of Metrology

Guojia Jingji Tizhi Gaige Weiyuanhui 国家经济体制改革委员会: Commission for the Reform of the Economic System

Guojia Linye Ju 国家林业局: State Forestry Administration

Guojia Liuxue Jijin Guanli Weiyuanhui 国家留学基金管理委员会: China Scholarship Council

guojia lüyou dujia qu 国家旅游度假区: national holiday resort

Guojia Lüyou Ju 国家旅游局: China National Tourist Office

Guojia Minzu Shiwu Weiyuanhui 国家民族事务委员会: State Ethnic Affairs Commission

Guojia Peichang Fa 国家赔偿法: State Compensation Law

Guojia Pinggu Celüe 国家评估策略: Country Assessment Strategy

Guojia Shehui Dang 国家社会党 (國家社會黨): State Socialist Party

guojia shui 国家税: national taxes

Guojia Tiyu Yundong Weiyuanhui 国家体育运动委员会: State Commission for Physical Culture and Sports

guojia tongji ju 国家统计局: National Bureau of Statistics, State Statistical Bureau

Guojia Tongyi Gangling 国家统一纲领: Guidelines for National Unification

Guojia Tongyi Weiyuanhui 国家统一委员会: National Unification Council

Guojia Waihui Guanli Ju 国家外汇管理局: State Administration of Foreign Exchange

Guojia Wenwu Ju 国家文物局 (國家文物局): State Administration of Cultural Heritage, State Bureau of Cultural Relics

Guojia Youzheng Ju 国家邮政局: State Post Bureau

Guojia zhishang 国家至上 (國家至上): The nation above all

guojia zhuquan 国家主权: national sovereignty

guojia zhuxi 国家主席: state president

Guojia Zongjiao Shiwu Ju 国家宗教事务局: State Religious Affairs Bureau

guojiaji fengjing mingsheng qu 国家级风景名胜区: national-class scenic regions

guojiao 国教 (國教): national religion

Guojun 国军 (國軍): Nationalist Army, Nationalist armed forces

Guoli Beiping Meishu Xuexiao 国立北平美术学校: National Beiping College of Art, National Beiping Art School

Guoli Beiping Tushuguan shanben shumu 国立北平图书馆善本书目 (國立北平圖書館善本書目): National Library of China rare book catalog

Guoli Beiping Yanjiuyuan 国立北平研究院: Peiping Academy

Guoli Dongnan Daxue 国立东南大学: National Southeast University

guoli gaodeng shifan 国立高等师范: national higher teachers' colleges

Guoli Gugong Bowuyuan 国立故宫博物院 (國立故宫博物院): National Palace Museum

Guoli Guofu Jinian Guan 国立国父纪念馆 (國立國父紀念館): Sun Yat-sen Memorial Hall

Guoli Hangzhou Xihu Yishuyuan 国立杭州西湖艺术院 (國立杭州西湖藝術院): National Hangzhou West Lake Art Academy

Guoli Hangzhou Yishu Zhuanke Xuexiao 国立杭州艺术专科学校: National Hangzhou Art College

Guoli Lishi Bowuguan 国立历史博物馆: National History Museum

Guoli Xiju Zhuanke Xuexiao 国立戏剧专科学校 (國立戲劇專科學校): National Academy of Dramatic Arts

Guoli Xinan Lianhe Daxue 国立西南联合大学 (國立西南聯合大學): National Southwest Associated University

Guoli Yishu Yuan 国立艺术院 (國立藝術院): National Academy of Art

Guoli Yishu Zhuanke Xuexiao 国立艺术专科学校: National Art Academy

Guoli Zhongshan Daxue 国立中山大学 (國立中山大學): National Sun Yat-sen University

Guoli Zhongyang Bowuyuan 国立中央博物院 (國立中央博物院): National Central Museum

Guoli Zhongyang Daxue 国立中央大学: National Central University (Nanjing University)

Guoli Zhongyang Zhengzhi Daxue 国立中央政治大学: National Central Political University

guomin 国民: the people

Guomin Canzheng Hui 国民参政会 (國民參政會): People's Political Council

Guomin Dahui 国民大会 (國民大會): National Assembly

guomin geming 国民革命 (國民革命): national revolution

"Guomin geming ge" 国民革命歌: National revolution song

Guomin Geming Jun 国民革命军 (國民革命軍): National Revolutionary Army

guomin jiaoyu 国民教育: citizen's education

Guomin Jun 国民军: Nationalist Army

Guomin Zhengfu 国民政府 (國民政府): Nationalist Government

Guomin zhengfu jianguo dagang 国民政府建国大纲 (國民政府建國大綱): Fundamentals of National Reconstruction

Guomin Zhengfu Zuzhi Fa 国民政府组织法 (國民政府組織法): National Government Organization Law

guomin zhi mu 国民之母 (國民之母): mothers of the nation

Guomindang 国民党 (國民黨): Nationalist Party, Kuomintang

Guomindang Geming Weiyuanhui 国民党革命委员会 (國民黨革命委員會): Revolutionary Committee of the Nationalist Party

Guomindang Linshi Xingdong Weiyuanhui 国民党临时行动委员会 (國民黨臨時行動委員會): Provisional Action Committee of the Nationalist Party

Guomin Jiaoyu Fazhan Huiyi 国民教育发展会议: National Education Development Conference

Guoqing Yanjiu Zhongxin 国情研究中心: Center for China Studies

guoshi 国史 (國史): state history

Guoshi Guan 国史馆 (國史館): History Office

guoshu 国术: martial arts

Guowen bao 国闻报: National news

guowu weiyuan 国务委员: state councillor

Guowu Yuan 国务院: State Council

Guowuyuan Jingji Tizhi Gaige Bangongshi 国务院经济体制改革办公室: State Council Office for the Reform of the Economic System

Guowuyuan Yanjiushi 国务院研究室: State Council Research Office

Guoxin Xunhu 国信寻呼: Guoxin Paging

Guoxue baocun hui 国学保存会: Society for the Preservation of National Learning

guoxue re 国学热 (國學熱): enthusiasm for Chinese studies

guoying qiye 国营企业: state-run enterprises

guoyou qiye 国有企业: state-owned enterprises

guoyu 国语 (國語): national language, Mandarin

Guoyu cidian 国语辞典 (國語辭典): Word dictionary of the national language

Guoyu Luomazi 国语罗马字 (國語羅馬字): a romanization system

guoyue 国乐: national music

gupai 骨牌: dominoes

gushi bian 古史辩 (古史辯): discussion of ancient history

Gushi xinbian 故事新编: Old tales retold

guwen 古文: classical, literary Chinese

guwen 顾问 (顧問): advisor

guwen jingxue 古文经学 (古文經學): old-text school, old-text studies

guwen yundong 古文运动: classical-prose movement, old-literature movement

guwu 古物: antiquities

Guwu Chenliesuo 古物陈列所 (古物陳列所): Gallery of Antiquities, Government Museum

guxue 古学 (古學): ancient learning

Guyuan 固原

Haba Xueshan 哈巴雪山: Haba Snow Mountain

Haerbin 哈尔滨: Harbin

"Hai de meng" 海的梦: Dreams of the sea

Hai langhua 海浪花: The foam of waves

Haibei 海北

Haidianqu 海淀区: Haidian District

Haidong 海东

Haier 海尔

haiguan 海关: customs house

Haiguan Shuiwu Si 海关税务司 (海關稅務司): Imperial Chinese Maritime Customs Service

Haiguan Yamen 海关衙门 (海關衙門): Imperial Chinese Maritime Customs Service

Haiguan Zong Shuiwu Sishu 海关总税务司署 (海關總稅務司署): Maritime Customs General Administration

Haiguo tuzhi 海国图志 (海國圖志): An illustrated treatise on the maritime kingdoms

Haihe 海河: Hai River

Haijun Hangkong Bing 海军航空兵: Naval Aviation Force

Haijun Luzhan Dui 海军陆战队: Marine Corps

Haijun Yamen 海军衙门 (海軍衙門): Admiralty

Haikou 海口

Haimen 海门

Hainan 海南

Haipai 海派: Shanghai school, Shanghai style

Haishang hua 海上花: *Flowers of Shanghai*

Haishang hua liezhuan 海上花列传: Lives of Shanghai Singsong Girls

Haishang huapai 海上画派 (海上畫派): Shanghai school of painting

Haishang molin 海上墨林: Ink forest of Shanghai

Haishang qishu 海上奇书: Marvelous Writings from Shanghai

Haishang Tijinguan Jinshi Shuhua Hui 海上题襟馆金石书画会 (海上題襟館金石書畫會): Shanghai Tijinguan Epigraphy, Calligraphy, and Painting Society

Haishu 海曙

Haixi 海西

Haixia Jiaoliu Jijinhui 海峡交流基金会: Strait Exchange Foundation

Haixia Liang'an Guanxi Xiehui Jigou 海峡两岸关系协会机构: Association for Relations across the Taiwan Strait

Haiyan 海盐

Haiyang Huanjing Baohu Fa 海洋环境保护法: Marine Environment Protection Law

Haiyuan 海原

Haizhu 海珠

Haizi wang 孩子王: *King of the Children*

Hakuba Kai 白馬会: White Horse Association

Hami 哈密: Qumul

Han 汉: Han ethnic majority

Han De 韩德: Pierre Heude

Han Fuju 韩复榘 (韓復榘) **Han Han** 韩寒

Han Jiaozhun 韓教準: Charlie Soong

Han Shantong 韓山童

Han Shaogong 韩少功 (韓少功)

Han Wenzhou 韩文洲

Han Xianchu 韩先楚

Han Xiaopeng 韩晓鹏

Han Yi 汉一

Han Ying 韩英

Han Yu 韩愈 (韓愈)

Hanchao 汉朝: Han dynasty

hang 行: trading companies (authorized foreign traders)

Hang Zhiying 杭稚英

Hangeijutsu 版芸術: The art of printmaking

hangshang 行商: chartered maritime traders

Hangzhou 杭州

Hangzhou Daxue 杭州大学 (杭州大學): Hangchow University

Hangzhou Wan 杭州湾: Hangzhou Bay

Hangzhou Yi Zhuan 杭州藝專: Hangzhou Academy of Art

Hanizu 哈尼族: Hani minority

hanjian 汉奸 (漢奸): traitor

Hanjiang 韩江: Han River

Hankou 汉口 (漢口) Hankow

Hanlin Yuan 翰林院: Hanlin Academy

Hanru tongyi 汉儒通义 (漢儒通義): Comprehensive meanings of Han scholars

Hanshou Daxue 函授大学: Open University

Hanshu 汉书: History of the former Han dynasty

Hanshui 汉水: Han River

Han-Tang Gudian Wudao 汉唐古典舞蹈: Han-Tang Dynasty Classical Dance

Hanxue 汉学 (漢學): Han learning, sinology

Hanyang 汉阳

Hanyeping 汉冶萍

Hanyeping Gongsi 汉冶萍公司: Hanyeping Company

Hanyeping Meitie Changkuang Gongsi 汉冶萍煤铁厂矿公司: Hanyeping Iron and Coal Company

Hanyu da cidian 汉语大词典: Chinese-language comprehensive word dictionary

Hanyu da zidian 汉语大字典: Chinese-language comprehensive character dictionary

Hanyu pinyin 汉语拼音: pinyin romanization

Hanzu 汉族: Han Chinese, Han majority, Han race

Hao Bocun 郝柏村: Hao Po-tsun

Haonan Haonü 好男好女: *Good Men, Good Women*

haoxian 耗羡: meltage fee

He Baosen 何寶森

He Changling 贺长龄 (賀長齡)

He Dun 何頓

He Duoling 何多苓

He Haohua 何浩华

He Hongshen 何鴻燊: Stanley Ho

He Houhua 何厚華: Edmund Ho

He Jingzhi 贺敬之

He Jiping 何冀平

He Lin 贺麟

He Long 贺龙

He Lüding 贺绿汀

He ni zai yiqi 和你在一起: *Together*

He Qifang 何其芳

He Ruzhang 何如璋

He Shaoji 何绍基

He Tianjian 贺天健

He Xian 何賢: Ho Yin

He Xiangning 何香凝

He Yong 何勇

He Youzhi 贺友直

He Yuan 何园: He's Garden

He Zhanhao 何占豪

He Zhen 何震

Hebei 河北

hebiao 河標: canal labor troops

Hechuan 合川

Hefei 合肥

hei'an mian 黑暗面: somber aspects

heibaihua niu 黑白花牛: Chinese black and white cows

Heibao 黑豹: Black Panther (band)

heihua 黑画: black painting

heijin zhengzhi 黑金政治: black-gold politics

Heilongjiang 黑龙江: Heilongjiang Provence, Amur River

Helin 和霖

Henan 河南: Ho Nam

Henan Bowuguan 河南博物館: Henan Museum

Heng bao 衡报 (衡報): Natural equality

heping fazhan 和平发展: peace and development

heping gongchu wuxiang yuanze 和平共处五项原则: five principles of peaceful coexistence

heping jueqi 和平崛起: peaceful rise

heping tongyi 和平统一: peaceful reunification

Hepingge 和平鸽: Doves of peace

hepingpai 和平派: peace advocates

Heqiaozhen 和桥镇: Heqiao Town

"Heshang" 河殇: River elegy

Heshen 和珅

hesuipian 贺岁片: New Year's movies

"Hetang yuese" 荷塘月色: The lotus pond by moonlight

Hetian 和田: Khotan

Hetong Fa 合同法: Contract Law, Unified Contract Law

hexie shehui 和谐社会: harmonious society

Heyuan 河源

Hezhou 河州

hezuo qiye 合作企业: cooperative enterprise

hezuo yiliao zhidu 合作医疗制度: cooperative medical system

Hirota Kōki 広田弘毅 (廣田弘毅)

Hong 洪

Hong 虹: *Rainbow*

Hong baoshu 红宝书: precious Red Book

Hong Er 洪二

Hong gaoliang 红高粱: *Red Sorghum*

Hong gaoliang jiazu 红高粱家族: *Red Sorghum: A Novel of China*

hong guang liang 红光亮: red, bright, vivid

Hon Hai 宏海: Foxconn

Hong Jun 洪鈞

Hong Liangji 洪亮吉

Hong mudan 红牡丹 (紅牡丹): *The Red Peony*

Hong Rengan 洪仁玕

Hong Shen 洪深

Hong Siguo 洪四果

Hong taiyang: Mao Zedong songge xin jiezou lianchang 红太阳: 毛泽东颂歌新节奏联唱: The red sun: A medley of songs praising Mao Zedong set to new rhythms

Hong Xiuquan 洪秀全

Hong Xuezhi 洪学智

Hong Ying 虹影

Hong Zhuan 紅塼: *Red Bricks*

hongbao 红包 (紅包): red packets containing cash

hongcha 红茶 (紅茶): black tea

Hongdeng ji 红灯记: The red lantern

Hongji 宏基: Acer

Hongjun 红军 (紅軍): Red Army

Hongkou 虹口: Hongkou ghetto

Honglou meng 红楼梦 (紅樓夢): *Dream of the Red Chamber*

Honglou meng tuyong 红楼梦图咏 (紅樓夢圖詠): Portraits of characters from *Dream of the Red Chamber*

Honglu 虹庐

hongqi 红契: sealed title deeds for land

Hongqi 红旗: Red flag

Hongqi geyao 红旗歌谣: Songs of the red flag

Hongqi xia de dan 红旗下的蛋: Eggs under the red flag

Hongqiao 虹桥

Hongse niangzi jun 红色娘子军: Red detachment of women

Hongshan 红山

Hongshan wenhua 红山文化: Hongshan culture

Hongsheng Huochai Gongsi 鸿生火柴公司: Hong Sung Match Company

Hongsou 虹叟

Hongweibing 红卫兵: Red Guards

Hongxian 洪宪

Hongyi 弘一

Hongzehu 洪泽湖: Lake Hongze

Hōten Kōha Dendai 奉天広播電台 (奉天廣播電台): Fengtian Broadcasting Station

Hou Bo 侯波

Hou Dejian 侯德建

hou menglong 后朦胧: post-misty

hou si Wang 后四王: the later Four Wangs

Hou Wenyi 侯文宜

Hou Xiaoxian 侯孝贤 (侯孝賢)

Hou Yi 后羿

houdang 后党 (后黨): faction of the empress dowager

Hougang 后冈

Houguan 侯官

Houmen 后门 (后門): Rear entrance

houxinchao 后新潮: post–new wave

Hu 沪: Shanghai

Hu Boxiang 胡伯翔

Hu Chunhua 胡春华

Hu Die 胡蝶

Hu Feng 胡风 (胡風)

Hu Guang zongdu 湖广总督: Governor-General of Hunan and Hubei

Hu Hanmin 胡汉民 (胡漢民)

Hu Jia 胡佳

Hu Jieqing 胡洁青 (胡絜青)

Hu Jinquan 胡金铨 (胡金銓): King Hu

Hu Jintao 胡锦涛

Hu Linyi 胡林翼

Hu Qiaomu 胡乔木

Hu Qili 胡启立

Hu Qiuyuan 胡秋原

Hu Ruihua 胡瑞华 (胡瑞華)

Hu She 湖社: Lake Society

Hu She yuekan 湖社月刊: Lake Society monthly

Hu Shi 胡适 (胡適)

Hu Shicha 胡石查

Hu Wanchun 胡万春

Hu Xiaolian 胡晓炼

Hu Yanlin 胡彦林

Hu Yaobang 胡耀邦

Hu Yepin 胡也频

Hu Yichuan 湖一川

Hu Yuan 胡遠

Hu Yufen 胡燏棻

Hu Yujuan 胡玉娟

Hu Zheng 胡正

Hua Guofeng 华国峰

Hua jingli 华经理 (華經理): Chinese representative

Hua Rui Fengdian Keji Youxian Gongsi 华锐风电科技有限公司: Sinovel Wind Co.

Hua Runchuan 华润泉 (華潤泉)

Hua Tianyou 滑田友

Hua Tuo 华佗

Hua yiban de zuie 花一般的罪恶: Flowerlike evil

Hua zhi si 花之寺: Temple of flowers

Huabei Daxue 华北大学: Huabei University

Huabei jianzhu 华北建筑 (華北建築): Journal of the Architectural Society of Northern China

Huabei jiebao 北华捷报 (北華捷報): North China herald

huabu 华埠 (華埠): Chinatown

huadan 花旦: coquettish-female role type in Peking Opera

Huadong Meikuang Gongsi 华东煤矿公司 (華東煤礦公司): East China Coal Mining Company

Huadu 花都

Huafa Yanjiuhui 画法研究会: Painting Methods Research Society

Huafa yaozhi 画法要旨: Essential painting techniques

Huafangzhai 畫舫齋: Huafang Studio

huagong 华工 (華工): Chinese unskilled labor

huaguxi 花鼓戏: flower-drum opera

Huaian 淮安

Huaibei 淮北

Huaihai 淮海

Huai-Hai Zhanyi 淮海战役 (淮海戰役): Huai-Hai Campaign

Huaihe 淮河: Huai River

Huaijiu 怀旧: Remembering

Huaiju shicun 槐聚诗存: Extant poems of Huaiju

Huaijun 淮军: Anhui Army

Huainian lang 怀念狼: Remembering wolves

Huamao Fandian 华懋饭店: Cathay Hotel

Huan Bohai Jingji Qu 环渤海经济区: Greater Bohai Economic Region

Huanan Nüzi Daxue 华南女子大学 (華南女子大學): South China Women's University

Huancheng 欢城

Huaneng Guoji Gufen Youxian Gongsi 华能国际电力股份有限公司: Huaneng Power International

huang 荒: crop failure

Huang Banruo 黄般若

Huang Binhong 黄宾虹 (黃賓虹)

Huang Chunming 黄春明

Huang di 黄帝: Yellow emperor

Huang di neijing 黄帝内经: The medical classic of the Yellow Emperor

Huang Dinghua 黄定华

Huang Ju 黄菊

Huang Junbi 黄君璧

Huang Kecheng 黄克诚

Huang Maozhi 黄懋质

Huang Qing jingjie 皇清经解 (皇清經解): Imperial Qing annotations on the classics

Huang Rui 黄銳

Huang She 黄社: Huang Society

Huang Tingjian 黄庭坚 (黃庭堅)

Huang tudi 黄土地: *Yellow Earth*

Huang Xiang 黄翔

Huang Xinbo 黄新波

Huang Xing 黄兴 (黃興)

Huang Yanpei 黄炎培

Huang Yao 黄尧

Huang Yongping 黄永砯

Huang Yongyu 黄永玉

Huang Yuan 黄源

Huang Zhi 黄质

Huang Zi 黄自

Huang Zongxi 黄宗羲

Huang Zunxian 黄遵宪 (黃遵憲)

Huang Zuolin 黄佐临

Huangchao jingshi wenbian 皇朝经世文编 (皇朝經世文編): Collected writings on Qing statecraft

Huangchuan 潢川

Huanggan 惶感: Bewilderment

Huanghai 黄海: Yellow Sea

Huanghe 黄河: Yellow River

"**Huanghe**" 黄河: Yellow River (the song)

Huanghe dahechang 黄河大合唱: Yellow River cantata

Huanghe gangqin xiezouqu 黄河钢琴协奏曲: Yellow River piano concerto

huanghuali 黄花梨: a type of rosewood

Huangjiao 黄教: *dge lugs* (Gelug) Tibetan Buddhism

Huangling 黄陵

Huangmei Xi 黄梅戏 (黃梅戲): Huangmei Opera

huangmin wenxue 皇民文学 (皇民文學): literature written by Chinese in Japanese

Huangnan 黄南

Huangni jie 黄泥街: Muddy street

Huangpu 黄埔: Whampoa

Huangpu Gongyuan 黄埔公园: Huangpu Park

Huangpu Junguan Xuexiao 黄埔军官学校 (黃埔軍官學校): Whampoa Military Academy

Huangpu Junxiao 黄埔军校 (黃埔軍校): Whampoa Military Academy

Huangpu Tiaoyue 黄埔条约 (黃埔條約): Treaty of Whampoa

Huangpujiang 黄浦江: Huangpu River

huangse yinyue 黄色音乐: pornographic (decadent) music

Huangshan 黄山: Yellow Mountains

Huangshan zhi lian 荒山之恋: *Love on a Barren Mountain*

huangtu 黄土: loess

huangyu 黄鱼: yellow croaker

huaniao 花鸟: flowers and birds

Huanjing Baohu Bu 环境保护部: Ministry of Environmental Protection

Huanjing Baohu Fa 环境保护法: Environmental Protection Law

Huanjing Baohu Ju 环境保护局: Environmental Protection Bureau

Huanjing Yingxiang Pingjia Fa 环境影响评价法: Environmental Impact Assessment Law

Huanmie 幻灭: Disillusion

huapian 画片: poster

huaping 花瓶: "flower vases"

Huaqiao 华侨 (華僑): Chinese citizens living abroad, Chinese overseas

Huaqiao Daxia 华侨大厦: Overseas Chinese Building

Huaren 华人 (華人): ethnic Chinese with foreign citizenship, Chinese people

Huashang 华商 (華商): Chinese traders

Huashang Liujiang Meikuang Tielu Gongsi 华商柳江煤矿铁路公司 (華商柳江煤礦鐵路公司): Liuchang Mining Company

Huashang Shanghai Shuini Gongsi 华商上海水泥公司 (華商上海水泥公司): Shanghai Portland Cement Works Company

Huawei Jishu Youxian Gongsi 华为技术有限公司: Huawei Technologies

Huaxi Daxue 华西大学 (華西大學): West China Union University

Huaxia luntan 华夏论坛: Huaxia forum

Huaxing Hui 华兴会 (華興會): China Revival Society

Huayang nianhua 花样年华 (花樣年華): *In the Mood for Love*

Huayi 华裔 (華裔): Chinese descendants

Huayuankou 花园口

Huazhong Daxue 华中大学 (華中大學): Central China University

Huazhong Shifan Daxue 华中师范大学 (華中師範大學): Huazhong Normal University

Hubei 湖北

Hubu 户部: Ministry of Revenue, Imperial Treasury, Board of Finance, Board of Households, Hoppo

"Hudie" 蝴蝶: Butterfly

hufa yundong 护法运动 (護法運動): constitution protection movement

Huguang 湖广

Huhehaote 呼和浩特: Hohhot

huhun tiantu qianzhai 戶婚田土錢債: household, marriage, land and monetary obligations

hui 會: association, brotherhood

"Hui jia lun" 毁家论: On destruction of the family

huidian 会典 (會典): collected statutes

huidian shili 会典事例 (會典事例): collected statutes with precedent cases

huidian zeli 会典则例 (會典則例): collected statutes with model cases

Huifeng Yinhang 汇丰银行: Hong Kong and Shanghai Banking Corporation

huiguan 会馆 (會館): merchant guilds, regional guilds, native-place halls

Huilan muke 迴澜木刻: Whirlpool woodcut

Huimie 毁灭: *The Rout*

Huimin Qiyi 回民起义: Panthay Rebellion

Huishen Gongtang 会审公堂 (會審公堂): Shanghai Mixed Court, International Mixed Court

Huishen Gongxie 会审公廨 (會審公廨): Shanghai Mixed Court, International Mixed Court

huishu 回贖: redeem

Huizhou 徽州

Huizong 徽宗: Emperor Huizong

Huizu 回族: Hui minority

hukou 户口: household registration, permanent residency

hukou zhidu 户口制度: household registration system

Hulanhe 呼兰河: *Tales of Hulan River*

Huli 湖里

Humen Tiaoyue 虎门条约 (虎門條約): Treaty of the Bogue

Hunan 湖南

Hunan hua 湖南话: Xiang dialects

"Hunan nongmin yundong kaocha baogao" 湖南農民運動考察報告: Report on an investigation of the peasant movement in Hunan

Hunan ren 湖南人: people from Hunan

Hunan Sheng Bowuguan 湖南省博物馆: Hunan Provincial Museum

Hunan Shengli Diyi Shifan 湖南省立第一师范学校: Hunan First Normal School

Hunyin Fa 婚姻法: Marriage Law

huodong 活动: movements

Huo shao Hongliansi 火烧红莲寺 (火燒紅蓮寺): *Red Lotus Temple on Fire*

Huodong bian renxing 活动变人形: Activities deform

Huohua 火花: Spark

huoju 火居: at-home (not living in a temple)

Huoju Jihua 火炬计划: Torch Program

Huoran kailang 豁然开朗 (豁然開朗): Gazing at the lake

Huoshan qingxie 火山情血: *Revenge by the Volcano*

Huozhe 活着: *To Live*

Huqiu 虎邱: Tiger Hill

Husheng huaji 护生画集 (護生畫集): Paintings to protect life

hushi 互市: tributary trade system; a system requiring foreign merchants to do business only with licensed Chinese merchants, who were obliged to pay foreign trade tax to the government

hutong 胡同 (衚衕): narrow back alleys, residential streets and alleys

Huxi Yuedui 呼吸乐队: Breathing (band)

Huxian 户县: Hu County

Huzhao Fa 护照法: Passport Law

Huzhou 湖州

huzhu 互助: mutual aid

Ichigō Sakusen 一号作戦: Operation Ichigō

Inukai Tsuyoshi 犬養毅

Ishiwara Kanji 石原莞尔

Ji Cheng 计成

Ji Xian 纪弦

Ji xiao duzhe 寄小读者 (寄小讀者): Letters to young readers

Ji Zheng 纪政 (紀政)

Ji'an 吉安

Jia 家: Family

jia 甲: a tithing in the *baojia* community self-defense system; **2.4 acres**

Jia Chunwang 贾春旺

Jia Lanpo 贾兰坡

Jia Liu 贾六

Jia Pingwa 贾平凹

Jia Qinglin 贾庆林

Jiafang yifang 甲方乙方: *The Dream Factory*

jiaguwen 甲骨文: oracle-bone script, writing

jiahao 架号 (架號): cangue, Chinese pillory

Jiahe 嘉禾: Golden Harvest Studio

Jiahu 贾湖

jiaju 家具: furniture

Jialing 嘉陵

jiamiao 家庙 (家廟): ancestor-worship halls

Jiamusi 佳木斯

Jian Youwen 简又文

Jian Zhen 鉴真

Jiancha Bu 监察部: Ministry of Supervision

Jiancha Yuan 检察院: Procuratorate

Jiancha Yuan 监察院: Supervisory Yuan

Jianchuan 剑川

Jianfu Gong 建富宫: Palace of Established Happiness

Jiang Baoling 蒋宝龄

Jiang Bibo 江碧波

Jiang Bingzhi 蒋冰之

Jiang Biwei 蒋碧微

Jiang Feng 江丰 (江豐)

Jiang Haicheng 蒋海澄 (蒋海澄)

Jiang Jieshi 蒋介石: Chiang Kai-shek

Jiang Jingguo 蒋经国 (蒋經國): Chiang Ching-kuo

Jiang Menglin 蒋梦麟

Jiang Qing 江青

Jiang Renjie 姜人杰

Jiang Tingfu 蒋廷黻

Jiang Wen 姜文

Jiang Wenye 江文也

Jiang Xin 江新

Jiang Yanyong 蒋彦永

Jiang Zemin 江泽民

Jiang Zhaohe 蒋兆和

Jiang Zhiyou 蒋智由

Jiang'an 江岸

Jiangbei 江北

Jiangdong 江东

Jianghe 江河

Jiangnan 江南

Jiangnan Zhizao Zongju 江南制造总局: Jiangnan Arsenal

Jiangnan Shuju 江南书局 (江南書局): Jiangnan Printing Office

Jiangning 江宁

Jiangsu 江苏

Jiangsu Haiyun quan'an 江苏海运全案 (江蘇海運全案): Complete records on Jiangsu sea transport

Jiangsusheng Bowuguan 江苏省博物馆: Jiangsu Provincial Museum

Jiangsusheng Jiaoyuhui Meishu Yanjiu Hui 江苏省教育会美术研究会: Jiangsu Provincial Education Committee Fine Art Study Society

Jiangwan 江湾

Jiangxi 江西

Jiangxi Gongchanzhuyi Laodong Daxue 江西共产主义劳动大学: Jiangxi Communist Labor University

Jiangzi 江孜: Gyantse

Jianhu nüxia 鉴湖女侠

jiankang xieshi 健康写实 (健康寫實): healthy realism

jianrong bingbao 兼容并包: tolerance and inclusion of all learning

jianshang 奸商: treacherous merchants

jiansheng 监生 (監生): student of the Imperial College, a purchased degree

jiantizi 简体字: simplified characters

jianwu 剑舞: sword dance

Jianxia zhuan 劍俠傳: Tales of knights at arms

jianzhi 剪纸: paper cuttings

Jianzhu Kexue Yanjiuyuan 建筑科学研究院: Institute of Building Science

Jianzhu xinfa 建筑新法 (建築新法): Building construction

Jianzhu yuekan 建筑月刊 (建築月刊): The builder

jiao 教: teaching, sect, religion, education

jiao 醮: Daoist ritual communal offerings

jiao xin yundong 交心运动: giving-of-hearts campaign

jiaoan 教案: missionary case

Jiaoao 胶澳

Jiaobinlu kangyi 校邠庐抗议: Straightforward discussion from the Jiaobin Studio

Jiaodian fangtan 焦点访谈: Focus

jiaohua 教化: moral education, cultural transformation

jiaohuaji 叫化鸡: beggar's chicken

jiaoshi jiaoyu 教师教育: teacher education

Jiaotai Dian 交泰殿: Hall of Mutual Ease

Jiaotong Yinhang 交通银行: Bank of Communications

Jiaoyu Bu 教育部: Ministry of Education

Jiaoyu Tongchou Weiyuanhui Diqihao Baogaoshu 教育统筹委员会第七号报告书: Education Commission Report No. 7

Jiaoyubu Liuxue Fuwu Zhongxin 教育部留学服务中心: Chinese Service Center for Scholarly Exchange

Jiaozhou 胶州

Jiaozhouwan 胶州灣: Jiaozhou Bay

Jiaqing 嘉庆 (嘉慶): emperor (r. 1796–1820)

jiashu 家塾: family school

jiating jiaohui 家庭教会: house churches

jiatou 甲头 (甲頭): head of a *jia* (tithing) in the *baojia* system

Jiawu Zhanzheng 甲午战争 (甲午戰爭): Sino-Japanese War of 1894–1895

jiaxi zhenchang 假戏真唱: to take pretend for real

Jiaxing 嘉興

jiaxun 家训: family instructions

jiazhuang 嫁妆: dowry

Jidao 几道

Jidong Fan-Gong Zizhi Zhengfu 冀东反共自治政府: East Hebei Anti-Communist Autonomous Government

Jidu hanleng 极度寒冷: *Frozen*

Jidujiao 基督教: Protestantism

jie 接: greeting

jie 界: constituency

jiebai xiongdi 结拜兄弟: sworn brotherhoods

jiedao banshichu 街道办事处: neighborhood committee or street office

Jiefang ribao 解放日报: Liberation daily

Jiefang Zhanzheng 解放战争 (解放戰爭): Chinese civil war, war of liberation

Jiefangjun 解放军 (解放軍): People's Liberation Army

Jiefangjun bao 解放军报: Liberation Army daily

Jiejue 解决: Solution

jiemei hui 姐妹会 (姐妹會): sisterhoods

jiemu 节母 (節母): virtuous mothers

"**Jieyan ge**" 戒烟歌 (戒煙歌): Opium-Quitting Song

Jieziyuan huapu 桔子园画谱 (桔子園畫譜): Mustard Seed Garden manual of painting

Jigu ma Cao 击鼓骂曹 (擊鼓罵曹): Scolding Cao Cao while beating the drum

Jihai za shi 己亥杂诗 (己亥雜詩): Miscellaneous poems of 1839

jihua 计划

jihua danlie shi 计划单列市: single planning municipality, central economic city

jihua shengyu 计划生育: planned parenting

jihua shengyu zhengce 计划生育政策: one-child policy

Jihuang 饥荒 (饑荒): Famine

jihuang 饥荒: famine

Jijie hao 集结号: *Assembly*

Jilin 吉林

Jiliu sanbuqu 激流三部曲: Torrents trilogy

Jilong 基隆: Keelung

Jimei 集美

jin 斤: catty

Jin Cheng 金城

"Jin Fen gu jianzhu yucha jilue" 晋汾古建筑预查纪略: A preliminary investigation of ancient architecture in Shanxi

Jin Feng Keji Gufen Youxian Gongsi 金风科技股份有限公司: Gold Wind

Jin Guidi 靳贵第

Jin He 金和

Jin Jialun 金嘉伦: King Chia-Lun

Jin Mao Daxia 金茂大廈: Jin Mao Tower

Jin Richeng 金日成: Kim Il-sung

Jin Shangyi 靳尚谊

Jin Shuren 金树仁

Jin Yunmei 金韵梅

Jin Zhaofeng 金兆丰 (金兆豐)

Jinan 济南

Jinan Daxue 暨南大学: Jinan University

Jinan Liujia gongfuzhen pu 济南刘家功夫针铺 (濟南劉家功夫針舖): Liu Needle Shop of Jinan

jinbiaozhuyi 锦标主义: championism

Jinbu Dang 进步党 (進步黨): Progressive Party

Jin-Cha-Ji huabao 晋察冀画报 (晉察冀画報): Jin-Cha-Ji pictorial

Jinchao 晋朝: Jin dynasty

Jincheng 晋城

Jincheng Yinhang 金城银行: Kincheng Banking Corporation

Jindaishi Yanjiusuo 近代史研究所: Institute of Modern History

jindun gongcheng 金盾工程: golden shield

jing 静: still

Jing chi 京尺: Beijing foot

Jing Xing 金星

Jing'an 静安 (靜安)

Jing'an Gongyuan 静安公园: Jing'an Park

Jingbao 京报 (京報): Beijing (Peking) gazette, Court gazette

Jingbao zuo meiren 警报作媒人 (警報作媒人): The air raid alarmist plays the role of a go-between

jingcha 警察: police

Jingdezhen 景德镇

Jingdian changtan 经典常谈: Lectures on the classics

jingfang 经方: classic formula

Jinggangshan 井冈山

jinghu 京胡: a Chinese bowed fiddle associated with Beijing

Jinghua yanyun 京华烟云 (京華烟雲): *Moment in Peking*

Jingji Hetong Fa 经济合同法: Economic Contract Law

jingji jishu kaifaqu 经济技术开发区: economic and technological development zone

jingji teke 经济特科: special examinations on public administration

jingji tequ 经济特区: special economic zone

Jingji zuangu 经籍纂诂: a dictionary of the Confucian classics

Jingji, Shehui, Wenhua Quanli Guoji Gongyue 经济、社会、文化权利国际公约: International Covenant on Economic, Social, and Cultural Rights

jingjie 境界: realm

Jingjixue zhoubao 经济学周报: Economics weekly

Jingju 京剧: Peking Opera

jingluo 经络: vessels

jingmi 粳米: japonica rice

Jingming Yuan 静明园 (靜明園): Jingming Garden

Jingpai 京派: Beijing school

Jingshan 景山: Scenic Hill

jingshen wenming 精神文明: spiritual civilization

jingshen wuran 精神污染: spiritual pollution

Jingshi 京师

jingshi 精實: streamline

jingshi 经世 (經世): statecraft

Jingshi Da Xuetang 京师大学堂 (京師大學堂): Imperial University of Beijing, Peking Imperial University, Imperial College

Jingshi Fang 敬事房: Office of Eunuch Affairs

Jingshi Jingcha Ting 京师警察厅: Capital Police Board

Jingshi Tongwen Guan 京师同文馆 (京師同文舘): Peking Foreign Language School

Jingshi Tushuguan 京师图书馆: Metropolitan Library of Beijing

jingshi zhixue 经世致学 (經世致學): statecraft learning

jingwai juezhan 境外决战 (境外決戰): offshore engagement

Jingwai Zhongguo Gongmin he Jiguo Anquan Baohu Gongzuo Buji Lianxi Huiyi 境外中国公民和机构安全保护工作部际联席会议: Interministry Working Meeting on Protecting the Safety of PRC Citizens and Organizations Overseas

Jingwu Xuetang 警务学堂: Police Academy

Jingxi 京戏 (京戲): Peking Opera

Jingxiong 竞雄

Jingyi Yuan 静宜园 (靜宜園): Jingyi Garden

Jingyuan 泾源

Jingzheng Nüxue 经正女学: Classic Uprightness Girls' School

Jingzhong ribao 警钟日报 (警鐘日報): Warning bell daily

Jingzhou Bowuguan 荆州博物馆: Jingzhou Museum

jinhua 进化: progress

Jinhua 金華

Jinhui Xueyuan 浸会学院 (浸會學院): Baptist College

Jining 济宁

Jinji Jiang 金鸡奖: Golden Rooster

Jinjiang 晋江: Jin River

Jinjibao 金积堡

Jinlanhui 金蘭會: Golden Orchid Association

Jinling 金陵

Jinling Daxue 金陵大学 (金陵大學): University of Nanking

Jinling Kejing Chu 金陵刻经处 (金陵刻經處): Jinling Sutra Carving Society, Jinling Woodblock Sutra Institute

Jinling Nüzi Daxue 金陵女子大学 (金陵女子大學): Ginling Women's College

Jinling Shuju 金陵书局 (金陵書局): Jinling Printing Office

Jinmen 金門: Quemoy

Jinnan 晉南

Jinniushan 金牛山

Jinqiao Gongcheng 金橋工程: Golden Bridge Project

Jinri shuofa 今日说法: Law today

Jinsha Bowuguan 金沙博物馆: Jinsha Museum

Jinshajiang 金沙江: Gold Sand River

jinshi 进士 (進士): presented scholar, metropolitan graduate; also the degree

jinshi 金石: metal and stone inscriptions

jinshi qi 金石气 (金石氣): bronze and stone epigraphic styles, epigraphic taste

jinshipai 金石派: epigraphic school

jinshixue 金石学 (金石學): the study of bronzes and stone stelae, studies of epigraphy, antiquarian studies, the epigraphic movement

Jintian 今天: Today

Jinwen jingxue 今文经学 (今文經學): New Text school; New Text, or New Script, Confucianism

Jinwu Shudian 金屋书店: Golden House Press

Jinxiugu zhi lian 锦绣谷之恋: *Brocade Valley*

jinyuan quan 金圆券 (金圓券): gold-pegged paper currency

jinzhang pingheng 紧张平衡: a tight equilibrium

Jinzhi Kuxing He Qita Canren, Bu Rendao Huo Youru Renge Daiyu Huo Chufa Gongyue 禁止苦刑和其他残忍，不人道或有辱人格待遇或处罚公约: Convention against Torture and Other Cruel, Inhuman, or Degrading Treatment or Punishment

Jinzhou 金州

Jishi he xugou 纪实和虚构: Reality and fiction

jishi sheying 纪实摄影: documentary photography

jishi wenxue 纪时文学: reportage fiction

Jissen Jo Gakkō 实践女学校: Jissen Women's School

Jissen Joshi Daigaku 实践女子大学: Jissen Women's University

jiti qiye 集体企业: collective enterprise

jiti tiliu 集体提留: collective withholding, a township and village levy

Jitong Tongxin 吉通通信: Jitong Communications

Jiu Fang Gao 九方皋

Jiu guo 酒国: *The Republic of Wine*

"Jiu hou" 酒后 (酒後): Flushed with wine

Jiu San Xueshe 九三学社 (九三學社): September Third Society

jiu shehui 旧社会: old society

jiucheng gaizao 旧城改造: old cities overhauled

Jiuduhui xiezhen 旧都会写真: Social images of the old capital

jiuer gongshi 九二共识: 1992 consensus

jiuguo 救国 （救国）: saving the nation

Jiuguo Hui 救国会 （救國會）: National Salvation Association

Jiuguo Tuan 救国团 （救國團）: China Youth Corps

Jiujiang 九江

Jiulongjiang 九龙江: Jiulong River

jiupai 旧派: old-style school

Jiuwang jue lun 救亡决论: A discussion of the remedy for national collapse

Jiuwen si pian 旧文四篇: Four old essays

Jiu-yiba ge 九一八歌: September 18 song

Jiu-yiba Jinian Bei 九·一八纪念碑: 9-18 (Mukden) Incident Memorial

Jiu-yiba Lishi Bowuguan 九·一八历史博物馆: 9-18 (Mukden) Incident Museum

Jiuzhaigou 九寨沟

Jiuzhang Lü 九章律: Statutes in Nine Sections

Ju Chao 居巢

Ju Lian 居廉

juan 卷: volume

juan cun 眷村: military village

juanguan 捐官: sales of official titles

juanxiang 捐饷: irregular business donation

Juedui xinhao 绝对信号: Absolute alarm

jueju 絕句: quatrain

Juelan She 决澜社 (決瀾社): Storm Society

juemai 絕賣: land sold outright

Julong 巨龙: a manufacturer of telecommunications equipment

jumin weiyuanhui 居民委员会: neighborhood committee

junfa 军阀 (軍閥): warlord

Junji Chu 军机处 (軍機處): Council of State, Grand Council

Junmin jinxingqu 军民进行曲: The soldiers advance

Junshi Weiyuanhui 军事委员会: Military Affairs Commission

Junxian ?县: Centralized bureaucratic monarchical rule

junzheng 军政 (軍政): military government, military rule

junzheng weiyuanhui 军政委员会 (軍政委員會): military-administrative committees

junzhu lixian 君主立宪: constitutional monarchy

junzi 君子

juren 举人 (舉人): recommended man, provincial graduate; **also the degree**

Jurong 裕廊

Juye 钜野

juyou Zhongguo tese de shehuizhuyi 具有中国特色的社会主义: socialism with Chinese characteristics

juzhang 局长: bureau leader

kaideng 开灯 (開燈): lighting-the-lantern ceremony

kaifang zhengce 开放政策: open-door policy

Kaifeng 开封

Kaiguo dadian 开国大典: *Founding Ceremony*

"**Kailu xianfeng**" 开路先锋: The pioneers

Kailuan Kuangwu Ju 开滦矿务局 (開灤礦務局): Kailuan Mining Administration

Kailuan Shoupinchu 开滦售品处 (開灤售品處): Kalian Sales Agency

Kai-Min Shengwang 开闽圣王 (開閩聖王): the sagely king who opened up Fujian

Kaiping 开平

Kaiping Kuangwu Ju 开平矿务局 (開平礦務局): Chinese Engineering and Mining Company

kaishu 楷书 (楷書): regular script, standard script

kang 炕: sleeping platform

Kang Baiqing 康白情

Kang Guangren 康广仁 (康廣仁)

Kang Keqing 康克清

kang Mei yuan Chao 抗美援朝: war to resist U.S. aggression and Aid Korea, the Korean War

Kang Sheng 康生

Kang Youwei 康有为 (康有為)

kangakusha 漢学者: Japanese sinologists

Kangba 康巴: Kham

Kangda 抗大: Resistance University

"**Kangqiao zaihui ba**" 康桥再会吧 (康橋再會吧): Farewell to Cambridge

Kangqu 康区: Kham

Kang-Ri Jiuguo Hui 抗日救国会 (抗日救國會): National Anti-Japanese Salvation Association

Kang-Ri jiuwang geyong yundong 抗日救亡歌咏运动: Singing for resistance against Japan and the national salvation movement

Kang-Ri Junzheng Daxue 抗日军政大学: Anti-Japanese Military and Political Academy

Kang-Ri Zhanzheng 抗日战争 (抗日戰爭): Anti-Japanese War, War of Resistance against Japan

Kang-Ri zhanzheng gequ jingxuan 抗日战争歌曲精选: Selection of songs of the War of Resistance against Japan

Kangxi 康熙: emperor (r. 1662–1722)

Kangxi zidian 康熙字典: Kangxi character dictionary

Kangzhan shenghuo 抗战生活: War of Resistance life

Kangzhan wenyi 抗战文艺 (抗戰文藝): Literature of national defense (journal)

Kangzhan zhong de Balujun 抗战中的八路军: Eighth Route Army in the War of Resistance

Kano Naoki 狩野直喜

Kanshangqu hen mei 看上去很美: It looks beautiful

Kantō 関東

Kao pan yu shi 考槃余事 (考槃餘事): Desultory remarks on furnishing the abode of the retired scholar

kaogu 考古: examining the past, archaeology

Kaogu tu 考古圖: Illustrated study of antiquity

Kaogu xuebao 考古学报: Acta archaeologica sinica

Kaogu Yanjiusuo 考古研究所: Institute of Archaeology

kaoju 考据 (考據): evidential research

kaojuxue 考据学 (考據學): evidential scholarship

Kaoshi Yuan 考试院 (考試院): Examination Yuan

kaozheng 考证 (考證): evidential research

kaozhengxue 考证学 (考證學): evidential learning, evidential research, examination of evidence and documents

Kashi 喀什: Kashgar

Kashige'er 喀什噶尔: Kashgar

Katsushika Hokusai 葛飾北齋

Kawabata Ga Gakkō 川端画学校: Kawabata Academy of Painting

ke 客: guest

ke 科: department

Ke Qunying 柯群英: Khun Eng Kuah

Ke Shaomin 柯紹忞

Kejia 客家: Hakka people and language

Kejia yanjiu daolun 客家研究导论: Introduction to Hakka studies

kejijie 科技界: circles of science and technology

keju 科举 (科舉): imperial civil-service examination

keting 客厅: the central guest room

kexue fazhan guan 科学发展观: scientific theory of development

Kezaisheng Nengyuan Fa 可再生能源法: Renewable Energy Law

kezhang 科长: division leader

kokuga 国画: traditional Japanese painting

kokusui hozon 国粹保存: preservation of the national essence

kōminka bungaku 皇民化文学 (皇民化文學): literature written by Chinese in Japanese

Kong fuzi 孔夫子: Confucius

Kong Guangsen 孔广森 (孔廣森)

Kong Jiesheng 孔捷生

Kong Luhua 孔璐華

Kong Qiu 孔丘: Confucius

Kong Xiangxi 孔祥熙: H. H. Kung

"**Kong Yiji**" 孔乙己: a short story by Lu Xun

Kong Zhongni 孔仲尼: Confucius

Kongcheng ji 空城计 (空城計): Ruse of the empty city

Kongzhong xiaojie 空中小姐: Air stewardess

Kongzi gaizhi kao 孔子改制考: Confucius as institutional innovator

Kongzi Xueyuan 孔子学院: Confucius Institute

Kosugi Hōan 小杉放庵

kuaiban 快板: clappertalk, Chinese rap

kuaikuai 块块: coordinate relationships

Kuanghuan de jijie 狂欢的季节: Season of ecstasy

"**Kuangren riji**" 狂人日记 (狂人日記): Diary of a madman

Kulian 苦恋: Unrequited love

Kulubaotejin 克鲁包特金: Kropotkin

Kunming 昆明

Kunning Gong 坤宁宫 (坤寧宮): Palace of Earthly Repose

Kunning Men 坤宁门 (坤寧門): Gate of Earthly Repose

Kunqu 昆曲 (崑曲): Kunqu Opera

kuping 库平 (庫平): standard of weight

Kuroda Seiki 黑田清輝

Lai Caishan 来财山 (來財山): Lai Choi San

Lai Changxing 赖昌星

Lai Shengchuan 賴聲川

laiwang 来往: comings and goings

Lan fengzheng 蓝风筝: *The Blue Kite*

Lan Ni 蓝妮

Lang Ping 郎平

lankou 懒口: lazy mouth

Lanting xu 兰亭序 (蘭亭序): Orchid Pavilion preface

Lanxi 兰溪

Lanyi She 藍衣社 (藍衣社): Blue Shirt Society

Lanzhou 兰州

Lao Can youji 老残游记 (老殘游記): The travels of Lao Can

Lao Foye 老佛爷 (老佛爺): Old Buddha

lao geming diqu 老革命地区: old revolutionary base areas

Lao Gui 老鬼

lao jiefang qu 老解放区: old liberated areas

Lao She 老舍

lao wei zhi 劳卫制: labor and defense qualification system

Lao Zhang de zhexue 老张的哲学 (老張的哲學): The philosophy of Lao Zhang

laoban jidutu 老板基督徒: boss Christians

laodong baoxian 劳动保险: labor insurance

Laodong Bu 劳动部: Ministry of Labor

Laodong Fa 劳动法: Labor Law

Laodong he Shehui Baozhang Bu 劳动和社会保障部: Ministry of Labor and Social Security

laogai 劳改 (勞改): reform through labor

laogequ 老歌曲: old songs

laojiao 劳教: reeducation through labor

laojiao changsuo 劳教场所: sites for reform through reeducation

laonian daxue 老年大学: continuing education for the elderly

Laonianren Quanyi Baozhang Fa 老年人权益保障法: Law for the Protection of Elders' Rights

laosanjie 老三届: students of the three older classes

Laoshao Zu 老少组: Oldsters and Youngsters

laosheng 老生: mature male role type in Peking Opera

Laoyuan baitai 老猿百态 (老猿百態): The numerous guises of the gibbons, Hundred gibbons

Laozi 老子

Lasa 拉萨: Lhasa

Lei Feng 雷锋

Lei Feng 雷锋: a play by Jia Liu

Lei Zhen 雷震

Leifeng si zhao 雷峰夕照: sunset glow at Leifeng Pagoda

Leiyu 雷雨: *Thunderstorm*

li 例: regulations

li 礼 (禮): propriety, moral ideals, rites

Li An 李安: Ang Lee

Li Bai 李白

Li Bihua 李碧华

Li Bin 李斌

Li Boyuan 李伯元

Li Bozhao 李伯钊

Li Changchun 李长春

Li Ching 利菁

Li Chun 李纯

Li Da 李达

Li Dazhao 李大钊 (李大釗)

Li Denghui 李登辉 (李登輝): Lee Teng-hui

Li Dongping 李東平

Li Dou 李斗

Li Feigan 李芾甘

Li Fen 李芬

li gai shui 利改税: changing profit into tax

Li Guoding 李国鼎: K. T. Li

Li Guyi 李谷一

Li Hanqiu 李涵秋

Li Hanxiang 李翰祥

Li Hanzhang 李翰章

Li Honggang 李红钢

Li Hongzao 李鸿藻

Li Hongzhang 李鸿章 (李鴻章)

Li Hongzhi 李洪志

Li Hua 李桦

Li Huang 李璜

Li Ji 李济 (李濟)

Li Jianqiang 李建强

Li Jinfa 李金发 (李金髮)

Li Jinghan 李景漢

Li Jinhui 黎锦辉

Li Kenong 李克农

Li Keqiang 李克强

Li Keran 李可染

Li Lianjie 李连杰 (李連杰): Jet Li

Li Liejun 李烈钧 (李烈鈞)

Li Lili 黎莉莉

Li Lisan 李立三

Li Ming 黎明: Leon Lai

Li Minghui 黎明晖 (黎明暉)

Li Minwei 黎民伟 (黎民偉): Lai Man-wai

Li Ning 李宁

Li Peng 李鹏 (李鵬)

Li Pingshu 李平书

Li Qiujun 李秋君

Li Rui 李锐

Li Ruihuan 李瑞环

Li Ruiqing 李瑞清

Li Ruzhen 李汝珍

Li Shan 李山

Li shang wanglai 礼尚往来: Etiquette requires reciprocity

Li Shanlan 李善兰

Li Shiming 李世明

Li Shizeng 李石曾 (李石曾)

Li Shizhen 李时珍

Li Shuang 李爽

"Li Shunda zaowu" 李顺达造屋: Li Shunda builds a house

Li Shutong 李叔同

Li Tieying 李铁映

Li Weihan 李维汉

Li Xianglan 李香兰 (李香蘭)

Li Xiannian 李先念

Li Xianting 栗宪庭

Li Xiaobin 李晓斌

Li Xiaojiang 李小江

Li Xiaolong 李小龙 (李小龍): Bruce Lee

Li Xing 李行: Lee Hsing

Li Xiongcai 黎雄才

Li Yaotang 李尧棠

Li Yimin 李逸民

Li Yinghai 黎英海

Li Yishi 李毅士

Li Yongcun 李永存

Li Youcai banhua 李有才板话: The rhymes of Li Youcai

Li Yu 李渔

Li Yuanhong 黎元洪

Li Yunchang 李蕴昌

Li Zehou 李泽厚 (李澤厚)

Li Zhengdao 李政道: Tsung-Dao Lee

Li Zhenguo 李珍国

Li Zhensheng 李振盛

Li Zhongsheng 李仲生

Li Zicheng 李自成

Li Zongren 李宗仁

Li'an quanshu 例案全书 (例案全書): Compendium of precedent cases

lian 脸: face

Lian Kafo 连卡佛: Lane Crawford

Lian'ai de jijie 恋爱的季节: Season of love

Lian'ai yu yiwu 恋爱与义务: *Love and Duty*

Lianchitan 蓮池潭: Lotus Lake

liang 两 (兩): tael, weight measure of silver, varies by touch, approx. 37.5 grams

Liang Bingjun 梁秉钧 (梁秉鈞): Leung Ping-kwan

Liang Dingming 梁鼎铭

Liang Qichao 梁启超 (梁啟超)

Liang Shanbo 梁山伯

Liang Shanbo yu Zhu Yingtai 梁山伯與祝英台: Butterfly Violin Concerto

Liang Shiqiu 梁實秋

Liang Shuming 梁漱溟

Liang Sicheng 梁思成

Liang Siyong 梁思永

Liang Xiaobin 梁小斌

Liang Xiaosheng 梁晓声

Liang Xihong 梁錫鴻

Liang Zhou jinwenci daxi tulu kaoshi 两周金文辞大系图录考释 (兩周金文辭大系圖錄考釋): An illustrated and annotated compendium of bronze inscriptions from the two Zhou dynasties

liang'an guanxi 两岸关系: cross-strait relations

liangdi chi 量地尺: builder's foot

"Liangge fanshi" 两个凡是: Two whatevers

"Liangge jiating" 两个家庭 (兩個家庭): Two families

liangge kouhao de lunzheng 两个口号的论争: polemic of the two slogans

liangguo lun 两国论: two-states theory

lianghe gongsi 两合公司: limited and unlimited joint companies

Liang-Huai 两淮: Huainan and Huaibei

Liang-Jiang 两江: Jiangnan and Jiangbei

Liangjiang Shifan Xuetang 两江师范学堂: Liangjiang Higher Normal School

Liangshan Yizu Zizhizhou 凉山彝族自治州: Liangshan Autonomous Prefecture

liangtiaotui zoulu 两条腿走路: walking on two legs (pursuing dual policies)

Liangyou huabo 良友画报: Young companion

Liang-Zhu 梁祝: butterfly lovers

Liangzhu 良渚

Liangzhu wenhua 良渚文化: Liangzhu culture

Lianhe huabao 联合画报: United pictorial

Lianhe Kangzhan 联合抗战: United Front

Lianheguo 联合国: United Nations

Lianheguo Huanjing Jihua 联合国环境计划: United Nations Environmental Program

Lianheguo Xianzhang 联合国宪章: United Nations Bill of Rights

Lianhua 联华: United Photoplay

Lianhua Yingye Gongsi 联华影业公司: Lianhua Film Company, United China Film Company

Lianhuan huabao 连环画报: Comics illustrated

lianhuan tuhua 连环图画 (連環圖畫): picture book or comic strip

Lianhuan tuhua Sanguo zhi 连环图画三国志 (連環圖畫三國志): The comic-book history of the Three Kingdoms

lianhuanhua 连环画 (連環畫): picture book, serial illustrations, storytelling books

liansuo dian 连锁店: chain store

Lianxiang 联想: Lenovo

Lianyungang 连云港

Liao Bingxiong 廖冰兄

Liao Chengzhi 廖承志

Liao Ping 廖平

Liao Zhongkai 廖仲恺 (廖仲愷)

Liaodong 辽东

Liaohe 辽河

Liaoning 辽宁

Liaoshen zhanyi 辽沈战役 (遼沈戰役): Liaoshen campaign

Liaoxi 辽西

Libu 礼部 (禮部): Ministry of Rites

Lienüzhuan 列女传 (列女傳): Biographies of exemplary women

Liexian jiupai 列仙酒牌: Immortals wine cards

Lifa Fa 立法法: Legislation Law

Lifa Yuan 立法院: Legislative Yuan

Lifan Yuan 理藩院: Court or Office of Colonial Affairs

Lihun 离婚 (離婚): *The Quest for Love of Lao Li*

Liji 礼记 (禮記): *Book of Rites*

Lijiang-shi 丽江市: Lijiang City

lijiao 礼教 (禮教): ethical teachings

Lijiazhuang de bianqian 李家庄的变迁: The changes in Li Village

lijin 厘金 (釐金): transit tax, tax on goods in transit, trade tax

lilong 里弄: neighborhood lanes

Lin Biao 林彪

Lin Changmin 林长民

Lin Fengmian 林风眠 (林風眠)

Lin Huaimin 林懷民

Lin Huiyin 林徽因

Lin Lepei 林乐陪: Doming Lam

Lin Puqing 林普青

Lin Qiaozhi 林巧稚

Lin Qing 林清

Lin Shengxi 林聲翕: Lin Shengshih

Lin Shu 林纾

Lin Shuangwen 林爽文

Lin Tianmiao 林天苗

Lin Wenzheng 林文铮 (錚)

Lin Xiling 林希翎

Lin Xu 林旭

Lin Yifu 林毅夫: Justin Lin

Lin Yong 林墉

Lin Yutang 林语堂 (林語堂)

Lin Zexu 林则徐 (林則徐)

Lin Zhaotang 林兆棠

Lin Zhengsheng 林正盛

Lin'an 临安

ling 令: administrative code

Ling Fupeng 凌福彭

ling qi luzao 另起炉灶: setting up a new stove

Ling Ruitang 凌瑞棠

Ling Shiwei Neidachen 领侍卫内大臣 (領侍衛內大臣): grand minister of the Imperial Household Department concurrently controlling the Imperial Guard

Ling Shuhua 凌叔华 (凌叔華)

Ling Yun 凌云

lingchi 凌迟 (凌遲): death by slicing

lingdao ganbu 领导干部: leading cadres

Linggusi 陵谷寺: Linggu Monastery

Lingnan 岭南

Lingnan Daxue 岭南大学 (嶺南大學): Lingnan University

Lingnan huapai 岭南画派 (嶺南畫派): Lingnan school of painting

Lingnan Huayuan 岭南画院: Lingnan Studio

Lingnan Xueyuan 岭南学院 (嶺南學院): Lingnan College

lingpai 灵牌 (靈牌): spirit tablets

Lingshan 灵山: *Soul Mountain*

Linji 临济

Linjia da wan 林家大湾: big village of the Lin Family

"Linjia puzi" 林家铺子: Lin family shop

Linqing 临清

Lintong 临潼

Linzhi Diqu 林芝地区: Nyingchi

Lishi Yuyan Yanjiusuo 历史语言研究所 (歷史語言研究所): Institute of History and Philology

lishu 隶书 (隸書): clerical script

Lishui 澧水: Li River

Lisuzu 傈僳族: Lisu minority

Litang daoting lu 里堂道听录 (里堂道听錄): Litang's scholarly notes

liu 流: exile

Liu Bannong 刘半农 (劉半農)

Liu Binyan 刘宾雁 (劉賓雁)

Liu Bocheng 刘伯承

Liu Boliang 刘伯良 (劉伯良)

Liu Buchan 刘步蟾 (劉步蟾)

Liu Changchun 刘长春

Liu Chunhua 刘春华

Liu Dabai 刘大白 (劉大白)

Liu Dehua 刘德华: Andy Lau Tak-Wah

Liu Dunzhen 刘敦桢 (劉敦楨)

Liu E 刘鹗 (劉鶚)

Liu Fenglu 刘逢禄 (劉逢祿)

Liu Fu 刘复

Liu Fuzhi 刘复之

Liu Guangdi 刘光第 (劉光第)

Liu Guochang 刘国昌 (劉國昌): Lawrence Ah Mon

Liu Guosong 刘国松 (劉國松)

Liu Haisu 刘海粟

Liu Hongji Zhangfang 劉鴻記帳房: Lieu Ong Kee Accounts Office

Liu Hongsheng 刘鸿生 (劉鴻生)

Liu Huan 刘欢

Liu Huaqing 刘华清

Liu Kaiqu 刘开渠

Liu Kunyi 刘坤一 (劉坤一)

Liu Li 刘莉

Liu Meng jiangjun 劉猛將軍: General Liu Meng

Liu Meng Jiangjun Miao 刘猛将军庙 (劉猛將軍廟): General Liu Meng Temple

Liu Mingchuan 刘铭传

Liu Na'ou 刘呐鸥 (劉呐鷗)

Liu Qingzhu 刘庆柱

Liu Shaoqi 刘少奇 (劉少奇)

Liu Shifu 刘师复 (劉師復)

Liu Shipei 刘师培 (劉師培)

Liu Sifu 刘思复 (劉思復)

Liu Tianhua 刘天华

Liu Wang Liming 刘王黎明

Liu Wenhui 刘文辉

Liu Xian 刘岘

Liu Xiang (1890–1938) 刘湘

Liu Xiang (b. 1983) 刘翔

Liu Xiaobo 刘晓波

Liu Xiaoqing 刘晓庆

Liu Xie 刘勰

Liu Xihong 刘锡鸿

Liu Xiji 刘锡基 (劉錫基)

Liu Xin 刘歆

Liu Xinwu 刘心武

Liu Xun 劉迅

Liu Yandong 刘延东

Liu Yang 刘洋

Liu Ying 劉瑩

Liu Yizheng 柳诒徵 (柳詒徵)

Liu Yongfu 劉永福

Liu Yongxing 刘永行

Liu Yulian 刘宇廉

Liu Zhidan 刘志丹

Liubukou 六部口

liudong renkou 流动人口 (流動人口): floating population

Liuhe Yeshi 六合夜市: Liuhe Night Market

Liuhua Binguan 流花宾馆: Liuhua Hotel

Liuku 六库 (六庫): Six Storehouses

Liulichang 琉璃厂

liumang wenxue 流氓文学 (流氓文學): hooligan literature

Liuqiu 琉球: Ryukyu

Liu-Si Dongluan 六四动乱: Tiananmen Incident (1989)

Liu-Si Shijian 六四事件: Tiananmen Incident (1989), Prodemocracy Movement (1989)

liutong 流通: circulation

liutong bumen 流通部门: distribution sector, circulation sector

liuxing yinyue 流行音乐: popular music

liuxue 留学 (留學): study abroad

liuxuesheng 留学生 (留學生): overseas students

liuxuesheng wenxue 留学生文学: student immigrant literature

Liuyang 浏阳

Liuyuan 留园

Liwan 荔湾

lixing huihua 理性绘画: rationalist painting

Lixing yu ganxing 理性与感性: *Sense and Sensibility*

lixue 理学 (理學): neo-Confucianism

Lixue Guan 礼学馆: Bureau of Rites

Liyuan Gongshe 梨园公社: Liyuan Commune

Lizu 黎族: Li minority

long 龙: zoomorphic serpent spirits

long de chuanren 龍的傳人: descendants of the dragon

Long Yingtai 龍應台

Long Yun 龍雲

Long Zhu 龙朱

Longgushan 龙骨山: Longgu Hill

Longhushan 龙虎山 (龍虎山): Mt. Longhu

Longjing 龙井

Longkan shoujian 龙龛手鉴 (龍龕手鑑): Handy mirror of the dragon shrine

Longshan wenhua 龙山文化: Longshan culture

longtang 弄堂: lane, alley

Longxingsi 龙兴寺 (龍興寺): Longxing Temple

Longxu Gou 龙须沟 (龍鬚溝): Dragon Beard Ditch

longyang 龙洋: dragon dollars

Longzhou 龙州

Lou Jiwei 楼继伟

lü 律: principle legal code

Lu Ban jing 鲁班经 (魯班經): Classic of Lu Ban

Lü Bicheng 吕碧城

Lu Danfeng 卢丹枫

Lü Dongbin 吕洞宾 (呂洞賓)

Lu Erkui 陆尔奎 (陸爾奎)

Lu Fusheng 卢辅圣 (盧輔聖)

Lu Guoji 卢国纪

Lu Hao 陆昊

Lu Haodong 陆皓东

Lu Hui 陆恢 (陸恢)

Lü Ji 吕骥

Lu Jingren 吕敬人 (呂敬人)

Lü juren Haoke 绿巨人浩克: *Hulk*

Lu Kun 卢坤

Lu Ling 路翎

Lu Muzhen 卢慕贞 (盧慕貞)

Lü Peng 吕澎

Lu Qinzhai 卢芹斋 （盧芹齋）: C. T. (Ching Tsai) Loo

Lu Rongting 陆荣廷

Lu Shaofei 鲁少飞 (鲁少飛)

Lü Shengzhong 吕胜中

Lu Shifu 卢施福

Lu Shoukun 吕寿琨 (呂壽琨): Lui Shou-Kwan

Lu Wenfu 陆文夫

Lu Xiaoman 陆小曼 (陸小曼)

Lu Xinhua 卢新华

Lu Xun 鲁迅 (魯迅)

Lu Xun Yishu Wenxuyuan 鲁迅艺术文学院: Lun Xun Academy of Art

Lu Xun Yishu Xueyuan 鲁迅艺术学院: Lu Xun Academy of Art

Lu Yanshao 陆俨少

Lü Yanzhi 吕彦直 (呂彥直)

Lu Yawen 卢雅文 (盧雅文): Marina Lu

Lu Yi 鲁艺

Lü Zhengcao 吕正操

Lu Zhengxiang 陆征祥

Lü Zhenyu 吕振羽

Lu Zhiwei 陆志韦

Lu Zun'e 吕遵谔

Lu Zuofu 卢作孚

luan 乱 (亂): social disorder, chaos

luban chi 鲁班尺: carpenter's foot

lücha 绿茶 (綠茶): green tea

Lüda 旅大

lüdi 绿地: Green Lots

ludi 芦笛 (蘆笛): reed pipe

Lugou Qiao 卢沟桥 (盧溝橋): Marco Polo Bridge

Luguhu 泸沽湖: Lugu Lake

Luhuan 路環: Coloanne

Lüliangshan 吕梁山: Lüliang Mountains

lun 论: essay

"Lun 'Renyan kewei'" 论〈人言可畏〉(論〈人言可畏〉): On "Gossip is a fearful thing"

"Lun nüxue" 论女学 (論女學): On female education

Lun shibian zhi ji 论世变之亟: A discussion of the urgent need for change

"Lun xiaoshuo yu qunzhi zhi guanxi" 论小说与群治之关系 (論少說與群治之關係): On the relation between fiction and governance of the people

"Lun zhengle yan kan" 论睁了眼看 (論睜了眼看): On Facing Facts

Lunchuan Zhaoshangju 輪船招商局: China Merchants' Steam Navigation Company

Lundun Zhongguo Yishu Gouji Zhanlanhui Choubei Weiyuanhui 倫敦中國藝術國際展覽會籌備委員會: Chinese Organizing Committee of the International Exhibition of Chinese Art (London)

Lunlixue de qiyuan he fazhan 伦理学的起源和发展: Ethics, origin, and development

Lunyu 论语 (論語): *Analects*

lunzhe 論者: people with judgment

Luo Dayou 罗大佑

Luo Ergang 罗尔纲 (羅爾綱)

Luo Fu (b. 1928) 洛夫

Luo Fu (1898–1976) 洛甫

Luo Gongliu 罗工柳

Luo Guangda 罗光达

Luo Hongyu 罗鸿玉

Luo Longji 罗隆基

Luo Ronghuan 罗荣桓

Luo Ruiqing 罗瑞卿

Luo Xianglin 罗香林

Luo Yonghui 罗永晖 (羅永暉): Law Wing-fai

Luo Zhenyu 罗振玉 (羅振玉)

Luo Zhongli 罗中立

Luo Zhufeng 罗竹风 (羅竹風)

Luodi shenggen 落地生根: Touch the soil and extend roots

luopan 罗盘: geomancy compass

Luotuo xiangzi 骆驼祥子 (駱駝祥子): *Rickshaw: The Novel L'o-t'o Hsiang Tzu*

Luoyang 洛阳

Luoye guigen 落叶归根: Falling leaves return to the roots

Lüse Changcheng 綠色長城: Green Great Wall

Lushan 庐山

Lushan Guojia Gongyuan 庐山国家公园: Lushan National Park

lüshi 律诗 (律詩): regulated verse

lushi 戮尸 (戮屍): desecration of the corpse

Lüshi Fa 律师法: Lawyers Law

Lüshun 旅顺 (旅順): formerly Port Arthur

Luxi 鲁西

Lüying 绿营 (綠營): Green Standard Army

m 唔: not (Cantonese)

ma 吗: question particle

Ma Bo 马波

Ma Bufang 马步芳 (馬步芳)

Ma Buqing 马步青

Ma Desheng 马德升

Ma Feng 马烽

Ma Fuxiang 马福祥

Ma Guiyuan 马桂源

Ma Hefu 马和福

Ma Heng 马衡

Ma Hongbin 马鸿宾

Ma Hongkui 马鸿逵

Ma Hualong 马化龙

Ma Jianmin 马建民

Ma Ke 马可

Ma Laichi 马来迟

Ma Lin 马麟

Ma Mingxin 马明心, 马明新

Ma Qi 马麒

Ma Sicong 马思聪

Ma Wenlu 马文禄

Ma Xiangbo 马相伯

Ma Xiangdong 马向东

Ma Xiaojun 马孝骏 (馬孝駿): Hsiao-Tsun Ma

Ma Xulun 马叙伦

Ma Yinchu 马寅初

Ma Yingbiao 马应彪 (馬應彪)

Ma Yingjiu 马英九 (馬英九): Ma Ying-jeou

Ma Youcheng 马友乘 (馬友乘): Yeou-Cheng Ma

Ma Youyou 马友友 (馬友友): Yo-Yo Ma

Ma Yuan 马原

Ma Zhan'ao 马占鳌

Ma Zhongying 马仲英

magua 马褂 (馬褂): man's riding jacket

Maguan Tiaoyue 马关条约 (馬關條約): Treaty of Shimonoseki

maiban 买办 (買辦): comprador

maiban zibenjia 买办资本家: comprador capitalist

Maiwei Jihua 买位计划: Bought Place Scheme

majia 马甲 (馬甲): man's vest

majiang 麻将: mah-jongg

Maliezhuyi Xueyuan 马列主义学院: Marxism-Leninism Academy

Man cheng jin dai huangjin jia 满城尽带黄金甲: *Curse of the Golden Flower*

Mancheng 满城

Mang Ke 芒克

mangliu 盲流: unregistered migrants

manhua 漫画 (漫畫): sketched drawing, comics

Manshū Eiga Kyōkai 满州映画协会 (滿州映畫協會): Manchurian Film Studios

Manshūkoku 满洲国: Manchukuo

Manshūkoku Kyōwakai 满州国协和会 (滿州國協和會): Manchukuo Cooperation Association

manyue 满月 (滿月): full-month celebration after birth

Manyun 蛮允: Manwyne

Manzhou 满洲: Manchuria

Manzhou Da Diguo 满洲大帝国: Great Empire of Manchuria

Manzhouguo 满州国 (滿州國): Manchukuo

Manzu 满族: Manchu

Mao cheng ji 猫城记 (貓城記): Cat country

Mao Dun 茅盾

Mao Dun shuxin ji 茅盾书信集: Letters of Mao Dun

Mao Dun Wenxue Jiang 茅盾文学奖: Mao Dun Literature Scholarship

Mao Lizi 毛栗子

Mao Xuhui 毛旭辉

Mao Yuanxin 毛远新

Mao Zedong 毛泽东 (毛澤東)

Mao Zedong Guju 毛泽东故居: Mao Zedong Museum

Mao Zedong xuanji 毛泽东选集: *Selected Works of Mao Zedong*

Mao Zhuxi Jinian Tang 毛主席纪念堂: Chairman Mao's Mausoleum, Mao Zedong's Mausoleum

Mao zhuxi qu Anyuan 毛主席去安源: *Mao Goes to Anyuan*

Mao zhuxi yulu 毛主席语录: *Quotations from Chairman Mao* (Mao's "Little Red Book")

Mao Zhuxi yuluge: Weiren songge yaogun lianchang 毛主席语录歌: 伟人颂歌摇滚联唱: Musical settings of quotations from Chairman Mao: A rock and roll medley of praise songs for a great man

"**Maomaoyü**" 毛毛雨: Drizzle

Maotouying 猫头鹰: The winking owl

maoxianzhuyi 冒险主义: adventurism

Matsui Iwane 松井石根

Matsuoka Yoshimasa 松岡義正

Mawangdui 马王堆: Mawangdui tombs

Mawangdui yihao Handai gumu 马王堆一号汉代古墓: Mawangdui Han tomb no. 1

Mawei 马尾

Maxongshan 马雄山

Mazu 妈祖 (媽祖): the patron goddess of seafarers

Mazu 马祖: Matsu

Mei Guangdi 梅光迪

Mei Lanfang 梅兰芳 (梅蘭芳)

Mei Ru'ao 梅汝璈

Mei wan mei liao 没完没了: *Sorry Baby*

Mei Yangfang 梅艳芳: Anita Mui Yimfong

Meiguo 美国: United States of America

Meihua xishenpu 梅花喜神谱 (梅花喜神譜): Manual of plum-blossom likenesses

Meiji 明治

Meijing Shuwu 梅景書屋: Meijing Study

Meili nanfang zhi xiari 美丽南方之夏日: The beautiful summer in the south

Meilidao 美麗島

Meilidao Shijian 美麗島事件: Meilidao Incident

Meipai 梅派: Mei school of Peking Opera

meiren 美人: beauties

meiren hua 美人画 (美人畫): pictures of beautiful women

meishu 美术: fine art

Meishu 美術: Art

Meishu congshu 美术丛书: Collectanea of the arts

Meishu Diaocha Chu 美术调查处: Fine Arts Research Branch (Education Ministry)

meishu gongyipin 美术工艺品: arts and crafts products

Meishu shenghuo 美术生活: Art and life

meishu sheying 美术摄影: fine-art photography

Meishu zazhi 美术杂志 (美術雜誌): Art magazine

Meishujia Lianmeng 美术家联盟: League of Left-Wing Artists

Meixian 梅县 (梅縣): Mei County

Meiye Gongzhan 煤業公棧: Coal Merchants' Wharf

"**Meiyou Gongchandang jiu meiyou xin Zhongguo**" 没有共产党就没有新中国: Without the Communist Party there would be no new China

Meizhou wenxue 每周文学: Weekly literature

meng 盟: league

Meng Dingsheng 孟定生

Meng hu 猛虎: Fierce tiger

Meng Jiangnü 孟姜女

Meng Jinghui 孟京辉

Meng Ke 梦珂

Meng Luding 孟禄丁

Meng Sen 孟森

Meng Xuenong 孟学农

"**Meng yu shi**" 夢與詩: Dreams and Poetry

Menggu 蒙古: Mongolia

menggubao 蒙古包: yurt

Mengguguo 蒙古国: Mongolia

Mengguzu 蒙古族: Meng minority, Mongolians

Mengjiang 蒙疆

menglong shi 朦胧诗 (朦朧詩): misty, obscure poetry

Mengmao 猛卯: Maingmaw

Mengzi 孟子: *Mencius*

Mengzu 蒙族: Meng minority, Mongolians

menshen 门神 (門神): door gods

Mi Gu 米谷

Mian Mian 棉棉

Mianbao yu ziyou 面包与自由: *The Conquest of Bread*

Mianzhu 绵竹

mianzi 面子: face

Mianzi wenti 面子问题 (面子問題): A problem of face

mianzi xiaofei 面子消费: conspicuous consumption

Miaozu 苗族: Miao minority

Midi Yinyue Xuexiao 迷笛音乐学校: Midi School of Music

Midi Yinyuejie 迷笛音乐节: Midi Modern Music Festival

Midian zhulin 秘殿珠林: a Qing art catalog

Mifeng huaji 蜜蜂画集: Bee pictorial

Mifeng Huashe 蜜蜂画社: Bee Painting Society

mimi banghui 秘密幫會: secret society

mimi huidang 秘密會黨: secret society

mimi shehui 秘密社會: secret society

mimi xiehui 秘密協會: secret society

min 民: citizens, people

Min 闽 (閩): ancient name of Fujian; **Min language group**

Min bao 民报 (民報): People's journal

Min sheng 民声 (民聲): Voice of the people

Minami Manshū Tetsudō Kabushiki Kaisha 南満洲鉄道株式会社: South Manchurian Railway Company

minban 民办: privately managed

minban xuexiao 民办学校 (民辦學校): popularly managed schools, village schools

minbing 民兵: militia

minfa 民法: civil law

Minfa Tongze 民法通则: General Principles of Civil Law

ming 名: given name

Ming Taizu 明太祖: the founding emperor of the Ming dynasty

Mingchao 明朝: Ming dynasty

Mingdao Nüxue 明道女学: Bright Path Girls' School

minge 民歌: folk song

mingjia 名家: famous painter

Minglang de tian 明朗的天: Bright skies

mingli 名例: section on names of punishments in the Qing Code

Minglü 明律: Ming Code

mingpai 名牌: famous brand

minguo 民国: citizens' country, republic

Minguo yuebao 民国月报: National monthly

Mingxing 明星

Mingxing Yingpian Gongsi 明星影片公司: Mingxing Film Studio

Mingyue Gewutuan 明月歌舞团: Bright Moon Song and Dance Troupe

Mingzhu Qiang 民主墙: Democracy Wall

minjian 民间: the private sector, society

minjian banhua 民间版画: popular woodcuts

minjian meishu 民间美术: folk art

minjian muke banhua 民间木刻版画: folk woodcut print

minjian qudao 民间渠道: nongovernmental channels

minjian xinyang 民間信仰: popular beliefs, popular faith

Minjiazu 民家族: Minjia nationality

Minnan hua 闽南话: Southern Min (a dialect)

minquan 民权 (民權): people's rights (one of the three principles of the people)

Minquan bao 民权报: People's rights (journal)

Minshangshi xiguan diaocha baogaolu 民商事习惯调查报告录 (民商事習慣調查報告錄): Report on investigations of civil and commercial customs

minsheng 民生: people's livelihood (one of the three principles of the people)

Minsheng Gongsi 民生公司: Minsheng Shipping Company

Minsheng Yinhang 民生银行: Minsheng Bank

Minshi Qisu Fa 民事诉讼法: Civil Procedure Law

Minshisan zhi Gugong 民十三之故宫: The Forbidden City in the thirteenth year of the Republic

Minxin 民新: China Sun

minyi 民意: public opinion

Minyue 闽越 (閩越): ancient kingdom

Minzheng Bu 民政部: Department of Civil Affairs

Minzheng Ju 民政局: Civil Affairs Bureau

Minzhong Geyong Tuan 民众歌咏团: Masses Singing Assembly

minzhu 民主: democracy

Minzhu Dang 民主党 (民主黨): Democratic Party

minzhu dangpai 民主党派 (民主黨派): democratic parties and groups

Minzhu Jinbu Dang 民主进步党 (民主進步黨): Democratic Progressive Party

minzhu jizhong zhi 民主集中制: democratic centralism

Minzhu Shehui Dang 民主社会党 (民主社會黨): Democratic Socialist Party

Minzhu Taipingyang Lianmeng 民主太平洋联盟: Democratic Pacific Union

minzu 民族: nationalism, self-determination (one of the three principles of the people); people, race, nationality, ethnic minority

minzu fengge 民族风格: national style

minzu geming zhanzheng de dazhong wenxue 民族革命战争的大众文学 (民族革命戰爭的大眾文學): mass literature of national revolutionary struggle

minzu gewutuan 民族歌舞团: minority song and dance troupes

Minzu Wenhua Gong 民族文化宫: Ethnic Cultural Palace, Nationalities Cultural Palace

minzu xiang 民族乡: nationality township, ethnic township

minzu xingshi 民族形式: national forms

minzu zibenjia 民族资本家: national capitalist

minzu zichan jieji 民族资产阶级: national bourgeoisie

minzuhua 民族化: nationalize

mishu 秘书: aide

Mitsui 三井

mixin 迷信: superstition

Miyajima Saichirō 宫岛佐一郎

Miyazaki Torazō 宫崎寅蔵

Miyazaki Yazō 宫崎弘蔵

Mizhi 米脂

MK Muke Yanjiuhui MK木刻研究会: MK Society

Mo Yan 莫言

moban 模板: stencil printing

Mochouhu 莫愁湖: Mochou Lake

mofan jiaoyu 模范教育: model learning

Mogao Ku 莫高窟: Mogao Caves

mogu 没骨 (沒骨): boneless style

Mojing Dang 磨镜黨: Rubbing-Mirrors Party

moshi 模式: model

Mosuozu 摩梭族: Moso minority

Mou Zongsan 牟宗三

Mozi 墨子

mu 亩: Chinese land area measure, 0.16 acre

Mu Dan 穆旦

Mu Guiying guashuai 穆桂英挂帅 (穆桂英挂帥): Mu Guiying takes command

Mu Ouchu 穆藕初

Mu Shiying 穆时英 (穆時英)

Mu Suixin 慕绥新

muban 木版: woodblock edition

muban nianhua 木版年画: New Year pictures

Mubanhua 木版画: Woodblock prints

mubing zhi 募兵制: voluntary recruitment system

Muchang'a 穆彰阿

Mudanjiang 牡丹江

mufu 幕府: private secretariat, personal staff

"Mujiewen" 墓碣文: Epitaph

Mulan congjun 木兰从军 (木蘭從軍): Mulan joins the army

Mulanxi 木兰溪: Mulan River

Muli Zangzu 木里藏族: Muli Tibetans

Muling muke yanjiuhui 木铃木刻研究会: Dumb Bell Woodcut Research Society

Muqin Yang Mo 母亲杨沫: My mother Yang Mo

"Muqin" 母亲: Mother

muyou 幕友: staff member

Na Ying 那英

nacai 納采: an exchange of wedding gifts

Nahan 呐喊: *Call to Arms*

Naitō Konan 内藤湖南

Nakamura Fusetsu 中村不折

Nakayama 中山

Nan Shui Bei Diao Gong Cheng 南水北调工程: South-North Water Transfer Project

Nanbei Jushe 南北剧社: South North Drama Society

Nanbei shupai lun 南北书派论 (南北書派論): Northern and southern schools of calligraphy

nanbeizong 南北宗: southern and northern schools of painting

Nanchang 南昌

Nanchizi 南池子

nandan 男旦: female impersonator in Peking Opera

Nandian 南甸

Nanfang dushi bao 南方都市报: Southern metropolis (newspaper)

Nanfang ribao 南方日报: Nanfang daily

Nanfang Yishu Qunti 南方艺术群体: Southern Art Salon

nanga 南画: Japanese literati painting

Nangang 南港

Nanguo Yishu Xueyuan 南国艺术学院: Académie du Midi

Nanguo zaijian, nanguo 南国再见, 南国 (南國再見, 南國): *Good-bye South, Goodbye*

Nanguoshe 南国社: Southern Society

Nanhai 南海

Nanhui 南汇

Nanjing 南京: Nanking

Nanjing Datusha 南京大屠杀 (南京大屠殺): Nanjing Massacre

Nanjing Daxue 南京大学 (南京大學): Nanking University

Nanjing Minguo Zhengfu 南京民国政府: Republican government at Nanjing

Nanjing Tiaoyue 南京条约 (南京條約): Treaty of Nanjing

Nanjinglu 南京路: Nanjing Road

Nanjō Bunyū 南条文雄

Nanling 南岭: southern range

Nanniwan 南泥湾

Nanpi 南皮

Nanputuosi 南普陀寺: Nanaputuo Temple

Nanqiao huiyi lu 南侨回忆录: Memoirs of Tan Kah Kee

Nantong 南通

Nantong Bowuyuan 南通博物苑: Nantong Museum

nanxun 南巡: southern tour

Nanyang Huaqiao Chouzhen Zuguo Nanmin Zonghui 南洋华侨筹赈祖国难民总会: South Seas Chinese Relief Fund Union

Nanyang Quanye Hui 南洋劝业会: Nanyang Industrial Exposition

Nanyang Xiongdi Yancao Gongsi 南洋兄弟烟草公司: Nanyang Brothers Tobacco Company

Natong 那桐

Naxizu 纳西族: Naxi minority

nei 内: inner sphere

Nei Lingding Dao 内伶仃岛: Lintin Island

Nei Menggu 内蒙古: Inner Mongolia

neibu 内部: internal circulation

Neicheng 内城: Inner City

Neijiang 内江

neiluan waihuan 内乱外患: internal disorder and external threats

Neiting 内廷: Inner Court

Neiwu Fu 内务府 (內務府): Imperial Household Department

Nenjiang 嫩江: Nen River

Ni banshi, wo fangxin 你办事我放心: With you in charge, I feel at ease

"Ni bobu meishu yijianshu" 拟播布美术意见书: A plan to disseminate the fine arts

Ni ming 匿名: *The Secret Name*

Ni Tuosheng 倪柝声 (倪柝聲): Watchman Nee

Ni wo 你我: You and I

Ni Yide 倪贻德 (倪貽德)

nianhua 年画 (年畫): Chinese New Year pictures

Nianjun 捻军 (捻軍): Nian Army, Nian rebels

Nianjun Qiyi 捻军起义 (捻軍起義): Nian Uprising

niao he longzi de guanxi 鸟和笼子的关系: like a bird in a cage (the relationship between the economy and administration)

Niaochao 鸟巢: Bird's Nest

Nie Er 聂耳

Nie Rongzhen 聂荣臻 (聶榮臻)

Nie Ying 聂嫈

Niehai bolan 孽海波澜: Waves of a sea of sin

Niehai hua 孽海花: A flower in a sinful sea

Nihon Nanga In 日本南画院: Japan Literati Painting Academy

nihonga 日本画: Japanese-style painting

niming hehuo 匿名合伙: dormant partnerships

Ningbo 宁波 (寧波)

Ningbo Shangye Yinhang 宁波商业银行: Ningbo Commercial and Savings Bank

Ninghai 宁海

ningju hexin 凝聚核心: coagulate core

Ningshou Gong 宁寿宫 (宁壽宮): Palace of Repose and Longevity

Ningxia 宁夏

Ningxia Huizu Zizhiqu 宁夏回族自治区: Ningxia Hui Autonomous Region

Nippon Hōsō Kyokai 日本放送協会: Japan Broadcasting Corporation

Nisu Yi 尼苏彝: Nosuo Yi minority

Niu Tianci zhuan 牛天赐传 (牛天賜傳): Heavensent

Niuzhuang 牛庄

nong 农: rural

nongcun 农村: rural areas

nongcun jishi 农村集市: rural markets

nongcun xinyong she 农村信用社: rural credit cooperatives

nongmin 农民: farmers, peasants

nongmin hua 农民画: peasant paintings

Nongmin Yundong Jiangxi Suo 农民运动讲习所: Peasant Movement Training Institute

nongye 农业: agriculture

Nongye Bu 农业部: Ministry of Agriculture

Nongye Fazhan Yinhang 农业发展银行: Agricultural Development Bank of China

Nongye xue Dazhai 农业学大寨: In agriculture, learn from Dazhai

Nongzheng quanshu 农政全书 (農政全書): A compendium on agricultural administration

Nuerhachi 努尔哈赤 (努爾哈赤): Nurgaci, Nurhachi

nügong 女工: womanly skills

Nujiang 怒江: Nu River

Nülan wuhao 女篮五号: Woman basketball player number five

Nüren 女人: Women

Nüshen 女神: Goddesses

Nüwa 女娲

Nüzhen 女真: Jurchens

Oga Seiun 小鹿青云

Okada Asatarō 岡田朝太郎

Okinawaken 沖縄県: Okinawa Prefecture

Ōmura Seigai 大村西崖

Ōsaka 大阪: Osaka

Ōtaka Yoshiko 大鷹淑子

"**Ouran**" 偶然: A chance encounter

Ouyang Jian 歐陽漸

Ouyang Jingwu 歐陽竟無

P'yŏngyang 平壤: Pyongyang

"**Pa man qingteng de muwu**" 爬满青藤的木屋: The ivy-covered wooden hut

pai 派: political group, school

pai 牌: a registration unit in the *baojia* community self-defense system; playing cards

paichu jigou 派出机构: provincial governments' delegated organ

paifang 牌坊: memorial archways

Paifangcun 牌坊村

paigou 派购: purchase by state quotas

paijiu 牌九: making nine (a domino game)

pailou 牌楼: memorial archways

paitou 牌头 (牌頭): head of a registration unit

Paiyun Dian 排云殿: Cloud Dispelling Hall

paizi 牌子: trademark

Pan Guangdan 潘光旦

Pan Jingshu 潘靜淑

Pan Shuhua 潘淑華 (潘淑华)

Pan Tianshou 潘天寿 (潘天壽)

Pan Yuliang 潘玉良

Pan Zuyin 潘祖蔭

Pang Tao 庞涛

Pang Xunqin 庞薰琹 (龐薰琹)

Panghuang 彷徨: *Wandering*

Panjin 盘锦

Panyu 番禺

Panzhihua 攀枝花

Pei Wenzhong 裴文中

Peligang wenhua 裴李岗文化: Peiligang culture

Peng Dehuai 彭德怀 (彭德懷)

Peng Pai 彭湃

Peng Shuzhi 彭述之

Peng Zemin 彭泽民

Peng Zhen 彭真

Penghu Qundao 澎湖群島: Pescadores Islands

pengtiao 烹调: cooking

Pengtoushan wenhua 彭头山文化: Pengtoushan culture

Pengyou shi zanshi de, liyi shi yongheng de 朋友是暂时的, 利益是永恒的: Friendship is temporary, only self-interest is forever

Pi Xirui 皮锡瑞 (皮錫瑞)

piaohao 票号 (票號): remittance business, an antecedent of private banking in China

pihuang 皮黄: a style of operatic singing

Pingdingshan 平丁山

Pinghuashe Shuhua Hui 萍花社书画会 (萍花社書畫會): Duckweek Blossom Society

Pingjiang 平江

pingjun diquan, jiezhi ziben 平均地权, 节制资本 (平均地權, 節制資本): equalizing landownership, restraining capital

pingmin jiaoyu 平民教育: mass education

Pingpuzu 平埔族: Lowland Tribes

pingtiao 平粜: below-market grain sales

Pingxiang 萍乡

Pingyao 平遥

pinjin 聘金: brideprice

pinli 聘礼 (聘禮): gifts for the bride to confirm a marital union

pinpai 品牌: brand

pipa 琵琶: Chinese lute

pizi wenxue 痞子文学 (痞子文學): hooligan literature

po Sijiu 破四旧: smash the Four Old's

Pochan Fa 破产法: Bankruptcy Law

popi 泼皮: cynical realism

Poyanghu 鄱阳湖: Lake Poyang

Pu Jin 蒲忻

Pu Quan 溥佺

Pu Xinyu 溥心畲

Puchengxian 蒲城县: Pucheng County

Pucun 朴存

Pudong Xinqu 浦东新区: Pudong New Area

puji 普及: popularization

pujitang 普济堂: poorhouses

Pukou 浦口

Pulandian 普兰店

Pumizu 普米族: Pumi minority

Putian 莆田

Putonghua 普通话: Mandarin, the common language, the vernacular language

Puyi 溥仪 (溥儀)

qi 旗: banner

qi 气 (氣): vital force; breath, energy; vitalities; human desires

Qi Baishi 齐白石 (齊白石)

qi chu 七出: seven outs

Qi Gong 启功

qi junzi 七君子: seven honorable gentlemen

Qi Longwei 祁龙威

Qi zhui ji 七缀集: Collection of seven patchings

Qian Binghe 钱病鹤 (錢病鶴)

Qian Huian 钱慧安

Qian Juntao 钱君陶 (錢君匋)

Qian Mu 钱穆 (錢穆)

Qian Qichen 钱其琛

Qian Shizhi 钱食芝

Qian Shoutie 钱瘦铁

Qian Songling 钱松龄

Qian Songyan 钱松岩

Qian Xiaodai 钱笑呆 (錢笑呆)

Qian Xingcun 钱杏邨 (錢杏邨)

Qian Xuantong 钱玄同

Qian xue 钱学: Qian studies

Qian Zhongshu 钱钟书

Qian Zhongshu yanjiu 钱钟书研究: Studies on Qian Zhongshu

Qian'an 倩庵

Qiandaohu 千岛湖

Qianfo Dong 千佛洞: Thousand Buddha Caves

Qiang Xuehui 强学会 (強學會): Self-Strengthening Society, Society for National Strengthening, Strength Study Society

qiangshou qi 强手棋: Monopoly

Qiangxue bao 强学报: Journal of self-strengthening studies

Qiangzu 羌族: Qiang minority

Qianjin fang 千金方: Essential formulas for emergencies worth a thousand pieces of gold

"Qianjin ge" 前进歌: Song of advance

Qianjin Tianzhutang 前金天主堂: Holy Rosary Cathedral

Qianjinzhong de Zhongguo Qingnian Meishu Zuopin Zhanlan 前进中的中国青年美术作品展览: Advancing Young Artists Exhibition

Qianlong 乾隆: emperor (r. 1736–1795)

Qianlongwang 钱龙网: Dragon Net

Qianmen 前门: Qian Gate

Qianqing Gong 乾清宫 (乾清宮): Palace of Heavenly Purity

Qianqing Men 乾清门 (乾清門): Gate of Heavenly Purity

Qianshou Guanyin 千手观音: Thousand-Hand Guanyin

Qiantangjiang 钱塘江: Qiantang River

Qianwan bie ba wo dang ren 千万别把我当人: *Please Don't Call Me Human*

qianwei xiaoshuo 前卫小说: avant-garde fiction

Qianxi Manbo 千喜曼波: *Millennium Mambo*

qianyin 铅印: lead type (for printing)

qianzhuang 钱庄 (錢莊): money houses, native banks, small local banks, an antecedent of private banking in China

Qiao 桥 (橋): The Bridge

qiaojuan 侨眷: overseas-Chinese dependents (residing in China)

qiaowu 侨务 (僑務): overseas Chinese affairs

qiaoxiang 侨乡: overseas-Chinese homeland communities, migrants' native areas

Qidao 奇岛 (奇島): *Unexpected Island*

Qie Gewala 切格瓦拉: Che Guevara

Qieyun 切韵 (切韻): a rhyming dictionary

qigai 乞丐: beggar

qigong 气功 (氣功): Chinese cultivation exercises, discipline of the vital force

qigong re 气功热: qigong boom

qigongjie 气功界: qigong world

Qijin 旗津: Cijin

qijuzhu 起居注: court diaries

Qimeng 启蒙: Enlightenment (journal)

"Qimeng" 奇梦: Strange dreams

Qin Hua Rijun Nanjing Datusha Yu'nan Tongbao Jinian Guan 侵华日军南京大屠杀遇难同胞纪念馆: Nanjing Massacre Memorial Hall

Qin Hui 秦晖

qin liugan 禽流感: avian flu

Qin Shi Huangdi 秦始皇帝: First Emperor of Qin

Qin Shouou 秦瘦鸥

Qin wang Li Shimin 秦王李世民: Li Shimin, prince of Qin

Qin Zihao 覃子豪

Qincheng Jianyu 秦城监狱: Qincheng Prison

Qinchuan Nanyang 秦川南陽

Qinding Hubu caoyun quanshu 钦定户部漕运全书 (钦定户部漕運全書): The Board of Revenue's complete book on grain transport

qing 情: care, empathy, fondness, friendship, forgiveness, respect, sentiment

Qing Bang 青帮: Green Gang

Qing gong yuan 清宫怨: *Malice of Empire*

"Qing he yibei suyoucha" 请喝一杯酥油茶: Drink a cup of buttered tea

Qing Niwakou 清泥洼口

Qing qinwang 庆亲王: Prince Qing

Qing shi 情史: A brief classification of stories about *qing*

Qing shi gao 清史稿: Manuscript history of the Qing dynasty

Qing yi bao 清议报 (清議報): Public opinion, The China discussion

qing yinyue 轻音乐: light music

qingcha 青茶: semifermented tea

Qingchao 清朝: Qing dynasty

Qingchuan 青川

Qingchun wansui 青春万岁: Long live youth

Qingchun zhi ge 青春之歌: *Song of Youth*

Qingdai tongshi 清代通史: A general history of the Qing period

Qingdao 青岛

Qingdao Daxue 青岛大学: Qingdao University

Qinghai 青海

Qinghongbang 青红帮: Green and Red Gangs

Qinghua Daxue 清华大学 (清華大學): Tsinghua University

Qinghua Daxue Gaodeng Yanjiu Zhongxin 清华大学高等研究中心: Institute of Advanced Studies at Tsinghua University

Qingjian 清涧

Qingjie Fazhan Jizhi 清洁发展机制: Clean Development Mechanism

qingjie shengchan celüe 清洁生产策略: cleaner production strategy

qingliu dang 清流党: purification clique

Qingming 清明: Spring

Qingming Jie 清明节 (清明節): Chinese All Souls' Day

Qingming qianhou 清明前后: Before and after the Qingming Festival

Qingming shang he tu 清明上河图 (清明上河圖): Along the River during Qingming Festival

Qingnian 青年: Youth

Qingnian gangqin xiezouqu 青年钢琴协奏曲: Youth piano concerto

Qingniantuan Ganbu Xunlianban 青年團幹部訓練班: Youth Corps Cadre Training School

Qingning Gong 清宁宫 (清寧宮): Pure Tranquility Palace

Qingong Jianxuesheng Tuan 勤工俭学生团 (勤工儉學生團): Movement for Diligent Work and Frugal Study

Qingpu 青浦

Qingqidui 轻骑队: Light cavalry (newspaper)

Qingwei Lingbao 清微灵宝 (清微靈寶): A lineage of elite Zhengyi Daoists

qingxu touzi 情绪投资: make investment decisions on the basis of emotion

qingyi 清议 (清議): moral leadership, disinterested counsel

qingyi 青衣: virtuous-female role type in Peking Opera

Qingyi Yuan 清漪园 (清漪園): Clear Ripples Garden

Qingyun Ge 卿云歌 (卿雲歌): Clouds of Hope

Qing-Zang Gaoyuan 青藏高原: Tibetan Plateau

Qing-Zang Tielu 青藏铁路: Qinghai-Tibet Railway

Qinhuaihe 秦淮河

Qinhuangdao 秦皇岛

Qinlingshan 秦岭山: Qinling Mountain

Qinmin Dang 亲民党 (親民黨): People First Party

Qinnan 秦南

Qinqiang 秦腔: Shaanxi Opera

Qinshihuang Lingmu 秦始皇陵墓: Mausoleum of the First Qin Emperor

Qinshui 沁水

Qiongzhou 琼州 (瓊州)

qipao 旗袍: Mandarin gown, cheongsam, traditional Chinese dress

Qi-qie chengqun 妻妾成群: Wives and concubines

Qiqihaer 齐齐哈尔

731 Butai 731部队 (731部隊): Unit 731

Qishan 琦善

Qitingqiao 屺亭桥

Qiu Fengjia 丘逢甲

Qiu Haitang 秋海棠

Qiu Jin 秋瑾

Qiu Ling 邱陵

Qiu Ti 丘堤

qiushen 秋审: autumn assizes

qiye danwei 企业单位: enterprise

qiye jituan 企业集团: enterprise group

Qiying 耆英

Qiyue 七月

qu 区: ward

qu 曲: aria

Qu Leilei 曲磊磊

Qu Qiubai 瞿秋白

Qu Xiaosong 瞿小松

Qu Yuan 屈原

Qu Yuan 屈原: a historical play

Quanguo Funü Lianhehui 全国妇联和会: All-China Women's Federation

Quanguo Furu Jiuji Hui 全国妇孺救济会: National Women's and Children's Salvation Society

Quanguo Gejie Jiuguo Lianhehui 全国各界救国联合会 (全國各界救國聯合會): National Anti-Japanese Salvation Association

Quanguo Jingji Weiyuanhui 全国经济委员会 (全國經濟委員會): National Economic Council

Quanguo Lishi Dang'an Ziliao Mulu Zhongxin 全國歷史檔案資料目錄中心: Union Finding-List Centers for Historical Archival Materials

Quanguo Nongye Zhanlanguan 全国农业展览馆: National Agricultural Exhibition Hall

Quanguo Renmin Daibiao Dahui 全国人民代表大会: National People's Congress

Quanguo Renmin Daibiao Dahui Changwu Weiyuanhui 全国人民代表大会常务委员会: Standing Committee of the National People's Congress

Quanguo Shengtai Huanjing Baohu Gangyao 全国生态环境保护纲要: Outline on National Eco-environment Protection

Quanguo Shengwu Wuzhong Ziyuan Baohu yu Liyong Guihua Gangyao 全国生物物种资源保护与利用规划纲要: Outline on Planning for the Protection and Utilization of National Species Resources

Quanguo Weiyuanhui 全国委员会: National Committee

Quanguo Zhengxie Wenshi he Xuexi Weiyuanhui 全国政协文史和学习委员会: Literature History and Study Committee

quanmian xiaokang shehui 全面小康社会: comprehensive small-welfare society

quanmin jie bing 全民皆兵: a nation under arms

quanmin waijiao 全民外交: people's diplomacy

Quanmin zongdongyuan 全民总动员 (全民總動員): Total mobilization

quanmindang 全民党: party for all the people

quanpan xihua 全盘西化: wholesale Westernization

Quanxue pian 劝学篇 (勸學篇): Exhortation to study

Quanzhen 全真: an order of Daoist clerics

Quanzhou 泉州

quanzong 全宗: fond, record group in archives

queguan 榷关: tax checkpoint

qun 裙: skirt

Qun bao 群报: The masses (newspaper)

qunsi 群祀: third tier of state cults

Qunyan 群言: Tribune

qunzhong gequ 群众歌曲: songs for the masses

qunzhong luxian 群众路线: mass line

qunzhong yishu 群众艺术: art for the masses

quyi 曲艺: dramatic folk literary forms

Quzhou 衢州

rangwai bi xian annei 攘外必先安内: pacifying within to resist without

Rao Shushi 饶漱石

Raosanling 绕三灵: festival

Rehe 热河

ren 仁: benevolence

Ren Bonian 任伯年

Ren Guang 任光

Ren Jiyu 任继愈

Ren shou gui 人·兽·鬼: Humans, beasts, and ghosts

Ren Wanding 任畹町

Ren Xia 任霞

Ren xiaoyao 任逍遥: *Unknown Pleasures*

Ren Xiong 任熊

Ren Xun 任熏

Ren Yi 任颐 (任頤)

Ren Yu 任预

Ren Zhongyi 任仲夷

rencai qiangguo 人才强国: a great power with talented people

Renjian shi 人间世 (人間世): The human world

Renjian Siyue tian 人间四月天 (人間四月天): April in the human world

renkou pucha 人口普查: census

Renli Ziyuan he Shehui Baozhang Bu 人力资源和社会保障部: Ministry of Human Resources and Social Security

renmin 人民: the people

Renmin Chubanshe 人民出版社: People's Press

Renmin Da Huitang 人民大会堂: Great Hall of the People

Renmin Daibiao Dahui 人民代表大会: People's Congress

Renmin Daxue 人民大学: People's University of China

renmin gongshe 人民公社: people's communes

Renmin huabao 人民画报: People's pictorial, *China pictorial*

Renmin Jiaoyu Chubanshe 人民教育出版社: People's Education Press

Renmin Jiefangjun 人民解放军 (人民解放軍): People's Liberation Army

Renmin Jiefangjun Haijun 人民解放军海军: People's Liberation Army Navy

Renmin Jiefangjun Kongjun 中国人民解放军空军: People's Liberation Army Air Force

Renmin Meishu Chubanshe 人民美术出版社: People's Fine Art Publishing House

Renmin Minzhu Tongyi Zhanxian 人民民主统一战线: Peoples' Democratic United Front

renmin minzhu zhuanzheng 人民民主专政: people's democratic dictatorship

Renmin ribao 人民日报: *People's Daily*

Renmin wenxue 人民文学: People's literature

Renmin Wuzhuang Jingcha Budui 人民武装警察部队: People's Armed Police

Renmin Yingxiong Jinian Bei 人民英雄纪念碑: Monument to the People's Heroes

Renmin yinyue 人民音乐: People's music (journal)

renmin zhanzheng 人民战争: people's war

Renmin Zhengzhi Huiyi 人民政治会议 (人民政治會議): People's Political Council

Renmin Zhisheng 人民之声: Voice of the People

Renminbi 人民币: the currency of China

renqing 人情: feelings of reciprocal obligation, human feelings, moral propriety

renquan 人权: human rights

Renshan 仁山

Renshen 妊娠: Pregnancy

Renshi Bu 人事部: Ministry of Personnel

Renshou Dian 仁寿殿 (仁壽殿): Bliss and Longevity Hall

renxing 人性: human nature

renxu 认许: permission

"Renyao zhi jian" 人妖之间: Between man and demon

"Rexue" 热血: Boiling blood

Ri Kōran 李香蘭

Riben 日本: Japan

Riben guozhi 日本国志 (日本國志): A treatise of the Japanese nation

Richu 日出: *Sunrise*

Ri-E Zhanzheng 日俄戰爭: Russo-Japanese War

Rikuchōha 六朝派: Six-Dynasties school

Rishengchang Piaohao 日升昌票号: a remittance firm

Rong Desheng 荣德生

rong er ru yu yilu 融而入于一炉: smelt together in single furnace

Rong Hong 容闳 (容閎): Yung Wing

Rong Hongyuan 荣鸿元

Rong Ruixing 荣瑞馨

Rong Yiren 荣毅仁 (榮毅仁)

Rong Zongjing 荣宗敬

ronghe 融合: fusion

ronghe Zhong Xi 融合中西: synthesizing the Chinese and the Western

Ronglu 荣禄

Roshiajin Jimu Kyoku ロシア人事務局: Bureau for the Affairs of Russian Émigrés

Rou Shi 柔石

Ru Zhijuan 茹志鹃

Ruan Agen 阮阿根

Ruan Fenggen 阮凤根

Ruan Lingyu 阮玲玉

Ruan Lingyu 阮玲玉: *Center Stage* (film)

Ruan Yuan 阮元

Ruan Yuying 阮玉英

Ruijin 瑞金

Rujiao 儒教: Confucianism

Rulin waishi 儒林外史: *The Scholars*

runli 润例: established profit margin

rusheng 入声: entering tone

"Ruwu hou" 入伍后: After entering the ranks

Ruxue 儒学 (儒學): Confucianism

ruzhui hun 入赘婚 (入贅婚): uxorilocal marriage

Ryūkyū Han 琉球藩: Ryukyu Domain

Sai Jinhua 赛金花 (賽金花)

Sai Jinhua 赛金花 (賽金花): a play

Sai xiansheng 赛先生 (賽先生): Mr. Science

Sai Zhenzhu 赛珍珠: Pearl S. Buck

Saidi Jituan 赛迪集团: CCID (China Center for Information Industry Development) Group

Saidi Zixun 赛迪咨询: CCID (China Center for Information Industry Development) Consulting

Saishang xing 塞上行: Journeys on the frontier

Saiyinsi xiansheng 赛因斯先生: Mr. Science

"San Ba Jie ganyan" 三八节感言: Thoughts on the March Eighth Festival

san buqu 三不去: three limitations

san he yi 三合一: three in one

San ji xiao duzhe 三寄小读者 (三寄小讀者): Still more letters to young readers

San mao 三毛: Three hairs

san Miao 三苗: three prehistoric Miao ethnic groups

san nong wenti 三农问题: three rural issues

san Qin 三秦: the three parts of the Qin empire

San si yi 三四一: Three, four, one

san tong 三通: three direct links

san tuchu 三突出: the three prominences

San ye ji 三叶集 (三葉集): Three leaves

sanba ganbu 三八干部: 1938 cadre

sanbailiushi hang 三百六十行: the 360 trades

Sanbaxiang 三坝乡: Sanba Township

sancong 三从 (三從): three obediences

Sandouping 三斗坪

Sanfan Wufan yundong 三反五反运动 (三反五反運動): Three-Anti's and Five-Anti's campaigns

Sang Tong 桑桐

Sange Daibiao 三个代表: Three Represent's

sange jueqi 三个崛起: three risings

Sange modeng nüxing 三个摩登女性: Three modern women

"Sange nanren he yige nüren" 三个男人和一个女人: Three men and a woman

sange shijie lilun 三个世界理论: three-worlds theory

sangji yutang 桑基鱼塘: mulberry tree and fish pond

Sanguo yanyi 三国演义 (三國演義): *Romance of the Three Kingdoms*

Sanguo zhi 三国志 (三國志): History of the Three Kingdoms

Sangyuanwei 桑园围: Mulberry Garden Enclosure

Sanhai 三海: Three Seas

sanheyuan 三合院: three-sided or u-shaped courtyard house

sanhua 三化: the three-pronged line

sanjue 三绝 (三絕): three perfections (poetry, calligraphy, and painting)

sanlei shangpin 三类商品: category-three goods

Sanliwan 三里湾: a novel

sanluan 三乱: arbitrary collection of fees, apportionments, and fundraising

Sanmenwan 三门湾

Sanmenxia 三门峡

Sanmenxia Guoguo Mudi Bowuguan 三门峡虢国墓地博物馆: Sanmenxia Guo State Tomb Museum

sanminzhuyi 三民主义 (三民主義): three principles of the people

Sanminzhuyi Lixing She 三民主义力行社 (三民主義力行社): Three People's Principles Earnest Action Society

Sanminzhuyi Qingnian Tuan 三民主义青年团 (三民主義青年團): Three People's Principles Youth Corps

Sanminzhuyi Yanjiusuo 三民主义研究所: Institute of Three Peoples' Principles

Sanshan Wuyuan 三山五园 (三山五園): Three Hills and Five Gardens

sanshi shuo 三世说 (三世說): three-age doctrine

Sanshui 三水

Sanwan 三湾

sanwen 散文: miscellaneous essay writing

sanwu 三无: three lackings, i.e., lacking proof of identity, lacking work, and lacking fixed residence

Sanxia Da Ba 三峡大坝: Three Gorges Dam

Sanxia Gongcheng 三峡工程: Three Gorges Project

Sanxiasheng 三峡省: Three Gorges Province

sanxian 三线: third front

Sanxian Jianshe 三线建设: Three Lines of Construction

Sanxingdui 三星堆

Sanya 三亚

Sanyi 三邑: Three Counties

Sanzi Aiguo yundong 三自爱国运动: Three-Self's Patriotic movement

Sanzi yundong 三自运动: Three-Self's movement

Satomi Katsuzō 里見勝蔵

Se, jie 色, 戒: *Lust, Caution*

seikei bunri 政経分離: separation of politics from economics

Seikyōsha 政教社: Society for Political Education

sengdao 僧道: Buddhist and Taoist clerics

Senggelinqin (Senggerinchin) 僧格林沁

Senlin Fa 森林法: Forest Law

Senoo Masahiko 妹尾正彦

sha 煞: vital force generated by destructive directions

Sha Ding 沙汀

Sha Fei 沙飞

Sha Mei 沙梅

Sha Yexin 沙叶新

Shaanbei 陕北

Shaanxi 陕西

Shaanxi Lishi Bowuguan 陕西历史博物馆: Shaanxi History Museum

"Shafei nüshi de riji" 莎菲女士的日记: Miss Sophie's diary

Shahekou 沙河口

shaizi 色子: dice

Shamian 沙面

Shan shang de xiao wu 山上的小屋: The cabin in the mountains

Shandong 山东

Shandong Chouzhen Hui 山东筹赈会: Shantung Relief Fund

Shandong Qilu Daxue 山东齐鲁大学 (山東齊魯大學): Shangtung Christian University

shang 商: merchants

Shang Qin 商禽

Shan-Gan-Ning bianqu 陕甘宁边区: Shaanxi-Gansu-Ningxia border region

shangbang 商帮: merchant groups

Shangbiao Fa 商标法: Trademark Law

Shangchao 商朝: Shang dynasty

shangfangzhe 上访者: petitioner

shangguan 商馆 (商館): factories

Shanghai 上海

Shanghai baiwan daheng 上海百万大亨 (上海百萬大亨): Monopoly

Shanghai bang 上海帮: Shanghai gang

Shanghai baobei 上海宝贝: Shanghai baby

Shanghai Baogang Jituan Gongsi 上海宝钢集团公司: Baosteel

Shanghai Baoxue She 上海报学社 (上海報學社): Shanghai Journalism Society

Shanghai Bowuguan 上海博物馆: Shanghai Museum

Shanghai Dianli Gongsi 上海电力公司: Shanghai Power Company

Shanghai Diyi Tequ Difang Fayuan 上海第一特区地方法院 (上海第一特區地方法院): First Special District Court of Shanghai

Shanghai Fa Zujie 上海法租界: Shanghai French Concession (La concession française de Changhaï)

Shanghai Gangtie Gufen Youxian Gongsi 上海钢铁股份有限公司: Shanghai Steel

Shanghai Gongbao 上海公报: Shanghai Communiqué

Shanghai Gongbuju 上海工部局: Shanghai Municipal Council

Shanghai Gonggong Zujie 上海公共租界: Shanghai International Settlement

Shanghai Guangfanyan Guan 上海广方言馆 (上海廣方言舘): Shanghai Foreign Language School

Shanghai Hezuo Zuzhi 上海合作组织: Shanghai Cooperation Organization

Shanghai hua 上海话: Shanghainese

Shanghai huabao 上海画报: Shanghai pictorial

Shanghai Huanqiu Jinrong Zhongxin 上海環球金融中心: Shanghai World Financial Center

Shanghai Jiaotong Daxue 上海交通大学: Shanghai Jiaotong University

Shanghai Manhua 上海漫画 (上海漫畫): Shanghai sketch

Shanghai Meishan Gangtie Gufen Youxian Gongsi 上海梅山钢铁股份有限公司: Meishan Steel

Shanghai Meizhuan 上海美专: Shanghai Art Academy

Shanghai Meishu Zhuanmen Xuexiao 上海美术专门学校: Shanghai Art College, Shanghai Art School

Shanghai poke 上海泼克 (上海潑克): Shanghai punch

Shanghai Shangye Yinhang 上海商业银行: Shanghai Commercial and Savings Bank

Shanghai Shuangnian Zhan 2000 年双年展2000: Shanghai Biennale 2000

Shanghai Shuhua Hui 上海书画会: Shanghai Calligraphy and Painting Society

Shanghai Shuhua Yanjiuhui 上海书画研究会: Shanghai Calligraphy and Painting Study Society

Shanghai Tuhua Meishu Yuan 上海图画美术院: Shanghai Pictorial Art School

Shanghai wenyi 上海文艺: Shanghai literature

Shanghai wuguo 上海五国: Shanghai five

Shanghai Ying-Mei Yancao Gongsi 上海英美烟草公司 (上海英美菸草公司): British American Tobacco Company

Shanghai Yinyue Xueyuan 上海音乐学院: Shanghai Conservatory

Shanghai Zhongguo Huayuan 上海中國畫院: Shanghai Painting Institute

Shanghai Zhongguo Shuhua Baocun Hui 上海中国书画保存会: Shanghai Chinese Calligraphy and Painting Preservation Society

Shanghai Zhonghua Yishu Daxue 上海中华艺术大学: Shanghai Chinese Arts University

Shanghaishi Zuojia Xiehui 上海市作家协会: Shanghai Writers' Association

shanghan 伤寒: cold damage

Shanghan lun 伤寒论: Treatise on cold damage

shanghen huihua 伤痕绘画: scar painting

shanghen meishu 伤恨美术: scar art

shanghen sheying 伤痕摄影: scar photography

shanghen wenxue 伤痕文学: scar literature, literature of the wounded

shanghen yishu 伤痕艺术: scar art

shanghui 商会 (商會): chambers of commerce

Shangmei Tu'an Guan 尚美图案馆 (尚美圖案館): Shangmei Design Studio

shangpin 商品: merchandise

Shangpin Jianyan Ju 商品检验局: Commodity Inspection Bureau

shangshan xiaxiang yundong 上山下乡运动: up to the mountains and down to the countryside movement

shangshen 商绅 (商紳): merchant-gentry

"Shangshi" 伤逝 (傷逝): Regret for the past

Shangshu 尚书 (尚書): Classic of history

Shangshu dazhuan, **"Yuxia zhuan"** 尚书大传·虞夏传: biography of Yuxia in the Book of History

shangsi 上祀: first tier of state cults

shangtou 上头 (上頭): hair-styling ritual in a wedding

Shangwu Bu 商务部: Ministry of Commerce

Shangwuyin Shuguan 商务印书馆 (商務印書館): Commercial Press

shangxia zhi tong 上下之通: communication between high and low

Shangxin Taipingyang 伤心太平洋: Grieving over the Pacific Ocean

Shangye Yinhang Fa 商业银行法: Commercial Bank Law

shangzhan 商战 (商戰): business warfare, commercial warfare

Shangzhou 商州

Shangzhou sanji 商州散记: Random notes on Shangzhou

Shanhai no onna 上海の女: A woman of Shanghai

Shanhaiguan 山海关

Shanqi 善耆

shanshu 善书: morality book

shantang 善堂: charity halls

Shantou 汕头: Swatow

Shanxi 山西

Shanxi Bowuguan 山西博物馆: Shanxi Museum

Shanxi Da Xuetang 山西大学堂: Shanxi University

Shanxi dangxun fukan 山西党讯副刊: Shanxi party newsletter supplement

Shanxiang jubian 山乡巨变 (山鄉巨變): Great change in a mountain village

shanyaodanpai 山药蛋派: mountain yam school

Shao Fei 邵飞 (邵飛)

Shao Keping 邵克萍

Shao shi xiongdi 邵氏兄弟: Shaw brothers

Shao Xunmei 邵洵美

Shao Yuanchong 邵元冲

Shaobohu 邵伯湖: Lake Shaobo

Shaonian Gong 少年宫: Children's Palace

Shaonian Kaige 少年凯歌: the youthful Kaige

Shaonian Zhongguo Xuehui 少年中国学会: Young China Association

shaoshu minzu 少数民族: minorities, minority nationalities

shaoshu minzu diqu 少数民族地区: minority areas

Shaoxing 紹興

Shaoxing Lü Hu Tongxiang Hui 绍兴旅沪同乡会: Shaoxing Compatriots Society in Shanghai

Shashi 沙市

"Shayangnala" 沙扬娜拉 (沙揚娜拉): Sayonara

shayingzui 杀婴罪: crime of infanticide

shehui tuanti 社会团体: social groups

shehuidiguozhuyi 社会帝国主义: social-imperialism

shehuizhuyi jiaoyu yundong 社会主义教育运动: socialist education campaign

shehuizhuyi xianshizhuyi 社会主义现实主义: socialist realism

shehuizhuyi xin shehui 社会主义新社会: new socialism

shehuizhuyi xueyuan 社会主义学院: institutes of socialism

Shei zhi guo 谁之过 (誰之過): Whose fault is this?

Sheji Tan 社稷坛 (社稷壇): Alters of Soil and Grain

Shekou Gongye Qu 蛇口工业區: Shekou Industrial Zone

Shen 申: Shanghai

Shen Baozhen 沈葆桢

Shen Bochen 沈伯尘 (沈伯塵)

Shen Congwen 沈从文 (沈從文)

Shen Dehong 沈德鸿

Shen Enfu 沈恩孚

Shen Jiaben 沈家本

Shen Junru 沈钧儒

Shen Manyun 沈曼云 (沈曼雲)

Shen Meishu 沈美叔

Shen Pengnian 沈彭年

Shen Shuyong 沈樹鏞

Shen Xingong 沈心工

Shen Yanbing 沈雁冰

Shen Yinmo 沈尹默

Shen Zengzhi 沈曾植

Shen Zurong 沈祖荣

Shenbao 申报 (申報): Shun Pao, Shanghai daily

Shenbaoguan 申报馆: a publishing house

Shenci Cunfei Biaozhun 神祠存廢標準: Standards for Determining Temples and Shrines to be Destroyed or Maintained

sheng 省: province

Sheng Shicai 盛世才

Sheng Xuanhuai 盛宣怀

Sheng Yuehan Daxue 圣约翰大学 (聖約翰大學): St. John's University

Sheng Zongliang 盛宗亮: Bright Sheng

"Sheng" 生: Living

shengchan dadui 生产大队: production brigade

shengchan dui 生产队: production team

Shengchan Jianshe Bingtuan 生产建设兵团: Production and Construction Corps

shengchan xiaodui 生产小队: production team

Shengchan yundong dahechang 生产运动大合唱: Production movement cantata

shengchanli lilun 生产力理论: productive-forces theory

shengcun quan 生存权: right to subsistence

shengguan tu 升官图 (升官圖): promotions chart (a board game)

Shenghuo de yishu 生活的艺术 (生活的藝術): *The Importance of Living*

Shenghuo zhoubao 生活周报 (生活周報): Life weekly

shengji 省级: provincial level

shengli 省例: provincial pronouncements, provincial regulations

Shengli Youtian 胜利油田: Shengli Oil Fields

Shengming de tuteng 生命的图腾: Totems of life

Shengming zhi liu 生命之流: Current of life (painting)

Shengshan tu 剩山圖: Surviving Mountain

Shengsi pilao 生死疲劳: Life and death are wearing me out

shengwairen 省外人: person from outside the province

Shengwu Duoyangxing Baohu Xingdong Jihua 生物多样性保护行动计划: Biodiversity Action Plan

Shengyu 圣谕 (聖谕): Sacred Edict

shengyuan 生员 (生員): licentiate, prefectural graduate, bachelor's degree

Shenji Shu 审计署: National Audit Office, National Auditing Administration

shenkui 腎虧: weakness of the kidney

Shenmei Shuguan 审美书馆: Aesthetics Bookshop

Shennong bencao jing 神农本草经: Shennong's classic of materia medica

Shennü 神女: *The Goddess*

shenpan ting 审判庭: adjudication chambers

Shenquan 神拳: Spirit Boxers

Shenquan 神拳: Invincible fist

shenshang 绅商: gentry and merchants

shenshi 绅士 (紳士): gentry

Shenwu zhi ai 神巫之爱: The shaman's love

shenxian 審限: deadline for a ruling

shenxiu 身修: moral character

Shenyang 沈阳: Mukden

Shenzhen 深圳

Shenzhen Daxue 深圳大學: Shenzhen University

Shenzhen Jingji Tequ 深圳經濟特區: Shenzhen Special Economic Zone

Shenzhen ren 深圳人: Shenzhen people

Shenzhou guoguang ji 神州国光集: The glories of Cathay

shenzhuan 審轉: judicial review and ratification

shequ 社区: communities

Shewai Jingji Hetong Fa 涉外经济合同法: Foreign Economic Contract Law

Shewai Wenhua Yishu Biaoyan ji Zhanlan Guanli Guiding 涉外文化艺术表演及展览管理规定: Regulatory Measures for Foreign-Related Cultural, Art, and Exhibition Activities

Shexian 歙县: She County

shexue 社学 (社學): community school

sheying xinchao 摄影新潮 (攝影新潮): photographic new wave

sheying yishu 摄影艺术: art of photography

Shezu 畲族: She minority

shi 士: scholar-official

shi 市: municipality

Shi 蚀: Eclipse

shi 诗: poetry

"**Shi bashou**" 诗八首 (詩八首): Eight poems

Shi Dakai 石达开

Shi ershiwushou 诗二十五首: Twenty-five poems

Shi Hui 施慧

Shi Jinbo 施金波: Shi Kumpor

Shi kan 诗刊: Poetry journal

Shi Liang 史良

Shi Liangcai 史量才

Shi Lu 石鲁

Shi lun 诗论 (詩論): On poetry

Shi Pingmei 石评梅

Shi Shaohua 石少华

Shi Weiliang 史惟亮

Shi Wu Zai 十五仔: Shap-ng-tsai

Shi Yi 施谊

Shi yu 石语: Words of Stone

Shi yuekan 诗月刊: Poetry monthly

Shi Zhaoji 施肇基

Shi Zhecun 施蛰存

Shibao 时报 (時報): Eastern times, Times, China times

"**Shibasheng dili lishi**" 十八省地理历史: Geography and history of the eighteen provinces

Shibasui chumen yuanxing 十八岁出门远行: Leaving home at eighteen

shibei 石碑: steles

Shida Kōtarō 志田鉀太郎

shidafu hua 士大夫画: scholar-official's painting

Shidai 时代 (時代): Modern miscellany (a pictorial)

Shidai butong le, nannü dou yiyang 时代不同了，男女都一样: The times have changed, yet men and women are the same

Shidai manhua 时代漫画 (時代漫畫): Time comics, Modern sketch

shidai qu 时代曲 (時代曲): modern songs, modern Chinese pop

shi'erzi fangzhen 十二字方针: twelve-words approach

shifan daxue 师范大学: normal university

shifan jiaoyu 师范教育: normal education

shifan xuexiao 师范学校: normal school

shifan xueyuan 师范学院: normal college

shifang 时方: contemporary formula

Shifenyi Hui 十分一会 (十分一會): Ten Percent Club

"**Shifou**" 是否: Yes or no

shifu hua 士夫画: scholar-official's painting

shigu 石鼓: stone drums

shigu wen 石鼓文: stone-drum script

Shihou 狮吼: Roaring lion

shihua 诗话: poetry critique

Shiji 史记 (史記): Records of the historian

shijian 诗笺 (詩箋): poetry paper

Shijiazhuang 石家庄

Shijie 世界: *The World*

shijie geming 诗界革命 (詩界革命): revolution in poetry

Shijie Renlei Ziran Yichan 世界人类自然遗产: World Heritage Sites

Shijie Renquan Xuanyan 世界人权宣言: Universal Declaration of Human Rights

Shijie ribao 世界日报: World daily

Shijie Shuju 世界书局 (世界書局): World Book Company

Shijing 诗经 (詩經): Book of songs, Book of odes, Classic of poetry

Shijingshan 石景山

Shijingshan Gongyuan 石景山公园: Shijingshan Park

shikumen 石库门: stonegate houses

Shimen 石門

Shimenwan 石门湾 (石門灣)

Shimian maifu 十面埋伏: *House of Flying Daggers*

shimin shehui 市民社会: civil society

Shimoda Utako 下田歌子

Shimonoseki Jōyaku 下関条約: Treaty of Shimonoseki

shimu 市亩: Chinese land-area measure

shin nanga 新南画: new literati painting

Shina kaiga shi 支那絵画史: History of Chinese painting

Shina kaiga shōshi 支那絵画小史: A concise history of Chinese painting

Shina no yoru 支那の夜: China Night

Shinbu Gakkō 振武学校: Shinbu Military School

Shinian yixunjian 十年一迅间: Flashback: A decade of changes, 1976–1986

shiping 时评: short editorials

Shiqikong Qiao 十七孔桥 (十七孔橋): Seventeen Arch Bridge

Shiqisui de danche 十七岁的单车: *Beijing Bicycle*

shiqu 市区: urban district, urban core

Shiqu baoji 石渠宝笈: a Qing art catalog

shiquan 十全: ten accomplishments of the Qianlong period

Shiro to kuro 白と黒: White and black

Shisan Yamen 十三衙门 (十三衙門): Thirteen Bureaus

shisanhang 十三行: hong merchants

Shisanjing zhushu 十三经注疏 (十三經注疏): Thirteen classics with commentary

shishen 士绅: scholar-gentry

Shishi manhua 时事漫画 (時事漫畫): a current-affairs comic

shishi qiushi 实事求是: seeking truth from facts

Shishi xinbao 时事新报 (時事新報): New current affairs daily

Shishido Tamaki 宍戶璣

"Shisi hanwei wuchan jieji wenhua dageming" 誓死捍卫无产阶级文化大革命: Pledge your life to defend the Great Proletarian Cultural Revolution

Shisihang ji 十四行集: Sonnets

Shitai de jijie 矢态的季节: Season of loss

Shitao 石涛 (石濤)

Shiwan 石湾

Shiwei 侍卫 (侍衛): Imperial Guard

Shiwu bao 时务报 (時務報): Chinese progress, Journal of current affairs

Shiwu guan 十五贯 (十五貫): Fifteen strings of cash

Shiwu Xuetang 事务学堂: School of Current Affairs

shixiaqu 市辖区: municipal districts

shixue 实学 (實學): practical studies, concrete studies

shiyan sheying 实验摄影: experimental photography

shiyan xiaoshuo 实验小说: experimental fiction

shiye danwei 事业单位: public institution, public sector

shiyi zhiyi 师夷制夷 (師夷制夷): Learn from the barbarians to rein them in

shiyin 石印: lithographic texts

shiyong 市用: commercial standard of weights and measures

shiyou 室友: roommate

shizhe shengcun 適者生存: survival of the fittest

Shizhi 食指

Shizhuzhai jianpu 十竹斋笺谱 (十竹齋箋譜): Decorated letter paper from the Ten Bamboo Studio

shizi peixun 师资培训: teacher training

Shizilin 狮子林: Lion Grove Garden

shizu 始祖: founding ancestor

shōka zōshin no zu 証果増進の図: promotions chart of accumulated karma

shougongye 手工业: handicraft

shouhui 手绘: hand painting on a print

shouhui jiaoyu quan yundong 收回教育权运动 (收回教育權運動): movement for reclaiming educational sovereignty

shouhui liquan 收回利权: recover sovereign rights, retrieve lost economic rights

Shouhuo 收获: Harvest

Shouji 手机: *Cell Phone*

Shouxihu 瘦西湖: Slender West Lake

Shouxun 寿勋

shouye 授业: to receive training in the tradition

Shu 蜀

Shu Han 叔翰

Shu Qi 叔齐 (叔齊)

Shu Qingchun 舒庆春 (舒慶春)

Shu Ting 舒婷

Shu Xincheng 舒新城

Shuangbai fangzhen 双百方针: Hundred Flowers campaign

shuanggui 双规: double rules

Shuangjianlou shanben shumu 双鉴楼善本书目 (雙鑒樓善本書目): Shuangjianlou rare book catalog

shudao 书道 (書道): epistle school of calligraphy

shuhao 书号: registration numbers for books and periodicals

shuhua 书画 (書畫): Chinese character paintings

Shui Hua 水华

Shui Wuran Fangzhi Fa 水污染防治法: Water Pollution Prevention Law

Shuihu Zhuan 水浒传 (水滸傳): *All Men Are Brothers, Outlaws of the Marsh, Water Margin*

shuili 水利: water management

Shuilifang 水立方: Water Cube

Shuiwu Ju 税务局 (稅務局): Revenue Board

Shuiwu Xuetang 税务学堂 (稅務學堂): Customs College

Shuixia Wenwu Baohu Guanli Tiaoli 水下文物保护管理条例 (水下文物保護管理條例): Regulations on the

Protection and Administration of Underwater Cultural Relics

shuixiu wu 水袖舞: water-sleeve dance

Shuizu 水族: Shui minority

Shuji Chu 书记处: Secretariat

shuji zhuanhuang 书籍装潢 (書籍裝潢): book design

Shujing 书经: Classic of history

shuju 书局 (書局): printing office

Shumu dawen 书目答问: Answers and questions on book catalogs

Shun 舜

Shundexian 顺德县: Shunde County

Shunzhi 顺治: emperor (r. 1644–1661)

shuo 说: essay

Shuoshuo changchang 说说唱唱: Reciting and singing

Shuowen jiezi 说文解字 (說文解字): Explanations of simple and compound characters

shushang 书商: book traders

Shushu de gushi 叔叔的故事: Story of an uncle

shuwang 书王: book kings

shuxue 书学 (書學): epistle school of calligraphy

Shuxue bao 蜀学报: Journal of Sichuan learning

Shuxue Hui 蜀学会: Society of Sichuan Learning

shuyuan 书院 (書院): academies, Confucian academies

si 死: death penalty

si 私: private, privacy

Si Outang 四歐堂

Si Wang 四王: the Four Wangs

Si Wang huapai 四王画派: orthodox school of the Four Wangs

si zi yuanze 四自原则: four self's principle

Sichou zhi Lu 丝绸之路: Silk Road

Sichou zhi Lu xiangmu 丝绸之路项目: Silk Road Project

Sichuan 四川

Sichuan Daxue 四川大学 (四川大學): Sichuan University

Sichuan Jiqi Ju 四川机器局: Sichuan Arsenal

Sichuan Wenchuan da dizhen 四川汶川大地震: Sichuan earthquake of May 12, 2008

sida mingdan 四大名旦: the four great female impersonators in Peking Opera

Sida Tianwang 四大天王: Four Heavenly Kings, 1990s Canto-pop singers

side 四德: four virtues

sidian 祀典: register of sacrifices

sifa weiyuanhui 司法委员会: committees on political and judicial matters

Sifa Yuan 司法院: Judicial Yuan

Sige Xiandaihua 四个现代化: Four Modernizations

siheyuan 四合院: traditional courtyard architecture

Sijiu 四旧: the Four Old's

sijue 四绝: the four perfections

Siku quanshu 四库全书 (四庫全書): Complete library of the four treasuries

sili 私立: privately established

Silu huayu 丝路花雨: Silk Road flower and rain

Sima Qian 司马迁

simiao 寺庙: temples

simin 四民: four classes of people

Siming Gongsuo 四明公所: Ningbo Commercial Guild

Siqin Gerile 斯琴格日乐

Sirenbang 四人帮: Gang of Four

Sisheng Nongye Yinhang 四省农业银行: Four Provinces Agricultural Bank

sishi tongtang 四世同堂: Four generations under one roof

Sishu 四书: the Four Books

sishu 私塾: traditional private schools, village and community schools

Sishu jizhu 四书集注: Selected Commentaries on the Four Books

Sishu Wujing 四书五经: the Four Books and Five Classics

Si-Wu Luntan 四五论坛: April fifth forum

sixiang jiben yuanze 四项基本原则: Four Basic Principles

sixiang jiefang 思想解放: emancipation of thought

Siyi 四邑: the Four Counties

Si-yiling Jiaoyu Gaige Shifan 四一〇教育改革示范: 4/10 Demonstration for Educational Reform

"Siyuan" 私愿: A secret wish

Xiziwan 西子湾 (西子灣): Siziwan

song 送: sending off

Song Ailing 宋蔼龄

Song Boren 宋伯仁

Song Chuyu 宋楚瑜: James Soong

Song Defu 宋德福

Song Huizong 宋徽宗

Song Jiaoren 宋教仁

Song Jiaoren Jinian Ta 宋教仁纪念塔: Song Jiaoren Memorial

Song Jiashu 宋嘉树 (宋嘉樹): Charlie Soong

Song Junfu 宋君复

Song Meiling 宋美龄: Mayling Soong

Song Ping 宋平

Song Qingling 宋庆龄 (宋慶齡)

Song Renqiong 宋任穷

Song Ruhai 宋如海

Song Shu 宋恕

Song xue 宋学 (宋學): Song learning

Song Ziliang 宋子良: T. L. Soong

Song Ziwen 宋子文 T. V. Soong

Songchao 宋朝: Song dynasty

Songhuajiang 松花江: Songhua River, Sungari River

"Songhuajiang shang" 松花江上: On the Songhua River

Songjiang 松江

Songjiangpai 松江派: Songjiang school

Songpan 松潘

Songshi xuanzhu 宋诗选注: An annotated selection of Song dynasty poetry

Soshū no yoru 蘇州の夜: Suzhou Night

Souhu 搜狐: Sohu

Su Bai 宿白

Su Bingqi 苏秉琦 (蘇秉琦)

Su Cong 苏聪 (蘇聰)

Su Di chun xiao 苏堤春晓: spring dawn at Su Causeway

Su Manshu 苏曼殊 (蘇曼殊)

Su Shi 苏轼 (蘇軾)

Su Tong 苏童

Su Wen 苏汶 (蘇汶)

Su Wonong 苏卧农 (蘇臥農)

Su Xuelin 苏雪林 (蘇雪林)

Su Yu 粟裕

Suao 苏澳

Subei 苏北

Suhua bao 俗话报 (俗話報): Vernacular magazine

Sui Jianguo 隋建国

Suichao 隋朝: Sui dynasty

suigan lu 随感录 (隨感錄): random thoughts

Suiyuan 綏遠

Suiyuan shidan 随园食单 (隨園食單): Menus of Suiyuan

suku 诉苦: recount suffering

suli 俗例: folk practice

Sulian 苏联: Soviet Union, Soviet

Sulian jianwen lu 苏联见闻录: Eyewitness account of the Soviet Union

Sulian zhi You She yinyue xiaozu 苏联之友社音乐小组: Soviet Friends Society

Sun Baoxin 孙宝信

Sun Benwen 孙本文 (孫本文)

Sun Chuanfang 孙传芳 (孫傳芳)

Sun Daolin Dianying Yishu Guan 孙道临电影艺术馆 (孫道臨電影藝術館): Sun Daolin Film Museum

Sun Duoci 孙多慈

Sun Ganlu 孙甘露

Sun Jianai 孙家鼐

Sun Mei 孙眉 (孫眉)

Sun Qian 孙谦

Sun Qingyuan 孙庆原 (孫慶原)

Sun Shaozhen 孙绍振

Sun Simiao 孙思邈

Sun Wen 孙文 (孫文): Sun Yat-sen

Sun Wenyao 孙文耀 (孫文耀)

Sun Wukong san da Baigujing 孙悟空三打白骨精: Monkey beats the White-Boned Demon

Sun Yirang 孙诒让 (孫詒讓)

Sun Yixian 孙逸仙 (孫逸仙): Sun Yat-sen

Sun Yu 孙瑜

Sun Zhigang 孙志刚 (孫志剛)

Sun Zhongshan 孙中山 (孫中山): Sun Yat-sen

suona 唢呐: a Chinese shawm

suoyang 缩阳 (縮陽): genital retraction syndrome [lit., retraction of yang]

Sushun 肃顺 (肅順)

suzhi 素质: quality

suzhi jiaoyu 素质教育: quality education

Suzhou 肃州: in Gansu Provence

Suzhou 苏州: in Jiangsu Provence

Suzhou Daxue 苏州大学 (蘇州大學): Suzhou University

Suzhou Gongye Yuanqu 苏州工业园区: Suzhou Industrial Park

Suzhou Xinqu 苏州新区: Suzhou New District

Suzhou Yishu Xuexiao 苏州艺术学校: Suzhou Art Training Institute

Suzhou zhi ye 苏州之夜 (蘇州之夜): Suzhou night

Suzhouhe 苏州河: *Suzhou River* (film)

suzhoujue 苏州撅: Suzhou hairdo

Taguchi Ukichi 田口卯吉

Taibei 台北: Taipei

Taibei Dangdai Yishuguan 台北当代艺术馆 (臺北當代藝術館): Museum of Contemporary Art, Taipei

Taibei Shili Meishuguan 台北市立美术馆 (臺北市立美術館): Taipei Fine Arts Museum

Taibei Shizhengfu Dushi Fazhan Ju 台北市政府都市发展局 (臺北市政府都市發展局): Taibei Bureau of Urban Development

Taierzhuang 台儿庄

Taierzhuang Huizhan 台儿庄会战 (臺兒莊會戰): Battle of Taierzhuang

Taihai guanxi 台海关系: cross-strait relations

Taihangshan 太行山: Taihang Mountains

Taihe Dian 太和殿: Hall of Great Harmony, Hall of Supreme Harmony

Taihu 太湖: Lake Tai

Taiji 太极: tai chi, Chinese martial exercises

Taiping Tianguo 太平天国 (太平天國): Heavenly Kingdom of Great Peace (Taiping Rebellion)

Taiping Tianguo Qiyi 太平天国起义 (太平天國起義): Taiping Uprising, Taiping Rebellion

Taiping Zhongwangfu 太平忠王府: a nineteenth-century palace

Taipingyang bao 太平洋报 (太平洋報): Pacific times

Taishan 台山: a coastal city in Guangdong Province

Taishan 泰山: Mt. Tai

Taiwan 台湾 (臺灣)

Taiwan Dushi Jihua Ling 台湾都市计画令 (台灣都市計畫令): Taiwan Urban Planning Ordinance

Taiwan Gaodeng Jiaoyu Pinggu he Jianding Weiyuanhui 台湾高等教育评估和检定委员会 (台灣高等教育評估和檢定委員會): Higher Education Evaluation and Accreditation Council of Taiwan

Taiwan Guanxi Fa 台湾关系法: Taiwan Relations Act

Taiwan Jiti Dianlu Gongsi 台湾集体电路公司 (台灣集体電路公司): Taiwan Semiconductor Corporation

Taiwan Minnanyu Yinbiao Xitong 台湾闽南语音标系统 (台灣閩南語音標系統): Taiwanese Southern Min Spelling System

Taiwan Minzhu Jijin Hui 台湾民主基金会 (台灣民主基金會): Taiwan Foundation for Democracy

Taiwan Minzhu Zizhi Tongmeng 台湾民主自治同盟 (台灣民主自治同盟): Taiwan Democratic Self-Government League

Taiwan Suliao Gongsi 台湾塑料公司 (台灣塑料公司): Formosa Plastics Corporation

Taiwan Tuanjie Lianmeng 台湾团结联盟 (台灣團結聯盟): Taiwan Solidarity Union

Taiwan wuqu 台湾舞曲: Taiwan dance, an orchestral piece

Taiwan yingzaojie 台湾营造界 (台灣營造界): Journal of the Taiwan building industry

Taiwanshi Yanjiusuo 台湾史研究所 (台灣史研究所): Institute of Taiwan History

Taixu 太虚

Taiyang he ren 太阳和人: Sun and man

Taiyang She 太阳社 (太陽社): Sun Society

Taiyang zhao zai Sangganhe shang 太阳照在桑干河上: The sun shines over the Sanggan River

Taiyuan 太原

Taiyuan Huizhan 太原会战 (太原會戰): Battle of Taiyuan

Taizhong 台中: Taichung

Taizhou 台州

taizi 太子: princeling (ordinary meaning: crown prince)

Takehisa Yumeji 竹久夢二

Takelamagan Shamo 塔克拉玛干沙漠: Taklamakan Desert

Takeuchi Seihō 竹内栖鳳

Talimu Pendi 塔里木盆地: Tarim Basin

tan 坛 (壇): Daoist family altar

Tan Dun 谭盾

Tan pai 谭派 (谭派): Tan school

Tan Shichang Xintuo Jijin 碳市场信托基金: Asia Pacific Carbon Fund

Tan Sitong 谭嗣同 (譚嗣同)

Tan Xiaolin 谭小麟

Tan Yankai 谭延闿 (譚延闓)

Tan yi lu 谈艺录: On the art of poetics

Tan Zheng 谭政

Tan Zhenlin 谭震林

Tan Zhonglin 谭钟麟

Tang Caichang 唐才常

Tang Guangzhao 唐光照

Tang hua 唐话: Tang speech

Tang Hualong 汤化龙 (湯化龍)

Tang Jingxing 唐景星: Tong King-Sing

Tang Jiyao 唐继尧

Tang Junyi 唐君毅

Tang Kunhua 唐昆华

Tang Qunying 唐群英

Tang Shaoyi 唐绍仪

Tang Xiangming 汤芗铭

Tang Xiong 唐熊

Tang'an Dongzu Shengtai Bowuguan 堂安侗族生态博物馆: Tang'an Dong Ecological Museum

tangbao 塘报: court gazette

Tangchao 唐朝: Tang dynasty; also Tang Dynasty (band)

tangfei 堂费: additional tuition charged by schools to build up their contingency funds

Tangren 唐人: men of Tang

Tangren jie 唐人街: Chinatown

Tangrenjie jiating 唐人街家庭: *Chinatown Family*

Tangshan 唐山

Tansuo 探索: Exploration

Tanxu 倓虚

Tao Menghe 陶孟和

Tao Xingzhi 陶行知

Tao Xisheng 陶希圣

Tao Yuanqing 陶元庆 (陶元慶)

Tao Zhiyue 陶峙岳

Tao Zhu 陶澍

Taohua qixue ji 桃花泣血记: *Peach Blossom Weeps Tears of Blood*

"**Taohuajiang**" 桃花江: Peach Blossom River

Taoli chunfeng 桃李春风 (桃李春風)

Taose de yun 桃色的云 (桃色的雲): Peach-Colored Cloud

taoyin banhua 套印版画: polychromatic woodcut

Taoyuanxian 桃园县: Taoyuan County

tebieshi 特别市: special municipalities

teji mofan jiaoshi 特级模范教师: superior model teachers

Teng Baiye 滕白也

Teng Ge'er 腾格尔

Teng Gu 滕固

Teng Haiqing 滕海清

Tengyue 腾越: Momein

Ti xiao jie fei 啼笑皆非: *Between Tears and Laughter*

Tian Fengshan 田凤山

Tian Han 田汉

Tian Heng wubaishi 田横五百士: Tian Heng and his five hundred retainers

Tian Xiaoqing 田晓青

Tiananmen 天安门 (天安門): Gate of Heavenly Peace

Tiananmen Guangchang 天安门广场: Tiananmen Square

Tiananmen Shijian 天安门事件: Prodemocracy Movement (1989), Tiananmen Incident (1989)

Tiandihui 天地會

Tianfeng Lou 天风楼: Heavenly Wind Pavilion

tianfu 天府: heaven's storehouse

tianfu zhengshi 田赋征实 (田賦征實): direct grain acquisition

"**Tiangou**" 天狗: Heavenly dog

Tianhe 天河

Tianhe Tiyu Zhongxin 天河体育中心: Tianhe Sports Complex

Tianjin 天津

Tianjin Bowuguan 天津博物馆: Tianjin Museum

Tianjin Gang Baoshuiqu 天津港保税区: Tianjin Port Free-Trade Zone

Tianjin Tiaoyue 天津条约 (天津條約): Treaty of Tianjin

Tianmahui 天马会: Heavenly Horse Society, Pegasus Society

Tianshan 天山

Tiantan 天坛 (天壇): Temple of Heaven

Tiantang suantai zhi ge 天堂蒜苔之歌: *The Garlic Ballads*

Tiantang yu wuyue 天堂与五月: Paradise and May

tianxia 天下: all under heaven, the empire, Confucian ecumene

Tianxia wu zei 天下无贼: *A World without Thieves*

Tianyan lun 天演论 (天演論): *Evolution and ethics*, On evolution

Tianyi bao 天义报 (天義報): Heaven's justice

Tianyi Yingpian Gongsi 天一影片公司: Tianyi Film Studio

Tianyunshan chuanqi 天云山传奇: Tianyun mountain legend

tianzai renhuo 天灾人祸: natural disaster and human calamity

tianze 天择: natural selection

Tianze Jingji Yanjiusuo 天则经济研究所: Unirule Institute of Economics

"Tianzhai" 田宅: Land and house

Tianzhujiao 天主教: Catholicism

Tianzhujiao 天竹教: Heavenly Bamboo movement

tianzu 天足: natural feet

Tianzu Hui 天足会 (天足會): Natural Foot Society

tiaokuai 条块: lines and blocks (sectoral administrative hierarchies and regional units)

tiaoli 条例 (條例): selected imperial edicts and notices from central government ministries directed at the governor of a province

tiaotiao 条条: vertical authority

ticao 体操: gymnastics and militaristic calisthenics

tidu jiumen 提督九门: commander of the nine gates

tie 帖: calligraphic model

tie fanwan 鐵飯碗: iron rice bowl (job security)

Tie Guniang 铁姑娘: Iron Girls

tie langtou 铁榔头: iron hammer

Tiedao Bing 铁道兵: Railway Construction Corps

Tieliang 铁良

Tiema banhua 铁马版画: Steel Horse prints

Tiema Banhua She 铁马版画社: Steel Horse Woodcut Society

Tieshan gongzhu 铁扇公主 (鐵扇公主): *Princess Iron Fan*

tiexue 帖学 (帖學): studies on calligraphic models, copybook script

tigao 提高: raising of standards

ting 厅: subprefecture

tingyi 庭议: court conference

Tingyun Shuhua She 停云书画社: Unmoving Clouds Calligraphy and Painting Society

tiqian 提前: to advance, advanced

Tixi 提喜

Tixiao yinyuan 啼笑姻缘: *Fate in Tears and Laughter*

tiyan shenghuo 体验生活: observing and learning from real life

tiyong 体用 (體用): Chinese essence, Western utility; Chinese learning for fundamental structure and Western learning for practical use

tiyu 体育: physical education, physical culture

Tiyu Fa 体育法: Law of Sports

Tiyu huanghou 体育皇后: *Queen of Sports* *"Tiyu zhi yanjiu"* 体育之研究: *A study of physical education

tizhi 体制: the system and institutions of society

tizhi gaige 体制改革: structural reform

Tōkyō 東京: Tokyo

Tōkyō Bijutsu Gakkō 東京美術学校: Tokyo School of Fine Arts

Tong Luo 仝洛

"Tong yinyuegongzuozhe de tanhua" 同音乐工作者的谈话: Talk to music workers

Tong Zhonggui 童中贵

Tong'anxian 同安县: Tong'an County

Tongcheng 桐城

Tongchengpai 桐城派: Tongcheng school

tongchou fei 统筹费: unified planning fee, a township and village levy

tonggou 统购: purchase under state monopoly

tonggou tongxiao 统购统销: unified purchasing and sales system

Tongguang ti 同光体: Tongguang style

Tongguang Tongzhi Zhanglao Jiaohui 同光同志长老教会 (同光同志長老教會): Tong-Kwang Light House Presbyterian Church

tongsheng 童生: apprentice candidates

Tongji Daxue 同济大学: Tongji University

Tongji Kexue Yanjiusuo Keti Zu 统计科学研究所课题组 (統計科學研究所課題組): Study Team of the Statistical Science Research Institute

Tongmeng Hui 同盟会 (同盟會): Revolutionary Alliance, United League

tongqian 铜钱 (銅錢): cash, copper or bronze coins

tongru yuan 通儒院: graduate schools (in the 1904 educational system)

Tongshan She 同善社: Fellowship of Goodness

tongshan tang 同善堂: united welfare agencies

tongshi 通事: linguist

tongshu 通书 (通書): a Chinese almanac

tongsu yinyue 通俗音乐: popular music

Tongwen Guan 同文馆 (同文館): Interpreters College, Interpreters School

tongxiang 同乡: fellow local; natives from the same village, town, or province

Tongxiang 桐乡

tongxiang hui 同乡会: hometown associations, native-place associations

Tongxin 同心: in Ningxia

tongxin 同心: friend, someone who shares my heart

tongxue 同学: classmate

tongyangxi 童养媳 (童養媳): little daughter-in-law

Tongyi Dang 统一党 (統一黨): Unification Party

Tongyi Jianguo Tongzhi Hui 统一建国同志会 (統一建國同志會): United National Reconstruction Comrades Association

Tongyi Zhanxian 统一战线: United Front

Tongyi Zhanxian Gongzuo Bu 统一战线工作部 (統一戰線工作部): United Front Work Department

Tongyi Zhanxian Gongzuobu Zongjiao Shiwuju 统一战线工作部宗教事务局 (統一戰線工作部宗教事務局): Religious Affairs Bureau of the United Front Department

tongyi Zhongguo 统一中国: reuniting China

tongzhi 同志: comrade, friend, someone who shares my life goal

Tongzhi 同治: emperor (r. 1862–1874)

Tongzhi Weixin 同治维新: Tongzhi Restoration

Tongzhi Zhongxing 同治中兴: Tongzhi Restoration

tongzhong 同种: single race

Tongzhou 通州

Tou shaoya 偷烧鸭 (偷燒鴨): Stealing the Roast Duck

Toufa luan le 头发乱了: *Dirt*

"**Touji fenzi**" 投机分子: Opportunists

Touming de hongluobo 透明的红萝卜: The transparent carrot

Tousheng 偷生: Ignominy

touzi 骰子: dice

Tōyō bijutsu shōshi 東洋美術小史: A concise history of Eastern art

Tōyō shi 東洋史: Asian history

Triads 三点会

Zeng Youhe 曾幼荷: Tseng Yuho

tu 徒: penal servitude

Tuanjie bao 团结报: Unity

tuanlian 团练 (團練): militia, irregular militias

tuanti geju 团体格局: organizational mode of association

Tudi Gaige 土地改革: Land Reform

Tudi Gaige Fa 土地改革法: Land Reform Law

Tudi Geming Zhanzheng 土地革命战争 (土地革命戰爭): Agrarian Revolutionary War

Tudi Guanli Fa 土地管理法: Land Administration Law

Tudi Shen 土地神: Earth God

Tudi Weiyuanhui 土地委员会: National Land Commission

tuhua 图画: drawing and painting

Tuhua zhoukan 图画周刊 (圖畫週刊): Pictures weekly

tui chen chu xin 推尘出新: weed through the old to bring forth the new

Tuibian 蜕变 (蛻變): Metamorphosis

Tuishou 推手: *Pushing Hands*

Tujiazu 土家族: Tujia minority

tuli 土例: local practice

tulou 土楼: fortified communal earth dwellings, found in Fujian Provence

Tulufan 吐鲁番: Turfan

Tumen 土门: Earth gate

Tumote 土默特: Tumed

tunken shubian 屯垦戍边: clear the land and protect the frontier

Tuo Delin 妥得璘

Tuo Ming 妥明

Tuoluocijizhuyi 托洛茨基主义 (托洛茨基主義): Trotskyism

Tushanwan 土山湾

tuwen guanggao 图文广告 (圖文廣告): display advertisement

Uchiyama Kakitsu 内山嘉吉

Uchiyama Kanzō 内山完造

ukiyo-e 浮世繪

Umehara Ryūzaburō 梅原龍三郎

Wafangdian 瓦房店

wai 外: outer, outer world

Waichao 外朝: Outer Court

Waicheng 外城: Outer City

waihuo 外货 (外貨): foreign products

wailai zhengquan 外来政权 (外來政權): foreign power

Waishang Touzi Tequan Xiangmu Zanxing Guiding 外商投资特权项目暂行规定: Provisional Regulations on Foreign-Investment Build-Operate-Transfer Projects

waishengren 外省人: outsiders

Waitan 外滩: Bund

Waiwu Bu 外务部 (外務部): Ministry of Foreign Affairs

waizi qiye 外资企业: wholly foreign-owned enterprise

Wan 万 (萬): a monk

Wan Jiabao 万家宝 (萬家寶)

Wan Li 万里 (萬里)

Wan Ren 万仁 (萬仁)

Wan Yanhai 万延海

Wang Anshi 王安石

Wang Anyi 王安忆

Wang Canzhi 王灿芝

Wang Chaowen 王朝闻

Wang Chonghui 王宠惠

Wang Daohan 汪道涵

Wang Dongxing 汪东兴

Wang Enmao 王恩茂

Wang Fangyu 王方宇

Wang Fei 王菲: Faye Wong

Wang Fuzhi 王夫之

Wang Guangqi 王光祈

Wang Guangyi 王广义

Wang Guowei 王国维 (王國維)

Wang Hongwen 王洪文

Wang Hui (b. 1959) 汪晖

Wang Hui (1632–1717) 王翚

Wang Huning 王沪宁

Wang Jian 王鉴

Wang Jiawei 王家卫 (王家衛): Wong Kar-wai

Wang Jiaxiang 王稼祥

Wang Jie 王杰

Wang Jinsong 王劲松

Wang Jingwei 汪精卫 (汪精衛)

Wang Jingwei zhuyi 汪精卫主义 (汪精衛主義): Wang Jingwei doctrine

Wang Jiqian 王己千

Wang Jiyuan 王濟遠

Wang Juntao 王军涛

Wang Kangnian 汪康年

Wang Keping 王克平

Wang Lequan 王乐泉

Wang Li 王礼 (王禮)

Wang Lun 王倫

Wang Luobin 王洛宾

Wang Mang 王莽

Wang Meng (b. 1934) 王蒙

Wang Meng xiaoshuo baogao wenxue xuan 王蒙小说报告文学选: Selected novellas, stories, and reportage of Wang Meng

Wang Ming 王明

Wang Ruoshui 王若水

Wang Shaoao 王绍鏊

Wang Shaoguang 王绍光

Wang Shen 王莘

Wang Shimin 王时敏

Wang Shiwei 王实味 (王實味)

Wang Shouren 王守仁

Wang Shuo 王朔

Wang Shusheng 王树声

Wang Sidao 王思禱

Wang Tao 王韬 (王韜)

Wang Tingjun 王廷钧

Wang Tongzhao 王统照

Wang Wenjuan 王文娟

Wang Wenxing 王文兴 (王文興)

Wang Wuya 王无邪: Wucius Wong

Wang Xia 王洽

Wang Xiang 王襄

Wang Xianqian 王先谦

Wang xiansheng 王先生: Mr. Wang

Wang Xianzhi 王献之 (王獻之)

Wang Xiaoni 王小妮

Wang Xizhe 王希哲

Wang Xizhi 王羲之

Wang Yang 汪洋

Wang Yangming 王阳明 (王陽明)

Wang Yinzhi 王引之

Wang Yirong 王懿荣

Wang Yiting 王一亭

Wang Yongjiang 王永江

Wang Yuande 王沅德

Wang Yuanlu 王圆箓

Wang Yuanqi 王原祁

Wang Zhaoguo 王兆国

Wang Zhaojun 王昭君: *The Consort of Peace*

Wang Zhaoqing 王赵卿

Wang Zhen 王震

Wang Zhengting 王正廷

Wang Zhenhe 王祯和 (王禎和)

Wang Zhiping 王志平

wangdao 王道: kingly way

Wangfujing 王府井

Wang-Gu huitan 汪辜会谈: Wang-Koo meeting

Wangjiao kamen 旺角卡门 (旺角卡門): *As Tears Go By*

Wanguo gongbao 万国公报 (萬國公報): Chinese global magazine, Review of the times

Wanguo gongfa 万国公法 (萬國公法): *Elements of International Law*

Wangxia Tiaoyue 望厦条约 (望廈條約): Treaty of Wangxia

Wanlong Huiyi 万隆会议: Bandung Conference

Wanmu Caotang 万木草堂 (萬木草堂): academy established by Kang Youwei

Wanquanhe 万泉河: Wanquan River

Wanr de jiu shi xin tiao 玩儿的就是心跳: *Playing for Thrills*

Wanshi liufang 万世流芳: *Eternity*

Wanshi shibiao 万世师表: Model teacher for ten thousand generations

wanshixieshizhuyi 玩世写实主义: cynical realism

Wanshoushan 万寿山 (万壽山): Longevity Hill, Wanshou Mountain

Wanxi Junfa 皖系军阀: Anhui Clique

wei 卫: guard station

Wei Daoming 魏道明

Wei Ershen 韦尔申

Wei gong, nong, bing fuwu 为工农兵服务: To serve the workers, peasants, and soldiers

Wei Hui 卫慧 (衛慧)

Wei Jiangong 魏建功

Wei Jingshan 魏景山

Wei Jingsheng 魏京生

Wei Juxian 卫聚贤

wei lishi 伪历史: false history

Wei Yuan 魏源

wei zengquan 伪政权 (偽政權): puppet government

Wei Zhongguo wenhua jinggao shijie renshi xuanyan 为中国文化敬告世界人士宣言 (為中國文化敬告世界人士宣言): Chinese culture manifesto

weianfu 慰安妇: comfort women

weiansuo 慰安所: comfort station

Weichang 渭长 (渭長)

Weichao 魏朝: Wei dynasty

Weicheng 围城: *Fortress besieged*

weida duoshou 伟大舵手: great helmsman

weida lingxiu 伟大领袖: great leader

Weifang 潍坊

Weihaiwei 威海衛 (威海卫)

Weihe 渭河: Wei River

weijing fafa 违警罚法: laws covering criminal offenses

Weiming muke xuan 未名木刻选: *Unnamed woodcuts*

weiqi 围棋 (圍棋): go (board game)

weiquan yundong 维权运动: rights-protection movement, defense of rights movement

Weisheng Bu 卫生部 (衛生部): Ministry of Health

Weisheng Ju 卫生局 (衛生局): Sanitary Bureau

weishi 唯识: consciousness only

Weiting 慰亭

weiwu bianzheng lun 唯物辩证论: dialectical materialism

weiwu lishi lun 唯物历史论: historical materialism

Weiwuer 维吾尔: Uygur

Weiyijun 威毅军: Valiant Army

weiyuanhui zhuren 委员会主任: commission chairpersons

wen 文: literary prose, the civil, writing, literature, culture, civilization

wen bai yi du 文白异读 (文白異讀): literary and colloquial readings of characters

Wen Jiabao 温家宝

Wen Lou 文楼: Van Lau

Wen Yiduo 闻一多 (聞一多)

wenbing 温病: febrile diseases

Wenchang 文昌

Wenchuan 汶川

wenda 文达: literarily accomplished

Weng Tonghe 翁同龢

Weng Wenhao 翁文灏

wenhua 文化: culture

Wenhua Bu 文化部: Ministry of Culture

Wenhua Geming 文化革命: Cultural Revolution

wenhua jidutu 文化基督徒: cultural Christians

wenhua re 文化热 (文化熱): culture fever

wenjian 文件: documents

Wenjin Ge 文津阁: Literary Ford Pavilion

wenke 文科: humanities and social sciences

Wenmeizhai baihua shijianpu 文美斋白华诗笺谱 (文美齋白華詩箋譜): Hundred flowers poetry-writing paper from the Wenmei Studio

wenming 文明: civility, civilization

wenming xi 文明戏 (文明戲): civilized drama, enlightened drama

wenren hua 文人画 (文人畫): literati painting

"Wenrenhua zhi jiazhi" 文人画之价值 (文人畫之价值): The value of literati painting

Wensu Ge 文溯阁: Imperial Library

wentan 文坛: literary scene

wenwu 文物: relics

Wenwu Baohu Fa 文物保护法 (文物保護法): Cultural Relics Protection Law

Wenxian Guan 文獻館: Bureau of Documents

Wenxiang 文祥

Wenxin diaolong 文心雕龙: The literary mind and the carving of dragons, a classic in literary criticism

Wenxing Tiaoli 问刑条例 (問刑條例): a secondary code of the Ming dynasty

Wenxuan 文选: Selections

Wenxuanpai 文选派: Wenxuan school

wenxue 文学 (文學): literature

Wenxue congbao 文学从报 (文學叢報): Literary gazette

"Wenxue gailiang chuyi" 文学改良刍议 (文學改良芻議): A modest proposal for literary reform

wenxue shetuan 文学社团 (文學社團): literary societies

Wenxue xunkan 文学旬刊: Literature thrice monthly

Wenxue Yanjiuhui 文学研究会 (文學研究會): Literary Research Association, Literary Association

Wenxue zhoubao 文学周报 (文學週報): Literature Weekly

wenyan 文言: classical Chinese

Wenyi bao 文艺报: Literary gazette, Literature and arts magazine

wenyi jiemu 文艺节目: literary and art program

Wenyijia xiehui 文艺家协会: Association of Chinese Literary Artists

Wenzhou 温州

Wenzhou hua 温州话: Wenzhou dialect

Wenzhou moshi 溫州模式: Wenzhou model

wenzi yishu 文字艺术: language art

"Wo ai weida de zuguo" 我爱伟大的祖国: I love the great homeland

Wo Cha 沃查

"Wo de jiaoyu" 我的教育: My education

Wo de qiansui han 我的千岁寒: My millennium

Wo de xiongdi jiemei 我的兄弟姐妹: *Roots and Branches*

Wo de zizhuan 我的自传: *Memoirs of a Revolutionist*

Wo hu cang long 卧虎藏龙: *Crouching Tiger, Hidden Dragon*

Wo neng bi ya 我能比呀: *I Can Compete*

Wo shi ni baba 我是你爸爸: I'm your father

"Wo zai Xia Cun de shihou" 我在霞村的时候: When I was in Xia Village

Wo zheyi beizi 我这一辈子 (我這一輩子): In my lifetime

Wo zouguo de lu 我走过的路: The road I walked

Wolong Guojiaji Ziran Baohuqu 卧龙国家级自然保护区: Wolong Wildlife Conservation Area

Woren 倭仁

Wu 吴: ancient state, dialect

wu 武: the military

Wu Bangguo 吴邦国 (吳邦國)

Wu Boxiong 吴伯雄 (吳伯雄)

Wu Changshi 吴昌硕 (吳昌碩)

Wu Changshuo 吴昌硕 (吳昌碩)

Wu Chuanyu 吴传玉

Wu Dacheng 吴大澄 (吳大澂)

Wu Guanzhong 吴冠中

Wu guo yu wu min 吾国与吾民 (吾國與吾民): *My Country and My People*

Wu Hongxun 吴鸿勋

Wu Hufan 吴湖帆 (吳湖帆)

Wu Huiming 吴慧明

Wu Jiayou 吴嘉猷 (吳嘉猷)

wu ke woniu yundong 无壳蜗牛运动 (無殼蝸牛運動): shell-less snail movement

Wu Kedu 吴可读 (吳可讀)

Wu Liande 伍连德 (伍連德): Wu Lien-teh

Wu Man 吴蛮

Wu Meichun 吴美纯

Wu Men 午门 (午門): Meridian Gate

Wu Mi 吴宓

Wu Peifu 吴佩孚 (吳佩孚)

"Wu qi gonghe ge" 五旗共和歌: Five-colored-flag republic song

Wu Shanzhuan 吴山专

Wu Shengli 吴胜利

Wu Shiguang 乌始光

Wu Shujuan 吴淑娟

Wu Tingfang 伍廷芳

Wu Tong 吴彤

Wu Wan 吴琬 (吳琬)

Wu Wenying 吴文英 (吳文英)

Wu Woyao 吴沃尧 (吳沃堯)

Wu Xingfen 吴杏芬

Wu Yi 吴仪

Wu Yifang 吴贻芳 (吳貽芳)

Wu Youru 吴友如 (吳友如)

Wu Yuru 吴玉如 (吳玉如)

Wu Yusen 吴宇森 (吳宇森): John Woo

Wu Yuzong 吴耀宗 (吳耀宗): Y. T. Wu

Wu Zetian zhuan 武则天传 (武則天傳): *Lady Wu*

Wu Zhihui 吴稚晖 (吳稚暉)

Wu Zhongxin 吴忠心

Wu Zijia 吴子嘉

wubao 五保: five guarantees

wubao 五宝: five treasures

Wubei Xuetang 武备学堂: [Tianjin] Military Academy

Wuchan Jieji Wenhua Da Geming 无产阶级文化大革命: Great Proletarian Cultural Revolution

Wuchang 武昌

wuchanjieji zhuanzheng xia jixu geming 无产阶级专政下继续革命: continuing the revolution under the dictatorship of the proletariat

wudan 武旦: military-female role type in Peking Opera

Wuhan 武汉

Wuhan Jingji Jishu Kaifaqu 武汉经济技术开发区: Wuhan Economic and Technology Development District

Wuhouci 武侯祠: Wuhou Temple

Wuhu 芜湖

Wuji 无极: *The Promise*

Wujiashan Taishang Touziqu 吴家山台商投资区: Wujiashan Taiwan Investment District

Wujing 五经 (五經): the Five Classics

wuju 舞剧: Chinese dance-drama

Wulanbatuo 乌兰巴托: Ulaanbaatar

Wulanfu 乌兰夫: Ulanhu

wulitou 无厘头 (無厘頭): moleitau screwball farce (Hong Kong humor)

Wulong Yuan 乌龙院 (烏龍院): Black Dragon Compound

Wulumuqi 乌鲁木齐: Ürümqi

wulun 无伦: the five cardinal relationships, the five cardinal dyadic ties

Wumenpai 吴门派: Suzhou school

Wuneng de liliang 无能的力量: Power of the powerless

wu-qi ganxiao 五七干校: May 7 cadre schools

Wuquan Fa 物权法: Property Rights Law

wusheng 武生: martial-male role type in Peking Opera

Wushou sumiao 五首素描: Five sketches for piano

wushu 武术: martial arts

"Wushui shang de feizao paomo" 污水上的肥皂泡沫: Soap bubbles in the dirty water

"Wu-si jinian aiguo ge" 五四纪念爱国歌: Patriotic song commemorating May Fourth

"Wu-si jinian ge" 五四纪念歌: May Fourth commemoration song

Wu-Si yundong 五四运动 (五四運動): May Fourth movement

Wusong 吴淞

Wusong Tielu 吴淞铁路: Wusong Railway

Wusulijiang 乌苏里江: Wusuli River

"Wutai jiemei" 舞台姐妹: Two stage sisters

Wutaishan 五台山: Mt. Wutai

Wuwei youjun 武卫右军: Right Division of the Military Defense Army

Wuwei zuojun 武卫左军: Left Division of the Military Defense Army

Wuweijun 武卫军: Military Defense Army

wuwo 无我 (無我): without a self

Wuxi 无锡

wuxia 武侠: martial-arts genre of literature

wuxian gongsi 无限公司: unlimited companies

wuxing 五刑: five punishments

wuxing 五行: five phases, five elements

Wuxing 吴兴

Wuxu 戊戌

Wuxu Bianfa 戊戌变法 (戊戌變法): Hundred Days' Reform

Wuxu Liu Junzi 戊戌六君子: Six Gentlemen

Wuxu zhengbian 戊戌政变 (戊戌政變): Coup of 1898

Wuya yu maque 乌鸦与麻雀: Crows and sparrows

Wuye Lan 午夜藍: Midnight Blue

Wuyi Shanmai 武夷山脉: Wuyi mountain range

Wuying Dian 武英殿: Hall of Martial Valor

Wuyishan 武夷山: Wuyi Mountains

Wuyue 五岳: Five Sacred Mountains

Wuyue Huahui 五月画会 (五月畫會): Fifth Moon Group

wuzei 乌贼: cuttlefish

wuzhi wenming 物质文明: material civilization

Wuzhishan 五指山: Mt. Wuzhi

Wuzhou 梧州

Wuzhuang Jingcha 武装警察: Armed Police

wuzi 物资: commodities

Xianshi Renshou Baoxian Gongsi 先施人寿保险公司 (先施人壽保險公司): Sincere Life Insurance Company

Xi Jinping 习近平 (習近平)

Xi Rong 西戎

Xi wang Chang'an 西望长安 (西望長安): Looking toward Chang'an

Xi wo hou 徯我后: Awaiting the deliverer

Xi Xi 西西

Xi Zhongxun 习仲勋

Xia Nai 夏鼐

Xia Yan 夏衍

Xia Zengyou 夏曾佑

Xiachao 夏朝: Xia dynasty

xiafang 下放: send down, downward transfer, demotion to manual labor

xiagang 下岗: laid-off workers who remained affiliated with their company, unemployed

Xiaguan 下关 (下關)

Xiamen 厦门 (廈門): Amoy

Xiamen Dada 厦门大大: art group

Xiamen Daxue 厦门大学: Xiamen University

Xiamen Huaqiao Bowuguan 厦门华侨博物馆: Xiamen Overseas Chinese Museum

Xi'an 西安

Xi'an Beilin Bowuguan 西安碑林博物馆: Xi'an Tablets Museum

Xi'an Gao Xin Jishu Chanye Kaifaqu 西安高新技术产业开发区: Xi'an High-Tech Industry Development Zone

Xi'an Jingji Kaifaqu 西安经济开发区: Xi'an Economic Development Zone

Xi'an Shibian 西安事变 (西安事變): Xi'an Incident

xian 县 (縣): county

xian 闲: free time, leisure

Xian furen 冼夫人: Madam Xian

xian qi liang mu 贤妻良母 (賢妻良母): virtuous wife and good mother

Xian Xinghai 冼星海

Xian Zuzhi Fa 县组织法: County Organization Law

Xiandai 现代 (現代): *Les contemporaines*

Xiandai banhua 现代版画: Modern prints

Xiandai Banhua Hui 现代版画会: Modern Prints Society

Xiandai meishu 现代美术 (現代美術): Modern art

xiandai minjian huihua 现代民间绘画: modern folk painting

xiandai nüxing 现代女性: modern woman

Xiandai shijie minghua ji 现代世界名畫集: Master paintings of the modern world (book series)

Xiandai xiaoshuo jiqiao chutan 现代小说技巧初探: A preliminary examination of modern fictional techniques

xiandai Zhongguo 现代中国

Xiandai Zhongguo huaji 现代中国画集: Modern Chinese painting pictorial

Xianfa 宪法 (憲法): the Constitution

Xianfeng 咸丰 (咸豐): emperor (r. 1851–1861)

xianfeng wenxue 先锋文学 (先鋒文學): avant-garde literature

xianfeng xiaoshuo 先锋小说: avant-garde fiction

xiang 乡: administrative village, township, rural township

Xiang Jingyu 向警予

Xiang Jun 湘军: Hunan Army

Xiang Nanjinglu shang hao Balian xuexi 向南京路上好八连学习: Emulating the good Eighth Company of Nanjing Road (a campaign)

Xiang xing san ji 湘行散记: Recollections of West Hunan

Xiang Ying 项英 (項英)

Xiang Zhongfa 向忠发

Xiangdao zhoubao 向导周报 (向導周報): Guide weekly

Xianggang 香港: Hong Kong

Xianggang Daxue 香港大学: University of Hong Kong

Xianggang Huaren Xiyi Shuyuan 香港华人西医书院: Hong Kong College of Medicine for Chinese

Xianggang Jinhui Daxue 香港浸会大学 (香港浸會大學): Hong Kong Baptist University

Xianggang Keji Daxue 香港科技大学: Hong Kong University of Science and Technology

Xianggang Nü Tongmeng 香港女同盟: Women's Coalition of Hong Kong

Xianggang Zhongwen Daxue 香港中文大学 (香港中文大學): Chinese University of Hong Kong

xianggui 乡规 (鄉規): folk usage

xiangji 乡级: township-level

Xiangjiaba Shuidian Zhan 向家坝水电站: Xiangjiaba Hydropower Station

Xiangjiang 湘江: Xiang River

Xiangjiang pinglun 湘江评论: Xiang River review

xiangjianpai 乡建派 (鄉建派): rural reconstructionists

"Xianglian" 乡恋: Nostalgia, Longing for home

Xiangpi ren 橡皮人: Rubber man

Xiangpu 湘浦

xiangqi 象棋: Chinese chess

Xiangrikui Yuehui 向日葵乐会: Sunflower Group

Xiangshan 象山

Xiangshan 香山: Fragrance Hill

Xiangshan Fandian 香山饭店: Xiangshan Hotel

xiangsu 乡俗 (鄉俗): folk usage

Xiangtan 湘潭

xiangtu 乡土: native-soil, regionalist, rural, homeland

xiangtu sheying 乡土摄影 (鄉土攝影): native-soil photography

xiangtu xieshi 乡土写实 (鄉土寫實): rustic realism

xiangtu ziranzhuyi huihua 乡土自然主义绘画: native-soil painting

Xiangxi 湘西: West Hunan

xiangxia 乡下: home village

xiangyan paizi 香烟牌子 (香煙牌子): cigarette card

Xiang-Yu xian 襄渝线: Xiangfan-Chongqing line

xiangzhen qiye 乡镇企业: township and village enterprises

xianji 县级: county-level

xianjishi 县级市: county-level municipalities

xianmi 籼米: indica rice

xianmu 贤母: worthy mother

Xiannong Tan 先农坛 (先農壇): Altar of Agriculture

Xianshi Baihuo Gongsi 先施百货公司 (先施百貨公司): Sincere Department Stores

Xianshi Baoxian Zhiye Gongsi 先施保险置业公司 (先施保險置業公司): Sincere Insurance and Investment Company

Xianshi yizhong 现实一种: A kind of reality

Xianshi Youxian Gongsi 先施有限公司: Sincere Company Limited

Xianxiang tu 现象图 (現象圖): a satirical painting

Xianyang 咸阳

Xianyang Jichang 咸阳机场: Xianyang Airport

xianzheng 宪政 (憲政): constitutional government, constitutional rule

xiao 孝: filial piety

Xiao Baozhuang 小鲍庄: *Baotown*

Xiao Ben Guanli Zixun Wenjian 校本管理咨询文件: School-Based Management Consultative Document

Xiao cheng zhi lian 小城之恋: *Love in a Small Town*

"Xiao Dou'er" 小豆儿: Sprout

Xiao Erhei jiehun 小二黑结婚: Xiao Erhei gets married

Xiao Fengxia 萧风霞: Helen Siu

Xiao ger lia 小哥儿俩 (小哥兒倆): Little brothers

xiao gongzhu 小公主: little empresses

Xiao Haichun 萧海春

Xiao Hong 萧红 (蕭紅)

xiao huangti 小皇帝: little emperors

Xiao Jingguang 萧劲光

Xiao Jiuhua Si 小九华寺: Xiao Jiuhua Temple

Xiao Jun 萧军 (蕭軍)

Xiao Le 萧乐: C. D. Siu

Xiao Ling Tong 小灵通: a mobile-telecommunications service provider

Xiao Lu 肖鲁

Xiao Penglai Shuhua Hui 小蓬莱书画会: Xiao Penglai Calligraphy and Painting Society

Xiao Qian 萧乾 (蕭乾)

Xiao Shan 萧珊

xiao si Wang 小四王: the minor Four Wangs

Xiao wanyi 小玩意: *Little Toys*

Xiao Wu 小武

Xiao Yishan 萧一山 (蕭一山)

Xiao Youmei 萧友梅

"Xiao" 笑: Smiles

xiaobao 小报: tabloid newspaper

Xiaochu dui Funü Yiqie Xingshi Qishi Gongyue 消除对妇女一切形式歧视公约: Convention on the Elimination of All Forms of Discrimination against Women

Xiaochu Yiqie Xingshi Zhongzu Qishi Guoji Gongyue 消除一切形式种族歧视国际公约: Convention on the Elimination of All Forms of Racial Discrimination

Xiaodaohui Qiyi 小刀会起义 (小刀會起義): Small Swords Uprising

"Xiaofangniu" 小放牛: Boys herding cattle, a traditional folk dance-drama

xiaogang shengchandui 小岗生产队: small production team

Xiaojing 孝经: Classic of filial piety

xiaokang 小康: small welfare

xiaokang shehui 小康社会: small-welfare society

xiaopin wen 小品文: little prose pieces

xiaorenshu 小人书 (小人書): children's book

xiaoshou 枭首 (梟首): display of the decapitated head

Xiaoshuo yuebao 小说月报 (小說月報): Fiction monthly, Short story magazine

Xiaotun 小屯

"Xiaoxue jiaoshi zhi qi" 小学老师之妻: The wife of a primary school teacher

Xiaozhai 小砦: Little stockade

Xiaozhen 孝镇 (孝鎮)

xiaozu 小组: party cells

Xiaxiang ji 下乡集: Going down to the countryside

xiaxiang qingnian 下乡青年: youth sent to the countryside

xiaxiang zhiqing 下乡知青: rusticated youth

Xibei Huangtu Gaoyuan 西北黄土高原: Northwest Loess Plateau

xibeifeng 西北风: northwest wind, a music style based on folk music of northwest China

Xibu da kaifa 西部大开发: great western development scheme

Xibu kaifa 西部开发: development of the West

Xidan 西单

Xidan minzhuqiang 西单民主墙: Xidan democracy wall

Xidanlu 西单路: Xidan Road

xie 邪: heterodox

Xie Bingying 谢冰莹

Xie Dongmin 谢东闵 (謝東閔)

Xie Fuzhi 谢富治

Xie Jin 谢晋

Xie Mian 谢冕

Xie Wanying 谢婉莹 (謝婉瑩)

Xie Xuehong 谢雪红

Xie zai rensheng bian shang 写在人生边上: Marginalia of life

Xie Zhiguang 谢之光

Xie Zhiliu 谢稚柳 (謝稚柳)

xiedou 械斗 (械鬥): interlineage battles

Xiehe Yixueyuan 协和医学院 (協和醫學院): Union Medical College

xiejiao 邪教: evil cults

xieyi 写意 (寫意): expressionistic brushwork, idea writing

xieyihua 写意画: spontaneous style painting

Xifanghua 西方化: Westernization

Xigang 西岗

Xihu 西湖: West Lake

Xihu Guoli Yishuyuan 西湖国立艺术院 (西湖國立藝術院): West Lake National Art Academy

xihua 西画 (西畫): Western-style painting

Xijiang 西江: West River, Xi River

Xikang 西康

Xikun 西崐

Xiling Yinshe 西泠印社: Xiling Seal Society, Xiling Association of Seal Carvers

Xiluodu Shuidian Zhan 溪洛渡水电站: Xiluodu Hydropower Station

Ximeng rensheng 戏梦人生 (戲夢人生): *Puppetmaster*

xin 信: trust; faithfulness to the original text

xin 心: heart

xin bihua 新壁画: new murals

Xin Changzhezng lushang de yaogun 新长征路上的摇滚: Rock and roll on the new Long March

Xin Dang 新党 (新黨): New Party

xin ganjuepai 新感觉派 (新感覺派): new sensationists

xin geju 新歌剧: new music theater

xin gelüshi 新格律诗 (新格律詩): new regulated poetry

Xin Gongsi Fa 新公司法: 1946 New Company Law

Xin Gudian Wutuan 新古典舞团: Neo-Classic Dance Company

xin guohua 新国画: new national painting

Xin Hua Chouzhen Hui 新华筹赈会: Singapore Chinese Relief Fund

xin huapai 新画派: new-style painting

Xin Hunan bao 新湖南报: New Hunan daily

Xin meishu 新美術: New art, New fine arts

Xin Meiti Xi 新媒体系: New Media Art Department

xin minzhuzhuyi 新民主主义 (新民主主義): new democracy

"Xin minzhuzhuyi de zhengzhi yu xin minzhuzhuyi de wenhua" 新民主主义的政治与新民主主义的文化: Politics and culture of the new democracy

xin minzhuzhuyi geming 新民主主义革命: new democratic revolution

"Xin minzhuzhuyi lun" 新民主主义论: On new democracy

Xin minzhuzhuyi shiqi de renmin minzhu tongyizhanxian 新民主主义时期的人民民主统一战线: People's Democratic United Front for the New Democratic Era

Xin nüxing 新女性: *The New Woman*

xin nüxing 新女性: new woman

Xin qingnian 新青年: La jeunesse, New youth

"Xin renkou lun" 新人口论: New population theory

xin Ruxue 新儒学 (新儒學): new Confucianism

xin shehuizhuyi nongcun 新社会主义农村: new socialist countryside

Xin Shenghuo yundong 新生活运动 (新生活運動): New Life movement

Xin shiji 新世纪: New century

Xin Shiji Tongyi Zhanxian 新世纪统一战线: New Century United Front

xin shiji wenxue 新世纪文学: fiction of the new age

Xin Shiqi Tongyi Zhanxian 新时期统一战线: New Era United Front

Xin shixue 新史学 (新史學): New historiography

xin shixue de kaishan 新史学的开山 (新史學的開山): pioneering modern historiography

xin shuimo 新水墨: new Chinese ink painting

xin shuimohua yundong 新水墨畫運動: new ink-painting movement

Xin Si Jun 新四军 (新四軍): New Fourth Army

Xin Taiwanren 新台灣人: New Taiwanese

Xin weishi lun 新唯识论: A new treatise on consciousness-only

Xin Wenhua yundong 新文化运动 (新文化運動): New Culture movement

xin wenrenhua 新文人画: new literati painting

xin wenxue 新文学 (新文學): new literature

Xin Wenxue shiliao 新文学资料: New Literature materials

xin xian zhi 新县制 (新縣制): new county system

xin xiaoshuo 新小说 (新小說): new fiction

xin yimin 新移民: new emigrants

Xin Yuan shi 新元史: New Yuan History

Xin Zhui 辛追: Lady Xin Zhui

xin zuopai 新左派: new left

Xi'nan Lianhe Daxue 西南联合大学: Southwest United University

xinchao 新潮: new wave

xinchao xiaoshuo 新潮小说: new-wave fiction

Xincheng Yinhang 信成银行: Xincheng Bank

Xinchun Huazhan 新春画展 (新春畫展): New Spring Art Exhibition

xinfang ju 信访局: complaint offices

xing 性: the nature of something

Xing she, xing zi? 姓社, 姓资? Is it socialist or capitalist?

Xing Zhong Hui 兴中会 (興中會): Revive China Society

xing'an huilan 刑案会览 (刑案會覽): conspectus of criminal cases

Xing'anling 兴安岭: Xing'an Mountains

Xingbu 刑部: Ministry of Justice

xingcunzai 性存在: sexuality

xingfa 刑法: criminal law

Xingfen laoren 杏芬老人

Xingfen nüshi 杏芬女士

Xinghuo liaoyuan 星火燎原: A single spark can start a prairie fire

Xingjiang Bayi Gangtie Youxian Gongsi 新疆八一钢铁有限公司: BaYi Steel

xingling 性灵 (性靈): character

Xinglongwa wenhua 兴隆洼文化: Xinglongwa culture

xinglü 刑律: laws relating to the Board of Punishment

xinglü caoan 刑律草案: draft of the criminal code

xingming muyou 刑名幕友: private legal secretaries

Xingshe 星社: Star Society

Xingshi Minshi Susongfa Caoan 刑事民事訴訟法草案: Draft Code of Criminal and Civil Procedure

Xingshi Susong Fa 刑事诉讼法: Criminal Procedure Law

xingshipai 形势派: forces and features school

xingshu 行书 (行書): semicursive script, running script

xingxiang 性相: sexuality

Xingxing 星星: Stars

Xingxing Huahui 星星画会 (星星畫會): Stars Painting Group

Xingxing Meizhan 星星美展: Stars Exhibition

Xingxing yundong 星星运动: Stars movement

Xingyi 兴义

xingyishi 性意识: sexuality

Xingzheng Chengxu Fa 行政程序法: Administrative Procedure Law

Xingzheng Chufa Fa 行政处罚法: Administrative Punishment Law

xingzheng cun 行政村: administrative rural area

Xingzheng Fagui Zhiding Chengxu Zanxing Tiaoli 行政法规制定程序暂行条例: Tentative Regulations on the Procedure for Enacting Administrative Laws and Regulations

Xingzheng Jiancha Fa 行政监察法: Administrative Supervision Law

xingzheng jigou zhiquan tiaozheng quan 行政机构职权调整权: administrative-organization adjustment right

Xingzheng Susong Fa 行政诉讼法: Administrative Litigation Law

Xingzheng Yuan 行政院: Executive Yuan

Xinhai Geming 辛亥革命: 1911 Revolution, Xinhai Revolution

Xinhua 新华: New China

Xinhua ribao 新华日报: New China daily

Xinhua She 新华社: New China News Agency

Xinhua Shudian 新华书店: New China Publishing House

Xinhua Yinhang 新华银行: Sin-hua Trust and Savings Bank

Xinhua Yishu Zhuanke Xuexiao 新华艺术专科学校: Xinhua Art College

Xinhua zidian 新华字典 (新華字典): New China character dictionary

Xining 西宁

xinjian 信笺 (信箋): letter paper

Xinjian Lujun 新建陆军: Newly Created Army

Xinjiang 新疆

Xinjiang Shengchan Jianshe Bingtuan 新疆生产建设兵团: Xinjiang Production and Construction Corps

xinjiao ziyou 信教自由: freedom of religious belief

Xinjiapo Fujian Hui 新加坡福建会: Singapore Fujian Association

Xinjiapo Zhonghua Zongshang Hui 新加坡中华总商会: Singapore Chinese Chamber of Commerce

Xinjiekou 新街口

Xinjing 新京

Xinjun 新军 (新軍): New Army, New Armies

Xinkedu Xiaozu 新刻度小组: New Measurement Group

Xinlang 新浪: Sina, Sina.com

xinmin 新民: new citizen

Xinmin congbao 新民丛报 (新民叢報): New citizen journal

Xinning 新宁

xinpai 新派: new-style school

xinren 新人: new man

xinsheng dai 新生代: newborn generation

Xinsheng Zhaodai Suo 新生招待所: New Life Institute

xinshi 新诗 (新詩): new poetry

Xinsijun Shibian 新四军事件 (新四軍事件): New Fourth Army Incident

Xintiandi 新天地

Xinwen Chuban Zongshu 新闻出版总署: General Administration of Press and Publication

Xinwen Chubanshu 新闻出版署: State Press and Publication Administration

Xinwen diaocha 新闻调查: News probe

xinwen sheying 新闻摄影: journalistic photography

Xinwenbao 新闻报: Newspaper

Xinwenju 新闻局: Government Information Office

xinwenzhi 新闻纸 (新聞紙): leaflets about things heard recently

Xinxi Chanye Bu 信息产业部: Ministry of Information Industry

Xinxihua Gongzuo Lingdao Xiaozu 信息化工作领导小组: National Information Infrastructure Steering Committee

xinxihua tiaojianxia jubu zhanzheng 信息化条件下局部战争: local wars under conditions of informationization

Xinxin Baihuo Gongsi 新新百货公司 (新新百貨公司): Sun Sun Department Store, Xinxin Company

xinxue 新学 (新學): new learning

Xinxue weijing kao 新学伪经考 (新學偽經考): Inquiry into the forged classics of the Xin period, Liu Xin's falsification of classics

Xinyang 信阳

Xinyue 新月: Crescent moon

Xinyue She 新月社: Crescent Moon Society

Xinyue Shudian 新月书店: Crescent Moon Press

xinzheng 新政: new policy, new deal [for the masses]

Xiong Bingkun 熊秉坤

Xiong Shili 熊十力

Xiong Xiling 熊希龄

Xiongdi 兄弟: Brothers

xipi 西皮: a style of operatic singing

Xishan 西山: Tay Son

xishi 細事: trivial cases

Xishi jian 析世鉴: A mirror to analyze the world

Xishuangbanna Guojiaji Ziran Baohu Qu 西双版纳国家级自然保护区: Xishuangbanna Wildlife Conservation Area

xisi 细丝: sycee (literally, pure silk), silver ingot

xiucai 秀才: cultivated talent, prefectural graduate; the degree

xiuding falü dachen 修訂法律大臣: commissioner of law revision

Xiuding Falü Guan 修订法律馆 (修訂法律館): Bureau for the Revision of Laws

xiuxian 休闲: leisure

xiuxian chanye 休闲产业: leisure industry

xiuxian wenhua 休闲文化: leisure culture

xiuzheng xinglü caoan 修正刑律草案: revised draft of the criminal code

Xiwang 希望: Hope

Xixia 西夏

Xiyan 喜宴: *Wedding Banquet*

Xiyin Shuyuan 惜阴书院: Xiyin Academy

Xiyou Manji 西游漫记 (西遊漫記): Journey to the West

Xiyouji 西游记 (西遊記): *Journey to the West*

Xiyuan 西园: West Garden (in Suzhou)

Xiyuan 西苑: Imperial Western Garden

Xiyucheng Yanliao zhuang 西裕成颜料庄: Xiyucheng Dye Company

Xizang 西藏: Tibet

Xizang Zizhiqu 西藏自治区: Tibetan Autonomous Region

Xu Beihong 徐悲鸿 (徐悲鴻)

Xu Bing 徐冰

Xu Changhui 许常惠

Xu Dazhang 徐达章

Xu Deheng 徐德珩

Xu Dishan 许地山

Xu Guangda 许光达

Xu Guangping 许广平 (許廣平)

Xu Guanjie 许冠杰 (許冠傑): Sam Hui

Xu Guansan 许冠三

Xu Guanwen 许冠文 (許冠文): Michael Hui

Xu Haidong 徐海东

Xu Jingya 徐敬亚

Xu Ke 徐克: Tsui Hark

Xu Lai 徐来 (徐來)

Xu Lei 徐累

Xu Maoyong 徐懋庸

Xu Naiji 许乃济 (許乃濟)

Xu San'geng 徐三庚

Xu Sanguan mai xue ji 许三观卖血记: Chronicle of a blood merchant

Xu Shen 许慎 (許慎)

Xu shi xiongdi 许氏兄弟 (許氏兄弟): Hui brothers

Xu Shichang 徐世昌

Xu Tong 徐桐

Xu Xiangqian 徐向前

Xu Xiaobing 徐肖冰

Xu Xilin 徐錫麟

Xu Xing 徐行

Xu Xingzhi 许幸之

Xu Yabao 徐亞保: Chu-apoo

Xu Yongqing 徐咏青

Xu Yongyue 许永跃

Xu Zhenya 徐枕亚

Xu Zhijing 徐致靖

Xu Zhimo 徐志摩

Xu Zhongshu 徐中舒

Xu Zhuodai 徐卓呆

Xuanchuan Bu 宣传部: Department of Propaganda

xuanchuan sheying 宣传摄影 (宣傳攝影): propaganda photography

xuan'gou 选购: selective purchases

Xuannan 宣南

Xuanqing 璿卿

Xuantong 宣统: emperor (r. 1909–1911), Puyi

Xuanwuhu 玄武湖: Xuanwu Lake

Xuanzang 玄奘

"Xue luo zai Zhongguo de tudi shang" 雪落在中国的土地上: Snow is falling on the land of China

Xue qing 雪晴: Clearing after the snow

Xue Rengui dongzheng 薛仁贵东征 (薛仁貴東征): Xue Rengui goes on an eastern expedition

Xue Wu 薛五

Xue Yue 薛岳

Xuebu 学部 (學部): Board of Education

xuebu 学部: academic division

Xuehai Tang 学海堂 (學海堂): Sea of Learning Academy, Xuehai Academy

xuehengpai 学衡派: critical review group

Xuesheng zazhi 学生杂志: The student magazine

xueshu 学术 (學術): "moral learning" in Wei Yuan's *Essays on Qing Imperial Statecraft*

xuetang ge 学堂歌: school songs

xuetang yuege 学堂乐歌: school songs

Xuexiao Guanli Xin Cuoshi 学校管理新措施: School Management Initiative

xueyuanpai 学院派: academist, academist painting

Xugu 虚谷

Xujiahui Bowuguan 徐家汇博物院: Siccawei Museum

xujun gonghe 虚君共和: titular monarchical republic

xun 埙: Chinese ocarina

Xun Kuang 荀况

xungen 寻根: seeking roots

xungen re 寻根热: roots fever

xungen wenxue 寻根文学 (尋根文學): root-searching literature, roots fiction

Xunhua 循化

xunhuan piao 循环票 (循環票): return ticket

Xunhuan ribao 循环日报 (循環日報): Daily circulator, Universal daily (Hong Kong newspaper)

xunyan yushi 巡盐御史 (巡鹽御史): salt censor

xunzheng 训政 (訓政): political tutelage, tutelage of governance, party tutelage

Xunzheng Gangling 训政纲领 (訓政綱領): Charter of Political Tutelage

Xunzheng shiqi 训政時期: period of political tutelage

Xunzi 荀子

Xuzhou 徐州

ya 雅: literary elegance

Ya Xian 瘂弦

Yadong 亚东: Yatung

Ya-Fei Huiyi 亚非会议: Asian-African Conference

yahang 牙行: government-licensed brokers

Yalujiang 鸭绿江: Yalu River

Yaluo Zhanzheng 亚罗战争 (亞羅戰爭): *Arrow* War

Yamaguchi Yoshiko 山口淑子

yamen 衙门: official quarters

Yan di 炎帝: Yan emperor, Shennong

Yan Fu 严复 (嚴復)

Yan Haiping 彦海平

Yan Han 彦涵

Yan Hui 颜回

Yan Jiaqi 严家其

Yan Lei 颜磊

Yan Li 严力 (嚴力)

Yan Lianke 阎连科 (閻連科)

Yan Wenliang 颜文樑

Yan Wenming 严文明

Yan Xishan 阎锡山 (閻錫山)

Yan Yangchu 晏阳初: Y. C. James Yen

Yan Yuan 颜元

Yan Zhenqing 颜真卿 (顏真卿)

Yan'an 延安

Yan'an Nüzi Daxue 延安女子大学: Yan'an Women's College

Yan'an Wenyi Zuotanhui 延安文艺座谈会 (延安文藝座談會): Yan'an Forum on Literature and Art

Yan'an Zhengfeng yundong 延安整风运动: Yan'an Rectification campaign

Yanbian 延边

yanda 严打: strike-hard campaign

yang 阳 (陽): active principle

Yang Chengye 杨成业

Yang Chongyi 杨崇伊

Yang Dechang 杨德昌 (楊德昌): Edward Yang

Yang Dezhi 杨得志

Yang Fudong 杨福东

Yang Hansheng 阳翰笙

Yang Hucheng 杨虎城 (楊虎城)

yang huiban 洋会办 (洋會辦): foreign inspector

Yang Jiang 杨绛

Yang Keyang 杨可扬

Yang Lian 杨炼

Yang Lüfang 杨履方

Yang Mingzhai 杨明斋

Yang Mo 杨沫 (楊沫)

Yang Naiwu 杨乃武

Yang Rui 杨瑞: Yang Rae

Yang Sen 杨森

Yang Shangkun 杨尚昆 (楊尚昆)

Yang Shanshen 杨善深: Yang Shen-Sum

Yang Shenxiu 杨深秀 (楊深秀)

Yang Shoujing 杨守敬 (楊守敬)

Yang Tingbao 杨廷宝 (楊廷寶)

Yang Wenhui 杨文会 (楊文會)

Yang Xiguang 杨曦光

Yang Xiuqiong 杨秀琼

Yang Xueyao 杨雪瑶

Yang Yang 杨扬

Yang Yanping 杨燕屏 (楊燕屏)

Yang Yiping 杨益平 (楊益平)

Yang Yunsong 杨筠松

Yang Zengxin 杨增新

Yang Zhenning 杨振宁 (楊振寧): Chen Ning Franklin Yang

Yang Zhuanguang 杨传广: C. K. Yang

yangban xi 样板戏 (樣板戲): model operas, model theater

yangge 秧歌: rice-seedlings folk song and dance form

Yangguang canlan de rizi 阳光灿烂的日子: *In the Heat of the Sun*

yanghang 洋行: trading companies (authorized foreign traders)

Yangjingbang she guan 洋泾浜设官 (洋涇浜設官): official installed north of the Yangjing Creek

yanglao di 養老地: land for nurturing the old

Yangliuqing 杨柳青

Yangmen nüjiang 杨门女将 (楊門女將): Women warriors of the Yang family

yangping liang 洋枰两: yangping tael, local weight measure of silver used in Fujian province

Yangpu 洋浦

Yangshan shenshui gang 洋山深水港: Yangshan deep-water port

Yangshao 仰韶

yanguan 言官: speaking official, censor

yangwu 洋务: foreign affairs

yangwu yundong 洋务运动 (洋務運動): foreign-affairs movement, Self-Strengthening movement, Westernization movement

Yangxin Dian 养心殿 (養心殿): Cultivating the Mind Hall

Yangzhou 扬州

Yangzhou Baguai 扬州八怪: the Eight Eccentrics of Yangzhou

Yangzhou huafang lu 扬州画舫录: Record of the painted boats of Yangzhou

Yangzhou huapai 扬州画派 (揚州畫派): Yangzhou school of painting

Yangzhou xuepai 扬州学派: Yangzhou school of learning

Yangzijiang 扬子江 (杨子江): Yangzi River

Yanji 延吉

Yanjing Daxue 燕京大学 (燕京大學): Yenching University

Yanjing Jushe 燕京剧社: Yenching Drama Society

Yanjingshe 眼镜蛇: Cobra (band)

yanke 盐课: salt tax

Yanke Tiju Si 盐课提举司 (鹽課提舉司): Salt Tax Supervisorate

yanlu 言路: avenue of words, road of speech

yanpiao 盐票 (鹽票): salt tickets

yanqing xiaoshuo 艳情小说: erotic fiction

yanrong 岩溶: karst

yanshang 盐商: licensed salt merchant

Yanshi 偃师

Yanshousi 延寿寺: Prolonging Life Monastery

yanshui 盐税: gabelle, salt tax

Yantai 烟台

Yantai Tiaoyue 烟台条约: Zhifu (Chefoo) Convention

Yanwu Jihe Zongsuo 盐务稽核总所 (鹽務稽核總所): [Sino-foreign] Salt Inspectorate

Yanye Yinhang 盐业银行: Yien Yieh Commercial Bank

yanyin 盐引 (鹽引): salt tickets, salt licensing

yanyun shi 盐运使 (鹽運使): salt distribution commissioner

yanyun si 盐运司 (鹽運司): salt distribution commission

yanzheng 盐政 (鹽政): salt administration

Yanzhi 胭脂: Rouge

Yanzhou 严州

Yao 尧 (堯)

Yao Hua 姚华

Yao Ke 姚克

Yao Ming 姚明

Yao Wenyuan 姚文元

"Yao" 药 (藥): Medicine

yaogun yinyue 摇滚音乐: rock music

Yaozu 瑶族: Yao minority

Yapian Zhanzheng 鸦片战争 (鴉片戰爭): Opium Wars

Yasui Sōtarō 安井曾太郎

Yayin Xiaoji 雅音小集: Yayin Opera Ensemble

Yazhou Kaifa Yinhang 亚洲开发银行: Asian Development Bank

Yazhou Minzhuhua Shijie Luntan 亚洲民主化世界论坛: World Forum for Democratization in Asia

yazu 押租: rental deposit

Ye Chengzhong 叶澄衷

"Ye de yan" 夜的眼: Eyes of the night

Ye Dehui 叶德辉

Ye Gongchuo 叶恭绰 (葉恭綽)

Ye Jianying 叶剑英 (葉劍英)

Ye Mingchen 葉名琛

Ye Qiangwei 野蔷薇: *Wild Rose*

Ye Qianyu 叶浅予 (葉淺予)

Ye Shengtao 叶圣陶 (葉聖陶)

Ye Shi 叶适

Ye Ting 葉挺

Ye yan 夜宴: *The Banquet*

Yebaihehua 野百合花: Wild lilies

Yecao 野草: Wild Grass

"Yelaixiang" 夜来香: Tuberose

Yesheng Dongwu Baohu Fa 野生动物保护法: Wild Animals Protection Law

Yesheng Zhiwu Baohu Tiaoli 野生植物保护条例: Wild Plants Protection Regulations

Yeshi ji 也是集: Also so collection

Yesui She 野穗社: Wild Grain Society

yezi xi 叶子戏 (葉子戲): card games

yi 义 (義): righteousness; obligation

Yi 易: Change (concerto series)

Yi ban shi huoyan, yi ban shi haishui 一半是火焰, 一半是海水: Half flame, half sea water

Yi Bingshou 伊秉绶

yi fa zhi guo 依法治国: rule the country by law

yi gong dai gan 以工代干: replacements of cadres with workers

yi gong dai zhen 以工代赈: food for work

yi ren wei ben 以人为本: people-centered development

yi shendao shejiao 以神道設教: instructing the people through the worship of the Gods

Yi sheng tan xi 一声叹息: *A Sigh*

yi wen hui you 以文会友: making friends through literature

Yi yao chifan, er yao jianshe 一要吃饭, 二要建设: Food first, construction second

Yiba yi she 一八艺社 (一八藝社): Eighteen Arts Society

yibian dao 一边倒: leaning to one side

yibian yiguo 一边一国: one country on each side of the Taiwan Strait

yibihua 意笔画: spontaneous-style painting

yichan 遗产: heritage

Yichang 宜昌

Yichang fengbo 一场风波: A crisis

"Yidairen" 一代人: A generation

yidui fufu zhi sheng yige haizi zhengce 一对夫妇只生一个孩子政策: one-child policy

"Yi-erba jinian ge" 一二八纪念歌: January 28 commemoration song

yifu yiqi 一夫一妻: monogamy

yige guojia, liangge zhidu 一个国家两个制度: one country, two systems

Yige he bage 一个和八个: *One and Eight*

Yige ren de shengjing 一个人的圣经: One man's bible

yige Zhongguo, ge zi biaoshu 一个中国, 各自标书 one-China policy, to be interpreted according to each party's perspective

yige Zhongguo yuanze 一个中国原则: one-China principle

yigou 议购: negotiated purchases

Yiguan 艺观: Arts overview, Art view

Yiguandao 一贯道 (一貫道): Persistent Way, Way of Penetrating Unity

yiguo liangzhi 一国两制: one country, two systems

Yihang 一行: First line

Yihe Yuan 颐和园 (頤和園): Summer Palace, Garden of Sustenance in Peace

Yihequan 义和拳: Boxers

Yihetuan 义和团 (義和團): Boxers

Yihetuan zhi Luan 义和团之乱 (義和團之亂): Boxer Uprising

Yihexuan Jielibu 怡和轩俱乐部: Ee Hoe Hean Club

Yijing 易经: Book of changes

1985 Xin Kongjian 1985新空间: New Space Exhibition

yijue 义绝 (義絕): breaking the bond

yikou tongshang 一口通商: Canton System

yilang 议郎: court gentleman for consultation

yilei shangpin 一类商品: category-one goods

yili 义理 (義理): ethics and metaphysics

Yili 伊黎 Ili

yimin 义民: righteous people, Boxers

yin 淫: illicit, lascivious, immoral

yin 阴 (陰): latent principle

Yin Chengzong 殷承宗

Yin Guangzhong 尹光中

Yin Rugeng 殷汝耕

Yin Xiuzhen 尹秀珍

Yin Zhongrong 尹仲容

Yinbingshi shihua 饮冰室诗话 (飲冰室詩話): Poetry talk from the ice drinker's studio

Yinchang 荫昌

Yinchao 殷朝: Yin dynasty, Shang dynasty

Yinchuan 银川

Yingguo Yazhou Wenhui Bei Zhongguo Zhihui 英国亚洲文会北中国支会: North China Branch of the Royal Asiatic Society

Yinghe 英和

Yinghua zhi ge 英华之歌: The song of blossoms

yingji min 英籍民: British subject

yingming lingxiu 英明领袖: clairvoyant leader

Yinguang 印光

Yingxiong 英雄: *Hero*

yingyang 鹰洋 (鷹洋): Mexican-minted silver coins

yingyu 盈余 (盈餘): quota surplus

yingzao 营造: construction, builder's standard of length

Yingzao fashi 营造法式 (營造法式): Building methods, Building standards

yinhang 银行: bank

Yinshi nannü 饮食男女: *Eat Drink Man Woman*

yinshuiren 引水人: pilots

yin-yang 阴阳 (陰陽): latent and active states

yinyuan 银元 (銀元): silver coins imported from Spanish America

Yinyue Jiangxi Hui 音乐讲习会: Music Discussion Society

Yinzhou 鄞州

yipian sansha 一片散沙: loose sheet of sand

Yishi bao 益世报 (益世報): Yishi daily

yishihui 议事会: local council

yishu pantu 艺术叛徒: traitor to art

yishu sheying 艺术摄影: art photography

Yitaixing Matou 義泰興碼頭: Nee Tai Shing Wharves

Yitaixing Meihao 義泰興煤號: Nee Tai Shing Coal Merchant

yitian liangzhu 一田两主 (一田兩主): one field, two owners; **dual land ownership**

yitiaobian 一条鞭 (一條鞭): single-whip method

Yitong zhi 一统志: National gazetteer

"**Yiwu suoyou**" 一无所有: Have nothing

yiwu yi 義務役: compulsory military service

yixi zhi di 一席之地: an important seat

Yixingxian 宜兴县: Yixing County

yixue 义学 (義學): charity school

"**Yiyongjun jinxingqu**" 义勇军进行曲: March of the volunteers, national anthem of the People's Republic of China

yiyuan 议院: parliament

yizheng wang 议政王 (議政王): prince counselor

Yizhou shuangji 艺舟双楫 (藝舟雙楫): Two oars of the boat of art

Yizu 彝族: Yi minority

yōga 洋画: Western painting, Western-style painting

Yokohama Shōkin Ginkō 横滨正金银行: Yokohama Specie Bank

Yokoyama Taikan 横山大観

yong bu jia fu 永不加赋: to never increase the tax

Yong shi wo ai 永失我爱: *Lost My Love*

Yong'an Baihuo Gongsi 永安百货公司 (永安百貨公司): Wing On Department Stores

Yongding Men 永定门 (永定門): Gate of Eternal Settlement

Yongdinghe 永定河: Yongding River

Yonghegong 雍和宫: a Tibetan Buddhist temple in Beijing

Yongjia shigong xuepai 永嘉事功学派: Yongjia utilitarian school of thought

Yongjiang 甬江: Yong River

Yongsheng Shangdian 永生商店: Yongsheng Company

yongying 勇营: mercenary armies

Yongzheng 雍正: emperor (r. 1723–1735)

you di shen ru 诱敌深入: lure the enemy in deep

You Dian Bu 邮电部: Ministry of Posts and Telecommunications

you hong you zhuan 又红又专: both red and professional, red and expert

you jihua de shangpin jingji 有计划的商品经济: planned market economy

You sheng yu wu 有生于无: Being itself is a product of nonbeing

you wo 有我: have a self

Youchai 邮差: *Postman*

youeryuan 幼儿园: kindergarten

youji shifan xuetang 优级师范学堂: advanced teachers' colleges

Youlian Yingpian Gongsi 友联影片公司 (友聯影片公司): Youlian Film Studio

Youling 又陵

youmin 游民: floating population

Youxi bao 遊戲報: *Entertainment*

youxian gongsi 有限公司: limited liability company

youxian guangbo 有线广播: line broadcasting

youyi 邮驿 (郵驛): postal service

youyi diyi, bisai dier 友谊第一, 比赛第二: friendship first, competition second

Youyi Ouzhou Shangcheng 友谊欧洲商城: Continental Emporium

Youzheng ChujinYinhang 邮政储金银行: Postal Remittances and Savings Bank

Youzheng Shuju 有正书局 (有正書局): Youzheng Publishing House, Youzheng Book Company

youzhiyuan 幼稚园: kindergarten

yu 欲: desire

Yu 禹

Yu Bingnan 余秉楠

Yu Dafu 郁达夫 (郁達夫)

Yu Fei'an 于非暗

Yu Feng 郁风

Yu Guangyuan 于光遠

Yu Hua 余华 (余華)

Yu Jianhua 俞剑华

Yu Kun 俞锟

Yu Lianyuan 余联沅

Yu Luoke 遇罗克

yu mi zhi xiang 魚米之鄉: land of rice and fish

Yu Pingbo 俞平伯

Yu Rizhang 余日章: David Yui

Yu Weichao 俞伟超

Yu Xiwei 于希渭

Yu Youhan 余友涵

Yu Yue 俞樾

Yu Zhengsheng 余正生

Yu Zhengxie 俞正燮

Yu Zhong 俞钟

Yu, shashasha 雨, 沙沙沙: *Gentle rain*

Yu'nan 豫南

yuan 园: garden

yuan 圆: unit of Chinese currency

Yuan Changying 袁昌英

Yuan Dahua 袁大化

Yuan Dexing 袁德星

Yuan Heping 袁和平: Yuen Woo-ping

Yuan Longping 袁隆平

Yuan Mei 袁枚

Yuan shi 元史: *Yuan history*

Yuan Shikai 袁世凯 (袁世凱)

yuan xushi 元叙事: metanarrative

yuanbao 元宝 (元寶): silver ingot

Yuanchao 元朝: Yuan dynasty

Yuanchao 院抄: Yamen courrier

yuandong bingfu 远东病夫: sickman of the Far East

Yuanjiang 沅江: Yuan River

yuanlou 圆楼: circular structures

Yuanming Yuan 圆明园 (圓明園): Old Summer Palace, Garden of Perfect Brightness

Yuanmingyuan Huajia Cun 圆明园画家村: Yuanmingyuan Artists' Village

Yuanqiang 原强: *On strengthening*

Yuanshan Fandian 圆山饭店 (圓山飯店): Grand Hotel

yuanshi 院士: academician, honorary member

yuanyang hudie pai 鸳鸯蝴蝶派: mandarin duck and butterfly school

yuanyang hudie xiaoshuo 鸳鸯蝴蝶小说 (鴛鴦蝴蝶小說): mandarin ducks and butterflies fiction

Yuanye 原野: *The Wilderness*

Yuanye 园冶: The craft of gardens

yuanzuo 缘坐 (緣坐): collective responsibility

Yuchanyan 玉蟾岩

Yuchi 尉迟

Yudai Qiao 玉带桥 (玉帶橋): Jade Belt Bridge

Yudaxiang 裕大祥: a company

Yuejing 乐经: Classic of music

Yue 粤: Yue (Cantonese) language group

Yue Fei 岳飞

yuefenpai hua 月份牌画 (月份牌畫): calendar poster

Yuehua Shuyuan 越華書院 (越华书院): Yuehua Academy

Yueju 粤剧 (粤劇): Cantonese Opera

Yuelu Shuyuan 岳麓书院: Yuelu Academy

"Yuexia xiaojing" 月下小景: Under moonlight

Yuexiu 越秀

Yueyar 月牙儿 (月牙兒): "Crescent Moon"

"Yueye ting qin" 月夜听琴: Listening to a Chinese lute on a moonlit night

Yuezun 乐傅

Yugu 玉姑

Yuhaixian 豫海县: Yuhai County

Yujun 通駿

yuke 预科: preparatory program

Yuli hun 玉梨魂: Jade pearl spirit

Yulin 榆林

yulu ge 语录歌: musical settings of the quotations of Mao Zedong

yumai 预买 (預買): prepurchase

Yumen Youtian 玉门油田: Yumen Oilfield

Yun Shouping 恽寿平

Yun'gang 云岗

yundong 运动: campaigns, movements

Yunmen Wuji 云门舞集: Cloud Gate Theatre Ballet Troupe

Yunnan 云南

yunpan 运判 (運判): second assistant salt controller

Yunyou 云游 (雲游): Wandering among the clouds

Yuquan Shan 玉泉山: Jade Spring Hill

Yushan 豫山

Yushima Shengtang 湯島聖堂: Yushima Temple

Yushu 玉树

Yusi 语丝 (語絲): Tattler

Yusuan Gongzuo Weiyuanhui 预算工作委员会: Budgetary Work Committee

yusuanwai shouru 预算外收入: extrabudgetary revenues

"Yuwai huihua liuru zhongtu kao" 域外绘画流入中土考: Research on the introduction of Western painting in China

Yuxiang 予向

Yuyao 余姚

Yuye Fa 渔业法: Fishery Law

yuyi 御医 (御醫): imperial physicians

Yuyuan Shuhua Shanhui 豫园书画善会 (豫園書畫善會): Yu Garden Charitable Association of Calligraphy and Paintings

Yuyue xianxian zhuan 於越先賢傳: Portraits and Biographies of Illustrious Forebears from Yuyue

Yuzhou feng 宇宙风 (宇宙風): Cosmic wind

"Zai bie Kangqiao" 再别康桥 (再別康橋): A second farewell to Cambridge

Zai ji xiao duzhe 再寄小读者 (再寄小讀者): More letters to young readers

"Zai jiulou shang" 在酒楼上 (在酒樓上): Upstairs in the tavern

Zai na yaoyuan de difang 在那遥远的地方: In that far-away place

"Zai Yan'an Wenyi Zuotanhui shang de jianghua" 在延安文艺座谈会上的讲话: Talks at the Yan'an Forum on Literature and Art

zaihuang 灾荒: natural disaster

Zaili Jiao 在理教: teaching of the abiding principle

zang xiang 藏象: visceral manifestation

zangfu 脏腑: organs

Zangshu 葬书: Book of burial

Zanxing xin xinglü buchong tiaoli 暂行新刑律补充条例: Provisional supplementary new laws and regulations

Zao yangfan shu 造洋饭书 (造洋飯書): Treatise on the preparation of Western meals

Zaojun 灶君: Stove God, Kitchen God

Zaoshen 灶神: Stove God, Kitchen God

Zatan Sulian 杂谈苏联: Talks on the Soviet Union

zawen 杂文 (雜文): satiric miscellaneous-style essay, feuilleton

"Ze ou ji" 择偶记: Choosing a wife

zeli 则例 (則例): model cases (collections of edicts and regulations extracted from precedent cases)

Zeng Guofan 曾国藩 (曾國蕃)

Zeng Liansong 曾联松

Zeng Ming 曾鸣

Zeng Peiyan 曾培炎

Zeng Pu 曾朴 (曾樸)

Zeng Qi 曾琦

Zeng Qinghong 曾庆红 (曾慶紅)

Zeng Xi 曾熙

Zeng Yefa 曾叶发 (曾葉發): Tseng Yip-fat

Zeng Youzhen 曾友贞

Zeng Zhuangxiang 曾壮祥 (曾壯祥)

Zengcheng 增城

zhaijidi 宅基地: residential-housing land

Zhan Tianyou 詹天佑

Zhan Wang 展望

zhang 杖: beating with the heavy stick

Zhang Ailing 张爱玲 (張愛玲): Eileen Chang

Zhang Aiping 张爱萍

Zhang Bao 张保 (張保)

Zhang Binglin 章炳麟

Zhang Bojun 章伯钧 (章伯鈞)

Zhang Cha 张察

Zhang Chonghe 张充和

Zhang Chongren 张充仁

Zhang Chunqiao 张春桥

Zhang Daqian 张大千 (張大千)

Zhang Dejiang 张德江

Zhang Fengyi 张丰毅

Zhang Geng 张庚

Zhang Guangren 张光人 (張光人)

Zhang Guangtian 张广天

Zhang Guangyu 张光宇 (張光宇)

Zhang Guangzhi 张光直: Chang Kwang-chih, K. C. Chang

Zhang Guorong 张国荣: Leslie Cheung

Zhang Guotao 张国焘 (張國燾)

Zhang Hanhui 张汉挥

Zhang Heng 张珩 (張珩)

Zhang Henshui 张恨水

Zhang Hongbao 张洪宝

Zhang Huimei 张惠妹 (張惠妹): Gulilai Amit

Zhang Huiyan 张惠言

Zhang Jian 张謇

Zhang Jiluan 张季鸾 (張季鸞)

Zhang Jingjiang 张静江 (張靜江)

Zhang Junli 张君励

Zhang Junmai 张君励 (張君勱): Carsun Chang

Zhang Kebiao 章克标

Zhang Kesha 张克莎 (張克莎)

Zhang Leping 张乐平 (張樂平)

Zhang Liangying 张靓颖: Jane Zhang

Zhang Lunying 张纶英 (張綸英)

Zhang Luoxing 张洛行 (張洛行)

Zhang Mojun 张默君 (張默君)

Zhang Peili 张培力

Zhang Ping 张平

Zhang Qun 张群

Zhang Shangpu 章尚璞

Zhang Shanzi 张善仔 (張善孖)

Zhang Shicheng 张师诚

Zhang Shu 张曙

Zhang Taiyan 章太炎

Zhang tianshi 张天师 (張天師): Zhang heavenly master

Zhang Tianyi 张天翼 (張天翼)

Zhang Wang 张望

Zhang Wenkang 张文康

Zhang Wentian 张闻天 (張聞天)

Zhang Xiangyu 张香玉

Zhang Xiaogang 张晓刚

Zhang Xinsheng 张心声 (張心聲)

Zhang Xiong 张熊 (張熊)

Zhang Xueliang 张学良 (張學良)

Zhang Xueyou 张学友: Jacky Cheung Hok-Yau

Zhang Xun 张勋 (張勳)

Zhang Yimou 张艺谋

Zhang Yin 张崟

Zhang Yingxu 张镆绪 (張鏌緒)

Zhang Yinhuan 张荫桓

Zhang Yonghe 张永和 (張永和): Yung Ho Chang

Zhang Youyi 张幼仪 (張幼儀)

Zhang Yuan (b. 1963) 张元

Zhang Yuan (1899–1983) 张猿 (張猿)

Zhang Yuguang 张聿光 (張聿光)

Zhang Yunyi 张云逸

Zhang Zai 张载

Zhang Zeduan 张择端 (張擇端)

Zhang Zhengquan 张正权 (張正權)

Zhang Zhidong 张之洞 (張之洞)

Zhang Zhizhong 张治中

Zhang Zhong 张中 (張中)

Zhang Zhongjing 张仲景

Zhang Zhongxing 张中行

Zhang Zhunli 张准立 (張准立)

Zhang Zizhong 张自忠 (張自忠): a play by Lao She

Zhang Zongchang 张宗昌

Zhang Zongyu 张宗禹 (張宗禹)

Zhang Zuolin 张作霖 (張作霖)

zhangcao 章草: archaistic forms of semicursive script

Zhanggeer 张格尔 (張袼兒): Jehangir

Zhanghua Maorong Fangzhi Gongsi 章华毛绒纺织公司 (章華毛絨紡織公司): China Wool Manufacturing Company

zhanghui xiaoshuo 章回小说: episodic novel

Zhangjiakou 张家口

Zhangwu zhi 长物志 (長物志): Treatise on superfluous things

Zhangzhou 漳州

Zhangzhuang 张庄: Longbow village

Zhanjiang 湛江

Zhantai 站台: *Platform*

zhanyou 战友: army comrade

zhanzhang 毡帐: felt tents

Zhao Erfeng 赵尔丰

Zhao Erxun 赵尔巽

Zhao Hongben 赵宏本 (趙宏本)

Zhao Lian 赵廉: moustache Zhao

Zhao Lisheng 赵俪生

Zhao Mengfu 赵孟頫

Zhao Shaoang 赵少昂 (趙少昂)

Zhao Shiyan 赵世炎 (趙世炎)

Zhao Shou 赵兽 (趙獸)

Zhao Shuli 赵树理 (趙樹理)

Zhao Wuji 赵无极 (趙無極)

Zhao Xingdao 赵行道

Zhao Yannian 赵延年

Zhao Yuanren 赵元任: Yuen Ren Chao

Zhao Zhiqian 赵之谦 (趙之謙)

Zhao Zichen 赵紫宸 (趙紫宸): T. C. Chao

Zhao Ziyang 赵紫阳

Zhao Ziyue 赵子曰 (趙子曰): a novel by Lao She

zhaojia 找价: supplementary payments

zhaotie 找贴: difference between land's original price and current value

Zhaozhuang 赵庄

Zhedong 浙東: eastern Zhejiang

Zhejiang 浙江

Zhejiang Daxue 浙江大学 (浙江大學): Zhejiang University

Zhejiang Diyi Shifan Xuexiao 浙江第一师范学校: Zhejiang First Normal School

Zhejiang Meishu Xueyuan 浙江美术学院: Zhejiang Academy of Fine Arts, Zhejiang Art Academy

Zhejiang Shiye Yinhang 浙江实业银行: Zhejiang Industrial Bank

Zhejiang Shuju 浙江书局 (浙江書局): Zhejiang Printing Office

Zhejiang Yunda Fengli Fadian Gongcheng Youxian Gongsi 浙江运达风力发电工程有限公司: Zhejiang Windey [sic.] Wind Generating Engineering Co.

zhen 镇: town, market town, nonadministrative town, urban township

Zhen ge dai dan 枕戈待旦: *The Vigil of a Nation*

Zhen xianshi lun 真现实论: The true realism

Zhenbaodao 珍宝岛: Zhenbao Island

Zhendan Daxue 震旦大学: Zhendan University

zheng 正: orthodox

Zheng Chang 郑昶

Zheng Chenggong 郑成功 (鄭成功)

Zheng Chouyu 郑愁予 (鄭愁予)

zheng fengsu 正风俗: reforming the customs

Zheng Guanying 郑观应 (鄭觀應)

Zheng He 郑和 (鄭和)

Zheng Jin 郑锦

Zheng Junli 郑君里 (鄭君里)

Zheng Kai 郑开 (鄭開)

Zheng Mantuo 郑曼陀 (鄭曼陀)

Zheng Shan 郑珊

Zheng Wanlong 郑万隆

Zheng Wuchang 郑午昌

Zheng Xuan 郑玄

Zheng Yi 郑一 (鄭一): a pirate

Zheng Yi (b. 1947) 郑义

Zheng Yi sao 郑一嫂 (鄭一嫂)

Zheng Yuxiu 郑毓秀 (鄭毓秀)

Zheng Zhenduo 郑振铎 (鄭振鐸)

Zheng Zhengqiu 郑正秋

zheng'e 正额: nonnegotiable tax

Zhengfa Weiyuanhui 政法委员会: Commission in Charge of Politics and Law, Political and Legal Commission

zhengfeng yundong 整风运动 (整風運動): rectification movement

Zhenghong qi xia 正红旗下 (正紅旗下): Under the plain red banner

zhengli guogu 整理国故 (整理國故): ordering the national heritage

zhengqi fenli 政企分开: separation of government and enterprises, separation of political and business functions

Zhengquan Fa 证券法: Securities Law

zhengshi yuangong 正式员工: formal employee

zhengshu 正书 (正書): standard script

Zhengwu Yuan 政务院: Administrative Affairs Council, Government Administrative Council

Zhengyang Men 正阳门 (正陽門): Due South Gate, Zhengyang Gate

Zhengyi 正一: Orthodox Unity order of Daoist clerics

Zhengzai xiang 正在想: Just now thinking

Zhengzhi guanbao zhangcheng 政治官报章程 (政治官報章程): Regulations for Official Political Newspapers

zhengzhi popu 政治波普: political pop

zhengzhi renwu 政治任务: political tasks

zhengzhi shiti 政治实体: political entity

Zhengzhi Xieshang Huiyi 政治协商会议 (政治協商會議): Political Consultative Conference

Zhengzhou 郑州

Zhenhai 镇海

Zhenjiang 镇江

zhenjie 贞节 (貞節): chastity

zhenjiu 針灸: acupuncture

Zhenwu Xuexiao 振武学校: Shinbu Military School

Zhenxiang huabao 真相画报: True record (art magazine)

Zhenzhen 贞贞

Zhepai 浙派: the Zhejiang school

Zhexi 浙西: western Zhejiang

zhi 志: treatise

zhi 智: wisdom

Zhi li wei gong 致力为公: Exert strength in the public interest

Zhian Guanli Chufa Tiaoli 治安管理处罚条例: Regulations on Security Administration and Punishment

Zhibao 直报: Zhili times

zhiduwai shouru 制度外收入: off-budgetary revenues

Zhifen shichang 脂粉市场 (脂粉市場): Rouge and powder market

zhifu 知府: prefect

Zhifu 芝罘: Chefoo

zhigong daibiao hui 职工代表会: workers' congresses

Zhigong Dang 致公党 (致公黨): Public Interest Party, Zhigong Party

zhigong renyuan 职工人员: [urban] staff and workers

Zhigong Tang 致公堂: Chinese Freemasons Society, Chee Kong Tong

Zhiheng Jingshe 祇洹精舍: Zhiheng Monastery

Zhihuang quanfa 治蝗全法: Complete methods to control locusts

Zhijiaopai 职教派 (職教派): Vocational Education Society

zhijie touzi 直接投资: foreign direct investment

Zhijie Zizhu Jihua 直接资助计划: Direct Subsidy Scheme

Zhili 直隶

zhili zhou 直隶州: autonomous department

Zhimo de shi 志摩的诗 (志摩的詩): Zhimo's poems

Zhina Nei Xueyuan 支那内學院: Chinese Inner Studies Academy

Zhina zhi ye 支那之夜: China Night

zhiqian 制钱: mint coins

Zhiqu Weihushan 智取威虎山: Taking Tiger Mountain by strategy

zhishi fenzi 知识分子: intellectuals, knowledgeable elements

zhishi qingnian 知识青年: educated youth

zhiti 治体 (治體): administrative fundamentals

zhiwai faquan 治外法权 (治外法權): extraterritoriality

Zhiwu Yanjiusuo 植物研究所: Institute of Botany

zhixian 知县 (知縣): county magistrate

zhixiashi 直辖市: municipalities under the jurisdiction of the central government, independent municipalities

zhiyin 知音: friend, someone who knows my sounds

zhizao ju 织造局 (織造局): imperial silk factories

Zhong Yao 钟繇 (鍾繇)

Zhongcai Fa 仲裁法: Arbitration Law

Zhongchangqi Kexue Jishu Fazhan Gangyao 中长期科学技术发展纲要: Medium to Long-Term Plan for the Development of Science and Technology

zhongdian 重点: key

zhongdian renkou 重点人口: targeted persons

Zhongdian Zangzu 中甸藏族: Gyalthang Tibetans

Zhong-Fa Zhanzheng 中法战争 (中法戰爭): Sino-French War

Zhonggong Zhongyang Xuanchuan Bu 中共中央宣传部: Central Propaganda Department

zhonggu lou 钟鼓楼: bell and drum towers

Zhongguancun 中关村

Zhongguancun Keji Yuanqu 中关村科技园区: Zhongguancun Science Park

Zhongguo 中国: China

Zhongguo binwei dongwu hongpishu 中国濒危动物红皮书: China red book on endangered faunas

Zhongguo Chukou Shangpin Jiaoyi Zhongxin 中国出口商品交易中心: Chinese Export Commodities Fair Center

Zhongguo da baike quanshu 中国大百科全书: Comprehensive encyclopedia sinica

Zhongguo Dang'an Xuehui 中國檔案學會: Chinese Organization of Archivists

Zhongguo de xibei jiao 中国的西北角 (中國的西北角): The northwest corner of China

Zhongguo Di'er Lishi Dang'an Guan 中国第二历史档案馆: Number Two Archives

Zhongguo Dianli Touzi Jituan Gongsi 中国电力投资集团公司: China Power Investment Corporation

Zhongguo Dianxin 中国电信: China Telecom

Zhongguo Dianzi Xinxi Chanye Fazhan Yanjiuyuan 中国电子信息产业发展研究: China Center for Information Industry Development

Zhongguo Diaoban Yinshua Bowuguan 中国雕版印刷博物馆 (中國雕版印刷博物館): China Block Printing Museum

Zhongguo Diyi Lishi Dang'an Guan 中国第一历史档案馆: Number One Archives

Zhongguo Ertong Fazhan Gangyao 中国儿童发展纲要: National Plans of Action for Children

Zhongguo Fazhan Yinhang 中国发展银行: Development Bank of China

Zhongguo Fojiao Hui 中国佛教会: Chinese Buddhist Association (Taiwan)

Zhongguo Fojiao Xiehui 中国佛教协会: Buddhist Association of China, Chinese Buddhist Association

Zhongguo Fuli Hui 中国福利会: China Welfare Institute

Zhongguo Gaige Fazhan Yanjiuyuan 中国改革发展研究院: China Institute of Reform and Development

Zhongguo Geming Bowuguan 中国革命博物馆: Museum of Chinese Revolution

Zhongguo Gongchandang 中国共产党 (中國共產黨): Chinese Communist Party

Zhongguo Gongchanzhuyi Qingniantuan 中国共产主义青年团: Chinese Communist Youth League

Zhongguo Gongmin Churujing Guanli Fa 中国公民出入境管理法: Law on the Administration of the Exit and Entry of Citizens

Zhongguo Gongshang Yinhang 中国工商银行: Industrial and Commercial Bank of China

Zhongguo gudai fushi yanjiu 中国古代服饰研究: Researches into ancient Chinese costume

Zhongguo gudai jianzhu shi 中国古代建筑史: A history of traditional Chinese architecture

Zhongguo gudai shehui yanjiu 中国古代社会研究 (中國古代社會研究): A study of ancient Chinese society

Zhongguo Guji Yizhi Baohu Xiehui 中国古迹遗址保护协会: International Council on Monuments and Sites, China

Zhongguo Guodian Jituan Gongsi 中国国电集团公司: National Power Group, China Guodian Corporation

Zhongguo Guoji Jingji Jishu Jiaoliu Zhongxin 中国国际经济技术交流中心: China International Center for Economic and Technical Exchanges

Zhongguo Guoji Jingji Maoyi Zhongcai Weiyuanhui 中国国际经济贸易仲裁委员会: China International Economic and Trade Arbitration Commission

Zhongguo Guojia Chubanju 中国国家出版局: China National Publishing Administration

Zhongguo Haiguan Zong Shuimu Si 中国海关总税务司 (中國海關總稅務司): Inspector General of the Chinese Imperial Maritime Customs Service

Zhongguo Haiguan Zong Shuimu Sishu 中国海关总税务司署 (中國海關總稅務司署): Office of the Inspector General of the Chinese Imperial Maritime Customs Service

Zhongguo Haishi Zhongcai Weiyuanhui 中国海事仲裁委员会: China Maritime Arbitration Commission

Zhongguo Haiyang Daxue 中国海洋大学: Chinese Ocean University

Zhongguo Hegongye Jituan Gongsi 中国核工业集团公司: China National Nuclear Corporation

Zhongguo hua 中国画: Chinese painting

Zhongguo Hua Hui 中国画会 (中國畫會): Chinese Painting Society

Zhongguo huaxue quanshi 中国画学全史: Complete history of Chinese painting

Zhongguo Huaxue Yanjiuhui 中国画学研究会 (中國畫學研究會): Society for the Study of Chinese Painting, Chinese Painting Research Society

Zhongguo huihua shi 中国绘画史 (中國繪畫史): A history of Chinese painting

Zhongguo Huihua Yanjiusuo 中国绘画研究所: Chinese Painting Research Center

Zhongguo Hulian Wangluo Xinxi Zhongxin 中国互联网络信息中心: China National Network Information Center

Zhongguo Jiankang Jiaoyu Yanjiusuo 中国健康教育研究所: China Health Education Research Institute

Zhongguo jianshe 中國建設: China reconstructs (magazine)

Zhongguo Jianshe Yin Gongsi 中国建设银公司: China Development Finance Corporation

Zhongguo Jianshe Yinhang 中国建设银行: China Construction Bank

Zhongguo jianzhu 中国建筑 (中國建築): Chinese architect

Zhongguo Jianzhu Gongcheng Zong Gongsi 中国建筑工程总公司: China State Construction Engineering Corporation

Zhongguo jianzhu shi 中国建筑史 (中國建築史): A history of Chinese architecture

Zhongguo Jianzhushi Xuehui 中国建筑师学会 (中國建筑師學會): Chinese Society of Architects

Zhongguo Jiaoyu Yanjiu Wang 中国教育研究网: China Education and Research Network

Zhongguo Jibing Yufang Kongzhi Zhongxin 中国疾病预防控制中心: Chinese Center for Disease Control and Prevention

Zhongguo Jinchukou Yinhang 中国进出口银行: Export-Import Bank of China

Zhongguo Jidujiao Sanzi Aiguo Yundong Weiyuanhui 中国基督教三自爱国运动委员会: National Committee of the Three-Self's Patriotic Movement of the Protestant Churches in China

Zhongguo Jingji Yanjiu Zhongxin 中国经济研究中心: China Center for Economic Research

Zhongguo Jingju Yuan 中国京剧院: China Peking Opera Institute

Zhongguo Jinshi Shuhua Yiguan Xuehui 中国金石书画艺观学会: Chinese Epigraphy, Calligraphy, and Painting Study Society

Zhongguo Junshi Kexue Yanjiuyuan 中国军事科学研究院: Chinese Academy of Military Sciences

Zhongguo Keji Daxue 中国科技大学: University of Science and Technology

Zhongguo Kexue Guanli Xiehui 中国科学管理协会: China Institute of Scientific Management

Zhongguo Kexue Jishu Guan 中国科学技术馆: Museum of Chinese Science and Technology

Zhongguo Kexue Jishu Xiehui 中国科学技术协会: China Association for Science and Technology

Zhongguo Kexue Yuan 中国科学院: Chinese Academy of Sciences

Zhongguo keyi shuobu 中国可以说不: China can say no

Zhongguo Lianhe Zhipian Gufen Gongsi 中国联合制片股份公司 (中國聯合制片股份公司): China United Productions

Zhongguo Liantong 中国联通: China Unicom

Zhongguo Lishi Bowuguan 中国历史博物馆: National Museum of Chinese History, Museum of Chinese History

Zhongguo lishi yanjiu fa 中国历史研究法 (中國歷史研究法): Methods for the study of Chinese history

Zhongguo Lüxing Jutuan 中国旅行剧团 (中國旅行劇團): China Traveling Drama Troupe, China Traveling Dramatic Company

Zhongguo Meishu Guan 中国美术馆: National Art Museum of China, China Art Gallery

Zhongguo meishu xiaoshi 中国美术小史: A concise history of Chinese art

Zhongguo Meishu Xueyuan 中国美术学院: China Academy of Art

Zhongguo Meishujia Xiehui 中国美术家协会: Chinese Artists Association, National Artists' Society

Zhongguo Minbing 中国民兵: People's Militia

Zhongguo minghua ji 中国名画集: Famous Chinese paintings

Zhongguo Minquan Baozhang Tongmeng 中国民权保障同盟: China League for Civil Rights

Zhongguo minshi xiguan daquan 中国民事习惯大全 (中國民事習慣大全): Corpus of civil customs of China

Zhongguo Minzhu Cujin Hui 中国民主促进会 (中國民主促進會): China Association for Promoting Democracy

Zhongguo Minzhu Dang 中国民主党: China Democracy Party

Zhongguo Minzhu Jianguo Hui 中国民主建国会 (中國民主建國會): China Democratic National Construction Association

Zhongguo Minzhu Tongmeng 中国民主同盟 (中國民主同盟): China Democratic League, Democratic League of China

Zhongguo Minzu Jiefang Xingdong Weiyuanhui 中国民主解放行动委员会 (中國民主解放行動委員會): China Liberation Action Committee

"**Zhongguo nan'er**" 中国男儿: Man of China

Zhongguo Nanyang Yinhang 中国南洋银行: China and South Sea Bank

Zhongguo Nonggong Minzhu Dang 中国农工民主党 (中國農工民主黨): Chinese Peasants and Workers Democratic Party

Zhongguo Nonggongye Yinhang 中国农工业银行: Agricultural and Industrial Bank of China

Zhongguo Nongye Kexue Yuan 中国农业科学院: Chinese Academy of Agricultural Sciences

Zhongguo Nongye Yinhang 中国农业银行: Agricultural Bank of China

Zhongguo Nü Xuetang 中国女学堂 (中國女學堂): Chinese Women's School

Zhongguo nü bao 中国女报: Chinese women's monthly

Zhongguo Nüzi Shuhua Hui 中国女子书画会 (中國女子書畫會): Chinese Women's Calligraphy and Painting Society

Zhongguo pengren 中国烹饪: Chinese cuisine

Zhongguo Qigong Kexue Yanjiuhui 中国气功科学研究会: China Qigong Scientific Research Association

Zhongguo qingnian bao 中国青年报 (中國青年報): China youth, Chinese youth

Zhongguo Qingnian Dang 中国青年党 (中國青年黨): China Youth Party

Zhongguo Qingnian Xinwen Jizhe Xuehui 中国青年新闻记者协会 (中國青年新聞記者協會): Chinese Young Journalists Society

Zhongguo Qiye Yinhang 中國企業銀行: China Development Bank

Zhongguo Renmin Geming Junshi Bowuguan 中国人民革命军事博物馆: Military Museum of the Chinese People's Revolution, Museum of Chinese Revolution, Chinese People's Military Museum

Zhongguo Renmin Yinhang 中国人民银行: People's Bank of China

Zhongguo Renmin Yinhang Fa 中国人民银行法: People's Bank of China Law

Zhongguo Renmin Zhengzhi Xieshang Huiyi 中国人民政治协商会议 (中國人民政治協商會議): Chinese People's Political Consultative Conference

Zhongguo ribao 中国日报: *China Daily*

Zhongguo Shangye Feiji Gongsi 中国商业飞机公司: Commercial Aircraft Corporation of China

Zhongguo Shehui Kexue Yuan 中国社会科学院: Chinese Academy of Social Sciences

Zhongguo Shehuizhuyi Qingnian Tuan 中国社会主义青年团: Chinese Socialist Youth League

Zhongguo sheying 中国摄影: Chinese photography

Zhongguo sheying sishi nian 中国摄影四十年: Forty years of Chinese photography

Zhongguo Sheying Xuehui 中国摄影学会: Chinese Association for Photography

Zhongguo Shiyou Huagong Gufen Youxian Gongsi 中国石油化工股份有限公司: Sinopec, China Petroleum & Chemical Corporation

Zhongguo Shudian 中国书店 (中國書店): Cathay Bookshop

Zhongguo tese shehuizhuyi 中国特色社会主义: Socialism with Chinese Characteristics

Zhongguo Tianzhujiao Aiguo Hui 中国天主教爱国会: Chinese Patriotic Catholic Association

Zhongguo Tongshang Yinhang 中国通商银行: National Commercial Bank, Imperial Bank of China

Zhongguo Touzi Youxian Zeren Gongsi 中国投资有限责任公司: China Investment Corporation

Zhongguo Wangtong 中国网通: China Netcom

Zhongguo wenhua 中国文化: Chinese culture

Zhongguo wenwu guji baohu zhunze 中国文物古迹保护准则: Principles for the Conservation of Heritage Sites in China

Zhongguo wenxue 中国文学: Chinese literature

Zhongguo Wenxue Yishu Jie Lianhehui 中国文学艺术界联合会 (中國文學藝術界聯合會): China Federation of Literary and Art Circles

"Zhongguo wenyi gongzuozhe xuanyan" 中国文艺工作者宣言: Manifesto of Chinese literature and art workers

Zhongguo Xiandai Yishu Zhan 中国现代艺术展: China Avant-Garde, Chinese Modern Art Exhibition

Zhongguo Xiaofeizhe Xiehui 中国消费者协会: Chinese Consumers' Association

Zhongguo xiaoshuo shilüe 中国小说史略 (中國小說史略): A Brief History of Chinese Fiction

Zhongguo Xinwenshe 中国新闻社: China News Service

Zhongguo yaogun yinyue 中国摇滚音乐: Chinese rock music

Zhongguo Yingzao Xueshe 中国营造学社 (中國營造學社): Institute for Research in Chinese Architecture, Society for the Study of Chinese Architecture

Zhongguo Yinhang 中国银行: Bank of China

Zhongguo Yinhangye Jiandu Guanli Weiyuanhui 中国银行业监督管理委员会: China Banking Regulatory Commission

Zhongguo Yinyue Dianshi 中国音乐电视: China Music Television

Zhongguo Youzheng 中国邮政: China Post

Zhongguo Zhanlüe yu Guanli Yanjiuhui 中国战略与管理研究会: China Institute of Strategy and Management

Zhongguo Zhengzhi yu Xingzheng Kexue Yanjiusuo 中国政治与行政科学研究所: Chinese Institute of Politics and Public Administration

Zhongguo zhexueshi dagang 中國哲學史大綱: Outline of the history of Chinese philosophy

Zhongguo Zhongxin Jituan Gongsi 中国中信集团公司: CITIC Group, China International Trust and Investment Corporation

Zhongguo Zuojia Xiehui 中国作家协会 (中國作家協會): China Writers Association

Zhongguoren 中国人: Chinese people

Zhongguoren 中国人: The Chinese

Zhongguo-Xinjiapo Suzhou Gongye Yuan 中国-新加坡苏州工业园: China-Singapore Suzhou Industrial Park

Zhonghe Dian 中和殿: Central Harmony Hall

Zhonghua da zidian 中华大字典 (中華大字典): Comprehensive Chinese character dictionary

Zhonghua Dianying Xuexiao 中华电影学校 (中華電影學校): China Film School

Zhonghua Fuxing She 中华复兴社 (中華復興社): Chinese Renaissance Society

Zhonghua Geming Dang 中华革命党 (中華革命黨): Chinese Revolutionary Party

Zhonghua Jiaoyu Wenhua Jijin Hui 中华教育文化基金会 (中華教育文化基金會): China Foundation for the Promotion of Education and Culture

Zhonghua Matou Gongsi 中华码头公司: Chung Hwa Wharf Company

Zhonghua Meiqiu Gongsi 中华煤球公司: China Coal Briquette Company

Zhonghua Duli Meishu Xiehui 中华独立美术协会 (中華獨立美術協會): Chinese Independent Art Association

Zhonghua Minguo 中华民国 (中華民國): Republic of China

Zhonghua Minguo Guojun 中華民國國軍: Nationalist Army

Zhonghua Minguo Minfa 中华民国民法 (中華民國民法): Civil code of the Republic of China

Zhonghua Minguo Nongye Yanjiusuo 中華民國農業研究所: National Agricultural Research Bureau

Zhonghua Minguo Xianfa 中华民国宪法 (中華民國憲法): Constitution of the Republic of China

Zhonghua Minguo Xingfa 中华民国刑法 (中華民國刑法): Republican Criminal Code

Zhonghua Minguo Zanxing Xin Xinglü 中华民国暂行新刑律 (中華民國暫行新刑律): Provisional New Criminal Code of the Republic of China

Zhonghua minzu 中华民族: Chinese nation, Chinese race

Zhonghua Nongmin Yinhang 中华农民银行 (中華農民銀行): Farmers Bank of China

Zhonghua Pingmin Jiaoyu Cujin Hui 中华平民教育促进会: National Association of Mass Education Movements

Zhonghua Quanguo Gongshangye Lianhehui 中华全国工商业联合会: All-China Federation of Industry and Commerce

Zhonghua Quanguo Guiguo Huaqiao Lianhehui 中华全国归国华侨联合会: All-China Federation of Returned Overseas Chinese

Zhonghua Quanguo Lüshi Xiehui 中华全国律师协会: China Lawyers' Association

Zhonghua Quanguo Mukejie Kangdi Xiehui 中华全国木刻界抗敌协会: The National Woodcut Society for Anti-Japanese War

Zhonghua Quanguo Tiyu Xiejinhui 中华全国体育协进会: Chinese National Amateur Athletic Federation

Zhonghua Quanguo Tiyu Zonghui 中华全国体育总会: All-China Athletic Committee

Zhonghua Quanguo Wenxue Yishu Gongzuozhe Daibiao Dahui 中华全国文学艺术工作者代表大会: All-China National Congress of Literary and Art Workers, Chinese Congress of Literary and Art Workers

Zhonghua Quanguo Wenxue Yishu Jie Lianhehui 中华全国文学艺术界联合会: Chinese Federation of Literary and Art Circles

Zhonghua Quanguo Wenyijie Kangdi Xiehui 中华全国文艺界抗敌协会 (中華全國文藝界抗敵協會): All-China Resistance Association of Writers and Artists

Zhonghua Quanguo Zong Gonghui 中华全国总工会: All-China Federation of Trade Unions

Zhonghua Renmin Gongheguo 中华人民共和国: People's Republic of China

Zhonghua Renmin Gongheguo dianxin tiaoli 中华人民共和国电信条例: Telecommunications Regulations of the People's Republic of China

Zhonghua Renmin Gongheguo yu Yazhou Kaifa Yinhang Fupin Hezuo Xieyi 中华人民共和国与亚洲开发银行扶贫合作协议: Agreement on a Poverty Reduction Partnership between the People's Republic of China and the Asia Development Bank

Zhonghua Shuju 中华书局 (中華書局): China Publishing House, Zhonghua Book Co.

Zhonghua Suweiai Gongheguo 中华苏维埃共和国 (中華蘇維埃共和國): Soviet Republic of China, Chinese Soviet Republic

Zhonghua Tiyu Xiejinhui 中华体育协进会: China National Amateur Athletic Federation

Zhonghua Wenhua Fuxing yundong 中华文化复兴运动 (中華文化復興運動): Chinese Cultural Renaissance movement

"Zhonghua xiongli yuzhoujian" 中华雄立宇宙间: China stands strong in the universe

Zhonghua Zhiye Jiaoyu She 中华职业教育社: China Vocational Educational Society

Zhonghuamen 中华门

Zhongli Shijian 中壢事件: Zhongli Incident

zhongqing 重情: cases of a grave nature

Zhongqu yishao 中衢一勺: Scooping out the thoroughfare

Zhong-Ri Jiawu Zhanzheng 中日甲午战争 (中日甲午戰爭): First Sino-Japanese War

Zhong-Ri Meishu Xiehui 中日美术协会 (中日美術協會): Sino-Japanese Art Society, Association of Sino-Japanese Art

Zhong-Ri meishu yuebao 中日美术月报: Sino-Japanese art monthly

Zhong-Ri Zhanzheng 中日战争: Second Sino-Japanese War

Zhongshan 中山

Zhongshan 锺山: Bell Mountain

Zhongshan Gongyuan 中山公园: Zhongshan Park

Zhongshan Ling 中山陵: Sun Yat-sen Mausoleum

Zhongshanxian 中山县 (中山縣): Zhongshan County

Zhongshan zhuang 中山装 (中山裝): Sun Yat-sen (Mao) suit

Zhongshanlu 中山路: Zhongshan Road

zhongsi 中祀: second tier of state cults

Zhong-Su Hu Bu Jinfan Tiaoyue 中苏互不侵犯条约 (中蘇互不侵犯條約): Sino-Soviet Nonaggression Pact

Zhong-Su Yinyue Xuehui 中苏音乐学会: music group of the Soviet Friends Society

Zhongwai gongbao 中外公报 (中外公報): Chinese and foreign news, Domestic and foreign information

Zhongwai hezi jingying qiye 中外合资 经营企业: joint venture

Zhongwen da cidian 中文大辞典 (中文大辭典): Chinese language encyclopedic dictionary

zhongxiao qiye 中小企业: small- and medium-scale enterprise

Zhongxing 中兴: restoration

Zhongxing Dianxin Shebei 中兴电信设备: Zhongxing Telecommunication Equipment

Zhongxing Meikuang Gongsi 中兴煤矿公司: Zhongxing Coal Mining Company

Zhongxue wei ti, Xixue wei yong 中学为体, 西学为用 (中學為体, 西學為用): Chinese learning for essence, Western learning for practical utility; Chinese learning for values, Western for use

Zhongyang Dang'an Guan 中央檔案館: Central Archives

Zhongyang Dianying Gongsi 中央电影公司 (中央電影公司): Central Motion Pictures Company

Zhongyang Diaocha Ju 中央调查句: Central Investigation Department

Zhongyang Gaizao Weiyuan 中央改造委員: Central Reorganization Commission

Zhongyang Gongyi Meiyuan 中央工艺美院 (中央工藝美院): Central Academy of Arts and Crafts

Zhongyang Gongyuan 中央公园: Central Park

Zhongyang Guangbo Dianshi Daxue 中央广播电视大学: Central Radio and TV University

Zhongyang Guangbo Diantai 中央廣播電台: Central Radio

Zhongyang Guji Baoguan Weiyuanhui 中央古迹保管委员会 (中央古跡保管委員會): Central Committee for the Protection of Monuments

Zhongyang Huaqiao Shiwu Weiyuanhui 中央华侨事务委员会: Central Overseas Chinese Affairs Commission

Zhongyang Huijin Touzi Youxian Zeren Gongsi 中央汇金投资有限责任公司: Central Huijin Investment Corporation

Zhongyang jilü Jiancha Weiyuanhui 中央纪律检查委员会: Central Discipline Inspection Commission

Zhongyang Junshi Weiyuanhui 中央军事委员会: Central Military Commission

Zhongyang Junshi Weiyuanhui Waishiju 中央军事委员会外事局: Central Military Commission Foreign Affairs Bureau

Zhongyang Meishu Xueyuan 中央美术学院 (中央美術學院): Central Academy of Fine Arts

Zhongyang Renmin Zhengfu Weiyuanhui 中央人民政府委员会: Central People's Government Council

Zhongyang ribao 中央日報: Central daily news

Zhongyang Shehui Bu 中央社会部: Central Social Affairs Department

Zhongyang Shuyuan 中央书院: Central School

Zhongyang Tongxun She 中央通讯社: Central News Agency

Zhongyang Xiju Xueyuan 中央戏剧学院 (中央戲劇學院): Central Academy of Drama, Central Drama Academy

Zhongyang Xuanchuan Bu 中央宣傳部: Central Propaganda Division

Zhongyang Yanjiuyuan 中央研究院: Academia Sinica

Zhongyang Yihao Wenjian 中央一号文件: No. 1 Central Document

Zhongyang Yinhang 中央银行: Central Bank of China

Zhongyang Zhengzhiju Changwu Weiyuanhui 中央政治局常务委员会: Politburo Standing Committee

Zhongyi Paiwei Jizhi 中一派位机制: Secondary School Place Allocation Scheme

Zhong-Ying Gengkuan Dongshihui 中英庚款董事会 (中英庚款董事會): Board of Trustees for the Administration of the Indemnity Funds Remitted by the British Government

zhongyuan 中原: central plains

Zhongyuan Daxue 中原大学 (中原大學): Chung Yuan Christian University

Zhongzhou 中州: central prefecture, ancient name for Henan

Zhonyang Zhengzhi Xuexiao 中央政治学校 (中央政治學校): Central Political Institute

zhou 州: prefecture

Zhou Bichang 周笔畅

Zhou Changgu 周昌谷

Zhou Chunya 周春芽

Zhou Enlai 周恩来 (周恩來)

Zhou Jielun 周杰伦: Jay Chou

Zhou li 周礼 (周禮): Rites of Zhou

Zhou Lianxia 周练霞

Zhou Libo 周立波

Zhou Lüyun 周绿云 (周綠雲): Irene Chou

Zhou Muqiao 周慕侨

Zhou Qiang 周强

Zhou Runfa 周润发 (周潤發): Chow Yun-fat

Zhou Shaozheng 周少正

Zhou Shoujuan 周瘦鹃

Zhou Shuqiao 周树桥

Zhou Shuren 周树人 (周樹人) Lu Xun

Zhou Sicong 周思聪

Zhou Wenzhong 周文中

Zhou Xian 周闲 (周閑)

Zhou Xiang 周湘

Zhou Xingchi 周星驰 (周星馳): Stephen Chow

Zhou Xuan 周璇

Zhou Yang 周扬 (周揚)

Zhou Yongkang 周永康

Zhou Yunfang 周云舫

Zhou Zhangshou 周樟寿 (周樟壽)

Zhou Zuoren 周作人

zhouchang 粥场: soup kitchen

Zhouchao 周朝: Zhou dynasty

Zhoukoudian 周口店

Zhoumo qingren 周末情人: *Weekend Lover*

Zhu Cheng 朱偁

Zhu Da 朱耷

Zhu De 朱德

Zhu Dequn 朱德群

Zhu Jia 朱加

Zhu Jiahua 朱家骅 (朱家驊)

Zhu Kezhen 竺可桢

Zhu Lao Zong 朱老总

Zhu Lian 朱琏 (朱璉)

Zhu Mao 朱毛

Zhu Qiqian 朱启钤 (朱啟鈐)

Zhu Qizhan 朱屺瞻

Zhu Rongji 朱镕基

Zhu Runzai 朱润斋 (朱潤斋)

Zhu Shilin 朱石麟

Zhu Tianwen 朱天文

Zhu Tianxin 朱天心

Zhu Xi 朱熹

Zhu Xiong 朱熊

Zhu Yingtai 祝英台

Zhu Yuanchu 朱鸳雏

Zhu Yuanzhang 朱元璋

Zhu Zhixin 朱执信

Zhu Zihua 朱自华

Zhu Ziqing 朱自清

Zhua da fang xiao 抓大放小: Keep control of the big ones, let the small ones go

"Zhua geming, cu shengchan" 抓革命促生产: Grasp revolution, promote production

zhuan bao 傳包: biographic packet

zhuan falun 转法轮: the revolving dharma wheel

zhuan'an jigou 专案机构: organs in charge of special affairs

Zhuang Cunyu 庄存与 (莊存與)

zhuang fen 撞粉: sprinkled powder

zhuang shui 撞水: splashed water

Zhuang Zedong 庄则栋

zhuangbao 状报: court gazette

Zhuanghe 庄河

zhuanghuang 装潢: decoration, graphic

zhuangyuan 状元: top scorers in the civil-service examination, scholar role (in opera)

zhuangyuan chou 状元筹 (状元籌): tallies for first on the list (a dice game)

Zhuangzi 庄子 (莊子)

Zhuangzi shi qi 庄子试妻 (莊子試妻): Zhuangzi tests his wife

Zhuangzu 壮族: Zhuang minority

Zhuanli Fa 专利法: Patent Law

zhuanshu 篆书 (篆書): seal script

zhufang zhidu gaige 住房制度改革: housing-system reform

"Zhufu" 祝福: New Year's sacrifice

Zhuge Wuhou Si 诸葛武侯祠: Shrine of Zhuge Liang

zhuguan zhandou jingshen 主观战斗精神 (主觀戰鬥精神): subjective fighting spirit

zhuguanzhuyi 主观主义 (主觀主義): subjectivism

Zhuhai 珠海

Zhuiqiu 追求: Pursuit

Zhujiang 珠江: Pearl River

Zhujiang Xin Cheng 珠江新城: Zhujiang New Town

Zhungaer Pendi 准噶尔盆地: Dzungar Basin

zhuo 拙: awkward

Zhuo Wenjun 卓文君

Zhuoni 卓尼: Choni

zhuxi 主席: state president (literally, chairman)

Zhuyin Fuhao 注音符号 (注音符號): phonetic symbols

zhuzi 诸子 (諸子): hundred schools of thought

Zhuzuoquan Fa 著作权法: Copyright Law

zi 字: courtesy name, style

"Zi jian Nanzi" 子见南子 (子見南子): *Confucius Saw Nancy*

ziban tielu 自办铁路: self-built railways

zibenzhuyi mengya 资本主义萌芽: sprouts of an indigenous Chinese capitalism

zichan guanli gongsi 资产管理公司: asset management company

zichou zijin, ziyou zuhe, zifuyingkui, zizhu jingying 自筹资金, 自由组合, 自负盈亏, 自主经营: self-financing, self-chosen partnership, self-responsibility for gains and losses, self-operation

zifei sheng 自费生 (自費生): self-sponsored students

Zigong 自贡

Zigong Konglong Bowuguan 自贡恐龙博物馆: Zigong Dinosaur Museum

Zijiang 资江: Zi River

Zijincheng 紫禁城: Forbidden City

Zijinshan 紫金山

Zikai manhua 子恺漫画 (子愷漫畫): comics by Zikai

zili gengsheng 自力更生: self-reliance

Zilin xibao 字林西报: North-China daily news

Zimei hua 姊妹花: Twin Sisters

Ziqiang yundong 自强运动 (自強運動): Self-Strengthening movement

Ziqiangjun 自强军: Self-Strengthening Army

ziran 自然: nature

Ziran Baohuqu Tiaoli 自然保护区条例: Nature Reserves Regulations

ziran cun 自然村: village composed of residents who live together

Ziran Ziyuan Zonghe Kaocha Weiyuanhui 自然资源综合考察委员会: Commission for Integrated Survey of Natural Resources

zishu 自梳: self-combed

Zishui 资水: Zi River

zitan 紫檀: a type of sandalwood

zixin 自新: self-renewal

Zixun Fenxi Huodong 谘询分析活动: Analytical and Advisory Activities

Ziye 子夜: *Midnight*

ziyiju 谘议局: consultative bureau, provincial assembly

ziyou ren 自由人: free man

Ziyou tan 自由谭: Free talk

Ziyou Zhongguo 自由中国 (自由中國): Free China

zizhen 自振: stir itself up

zizhengyuan 资政院: national assembly

zizhi 自治: self-government

zizhi yanjiusuo 自治研究所: self-government school

zizhiqi 自治旗: autonomous banner

zizhiqu 自治区: autonomous region

zizhixian 自治县: autonomous county

zizhizhou 自治州: autonomous prefecture

Zong Zhengzhi Zuozhan Ju 总政治作战局 (總政治作戰局): General Political Warfare Department

Zong Zhuangbei Bu 总装备部: General Armament Department

zongcai 总裁 (總裁): supreme leader (referring to Chiang Kai-shek)

zongdu 总督 (總督): governor general

Zongguan Neiwufu Dachen 总管内务府大臣 (總管内務府大臣): ministers of the Imperial Household Department

Zonghe Dang'an Guan 综合档案馆: Comprehensive Archives

Zonghe Kaifa Yanjiuyuan 综合开发研究院: China Development Institute

zongjiao 宗教: religion

zongli 总理 (總理): premier, head of government and party, supreme leader (referring to Sun Yat-sen)

Zongli Geguo Shiwu Yamen 总理各国事务衙门 (總理各國事務衙門): Office for the General Management of Foreign Affairs

Zongli Yamen 总理衙门 (總理衙門): Abbreviated form of Zongli Geguo Shiwu Yamen [see above]

zongpai 宗派: lineage

Zongshan Daxue 中山大學: Sun Yat-Sen University

zongzi 粽子: rice ball wrapped in a bamboo leaf

zongzu 宗族: lineage

Zou An 邹安

Zou Rong 鄒容

Zou Taofen 邹韬奋 (鄒韜奮)

zougou 走狗: running dogs

Zoumalou 走马楼

Zoupingxian 邹平县: Zouping County

zudakang 租大炕: underground brothels

"**Zuguo ge**" 祖国歌: Song of the homeland

"**Zui baogui de**" 最宝贵的: The most precious thing

Zuidi Shenghuo Baozhang Zhidu 最低生活保障制度: Minimum Living Standard Guarantee System

Zuigao Guowu Huiyi 最高国务会议: Supreme State Conference

Zuigao Renmin Fayuan 最高人民法院: Supreme People's Court

Zuigao Renmin Jiancha Yuan 最高人民检察院: Supreme People's Procuratorate

Zuihao de shiguang 最好的时光: *Three Times*

Zuihou de guizu 最后的贵族: The last aristocrat

Zuihou yige Xiongnu 最后一个匈奴: The last Xiongnu

Zuixin guowen jiaokeshu 最新国文教科书: China national readers

Zuixin zhongxue Zhongguo lishi jiaokeshu 最新中学中国历史教科书 (最新中學中國歷史教科書): Newest middle school textbook of Chinese history

Zunyi Huiyi 遵义会议 (遵義會議): Zunyi Conference

Zuo Shunsheng 左舜生

Zuo Zhuan 左传 (左傳): Zuo commentary on Spring and Autumn Annals

Zuo Zongtang 左宗棠

zuobang dianying 左帮电影: left-wing film

Zuojia Xiehui 作家协会 (作家協會): Writers Union

Zuojiang 左江: Zuo River

zuoren 做人: be fully human

Zuoyi Meishujia Lianmeng 左翼美术家联盟 (左翼美術家聯盟): League of Leftist Artists

Zuoyi Zuojia Lianmeng 左翼作家联盟 (左翼作家聯盟): League of Left-Wing Writers

Zuoying 左营 (左營)

zuoyuezi 坐月子: recuperate for a month after childbirth

zupu 族谱: lineage genealogy

zutang 祖堂: ancestral trust

zuxue 族学: clan school

zuzhang 族长 (族長): lineage head

Zuzhi Bu 组织部: Organization Department

Zuzhibu laile ge nianqingren 组织部来了个年轻人: The young newcomer in the Organization Department

zuzong geming 祖宗革命: ancestor revolution

Index

Humans, Beasts, and Ghosts (Qian), 3:227

Hunan and Hubei, **2:271–275,** *275,* 4:97

Hunan Army, 1:391, 4:139

"Hunan Report," 1:221

Hunan Self-study University, 1:3

Hundred Days' Reform, **2:275–276**
    Cixi, Empress Dowager, 1:275
    Confucianism, 1:348
    institutional changes, 3:251
    Kang Youwei, 2:210, 401, 402
    Richard, Timothy, influence of, 3:274
    Sino-Japanese War, 3:408
    Zhang Zhidong, 4:151

Hundred Flowers campaign, **2:276–278**
    Chinese Communist Party, 1:326
    Chinese People's Political Consultative Conference, 1:183
    Democratic League of China, 1:404
    democratic parties, 1:401
    Federation of Literary and Art Circles, 2:29
    Hu Yaobang, 2:261
    intellectuals, 2:217
    Liu Binyan, 2:512
    Mao Zedong, 2:557
    mass movements, 1:231
    "On the Correct Handling of Contradictions Among the People" (Mao), 4:228–230
    propaganda and mass mobilization music, 2:645

Hundred Regiments campaign
    Deng Xiaoping, 1:408
    Eighth Route Army, 3:105
    Peng Dehuai, 3:94–95
    Zhu De, 4:168

Hundred schools, 1:280–281

Hung Wu, 1:89

Hungary, 3:596

Hunger, 3:171

"Hunger Strike Manifesto" (Liu), 4:285–287

Hunger strikes, 2:521

Huozhe (film), 1:124

Hupeh. *See* Hunan and Hubei

Hupei. *See* Hunan and Hubei

Hurley, Patrick, 3:17, 4:123

Huters, Theodore, 3:228

Hutong, **2:278–280,** *279*

Huxley, Thomas H., 1:285, 3:10, 4:121

Hydrological power, 1:518–520

Hydropower, 3:240, 279

Hyperinflation, 1:362–363, 3:15

Hyperrealism, 3:35

I

I Ching, 2:650

Ibsen, Henrik, 3:596

Ice and Snow Festival, *2:179,* 180

Ichi-Go offensive, 1:408

Iconography, Maoist. *See* Cult of Mao

Idea writing, 2:501

Identification and belonging, **2:281–283**

Identification cards, 1:254, 2:246

Identity, **2:283–287,** *285*
    autonomous regions, 3:208–209
    Chinese overseas, 1:235, 237
    collective identity, 3:82
    film, 2:449
    Hakkas, 2:173–174
    Muslims, 2:370
    origins and development of Chinese civilization, 1:45–46
    peasants, 3:82
    Taiwan, 3:539–540
    Zhuang, 3:209

Ideological education, 1:495

Ido Reizan, 1:86

Illegal aliens, 2:422

Illegal land transfers, 2:476, 3:313

Illiteracy and literacy, **2:287–288**
    adults, 1:489, 490
    baojia system, 1:136
    examination system, 1:541
    funding, 1:498
    peasantry, 3:80
    rural areas, 1:473
    sishu schools, 1:463
    Taiwan, 3:545
    United Nations Development Programme Report, 1:451
    villages, 4:36
    women, 1:462, 493, 494f
    Zouping County, 1:469

Image and Phenomena (exhibition), 1:91

Imamura Shiko, 2:319

Imla Convention, 3:104

Immigrants
    Korean labor, 2:406
    social welfare, 3:452
    Taibei, 3:518
    Taiwan, 3:529–530, 540, *3:540*

Immigration policy, 1:235, 256–257

Immunity, legal. *See* Extraterritoriality

Imperial art collections, 2:199–200

Imperial-audience questions, 4:44

Imperial Bank of China, 2:622

Imperial collections, 1:306–307, 2:68, 635–636

Imperial commissioners
    Lin Zexu, 2:491–492

Imperial gardens, 2:111–112

Imperial Household Department, 2:62, 129, **288–289,** 3:331

Imperial Maritime Customs Service. *See* Chinese Maritime Customs Service

Imperial orthodoxy, 1:277

Imperial palaces, **2:289–293**

Imperial physicians, 2:182

Imperial University of Beijing, 1:479

Imperialism, **2:293–297,** *294*
    capitalism, link with, 1:222
    consumption and consumer culture, 1:358
    extraterritoriality, 1:542–543
    foreign settlements, concessions and leased territories, 2:71–72
    nationalism, 2:281, 352, 3:10
    police, 3:140
    radio, 3:243–244
    railways, 3:603–604
    scramble for concessions, 2:350–351
    treaty ports, 3:612–614
    Western explorers, 1:40
    Xinjiang, Qing conquest of, 4:111–112
    Yuan Shikai, 2:138

"Implementing 'The Three People's Principles'" (Jiang), 4:282–283

Import liberalization, 2:89

Imports
    arms, 1:74
    coal, 1:516
    consumption and consumer culture, 1:358–359
    oil, 1:517
    shops, 3:395
    telecommunications equipment, 3:609
    textiles, 2:175
    See also Foreign trade

Imprisonment, 3:91, 93

In the New Era: Revelation of Adam and Eve (painting), 3:34–35

Inauguration of Barack Obama, 2:539

Incentives
    agricultural production, 1:15–16
    central planning, 1:177–178
    economic incentives and gradualism, 1:459
    one-child policy, 3:168
    special economic zones, 3:475, 476

Income, 1:444f, **2:297–299,** 298f
    Agrarian Reform Law, 3:301
    farmers, 3:316–317
    financial markets, 2:54
    gradualism, 1:461
    Great Leap Forward, 3:305
    Guizhou, 2:164

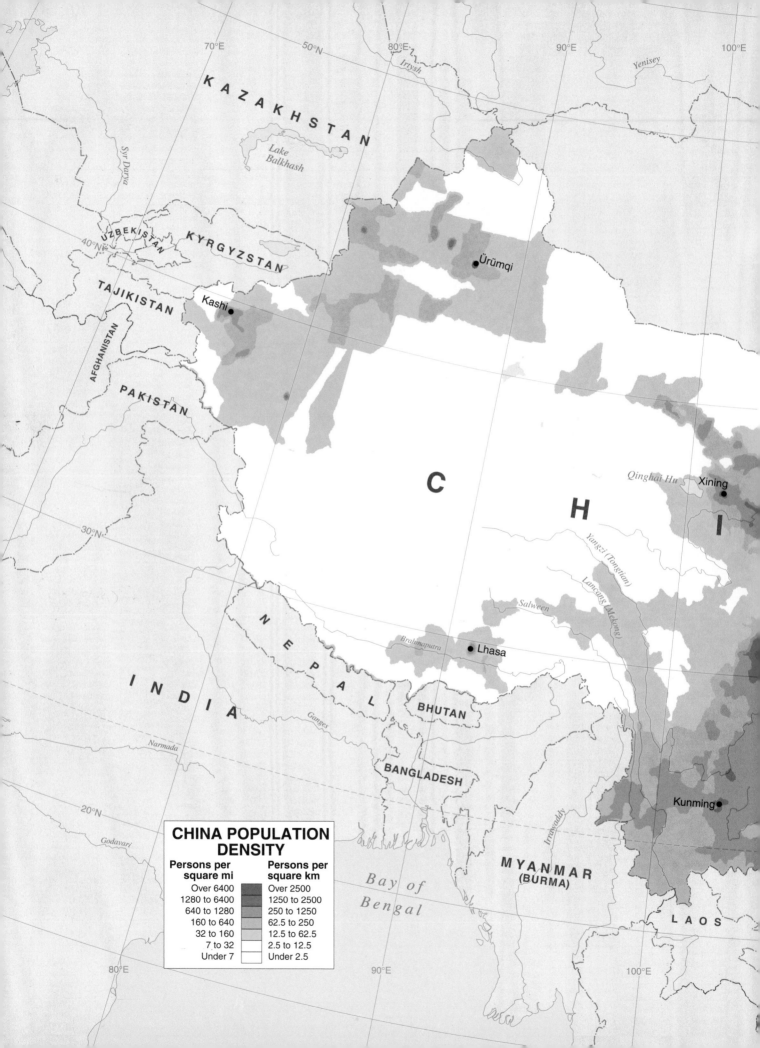

CHINA POPULATION DENSITY

Persons per square mi	Persons per square km
Over 6400	Over 2500
1280 to 6400	1250 to 2500
640 to 1280	250 to 1250
160 to 640	62.5 to 250
32 to 160	12.5 to 62.5
7 to 32	2.5 to 12.5
Under 7	Under 2.5